PC

CONFIGURATION

HANDBOOK

A Complete Guide to Assembling, Enhancing, and Maintaining your PC

PC CONFIGURATION HANDBOOK

A Complete Guide to Assembling, Enhancing, and Maintaining your PC

2nd Edition

John Woram

BANTAM BOOKS

TORONTO · NEW YORK · LONDON · SYDNEY · AUCKLAND

THE PC CONFIGURATION HANDBOOK, 2ND EDITION
A Bantam Book/November 1990

0 9 8 7

To Christina Marie,
who has her own definition
of IBM compatibility

Contents

11 Monitors and Adapters 445

Preface

Even if you've never been behind the scenes at a computer service center, no doubt you have an image of what it's like: white lab coats, exotic test equipment, a soldering iron at every hand, and wastebaskets full of expired microchips. A fascinating place to visit, but you wouldn't want to work there, would you?

You would? Then you won't be very happy reading this book. Here, test equipment isn't even mentioned (except once, but you probably won't even notice). As for tools, if you can find a screwdriver down in the basement somewhere, you're well equipped for all that follows.

Well, almost all. If you decide to pull a chip or two you'll want a chip puller, although if you're careful you can make do with that screwdriver. Just be sure the blade isn't magnetized, by trying to pick up a paper clip with it; if it clings, find another screwdriver—or buy that chip puller. (And get rid of the paper clip.)

Well then, who is this book for? Mostly, for me. In the course of my day-to-day work, I manage to keep three IBM computers up and running (well, most of the time). But since stamp collections and computer systems are never really complete, there's always just one more little something that needs to be added. There's really nothing to it: I just turn the power off, insert the new toy, turn the power back on again, and away we go. If you believe that, this book is also not for you.

Now then, for the rest of us. This book is for you, too, if:

Your system doesn't recall how much memory it has.

Your keyboard can't type very well.

Your disk drives haven't learned how to write.

Your display colors are black-on-black.

Your modem isn't feeling communicative.

Your printer won't take a letter.

Your system has recently discovered some new way to frustrate whatever it is you're trying to do.

Or am I the only one? I certainly hope not. Usually after the requisite few hours of blaming the computer for fouling up, plus a phone call to someone who knows all about these things, it's discovered that either some switch is in the wrong position, or perhaps a memory chip has failed, or maybe the program is flashing a message to a screen that isn't really there.

Unfortunately for professional dignity, it's never the computer's fault. It's doing just what I told it to do, even if it should have known that what I really meant was . . .

Sometimes the computer tries—half-heartedly it may seem—to help out by flashing an informative (?) display on the screen, such as,

2C 301, or perhaps

040002 0800, or maybe even

Device Timeout in 130.

Any one of these or countless other codes, messages, or audio beeps will tell the trained specialist just where the problem is. Of course, if it really is a problem (it happens), then you may need that specialist. But in most cases, it's something you can fix yourself in less time than it takes to have someone else do it for you.

For example, the messages seen above tell you that a key is stuck, a memory chip has failed, and that you forgot to turn something on. You just have to know how to read between the numbers. It's not that the computer wants to keep you guessing, but with all those keys, chips, and the external devices you've got plugged in, the terse message becomes a very efficient way of pointing to the trouble spot. Armed with that screwdriver and this book, you should be able to find the problem and fix it quickly.

Many problems show up when some new device is added to your system. As a typical example, a new memory option is installed and now nothing works right anymore. The solution? Just a few switch settings, or on a newer system, an automatic configuration routine. In some cases, it's tempting to reach for the phone. But before dialing, consider the following. Unless your friend the expert already knows your system's innards, you'll have to supply a little information. And if you can supply the right information, you probably don't need to make that call anyway.

In order to get that information, you have to "know the system." But you really don't have to give up your day job to put in long hours learning all the details. Instead, an hour or so here and there throughout these chapters should do it. And then you can fix it on your own, and maybe even answer a few calls yourself if the word gets out.

This book parts company with many other up-and-running type books, by making a basic assumption. It's assumed you are not a computer whiz and don't expect to be. Before buying your PC, you probably already owned a car, perhaps a tape recorder, and maybe even an air conditioner. But that didn't mean you were an internal-combustion specialist, an audio engineer, and a cooling-system technician. You just have to know a little something about each of these machines so you can get them to do what you want them to do. Don't forget about gas and oil, put a tape in the recorder, and make sure the thermostat is set. There's a little bit more to it, but not really that much more.

So it is with the computer. It's new, and it's different. But with just a bit of time, you can get it to behave just as reliably as any of the above.

Here and there, this book sneaks in a little theory of operation. Not enough to turn it into a text book, but perhaps just enough to give you a basic idea of what's going on in there. You don't have to take a degree in computer science to flip a switch, but it does make a bit more sense if you know why you're doing it. The little bit of extra information may even help keep your system out of trouble the next time something is changed.

As well as possible, the book is designed to stand alone. No prior knowledge is assumed, beyond a general familiarity with your PC. Chapter 4 offers some programming tips to help keep your system up and running, and here and there a small BASIC program is inserted to check various system features. However, these are not essential to the flow of the material covered, and may be safely ignored by readers who are not interested in programming.

Now and then a chart or other illustration may err on the side of giving too much information. Some of this was inserted just to make the book more valuable later on, after more experience has been acquired. So if some bit of information thus encountered doesn't seem to be useful, forget about it. Perhaps it will come in handy next time around.

As Exhibit A in the too-much category, consider Appendix C: a fairly complete list of error codes, most of which will never be seen. Some reviewers have pointed out that these have no place in a nonspecialist book. Perhaps they're right: does it help to know that a code 1126 means all modem status register bits cannot be set? Or that code 1127 means they can't be reset? Again, if either code means something to you, then perhaps this is not the book to be reading.

What matters to this book's readers is that a four-digit code beginning with 11 means trouble at the Asynchronous Communications Adapter. Anything beyond that is a potential confusion factor, unless the information is in the hands of a trained specialist. So please don't go about trying to set or unset those bits—just make a note of whatever error codes you see, report them to the service center, and sneak a peek at Appendix C if you like.

Chances are, this won't be necessary. Except for various memory-related error codes, you won't see much beyond a general error code, which is any code ending in 01. And as for those memory errors, they're not listed in Appendix A anyway (you'll have to buy the book and read Chapter 7 to find out more on this though).

Although an author's preface comes at the front, it's written at the back, that is, after everything else is done, and while waiting for the page proofs to come from the printer. So I already know what you're about to discover. I learned most of it the same way you will: by plugging something in and expecting it to work right the first time. And then, when all else fails, by reading the directions.

But even directions fail sometimes, when they describe the device but not the system into which it's about to go. That's a tough call—every system is different. If you doubt it, count the adapter slots on your own system board, and the number of installable options available at your local PC dealer. Then try to guess which ones are in the system next door, and write an instruction manual that covers all bases.

Perhaps that's the trouble with the PC. A car is to drive, a cassette recorder is to record, an air conditioner is to keep cool, and a personal computer is to do just about anything else. And depending on what you want it to do, you've put together a system that's a bit different from the one in the next office or the one at your neighbor's. Or if you haven't, you will soon.

So the PC's own Guide to Operations can only go so far. After that, it's up to you, and to this book about keeping your system up-and-running. To keep things simple (for me at least), the discussion uses IBM computers and a handful of very-compatible accessories as its frame of reference. Thanks to the PC's open architecture and overwhelming third-party support, there are just too many independent variables out there to be covered within a single text. Although many of these installable options can be discussed generically, some can't. Memory configuration switches are a good example. Because a combination seen here works for the adapter being described, it can't be assumed that the same settings mean the same thing on every other memory board. Because a device is IBM compatible, plug-compatible, or has the same general physical appearance, it can't be assumed that its everything-else is also the same.

The above is certainly not another little plug for buying Big Blue. It's simply to emphasize that with all the diversity out there, there's no such thing as a standard for switch settings or configuration routines. And where there are standards, not everyone follows them. Or, as someone once said,

> All IBM-compatible computers are compatible, but some
> compatibles are more compatible than others.

Well, that's not *quite* the way George Orwell put it, but it does describe the compatibility situation. Thanks to IBM's policy of open architecture, the PC user may choose from a bewildering variety of options—both as additions to an IBM PC and as the basic PC itself. Almost all are proclaimed "IBM Compatible" by their manufacturer.

But true Big-Blue compatibility is a sometime thing, and sometimes the thing does and sometimes it doesn't. That means some of the directions found here may take a bit of adaptation on a non-IBM system. As an obvious example, IBM systems use an extensive series of numeric error codes and self-testing procedures to help you find a trouble spot. As appropriate, these codes are found throughout this book. However, they may not be found in your non-IBM system. Specific error messages (those terse phrases that let you know something's wrong, without telling you what it is) may also vary from what is found here. So if you're working with a PC that is not 100 percent IBM, don't take all the instructions found here too literally. However, the basic theories still apply. Memory must be contiguous (again, Chapter 7), and don't plug anything in while the power is on.

Read the directions, find the appropriate chapter here, and you should be up and running in no time. Now if someone can help me figure out this hyper-VGA card that just arrived . . .

John M. Woram
Rockville Centre, New York
October 15, 1990

Acknowledgments

Well, of course, my first-place thanks go to IBM for building a series of personal computers that captured the fancy of the PC-buying market—in fact, that helped define the market. Coming in second, thanks to IBM for supplying said computers with lots of documentation—obscure perhaps, but nevertheless it's there, just crying out for translation into English. And in third place, a special thanks this time to Big Blue, for abandoning the PC series just as the first edition of this work was nearing completion. I'm sure they had loftier goals in mind than just my welfare, but still, it did create a nice little market niche for a "what do I do now?" kind of book (like this one).

By comparison with IBM's first round of personal computers, the PS/2 generation is still relatively new. In fact, several additions to the series were introduced during this edition's production cycle, and it would have been difficult, if not impossible, to keep up with all this without a little inside support. Yet IBM is not known to part with information easily, and it has been said that "no comment" is (or should be) a company trademark. Despite the wealth of documentation, tracking down a specific piece of information is no task for the weak, and were it not for the kindness and enthusiastic support of a few IBMers, there would be a lot more white space in this book. And so, a special thank-you to Elaine C. Schapker, who knows the meaning of the word "communications," and to Sheila Shanahan for valuable help with PS/2 hardware. Dick Conklin, editor of the *IBM Personal Systems Developer* and general goodwill ambassador to the fourth estate, offered his continuing support and encouragement, without which it would have been tempting to walk away from some of the more difficult aspects of this project. And there were others on the inside who cannot be named here.

Of course, there is one sure way to get reliable information about IBM hardware: just go out and buy one of everything and study the manuals. It's not cheap, but it is effective. Fortunately, I discovered a better way. Jim Barry, ex-IBMer and present manager of the Nynex Business Center in Hicksville, New York, let me pretend to be a potential power buyer, come to examine every IBM product in the store. Operations manager Leo Byron and technician Alex Corsini were always available to offer expert assistance, as needed. Without their help, I'd still be looking for a few stray model bytes and other exotica.

Since this book is about more than just IBM hardware, you'll find here and there a photo or text mention of hardware and software designed to support the IBM architecture. If you could look behind each such picture or word you'd find a long series of fact-checking phone conversations, and I hope the photo or other reference found here will serve as a quiet thank-you note to the supplier of same.

Now and then the assistance went a bit beyond just getting the facts straight, and I'd like to acknowledge my debt to the following folks (and to hope that I haven't overlooked anyone).

For help with power-related problems, including a heart transplant for an ancient PC, thanks to Doug Dodson at PC Cooling Systems.

The new material in Chapter 6 would have gone a lot slower were it not for the technical support of folks like Clyde Washburn at AMI (American Megatrends, Inc.) and Ken Plotkin at Hauppauge Computer Works. For a little hands-on experience with EISA hardware, my thanks to Roberta Frye at ALR (Advanced Logic Research) for making an i486 PowerVEISA computer available, and to Sia Maher in tech support for always answering the phone.

Kevin Goldstein and Brian Kingsbury at Peter Norton Computing were a great help in polishing up some of the finer points on hidden sectors and in clarifying the arcane mysteries of hard disk lore.

At Personics, John Jurewicz was a continuing source of help in sorting out all the vagaries and variables of video. And a special thanks to Jan Shepherd at VESA (Video Electronics Standards Organization) for rushing the proposed VESA standards to me, almost as the book went to press. For the first edition, Andy Fischer at Hercules Computer Technology lent a hand in clarifying a few graphics points, especially as related to you-know-what.

Sharon O'Brien at Hayes let me read some of the first-edition modem test procedures to her over the phone (voice transmission). She was kind enough to call back after checking the facts with the tech support crew (who needed a good laugh anyway). And thanks again to Hayes for permission to reproduce a page from their manual, as Figure 12.2(c).

Microsoft DOS 5.0 should be making its debut at about the time this book hits the stands. Thanks to Tanya vanDam, a beta version was made available on short notice so that some of the key features could be included here, as Appendix A.

During the early production stages of the first edition, Paul Farrell and Glen Hartley provided lots of much-appreciated editing expertise. And finally, thanks to Bantam Books—and especially to Steve Guty—for the enthusiastic early support, which continued through this new edition.

1

An Introduction to Computer Diagnostics

No matter what your level of computer literacy, there is little likelihood that the following phrase needs to be explained: "The computer is down."

We've all heard it, and probably more than once. The words conjure up visions of a petulant machine gone on the microequivalent of a sit-down strike. Perhaps it will be up and running later on, once some gifted technician can be found, one who can persuade the machine to behave itself.

Eventually we learn that the computer is once again back in operation. What we don't learn is that the trouble really wasn't the computer's fault at all. Instead, some operator error caused it to perform in an unexpected manner. Then it became necessary to shut down the system while that error was traced, isolated, and corrected. Meanwhile, the machine took the blame.

It's conceivable that the computer really was down, but the odds are overwhelmingly against it. In fact, during the preparation of the first and second editions of this book, a number of IBM and other computers—ranging in sophistication from the ancient PC to the latest PS/2 and EISA systems—were subjected to all sorts of physical abuse, in order to better describe the symptoms of just about anything that could go wrong. Without exception, every machine bounced right back into service as soon as the deliberately induced error was removed.

In fact, the computer is one of the most reliable machines ever made. It has almost no moving parts, so there's very little to get out of alignment. Its electronic components do not demand periodic adjustment. And since it really has no brain of its own, it just can't make its own mistakes. In fact, it can't make its own anything. It does only what it's told, nothing more and nothing less. Given a minimal amount of care and a decent operating environment, it should provide years of trouble-free, error-free service.

Of course, no one can say that computers never break down. Some components may indeed fail now and then, yet far more often a "computer is down" problem can be traced to human error. And while that may make the problem no less frustrating, it does make it much simpler to solve. Needless to say, an actual hardware failure may require the services of a skilled service person. However, an apparent failure may require nothing more than a moment's attention by the user.

Architecture of the PC

For better or worse, when IBM discovered all the PC gold that Apple had been happily mining for years, it jumped into the bit stream with all its marketing weight, leading at least some industry watchers to speculate whether the big blue elephant could learn to dance to the fast-paced rhythm of personal computing. Soon enough it was discovered that even if this corporate behemoth was no leader on the high-tech dance floor, it was at least a reasonable follower. The famous PC soon became a de facto industry standard, and was followed by the XT and the AT. The machines were for the most part upwardly compatible, and a legion of supporting manufacturers jumped in to support the IBM design, thanks to the company's policy of open architecture. Before long, "IBM compatible" was the password to success in the marketplace.

The open architecture policy had its good and bad points. Tremendous industry support helped IBM move a lot of machines out of its warehouses. But Big Blue's supporters were not long content to supply peripheral equipment, and a flourishing clone industry was soon supplying IBM-compatible computers, usually cheaper and often better than those of the leader.

While all this was happening, the first edition of this book was in production. The ink had hardly dried when, much to the author's delight, IBM decided to try a little something new: the IBM PS/2 system of computers was announced. The PC, XT, and AT systems were abandoned one by one, as was the system architecture they all shared, and which we now call ISA, or Industry Standard Architecture—because that's what it was. An all-new MCA, or Micro-Channel Architecture, system was announced for the PS/2 system. And for better or worse, it was incompatible with ISA. Given the tremendous number of suddenly obsolete machines out there, it was a good time for a book that showed how to keep them up and running.

But time passes, and PS/2 systems are showing up in more and more places. But not everywhere, for in the judgment of at least a few manufacturers, there are other ways to build a computer that may be better. In fact, a consortium of manufacturers, sometimes referred to as "the gang of nine," have announced their support for EISA, or Extended Industry Standard Architecture. No lightweights here, the original EISA gang comprised AST, Compaq, Epson, Hewlett-Packard, NEC, Olivetti, Tandy, Wyse, and Zenith. As this edition is being written, the first EISA machines are showing up, to generally favorable reviews. And not the least of their attractions is that they are IBM-compatible, that is, *ISA* IBM-compatible. That means anyone with an old PC, XT, or AT does not have to consign the whole works to the scrap heap in order to keep up with the high-tech times. Most, if not all, components from an ISA machine will fit and work happily in an EISA system, at least till they can be replaced by something newer. And for the purposes of getting through the other chapters of this book, most of the ISA information pertains as well to EISA systems.

Which brings us back to IBM. As noted, PS/2 (models 50 through 80) introduced the MCA system to the marketplace. The marketplace reacted, but with not quite the enthusiasm that IBM had expected. A lot of people were quite happy with ISA and saw no reason to jump ship in favor of the new line. Perhaps sensing they had missed their own boat, IBM introduced the PS/2 models 25, 30, 30 286, and as this edition goes to press, the 25 286. All support the old ISA system.

As a result of all this, we now have the following machines to contend with: the new PS/2 MCA (IBM models 50 through 80) and EISA (gang-of-nine) systems, the old ISA (PC, XT, AT) systems, and the new/old PS/2 ISA (IBM models 25 and 30 and their 286 versions).

The proliferation puts a bit of a strain on "IBM compatible," especially among IBM's own. For example, a hard disk drive taken from a model 30 286 will not fit in a model 70, and the memory modules from one model will not generally fit in another model. PS/2 ISA systems can borrow adapter cards from the older XT and AT systems, but not memory chips. Except for the model 25, IBM post-XT systems use a 64-byte CMOS section to store configuration data, but the configuration of the CMOS itself varies from ISA to MCA. The required battery may now be found on top of the speaker module, soldered to an adapter card, or concealed in a clock chip. There's a hard disk (IBM calls it a fixed disk) drive parameter table in the ROM BIOS module, but its starting address varies from one model to another.

All this works out nicely for anyone in the business of selling spare parts, but is not apt to please the manager of a large multisystem operation. So once again, there's a need for a unified source of information—not about discontinued models, but now about the differences between currently available systems.

Perhaps the first order of business is to briefly review the similarities and differences between the three systems now found in the computer marketplace. The pros and cons of the contending systems are given no attention here, except to point out that of all three systems, it has recently been proved that each one is superior to the others. Also ignored are the finer points of bus structure, interrupt requests, and such. No doubt all that means something to someone, but not to the reader who is trying to contend with a dead or dying system.

However, a few points on intersystem compatibility are briefly reviewed here, followed at last by that introduction to computer diagnostics. Refer to Chapter 6 for further details about the physical characteristics of ISA, MCA, and EISA system hardware.

ISA/MCA Compatibility Upward compatibility is good, but not great. That is, most external devices—displays, printers, modems, etc.—will work with both ISA and MCA systems. However, any adapter card used to interface an external device to either system will not work in the other system. However, a few potential compatibility problems are avoided, since PS/2 MCA systems contain built-in video, parallel, and serial connectors, together with the required circuitry.

EISA/MCA Compatibility The conditions just described apply as well to EISA and MCA systems.

ISA/EISA Compatibility One of the major attractions of the EISA standard is that it supports ISA system hardware; that is, an ISA adapter will work in an EISA system. At the physical heart of the EISA system is an adapter slot containing all the ISA connections, plus the additional connections required by EISA devices. The slots are designed so that an EISA device makes contact with all the pins. However, several barrier keys prevent an ISA device from fitting all the way into the slot, thus ensuring that it interfaces with the ISA pins only.

Since an ISA adapter fits an EISA slot, it follows that an EISA adapter will likewise fit an ISA slot. But that's the extent of the compatibility: an EISA adapter will not function in an ISA system, and the system itself may not function if an EISA card is installed in it. Although the latter's ISA pins may make good contact within the ISA slot, the adapter's EISA pins will be useless, or worse, may make contact with a nearby ISA connector. In either case, the adapter won't work, and there is always the possibility that the adapter and/or the system may be damaged.

A Preliminary Diagnostics Check List

When making a list of all the things that can go wrong, we mustn't forget to put ourselves at the head of the list. Next in line are various external devices, followed by internal devices with moving parts. After that, it's apt to be the display. Finally, when all else fails—or rather, when we have carefully verified that all else has *not* failed—only then can we begin to suspect the computer itself. So our prioritized Suspect List may look something like this:

1. Human error (oops! forgot to turn the power on, plugged the display into the wrong socket, etc.)
2. External device (printer out of paper, coffee spilled on diskette, etc.)
3. Internal moving parts (look to the diskette or hard-disk drives)
4. Display device (check the monochrome or color display)
5. The computer itself (most likely, a faulty chip)

As we proceed through the rest of this book, we'll try to point out the places where human error can be a factor. For example, one serviceman's log reports a panic-stricken client who insisted his system had failed overnight. As evidence, he cited the payroll program that had run flawlessly on Thursday evening. On Friday, the computer produced nothing but error messages.

"Fix it!" demanded the customer.

"It isn't broken," suggested the field engineer.

Much of the ensuing dialogue is unprintable, but it turned out that a magnetized paper clip had been used to affix a memo to the diskette, so the morning-shift operator would know just where to begin. At the client's demand (and at the usual hourly rate) the field engineer eventually proved that the now-missing paper clip had left its magnetic footprint on the diskette—in place of some data that had been there the night before. The client is now a little poorer and a lot wiser, or worse yet, vice versa. But the next time there's a system failure, we can be sure he'll check the "everything else" factor before reaching for the phone.

That's what much of this book is all about. It explains how to make a sound diagnosis of just about anything that can go wrong with a personal computer. Since most failures are easily traced, it is usually possible to identify the problem, locate the faulty device, and quickly remove and replace it—all this without losing the use of the entire system while the fault itself is being remedied.

Once we've accurately diagnosed the problem as originating on, say, a specific printed circuit board, one more question must be answered: Shall we investigate the various components on the board to try to find the one that has failed?

The definitive answer comes later. As we shall see, a failing memory chip can easily be removed and replaced; the job's not that much more difficult than performing the same operation on a light bulb. But a burned-out resistor hidden somewhere in the dense jungle of a logic circuit may be all but impossible to find or, once found, may be too difficult to remove without causing even more damage.

Nor should the nontechnical reader even try—for at least two very good reasons. First, doing so will surely void the warranty. Second, making such a repair is usually just too expensive. Even the best-equipped service facility will often prefer to replace an entire subsection, rather than spend countless hours—and dollars—trying to locate and replace the 50-cent part that failed. It's a lot more efficient and cost-effective to simply replace the entire unit—usually, a printed circuit board.

The Importance of PC Diagnostics

Even if you would prefer not to make any repairs yourself, your ability to make a well-informed diagnosis will go a very long way toward helping to get your computer back up and running quickly. Whatever diagnostics work you do yourself is more or less the PC equivalent of seeking medical help for a very specific ailment, as opposed to saying nothing and letting the doctor figure out what's wrong all by himself. In time, perhaps he will. But it's your time too, and no doubt you have better things to do with it. You might also wish to save your money and spend it on something more important, perhaps a little extra memory or a new display for your PC.

A BRIEF INTRODUCTION TO ERROR DETECTION

Fortunately, most personal computers are rather well equipped for the diagnosis, if not the cure, of most of their internal ailments. As a diagnostic aid, a problem within the system is usually accompanied by the screen display of a numeric error code. For example, the code 4E 301 indicates a problem with the rightmost "+" key. Knowing nothing more than this is, in itself, valuable. You are now able to make an informed decision about what to do. If you rarely use this key, you may decide that its repair may be put off until a more convenient time. On the other hand, trouble with a letter key will probably demand priority attention.

To many users, a displayed error code is easy to overlook and not very informative even when seen. However, letting the service person know that when you turn on your PC, this, or some other number, appears on the screen will help get your system in and out of the shop in the least possible time. Better yet, the number that appears may indicate that a trip to the shop isn't even needed. Now that you know what the trouble is, you may be able to fix it yourself in less time than it takes to have someone else do it.

By the end of this book, you will have discovered that the lion's share of the problems encountered can be fixed within a very short time. And for those that can't, you'll be able to make a more enlightened report than our friend with the paper clip did. And so with all of this in mind, it's time to begin learning how to become a PC diagnostician.

How Much Do We Need To Know?

There are those who will insist that in order to be trusted with a personal computer, the user must be on intimate terms with ROM and RAM, know how to multiply binary numbers mentally, and be fluent in at least three computer languages. And as for making modifications or repairs, nothing short of a degree in computer science will do.

This simply isn't true. One doesn't need to study brain surgery in order to cure a routine headache, nor is anyone expected to design an automobile before driving across town. In most such cases, the layperson's knowledge, coupled with a little common sense, is more than enough to tell when to take an aspirin and when (and how) to drive to the doctor's office to seek the help of a specialist. The same level of expertise that gets us through most minor mishaps will be more than enough to help us cope with computer problems.

Removing the Psychological Stumbling Block

Of course, headache remedies and automobiles have been with us for years, and we've long since come to take them for granted. In contrast, the personal computer is a comparatively recent addition to our lives, and there's still a reasonable amount of technological mystery surrounding it.

But the computer is not nearly as sophisticated as our very own brain, for whose immediate comfort we don't hesitate to take that pill. And not only does the computer have fewer moving parts than the family car, it also demands far less maintenance to keep it running dependably for years.

However, a personal computer does deserve at least a minimal amount of attention if it is to faithfully serve us over the years. Again comparing the computer to the car, we don't wait to see smoke coming from under the hood before changing the oil filter. So let's not wait for the microequivalent of an overheated engine before turning our attention to routine maintenance procedures.

The first part of Chapter 2 describes the routine preventive-maintenance procedures that will help keep your personal computer up and running. It will be assumed that your computer has already been put into service, is fully operational, and has no present malfunction. That being so, the material found in Chapter 2 will help you keep future trouble to a minimum, while that in Chapter 3 shows how to conduct regular routine diagnostics procedures. The remainder of the book describes the various components of the total PC system in some detail to help you whenever you encounter a problem that demands immediate attention.

Introduction to Computer Jargon

A fair amount of computer jargon will be encountered throughout this book, with most terms explained just before their official introduction in the text. In many cases, a term will seem to have been chosen simply because it conveys no useful information. In other cases, the word is one that may be easily confused with another word that means something entirely different. As a preview of things to come, here are a few samples of terms that will show up over and over again, both here and elsewhere.

Bits and Bytes. A *bit* (binary digit) represents the smallest possible storage unit used in a computer system. Each bit can represent either a binary 0 or a binary 1. The term *bit* should not be abbreviated as *b* or *B* for two reasons: the word itself is already an abbreviation, and its initial letter has more important things to do. For example, the term *byte* is used to describe a quantity of eight bits. This book follows the general engineering practice of using lowercase letters for units not named after people, so here byte is abbreviated as *b*.

Kilobytes and Kbytes. In most fields of engineering, the lowercase letter "k" (kilo) denotes 1,000. Thus, a frequency of, say, 15 kHz is understood to be 15,000 Hz (formerly 15,000 cycles per second).

Since computers deal in powers of two, the number closest to 1,000 is 2^{10} = 1,024. The numeric difference is trivial, so it's no great crime to borrow the letter "k" to describe this quantity too, as is in fact the case in the computer industry. However, when one wants to discuss both the frequency at which a display operates (in kHz) and its required video memory (in Kbytes), things can get mildly confusing.

This book tries to keep the confusion factor low by using the lowercase letter "k" *only* when the quantity is literally a multiple of 1,000. Thus, the horizontal frequency of a certain display may be represented as 15.432 kHz, that is, 15,432 Hz. Note there is *always* a space between the number and the unit symbol, and that *xx k* of anything is always *xx* thousand, literally.

On the other hand, when one has a computer with 640 Kbytes of system memory, this is not 640,000 bytes, but 640 × 1,024 bytes = 655,360 bytes. Where space or context does not permit spelling out *bytes*, the same quantity is represented as 640Kb (no space) to help make the distinction between k = 1,000 and K = 1,024.

Elsewhere, this distinction is not always carefully made, and the reader is left to guess what the quantity really is. Usually the context makes this clear, but sometimes it doesn't.

Megabytes and Mbytes. Here, an uppercase letter "M" (mega) means 1,000,000 (one million) to the engineer, but 2^{20} = 1,048,576 to the computer maven. Therefore, a hard disk with a capacity of 25Mb really has room for 26,214,400 bytes, while a 25-MHz crystal oscillator is crawling along at only 25,000,000 Hz.

PRELIMINARY PROBLEM-SOLVING SUGGESTIONS

If you have already discovered a problem and aren't sure how to proceed, then follow the appropriate instructions given below.

System Not Yet in Service

Follow the specific installation and setup instructions that accompany your system. If you are having difficulty installing some option or adapter, you may want to review the chapter in this book that discusses that particular component.

System Not Fully Operational

If some newly installed option does not operate properly in an otherwise-functioning computer, chances are the system needs to be reconfigured to take that option into account. System configuration is done in one of the following ways:

Computer type	System configuration is via
PC and XT	system board switches
AT	Diagnostics diskette
PS/2	configuration software on the Starter or Reference diskette
IBM-compatible PC	switches, configuration software embedded in ROM
EISA system	configuration software embedded in ROM

In addition to the above, some installable options contain switches and/or jumpers that must be set. The correct setting usually depends on the specific system in which the option is to be installed. Obviously, the instructions accompanying any new option will be the last word, but if these are missing, or written in a language that bears only a passing resemblance to English, then consult the appropriate chapter of this book for additional help.

System Malfunctioning

If, in the middle of a lengthy project (e.g., while working with a spreadsheet or a word processor), the entire keyboard suddenly quits functioning, this would certainly appear to be a serious malfunction. If the action—or worse, the inaction—is indeed the result of a malfunction, then routine preventive-maintenance procedures will be of no use. However, the odds in this case are overwhelmingly against an actual hardware failure. Chances are the program is just busy doing something important and doesn't want to be disturbed. More often than not, the cure is just a little patience. In a moment or two, or perhaps in a few minutes, your control of the keyboard will be restored and you may continue.

If you believe your personal computer is not operating properly because of an actual system failure, but are not yet sure of the precise location of the problem, Chapter 3 is probably the best place to start. But if you are not yet sure whether the problem is attributable to hardware or software, the following sections may be of some help.

Every now and then a software problem will cause a system crash. Although the phrase suggests metal fragments all over the place, it's the in-memory program that crashes, not the hardware itself. Though frustrating enough, the cure requires nothing more complicated than the system reboot described immediately below. The head crash is quite another matter, about which more in Chapter 9.

Boot and Reboot Procedure

A personal computer is said to boot itself on because when power is first applied, a small program is automatically loaded into memory. The small program loads a larger program, and the system pulls itself up by its own electronic bootstraps. Unfortunately, when some software goes awry, the system must be rebooted to restore normal operation. This is accomplished in one of two ways.

Warm Reboot. Holding down the Control and Alternate keys while pressing the Delete key is often sufficient to restart the system. The three-way key press is often abbreviated as Ctrl + Alt + Del. Since it's not necessary to turn the power off, the procedure is known as a warm reboot. Once the warm reboot has been accomplished, it's time to start all over again, but this time, try to avoid whatever it was that caused the crash in the first place. When working with finicky software, this is easier said than done—a strong argument for even more frequent backups when working with untried new software.

Cold Reboot. If the three-way key press has no effect, then it's necessary to turn the computer off, wait at least five seconds, and then turn it back on again.

With either a cold or warm reboot, you will a.) lose all data not saved prior to the crash and b.) learn to make those backups more often from now on.

After the boot/reboot, resumption of normal operation is your assurance that hardware repair is not required. But if normal operation is not restored, then it's time to turn to Chapter 3 for help in locating the problem area. But for now, let's assume that all's well and get on with an important first step in routine maintenance.

SETTING UP THE WORK AREA

A little careful attention to setting up the computer workspace will go a long way toward ensuring that your system will function properly for years without requiring more than a little preventive maintenance.

In many large corporations, the computer room looks like an intimidating environment. The machine and its attendants are behind glass, breathing specially filtered air, and the attendants are not permitted to even *think* about on-the-job food or drink.

Meanwhile, out in the regular office space, the personal computer shares its desk with an ash tray, coffee cup, and now and then a cheese danish. The area is an accident just waiting to happen; for although the smaller machine does not demand a rigorously controlled environment to ensure dependable operation, it probably does need a little more attention than it may be getting.

Some machines deteriorate gracefully, or at least gradually. For example, with a little routine neglect, the office typewriter slowly accumulates a layer of grime, and its letters become less and less crisp. It issues progressively more visible cries for attention. In contrast, the computer operates flawlessly—until one day when it doesn't operate at all. There is no transition period between "go" and "no go."

The great lawgiver Edsel Murphy has left us one of his many laws on computer failure: The probability of failure is inversely proportional to the amount of time in which the project must be completed. It's really quite a simple matter to verify the validity of this law—just ignore the rest of this book.

As a rule of thumb, if the operator is comfortable in the workspace, the computer will be too. In fact, on some counts the computer may be even less finicky than its human companion, since such amenities as ambient lighting and chair height are of no importance to it. However, food, drink, and good ventilation are vitally important, as is a reliable source of electric power.

Food, Drink, and Smoking Taboos

As for food and drink, it is their complete absence that is important. For as Murphy has also taught us, all liquids seek their own level, which is usually found somewhere inside the keyboard. In a similar manner, food crumbs are attracted by magnetic media, while cigarette ashes and smoke are irresistibly drawn toward diskette drives.

On a desktop, the coffee spill may be easily wiped up with a sponge; on an important stack of papers, some retyping will be required. But when the keyboard serves as the sponge, you can count on a trip to the service center, and perhaps a new keyboard.

So much for the good news. At some expense, one simply buys a new keyboard and remembers to go to the cafeteria on the next coffee break. But what happens when the spill flows over a diskette? At how much expense can a damaged diskette be replaced? While a new diskette costs only a few dollars, consider the thousands of dollars' worth of time and effort needed to replace the data that's had cream and sugar added.

Ventilation Requirements

Although the typical personal computer doesn't have any extraordinary ventilation requirements, remember that it is an electronic device and that some of its components generate a fair amount of heat. The computer should be placed in a reasonably clear work area, so that air circulation is not restricted or cut off. The low-level sound heard while the computer is on indicates that the internal fan is doing its job, drawing in fresh clean air to circulate through the system. Given unobstructed ventilation, the computer's metal cabinet will dissipate internal heat. Simply feeling the outside of the chassis is usually enough to assure you that all's well inside.

System Unit Ventilation. For proper ventilation, make sure there is a blank bracket covering the rear-panel access slot for each unoccupied adapter. Circulating air enters the system unit through the front panel slots and leaves through the exhaust fan at the rear, and there should be no other path by which air may enter or leave the system.

Display Ventilation. Avoid the temptation to use the top of the display unit as a convenient location for storing paperwork. The open grillwork there is not decorative: it allows warm air to rise out of the display, and if blocked by papers, the display interior may become too hot.

Power Requirements

For most routine PC setups, the familiar three-prong, grounded wall outlet at home or in the office should be more than sufficient to accommodate the needs of any personal computer. However, if the computer is to become the nucleus of an extensive work station, consisting of one or more printers, displays, and other computer-related devices, then the current-handling capacity of the electrical service should be verified before installing the equipment.

Chapter 5 should be consulted for specific information regarding electrical power considerations, including surge protectors and uninterruptible power supplies, as well as power-on and power-off procedures, and so on.

Static Electricity

Beyond electrical power considerations, careful attention should be given to the matter of static electricity. Anyone who has walked across a carpeted room on a dry day has discovered static electricity when reaching for a metal doorknob. A startling zap is felt at the fingertips. While certainly not enough for an electrocution, the electricity generated is more than enough for data demolition if it's the computer instead of the doorknob that receives the discharge. Now and then, the current discharge may even be great enough to destroy some component within the computer itself.

Antistatic Mats. It may be worthwhile to consider an antistatic mat for table and/or floor, especially in a low-humidity, carpeted area. A ten-second walk across a carpet can generate 20,000 to 30,000 volts of electrostatic energy, and discharging as few as 2,000 of these into your computer system can cause data loss.

Some mats drain off static electricity by means of an electrically conductive grid which is fusion-bonded to a vinyl base and attached to a ground cord. A shock-absorbing rug may dissipate static electricity into a conductive fabric that serves as backing for the rug's nylon exterior. A table mat works well in areas too small for a floor mat or rug, and it may offer added insurance, since rubber- or synthetic-soled shoes will electrically isolate the user from a floor mat, thus rendering it ineffective as a static drain-off. Touching the mat before switching on the computer—or after returning to an operating computer—effectively dissipates static. If static problems persist despite the use of mats, an antistatic spray may also prove useful.

Smoke and Water Damage

If your computer appears to have survived a fire in the building without visible damage, it should nevertheless be thoroughly checked out by a reputable service center before it is used again. The slightest trace of smoke-and-water grime on the outside is an almost certain indication that drive heads and other internal components need a thorough cleaning. Even if there are no external traces of damage, remove all doubt by making a careful inspection of all components. In most cases, a user's attempt to clean up this sort of damage will void any warranty that is in effect.

Service Contracts

For the reader who prefers outside help with service-related problems, IBM and other manufacturers offer a variety of service plans. However, it's a good idea to read through this book even if you prefer to leave your repairs to others. When things go wrong, it's possible to save a great deal of time, money, or both, just by being able to provide the service facility with a little extra information that will help them to diagnose and cure the problem.

2

PREVENTIVE AND CORRECTIVE MAINTENANCE

Maintenance of any complex system—electronic, mechanical, even human—may be divided into two categories: preventive and corrective. A little of the former goes a long way toward preventing a costly experience with the latter. But unfortunately, the tired old aphorism about an "ounce of prevention" is too often ignored. We put off seeing the dentist or oiling the engine until we feel the pain or see the smoke. By then the damage is done, and we try to remember to do better next time.

The personal computer is no exception to the laws of prevention and correction. However, the demands of preventive maintenance are quite modest: lubrication is never required, moving parts are at an absolute minimum, and nothing needs to be cleaned out after a certain number of bytes have passed through the system. But that does not mean preventive maintenance can be entirely ignored.

Preventive Maintenance Procedures

The trouble with routine preventive maintenance is that it's . . . well, it's just so *routine.* When everything is working properly, it's tempting to ignore it. Then one day we hear a funny little clicking noise and realize that our data has just gone up in smoke. Too late, we remember what we should have been doing all these months—spending a minimal amount of time on preventive maintenance to help avoid spending a longer time on corrective maintenance.

• **Preventive Maintenance Caution.** Since routine maintenance may involve moving or unplugging one or more components, make sure the power is turned off before proceeding. If any connector is plugged in or removed while power is on, there's a definite possibility of causing permanent damage to the computer. Also, remember to read all instructions concerning a given test before you actually run that test.

Keyboard

Assuming the keyboard is functioning properly, a little care will keep it working that way. A soft-bristle paintbrush will help remove dust buildup between the keys, or a small vacuum cleaner, such as the one seen in Figure 2.1, may be used for this purpose. Alternatively, a small compressed-air sprayer may be used to blow away dust, but be sure that it is aimed away

Figure 2.1. A vacuum cleaner designed for cleaning those difficult-to-reach areas. (#440 System Sweeper courtesy Microcomputer Accessories, Inc.)

Figure 2.2.   Keyboard detail, with two key caps removed to show captive springs.

from the diskette drives and the ventilation panel on the front of the system unit.

If that can of soda or cup of coffee gets spilled on the keyboard while the computer is in use, turn the machine off immediately and unplug the keyboard connector at the rear of the system unit. Move the keyboard away from the PC and remove all the key caps in the vicinity of the spill by gently prying up on either side of each cap. Make sure that the spring underneath is not damaged, or if removed, that it does not get lost. The key spring is shown in Figure 2.2. Do not try to remove the space bar on an IBM keyboard, as it's just about impossible to reconnect it properly.

The caps may be cleaned in warm soapy water, rinsed, and set aside to dry. Unfortunately, the keyboard housing will require much greater care. A combination of cotton swabs, denatured alcohol, and clean damp rags may be used to carefully clean up the sticky residue. After making sure that all components are cleaned, dried, and replaced, return the keyboard to the computer, plug it in, and test it.

Depending on the extent of the spill and the success of the cleanup, there may be no lasting aftereffects. However, if any liquid has managed to penetrate beyond the mechanical parts of the keyboard, one or more keys may eventually perform erratically or fail completely, in which case it will probably be necessary to replace the entire keyboard.

Display Screen

Because of static buildup, the screen on any display attracts and holds a fair share of grime and dust particles. Here, a clean damp cloth and glass cleaner or an antistatic screen-cleaning solution may be used. To avoid further static buildup, wipe the screen gently and slowly, making sure the computer is off while doing so. Also make sure that all cleaning solutions are kept well away from the diskette drives.

Diskette Drive

Just like the heads on an audio tape recorder, those in a diskette drive come into direct contact with the recorded medium. In time, a residue of magnetic oxide may accumulate on the head, which will then need to be cleaned in order to maintain correct operation.

Since the drive heads are not readily accessible without disassembling the system, a head-cleaning diskette may be used for this purpose. This

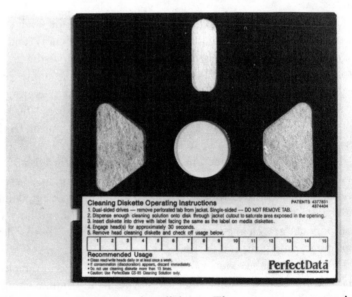

Figure 2.3. Head-cleaning diskette. The customary magnetic medium is replaced here by an absorbent cloth disk.

diskette superficially resembles the conventional data diskette, except that there are large cutout slots on one side of the jacket, as seen in Figure 2.3. The diskette itself is made of a porous, nonmagnetic material, and the user pours a cleaning solution onto the area exposed by the cutouts. For use with a double-sided drive, a cutout tab on the opposite side of the diskette jacket should be removed so that both heads are cleaned. Once the tab has been removed, do not use the cleaning diskette in a single-sided drive, since the moistened diskette will clog the pressure pad which takes the place of the second head inside the drive mechanism.

As another exception to a rule, the computer must be on in order to use the cleaning diskette for preventive maintenance. Place the diskette in the drive in the usual manner and type any command that will attempt to read the diskette—for example, DIR from DOS or FILES from BASIC. Of course, an error message will be seen on screen, but while the computer searches the diskette for useful information, the diskette supplies the head with a good cleaning instead of with data. Repeat the process until the heads have been cleaned for about 30 seconds.

A head-cleaning solvent works by dissolving and washing away any magnetic oxide particles that have become attached to the head and are thereby interfering with read/write operations. Therefore, if a solvent-saturated head-cleaning diskette is used, do not insert a regular data diskette until sufficient time has passed for the solvent to evaporate completely. (Check to see if the head-cleaning diskette is dry.) If the drive head is still wet when a data diskette is inserted, it will partially wipe the data right off the diskette and again foul the head with magnetic oxide. Although the head may be recleaned, the diskette is permanently ruined—and, of course, the data is gone forever.

Diskettes

The diskette is a physically delicate medium, far more fragile than, say, a sound-recording cassette tape. To illustrate just how sensitive the surface magnetic coating is, consider that a 360Kb double-sided diskette must reliably store and retrieve 1,474,560 data bits in the 40 concentric tracks on each side of the diskette.

Without going any farther, it should be clear that each recorded data bit occupies a very small area of the total diskette surface. By comparison, as Figure 2.4 illustrates, a minute dust particle or the smudge of a misplaced fingerprint is a huge obstacle to be negotiated by the disk drive's read/write mechanism. In many cases, the contaminated area becomes useless, which

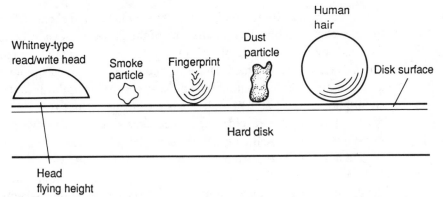

Figure 2.4.   The relative size of assorted diskette contaminants. Even the faintest fingerprint can cause data loss, since the read/write head tends to skip over the soiled area.

is inconvenient on a new diskette, and disastrous on one that already contains important data.

A word—or these few paragraphs—to the wise should be sufficient: Treat the diskette with extreme care. Like any other magnetic storage medium, it must be kept well away from any object or device, other than a diskette drive, that may produce a magnetic field. Otherwise, the interfering magnetic field may write its own data to the diskette, thereby replacing useful information. Needless to say, the new "information" will be worse than useless. Magnetic memo and copy holders, magnetized scissors and paper clips, and the magnets inside many telephones are all potential troublemakers.

When the diskette is handled by the user, the most critical area is, of course, in the vicinity of the head-access slot, which may be seen in Figure 2.5. Here a small portion of the diskette's magnetic surface is exposed so that the read/write head can make contact with the magnetic oxide. When handling the diskette, take care not to touch this area, and when a 5.25-inch diskette is not in use, take the time to return it to its cardboard jacket, making sure the head-access slot area is protected by the jacket.

On a 1.2Mb high-capacity diskette, the data density is of course even greater, as is the potential for data loss because of a casually placed fingerprint. By contrast, the 3.5-inch 720Kb diskette also seen in Figure 2.5 is physically more robust, with the entire diskette surface protected by the plastic cartridge. A sliding door exposes the surface only as the diskette is placed in the drive system.

Further specifications for various diskette media are given in Chapter 8.

Figure 2.5 5.25-inch and 3.50-inch diskettes. Keep stray fingers and other contaminants well away from the head-access slot on the 5.25-inch diskette. On the 3.50-inch diskette, the slot is protected by a sliding metal cover (shown open in the illustration).

Hard Disk Drives

On a hard disk drive system, the magnetic medium is placed within a sealed enclosure, thus protecting it against outside contaminants. The drive system requires no routine maintenance.

System Unit and Adapters

Here the rule is, "If it's not broken, don't fix it." In other words, routine maintenance does not require the removal of the system unit's metal cover. The diskette drives may be maintained from outside the system, and there are no internal parts that require routine attention.

Of course, for every rule there is the exception. If some part of the complete system is performing erratically or not at all, the problem might be traced to a loose connection. This could be at one of the connector plugs at the back of the chassis, or it's possible that one of the plug-in adapters inside is not seated firmly in its slot. This sort of problem is not likely to occur during the course of normal operations. However, if the computer has recently been modified or moved, it's a good idea to make a routine check of all connections.

Before checking any adapter, turn the power off and unplug all connecting cables, making careful note of which cable goes to which adapter, especially in those cases where it's physically possible to connect the same cable to more than one adapter connector. For example, make sure the monochrome display cable will be replugged into the monochrome adapter.

Removing the Cover. To remove the system unit cover, first unplug the AC power cord (as a safety precaution) and then remove the five (two, on early-model PCs) cover-mounting screws on the rear panel. If your display sits on top of the system unit, unplug and remove it. The keyboard may also have to be moved to one side. When removing an AT or PS/2 cover, also make sure the key lock is in its unlocked position, freeing the cover for removal.

Checking the Adapters. Once the cover is removed, the various plug-in adapters are accessible for checking. Note that in this chapter the specific function of each adapter, and of the system board itself, is not discussed. At this point, all that is called for is a routine inspection of each adapter's physical placement in its socket. For specific details about any adapter, consult the appropriate chapter later in this book.

To remove an adapter, first disconnect any cable that leads to it from an external device. Then remove the screw that fastens the adapter bracket to the system-unit chassis on pre-PS/2 systems. Take care that this screw does not fall onto the system board. When it does so anyway, carefully retrieve it with a pair of long-nosed pliers, not a magnet or magnetized screwdriver. Unless you are very lucky, the magnet will not only fetch the screw but will also demolish one or more nearby components.

With the screw removed and placed safely out of the way, work the adapter loose from its slot. As it comes free, carefully disconnect any cables leading to internal devices. When the adapter is removed from the system, examine the metallic prongs that make contact with the slot on the system board. If there is any doubt about the cleanliness of the prongs, clean them with a pencil eraser or a contact cleaner. Do this cleaning well away from the system unit, and then carefully replace the adapter in its slot, making sure it is seated firmly. If you disconnected any internal cables, make sure you reconnect them. Then replace the screw that holds the adapter in place, and repeat the procedure for the other adapters. Next, replace the system unit's metal cover. Finally, reinstall all cable connectors at the rear of the system unit, again making sure that each is connected to the proper adapter.

Cable and Adapter Connectors

In most cases, plugs and sockets that remain connected do not need to be separated for routine cleaning of their metal contacts. However, the contacts on any plug, socket, or adapter card that has not been in regular use may acquire a film of grime, especially if it has been long exposed to the surrounding environment. In such cases, a commercially available contact cleaner may be sprayed onto the contacts before the device is put into service.

Impact Printers

Since the PC is compatible with a wide variety of printers, the instructions given here must be limited to general suggestions, plus the obvious: Carefully read and follow the instructions for cleaning your printer that are found in the printer's guide to operations or user's manual.

Depending on the paper stock used by the printer, a certain amount of paper fragments may settle inside the printer housing. This area should be periodically vacuumed, using a small vacuum cleaner such as the one seen in Figure 2.1. Use a soft brush to help loosen dirt particles in the path of the vacuum cleaner. Before vacuuming, remove the printer's ribbon to prevent its being drawn into the vacuum.

Cleaning the Printer Cover. Clean the printer's outer cover with a damp cloth and mild soap. For stubborn ink stains on but not inside the cover, use a commercially available mechanic's hand cleaner.

Choosing Printer Ribbons. For the impact printer which uses a replaceable ribbon cartridge, there are usually two types of cartridges available. The carbon ribbon offers highest-quality, crisp character printing by transferring carbon from the ribbon to the paper. After one or two passes in each direction, the cartridge must be replaced. The inked fabric ribbon has a longer useful life than the carbon ribbon, achieved at the cost of some loss of crispness.

Often a specific characteristic of a ribbon is identified by a word or phrase that is either uninformative or, even worse, somewhat misleading—as, for example, describing as "multistrike" a ribbon that may not actually be struck as many times as a fabric ribbon. Generally speaking, ribbons that offer crisp, well-defined printing similar to that obtained on a carbon typewriter ribbon are described as Mylar-coated, film, or multistrike. Ribbons described as nylon, fabric, or inked offer less crispness but are longer lasting.

For purposes of routine maintenance, it is well to remember that both Mylar and nylon ribbons leave a distinctive residue behind them, the first in the form of minute carbon particles and the other in the form of ink stains. To clean either type of residue from the platen (the hard-rubber cylinder in some printers around which the paper travels) use a commercially available platen cleaner. Do not use alcohol to clean the platen or any plastic parts. Doing so may deform the component thus cleaned.

Cleaning the Print Head. After extended use, a coating of grime may build up on the print head of a thermal-transfer printer, with a resulting deterioration in print quality. For some printers, a special print-head-cleaning cartridge is available. Remove the regular ribbon, install the cleaning cartridge in its place, and follow the specific cleaning procedure for your printer. Then put the ribbon back in place and verify that print quality is again satisfactory. If it is not, then the print head itself, or some other component, may need to be replaced.

Laser Printers

In addition to the general cleaning requirements described above, there are a few areas unique to the laser printer that should be cleaned as part of a routine maintenance procedure. Remember that some areas inside the laser printer get quite hot, so try to give the printer time to cool down before scheduling routine cleaning.

The procedures given here are based on the components found in a Hewlett-Packard LaserJet II, and the descriptions may need to be modified for other laser printers. As elsewhere, the user's manual should be consulted for specific system-cleaning details.

Transfer Corona Wire. This very fine wire is found in a metal channel that runs the entire width of the paper feed path inside the printer. There are usually several diagonal filament wires that run across the top of the channel. These wires should be cleaned carefully with a cotton swab dipped in alcohol until all dirt is removed. As elsewhere, make sure the alcohol does not make contact with any plastic elements.

Transfer and Paper Feed Guides. These areas should be wiped off with a clean cloth dampened with water (not alcohol). Refer to your user's manual for illustrations of the specific areas that need attention.

The Fixing-Roller Cleaner. The printer's fixing roller rotates under a long removable cleaning bar with a self-cleaning pad attached to it. As the roller rotates, the pad clears away debris. A new pad is usually included with the toner cartridge described below.

If black spots begin appearing on your paper, there may be some debris on the roller that has not been wiped away by the pad on the cleaning bar. If so, remove the bar and examine the roller for black spots. If any are seen, try to remove them by wiping the roller with a new cleaning bar, which should have a smaller disposable pad at one end. Be very careful. The fixing roller is an integral part of the printer, and if it is damaged it will have to be replaced.

Toner Cartridge. Just as the conventional printer ribbon needs to be replaced at regular intervals, the laser printer's toner supply must be replenished from time to time. In most cases, a front panel readout will advise with a "TONER LOW" or similar display. However, this is just a warning that the supply is running out: there is no need to actually replace the toner cartridge until the print quality begins to deteriorate. The first visible symptom may be a series of white streaks appearing on your printed sheets. As a temporary fix, remove the toner cartridge, tilt it back and forth a few times to redistribute the remaining toner, and reinsert it in the printer. The cartridge should now be good for another 100 or so pages.

Primary Corona Wire. In addition to the transfer corona wire which is part of the printer itself, the toner cartridge contains its own *primary corona wire.* The wire is not exposed to the surrounding environment and should not need routine cleaning. However, if black streaks appear on your paper, clean the corona wire using a wire-cleaning brush, usually supplied with the printer.

Print Density. On most laser printers, a *print density* control allows the relative blackness of the printed characters to be adjusted. At one extreme setting, characters may take on a heavy look; at the other, solid black areas may not be completely filled in. To conserve toner, try lightening the print density until characters are too light, then increase it slightly to print a good crisp black character with no unfilled areas.

Note that the markings on the control are not always consistent with common sense: the Hewlett-Packard LaserJet II control is labeled 1 through 9, with 1 as the darkest setting.

Corrective Maintenance Procedures

In the next chapter we begin our examination of the various components that make up a typical personal computer. As we shall soon discover, many maintenance problems may be resolved by the user with little or no difficulty.

Some problems will almost fix themselves, or at least will be so easily solved that you'll find it far simpler to take care of them yourself rather than take the system to an authorized service center. As an obvious example, a problem caused by an improperly connected plug will vanish if all connectors are unplugged prior to shipping the system out for servicing. At the service center, the staff will reassemble the system properly, discover no problem, and return it to you. Worse yet, only an educated guess can be made as to what the problem may have been in the first place. You may be left worrying that your PC has a mysterious problem so exotic that it managed to elude even the trained specialist, when all along the mystery is only over which cable had the loose connection.

In fact, since the overwhelming majority of system errors may be easily traced and remedied on the spot, a trip to a repair shop should be considered only as a last resort. Of course, if you are sure that the problem is indeed due to an actual system failure, then it is probably time to take that trip.

Your level of expertise and the specific part that has failed will have much to do with whether you can make the repair yourself. As noted in Chapter 1, replacing a plug-in memory chip is easy and inexpensive, and it's far more economical—in terms of both time and money—to do the job yourself. However, when going further, remember the precaution about attempting any repair that might void a warranty. Also bear in mind that some repair work may be physically dangerous, such as those repairs that would require opening the display cabinet.

While opening the display cabinet can be dangerous, every PC owner will sooner or later want to open the system unit, if only to get a better feel for what's inside. This need be no more intimidating than having a look under the hood of your automobile. You may not care to change the oil or replace a spark plug, but at least you'll know where to find these items.

Of course, even the least adventurous tinkerer won't object to adjusting the car's radio or air conditioning, or even to filling the tank every now and then. Such tasks are hardly considered maintenance at all; they're just part of keeping the vehicle up and running. And so it is with the PC. Within reason you may keep this vehicle up and running indefinitely with no more outside help than consulting the appropriate chapter in this book.

Which chapter is appropriate? That, of course, depends on the nature of the problem encountered. Some problems have an obvious source, and some don't. For example, when pressing a key produces no visible result, the problem may lie with the keyboard or with the display. Or some other factor may be adversely influencing both devices.

General Problem-Isolation Suggestions

Although the rest of this book will help identify and solve many computer problems, a few suggestions made here may make it a bit easier to clarify the actual source of the trouble. Then if more help is needed, turn to the appropriate chapter to continue.

Hardware Problems. A little experimentation will often go a long way toward localizing a hardware problem. Turn up the brightness and/or contrast controls on the display. If nothing happens, the display probably needs attention. Quickly press any key more than fifteen times. If a warning beep is heard, that's an indication your key presses are being received. Pressing Ctrl + Alt + Del should reboot the system, which is another indication that the keyboard works.

If the DOS A> or C> prompt is seen (or if it is not seen and you think it should be), type a few random characters and press the Enter key. If the drive's in-use light comes on, that's an indication your keystrokes were understood to be the name of a program on a diskette in the drive. Although the program doesn't exist, it appears as though the keyboard and the diskette drive system are in order. If the drive's in-use light does not come on, then the problem probably does lie somewhere between the keyboard and the drive, and the display may not be at fault.

Of course, none of these techniques are definitive tests. If the device passes the test, it obviously works. But if it doesn't, it may be because of some other factor. In some cases, a unique keystroke combination will cause the software to lock up the system. What may have happened is that the computer has been instructed to perform some never-ending chore—one which cannot be interrupted by the keyboard and which does not produce a screen display. While the computer works away behind the scenes, it appears to be dead. The only cure is to turn it off, wait five seconds, and turn it back on again. If this clears up the problem, then the computer itself is not at fault.

Software Problems. Not much can be said here about software corrective maintenance, which usually means isolating a programming bug and then rewriting the software to get rid of it. Many companies issue periodic software updates, sometimes to offer an additional feature, sometimes to debug an old feature that doesn't work properly. The user's first line of defense is to verify that a problem is indeed software-related, and then to hope the manufacturer has already issued an update.

If a problem is clearly a function of some commercially available software, then it's time to get in touch with the manufacturer. Otherwise, consult the Software Error Message section of Chapter 3 (page 73) for some general suggestions on getting to the bottom of such problems.

3

SYSTEM DIAGNOSTICS

Diagnostic procedures may be divided into three separate categories, each of which will be discussed in detail in this chapter, following a discussion of modification considerations.

System Modification Considerations

When an IBM or compatible personal computer is modified—for example, by changing a display, adding a new component or adding memory—the system must be reconfigured so that the new component is properly tested during the routine diagnostics procedures (described in this chapter) and properly used during routine computer operations.

If you have just made a modification, reconfigure your system before continuing with this chapter. System configuration is described in Chapter 6, with supplementary instructions found in the chapter associated with each device that is added to, or removed from, the system.

• **Power-On Caution.** If you are about to turn on the power after a modification or reconfiguration—especially one that involves the display—be particularly attentive to unusual sounds and screen displays. In the case of either, turn the power off immediately. A high-pitched whistle or an erratic screen display could indicate a condition that will cause permanent damage to the display. If you have any doubts about the installation of your display, read Chapter 10 before continuing.

Diagnostic Categories

There are three diagnostic categories discussed in this chapter:

1. The POST (Power-On Self-Test) procedure
2. Routine diagnostics
3. Troubleshooting diagnostics

Each of these diagnostic categories describes procedures that will help you keep your personal computer up and running.

The POST Procedure

Every time the power switch is turned on, the computer automatically begins the diagnostic procedure known as POST, or *Power-On Self-Test*, in which various system components are tested. If POST discovers a problem, a message is issued to the user. This message may be an on-screen display, a series of beeps, or both, as indicated here.

Error code	a two- to five-digit number
Error message	a brief message in English (more or less) that describes the problem
Beep code	a series of beeps

POST includes an examination of all memory, so the duration of the test varies depending on how much memory is installed. However, POST does not check all installed options, such as printers, modems, communications adapters, and the math coprocessor. Some of these devices may be checked with a diagnostics diskette, as described later in this chapter.

Note: For ISA computers, IBM supplies very little routine information about POST, and even less for PS/2 systems, where the procedure is only referred to as an "internal self-test."

POST Procedures

The system tests within POST are executed in the order given here. Unfamiliar terms in this section may safely be ignored, as they are presented here mostly for the sake of future reference.

Test 1: Basic System. This test verifies that the system's MPU (microprocessor unit) is operating properly. It also tests the segment of memory containing the POST program itself, part of the system board memory, and the system buses (that is, the conductors used for transmitting signals or power throughout the system).

Test 2: Extended System. The ROM BASIC interpreter, if one exists, and the system timer are checked.

Test 3: Display. The memory on the default display adapter and the video signals which drive the display are tested. If a secondary display is installed in the system, it is not checked during the POST procedure.

Test 4: Memory. The POST procedure tests all memory by writing data, then reading it back and checking for errors. On XT, AT, and PS/2 systems, the number in the upper left-hand corner of the screen indicates the amount of memory that has been checked so far. During the POST memory-write test the number slowly increases, up to the total installed memory. This is followed by the somewhat faster memory-read test, during which the display sequence is repeated. On PS/2 MCA systems, (models 50 through 80), only one display sequence is seen.

Test 5: Keyboard. The keyboard interface is checked and then the keyboard itself is examined for stuck keys.

Test 6: Cassette Data Wrap. The cassette recorder interface is checked (PC only).

Test 7: Drive. The test determines whether a disk drive is installed in the system. If so, the drive status is checked. If not, the test is bypassed.

Additional MCA System Tests During POST

In MCA systems (i.e., PS/2 models 50 through 80), the POS (Programmable Option Select) feature enables the system board to recognize and configure various adapter cards whenever these are installed. If such a card is present in the system, a ROM module on the card may add an additional test to the POST procedure.

Error Messages During POST

If an error is encountered during any part of the POST procedure, one of the actions described below and/or listed in Table 3.1 will occur. Note that a failure during tests 1 or 2 halts the system. This is because an error at either of these early stages is too severe to permit reliable system operation.

Errors encountered during tests 3 through 7 do not halt the POST, since it may still be possible to operate the rest of the system despite the error.

Test 1: Basic System Error. The system halts with no visible display and no beep, although the cursor may be seen.

Test 2: Extended System Error. The system emits one long beep followed by one short beep, and execution of the POST halts.

Test 3: Display Error. The system emits one long beep followed by two short beeps, and the POST continues with the next test.

Test 4: Memory Error. The screen displays a numeric error code. Error codes are described in detail later in this chapter. Additional information on memory-related errors is found in Chapter 7.

Test 5: Keyboard Error. A numeric error code is displayed on screen. Additional information on keyboard-related errors is found in Chapter 10.

Test 6: Cassette Data Wrap Error. The numeric error code 131 is displayed on screen, and POST continues with the next test.

Test 7: Drive Error. The numeric error code 601, 1780, or 1781 is displayed on screen. Drive-related errors are discussed in Chapter 8 and 9.

During the POST procedure, any beep code other than a single short beep indicates that a problem exists. Keep in mind that no beep at all is also an indication of an error. As indicated in Table 3.1, the missing beep may indicate a power problem, or simply a disconnected or inoperative speaker. Again, diagnostics testing is indicated.

A beep code that indicates a display problem may be verified by observing the screen display itself. However, if the beep code indicates some other

Table 3.1 POST Audio Error Signals

Audio (beeps)	Video display	Problem area	refer to Chapter
none	none	power	5
none	cursor only	power	5
none	DOS prompt	speaker defective	6
•	DOS prompt	none; normal startup	
•	PC BASIC screen	diskette	8
• —	none	monitor	11
• •	incorrect or blank	monitor	11
• •	an error code	refer to Table 3.5	
repeating short beeps	305 error code	keyboard fuse	10
repeating short beeps	anything else	power	5
continuous beep		power	5
— •		system board	6
— • •		monitor	11
— • • •		monitor	11

   • = short beep
   — = long beep

problem, the nature of the video display is unimportant, since the beep code takes precedence.

POST Video Error Code

If a beep code is heard during POST, it may be accompanied by the video display of an error code number. Quickly jot down any such number that appears, since it may be erased by the next screen display.

A POST Error Simulation

To familiarize yourself with what might happen if POST encounters an error, simulate one by holding down any key during the POST interval. For example, depress the C key to produce the following POST error display, accompanied by two beeps:

```
2E 301
```

The hexadecimal 2E is the scan code for the bottom-row third letter key (C or c), and the number 301 is the keyboard error code. Therefore, the message identifies the stuck key, and that the error is related to the keyboard.

If the keyboard were unplugged from the system unit, or otherwise nonoperational, only the keyboard error message—301—would be seen. If either of these error codes is seen during POST, consult Chapter 10 for further details, including an explanation of the scan code.

POST Summary

Assuming POST uncovers no problem serious enough to halt the system, the following sequence is observed at its conclusion:

1. A short single beep is heard at the completion of POST. (Note that on some IBM-compatible systems, *two* beeps are heard.)
2. A blinking cursor is seen. On PS/2 systems in which the password function is enabled, a key symbol is seen in place of the blinking cursor, and you must enter your password in order to continue. For further details, see the Password section in Chapter 6.
3. One of the displays shown in Figure 3.1 appears on screen.

Note that the latter two displays in Figure 3.1 do not indicate a drive-related POST error. Such an error would have simply displayed the error code number 601 before the POST concluded. The incorrect displays seen in Figure 3.1 indicate that although POST encountered no error during its drive test, some other problem exists, as indicated by the displayed message. For example, if the system goes into the Cassette BASIC mode despite the presence of a valid DOS diskette in the A drive, refer to Chapter 8 for further assistance before continuing here.

PS/2 Note. The screen display shown in Figure 3.2 will appear at the successful completion of POST, if the system is not configured to boot from the hard disk and there is no diskette in drive A. The display prompts you to insert a DOS diskette in drive A and then press the F1 function key. If you simply press the F1 key without inserting a DOS diskette in the drive, the system goes into the Cassette BASIC mode (so-called even though the option to save on cassette was discontinued long before the PS/2 was introduced). However, if this screen display is preceded by a three-digit number in the upper left-hand corner of the screen, just below the xxxxx KB OK legend, then refer to the Configuration Problem paragraphs in the POST Failure section immediately following.

Screen Display Meaning

`A>`
        A diskette containing the operating system is properly installed in the default drive.

`C>`
        The hard disk is the default drive.

The DOS shell menu
        Your system is configured to use the DOS shell feature (described in Chapter 4).

`Current date is` (*current date*)
`Enter new date (mm-dd-yy):`
        An AUTOEXEC.BAT file is not present on the diskette in drive A or on hard disk drive C. You must therefore enter the date, or simply press Enter if the displayed date is correct. The date prompt is followed by:

`Current time is` (*current time*)
`Enter new time:`
        Enter correct time or press Enter if the displayed time is correct. The DOS prompt should now appear on screen.

Some other valid message
        An AUTOEXEC.BAT file is present on the diskette in drive A or on hard disk drive C. A line in this file is automatically executing the program that creates the displayed message. For the purposes of this chapter, exit the program and return to the DOS prompt. See Chapter 4 for information about batch files.

`The IBM Personal Computer Basic`
`Version C1.00 Copyright IBM Corp 1981`
`xxxx Bytes free`
`Ok`
        System is not set up for hard disk default and either there is no diskette in drive A or the drive door has been left open. The PC is now in the Cassette BASIC mode. Note that in BASIC, the function key directory appears at the bottom of the screen display.

`Non-System disk or disk error`
`Replace and strike any key when ready`
        The diskette in drive A is not a valid DOS system diskette.

Figure 3.1.   Screen displays at the successful completion of the POST procedure.

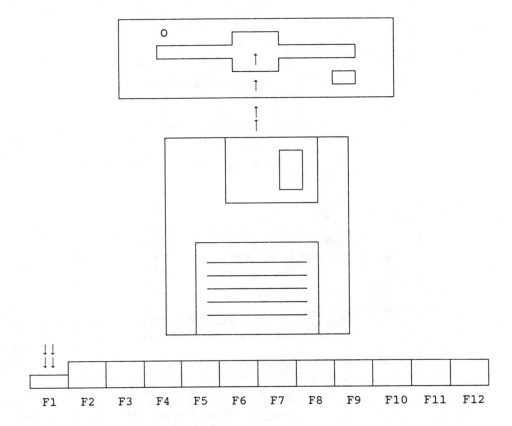

Figure 3.2. PS/2 screen display prompts user to insert diskette in drive and press function key F1 if system is not configured to boot from a hard disk and there is no diskette in drive A.

POST Failure

If the on-screen display is something other than what has been described so far, then either system configuration or troubleshooting diagnostics are required. Typically, the screen will display a brief error message indicating the nature of the problem, or a three-digit error code will be seen. A beep code other than a single beep is also heard. Error messages, error codes, and beep codes are all described below. If any of these indications of an error is noted, then take the appropriate action, as described here.

Configuration Problem. A system configuration error is indicated by a three-digit number $16n$ (n = 1 to 9) displayed on the screen, possibly preceded by another number which identifies the specific area in which configuration is required. This display is most often seen when some new device has been added to the system, or when a previously installed device has been removed (a diskette drive, for example). In either case, the system must be reconfigured to take the change into account. Refer to Chapter 6 for the appropriate configuration instructions (page 169).

MCA System Note. If necessary, it may be possible to run the system despite the configuration problem. Again using a diskette drive as the example, if drive A is disconnected, the system will display a 601 (diskette drive) error code, followed by a 162 (configuration) error code. Or, if drive A is operational and there is some other configuration problem, a 16x error code will be displayed. On some systems this is accompanied by a graphics symbol (a circled "OK" with a backslash through it), followed by an arrow pointing to an IBM manual.

In either case, press the F1 function key and after a short delay the DOS C> prompt should be seen (assuming a hard disk drive is properly installed). You may now operate the computer as before, except of course for the component causing the unresolved error. However, it would be better to take one of the following actions:

1. Investigate the source of the error by consulting the Troubleshooting Diagnostics section of this chapter (page 73)
2. Configure the system, as described in Chapter 6 (page 178).

Other POST Failures. In the event of any indication of failure other than the 16n configuration error code, refer to the Troubleshooting Diagnostics section of this chapter (page 73) and then to the chapter covering the device that has failed.

On PS/2 systems which use a replaceable real-time clock module (30 286 and 65 SX), a defective module may create an endless memory-check loop during POST, a system lockup with total memory displayed on screen, or some other indication that POST has failed. Make sure the clock module is properly seated and if the trouble persists, the module should be replaced and the system reconfigured. See the Configuration After Battery Failure section of Chapter 6 (page 177) for details about the clock module.

ROUTINE DIAGNOSTICS

As an important supplement to the POST procedure described above, a more extensive set of routine diagnostic procedures is used to

Verify system configuration

Change the system configuration (AT and PS/2)

Format a diskette for diagnostics use only

Copy the diagnostics or Starter/Reference diskette

Prepare the system for moving (required for hard disks lacking an automatic head-parking utility)

Run a series of diagnostics tests

To perform these procedures, routine diagnostic programs are supplied with every IBM personal computer. As the original PC gave way first to the XT, then the AT, and more recently to the PS/2 series of computers, these procedures have of course been modified to keep pace with each new system. Nevertheless, the basic diagnostic structure remains essentially the same. To the user, the most noticeable differences are in nomenclature, screen displays, and actual location of the diagnostic programs.

The procedures are described here in the order in which they appear as choices or options in the various screen menu displays. This is not necessarily the order in which you will want to use them, and in at least a few cases you *must* perform, say, Option 2 before Option 0. Therefore, it's a good idea to read this section in its entirety before doing any actual hands-on work.

For pre-PS/2 systems, the term *diagnostics* is used to describe both the test programs themselves and the diskette on which they are found. For PS/2 systems, the term has been gradually phased out (user-unfriendly?) in favor of *testing*. The diagnostic/testing programs may be found in the following places:

Computer	Program location
PC, XT, AT	A special diagnostics diskette is found in back of the GTO (*Guide to Operations*) manual.
PS/2	Testing procedures are an integral part of the Starter or Reference diskette. See the Main Menu description later in this chapter for further details.

Diagnostics Nomenclature

A few terms that will be used in the following discussion are given brief definitions here.

Scratch Diskette. During the diskette drive test procedure, you will need a scratch diskette for each drive to be tested. A scratch diskette is defined as any diskette whose present contents need not be saved. Before assigning any diskette to this category, make *sure* there is nothing on it that you really didn't mean to destroy.

Diskette Media. In the period between the introduction of the first PC and the last AT, both the diagnostics diskette and the GTO were periodically revised to incorporate the latest system modifications. Therefore, you may find some variance between the general discussion given here and the more system-specific instructions found on your own diskette and/or in your GTO manual.

The diagnostics program uses the following terms to describe various drive and/or diskette configurations:

5.25-inch media
    Single Sided   single-sided 160Kb drive/diskette
    Double Sided   double-sided 320Kb or 360Kb drive/diskette
    High Capacity   double-sided 1.2Mb drive/diskette
3.5-inch media   listed according to capacity (720Kb or 1.44Mb)

Note that although a high-capacity system is also double-sided, the specific "double-sided" nomenclature refers only to 320Kb and 360Kb systems.

When using diagnostics diskette version 2.00 or greater with a PC or XT, each installed option will be preceded by the letter S or E to indicate the listed device is installed in the system unit (S) or in an expansion unit (E).

• **Diagnostics Diskette Caution.** There are several versions of ISA system diagnostics diskettes. The diskette labeled "Diagnostics" is for use with the IBM PC and XT, while the diskette labeled "Diagnostics for IBM Personal Computer AT" is for use with the AT. A more recent diagnostics diskette (version 2.04) was labeled for use with both the AT and the XT model 286 only.

Although these diskettes are alike in concept, they are not identical, so make sure each is used only with the intended system. If the wrong diagnostics diskette is used, many of the test procedures will be invalid. Furthermore, hard disk data may be destroyed if the wrong diagnostics diskette is used to prepare the drive for relocation. For further details, see the Relocation Notes section in Chapter 9 (page 366).

Supplementary Diagnostics Diskettes

Of course, any version of the diagnostics diskette can only test devices that were available prior to the release of that diskette. Therefore, certain IBM accessory devices may come with a diagnostics diskette which includes all the old diagnostics programs, plus additional diagnostics for the new device.

Other devices are supplied with a diskette containing a diagnostics program just for the device itself. The diagnostics program(s) on such a diskette should be merged with the regular diagnostics diskette, as described in the next section of this chapter.

Still other devices may be supplied with no diagnostics program, if the device does not lend itself to diagnostics testing.

As a final example, a non-IBM device may be supplied with its own diagnostics diskette. Unless otherwise noted, the program(s) on such a diskette should *not* be merged with the IBM diagnostics diskette, but should be run separately, following the manufacturer's instructions.

Typical examples of each category are given here.

Enhanced Graphics Adapter. This device is accompanied by an entirely new diagnostics diskette for the PC and XT, which replaces all previous versions. The regular AT diagnostics diskette already contains enhanced graphics diagnostics.

Internal Modems. IBM internal modems are supplied with a supplementary diskette containing two diagnostic programs that should be merged with your main diagnostics diskette, as described in the next section. The modem diagnostics procedure itself is covered in detail in Chapter 12.

External Modems. In contrast to the internal modem, IBM external modems have a series of front-panel test switches and do not use a diskette-based diagnostic program at all.

Hercules Graphics Card. There are two diagnostic programs on the Hercules diskette accompanying the Graphics Card. The Hercules diagnostics procedure is described in Chapter 11.

Diagnostics Diskette Preparation

The following section describes how to prepare a single diskette for use in the diagnostic/testing procedures. To help keep things confusing, IBM refers to the required steps as *Copy* and *Merge* for the PC, XT, and AT, and as *Backup* and *Copy an Option* for PS/2 systems. In either case, their purpose is to prepare a single diskette containing all your diagnostic programs. To help simplify the explanation of how to proceed, the following terms will be used here:

Main diskette	The ISA diagnostics diskette found in the back of the Guide To Operations manual, or the PS/2 Starter or Reference diskette
Copy diskette	A copy of the main diskette
Supplementary diskette, or Option diskette (PS/2)	A diskette that accompanies a newly acquired device and contains diagnostics for that device only (such as the diskette accompanying the Internal Modem 1200 mentioned above)
DOS diskette	The regular IBM system diskette

ISA System Copy and Merge Procedures

Use option 2, COPY DISKETTE, as described on page 55. (Note: do *not* use the DOS DISKCOPY command to make this copy.) After you have done this, if you have supplementary diagnostics diskettes, prepare a merged diagnostics diskette by performing the following steps:

1. Log on to drive A and insert the supplementary diskette in this drive.

2. Temporarily remove the write-protect tab from your copy diskette and place this diskette in drive B. On a single-drive system, simply have the copy diskette ready and follow the diskette-swapping instructions as they appear on screen.

3. Copy the supplementary diskette's diagnostics file(s) onto the copy diskette in drive B by typing the following command:

```
COPY A: *.DGS B:↵
```

The DGS extension is used to indicate a diagnostic file. The copy diskette in drive B now contains all diagnostic files from both the main and supplementary diagnostics diskettes. Some of the latter may overwrite earlier versions of specific files, while one or more others will be completely new. Therefore the number of files with the DGS extension seen on the drive B diskette may not quite equal the sum of those on the main and supplementary diagnostics diskettes.

4. Remove the merged diagnostics diskette from drive B, restore its write-protect tab, and relabel the diskette to indicate that it is now to be used for all future diagnostics work.

Updated ISA Diagnostics Diskettes

An updated diagnostics diskette can be used as a direct replacement for earlier versions you may have on hand. However, before discarding an earlier diagnostics diskette, make sure the updated version you have just received contains all the supplementary diagnostics programs you have already acquired and merged with your original diagnostics diskette. If it does not, then these should be merged with the new diskette, as described in the merge procedure above.

COMMAND.COM and Format Programs on ISA Diagnostics and MCA Starter/Reference Diskettes

The COMMAND.COM program on a diagnostics or Starter/Reference diskette is not suitable for use elsewhere. In case of future doubt about which version of COMMAND.COM is on any diskette, type DIR and note the number of bytes this file occupies. Check this figure against the versions of COMMAND.COM on your original DOS and diagnostics diskettes to find the one it matches. For reference purposes, Table 3.2a lists the lengths of various COMMAND.COM programs.

The same precaution applies to the diagnostics FORMAT.COM program, which is named DFORMAT.COM on ISA and PS/2 Starter diskettes. On the MCA Reference diskette, formatting for testing purposes is an integral part of the BACKUP.COM program and a separate format program is not found on the diskette.

The VER Command. On DOS diskettes, version 2.00 and above, the VER (version) command displays the DOS version number. Remember, however, that this command displays the DOS version that was last used to boot the system, which is not necessarily the version on the diskette you are currently checking.

DOS 4.01 Note: On IBM system diskettes, the VER command incorrectly identifies DOS 4.01 as IBM DOS Version 4.00, although the diskette label itself does show the correct 4.01 identification. But of course this identification gets lost when either version is transferred to hard disk or to a copy diskette. To further complicate matters, the date and length of the COMMAND.COM file are identical on both versions; the changes take place in the hidden IBMBIO.COM and IBMDOS.COM files. To distinguish copies of the original version 4.00 from the bug-corrected version 4.01 (and

Table 3.2a Length of IBM COMMAND.COM Files

COMMAND.COM	Date	Version	Comments
943	02–09–82	1.02	PC, XT diagnostics
3231	08–04–81	1.00	IBM PC DOS
3566	02–28–83	2.02	PC, XT diagnostics
3582	10–21–83	2.05	PC, XT diagnostics
3612	06–12–84	2.07	PC, XT diagnostics
3614	03–26–85	1.00	Internal Modem diagnostics
4959	05–07–82	1.10	IBM PC DOS
11182	08–01–88	1.01	Starter Diskette, model 30 286
11310	12–11–87	1.03	Reference Diskette, model 70/80
11598	10–01–87	1.02	Reference Diskette, model 50/60
17664	03–08–83	2.00	IBM PC DOS
17792	10–20–83	2.10	IBM PC DOS
22040	08–14–84	3.00	IBM PC DOS
23210	03–07–85	3.10	IBM PC DOS
23791	12–30–85	3.20	IBM PC DOS
25307	03–17–87	3.30	IBM PC DOS
29488	03–01–84	1.00	AT diagnostics
30352	06–13–84	1.02	AT diagnostics
37xxx †	06–17–88	4.0x	IBM PC DOS

† See Table 3.2b

subsequent revisions), refer to Table 3.2b or 3.2c for the length and date information needed to tell one from the other.

The easiest way to read the date and file size of either hidden file is with a program such as the Norton Utilities. The DOS DEBUG program can also be used to track down the desired information, though not with the same ease. For example, to read the date of the IBMDOS.COM file on a diskette in drive A, type in the lines below which end with a ↵ (the symbol for the Enter key). The lines beginning with 1E9E: will be displayed as indicated, although both the 1E9E: and the four digits immediately following will vary from one system to another.

Comments

```
C>C:\DOS\DEBUG↵        Execute the DEBUG program.
-L CS:0 0 1 20↵        From drive 0 (A) sector 1, load 20 (hex) sectors.
-S CS:0 4000 "IBMDOS"↵ Now search for the IBMDOS file.
1E9E:0F20              IBMDOS found at this address.
-D CS:0F20 ↵           Dump (i.e, display) the data at 1E9E:0F20.
1E9E:0F20 49 42 4D 44 4F 53 20 20-43 4F 4D 27 00 00 00 00  IBMDOS  COM'....
1E9E:0F30 00 00 00 00 00 00 00 60-03 11 43 00 A0 8C 00 00  .......'..C.....
1E9E:0F40 43 4F 4D 4D 41 4E 44 20-43 4F 4D 20 00 00 00 00  COMMAND COM'....
```
(Five more lines of code appear here.)
```
-Q↵                   Type this when you are ready to quit DEBUG.
```

Table 3.2b IBM PC-DOS Version 4.00 and 4.01 Files *

COMMAND.COM bytes	date	IBMBIO.COM bytes	date	IBMDOS.COM bytes	date	DOS/ CSD **	release date
37637	06-17-88	32810	06-17-88	35984	06-17-88	4.00	06-17-88
37637	06-17-88	32816	08-03-88	36000	08-03-88	22624 & 4.01	08-15-88
37652	11-11-88	32816	08-03-88	36000	11-11-88	24270	03-27-89
37652	11-11-88	33901	04-06-89	37136	04-06-89	25066	05-10-89
37765	03-20-90	34660	03-20-90	37248	02-20-90	29015	03-20-90
37765	06-29-90	34660	03-27-90	37264	05-21-90	31300	07-25-90

   * The DOS VER command displays *IBM DOS Version 4.00* for all versions listed in this table.

   ** A CSD (Corrective Service Diskette) will update *all* prior versions of DOS 4.0x to provide the byte counts and dates given here. Note that COMMAND.COM data alone is insufficient for positive identification of the DOS version or CSD update.

Table 3.2c Microsoft MS-DOS Versions 4.0x and 5.00 Files

COMMAND.COM bytes	date	IO.SYS bytes	date	MSDOS.SYS bytes	date	DOS VER command *
37556	10-06-88	33321	10-06-88	37376	10-06-88	4.00
37557	04-07-89	33337	04-07-89	37376	04-07-89	4.01
41765	08-15-90	32297	08-15-90	36748	08-15-90	5.00 †
46246	12-13-90	33044	12-30-90	37506	‡	

   * The VER command correctly displays *MS-DOS Version 4.00, 4.01* or *5.00*.

   † Beta versions. Values subject to change prior to release date.

   ‡ MSDOS.SYS date is date of DOS installation on system.

Make sure the first line of sixteen hexadecimal numbers (bytes 0 through 15) is followed by the equivalent ASCII characters IBMDOS and COM at the right of the screen. The information of interest is in the second line, where the date bytes (24 and 25) are underlined in this example, though not on the screen, of course. To decode the date, write the numbers in the reverse sequence and then convert them to a binary string. The first seven bits contain the year (add 1980 to it), the next four the month, and the last five the day. Thus

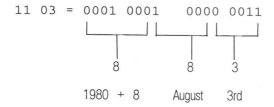

The numbers you may find in the underlined positions 24 and 25 are

24	25	25	24	Binary string	Date	DOS version
D1	10	10	D1	0001 0000 1101 0001	June 6, 1988	DOS 4.00
03	11	11	03	0001 0001 0000 0011	August 3, 1988	DOS 4.01
6B	11	11	6B	0001 0001 0110 1011	November 11, 1988	CSD 24270
86	12	12	86	0001 0010 1000 0110	April 6, 1989	CSD 25066
54	14	14	54	0001 0100 0101 0100	February 20, 1990	CSD 29015

If you still have version 4.00, your dealer should be able to provide an updated version for you. (See Table 3.2b for explanation of the CSD nomenclature.)

SYSLEVEL Command. This new DOS command, introduced with the CSD 29015 update, displays the following lines:

```
DOS Version: 4.00 U.S. Date: 06/17/88
CSD Version: UR29015 U.S. Date: 03/20/90
```

The final column in each row gives the date at which the listed version became available.

Main Menu (all PS/2 systems)

PS/2 system diagnostics are accessed via one of the main menus shown in Figure 3.3. To access this menu, place the Starter/Reference diskette in drive A and reboot the system. When the IBM logo appears on screen, press the Enter key to display the main menu, then select the desired menu choice. The choices are listed here, with diagnostics-related options discussed in this chapter and the other options covered in Chapter 6, where the menu is repeated as Figure 6.12.

Main Menu Notes. For reasons best known to themselves (one hopes), IBM varies the number and wording of some menu options on some Starter and Reference diskettes. The choices described below are based on currently available diskettes. In case of variations from the format seen here, follow

(a)

```
┌─────────────────────────────────────────────┐
│ Main Menu                                     │
├─────────────────────────────────────────────┤
│   1. Learn about the computer                 │
│   2. Backup the Reference Diskette            │
│   3. Set configuration                        │
│   4. Set features                             │
│   5. Copy an option diskette                  │
│   6. Test the computer                        │
│                                               │
│                                               │
├─────────────────────────────────────────────┤
│ Use↑or↓to select. Press Enter.                │
│ Esc=Quit    F1=Help                           │
└─────────────────────────────────────────────┘
```

Note the following variations on the Main Menu:
model 30 286
```
  2. Backup the Starter Diskette
  5. Move the system
  6. Test the system
```

model 50/60
```
  6. Move the computer
  7. Test the computer
```

(b)

```
IBM Personal System/2 Model 25 (or 30)
STARTER DISKETTE
Version 1.00

(C) Copyright IBM Corporation, 1987

STARTER DISKETTE MAIN MENU

1.   LEARNING ABOUT YOUR SYSTEM
2.   SERVICES
        System Checkout
        Format Diskette
        Copy Diskette
        Prepare System for Moving
        Set Time and Date

Select a Number and Press ENTER

ESC=Quit
```

Figure 3.3. PS/2 diagnostic main menus: (a) models 25 286, 30 286, and all MCA systems; (b) models 25 and 30.

the on-screen menu choice that comes closest to that given below. On PS/2 models 25 and 30, only options 1 and 2 are available.

Option 1. Learning About Your System   (models 25 and 30)
                Learn About the System   (model 30 286)
                Learn About the computer   (MCA systems)

This option is described in Chapter 6 (page 181).

Option 2. Services   (models 25 and 30)

An intermediate display (not shown here) explains the purpose of this option. Press the Enter key to display the Services menu itself, which is shown in Figures 3.4(c) and 3.4(d). The diagnostic menu choices are described in the Select an Option or Services Menu section (page 55). The Set Time and Date option (4) is described in Chapter 6 (page 181).

Option 2. Backup the Starter Diskette   (model 30 286)
                Backup the Reference Diskette   (MCA systems)

Use this option to prepare a copy of the diskette for use in the future. Begin by inserting your Starter or Reference diskette in drive A. Press the Enter key and follow the on-screen directions. On a system with two drives, you are prompted to identify the drives containing the original Starter/Reference diskette and the target diskette, that is, the diskette which will eventually contain the copy. You may copy A-to-B or B-to-A. Use the cursor keys to move between selections, type in the desired drive letters, and then press the Enter key. If you elect to copy to the same drive containing the original diskette, or if you have a one-drive system, you will be prompted to swap diskettes as required during the copy procedure.

The target diskette is formatted during the backup procedure. Therefore, make sure it contains no useful files before using it for this purpose. When you are finished, store the original diskette in a safe place and use the backup copy. Save your own system configuration on this backup copy, as described in Chapter 6 under the Set configuration option (page 181).

Option 3. Set Configuration   (model 30 286 and MCA systems)
Option 4. Set Features

These options are both described in Chapter 6 (pages 181 and 188).

Option 5.   Move the System   (model 30 286)
Option 6.   Move the computer   (models 50/60)

Select this choice to park the hard disk heads prior to moving your computer. But before doing so, be sure to make a backup copy of all fixed disk files, as described in Chapter 9 (page 368).

If this choice is selected on a system that does not have a hard disk, or if the hard disk has been disconnected, the screen will display an error message pointing out that fact. If the message is seen on a system that does have a hard disk installed, then select the Test the System option (6 or 7) to determine the cause of the problem.

The Main Menu's Backup the Starter Diskette option (2, above) is *not* usable for this purpose. See Chapter 9 (page 366) for further details about moving a system containing a hard disk. (Note that IBM refers to a hard disk system as a fixed disk, and occasionally, as a hardfile.)

Option 5.   Copy an Option Diskette   (MCA Systems)

In you have an option diskette on hand, select this menu choice and follow the on-screen instructions to transfer the new option diagnostics to your copy diskette. At the conclusion of this procedure, your copy diskette will contain all the diagnostics from the main diskette, plus the new diagnostics from the option diskette. Again, store the option diskette in a safe place and use the copy diskette from now on.

Option 6.   Test the System   (model 30 286)
                 Test the Computer   (models 70/80)
Option 7.   Test the Computer   (models 50/60)

This menu choice is described in the Start Routine Diagnostics section immediately following. Follow the directions for the desired system.

Start Routine Diagnostics (All Systems)

To begin routine diagnostics, follow the appropriate procedure below. The page sequence that is presented here follows the sequence of the PC family diagnostics. A few minor changes in sequence for PS/2 system testing are described at the appropriate points in the text.

PC, XT, AT Systems. Insert the diagnostics diskette in drive A. Turn the power on, or if it is already on, press the Ctrl + Alt + Del keys, as described in the Warm Reboot section of Chapter 1 (page 11). When the Select an

Option menu is seen, follow the instructions in the Select an Option or Services Menu section seen below. If the menu is not seen, then continue reading here.

PC, XT, AT Systems with an Accelerator Board Installed. Follow the procedure just described. However, keep in mind that some IBM diagnostic tests are speed-sensitive, and may fail on a system running at an accelerated clock rate. In case of doubt, run the diagnostic tests at the normal clock rate before concluding that a device is indeed faulty. Refer to Chapter 6 for general details on accelerator devices (page 211).

IBM-Compatible ISA Systems. The IBM diagnostics diskette is of course designed for use with IBM's own series of personal computers. When the diskette is used with a non-IBM personal computer, it may or may not work, depending on the computer's level of compatibility. As a typical example, if the IBM procedure described above causes a system crash, try the following alternative:

1. Insert the normal DOS system diskette and turn the power on.
2. Verify that the DOS A> prompt is seen.
3. Remove the DOS diskette and insert the diagnostics diskette in its place.
4. Type COMMAND↵

If the Select an Option menu is seen, then the diagnostics program has been successfully loaded into memory. However, it's still possible that some of the tests may not work properly. The best course of action is to try them all, on a system known to be good.

For future reference, make a note of all tests that conclude successfully. If a specific test consistently fails even though the tested device is known to be good, see if the name of that device is listed in Table 3.3. If the name appears there, then the name of the diagnostics program that checks that device is also seen in the table. Use the DOS RENAME command to change its DGS suffix to anything else. For example, to customize the diagnostics diskette to ignore the diskette drive test, type

```
RENAME US1DSK.DGS US1DSK.XYZ
```

Now the diskette drives will not be tested when the diagnostics diskette is used in the future, nor will the drives appear in the list of installed devices.

Table 3.3 Installed Devices Recognized by IBM Diagnostics Diskettes

Device (IBM Adapter)	PC, XT	XT 286, AT	PS/2
Adapter			
3117			GFDR
3119			GFGR
Asynchronous			
Adapter, Dual			ASYNC
Communications		ASYNC (XT 286 only)	
plus Compact Printer	US1SRL		
Port, System Board			ASYNC
BSC (Binary Sync. Comm.)	US0BSC	BSC03	
Channel Emulator, S/370			S370CHAN †
Cluster	US1PCL	CLUSTER1	
Connection, 3270			IBMCONN †
Coprocessor, Math	US0M87	COPROC	COPROC
Data Acquisition Adapter	US1DAC		US1DAC
Device Channel, IBM 4684			US4684 †
Display Adapters			
8514			EF7F
C/GA, MD&PA	US1CDG		
C/GA, EGA, MD	US1ADG2	DISPLAY1	
MCGA			DISPLAY
Prof. Graphics Controller	US1PGC		
Video Graphics Array			VGA
Drives, diskette			
3½"	EXTDRV2	US1EDRV	DISKETTE (MCA)
			DISK1 & DSKT1 (ISA)
5¼"	US1DSK	EDSDSKT1	
5¼" adapter			DSKTS
5¼" external drive adapter			DISKETTE †
Drives, hard (Fixed)	US1FDK	EDSFD1	
ESDI Fixed Disk Controller			ESDI
Integrated Fixed Disk Controller		HARDFILE	
Expansion Option	US0EXP		
Game Control	US0GCTL	GAME	GAME0
GPIB (General Purpose Interface Bus)		US1GPIB	US1GPIB
High-Speed Adapter			HSAR
InfoWindow			
GPIB card			DFFC †
VGA Control Card			EFBF †
Interface Coprocessor			MPORT †
Keyboard	US0KBD	KYBD	KYBD, US01MAIN
Memory	US0STG	STORAGE	MEMORY
Expanded Memory Adapters, 80286			XMA
Expansion Options, 80286			XEXPMEM

Table 3.3 Installed Devices Recognized by IBM Diagnostics Diskettes (continued)

Device (IBM Adapter)	Diagnostic file name (.DGS extension)		
	PC, XT	XT 286, AT	PS/2
Memory, continued			
Expansion Options, 80386			MEMORY
2-4Mb module kits for above			FDDF
Modem			
External	none	none	
Internal 300/1200	US1M212 †	US1M212 †	MODEM
Internal 300/1200/2400			MODEM24
Mouse Port			MOUSE
Multiprotocol Adapter(s)			MPCA
Music Feature Card			US1MUSIC
Network Adapter	USOPCN	USOPCN	NETWORK, USOPCN
Optical Disk Controller, IBM 3363		USOPDIAG	
Parallel Port			PARA
Personal Pageprinter Adapter			EFF6
Printers	none	none	
Color/Graphics	US1CPRT	CPS200	
Compact	US1SRL		
Matrix	USOPRT	CPS80	
Parallel	US1PAR	PARA1	
plus C/GA, MD	US1CDG		
Pro 200			PRO200
Realtime Interface Coprocessor Adapter			DEV141 †
Multiport/2			MPORT
SDLC (Sync. Data Link Control)	US1SDL	SDLC03	
Serial/Parallel	n/a	ASYNC & PARA1	
Speech Adapter			USTKR0
Storage (test)	STORAGE		
Store Loop Controller			USSLOOP †
Streaming Tape Drive Adapter, 6157		TAPEADAP	
System Board	USOCPU	SYSTEST	PLANAR, CPU0
System 36/38 Work Station Emulation Adapter			FFF8
Token Ring Network Adapters			E000
Voice Communications	VOICE17		
3278/79 Emulation	USOCUA † or USO78EA †		

† Diagnostics file is on supplementary diskette, supplied with device.

If none of the above suggestions work, then it may be assumed there is sufficient incompatibility between the non-IBM PC and the IBM diagnostics diskette to preclude the diskette's use. As an alternative, non-IBM diagnostics diskettes are commercially available for testing PCs with varying levels of IBM compatibility, as well as for testing many installed devices that are not supported by the IBM diagnostics diskette.

If you are able to successfully load the diagnostics program, then follow the procedures given below.

PS/2 Systems (except models 25 and 30). Insert the ISA Starter diskette or the MCA Reference diskette in drive A. Turn the power on, or if it is already on, press the Ctrl+Alt+Del keys, as described in the Warm Reboot section of Chapter 1 (page 11). When the IBM logo is seen, press the Enter key to display the Starter/Reference diskette Main Menu, which was illustrated above in Figure 3.3.

To begin testing move the highlighted bar down to the Test the System (model 30 286) or Test the Computer (MCA systems) line and then press the Enter key, or simply press key 6. Then follow the instructions immediately below for the specific PS/2 system of interest.

PS/2 ISA System (model 30 286). The following advisory message is now displayed:

```
YOU WILL NEED A BLANK FORMATTED DISKETTE FOR EACH
DISKETTE DRIVE IN THE SYSTEM. SELECT THE "FORMAT
DISKETTE" OPTION TO FORMAT THE DISKETTE(S) BEFORE
SELECTING "SYSTEM CHECKOUT."

PRESS ENTER TO CONTINUE

?_
```

The "format diskette" message refers to an option that will be seen the next time you press the Enter key. Do so now, and then continue reading here.

PS/2 MCA Systems (models 50 through 80). Since neither the Select an Option nor the Services menu is implemented in these systems, turn directly to the Run Diagnostics/Testing Routines section (page 59) to continue.

The Select an Option or Services Menu

Figure 3.4 illustrates the menu which should now be displayed on screen. Note that on PC, XT, and AT systems, the menu is labeled Select an Option, and on the PS/2 models 25, 30, and 30 286 it is simply called Services. In either case, each option is described immediately below. Because the options are not necessarily used in the sequence in which they appear, it is important to review all options before actually selecting any one of them. Note that some options are not included in PS/2 menus, but appear instead in the Starter diskette Main Menu shown in Figure 3.3 (page 48).

Option 0.   Run Diagnostics Routines   (PC, XT)
　　　　　　　 System Checkout   (AT, PS/2 ISA systems)

The routine diagnostic procedures begin when this option is selected. But first, use option 1 to prepare a formatted diskette for each drive. For PC, XT, and AT systems and PS/2 models 25 and 30, also use option 2 to make a copy of the master diagnostics diskette. For the PS/2 model 30 286, make this copy by using the Backup the Reference (or Starter) Diskette option (2) described earlier in the Main Menu section (page 47).

When you are ready to begin diagnostic testing, select this option and turn to the section entitled Run Diagnostics/Testing Routines (page 59).

Option 1.   Format Diskette   (all ISA systems)

All diskette drives are tested during the system checkout procedure, which requires a formatted diskette for each drive. Use this option to format these diskettes, following the directions seen on screen. Set the formatted diskettes aside until you are prompted to insert them in the drives during the system checkout procedure.

It is important to remember that the formatting program on the diagnostics diskette is significantly different from that found on the regular IBM DOS diskette. Therefore, a diskette formatted during diagnostics is not suitable for use elsewhere, and vice versa. Prior to use in a nondiagnostics application, a diskette must be reformatted using the FORMAT.COM program on the DOS diskette.

Option 2.   Copy Diskette   (PC, XT, AT, PS/2 models 25 and 30)

Because of the differences between the DOS and the diagnostics COM-MAND.COM programs, the diagnostics diskette should not be copied using DOS's normal COPY or DISKCOPY commands. Instead, select this option

(a)

```
SELECT AN OPTION

0 - RUN DIAGNOSTIC ROUTINES
1 - FORMAT DISKETTE
2 - COPY DISKETTE
3 - PREPARE SYSTEM FOR RELOCATION
9 - EXIT TO SYSTEM DISKETTE

ENTER THE ACTION DESIRED
? _
```

(b)

```
SELECT AN OPTION

0 - SYSTEM CHECKOUT
1 - FORMAT DISKETTE
2 - COPY DISKETTE
3 - PREPARE SYSTEM FOR MOVING
4 - SETUP
9 - END DIAGNOSTICS

ENTER THE ACTION DESIRED
? _
```

(c)

```
SERVICES

0 - SYSTEM CHECKOUT
1 - FORMAT DISKETTE
2 - COPY DISKETTE
3 - PREPARE SYSTEM FOR MOVING
4 - SET TIME AND DATE

9 - END SERVICES

Select a Number and press ENTER
? _
```

(d)

```
SERVICES

0 - SYSTEM CHECKOUT
1 - FORMAT DISKETTE

9 - END SERVICES

Select a Number and press ENTER
? _
```

Figure 3.4.   The Select an Option and Services menus: (a) PC and XT, (b) AT, (c) PS/2 models 25 and 30, (d) PS/2 models 25 286 and 30 286.

and follow the directions seen on screen. It is not necessary to format the diskette, since this is automatically done during the copy process.

When you have finished making the copy, put the master diagnostics diskette away and use the copy in its place. But before you use it, make sure you place a write-protect tab on it. Otherwise the diagnostics program will be destroyed if the diskette is inadvertently left in the drive during testing. But since at this point the diagnostics program is already in memory, the tests will continue to run, with no indication of what has happened until the next time you attempt to use the same diskette. Since diskette-writing tests were made during the former diagnostics procedure, all previously stored data will have been lost, and the following message will be displayed:

```
Non-System disk or disk error
Replace and strike any key when ready
```

If you see this message, use your master diagnostics diskette to make another copy diskette.

Option 3.   Prepare System for Relocation   (PC, XT)
Prepare System for Moving   (AT, PS/2 models 25 and 30)

This option parks the hard disk read/write head in the proper physical location for shipment, after which one of the following messages is displayed on screen:

```
SYSTEM PREPARED FOR MOVING
```

or

```
SYSTEM READY FOR RELOCATION
```

or

```
FIXED DISK(S) READY FOR SHIPPING
```

For further details, see the Relocation Notes in Chapter 9.

•**Option 3 Cautions**
1. To avoid data loss, make sure to use only the main diagnostics diskette that is specifically intended for use with your computer.
2. If the supplementary diagnostics diskette accompanying the IBM internal modem 1200 is used independently—that is, not merged with the main diagnostics diskette—its menu will also display the reloca-

tion option. However, loss of data may occur if this option is used on an IBM AT with a 30Mb hard disk drive. Therefore, when preparing such a system for relocation, make sure to select option 3 on the main diskette, not on the supplementary one. To guard against accidental use, change the file name on the internal modem diagnostics diskette from SHIPDISK.COM to XHIPDISK.COM.

Option 4.   Setup   (AT only)
              Set Time and Date   (PS/2 models 25 and 30)

This option is used to configure the AT system, and also to set the correct time and date, as described in Chapter 6 (page 175).

An AT Diagnostics Note. If version 2.0 or 2.1 of the AT diagnostics diskette is run in the multiple-test mode described below, the clock will be automatically reset to 13:00. In this case, use option 4 to reenter the correct time before exiting diagnostics. This extra step should be unnecessary in subsequent versions of the diagnostics diskette.

Options 5 through 8

These options have not been implemented by IBM.

Option 9.   Exit to System Diskette   (PC, XT)
              End Diagnostics   (AT)
              End Services   (PS/2 models 25, 30, and 30 286)

Select this option when you are finished using the diagnostics diskette or the diagnostic services on the Starter diskette. When you do, the next message will advise you how to resume normal operations. The message format varies from one system to another, but in any case the general procedure is the same:

   To continue with more diagnostics/testing, leave the diagnostics or Starter/Reference diskette in place.
   To reboot from drive A, replace the above diskette with your regular system diskette.
   To reboot from drive C, remove the above diskette and leave drive A empty.

Now when you press the Enter key, the system reboots and is once again ready for routine operation.

Run Diagnostic/Testing Routines

PC, XT, AT, and PS/2 Model 30 286. When option 0 is chosen from the Select an Option or Services menus seen in Figure 3.4, the diagnostics program takes a few seconds to load, and then a series of questions appears on screen. Answer each question as it appears (Y or y, N or n, followed by pressing the Enter key), and write down any error messages that occur. If more than one display adapter is installed, you will be asked if a monitor is attached to each one. Keep in mind that if you answer yes, but do not actually turn each display on, the tests for that display will not be seen.

The next display is the List of Installed Devices, described below.

PS/2 Models 25 and 30. When option 0 is chosen from the Services menu (Figure 3.4c), the screen displays a list of installed devices, as described below.

MCA Systems. When option 6 on the Main Menu (Figure 3.3) is selected, the testing procedure goes directly to the List of Installed Devices described immediately below.

List of Installed Devices. The next display is shown in Figure 3.5. If you have properly installed any of the devices listed in Table 3.3, the name of that device should automatically appear in the screen display seen in Figure 3.5. In addition, devices represented by merged diagnostics files should also appear, provided the device is still present in your system. If such a device is subsequently removed, it is not necessary to remove its diagnostics program from your diagnostics diskette.

If the name of an installed device does not appear on screen, carefully review your installation, following the appropriate chapter in this book and the instructions that came with the option. If the installation appears to be in order and the device name still does not appear in the list, then servicing is indicated.

Don't overlook the possibility of device conflicts in which two devices are accidentally configured to occupy the same logical space. For example, if two communications adapters are installed, one must be configured as COM1 and the other as COM2. Instructions for doing this are given in Chapter 12 (page 533). If the configuration is incorrect, only one COM device may show up on the list. In a properly configured system, the COM2 device is displayed with the prefix ALT, as seen in this excerpt from a list of installed devices:

```
ASYNC COMMUNICATIONS ADAPTER
ALT. INTERNAL MODEM 1200
```

The first listing is the COM1 device and the second is the COM2.

Of course, devices not supported by a diagnostics program (such as the external modem) will not appear under any circumstances.

(a)

```
THE INSTALLED DEVICES ARE

SYSTEM BOARD
XXXKB MEMORY
KEYBOARD
MONOCHROME & PRINTER ADAPTER
COLOR/GRAPHICS MONITOR ADAPTER
2 DISKETTE DRIVE(S) AND ADAPTER

IS THE LIST CORRECT (Y/N)?
```

(b)

```
  System Unit
 1920Kb Memory
  Keyboard
  Parallel Port
1 Diskette Drive(s)
  Math Coprocessor
  System Board Async Port
  Video Graphics Array
  Mouse Port
1 ESDI Fixed Disk(s)
```

```
┌──────────────────────────────────────────────┐
│ Question                      Page    1 of 1   │
├──────────────────────────────────────────────┤
│ This list shows the devices that the           │
│ testing program sees as being installed        │
│ in your computer.                              │
│                                                │
│ Is this list correct?                          │
├──────────────────────────────────────────────┤
│ Press Y or N                                   │
└──────────────────────────────────────────────┘
```

Figure 3.5.   The List of Installed Devices menus: (a) all ISA systems, (b) all MCA systems.

Installed Devices Review. Be especially on the lookout for an inaccurate assessment of the amount of installed memory (*xxxx*Kb) and for incorrect information concerning diskette and hard disk drives.

If the list of installed devices is correct, respond to the "Is the list correct?" question by pressing Y and then refer to the following section:

Computer	Chapter Section
PC, XT, AT	System Checkout Menu
PS/2 (all)	Test Notes

However, if you answer no (N), you will see a display that looks like one of the following displays:

ISA Systems

```
hh:mm:ss
ERROR - INSTALLED DEVICES LIST 199
PRESS ENTER TO CONTINUE
?
```

The 199 error code is simply a reminder that you have noted a discrepancy in the list. Now press the Enter key and then refer to the System Checkout Menu section below.

MCA Systems

```
If there is an IBM device installed
that is NOT on the list, have the
system unit serviced. Press Esc to
test the devices that are listed.

Esc=Quit
```

The message will partially overwrite the list of installed devices displayed on your screen.

Ignore the misleading Esc = Quit message in the last line, and simply press the Escape key to begin testing, and then refer to the Test Notes section (page 64).

The System Checkout Menu (PC, XT, AT only)

The System Checkout menu shown in Figure 3.6 allows you to modify the tests to run once or multiple times, to log test errors, and to return to the previous menu. Again, do not choose an option until you have read descriptions of all the options. When you are ready to run the tests, refer to the Test Notes section (page 64).

```
SYSTEM CHECKOUT

0 - RUN TESTS ONE TIME
1 - RUN TESTS MULTIPLE TIMES
2 - LOG UTILITIES
9 - EXIT DIAGNOSTIC ROUTINES

ENTER THE ACTION DESIRED
? _
```

Figure 3.6.   The System Checkout menu for the PC, XT, and AT.

Option 0.   Run Tests One Time

This option executes a routine of procedures for a one-time check of system memory, keyboard, display(s), and installed options. Some tests require a user response to verify the status of the test.

Option 1.   Run Tests Multiple Times

This option is available only on PC and XT diagnostics prior to version 2.20 and on AT diagnostics prior to version 2.00. If you'd like to get a general idea of what to expect from the test procedure, select this option. In response to the questions that appear, have the tests run once, with a pause whenever an error is encountered.

Some Option 1 Limitations.   In order for the procedure to run multiple times without continually pausing for user input, tests that require a user response are omitted. Furthermore, the tests assume your list of installed devices is correct. Installed devices that do not appear in your list are not tested.

The selection of the multiple-tests option is handy for uncovering certain intermittent problems that otherwise would be difficult to localize. Remember, however, that some tests are disabled in this mode, precluding, for example, the complete keyboard test, which requires the user's presence.

Option 2.   Log Utilities

Obviously, the ideal way to identify an error is to catch it in the act of happening. But in the case of some intermittent problems, the suspect device may behave properly during the test interval, only to fail again later on. The test may need to be repeated over and over again, until it finally coincides with an occurrence of the error. Of course, this is the purpose of option 1 above, and in such cases the Log Utilities function may be of some use, depending on the specific nature of the error.

For technically inclined readers, a two-volume *IBM Hardware Maintenance and Service Manual* provided an advanced diagnostics diskette with a thorough multiple-run testing procedure. However, this two-volume set was later supplanted by a single *Hardware Maintenance Service Manual* with advanced diagnostics diskettes, plus a separate *Hardware Maintenance Reference Manual.*

Under the advanced diagnostics Log Utilities option, a printed log of all errors may be prepared. Alternatively, the log may be written to diskette. As a convenience to those who do not need such extensive logging facilities, a limited log-to-diskette option was included on early versions of the regular diagnostics diskette under discussion here. However, the logistical problems of maintaining this log outweigh its practical value to the user. This is because both diskette drives are automatically tested during the diagnostics procedure, thereby obliterating previous data, including the error log itself.

The choice of logging to printer or diskette was therefore deleted from later versions of the diagnostics diskette. Users whose diagnostics diskette still offers this choice should select the log-to-printer option. Then the error log will print out the time and nature of all errors encountered during the Option 0 or Option 1 tests. Subject to the limitations discussed under Option 1, the user may leave the system unattended and return later to review the printed error log.

Briefly stated, the error-logging procedure is as follows:

1. Turn on the printer.
2. Select the Log Utilities option and begin the error log.
3. Select the desired Run Tests (Option 0 or 1).
4. Review the printed error log.

The Log Utilities Menu. To begin, select Option 2, and the Log Utilities menu seen in Figure 3.7 will be displayed on screen. To maintain a printed log of all errors as they are encountered, select Option 0 (Start Error Log) and then press the Enter key. If the prompt

```
LOG TO DISK, CASSETTE OR PRINTER (D C P)?
```

appears, select P and the menu seen above is redisplayed. If this prompt is not offered, the Log Utilities menu simply remains on the screen and the log will automatically be sent to the printer.

```
LOG UTILITIES

0 - START ERROR LOG
1 - STOP ERROR LOG
2 - LIST LOG
3 - SET TIME OF DAY
4 - DISPLAY TIME OF DAY
9 - RETURN FROM UTILITIES

ENTER THE ACTION DESIRED
? _
```

Figure 3.7.　The Log Utilities menu for the PC, XT, and AT.

If you have already printed an error log and now wish to run more tests without printing another log, select Log Utilities menu (Option 1—Stop Error Log) to discontinue the printed log.

The next step is to select Option 9 of the Log Utilities menu, Return from Utilities, and then Option 0 or 1 of the System Checkout menu. If you select Option 1, choose a suitable number of times for the tests to be repeated, and do not choose to have the test pause at each error. Now the diagnostics will run continuously, with errors printed as they are encountered. To make sure the procedure is properly set up, you may wish to leave one of the diskette drive doors open during the first pass through the test sequence. This should produce printed TIME OUT and SYSTEM UNIT error messages.

Option 9. Exit Diagnostic Routines

If your displayed list of installed devices was incorrect, choose this option and then make the necessary changes to the system configuration, as described in Chapter 6 (page 175). Once this is done, rerun the diagnostics diskette, verify that the list of installed devices is now correct, and then select one of the other options listed above.

Also choose this option when you have finished running the diagnostics program. This redisplays the Select an Option menu shown earlier in Figure 3.4. If you are ready to return to routine system operation, select Option 9 of that menu and you will be prompted to insert the system diskette (that is, your regular DOS boot diskette), as described earlier in this chapter.

Test Notes (all systems)

As the tests proceed, each system component is examined in turn, and various code numbers and messages are displayed on screen. A code number ending in 00 indicates the successful completion of a test in which no error was encountered.

A few of those tests requiring a user response are briefly described here. The error code number in parentheses is seen if you answer no (N) to a question related to the indicated test. This serves as a reminder of the error and on pre-PS/2 systems may be of use if you decide to log these error messages to the printer for future reference, as described in the section on Log Utilities (page 62). The described test will not be executed if any of the equipment listed below is not present in your system, or if you have eliminated the corresponding diagnostics program by renaming it, as described above in the section on IBM-Compatible ISA Systems (page 51).

System Board Test (199).   You are asked to verify that the list of installed devices is correct.

Keyboard Test (302).   During the keyboard test, you will be asked to press each key once and then to indicate whether all keys are properly functioning. The PS/2 keyboard test begins by asking you to identify the shape of the Enter key on your keyboard. The keys may be tested in any sequence. On ISA systems, conclude the test by pressing Y or N immediately followed by the Enter key. On PS/2 systems, press F1 or F2 to conclude.

Monochrome Display Test (4xx).   Table 3.4 lists various monochrome screen characteristics that are sequentially displayed. At each new screen display, you are asked to verify that the display is correct. If you answer no,

Table 3.4 Display Diagnostics Error Codes

Test failure	Monochrome	color	EGA, VGA
none; test concluded successfully	400	500	2400
Hercules conflict with EGA	401 †	–	–
display attributes	408	508	2408
character set	416	516	2416
80 × 24 mode	424	524	2424
parallel port	432	–	–
40 × 24 mode	–	532	2432
320 × 200 graphics mode	–	540	2440
640 × 200 graphics mode	–	548	2448
light pen	–	556	2456
screen pages	–	564	2464

† See Chapter 11 for further details

the error code seen in the Monochrome column is displayed, the Monochrome Display Test concludes, and the next test begins.

If a Hercules Graphics Card is installed in a system containing an Enhanced Graphics Adapter, this test may fail and a 401 error code will be seen. To run the test, either remove the EGA or temporarily reconfigure it as a conventional color/graphics adapter by setting its rear-panel switches in positions 0001 or 0111. (See Table 11.9 for further details.)

The Monochrome Display Test may also fail if the system is running at an accelerated clock rate. In this case, a 401 error code is displayed, the Monochrome Display Test concludes, and the next test begins. If this happens, try returning to the normal clock rate and running the test again. If the 401 error code continues to be seen, then the device is indeed defective. Otherwise, the error was speed-related and can be ignored, provided of course that the display functions properly during routine operations.

Color/Graphics Display Test (5xx). Table 3.4 also lists the color/graphics tests, and the appropriate error code for each test. Again, you are asked to verify that each display is correct. As with the Monochrome Display Test, the Color/Graphics Display Test may fail if the system is running at an accelerated clock rate. Again, the solution is to run the test at normal speed.

Diskette Drive Test (6xx). The diskette drives are tested, and various error codes indicate write-protected, door open, or other diskette- and drive-related errors. On all ISA systems, you must have a previously formatted scratch diskette available (see Option 1, page 55). On MCA systems, the scratch diskette will be formatted during the test procedure itself, so it need not be formatted in advance.

Asynchronous Communications Adapter Test (1101). Test 1100 checks the serial port on the Asynchronous Communications Adapter and the cable which may be attached to the card. However, it does not test the device attached to the other end of the cable. If this device—for example, an external modem—is on during the test period, the device itself may produce an 1101 error code, which may be considered erroneous and ignored. Better yet, disconnect the external device and in its place install the wrap plug that comes with each IBM communications adapter cable. See Chapter 12 for further details.

Enhanced Color Display Test (24xx). If the system is configured for an enhanced color display, this display is checked for the various screen characteristics listed in Table 3.4 above. As with the Monochrome and Color/Graphics tests, you are asked to verify that each screen display is correct. If not, the appropriate error code is displayed, this test concludes, and the next test begins.

For details about a speed-related test failure, the comments in the Monochrome and Color/Graphics Display Tests apply to this test as well.

Other Tests. A series of other tests may be executed, depending on which options are installed in your system.

As each test is completed, a message such as SYSTEM UNIT *xxx* appears on screen. Again, the *xxx* refers to the specific test that just concluded, and not to the one that is currently in progress. The last two digits should be 00, indicating the completion of a successful test. Note that the term SYSTEM UNIT may apply to devices connected to the system unit, as well as to the system unit itself. Consult the error code guide given in Table 3.5 for the name of each test, and see Appendix C for a more extensive listing of error codes.

A System Unit Test Note. As a possible point of confusion, a message such as the following is seen at the beginning of certain ISA system tests:

```
SYSTEM UNIT x00
THIS TEST TAKES UP TO TWO MINUTES
PLEASE STAND BY
```

Other messages also appear in various displays whose first line is always SYSTEM UNIT *x*00 (where *x* is a test number).

Despite what the display appears to signify, the messages refer not to Test *x*00, which has already concluded, but to the test that follows it. In the case of the System Board Test (Test 100), the next test is always of system memory (Test 200). However, at the conclusion of the Drive Test (Test 600), the next test depends on what options are installed.

On the PC, XT, and AT, this makes for a rather confusing display, in which a message is seen that has nothing to do with the test currently under way, followed by other messages that refer to a test that is not identified. It may help to jot down the sequence of test numbers the first time the diagnostics diskette is run. Next time, you may refer to this list to determine the identity of the test that is now under way.

On PS/2 systems, the messages seen during each test are more informative, so there should be little doubt as to what test is currently under way.

Table 3.5a Guide to Error Codes and Error Messages

Error code	Problem location	refer to Chapter
x or *xx* = any number †		
02*x*	Power	5
1*xx*	System board	6
2*xx*	Memory	7
nn 2*xx*	Memory (*nn* indicates specific memory chip)	7
3*xx*	Keyboard	10
nn 3*xx*	Keyboard (*nn* is scan code for faulty key)	10
4*xx*	Monochrome Display and/or Adapter	11
5*xx*	Color/Graphics Display and/or Adapter	11
6*xx*	Diskette drives and/or adapter	8
7*xx*	Math Coprocessor	6
8*xx*	reserved for future use	
9*xx*	Printer Adapter	13
10*xx*	Alternate Printer Adapter	13
11*xx*	Asynchronous Communications Adapter	12
12*xx*	Alternate Asynchronous Communications Adapter	12
13*xx*	Game Control Adapter	
14*xx*	IBM Graphics Printer	13
15*xx*	SDLC Communications Adapter	12
16*xx*	reserved for future use	
17*xx*	Fixed disk drive and/or adapter	9
18*xx*	Expansion Unit (PC, XT)	
19*xx*	reserved for future use	
20*xx*	Bisync Communications (BSC) Adapter	12
21*xx*	Alternate Bisync Communications (BSC) Adapter	12
22*xx*	Cluster Adapter	
23*xx*	reserved for future use	
24*xx*	Enhanced Graphics Display and/or Adapter	11
25*xx*	Alternate Enhanced Graphics Display and/or Adapter	11
26*xx*	reserved for future use	
27*xx*	reserved for future use	
28*xx*	3278/79 Emulator Adapter (PC, XT)	
29*xx*	IBM Color/Graphics Printer	13
30*xx*	Local Area Network Adapter	
31*xx*	Alternate Local Area Network Adapter	
32*xx*	reserved for future use	
33*xx*	Compact Printer	13
34*xx*	reserved for future use	
35*xx*	reserved for future use	
36*xx*	IEEE 488 Adapter	
37*xx*	reserved for future use	
38*xx*	Data Acquisition Adapter	
39*xx*	Professional Graphics Display and/or Adapter	

Table 3.5a Guide to Error Codes and Error Messages (continued)

Error code	Problem location	refer to Chapter
48*xx*	Internal Modem	12
49*xx*	Alternate Internal Modem	12
71*xx*	Voice Communications Adapter	
73*xx*	3.5–inch External Diskette Drive	8
74*xx*	Display Adapter 8514/A	11
84*xx*	PS/2 Speech Option	
86*xx*	Mouse	10
100*xx*	Multiprotocol Adapter	
104*xx*	ESDI disk drive or adapter	9

† If $x = 0$ or $xx = 00$, the device tested successfully, with no errors.

Table 3.5b Guide to Error Codes and Error Messages, continued

Error message	Problem location	refer to Chapter
CC0000 ROM	PC Network Adapter	
IO ROM CC0000	PC Network Adapter	
PARITY CHECK 1 *xxxx*	System–board parity error address *xxxx*	7
PARITY CHECK 2 *xxxx*	Memory–card parity error at address *xxxx*	7
PARITY CHECK *x* ?????	Parity error ($x = 1$ or 2) at unknown address	7
PARITY ERROR *xxxx:yyyy*	Memory error at indicated segment:offset	7
110	System board parity check (PS/2)	7
111	Memory adapter parity check (PS/2)	7
ROM ERROR	Checksum error in read–only memory (servicing required)	

Conclude Routine Diagnostics

This concludes the routine diagnostics section. On ISA systems, refer to Option 9 above (page 64) to end the diagnostics procedure. On MCA systems, an onscreen message appears after the last test, advising you to remove the Starter or Reference diskette in drive A and then press the Enter key to continue—that is, to reboot the system.

If you have encountered any unexplainable error messages, consult the Troubleshooting Diagnostics section which follows (page 73), and then turn to the appropriate chapter for further details.

MCA Advanced Diagnostics

An undocumented feature on MCA Reference diskettes makes available the following advanced diagnostic features:

Test selected devices.

Run single or continuous test of selected devices.

Maintain a log of test errors.

Low-level format a hard disk drive.

To gain access to these features, boot the system with the Reference diskette in drive A. At the IBM logo, press the Enter key to display the Main Menu (Figure 3.3) described earlier in the chapter. Now press Ctrl + A to display the Advanced Diagnostic menu shown in Figure 3.8. A description of the advanced diagnostics options follows.

Option 1: System checkout. The list of installed devices described earlier (Figure 3.5) is again displayed, and the on-screen question box asks

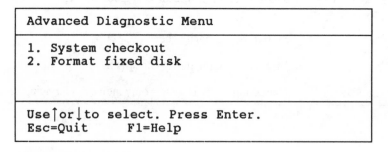

```
Advanced Diagnostic Menu

1. System checkout
2. Format fixed disk



Use↑or↓to select. Press Enter.
Esc=Quit      F1=Help
```

Figure 3.8.   The Advanced Diagnostics menu is accessed from MCA Reference diskettes by pressing Ctrl+A at the Main menu.

```
┌─────────────────────────────────────────────────────┐
│ Test Selection Menu                                   │
├─────────────────────────────────────────────────────┤
│ 1. Run tests one time                                 │
│ 2. Run tests continuously                             │
│ 3. Log or display errors                              │
│                                                       │
│                                                       │
├─────────────────────────────────────────────────────┤
│ Use↑or↓to select. Press Enter.                        │
│ Esc=Quit      F1=Help                                 │
└─────────────────────────────────────────────────────┘
```

Figure 3.9. For MCA systems, the Test Selection menu offers greater testing flexibility.

once more if the list is correct. However, you may now delete items from the list prior to testing by answering *no*. This option is helpful if you wish to run an extended test of selected items without wasting time testing the entire system. If you wish to test one device only, simply answer *yes* and proceed to the Test Selection menu described next.

After you modify the list of installed devices, the Test Selection menu shown in Figure 3.9 offers Option 1, Run Tests One Time, and Option 2, Run Tests Continuously. If either of these options is selected, the Device Test menu shown in Figure 3.10 allows you to test all devices or to select a single device for testing. In either case, the test(s) keep repeating until you press Ctrl + C.

Option 3, Log or Display Errors, is used to maintain an error log on diskette or to log all errors to your printer. An Error Log menu (not shown here) and on-screen instructions prompt you on how to proceed.

Option 2: Format Fixed Disk. Low-level formatting is described in Chapter 9 (page 384).

Examples of a Test Failure

To illustrate the general style of message seen when a test failure occurs, you can simulate a write-protect error by inserting a write-protected diskette in a drive when you are prompted to insert a scratch diskette. In this case the drive will not be completely checked and the diagnostics routine will proceed to the next drive, or to the next test, as appropriate. System-specific screen displays are illustrated below.

```
┌────────────────────────────────────────────────────────┐
│ Device Test Menu                                         │
├────────────────────────────────────────────────────────┤
│     Test All Devices                                     │
│     System Unit                                          │
│   xxxxKb Memory                                          │
│     Keyboard                                             │
│     Parallel Port                                        │
│   1 Diskette Drive(s)                                    │
│     Math Coprocessor                                     │
│                                                          │
│   (other devices listed here)                            │
│                                                          │
│                                                          │
├────────────────────────────────────────────────────────┤
│ Use↑or↓to select. Press Enter.                          │
│ Esc=Quit        F1=Help                                  │
└────────────────────────────────────────────────────────┘
```

Figure 3.10. The Device Test menu allows selected devices to be tested on MCA systems.

PC, XT, AT Systems. After both drive tests are concluded, the screen will look like this:

```
SYSTEM UNIT 500
hh:mm:ss
ERROR - 07 WRITE PROTECT
DISKETTE A: IS A xxxKb DRIVE (or DISKETTE DRIVE A: IS SINGLE SIDED)
DISKETTE B: IS A xxxKb DRIVE (or DISKETTE DRIVE B: IS SINGLE SIDED)
hh:mm:ss
ERROR - SYSTEM UNIT 601
```

The first line indicates the successful completion of the previous test, which in this case was of the color/graphics display. This is followed by the time the drive-related error occurred and the nature (07 WRITE PROTECT) of that error. The next two lines describe the diskettes found in each drive, not the drive itself. The final line lists the error code associated with the system just tested.

PS/2 Systems. At the beginning of the diskette drive test, you are asked to insert a scratch, high-density diskette in drive A and then press the Enter key to continue testing. If the diskette is in fact write-protected, the following message is seen after the successful conclusion of the speed test:

```
Verify diskette is not write-protected
Enter=Continue
```

This is your cue to replace the write-protected diskette with a formatted scratch diskette. However, leave the write-protected diskette in the drive and press the Enter key to display the following message:

```
hh:mm:ss Slot = 0
1 Diskette Drive(s) 659
Write-protect error on drive A.
Make sure the diskette is not
write-protected. If it is not write-
protected, have your system unit
serviced. Refer to the "Quick Reference"
for write-protect information.

Esc=Quit
```

As before, the Esc=Quit message *really* means press Escape to *continue* testing.

Diagnostics on IBM-Compatible Systems

Extensive diagnostic test routines are often built into the ROM BIOS in IBM-compatible computers. Due to the wide variety currently available, these tests are not described in detail here, although two typical screen displays are shown in Figure 3.11 simply to illustrate the options that are available. In these examples, the cursor movement keys are used to highlight the desired tests.

Since the testing procedures are contained within the ROM BIOS module itself, a separate diagnostics diskette is not required.

Troubleshooting Diagnostics

As a diagnostics aid, the IBM personal computer may indicate an error by a screen display in one of the following categories (as shown in the table at the top of the next page).

Each error category is described immediately below.

Software Error Message

These messages are program-related and indicate a problem that may be traced either to the software in use at the time the message is displayed or to your system configuration. If the message content itself does not give you

Error Category	Typical example
Software	`Bad command or file name`
	`Disk not ready`
	`Internal error`
	`Overflow`
Configuration	Configuration too large for memory
Error code	`201 ERROR - SYSTEM UNIT`
	`601 PARITY CHECK x`
	When an error code is displayed, the system may also lock up.
System lockup	The system simply locks up so that the keyboard no longer functions.

sufficient information to resolve the problem, then try the following procedure to localize the problem.

First, identify the source of the error message. If it occurs after you have typed something at the DOS prompt, then the error is of course DOS-related. Likewise, a BASIC or other language problem may be localized to a programming error. In either case, further information about the error message may be found in one of the following manuals.

Manual	Section	Title
DOS 2.xx	Chapter 8	Messages
DOS 3.xx	Appendix A	Messages
DOS 4.xx	Appendix D	Messages
DOS 5.xx	Appendix B	Messages
IBM BASIC	Appendix A	Error Messages

If the error message is unique to, say, your word processor or spreadsheet, then of course you should pull out the appropriate user manual and hope there is a chapter or appendix of error messages. If there is no such section, try the index. If there is no index, think about moving on to some better-documented product as soon as you can.

But if neither the DOS nor the software documentation allows you to resolve the problem, don't overlook the possibility that your system configuration is at fault. Since many such problems can be traced to, and corrected by, a CONFIG.SYS or AUTOEXEC.BAT file, the next chapter of this book is devoted to an overview of both. The addition of a few program lines to either file may go a long way toward eliminating program-related problems.

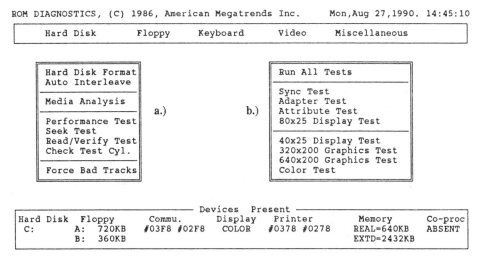

Figure 3.11. Extensive diagnostic facilities are often embedded in third-party ROM BIOS modules. In this AMI BIOS example, the desired test menu is accessed by highlighting a selection in the upper bar of the screen display: (a) hard disk format and testing menu, (b) video test menu.

Configuration Error Message

At the conclusion of the POST procedure on a system with a minimal memory configuration, the following error message may be seen:

```
Configuration too large for memory
```

This indicates that the total base memory is not sufficient to load COM-MAND.COM and the two hidden files (IBMDOS.COM and IBMBIO.COM). As a typical example, the message would be seen when attempting to boot an old 64-Kbyte system with DOS 3.2, which requires almost 70 Kbytes. The solution is to install more memory or use an earlier version of DOS. For further information about memory-related problems, refer to Chapter 7.

Error Code

The error code, and a brief review of the chapter that covers the problematic part, may help you to determine whether the problem can be easily resolved or requires the assistance of a competent service facility. For example, some keyboard errors may be cured simply by cleaning the area around the key and exercising it a few extra times. You may also feel comfortable replacing the occasional failed memory chip. Or if the error is clearly localized to drive A, you may want to remove it for servicing, while temporarily using drive B in its place.

If the error is traced to an adapter, chances are the adapter may be removed for servicing without losing the use of the rest of the system. On the other hand, a failure on the system board will almost undoubtedly require a trip to a service facility.

During POST, an error code may appear on screen briefly and then be erased by the BASIC screen display. In case of doubt, turn the system off and back on again. Watch carefully for an error code and jot it down before it disappears, or press the Control and Number Lock keys to halt POST, leaving the code displayed on screen. If a printer is available, turn it on and then press the Shift and PrtSc (Print Screen) keys to send all error messages and codes to the printer.

In any case, the error codes seen in Table 3.5, in Appendix C, and in the appropriate chapters in this book will help you to make the most informed choice. Take careful note of any error messages that are displayed, and in case outside help is indicated, carefully describe all error messages and codes that were seen or heard. This will help the service facility to diagnose and cure the problem quickly.

If the problem is related to the video display itself, it's quite likely that an error message will not be seen. For example, a distorted screen display presents a distinctive error message of its own, for which a code number is neither necessary nor possible.

Of course, no error messages will be seen or heard at all if the computer is incapable of supplying them. As an obvious example of an error that won't be reported by the system, consider what will—or rather, what won't—happen if the power cord is not plugged in! So in the event of no messages at all, look for the obvious at both ends of the power cord. If this doesn't turn up the problem, then refer to Chapter 5.

System Lockup

A system lockup is also a form of error message. Although not quite as informative as the other examples, it nevertheless does indicate a problem somewhere, and chances are this originates in the software. To begin the diagnosis, don't overlook the fact that the lockup may be nothing more than a pause while the program is doing something else, or while it awaits an unprompted user input. Unfortunately, some programs don't keep the user as informed as they should, and the solution to the problem turns out to be nothing more than waiting a few moments, or noting that a user input is expected.

But if neither waiting nor striking a few keys gets the system moving again, then reboot and try to duplicate the problem, while making a note of all keystrokes. If the lockup consistently occurs after a certain combination of keystrokes, or at a specific point in one program only, then the problem is indeed software related.

On the other hand, a system that locks up either at random intervals, at turn on, or after a specific numbered error message does indicate a hardware failure. If the remainder of this chapter does not suggest an appropriate course of action, then outside servicing is indicated.

Frequently Encountered Error Codes

Table 3.6 lists a few of the error codes that may be encountered during routine diagnostics testing. It's best to correct the condition causing the error and run the test once again.

Erroneous Error Codes

In a few isolated cases, an error code that is apparently incorrect may be encountered. In this case there are several possibilities that should be considered.

Table 3.6 Frequently Encountered Error Codes

Error code	Problem location
x = any number	
10x	System board
16x	System options not set
163	Time and date not set
164	System memory configuration
199	Reminder that list of installed devices is incorrect
20x	Memory – related
30x	Keyboard
401	Monochrome Display
432	Parallel printer is not turned on
501	Color/Graphics Display
601	Diskette drive
1101	External modem has been left on during test
178x	Hard disk
2401	EGA or VGA
2501	EGA or VGA

Memory Error. If the error code indicates a memory location that does not exist in your system, one or more memory configuration switches may be improperly set. Check all switch settings using the information given in Chapter 7.

Non-IBM Device Conflict. There is a possibility that an error code may be caused by the presence of an installed non-IBM device. In this case, the error code may be erroneous, and neither the device nor the rest of the system necessarily has a problem. To double-check this, temporarily remove all non-IBM devices and retest.

Other Misleading Error Codes A small handful of other error codes are given below. If you find one of the codes listed here, follow the instructions given. If the instructions given here do not clear up the problem, then further servicing is indicated.

164 or 201 POST Error Code (model 25 only, with installed option adapters). Remove all adapter cards and run automatic configuration (as described in Chapter 6, page 188). Then reinstall removed adapter cards.

622 through 626 (PC only).   If these errors occur while testing a diskette drive, use the diagnostics diskette to reformat the diskette that was in use at the time the error code was displayed.

06xx Errors While Formatting. These errors occur on an XT with DOS 2.0 or 2.1 only. Before assuming the diskette drive or adapter is defective, insert the following line in the CONFIG.SYS file: BUFFERS= xx where xx is any number from 1 to 99. If this line already exists in your CONFIG file, try changing the number to a higher value. (See Chapter 4 for further details about creating and/or editing a CONFIG.SYS file.) Revising the number of buffers in use shifts the memory location at which the format command operates, and this may clear up the problem.

1701 or 1712 (AT only). Turn the system power off, insert the original diagnostics diskette, and turn the power back on again. Do not reboot by pressing Ctrl + Alt + Del. Make a copy of the diagnostics diskette by selecting Option 2, Copy Diskette, in the Select an Option menu (do not use the usual DOS COPY *.* or DISKCOPY commands), and then use this diskette for subsequent testing.

Write-Protect Error Reading Drive A. This error, which may occur on the AT when attempting to format a 1.2-Mbyte diskette, may be caused by a non-IBM device driver or other program that is loaded into memory when the system is powered on. The name of the program causing the problem is probably found in an AUTOEXEC.BAT or CONFIG.SYS file on your boot diskette. Reboot using the original DOS diskette—that is, one without an AUTOEXEC or CONFIG file—and once again attempt to format a 1.2-Mbyte diskette. If the format succeeds, then the problem is indeed caused by a program whose name appears in one of these files.

If you are unsure about how to further localize and correct the problem and are experiencing no other difficulties, you may prefer to simply format one or more 1.2-Mbyte diskettes using the DOS diskette, then return to your own boot diskette once the formatting is done.

4

CONFIGURATION AND BATCH FILES

With the exception of what you are about to read, this is not a book about programming. There are no routine programming techniques that need to be followed on a regular schedule in order to keep your personal computer up and running. Furthermore, it is not possible to damage the computer by entering some lethal combination of keystrokes or by inserting an improperly prepared or otherwise incompatible diskette into a drive. Therefore, it might not seem appropriate to discuss programming and system diagnostics in the same book.

However, it is quite possible for a program to cause an *apparent* system failure, especially if it makes certain erroneous assumptions about how the PC is set up. For example, the program may attempt to write data to a file on a drive that doesn't exist, to read a file that it can't find, to do color graphics on a monochrome display, or to print a 132-column spreadsheet on a printer set for 80 characters per line.

In all of these cases, the user ends up looking at some sort of error message, and a bit of diagnostics work is required to track down the problem and rule out an apparent system failure.

Many of these problems occur during the brief interval between the successful completion of the POST procedure and the start of the day's programming, word processing, or spreadsheeting.

The failure occurs because in the absence of explicit instructions to the contrary, the computer makes a certain number of default assumptions.

81

Needless to say, these are not always appropriate to the job at hand, and some may indeed get in the way of whatever it is you want to do next.

For example, if there are two displays installed, the computer selects one of them as the default display, that is, the display whose screen is to be used for the day's programming. Murphy's Law clearly states that the other display is the one needed this time. In another case, you want to use a diskette in drive B; the computer assumes you want to use the hard disk that is designated drive C.

These are but two of the many examples of what you want and what you get if you don't ask. And so, this chapter. Here we'll examine a few programming techniques that will help you to get your computer up and running quickly and in the manner in which you want it to work. By giving some attention to these details here and now, a lot of time can be saved later on, since there will be less likelihood of having to waste time diagnosing some unpredictable system behavior.

This chapter briefly looks at four potentially confusing aspects of computer use: the configuration file, the device driver, the tree-structured directory, and the batch file. The treatment here is necessarily brief but should be sufficient to give you a basic understanding of these topics. For further details, consult the chapters and sections of your DOS Manual as listed in Table 4.1. Readers who are already familiar with these subjects may safely skip this chapter without fear of missing anything important.

THE CONFIGURATION FILE

At the conclusion of the POST procedure, DOS searches the default drive for a text file called CONFIG.SYS (Configure System). The file gives DOS

Table 4.1 Pertinent Sections of IBM DOS Manuals

Topic	DOS 3.00	DOS 4.00
ANSI.SYS	4-14	75-78
Batch files	7-24 – 7-42	Chapter 5
CONFIG.SYS	Chapter 4	Chapter 4
Device drivers	4-13 – 4-18	75-98
LASTDRIVE	4-24	104
MODE	7-132	145-146
PROMPT	7-149	47-48
SUBST	7-172	151
TREE		53
Tree-structured directories	Chapter 5	
VDISK, electronic disks	4-14 – 4-18	84-87

instructions on how to configure the system and load certain files to meet your specific needs. The CONFIG.SYS file is usually created automatically the first time you install DOS. Later on, you may modify the file to suit your changing requirements.

Creating a CONFIG.SYS File

Creating a configuration file, or the batch file described later on, is really quite easy. Either one may be written with any word processor that will save a file in ASCII mode (American National Standard Code for Information Interchange). Alternatively, the EDLIN program described in the DOS manual may be used, or, better yet, the new DOS 5.0 EDIT utility. Or you may write a short file by entering the following line at the DOS prompt:

```
COPY CON CONFIG.SYS
```

In other words, COPY the keystrokes which are about to be entered at the CONsole, or keyboard, to a file named CONFIG.SYS that is to be written to a diskette in the default drive or to the hard disk drive C. To write a small configuration file, enter the program lines seen below and press the Enter key at the end of each line. More detailed explanations of each line follow the listing.

Program line	Explanation
COPY CON CONFIG.SYS	Name the file CONFIG.SYS.
LASTDRIVE= x	Provide space for additional drives, where x is the letter (F through Z) of the last drive.
SHELL=C:\DOS\COMMAND.COM /p /e: xxx	Install COMMAND.COM permanently.
INSTALL=SHARE.EXE	Install the SHARE utility (DOS 4.xx).
DEVICE=ANSI.SYS	Load the ANSI.SYS device driver.
DEVICE=VDISK.SYS 1536 512 128 /E	Load the VDISK.SYS device driver with the parameters described below.
^Z	Press function key 6, then press ↵ to quit and save the file.

Once your configuration file is entered and saved, the installed programs and listed devices become part of the total system every time the computer is rebooted. Add a separate line to your own CONFIG.SYS file to accommodate each device that requires its own driver. Of course, each device-driver file listed in your configuration file must either be present in the current directory or have its path specified in its instruction line. (The PATH command is described on page 94.)

LASTDRIVE. Under normal conditions, DOS provides space for five drives, labeled A through E. But when making extensive use of the SUBSTitute command described below, or logical drives (see Chapter 9, page 348), you may want to designate additional drives as F, G, and so on, up to the letter Z. To do so, the system must be configured to take into account the last drive letter you wish to use. This is easily done by adding the LASTDRIVE line seen above.

SHELL. If COMMAND.COM is located in the DOS (or some other) subdirectory and is not also present in the root directory, then the SHELL command seen above must be entered in your configuration file, followed by the path to the directory in which COMMAND.COM is located. The parameters following it are

/p	If the SHELL command is used, it must be followed by the /p parameter in order for your AUTOEXEC.BAT file (see page 92) to be executed. Refer to the DOS manual for other details.
/e:xxx	This parameter defines the number of bytes set aside for the DOS environment. The default value is 160 bytes. The DOS environment is described later in the chapter.

INSTALL. This new command is available starting with DOS version 4.00. In the example seen above, it is used to load the SHARE.EXE program, which is required if a hard drive is to support partition sizes greater than 32Mb. See Chapter 9 for more details about partitions (page 348). Prior to DOS 4.00, the SHARE program or similar programs would have to be loaded via the AUTOEXEC.BAT file described later on in this chapter.

DEVICE. This command is used to load any device drivers required to properly configure the system. The following section gives more details.

THE DEVICE DRIVER

In computer jargon, a device is any one of a number of physical or logical attachments to the personal computer system. Typical devices include your PC's keyboard, display, printer, standard diskette and disk drives, communications ports, an electronic disk, and so on. Each such device requires its own device driver, which is a special program providing the required logical interface between the device and the total system.

Resident Device Drivers

The drivers for some devices are provided and automatically loaded into memory by DOS, and the user need not be concerned with them. These resident drivers include all the devices just mentioned, with the exception of the electronic disk.

Additional IBM Device Drivers

However, some additional devices require device drivers that are not routinely loaded into memory when the system is turned on. Typical examples include the drivers needed for an electronic disk, for various extended screen and keyboard enhancements, for expanded memory, and for many external devices. Some of these driver programs are found on the DOS diskette, while others are separately supplied with the devices that require them. Since they are not automatically loaded when the system is turned on, their file names must be included in a device line in the configuration file. Since DOS must be able to find the driver in order to load it, the device line must specify the path (if any) to the driver. For example, if you keep all your device drivers in a DRIVERS subdirectory, each line would read as follows:

DEVICE=C:\DRIVERS*driver name* (and parameters, if any)

A few frequently used device drivers are described here. For further details, consult the DOS manual.

ANSI.SYS. This driver is found on the DOS system diskette and must be loaded in order to use various features such as the PROMPT command described later in this chapter.

DRIVER.SYS and EXDSKBIO.DRV. The first of these two device drivers is used with the IBM 3.5-inch diskette drive for the PC, XT, and AT, and may be found on the IBM system diskette, starting with DOS version 3.2. The AT requires the second driver as well, and this is supplied on a separate diskette packaged with the drive itself.

IBMCACHE.SYS. In the jargon of the PC, a cache—that is, a hiding place—is a reserved section of RAM in which frequently accessed disk/diskette sectors are stored. Given the appropriate software, the cache is searched first, and if it holds the desired data, access is faster than in a conventional disk-read operation. Apparently IBM takes the definition of cache seriously, for the driver itself is a hidden file on MCA Reference and ISA model 30 286 Starter diskettes and it is not described in the DOS manual. Instead, a separate single-sheet binder insert provides the necessary documentation.

A cache installation utility (also hidden) is also on the diskette. To install the cache, insert the Reference diskette in drive A *after* the system has already booted. At the DOS prompt type A:IBMCACHE ↵ and then select the Install Disk Cache option from the Main Menu. Doing so adds a cache driver line to your configuration file, followed by the three cache parameters seen here:

```
DEVICE=IBMCACHE.SYS C /m /Pn
```

Parameter and definition	Units	Range	Default
C cache size	Kb	16–512 with /NE	64Kb
		16–15360 with /E	64Kb
/m *m* = NE		use low memory (NE = not Extended)	
	m = E	use Extended memory	NE
/Pn page size	sectors	2, 4, 8	4

Once the IBMCACHE line has been added to your configuration file, the default parameter values may be changed by again running the installation utility and this time selecting the Change Disk Cache Settings option. The cache utility requires DOS version 3.3 or greater.

VDISK.SYS. DOS versions 3.0 and beyond provide the means to create an electronic, or RAM, disk, which IBM documentation calls a virtual disk or VDISK. The VDISK.SYS device driver instructs DOS to set aside a portion of unused system memory to function as though it were an actual disk or diskette. Since this reserved memory has no moving parts, data moves back and forth in a fraction of the time required when a physical drive is involved.

The electronic disk automatically assumes the next available drive letter and functions as though it were an actual physical drive. Thus in a PC containing two diskette drives, A and B, and one hard disk drive, C, the electronic disk becomes drive D.

Your PC may be configured to utilize the electronic disk by adding the appropriate device driver to your configuration file. The driver itself is found on the DOS diskette. In use, VDISK.SYS may be followed by three numeric parameters and a software switch, as shown here.

```
DEVICE=VDISK.SYS D S F /m:n
```

Parameter and definition		Units	Range	Default
D	disk size	Kb	1Kb–16Mb	64Kb
S	sector size	bytes	128, 256, 512	128
F	max directory entries	files	2–512	64
/m:n	m = E		use Extended memory	
	m = X		use eXpanded memory (DOS 4.00)	
	n = number of sectors to be transferred at one time	sectors	1–8	8

Notes. The extended/expanded memory option is for AT and PS/2 systems only. If the /X:n option is used, the following line must appear in your configuration file *before* the VDISK.SYS line:

```
DEVICE=XMA2EMS.SYS
```

In addition, the /X parameter must be appended to the BUFFERS command in the configuration file (see DOS manual for further details).

• **Electronic Disk Caution.** Since the electronic disk is, in fact, nothing more than a segment of RAM, its contents will of course be lost when the system is turned off. Therefore, it is a good idea to periodically copy work in progress to a physical drive, and it is absolutely essential to do this before turning the system off.

XMAEM.SYS. Installation of this driver permits extended memory (at starting address 1,024Kb) to be used for expanded memory applications. It requires DOS 4.00 and an 80386 system such as PS/2 models 70 and 80, and it must be followed in the configuration file by the XMA2EMS.SYS driver described below.

Assuming the driver remains in the DOS subdirectory, the required line in the configuration file is

```
DEVICE=C:\DOS\XMAEM.SYS n
```

where *n* is the number of 16Kb pages to be accessed. If the *n* parameter is omitted, XMAEM.SYS will use all the extended memory that is available. Otherwise, *n* may be any value from a minimum of 64 (× 16Kb = 1,024Kb) to the maximum available extended memory in the system. This driver must be installed before the XMA2EMS.SYS driver described next.

XMA2EMS.SYS. This driver supports the LIM Expanded Memory Specification (version 4.00) and requires DOS 4.00. Hardware requirements are as follows:

80286 system	an expanded memory adapter
80386 system	a minimum of 1Mb extended memory and the prior installation of the XMAEM.SYS driver in the configuration file.

The required configuration file line is

```
DEVICE=C:\DOS\XMA2EMS.SYS FRAME=nnnn P254=nnnn P255=nnnn /X:xx
```

Parameter	Definition
FRAME	any 64Kb block of memory within the reserved memory area
P254 & P255	two 16Kb memory pages required for DOS 4.00
nnnn	the segment address at which each of the above memory blocks begins
/X:xx	*xx* is the number of 16Kb pages to be accessed. The minimum is 4, the maximum is the amount of available memory.

For further details, refer to the Expanded Memory and Expanded Memory Diagnostics sections of Chapter 7.

Non-IBM Device Drivers. In addition to the above device drivers, the user may have a non-IBM device that comes with its own device-driver program. The names of a few such drivers, as well as those mentioned above, are listed in Table 4.2. The listing is by no means complete, and is intended only to give an idea of the probable need for additional device drivers when adding various options to a PC.

Table 4.2 Typical Device Drivers *

Driver name	Extension	Product
A10 – 20	COM	Iomega 10Mb Bernoulli Box
AMDEK	SYS	Amdek CD – ROM LaserDrive – 1
ANSI	SYS	for extended screen and keyboard control
ATDOSHC2	SYS	Plus Development Hardcard II
DRIVER	SYS	IBM 3.5 – inch External Diskette Drive
EGA	SYS	Microsoft Windows
EXDSKBIO	DRV	IBM 3.5 – inch External Drive for AT
IDRIVE	SYS	Iomega 20Mb Bernoulli Box
INVOC	SYS	Intel Inboard 386/AT
MOUSE	DRV	Microsoft Windows mouse driver
MOUSE	SYS	Microsoft DOS – level mouse driver
PCM100	DRV	Philips CM100/CM155 CD – ROM drive
RCD	SYS	Iomega 44Mb Bernoulli Box
SMARTDRV	SYS	Microsoft Windows disk caching program
SPEED	SYS	Intel Inboard 386/AT
SSTOR	SYS	Storage Dimensions SpeedStor utilities
VDISK	SYS	IBM virtual disk
XMA2EMS	SYS	IBM DOS 4.00 expanded memory support

* Some device drivers require additional parameters following the driver
name and extension. Consult the manufacturer's documentation for
specific details.

TREE-STRUCTURED DIRECTORIES

In early versions of DOS, typing the DIRectory command displayed the
name of every program on the diskette in the default drive. But as storage
capacity on diskette media and hard disks continued to expand, more and
more programs shared the same disk surface. It soon became difficult to
find whatever file you wanted when it was buried deep in a list of unrelated
other files.

Root and Subdirectories.

Figure 4.1 illustrates a tree-structured directory system. With typical PC
perversity, the *root directory* is the only directory in the tree that does not
resemble a root, while the directories that do look like roots are called
subdirectories. But notwithstanding the confusing nomenclature, the system makes it convenient to assign your programs to various subdirectories,
sub-subdirectories, and so on. Then, by looking at the files contained in just
one of these subdirectories, all the other files in all the other directories can,
for the moment, be ignored.

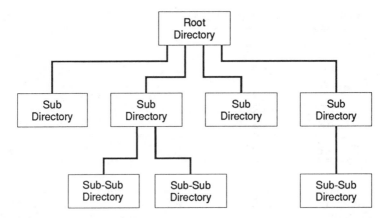

Figure 4.1. An example of a tree-structured directory. Although the subdirectories branching out from the main directory are like the roots of a tree, computer jargon confuses the issue by calling the main directory the root, while all the others are known as subdirectories.

As an example, you might have a subdirectory for all your BASIC programs. This can be further divided into sub-subdirectories of game programs, scientific programs, financial programs, and so on. Elsewhere on the same diskette there might be an extensive collection of document files, subdivided into scientific, financial, and legal categories. In fact, two or more such directories might be in place, one for each person who uses the same computer.

When all this is done, Ms. Ortiz can look at her own financial documents relating to mortgages without having to search through Mr. Hartley's scientific files in order to find them. In fact, she can even ignore her own financial files on income tax, which are in a separate subdirectory.

Accessing a Subdirectory

When the PC is first turned on, the default directory is, of course, the one on either drive A or drive C. Therefore, in order for Ms. Ortiz to get to her mortgage files on the hard disk in drive D, she must type

D:	to log on to drive D
CD \ORTIZ\FINANCE\MORTGAGE	to change to the indicated directory
DIR	to display a directory listing

Of course, there's a trade-off. For the convenience of working within a directory of manageable size, it becomes awkward to reach a file in another directory several levels removed from the current one. Ordinarily, in order to reach a program on a diskette in, say, drive B, it's only necessary to include the required drive letter as a prefix to the file name. Thus

`FILENAME.XYZ`

becomes

`B:FILENAME.XYZ`

But if that file is tucked away in a subdirectory, then the lengthy series of keystrokes described above must be entered in order to reach it. The task is certainly not impossible, but it is tedious, especially if it must be done with any kind of regularity.

This is just the sort of task that a batch file can handle, either automatically when the system is turned on, or as required during the course of the work day. Both kinds of batch files are described in the following sections.

THE BATCH FILE

Whenever it's necessary to change displays, diskette drives, directories, and so on, a certain amount of keyboarding will usually produce the necessary changes. However, the required keystrokes may be rather cryptic, and it's easy to make an error. For example, to display the current disk drive, path, and time of day in the upper right-hand corner of the screen, the following keystrokes are required:

`PROMPT $e[s$e[1;49H$e$p$b$t$e[u$n$g`

Before trying out this command, you must first include the ANSI.SYS file in your configuration file, as described earlier in this chapter.

It is unlikely that anyone would care to type the PROMPT line seen above every time the computer is turned on. And it is even more unlikely that it will be typed flawlessly at every attempt. On a lesser note, it is simply annoying to be asked by your PC for today's date and the correct time whenever you turn it on, although those whose computers lack an internal system clock will have to continue being annoyed. To circumvent these tedious chores, you can write a little program that contains your routine start-up instructions. Then every time you turn the PC on, it will automatically seek out this program and execute your wishes without being asked.

This type of program is known as a batch file, because it contains a batch of instructions that are to be executed in sequence.

The AUTOEXEC.BAT File

When the PC is turned on and the POST procedure is successfully completed, the system searches the default drive for the configuration file described earlier in this chapter, and then for a batch file called AUTOEXEC.BAT. The distinctive file name tells the system to AUTOmatically EXECute the BATch of instructions in the file before doing anything else. In fact, the batch file is really nothing more than a series of commands that are read from a diskette or hard disk, instead of from the keyboard. These may consist of all those tedious keystrokes that are required to get the computer up and running and doing whatever it is you want it to do.

Depending on the particular configuration of your system, the presence of the AUTOEXEC.BAT file may obviate the need to enter the date and time whenever the system is turned on. In AT and PS/2 systems (except model 25), an internal battery-operated clock keeps track of the correct date and time. On turn-on, if a batch file is detected, the system automatically assumes that the date and time are correct, regardless of the contents of the batch file. However, if a batch file is not found, the user is asked to verify the date and time.

In other personal computers, an optional adapter may contain a similar type of battery-operated clock. In this case, the batch file will require an instruction in order for the system to accept that clock's date and time information. The user's manual accompanying the card should list the appropriate instruction for you to write into your AUTOEXEC.BAT file.

Multipurpose Batch Files

The AUTOEXEC.BAT file described above will automatically perform a single set of tasks each time the computer is turned on. However, it's more likely that you'll want to do one of several sets of tasks and that you'll also want to change to a different setup during the course of the work day. In this case, each set of instructions can be written into its own batch file and be given a distinctive name.

Creating and Saving a Batch File

To write a batch file, begin by typing COPY CON AUTOEXEC.BAT using the same general procedure that was described earlier for writing a configuration file. Next, enter each instruction that you would like to have executed and press the Enter key at the end of each line. For example, a batch file containing the following lines will perform the following functions:

Program line	Explanation
MODE MONO	MODE executes MODE.COM program on DOS diskette. MONO tells MODE.COM to switch to monochrome display.
MODE LPT1: 132, 8	MODE.COM is instructed to change printer's default parameters to print 132 characters on each line, with vertical spacing of 8 lines per inch. The printer's default parameters are usually 80 characters per line, 6 lines per inch.
D:	Signals change to drive D.
CD\ORTIZ\FINANCE\MORTGAGE	Changes current directory as indicated.
YOURPROG	Executes program with this name found in current directory.
C:	Signals a return to drive C.
MODE CO40	MODE.COM program is executed and changes display to color display, with 40-character line width. The previously set printer parameters remain in place.
^Z↵	Pressing function key 6 places the ^Z characters on screen and writes the batch file to the diskette or hard drive.

Notes. Use of the MODE command assumes that the MODE.COM file is in the current directory on the default drive. If it is not, the PATH command described later on may be of use. When YOURPROG is executed, the remaining batch file instructions (C: and MODE CO40) are not implemented until you exit YOURPROG. The next time the computer is turned on or rebooted, all of the above instructions will be executed automatically.

The advantage of an automatically executed batch file is obvious. A lengthy series of keystrokes may be written once, saved in the file, corrected or modified as required, and then ignored. Once again, the personal computer takes over another little bit of drudgery, freeing the user for more important tasks.

Batch File Enhancements

As noted above, in order to execute a batch file other than AUTOEXEC.BAT, you must type its name (it's not necessary to enter the BAT extension) and then press the Enter key. All the batch files might be kept in a subdirectory on drive A called BATFILES, and a return to this directory could be written as the last line of every batch file. Using Ms. Ortiz's batch file as an example, the last few lines become

```
MODE CO80
A:
CD \BATFILES
```

Here, the color display is turned back on again, drive A is selected, and the current directory is changed to BATFILES. The next user merely needs to enter his or her name, or whatever else the batch file of interest may be called.

Additional enhancements such as the PATH, SET, and SUBST commands can make batch files even more useful, as briefly described here. For further information on these commands, refer to your DOS manual.

PATH Command. Earlier it was assumed that the MODE.COM program was in the current directory. But in a complex directory system, every program that may be needed obviously can't be in the current directory. Therefore, the PATH command may be used to instruct the system to look elsewhere for any program that can't be found in the current directory. This saves the user the bother of having to recall and accurately enter the path that is needed to reach various programs. In the present case, a line such as the following could be written into the AUTOEXEC.BAT file:

```
PATH=C:\THESE;D:\THOSE;E:\UTILITY
```

With the addition of this line, if YOURPROG is not found in the current directory, DOS will look for it in three other places—in directories with the unlikely names of C:\THESE and D:\THOSE, and then in your UTILITY directory on drive E. Note that a semicolon separates each path that is to be searched, and that the complete path may not exceed 127 characters. (A second PATH command will cancel all paths in the first line.)

In the case of the MODE.COM program described earlier, its path is probably well known, so there is an alternative way to get to it. For the sake of the example, let's assume it's in a subdirectory called UTILITY on hard drive C. If so, just enter the appropriate line in the batch file, either

```
C:\UTILITY\MODE MONO
```

   or

```
C:\UTILITY\MODE LPT1: 132, 8
```

or whatever it is that you want MODE to do.

The PATH command is especially helpful in finding executable files—those with a COM, EXE, or BAT extension—that may be buried several layers down in a directory tree. For example, among your miscellaneous program files—MISCPROG—there are a number of scientific programs arranged by division, department, and engineer. To execute the SMITH.COM program stored at the bottom of this path, you would have to type

```
D:\MISCPROG\SCIENTIF\AEROSPAC\MISSILES\SMITH
```

Of course, that's not impossible to do, but it's far easier to simply enter

```
SMITH
```

and this can be done if a suitably written PATH command is in the AUTOEXEC.BAT file. Not finding SMITH on the default drive, DOS will search for it along all the paths indicated in the PATH command. For this reason, it is usually a good idea *not* to include a diskette drive in the PATH command line, or if such a drive is included, to make it the last entry in the path. In either case, if there is no diskette in the drive, an *Abort, Retry, Fail?* message will be seen when DOS attempts to search that part of the path.

SET Command. At the conclusion of some programs, DOS will look in the default directory for the COMMAND.COM file, which it must reload into system memory. If DOS cannot find the file, the system locks up and the following error message is seen:

```
Cannot load COMMAND, system halted
```

In order to avoid this error, use the SET command to tell DOS where to look for the COMMAND.COM file. Assuming the file is located in, say, your UTILITY subdirectory on drive E, enter the following instruction line into your AUTOEXEC.BAT file:

```
SET COMSPEC=E:\UTILITY\COMMAND.COM
```

Note that the SET command is required even if a PATH command specifies a path which should lead to the COMMAND.COM file (as in the description of the PATH command given above).

SUBST Command. For users with DOS version 3.2 or later, another convenient way of accessing a complete subdirectory that is several levels down is to temporarily assign a unique drive letter to it. For example, if the actual last drive in the PC is drive C, then by use of the SUBST (SUBSTitute) command, drive letters D or E can be assigned to a specific subdirectory by entering the following line in the batch file:

```
SUBST E: C:\ORTIZ\FINANCE\MORTGAGE
```

This subdirectory may now be accessed simply by typing E: instead of the longer sequence seen above. Any number of drive letters, up to and including Z, may be used. However, if letters beyond E are required, the LASTDRIVE command must be inserted in a configuration file, as described earlier in this chapter.

A Batch File/Electronic Disk Application

Once the electronic disk described earlier is installed, files may be copied to it, worked on, and then returned to permanent storage on diskette or hard disk before the system is turned off. As a typical example, let's assume the name of your word-processing software is WP.EXE and that it is stored on the hard disk in drive C in a directory which you have called WORDPROC. Your file of documents is stored on a diskette in drive A, and you want to revise your recent letter to Paul Farrell.

The following batch file will accomplish all of this. The first and last line are not part of the file itself, but simply serve to name the file and then write it to disk.

Program Line	**Explanation**
COPY CON WP.BAT	Copy the following lines into a file named WP.BAT.
D:	Signals a change to drive D, the electronic disk.
IF EXIST WP.EXE GOTO START	If WP.EXE is already installed on drive D, program execution jumps to the :START line below.
COPY C:\WORDPROC\WP.EXE	Copy your word-processing software to the electronic disk.
COPY C:\(*other programs*)	Copy any other programs (dictionary, thesaurus, etc.) that are used with your word processor.
:START	From above, execution jumps to this line if WP.EXE already exists on drive D.
COPY A:%1	Copy %1 file to drive D. The %1 is automatically replaced by whatever you type after WP when you execute the batch file later on.
WP %1	Execute WP.EXE and open %1 file.
COPY %1 A:	Copy %1 file back to drive A.
C:	Return to drive C.
CD\BATFILES	Orders a change to batch file directory.
^Z	Press function key 6, then press ↵ to quit and save program.

To work on the letter to Mr. Farrell, just type

```
WP FARRELL.LTR
```

and the %1 in the batch file automatically becomes FARRELL.LTR, so that the COPY A:%1 instruction copies the file named FARRELL.LTR from drive A to the electronic disk. The next line executes the word-processor program and opens the FARRELL.LTR file you specified. The following line copies the revised letter back to drive A for permanent storage. The line is automatically executed when you exit the word-processor program, thus returning your revised letter to drive A for permanent storage.

A batch file such as this enables you to effortlessly transfer the necessary files to the electronic disk to enjoy its speed advantages, and also protects against accidental loss of the edited document. But keep in mind that the COPY %1 A: line will automatically copy *only* the file you specified when you first executed the WP batch file. If you transfer and edit other documents on your electronic disk before exiting the word processor, then these must also be copied back to diskette or hard disk before turning off the power.

Keep in mind too that all files saved only on electronic disk will be lost in the event of a power failure. If you do not have a backup power supply, make sure to frequently copy such files back to diskette or hard disk for safekeeping. The backup power supply is described in Chapter 5.

CONFIGURATION AND BATCH FILE DIAGNOSTICS

In writing the configuration and batch files described above, it's easy enough to create a file that, when executed, displays one or more error messages. Such errors may be caused by a problem with the DOS environment or by a faulty line in either file. A few examples of typical errors are given here.

The DOS Environment and Environment Space Error

This one has nothing to do with rain forests or toxic waste, yet it's still important to the PC ecosystem. The *master DOS environment block* (or simply, "the environment") is a memory block located just above COM-MAND.COM in which the system stores critical information created by the CONFIG.SYS and AUTOEXEC.BAT files described in this chapter. To view the current environment, type SET at the DOS prompt, which should display lines such as

```
COMSPEC=C:\DOS\COMMAND.COM
PATH=C:\DOS; (additional paths listed here)
PROMPT=(your prompt, if any)
```

By default, DOS sets aside 160 bytes to store the master environment.

Environment Blocks. In addition to the master DOS environment, each executable program loaded in memory is accompanied by its own *environment block*, which is loaded ahead of the program itself. Later in Chapter 7 (page 280 and Table 7.14), we see how to use the DOS 4.01 MEM/PRO-GRAM to examine the contents of memory, and in so doing, to reveal the location of these blocks, which may be displayed by using the debug utility or by returning to the DOS prompt from within an application program and typing SET, as just described.

Out of Environment Space. This error message is seen if the current environment space is too small, as may be the case if your PATH length is quite long (maximum, 127 bytes) and with other environment data, the total length exceeds the system default of 160 bytes.

To set aside more space for the environment, edit the CONFIG.SYS file to include or modify the following line:

```
SHELL=C:\DOS\COMMAND.COM /p /e:xxx
```

where /e:*xxx* is the amount of space set aside for the environment, rounded up to the nearest paragraph (16-byte) boundary. Increase the value of *xxx* and reboot the system. If the error message is repeated, increase the value again.

For information about the /p parameter and the SHELL command itself, refer to the SHELL command described earlier in this chapter (page 84).

Other CONFIG.SYS and AUTOEXEC.BAT Errors

As with any other executable program, there are all sorts of things that can cause errors in configuration and batch files. A few examples are mentioned here.

```
Unrecognized command in CONFIG.SYS
Error in CONFIG.SYS line x.
```

Here, the configuration file cannot execute a command found on line *x* of the file. However, the remainder of the configuration file is executed, followed by the AUTOEXEC.BAT file (if any).

Make a note of the displayed line number and at the DOS prompt, type the following line:

```
TYPE CONFIG.SYS
```

With the file contents displayed on screen, count down to the appropriate line number and note the error. Then use EDLIN or an ASCII editor to correct the line, as required.

```
Bad or missing (drive letter):(path)\(file name)
Error in CONFIG.SYS line x.
```

This error message will be seen if a DEVICE= line is followed by a path and/or device driver name that does not exist. As above, check the indicated line and make the necessary correction. If the line is typed correctly, then the indicated file is probably found elsewhere on your boot diskette or hard drive. Either move the file to the proper location, or change the instruction line in the configuration file.

```
Bad command or file name.
```

This error message may be seen if the system can't find a program listed in the AUTOEXEC.BAT file. The message does not specify which command or file name is bad, so if an inspection of the file does not immediately reveal the problem, you may want to insert a few PAUSE commands in the file and reboot the system. At each pause, press any key to continue. When the error message reappears, you know the problem lies somewhere after the last "Press any key" message. Insert additional PAUSE commands as required, until the specific problem line is isolated. Then try executing that line directly at the DOS prompt. If the indicated program executes correctly, then there is probably an error in the line as it appears in the batch file. But if the *Bad command* error continues to be seen, then either the program is missing or the command itself is invalid.

Problems with INSTALL Utilities. Some software comes with an automatic installation utility program. To configure your system, you type INSTALL↵ (or similar) and then answer a series of on-screen questions. Depending on the sophistication of the software vendor, the install program will either skillfully modify your CONFIG.SYS and/or AUTOEXEC.BAT files to include the necessary instructions, or trash one or both of them, leaving you with a system that operates the new software but nothing else. As a precaution, some installation programs save your old files by giving them BAK (backup) suffixes, while others don't. So with the wrong kind of luck, you'll have to reconstruct your older files from memory if the new installation doesn't work the way you thought it would.

If you have any doubts about what an install program will or won't do, take the time to make a protection copy of your configuration and batch files, so that you can recover any information that gets lost during a new installation.

After the installation utility has done its work, examine your CONFIG.SYS and AUTOEXEC.BAT files *before* rebooting, just to make sure there will be no little surprises after you press the Ctrl + Alt + Del keys.

Make sure your original PATH command (if any) remains intact, and that a new PATH command is not found later in the file, thereby canceling the earlier line. If this has happened, delete the new PATH line and append its contents to your original line.

Assuming the install program has inserted new command lines in your AUTOEXEC.BAT file, make sure these lines are located where they can be found. For example, some installation programs copy your existing batch file and append new lines at the end. These lines may never be executed if some command in your original file transfers execution to another file, or if some other condition otherwise isolates the new lines.

CONFIGURATION AND BATCH FILE SUMMARY

As noted at the beginning of this chapter, the information found here may not seem to fit under anyone's, except the author's, definition of routine maintenance. However, a lot of the apparent system failures that pop up every now and then—usually during those first few minutes of operation—may be traced to an error made while entering one or more lines of not-very-informative keystrokes, such as the PROMPT command noted earlier in this chapter.

Putting the names of all the required device drivers into a CONFIG.SYS file and using an AUTOEXEC.BAT file as described here will go a long way toward relieving the operator of having to wade through a long series of complex instructions every time the system is turned on.

Remember that any program name included in a configuration or batch file must be accounted for in one of the following ways:

If just the program name is given (for example, MODE.COM), the program must actually be present in the current directory.

If the program is in another directory, its name must be prefixed by the path to that directory (for example, C:\DOS\MODE.COM).

If neither of these conditions is met, then a PATH command must be used to show DOS how to find the program (for example, PATH=C:\DOS). The PATH command can also include other paths that may be taken to find a program, with each path separated from the preceding one by a semicolon.

To help distinguish the CONFIG.SYS from the AUTOEXEC.BAT file, note that the former contains configuration instructions that (with the exception of INSTALL) cannot otherwise be executed. By contrast, the AUTOEXEC.BAT file contains nothing other than instructions that could also be entered at any DOS prompt by typing them in one line at a time.

Once the CONFIG.SYS and AUTOEXEC.BAT are written and debugged, their presence will help avoid many apparent errors which might otherwise suggest that some part of the system is malfunctioning.

5

ELECTRIC POWER
AND THE POWER
SUPPLY UNIT

After setting up your personal computer, it's tempting to simply plug it in, turn it on, and begin using it with no further thought about external electrical requirements. But since successful routine operation depends on supplying the computer with a reliable source of power, this chapter will begin with a look at what's required and how to anticipate potential power problems before they occur.

Electrical Terminology

Throughout this chapter you will encounter a handful of common electrical terms. Several of these are given a brief, informal definition here.

Term	Definition
current	Measure of rate at which electricity flows through a circuit; measured in amperes (A), popularly abbreviated as amps. Amount of current varies according to electrical requirements of system. The larger the system, the greater the total current flow.
frequency	The number of alternating-current cycles per unit of time. Cycles per second is now expressed as hertz (Hz).

Term	Definition
power	Measure of electrical energy consumed by a device; measured in watts (W).
voltage	Measure of difference in electric potential between two conductors in a power line; measured in volts (V) or kilovolts (kV).

VOLTAGE REQUIREMENTS FOR IBM PCS

All IBM personal computers are designed to work within one of two alternating-current (AC) electrical ranges. But, using products marketed in the United States as an example, there seems to be little agreement on how to specify a voltage requirement. For example, the old IBM PC Monochrome Display was described as a 110-volt device, whereas the Color Display was said to operate at 120 volts. In fact, both devices, and most others, operate over a voltage range from about 100 volts to 125 volts. This is often referred to as the "115-volt range" and is abbreviated in electrical charts as 120. Outside this country, electric service of 200 to 240 volts (230-volt range) is frequently encountered.

PC and XT. The 115-V range was standard, and the 230-V range was available as an option, or as standard in countries in which that voltage range is normally used.

AT. The voltage range is selected by setting a slide switch immediately above the power cord plug on the system unit rear panel, as seen in Figure 5.1. Therefore, it is important to make sure that this switch is set to the voltage supplied by the electric wall socket in use. If the computer is already set up and in use, it can be assumed that the switch is in its correct position. Otherwise, it's worth the time to double-check before powering on for the first time.

PS/2 Systems. Although all PS/2 computers operate within either voltage range, some systems follow the AT example, while others automatically switch to the correct range every time power is applied. Refer to the *AC Select* listing given later on in Table 5.5 for specific system information.

• **Input Voltage Cautions.** Other than the PS/2 MCA systems, if any of the above IBM personal computers are plugged into an electric outlet delivering the wrong voltage, one of two effects will be noted. If 115 volts is supplied to a 230-volt computer, no damage will occur, but the system

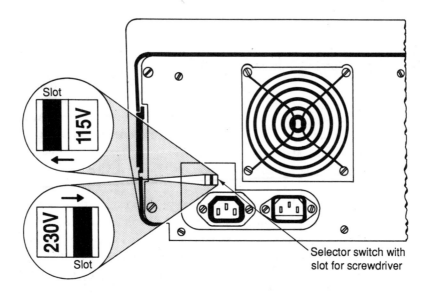

Figure 5.1.   The rear-panel voltage-selector switch on the AT. A similar switch is found on PS/2 models 25, 25 286, 30 286, and 55SX.

will not function. If the computer is an AT, the power-on light will come on, the fan will turn, and the in-use light on drive A may also be illuminated. If 230 volts is supplied to a 115 volt computer, the internal power supply system will be damaged and will have to be replaced. Note that IBM PS/2 monitors do *not* include the automatic voltage-switching feature described above. Therefore a monitor must be selected to meet the voltage requirements of the country in which it will be used.

Power versus VA Rating

A power specification may be given in terms of an actual power rating or as a product of voltage and current. Both methods are briefly described here.

Actual Power Rating.   Power is usually found by multiplying the applied voltage by the current drawn by the device being measured, as seen in the following equation:

$P = E \times I$

where
P is power, in watts,
E is voltage, in volts, and
I is current, in amps.

Power Factor. For greater accuracy, the $E \times I$ product should be multiplied by a power factor, usually a value slightly less than 1.00, but beyond the scope of this discussion. For routine power calculations, the simple product found by multiplying *E* and *I* errs on the side of safety, giving a value that may be slightly higher than the actual power consumed by the device.

VA (or kVA) Rating. In some cases a power rating is published with either a VA (volt-ampere) or a kVA (kilovolt-ampere) suffix, instead of W (watts). This is done to indicate that the value seen is the simple product of voltage times current and does not take the power factor into account, as would be required for the more accurate, but more difficult to measure, actual power rating.

Electrical Service Overseas

For the benefit of readers who may need to ship a personal computer overseas, Table 5.1 lists the nominal voltages now in use in various areas worldwide. For a more complete list, the U.S. Department of Commerce publishes *Electric Current Abroad.* This booklet lists frequency, phase,

Table 5.1 Voltages and Line Frequencies at Selected Locations Worldwide

Location	Voltage (V)	Frequency (Hz)
Canada	120/240	60
Europe	220/380	50
Israel	230/400	50
Japan	100/200	50/60
Latin America †		
Mexico	127/220	60
Middle East	220/380	50
United Kingdom	240/415	50
United States	120/240	60

† Wide variation between cities, countries

nominal voltage, number of conductors, frequency stability notes, and other information for just about every city in the world. If you are going someplace not listed, you might want to consider taking a steno pad along and leaving your computer at home.

System-Specific Power Requirements

Table 5.2 lists the current ratings of several typical IBM personal computer configurations, as observed during a series of field measurements (VA ratings can be computed as indicated in the table). The values given may be used as a very general guideline to anticipating your own system's power requirements, but should not be interpreted as being definitive.

For comparison, Table 5.3 lists the PC's electric current requirements along with those of various other popular appliances. You can see that the personal computer consumes less power than many other commonly used electric devices. With the exception of the cautions listed here, there is no danger of installing more options than the system is capable of supplying with power.

Color Displays. All color displays must be plugged into a separate AC outlet, not into the outlet on the rear of pre-PS/2 system units. This outlet is reserved for the monochrome display only, as explained later in this chapter.

PC Hard Disk Drive. In the PC system only, the hard disk drive must be placed in the expansion unit, which has a separate power supply capable of supplying the requisite power. Alternatively, a larger power supply may be installed in the PC, as described at the end of this chapter.

PS/2 Hard Disk Drive. When adding or replacing a hard disk drive in a PS/2 system, make sure the new drive does not exceed the capabilities of the system power supply. Table 5.4 lists the power requirements of representative IBM hard disk drives and adapters. If you plan to install a third-party drive in a PS/2 computer, make sure it does not draw significantly more power than the equivalent IBM drive.

Non-IBM Adapters. Due to the impressive variety of second-source support, it is not possible to know which of these devices may exceed the power limits of an IBM personal computer.

Table 5.2 Current Drawn by Various Representative System Configurations Powered from a Standard 120-volt Line

Components	PC per device	PC cumulative	AT per device	AT cumulative	PS/2 30 286 per device	PS/2 30 286 cumulative	PS/2 70 386 per device	PS/2 70 386 cumulative
The basic system, with keyboard:								
64Kb RAM	0.22	0.22	- -	- -	- -	- -	- -	- -
512Kb RAM	- -	- -	0.80	0.80	- -	- -	- -	- -
0Kb RAM	- -	- -	- -	- -	0.25	0.25	0.65	0.65
Add the following options:								
RAM: 512Kb (30), 1024Kb (70)	- -	- -	- -	- -	0.02	0.27	0.04	0.69
diskette drive adapter, one drive	0.16	0.38	0.13	0.93	- -	- -	- -	- -
PS/2, first drive	- -	- -	- -	- -	0.01	0.28	0.01	0.70
second drive	0.05	0.43	0.03	0.96	- -	- -	0.01	0.71
hard drive †	- -	- -	- -	- -	0.10	0.38	0.06	0.77
internal modem	0.05	0.48	0.05	1.01				
256Kb RAM on adapter card	0.05	0.53	- -	- -				
1Mb RAM on adapter card	- -	- -	0.09	1.10				
Add display:								
Monochrome adapter card	0.09	0.62	0.09	1.19				
Monochrome display	0.23	0.85	0.23	1.42				
or								
Color/graphics adapter	0.08	0.61	0.08	1.18				
Color/graphics display	0.50	1.11	0.50	1.68				
or								
Enhanced graphics adapter	- -	- -	0.05	1.15				
Enhanced graphics display	- -	- -	0.65	1.80				
Model 8513 display	- -	- -	- -	- -	0.48	0.86	0.48	1.25
Printers:								
IBM Proprinter (in use)	0.50							
NEC Thimble Printer (in use)	1.05							
Hewlett-Packard LaserJet series II ‡	5.50							

Current drawn, in amps *

* To find the VA (volt-ampere) rating, multiply each figure by 120.
   To estimate the approximate actual power dissipated, multiply the VA rating by about 0.80.
† Hard disk drives: AT, Seagate 80Mb; model 30 286, IBM 20Mb; model 70, IBM 60Mb.
‡ Printer draws this momentary current at intervals of about 25 seconds.

Table 5.3 Comparison of Current Used by Personal Computers * and Common Household Appliances

Electric device	Current (amps)	VA rating
PC – 1 64Kb system unit only	0.22	26
PS/2 model 30 286, no display	0.38	46
50 – watt light bulb	0.40	48
13 – inch RGB monitor	0.50	60
Thimble printer, on but not printing	0.75	90
PS/2 model 70 386, no display	0.77	92
AT 512Kb system unit only	0.80	96
100 – watt light bulb	0.80	96
PC with monochrome display	0.85	102
PS/2 model 30 286 with 8513 display	0.86	103
Thimble printer, while printing	1.05	126
PC with color/graphics display	1.11	133
150 – watt light bulb	1.20	144
Color television set	1.25	150
PS/2 model 70 with 8513 display	1.25	150
AT with monochrome display	1.42	170
AT with enhanced graphics display	1.80	216
AT with monochrome and EGA displays	2.12	254
Hewlett – Packard LaserJet series II printer	5.50	660
Vacuum cleaner	5.50	660
Electric toaster	10.00	1,200
Microwave oven	12.50	1,500

* IBM system configurations are taken from Table 5.2.

Power Supplies in IBM Personal Computers

For reference purposes, Tables 5.5 and 5.6 list the electrical specifications of the power supplies found in IBM personal computers. Note the important functional difference between the power supply found within each PC's system unit and a backup power supply. While the former furnishes the required voltages within the system, the latter serves quite a different function, as described in the section on Backup Power Supplies (page 117).

POWER-LINE CONSIDERATIONS

The following section presents a brief review of some power-related factors that may influence the performance of a personal computer.

Table 5.4 Power Requirements for Selected PS/2 Hard Disks and Adapters

	Power range	
Component	min. (watts)	max. (watts)
3.5" hard disks		
20Mb	15.7	17
30Mb	12	14
60Mb	13	19
120Mb	13	19
5.25" hard disks		
44Mb	31	39
70Mb	31	39
115Mb	31	39
314Mb	35	42
MCA Adapters		
16 bit	7	10
32 bit	7	13

On/Off Voltage Transients

Perhaps the most common cause of failure in electric devices is the transient condition that occurs as each device is turned on and off. In many highly complex electronic systems, power is turned on once and stays on continuously for the life of the device. This is because the continuous-power expense is far less than the cost, both in money and in time, of power on/off failures.

As shown in Table 5.3, even a fully equipped IBM personal computer does not draw a lot of current. Therefore, it's best to leave your PC on until you're completely done using it for the day. However, to avoid damage to your display screen, turn down the brightness and contrast when you will be away from the unit for longer than half an hour. Or better yet, use a screen-blanking utility which blanks the screen after five or so minutes of inactivity. Generally, pressing any key will turn the screen back on again.

Use of a Master Power Switch

In any system employing a wide variety of devices—more than one display, printer, or other external devices—it is not a good idea to turn the complete system on via a single master switch. Doing so may cause an excessive power-surge demand, since many devices, especially printers,

Table 5.5   IBM Personal Computer Power Supply Specifications

Computer	PC		XT		XT 286		AT	
Power (watts)	63.5		130		157		192	
AC select	fixed		fixed		automatic		switch	
Supply voltages (VDC)	Under-voltage and Current (VDC) (amps)		Under-voltage and Current (VDC) (amps)		Under-voltage and Current (VDC) (amps)		Under-voltage and Current (VDC) (amps)	
+5	+4.0	7	+4.5	15	+4.5	20	+4.5	19.8
-5	-4.0	0.3	-4.3	0.3	-4.3	0.3	-3.75	0.3
+12	+9.6	2	+10.8	4.2	+10.8	4.2	+10.8	7.3
-12	-9.6	0.25	-10.2	0.25	-10.2	0.25	-10.4	0.3

Computer	25		25 286		30		30 286	
Power (watts)	90 (monochrome) 115 (color)		124.5 (color only)		70		90	
AC select	manual		manual		automatic		manual	
Supply voltages (VDC)	Under-voltage and Current (VDC) (amps)		Under-voltage and Current (VDC) (amps)		Under-voltage and Current (VDC) (amps)		Under-voltage and Current (VDC) (amps)	
+5	+3.2	7	+4.5	9.0	+4.5	9	+4.5	13
-5	-2.4	0.10	-4.3	0.11	-4.3	0.11	-4.3	0.11
+12	+10.5	1.7	+10.8	1.7	+10.8	1.8	+10.8	1.8
-12	-8.6	0.25	-10.2	0.55	-10.2	0.30	-10.2	0.30
+12 †		0.22		0.3				
+39 ‡		0.80						
+115 †		0.45		0.45				

† for built-in color or monochrome display
‡ for built-in model 25 monochrome display only

require considerable, though brief, extra power during the turn-on interval. If all such devices make their power-on demands at the same instant, the combined power requirement may be excessive. In extreme cases, a device may fail during power on and will have to be turned off and back on again to restore normal operation.

Power-Line Irregularities

For a variety of reasons, from electrical storms to excessive power demands on the local utility plant, measured line voltage may vary from time to time, causing the effects described here.

Table 5.5   IBM Personal Computer Power Supply Specifications (continued)

Computer Power (watts) AC select		50, 50Z 94 auto	55 SX 90 manual	60-041 207 auto	60-071 225 auto	65 SX 250 auto
Supply voltages (VDC)	Under- voltage (VDC)	Current (amps)	Current (amps)	Current (amps)	Current (amps)	Current (amps)
+5	+4.5	12.9	13.0	23.65	27.25	30.75
+12	+10.8	2.1	1.8	7.00	7.00	7.00
-12	-10.2	0.41	0.30	0.39	0.39	1.00

Computer Power (watts) AC select		70 132 auto	P70 85 auto	80-041 207 auto	80-071 225 auto
Supply voltages (VDC)	Under- voltage (VDC)	Current (amps)	Current (amps)	Current (amps)	Current (amps)
+5	+4.5	19.2	8.8	23.65	27.25
+12	+10.8	3.21	0.9	7.00	7.00
-12	-10.2	0.30	0.1	0.39	0.39

Brownout. The line voltage falls below the level required by the computer. During a brownout, lights dim, appliance motors slow down, and the display on the computer screen may shrink noticeably.

Voltage Spikes. Transient high-voltage surges in the power line. They generally pass unnoticed by lights and most electrical appliances but may be sufficient to destroy one or more integrated circuits within a computer.

Power Failure. The complete interruption of electric power for more than a fraction of a second.

Ill Effects of Power-Line Irregularities

Unfortunately, the ill effects of some power-line irregularities go beyond the inconvenience of interrupted operations. The most apparent problem is, of course, the loss of data that had not been saved before the power was

Table 5.6 Power Supply Output Voltages *

ISA Systems: Multi-lead cables (all models)					model 25 286	
PC, XT, AT		model 25		model 30	model 30 286	
P1 (PS8 on AT)	J7		P3		J7	same as
1 power good †	1	power good †	1	power good †		model 25
2 n.c. (AT, +5V)	2	ground	2	ground		
3 +12 V	3	+12 V	3	+12 V		
4 −12 V	4	−12 V	4	−12 V		
5 ground	5	ground	5	ground		
6 ground	6	ground	6	ground		
	7	ground				
P2 (PS9 on AT)	8	ground	P4		J14	
1 ground	9	−5 V	1	ground	1	ground
2 ground	10	+5 V	2	ground	2	ground
3 −5 V	11	+5 V	3	−5 V	3	+5 V
4 +5 V	12	+5 V	4	+5 V	4	+5 V
5 +5 V			5	+5 V	5	+5 V
6 +5 V			6	+5 V		sense

Note: P*n*, PS*n* and J*n* are connector labels on system board. Pin 1 is pin
closest to rear of system unit.

MCA Systems with Type 1 ** Power Supply (PS/2 models 50 & 70)			
Single edge connector built into power supply, with pinouts as indicated			
odd numbers		even numbers	
1	−12 V	2–48	ground
3–13	+12 V	50	power good †
15–47	+5 V		
49	system status ‡		

interrupted. If the power interruption occurs during certain disk-write
operations, data already written to disk may be damaged. In such a case,
some of the previously written data may be recoverable by using one of the
file-recovery techniques described in Chapter 8 (page 331). Fortunately, an
interrupted disk-read will not cause a data-loss problem.

Occasionally, a power interruption that is not otherwise noticeable to an
operator may cause a system lockup. In this case, the system must be turned
off and then back on again. In some other cases, the interruption interval
may be such that the system will shut down and immediately reboot as
power is restored. Again, the interval may be so brief that the operator is
not otherwise aware of the problem.

When power is restored after a power failure, you have probably noticed
all sorts of momentary effects on electric appliances. Lights flicker a few

Table 5.6 Power Supply Output Voltages (continued) *

MCA Systems with Type 2 ** Power Supply (PS/2 models 60 & 80)
One 15-lead cable to system board, two 4-pin sockets built into power supply

15–pin connector		4–pin sockets	
1	+5 V	1	+12 V
2	ground	2	ground
3	+12 V	3	ground
4	+5 V	4	+5 V
5	ground		
6	ground		
7	+5 V		
8	ground		
9	−12 V		
10	+5 V		
11	ground		
12	power good †		
13	+5 V		
14	ground		
15	system status ‡		

MCA Systems with Type 3 ‡ Power Supply (PS/2 model 55 SX)
One 12-lead cable, one 5-lead cable to system board

J7		J14	
1	power good §	1	ground
2	ground	2	ground
3	+12 V	3	+5 V
4	−12 V	4	+5 V
5	ground	5	+5 V
6	ground		
7	ground		
8	ground		
9	no connection		
10	+5 V		
11	+5 V		
12	+5 V		

    *   All voltages are DC.

  **   Types 1, 2 and 3 refer here to power supply type *only*. Thus, all model 50 and 70 computers (i.e., types 1 and 2) use a Type 1 supply.

   †   Power good signal is 2.4 to 5.25 V (2.4 to 5.5 V on PC & XT) in normal operation.

   ‡   System status illuminates front panel LED when hard drive is active.

times, the radio fades in and out, and the refrigerator clicks on and off. Most of these devices are sufficiently robust to take these momentary power-line irregularities, and within reason, so is the computer. Power fluctuations of ten to twenty percent should cause no problems, nor should everyday "glitches"—momentary high-level electric surges—do any damage. But not every power-line surge may be counted on to fall within safe limits for a computer. Now and then an irregularity that goes unnoticed elsewhere may be enough to destroy some internal components, making their replacement necessary.

Although such surges may take place at any time without warning, they are especially prevalent in the interval during which power is restored. When a power failure does occur, you may not get the chance to switch the computer off and leave it off until after normal power is restored. In many cases, the power goes off and back on again before you have the chance to realize what has happened, and the damage is done before the switch gets flipped.

POWER-CONDITIONING DEVICES

To help minimize power-line-related problems, surge protectors and backup power supplies are often employed. Both devices are described here.

The Surge Protector

Simply stated, the surge protector filters out potentially harmful power-line irregularities so that these do not reach and damage the computer. For systems making use of a modem, similar devices may be inserted in the telephone line for the same reason.

Some areas of the country are more prone to power-line problems than others. In a densely populated metropolitan area plagued with frequent momentary power interruptions, a surge protector should be considered mandatory. But no matter where you live, it is still a very inexpensive disaster insurance policy. Figure 5.2 illustrates a few representative surge-protection devices that may be used with a PC system installation.

But remember that the surge protector just protects against surges; it can't help when the power drops or dies completely.

Figure 5.2. Surge protectors filter out potentially harmful power-line irregularities. (a) In this example, the surge protector is built into the wall receptacle (5252-IS Surge Suppression Receptacle courtesy Hubbel, Inc.). (b) Outlet strips with built-in surge suppression. (c) Modem and fax protection devices (Power Tree outlet strips and modem/fax protectors courtesy Kensington Microware Ltd.)

The Backup Power Supply

For even more peace of mind, a backup power supply may be considered. A typical backup power supply is shown in Figure 5.3. As its name implies, the device furnishes the computer with a continuous source of electric power, regardless of what happens on the power line. This auxiliary power is furnished by a set of batteries within the backup power supply.

The batteries are kept charged while normal alternating current is supplied to the unit, and their low-voltage direct current is in turn converted to the 115- or 230-volt alternating current required to keep the computer operating during a power failure.

But if power is not eventually restored, the batteries in the backup supply unit will gradually discharge and the computer will then shut down. Depending on the nature of the facility and the work requirements, a backup supply may be selected that permits work to continue for several hours, or one may

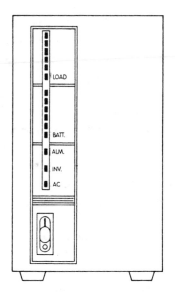
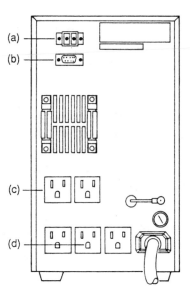

Figure 5.3. A backup power supply furnishes the PC with a continuous source of electricity during a power failure. The illustrated unit provides (a) remote alarm contacts, (b) system interface for automatic shutdown, (c) filtered non-backup outlets, (d) uninterruptable power outlets. (PC-2400 Uninterruptible Power System courtesy Clary Corp.)

be chosen that only allows sufficient time to save work in progress and make an orderly shutdown until normal power is restored.

Even if outside power has been cut off, a fully charged backup power supply must remain plugged into a well-grounded wall outlet at all times. This keeps its chassis at ground potential, minimizing the possibility of electric shock.

Two types of backup power supplies are commonly available—standby and uninterruptible.

Standby Power Supply. In the event of a brownout or total power failure, the standby power supply switches over to its internal batteries, typically within 40 milliseconds. But in some cases, the computer's own fast-acting internal power supply may shut down before the standby power supply has the chance to switch over to its batteries. This does not necessarily indicate a problem with the standby device but is a function of the computer's own power supply, which has been designed to provide optimum voltage regulation while consuming considerably less power and dissipating less heat.

Uninterruptible Power Supply. The   switching   interval   problem described above is unique to standby power supply units and will not be encountered with an uninterruptible power supply unit, since this device does not switch back and forth between battery and regular line voltage. Instead, the computer is always powered by the backup supply's internal batteries, regardless of the condition of the incoming power line. Therefore, there is no switching interval to contend with whenever the external power source fails.

Before purchasing any type of backup power supply system, it's a good idea to determine with certainty its manner of operation. For example, some switching-type supplies are labeled as uninterruptible, since when used with devices other than computers they may indeed seem to be so. While some of these devices make the switch so quickly that there are no problems, others have a relatively long interval before switching from power line to battery, and that delay may present a problem for the computer.

To avoid future problems, make sure the device is a true uninterruptible power supply, or test the device with your computer to be sure the switching interval does not create a problem.

In selecting a backup power supply, keep in mind that for most routine operations it is not necessary to go to the expense of providing backup power for the printer or for more than one display.

If communications is a vital part of your work, you may also want to power an external modem from the backup supply. An internal modem receives its power from the system power supply and so is automatically protected by the backup supply.

The VA ratings given in Table 5.3 may be of some assistance in determining the proper size for a backup power supply for your system.

Backup Supply Units and Power Surges

Although some standby power supply devices may also feature a built-in surge protector of the type described earlier, others are not designed to protect the computer against momentary power-line irregularities. By contrast, the uninterruptible power supply continuously isolates the computer from the power line and therefore serves as protection against momentary irregularities in the line.

Pre-Power-On System Checkout

The very first step in helping to minimize power-related problems is to make sure the computer is plugged into a three-hole grounded electric outlet. In a modern office building, the presence of the three-hole outlet is usually, but not always, an indication that the power service is properly wired. If there is any doubt about this, have the outlet checked first.

In the presence of an older, two-hole electric socket, a commercially available 3-to-2–prong adapter may be used with caution. The pigtail wire on the adapter must be secured to the screw on the outlet's cover plate. The screw and the plate itself must be metal and must be securely fastened to the metal outlet box, which in turn must be properly connected to the building's internal wiring ground.

It's really best to have the two-hole outlet replaced with a three-hole one by a competent electrician who can assure you, in writing, that the outlet is now properly grounded. This is doubly essential if a backup power supply is to be used.

Rear-Panel AC Outlet

The AC outlet on the rear panel of older IBM system units should only be used to supply power to the IBM ISA monochrome display (model 5151). A nonstandard plug/socket combination is employed here for two reasons: (1) to prevent the accidental use of the outlet in conjunction with other devices and (2) to prevent the monochrome display from being plugged into a standard wall socket.

These precautions have been taken because IBM system design considerations require (1) that the monochrome display adapter be on and (2) that the monochrome display be physically connected to the adapter before the monochrome display itself is turned on. If these conditions are not met, the monochrome display may be damaged. By making sure this display is only plugged into the outlet on the rear of the system board, the potential danger is eliminated.

As a further consideration, the designated outlet supplies a maximum current of 0.75 amps, which is suitable for the monochrome display but will not usually be sufficient for color displays, as seen by the values given here:

Device	Maximum current (amps)
Monochrome Display	0.40
Rear-panel outlet	0.75
Color/Graphics Display	0.95
Enhanced Graphics Display	1.00

Before attempting to plug some other display into this outlet, make sure it does not draw more current than the outlet is capable of providing.

DIAGNOSTICS PROCEDURES FOR POWER-RELATED PROBLEMS

When an IBM personal computer is turned on, the normal responses are those given in the power-on checklists below. A response other than one of those described here is an indication that a problem exists.

For the PC, the response sequence is as follows:

1. Diskette drive lights blink once.

2. Blinking cursor appears in top left corner of screen.

3. One short beep is heard at end of POST.

4. Drive A spins briefly.

5. DOS prompt (A> or C>) or IBM PC BASIC screen is displayed.

For other IBM personal computers, the response sequence is as follows:

1. Keyboard status lights blink on and off.

2. Memory size is displayed in top left corner of screen, increasing in 64K increments until all memory is tested.

3. Keyboard status lights blink on and off again, or Num Lock status light comes on and stays on.

4. One short beep is heard at end of POST.

5. Each drive spins briefly.

6. DOS prompt (A> or C>) or IBM PC BASIC screen is displayed.

Power-related problems may be divided into two categories; those that are noted when the system is first turned on at the beginning of the work day, and those that occur while the system is in operation. Each category is discussed below.

We will attempt to solve power-related problems in both categories by isolating the defective element by means of a trial-and-error process. We will physically remove various groups of components from the system to see if their removal has an effect on the problem. If it does, we can assume one or more of the removed devices is causing the problem. If it doesn't, the removed devices can be presumed innocent, and we can turn our attention to whatever remains in place.

Start-Up Problems

The following checklist indicates likely sources of power-related problems that occur when the system is first turned on. The various possibilities are listed more or less in the order in which each might be suspected of being the troublemaker.

1. The room's electric service (e.g., wall outlet, circuit breaker)

2. The computer's AC power cable

3. An external device (e.g., printer, modem)

4. An internal plug-in option

5. The system board

6. The computer's internal power supply unit itself

In order to ascertain which of these devices might be at fault, it is necessary to evaluate the symptoms exhibited by your personal computer. Generally, when an error is encountered as the system is turned on, one of the following symptoms is observed:

1. No response at all

2. System shuts itself off almost immediately

3. Incorrect audio or video response noted

4. Error code other than 02x appears

Each of these responses is briefly described and explained in the paragraphs below.

No Response upon Turning Power On. If there is absolutely no audio/video response, it is not immediately obvious whether the computer itself is at fault or whether it is simply not receiving power. Remember that any response at all from the PC is an indication that the computer is receiving power. The mere presence of an error message is usually sufficient evidence to rule out an external power supply problem, because in order for a message to be displayed or for most—but not all—audio beep codes to be heard, the power supply must be functioning properly.

If no beep is heard, but otherwise the system appears to be operating normally, it is probably just the speaker that is defective. In that case, consult Chapter 6 for further instructions (page 208).

Even if there is neither an audio nor a video response, you should listen carefully for the sound of the PC's internal fan. If the fan is not heard, then the problem may lie outside the computer itself, perhaps in the room's electric service or in the computer's AC power outlet. If the fan is heard, than the computer is obviously receiving power, and those two items may be eliminated from the list of suspects.

Make a quick inspection of the power cord leading from the wall outlet to the PC. Make sure that it is firmly plugged into the wall socket and that the other end has not worked loose from the system unit. Next, make sure that the wall outlet itself is operating. This can be quickly verified by plugging a functioning lamp or other device into the same outlet used for the computer. If this device also fails to work, then look for a tripped circuit breaker or a problem with the outlet.

Assuming these quick tests don't turn up the problem, examine the power cord a little more carefully. If possible, swap the cord with a similar one from a printer or other appliance.

System Shuts Itself Off. This may happen if the power supply attempts to exceed its maximum-current limit. The first thing to suspect is that the addition of some new option is creating an excessive demand on the power supply. Such an adapter may work quite well in a system that is not fully populated with adapters, but as more adapters are added, the total current draw eventually exceeds the limit, and the system shuts down. In such a case, the last adapter added is not necessarily the actual source of the trouble.

To isolate the problem, remove some adapters and then replace them one by one until the condition is repeated. Don't forget to turn the power off before removing or reinstalling each adapter. Again, it may not be the last adapter that is causing the problem in and of itself. The sum of the currents drawn by all the adapters may simply be excessive.

There is also the possibility that a defect on an adapter is causing it to draw current beyond its normal requirement. In this case, the adapter may shut down the system even if there are very few other adapters in place. Depending on the specific adapter and the nature of the fault, an error code may be seen when the total current draw is not yet sufficient to turn the system off.

If none of the above procedures helps to identify the system turn-off problem, then outside servicing is needed. However, if the problem is simply that the total current demand of all the installed options exceeds the limit of the power supply, then a higher-capacity replacement power supply might be worth considering, as described in the Power Supply Replacement section at the end of this chapter (page 127).

If the system continues to shut itself off despite the removal of all adapters, then there is either a problem on the system board or within the power supply itself. In either case, outside servicing is probably required.

Response Is Incorrect. If the system does come on and it stays on, then a power-related problem may be indicated by one or more of the following incorrect responses:

Continuous beep
Series of more than two short beeps
02x error message

One or more of these responses suggest that although the power supply itself may not be defective, some other device is preventing the proper distribution of power to the rest of the system. If this is the case, correct operation may be restored by isolating and removing the defective device. The section on problem-isolation techniques will help to pinpoint the source of the power-related problem.

Note that in the three-character 02x error code, x is any single hexadecimal number; a character code such as 2xx indicates a memory-related, rather than power-related, error. If an error code other than 02x is seen, it may be assumed that the problem is not related to the power supply. Refer to Chapter 3 or Appendix C for an interpretation of the observed error code, and then consult the appropriate chapter for further details.

Problem-Isolation Techniques

If the problem has not yet been identified, then it is time to investigate various external and internal components to find the one that is causing the trouble.

Checking External Devices. Turn the power off and prepare to disconnect all cables leading to external devices, such as printers, modems, and a second video display. Disconnect the devices one at a time, turning the PC back on again after each cable has been removed. Disconnect each cable where it attaches to the rear of the system unit, not at the other end, thus removing both the device and the cable.

If this procedure eventually solves the problem, then the last device removed, or its cable, is defective. Set the device and cable to one side and reconnect everything else that was removed. As a double check, turn the power back on again, and verify that the rest of the system now functions properly. Depending on the device that was removed, the system may have to be reconfigured to account for the missing component.

Cable Test. If you are uncertain whether it is the external device or the cable itself that is defective, reconnect the cable to the computer, disconnect the other end from the external device, and turn on the computer. If the fault is within the cable, the computer will once again exhibit the trouble symptom. If not, it may be assumed that the cable is not at fault and it is the external device itself that requires servicing. Note that this test only identifies a cable with an internal short circuit between conductors. An open-circuit cable cannot be spotted this way. However, such a problem will not create a power-related symptom anyway.

Checking Internal Options. If no external device is at fault, then the various adapters installed in the system board slots should each be checked. If a math coprocessor chip is installed, this should also be checked in the same manner. Always remember to turn the power off before disconnecting anything and before each reconnection is made. Failure to do so may cause additional damage to the system or to a component.

If a 02x error code was seen earlier, there is of course no need to check either the display on which the error code is seen or its adapter, since both obviously work. However, if no error code was seen, the display adapter may be suspected, and it should be removed first. If the adapter is for the monochrome display, don't forget to also unplug the monochrome display's power plug from the rear-panel AC outlet.

• **Display Caution.** If a second video display is among the options removed from a PC or XT, make sure the system-board configuration switches are properly reset before turning the system on again. Failure to follow this precaution may damage the remaining display. See Chapter 11 for further directions concerning displays.

When the power is turned back on again, listen for one of the following beep codes:

Beep code	Meaning
•	System now functioning properly
—··	System functioning properly, except that the missing display adapter has been detected
anything else	A remaining adapter probably needs servicing or replacement

In the case of the first two examples, the problem has been narrowed down to the removed display adapter and its related display. To determine which one is faulty, replace the adapter but leave the display disconnected. Turn the system power back on and note the audio signal. If there is no change, then the adapter functions properly and the display itself is faulty. But if the audio signal is again the same as that heard earlier, then the adapter is defective and needs to be serviced.

If either of the first two signals (· or —··) is noted, the display and its adapter are probably OK. At this point, you may wish to reinstall them both so that any subsequent error codes may be seen. Next, remove every other adapter, except for diskette and hard disk drive adapters, and turn the system back on again. If it now functions properly, then one of the removed adapters is defective. However, the system may also need reconfiguration, as indicated by two beeps and an on-screen message. But before doing so, if you have removed more than one adapter, try replacing them one at a time until the original beep code error is again heard. First, replace any adapter whose absence would account for the configuration error message—a board with additional memory, for example. If the system eventually resumes normal operation, then the problem has been localized to some adapter that has not been reinstalled, but at least it's one that has no effect on system configuration.

On the other hand, if the removal of all the adapters just mentioned has no effect on the beep code, then the problem is related to the drive system. To isolate the specific drive-related failure, disconnect all four-conductor power leads to all drives (but do not do this for leads connected to a dummy

used for data, then unplug each flat ribbon-cable connector at the drive end
of the cable, or disengage each drive by sliding it away from its mating
connector, as appropriate for your specific system. Also remove the drive
adapter card itself (if any). See Chapter 9 for further details about drive-related cables and adapters.

Now turn the system back on again. With all drives disconnected, the
BASIC screen display should appear at the conclusion of the POST procedure. If it does not appear and a continuous beep, or a series of beeps, is still
heard, then the trouble is either on the motherboard or within the power
supply itself. In either case, outside servicing will be required.

But if the BASIC screen display does appear, then one of the removed
components is indeed faulty. Replace them one at a time, being careful to
turn the system off before and on again after, each replacement.

Once a defective adapter or a drive has been isolated and identified, it
will probably have to be returned for repair or replacement. However,
further on-the-spot testing may be appropriate, depending on the specific
adapter that is causing the problem. For further directions, consult the
chapter of this book that discusses the device in question.

In-Operation Problems

As already noted (page 109), various power-line problems may occur
during routine system operation. These may or may not be sufficient to
affect other devices in the area. As an obvious example, if the lights flicker
at the same time the computer exhibits a problem, the cause is surely related
to external power. But if the lights don't flicker, the problem may still be
an external one, the duration of which was too brief to affect the lights.

If the problem is accompanied by a flash of lightning (hopefully outside),
there's little doubt as to its cause. But often a more subtle power-line
disturbance may be at the root of the problem, with one of the following
symptoms manifesting itself.

System Locks Up. Although this is usually a software-related symptom,
from time to time a power-line irregularity may cause the system to lock
up. If so, the computer will have to be turned off and then back on again.

System Reboots Itself. Again, a momentary power-line disturbance is
probably the cause of the problem. However, if the problem occurs with
regularity, the power supply unit itself is probably faulty and will have to
be replaced.

System Shuts Down During Routine Operation. Assuming power is still on elsewhere in the room, this is a clear indication that some internal power supply component is failing after an initial warm-up period. Depending upon which specific part has failed, the system may turn itself back on again after the component cools off. But in any case, the PC should be returned for repair.

Intermittent Failure of an Option. Generally, an installed option either works or it doesn't. Of course, there may be the occasional intermittent problem with a particular device, but if several such devices seem to fail at random, the problem may be with one of the direct-current voltages routed through the system. Since the power supply unit itself rarely fails intermittently, the problem may be nothing more serious than a loose connection. To investigate this possibility, turn the system off, remove the system unit cover, and check all connections—especially those on suspect devices—for physical integrity.

Power Supply Removal and Replacement Procedure

Figure 5.4 shows typical power supply units found in IBM ISA and MCA systems. The units in the XT and AT are similar to the PC supply, though of course larger in capacity. The power supply in a PS/2 model 70 may be seen in Chapter 6, Figure 6.2(a).

To remove the power supply from the system unit, turn the power off and unplug the power cable at the rear of the computer. Disconnect and move the display well away from the system unit and then slide the system unit cover off.

Table 5.7 lists the cables and connectors associated with each type of power supply. Disconnect each such cable, remove the screws holding the power supply in place, and then carefully remove the supply from the system.

Reverse the procedure to install a new power supply, such as the PC replacement supply seen in Figure 5.5. And of course, make sure the dimensions of the new power supply allow it to fit in place of the old one.

Power Supply Servicing Notes

Due to the shock hazard, most personal computer power supplies—IBM's included—are not designed for casual servicing. To help discourage the inexperienced user from even trying, the screws which hold the power supply cover in place are often removable only with a special tool. There-

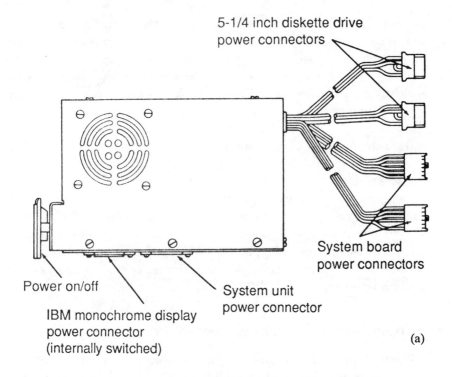

5-1/4 inch diskette drive
power connectors

System board
power connectors

Power on/off

System unit
power connector

IBM monochrome display
power connector
(internally switched)

(a)

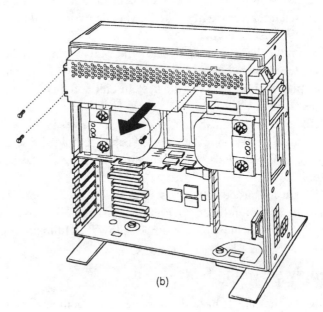

(b)

Figure 5.4.   Internal power supplies in IBM personal computers. (a) PC, (b) PS/2
models 60 and 80.

Table 5.7 Power Supply Connections to System Board and Drives

Computer	Power supply connection to system board *	Power supply connection to each drive
PC, XT, AT	two 6 – conductor sockets	one 4 – conductor socket one ground wire
25	one 12 – conductor socket	none †
30	two 6 – conductor sockets	none †
30 286	one 12 – conductor socket & one 5 – conductor socket	none †
50	one 50 – pin edge connector	none †
60, 65 SX	one 15 – conductor socket	two 4 – conductor sockets ‡
70	one 50 – pin edge connector	none †
80	one 15 – conductor socket	two 4 – conductor sockets ‡

* Except as otherwise noted, each socket connects multiple single – conductor leads to system board or drive.
Edge connector is integral part of system board, with matching socket built into side of power supply.
† Each drive is powered via multiconductor ribbon cable from system board.
‡ Sockets built into side of power supply (for hard disk drives only). Diskette drives powered via multiconductor ribbon cable from system board.

Figure 5.5. A 150-watt replacement power supply for IBM PC, XT, and other ISA personal computers. (Silencer 150 courtesy PC Power & Cooling Systems, Inc.)

fore, although the supply itself may be easily removed and replaced, it may not be serviced with the same ease. In fact, even the power-line fuse in some PS/2 supplies is mounted internally and cannot be replaced by the user. The fuse found on some PS/2 system boards is for the keyboard, and has nothing to do with the system's AC power supply.

6

PC SYSTEM CONFIGURATION

The first part of this chapter takes a close look at the personal computer system board, to get an idea of where it is and what it does. The peripheral components connected to the system board are briefly described, as are the adapter slots on the system board itself.

System configuration procedures are described next, followed by routine system diagnostics and troubleshooting. The chapter concludes with an overview of various personal computer system enhancements. This coverage is by no means definitive, but is intended to give a general idea of what is available, the implications of trying to exceed a computer's original performance specifications, and a description of some of the problems that may be encountered when exceeding the posted speed limit.

SYSTEM BOARD DESCRIPTION

Since a system board is at the heart of every personal computer, we need to discuss this important component in some detail before moving on to all those devices which are eventually connected to it. If you have not already done so, now is the time to remove the system unit's cover to have a look under the hood. To do so, turn the power off and remove the screws (or loosen the thumb screws) that secure the cover. On table model system units, slide the cover forward and off. For tower units, remove the cover plate, or

131

if the cover is hinged, simply open it to gain access. If more information is needed, follow the specific instructions found in your Guide to Operations, Quick Reference manual, User's Manual, or whatever it's called for your system.

In almost every PC, the system board occupies the entire left side of the chassis and extends to the right as far as the power supply. The power supply is located in the upper right-hand quadrant of the chassis, or in some PS/2 systems, along the entire right-hand side of the system board.

Tables 6.1 through 6.3 summarize system board and other features of various models of IBM personal computers.

PC, XT, AT System Disassembly

Figure 6.1 shows PC, XT, and AT system boards. In the PC, a diskette drive installed in the left-hand drive area will cover the lower right-hand quadrant of the system board. In the XT and AT, an internal hard disk drive will occupy that same space. In either case there are no user-serviceable components in the system board area obstructed by the drive. However, if either drive needs to be removed for servicing, refer to Chapter 8 (page 338) or 9 (page 409) for details.

PS/2 System Disassembly

Much of the system board may be underneath the various diskette and hard drive systems. Consequently, one or more drives may have to be removed to gain access for installation or removal of some memory option cards.

Since each PS/2 system seems to have been designed by a different committee, no system-specific instructions can be given here, other than to refer to the appropriate *Guide to Operations*. However, Figure 6.2 does show some details for the model 70, which like some other PS/2 systems may be disassembled in minutes.

Figure 6.2(a) shows the layout of the system board. The memory module slots are seen in the lower right-hand corner of the board and again in the detail view in Figure 6.2(b). The figure also shows one of several round pegs which support a platform (not shown) for the two diskette drives and a single hard drive. The close-up view of the speaker/battery assembly (Figure 6.2(c)) shows the plastic key used to pop the captive mounting buttons in and out of the pegs, allowing almost effortless disassembly. The key is supplied by IBM, and when not in use is stored directly under the speaker. Finally, Figure 6.2(d) shows the drive adapter card in place, with

Table 6.1 IBM Personal Computer System Identification

System name	Model byte *	Sub-model	Rev. no.	BIOS date	MP type	Clock (MHz)	Machine numbers, comments **
PCjr	FD	–	–	06–01–83	8088	4.77	4, 67
PC1	FF	–	–	04–24–81	8088	4.77	104, 114, 164, 174
		–	–	10–19–81			BIOS for expansion unit
PC2		–	–	10–27–82			166, 176
PC Convertible							
	F9	–	–	09–13–85	80C88	4.77	2, 22
PC Portable							
	FE	–	–	11–08–82	8088	4.77	68, 76
XT	FE	–	–	08–16–82	8088	4.77	68, 78, 86, 87, 88
		–	–	11–08–82			PC 3270 Workstation
	FB	00	01	01–10–86			89, 267, 268, 277, 278
	FB	00	02	05–09–86			
XT 286	FC	02	00	04–21–86	80286		286
AT	FC	–	–	01–10–84	80286	6	68, 99, 239
		00	01	06–10–85			same
		01	00	11–15–85		8	319, 339

PS/2 models

System name	Model byte *	Sub-model	Rev. no.	BIOS date	MP type	Clock (MHz)	Machine numbers, comments **
25	FA	01	00	06–26–87	8086	8	all (see Table 6.3)
25 286†	FC	09	00	08–25–88	80286	10	all (see Table 6.3)
30	FA	00	00	09–02–86	8086	8	001, 002, 021
		00	01	12–12–86			
30 286†	FC	09	00	08–25–88	80286	10	E01, E21, E31
50	FC	04	00	02–12–87	80286	10	[1] 021
50Z			03	01–28–88			[2] 031, 061
55 SX	F8	0C	00	11–02–88	386 SX	16	031, 061
60	FC	05	00	02–13–87	80286	10	041, 071
65 SX	F8	1C	00	02–08–90	386 SX	16	061, 121

Table 6.1 IBM Personal Computer System Identification (continued)

System name	Model byte *	Sub-model no.	Rev. no.	BIOS date	MP type	Clock (MHz)	Machine numbers, comments **
70 386	F8	04	00	01-29-88		20	[2] 061, 121
		09	00	01-29-88	386 DX	16	[1] E61
			02	04-11-88		16	[1] E61
		OD	00	02-20-89		25	[3] A21, A61
P70 386	F8	0B	00	01-18-89	386 DX	20	061, 121
			01				same
						16	031
70 486	F8	1B	00	09-29-89	i486	25	B21, B61
80 386	F8	00	00	03-30-87	386 DX	16	041, 071
		01	00	10-07-87		20	111, 121, 311, 321
		08	01	11-21-89		25	A21, A31

*   The IBM model byte is located in ROM BIOS at F000:FFFE in all systems.
    Submodel and revision numbers are accessed via Interrupt 15H.
** [*n*] is a type number, used in some IBM documentation.
†   models share same model, submodel, revision bytes & BIOS date.

(a)

Figure 6.1.   System board layouts in early ISA computers: (a) PC, (b) XT, (c) AT.

(b)

(c)

(a)

(b)

Figure 6.2.   The system board in a PS/2 model 70. (a) System unit with cover removed, showing system board and power supply. (b) Slots for memory modules, with module inserted in second slot. (c) Speaker module, showing battery on top. Removable plastic tool at right of speaker is used to pop out retaining pins which lock system components in place. (d) Drive adapter card plugs into dedicated slot on system board. One diskette drive is installed, with supporting platform removed to show system board.

(c)

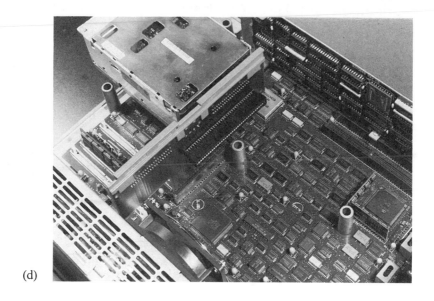

(d)

Figure 6.2   (Continued)

Table 6.2 IBM Personal Computer System Identification

Model byte *	Sub-model	Rev. no.	BIOS date	System name	Clock (MHz)	Machine numbers
F8	00	00	03-30-87	PS/2 80 386	16	041, 071
	01	00	10-07-87		20	111, 121, 311, 321
	04	00	01-29-88		20	121
	08	01	11-21-89		25	A21, A31
	09	00	01-29-88	PS/2 70 386	16	E61
		02	04-11-88		16	E61
	0B	00	01-18-89	PS/2 P70 386	20	061, 121
	0C	00	11-02-88	PS/2 55 SX	16	031, 061
	0D	00	02-20-89	PS/2 70 386	25	A21, A61
	1B	00	09-29-89	PS/2 70 486	25	B21, B61
	IC	00	02-08-90	PS/2 65 SX	16	061, 121
F9	–	–	09-13-85	PC Convertible	4.77	2, 22
FA	00	00	09-02-86	PS/2 30	8	001, 002, 021
		01	12-12-86			
	01	00	06-26-87	PS/2 25	8	all
FB	00	01	01-10-86	XT	4.77	89, 267, 268, 277, 278
	00	02	05-09-86			268, 269
FC	–	–	01-10-84	AT (original)	6	68, 99, 239
	00	01	06-10-85	AT		same
	01	00	11-15-85	AT (30 Mb drive)	8	319, 339
	02	00	04-21-86	XT 286	6	286
	04	00	02-13-87	PS/2 50	10	021
		01	05-09-87	PS/2 50		
		03	01-28-88	PS/2 50Z	10	031, 061
	05	00	02-13-87	PS/2 60	10	041, 071
	09	00	08-25-88	PS/2 25 286	10	all
				PS/2 30 286	10	E01, E21
FD	–	–	06-01-83	PCjr	4.77	all
FE	–	–	08-16-82	XT (original)	4.77	68, 78, 86, 87, 88
	–	–	11-08-82	3270 Workstation		
	–	–	11-08-82	PC Portable	4.77	68, 76
FF	–	–	04-24-81	PC1 (original)	4.77	104, 114, 164, 174
	–	–	10-19-81	PC1 (exp. unit)		same
	–	–	10-27-82	PC2 (256Kb)		166,176

*   The IBM model byte is located in ROM BIOS at F000:FFFE in all systems. Submodel and revision numbers are accessed via Interrupt 15H.

Table 6.3 IBM Personal Computer Model Number Cross-Reference

System model number	Model no. suffix	Exp. slots	System board RAM (Kb) min	max	Hard disk (Mb)	System controller type	Diskette drive *	Keyb. number of keys
PCjr	4		64	512	none	none	none	64
	67		128	512			1 DS	
PC1	104	5	16	64	none	none	none	83
	114						1 SS	
	164						1 DS	
	174						2 DS	
PC2	166	5	64	256	none	none	1 DS	83
	176						2 DS	
PC Convertible 2			256	512	none	none	2 720Kb	78
	22							
PC Portable	68	7	256	640	none	none	1 DS	83
	76						2 DS	
XT1	68	8	128	256	none	ST-506	1 DS	
	78				none		2 DS	
	86				10		1 DS	
	87				10		1 DS	83
	88			640	20		1 DS	
	89				20		1 DS	101
	267			256	none		1 DSH	
	268				none		1 DSH	101
	277				none		2 DSH	
	278				none		2 DSH	101
XT2	286	8		640	20	ST-506	1 HC	101
AT	68	8	256	512	none	ST-506	1 HC	84
	99			512	20		1 HC	
	239				30		1 HC	
	319				30		1 HC	
	339				30		1 HC	101

PS/1 ISA systems †

2011	M01	3	512	1024	none		1 1.44Mb	101
	M34		1024		30	ESDI		
	C01		512		none			
	C34		1024		30	ESDI		

Table 6.3 IBM Personal Computer Model Number Cross-Reference (continued)

System model number	Model no. suffix	Exp. slots	System board RAM (Kb) min	max	Hard disk (Mb)	System controller type	Diskette drive *	Keyb. number of keys
PS/2 ISA systems								
25 †	001, 004	2	512	640	none	ST-506	1 720Kb	84
	C02, C05		640	640			2 720Kb	84
	G01, G04		512	640			1 720Kb	101
	K02, K05		640	640			2 720Kb	101
	L01, L04							
	W04, WTR		512	640			1 720Kb	
25 286	006, G06	2	512	4096	none	ST-506	1 1.44Mb	
	036, G36	2	1024		30			
30 †	001	3	640	640	none	ST-506	1 720Kb	101
	002, R02						2 720Kb	
	021, R21				20		1 720Kb	
30 286 † ‡	E01, E0R	3	1024	4096	none	ST-506	1 1.44Mb	101
	E21, E2R				20			
	E31				30			
PS/2 MCA systems								
50 †	021, R21	3	1024	1024	20	ST-506	1 1.44Mb	101
50Z	031	3	1024	2048	30	ST-506	1 1.44Mb	101
	061				60	ESDI		
55 SX †	031, R31	3	2048	4096	30	ST-506	1 1.44Mb	101
	061, R61				60	ESDI		
60	041	7	1024	1024	44	ST-506	1 1.44Mb	101
	071				70	ESDI		
65 SX	061	8	2048	8192	60	SCSI	1 1.44Mb	101
	121				120			
70 386	061	1/2 §	2048	6144	60	ESDI	1 1.44Mb	101
	121				120			
	A21		2048	8192				
	A61				60			
	E61 ‡		2048	6144	60			

Table 6.3 IBM Personal Computer Model Number Cross-Reference (continued)

System model number	Model no. suffix	Exp. slots	System board RAM (Kb) min	max	Hard disk (Mb)	System controller type	Diskette drive *	Keyb. number of keys
70 486	B21	1/2 §2048		8192	120		1 1.44Mb	101
	B61				60			
P70 386	031	1/1 §4096		8192	30		1 1.44Mb	101
	061				60	ESDI		
	121				120			
80 386	041	4/3 §1024		2048	44	ST-506	1 1.44Mb	101
	071		2048	2048	70	ESDI		
	111		2048	4096	115			
	121				120	SCSI		
	311	4/4 §			314	ESDI		
	321				320	SCSI		
	A21		4096	8192	120			
	A31				320			

* diskette drive abbreviations (see Table 8.1 for additional details)
    DS   double-sided, full height
    DSH   double-sided, half height
    HC   high-capacity
    SS   single-sided
† additional model details (*nn* = any numbers)
    001, C02, W*nn*   space-saving keyboard, built-in monochrome display
    004, 006, 036, C05
                        space-saving keyboard, built-in color display
    C*nn*   (PS/1) color display, expansion slots on optional adapter
                        card, mouse, internal modem
    G01, K02   standard keyboard, built-in monochrome display
    G04, G06, G36, K05
                        standard keyboard, built-in color display
    L01   same as G01, plus token-ring network PC adapter
    L04   same as G04, plus token-ring network PC adapter
    M*nn*   (PS/1) monochrome display, expansion slots on optional
                        adapter card, mouse, internal modem
    R*nn* or *nn*R   same as 0*nn* or *nn*1, except supplied with 50-key function
                        keyboard for banking application programs
‡ Minimum standard memory half this amount before Sept. 1989.
§ *a/b*   *a* = 16-bit slot(s); *b* = 16/32-bit slot(s)

one diskette drive installed. The hard drive (not shown) slides into the rear-pointing socket. Again, the support table itself has been removed for purposes of illustration.

Each diskette drive is easily removed by pressing a tab at the front underside of the drive and sliding it forward. To remove the hard drive, press down on two plastic keys and slide the drive away from its connector. The keys holding the drive in place are an integral part of the supporting table.

On some PS/2 systems (model 30 286, for example), a small plastic peg locks the front-mounted hard disk drive in place, and must be removed in order to slide the drive forward and out of the system.

In the PS/2 models 60 and 80, the system board is mounted in a floor-standing tower unit. The system unit cover plate may be easily removed by turning the key in the lock and loosening the two screws which secure the plate.

EISA System Disassembly

EISA systems are available in both table-top and floor-standing models. For disassembly, follow the general procedures already described, and refer to the user's manual for more specific instructions.

System Board Component Description

With the exception of the random-access memory modules briefly mentioned below and described in greater detail in Chapter 7, most of the IC chips on the system board do not require the routine attention of the user. If it does become necessary to remove one or more modules or chips from either the system board or from one of the option cards, follow the chip-handling procedure described later on in this chapter (page 225). The various PC, XT, and AT system board components described here are all seen in Figure 6.3, and Table 6.4 lists most of these components.

On PS/2 and EISA systems, most components are soldered in place on the system board, the notable exceptions being the ROM BIOS modules, MPU, and math coprocessor. Furthermore, the location of similar components varies greatly from one model to another.

ROM BIOS Modules. One or more ROM BIOS (Basic Input/Output System) chips on the PC, XT, or AT system board may need to be replaced when certain new options are added. Table 6.5 lists various dates that determine whether a replacement is required.

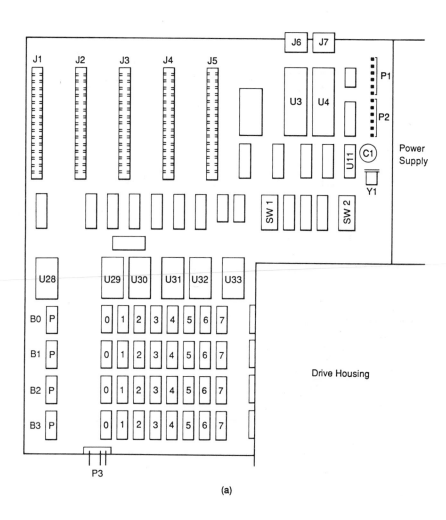

Figure 6.3. System board details for the (a) PC, (b) XT, and (c) AT. (d) Detail view of the AT RAM jumper, speaker, and keylock connectors.

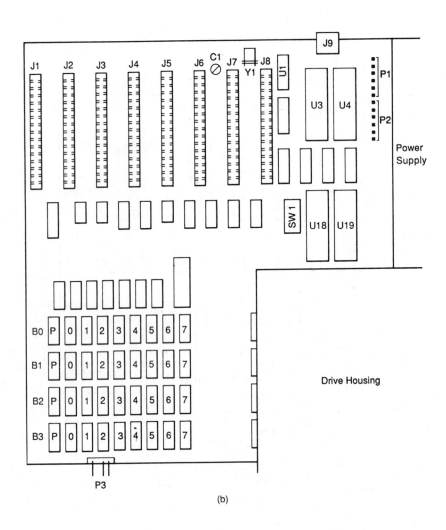

(b)

Figure 6.3. (Continued)

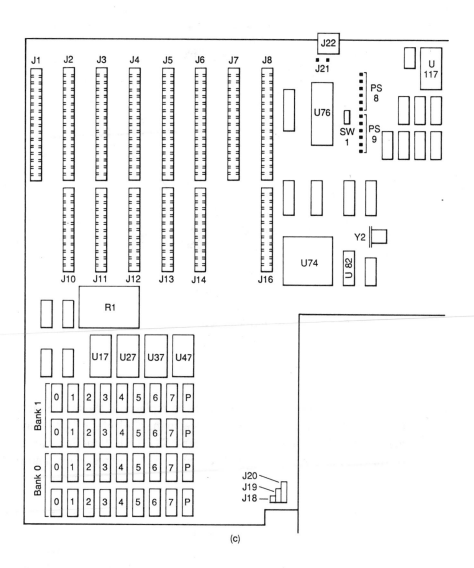

(c)

Figure 6.3. (Continued)

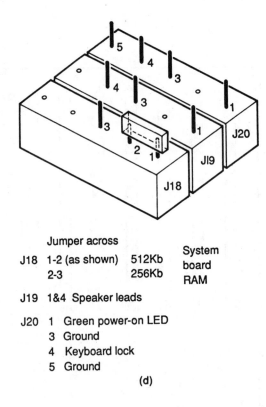

Jumper across

J18	1-2 (as shown)	512Kb	System
	2-3	256Kb	board RAM

J19   1&4   Speaker leads

J20   1   Green power-on LED
      3   Ground
      4   Keyboard lock
      5   Ground

(d)

On the PC system board, the chip to be replaced is the one in the socket labeled U33. This is the rightmost socket in the bank of six ROM (read-only memory) sockets shown in Figure 6.3(a). ROM BIOS modules for the XT (U18, U19) and AT (U27, U47) are shown in Figures 6.3(b) and 6.3(c), respectively.

ROM Date Programs. Run the short BASIC program given in Listing 6.1(a) to display the revision date of the ROM BIOS on the system board. Listing 6.1(b) modifies the program to display the IBM copyright notice, and Listing 6.1(c) displays the copyright notice and date for the Enhanced Graphics Adapter.

In the case of non-IBM BIOS, or of an IBM-compatible EGA, the BASIC program may display a fragment in which the magic initials "IBM" are seen. In each case, vary the numbers in line 110 as required to display the complete message. In some cases, it may be necessary to vary line 100 as indicated in Listing 6.1(d), and then change the values in line 110 until just the necessary information is seen. For example, the ALR PowerVeisa system displays

Table 6.4 PC, XT, AT System Board Configurations

Part		PC	XT	AT	Description
Hardware interface					
Adapter slots		J1-J5	J1-J8	J1, J7	62-pin sockets
			J2-J6, J8	Dual slots with 62- and 36-pin sockets	
battery		—	—	J21	4-pin Berg strip
cassette		J7	—	—	5-pin DIN connector
keyboard		J6	J9	J22	5-pin DIN connector
power supply		P1, P2	P1, P2	PS8, PS9	Two 6-pin connectors
RAM jumper		—	—	J18	3-pin Berg strip
speaker		P3	P3	J19	4-pin Berg strip
Circuit components					
clock generators		U11	U1	U82	
			U18 (for CGA color)		
CMOS RAM		—	—	U117	
crystal		Y1	Y1	Y2	
			Y1 (for CGA color)		
math coprocessor		U4	U4	U76	
microprocessor		U3	U3	U74	
Memory					
RAM (Bank)	(0)	U37-45	U30-U38	(1) U4,10, 16, 22, 26, 31, 36, 42, 46	
	(1)	U53-U61	U46-U54	(1) U3, 9, 15, 21, 25, 30, 35, 41, 45	
	(2)	U69-U77	U59-U67	(0) U2, 8, 14, 20, 24, 29, 34, 40, 44	
	(3)	U85-U93	U75-U83	(0) U1, 7, 13, 19, 23, 28, 33, 39, 43	
ROM *		U28		U17, U37	Unoccupied
		U29-U32	U18	U27, U47	BASIC
		U33	U19	U27, U47	BIOS
Adjustments					
capacitor		C1	C1	R1	CGA/TV color trim
switch blocks		SW1	SW1	none	system configuration
		SW2	—	—	system memory
		—	—	SW1	default display

* **ROM address notes:**

Chip location			**Starting address**
PC	**XT**	**AT**	**Segment:Offset**
		U17	E000:0000 even addresses
		U37	E000:0001 odd addresses
		U27	F000:0000 even addresses
		U47	F000:0001 odd addresses
U28			F400:0000
U29	U18		F600:0000 low addresses
U30			F800:0000
U31			FA00:0000
U32			FC00:0000
U33	U19		FE00:0000 high addresses

Table 6.5 PC, XT, AT ROM BIOS Date Reference Guide

Installed device *	PC	XT	AT **
Cluster Adapter	10-27-82		
Crystal limit of 12 MHz			11-15-85
Emulator Adapter 3278/79	10-27-82		
Enhanced graphics adapter	10-27-82		
Keyboard		01-10-86	11-15-85
Expansion Unit	10-19-81		
Hard Disk Drive	10-27-82		
Hard Disk Drive (30Mb AT)		11-15-85	
Memory above 544Kb	10-27-82		
PC Network Adapter	10-27-82		
RAM: 256Kb chips	10-27-82		

ROM BIOS dates

04-24-81	PC original
10-19-81	PC revision
10-27-82	PC with hard disk and/or 256Kb RAM chips
08-16-82	XT original
11-08-82	XT revision, PC 3270 Workstation
01-10-84	AT original
06-10-85	AT revision
11-15-85	AT with 12 MHz crystal limitation, 30Mb drive support, enhanced keyboard
01-10-86	XT 286 original (enhanced keyboard)

* In order to use the listed device, the ROM BIOS must be dated as indicated, or later.

** Note that the same AT ROM BIOS that supports the enhanced keyboard and 30Mb hard disk drive also limits the system to operation at 6 MHz (12 Mhz crystal).

"RESERVED FOR IBM COMPATIBILITY" (X = 17 TO 46). Once the necessary values are found, the program can be simplified to follow the format of the previous listing.

In the examples, note that the copyright notice and the BIOS revision date are not located in the same general area. And of course, a non-IBM BIOS date cannot be checked against the information in Table 6.5, which applies to IBM computers only. In case of doubt about device compatibility, consult the manufacturer of either the computer or of the device to be installed.

The DOS debug utility can also be used to show the dates just described. Log on to the directory containing DEBUG.COM and type DEBUG↵. At the debug prompt (a hyphen), simply type the single line shown in the right-hand column of each program in Listing 6.1. The date in question should be displayed in the upper right-hand corner of the screen. If neces-

Listing 6.1 A BASIC ROM Date-Finding Program

BASIC   **DEBUG**

(a) For IBM ROM BIOS revision date

```
100 DEF SEG = &HFFFF              D F000:FFF0
110 FOR X = 5 TO 12
120 PRINT CHR$(PEEK(X));
130 NEXT X
```

(b) For IBM Copyright Notice

```
100 DEF SEG = &HFE00              D F000:E000
110 FOR X = 8 TO 21
120 PRINT CHR$(PEEK(X));
130 NEXT X
```

(c) For IBM EGA

```
100 DEF SEG = &HC000              D C000:0000
110 FOR X = 17 TO 37
120 PRINT CHR$(PEEK(X));
130 NEXT X
```

(d) For IBM – Compatible ROM BIOS *

```
100 DEF SEG = &HF?00              D F?00:0000
110 FOR X = 0 to 255
120 P = PEEK(X)
130 IF P < 32 THEN P = 46
140 PRINT CHR$(P);
150 NEXT X
```

    * Try replacing the ? in line 100 (or in the DEBUG line) with A–F, then with
      0–9 until a recognizable copyright/date message is displayed. Line 130
      prevents non–printable codes from garbling the display.

sary, press D↵ to display additional lines of text, and press Q↵ when you
are ready to quit.

Microprocessor (MP). Depending on your favorite computer dictionary,
the term *microprocessor* can mean just about anything you like, from a
complete PC (which, compared to a mammoth mainframe system, certainly
is micro), to the chip set that does most of the real computing work, to the
single chip whose last two numbers are usually 86. This book steers the last
course: the microprocessor is the large integrated circuit chip that receives and
executes instructions. Figure 6.4(a) shows two of the microprocessors

(a)

Figure 6.4. Typical microprocessors used in PS/2 and similar personal computers: (a) Intel 386 DX and i486. Microprocessor packaging styles: (b) plastic leaded chip carrier, (c) leadless chip carrier, (d) pin grid array. (photos and drawings courtesy Intel Corp.)

used in recent IBM and IBM-compatible personal computers. In addition to the obvious performance differences between one generation and another, most microprocessors are now available in several physical packages. For example, Figure 6.4b shows examples of an 80286 microprocessor (MP) in three configurations:

Microprocessor	Configuration description
Plastic leaded chip carrier	The MP leads are soldered to the system board.
Leadless chip carrier	The MP plugs into a socket mounted on the system board.
Pin grid array	Same, except the socket comprises multiple rows of pin sockets.

The Intel i486 microprocessor shown on the cover is in the pin grid array format, and another pin grid array socket is also seen just above it.

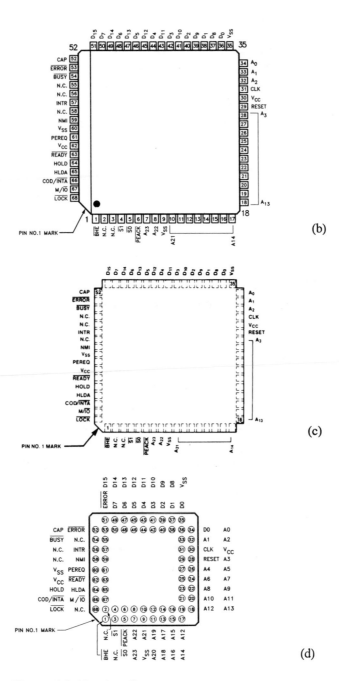

(b)

(c)

(d)

Figure 6.4. (Continued)

Math Coprocessor. On all IBM and most other personal computers, an optional math coprocessor may be installed in a socket located in the upper right-hand quadrant of pre-PS/2 system boards, and just about anywhere else on EISA and PS/2 systems. If you have installed a coprocessor, it should be treated similarly to any other added option if it becomes necessary to diagnose a power-related problem, such as those discussed in Chapter 5. That is, the chip may need to be removed to see if its presence is causing a power supply failure.

Table 6.6a is a cross-reference guide between microprocessors and math coprocessors. The table also lists the NEC (Nippon Electric Company) V series microprocessor that may be used as a direct plug-in replacement for an 8086 or 8088. The NEC device offers a slight performance improvement.

When installing a math coprocessor, make sure its notch or beveled edge is correctly oriented.

The IBM math coprocessor option kit for the PC and XT included an 8087-2 coprocessor and a matched 8088-2 microprocessor, which had to be installed in place of the regular 8088-3 chip. If the 8088 processor is soldered in place, a new system board with a plug-in socket will be required.

80287 Coprocessors. On some (but not all) 80286 system boards, the math coprocessor runs at two thirds the speed of the MPU, which is one third the crystal speed. For example, on a system with a 10-MHz microprocessor (20-MHz crystal), the maximum coprocessor speed is two thirds of 10 MHz, or 6.66 MHz. The closest available coprocessor is an 8-MHz 80387-8. There is no point to installing a "matching" 10-MHz coprocessor, since even the 8-MHz device exceeds the system's built-in speed limit.

Central Processing Unit (CPU). Although the term is sometimes used as a synonym for the microprocessor, the *central processing unit* actually comprises the MP, the math coprocessor (if any), and associated circuitry (at least it does in this book). To help further complicate the nomenclature, the Intel i486 microprocessor incorporates an 80387 math coprocessor in the same package, as well as an 8-Kbyte cache, possibly making it both a microprocessor and a CPU (even in this book).

Variable Capacitor. An adjustable color trimmer capacitor is the only user-variable control to be found on the system board (PC, XT, AT). Its use is described in Chapter 11.

Table 6.6a Microprocessor/Coprocessor Cross-Reference Guide

Microprocessor Intel *	NEC	Clock (MHz)	Coprocessor Intel *	Clock (MHz)	Crystal (MHz)	Notes
8088	V20		8087			
none, −3	−5	5	−3	5	10	(a)
−2	−8	8	−2	8	16	(b)
−1		10	−1	10	20	
80C88			none			
none		5			10	(a) PC Conv.
−2		8				
8086	V30		8087			
none	−5	5	−3	5	10	
−2	−8	8	−2	8	10	(c) PS/2 25 & 30
−1	−10	10	−1	10	20	(d)
80C86			none			
none		5				
−2		8				
80286			80287			(e)
−6		6	−3 or −6	4	12	(f) XT 286
−8		8	−6	5.33	16	AT 319, 339
−10		10	−8	6.66	20	Tandy 4000
			−10	10	20	(g) 25 & 30 286, 50, 60
−12		12	−8	8	24	
80C286			80C287			
−12			−12	12	24	(h) Toshiba 1600
	Hauppauge (replacement system board)					(i)
386 DX	AT		387 DX			(j)
−16	16	16	−16	16	32	PS/2 70 & 80
−20	20	20	−20	20	40	PS/2 70 & 80
−25	25	25	−25	25	50	PS/2 70
−33	33	33	−33	33	66	Compaq 386/33
386 SX	none		387 SX			
none, −16		16	none, −16	16	32	PS/2 55 SX
−20		20	−20	20	40	
i486	4860		none			(k)
−25	AT25	25			50	
−33	AT33	33			66	

Table 6.6a Microprocessor/Coprocessor Cross-Reference Guide (notes)

  *   Model number suffix omitted from some early chip labels, but added later. For example, 386 SX and 386 SX-16 are both 16 MHz devices.

(a) 4.77 MHz clock, 14.318 MHz crystal in PC, PC convertible, XT.

(b) MP bundled with some accelerator boards as swap for 8088-3 on system board.

(c) PS/2 crystal speed is 48 MHz.

(d) MP mounted on some accelerator boards replaces system board 8088-3.

(e) 80286 systems run coprocessor at 2/3 MP speed. See (g, h) for exceptions.

(f) original AT MP. Early coprocessor -3 suffix changed to -6 to reflect actual capability.

(g) Indicated PS/2 models run coprocessor at same speed as MP.

(h) Coprocessor pins are electrically incompatible with standard 80287 socket. Use only in systems specifically designed for this chip.

(i) equivalent replacement system board for updating PC, XT, AT systems.

(j) 80386 & 80387 changed to 386 DX & 387 DX after the 386 & 387 SX series was introduced. 386 and 387 are Intel trademarks.

(k) i486 is Intel preferred nomenclature for their 80486 MP.

Table 6.6b Microprocessor Bus Structure

Microprocessor	Bus width (bits) internal	external
8088	8	16
8086	16	16
80286	16	16
386 SX	16	32
386 DX	32	32
i486	32	32

Memory Modules

PC, XT, AT Systems. In the lower left-hand quadrant of the system board, four rows of nine sockets each are used to hold the RAM (random-access memory) chips.

PS/2 systems. On the models 25 and 30, the first 128 Kbytes of RAM chips are mounted on the system board. The chips are mounted in sockets on the model 25 and soldered in place on the model 30. Additional RAM for these models and *all* RAM for all other PS/2 systems are mounted on removable modules, varying in capacity from 256Kb to 4Mb. In Chapter 7, Figure 7.1 shows a few RAM modules for PS/2 systems.

EISA Systems. System board RAM is also installed in modules similar to those used for IBM PS/2 systems.

System Board Adapter Slots

In the upper left-hand quadrant of the system board there are five or more multipin slots into which various adapters may be inserted. Each model of IBM computer has a slightly different adapter-slot configuration, as was seen in the PC, XT, and AT examples in Figure 6.3. A comparison of IBM ISA and MCA adapter slots is shown in Figure 6.5.

On pre-PS/2 ISA systems, there are probably at least two adapters already in place in these slots. One is used in conjunction with the diskette and hard disk drives, the other is the one used for the primary display. On PS/2 systems, both of these functions are built into the system board itself. On EISA systems, the video adapter is usually a separate card, and the diskette controllers are built into the system board.

Slot 8 on the XT System Board. IBM documentation points out that this slot on the XT system board is "slightly different" from the others. An adapter inserted in slot 8 is expected to provide a "card-selected signal." The IBM Asynchronous Adapter may be configured to provide this signal, via a jumper (J18). With the jumper in place, the adapter may be installed in Slot 8.

Some other adapters also provide a jumper position that allows them to be installed in Slot 8. If an adapter does not provide this jumper, or is not otherwise specifically designed to work in Slot 8, then it should be located elsewhere.

Adapter Compatibility

Figure 6.5 compared the adapter card sockets on ISA and MCA system boards. Note that the configurations are quite different and that any ISA or MCA adapter card will therefore fit (and work) *only* in the system for which it is designed. Within either system, almost any adapter that may be plugged into a system board socket will work properly.

In the PS/2 system, the length of an adapter's edge connector may fall somewhat short of a system board socket, and yet the adapter will nevertheless work properly in that socket. For example, the edge connectors on

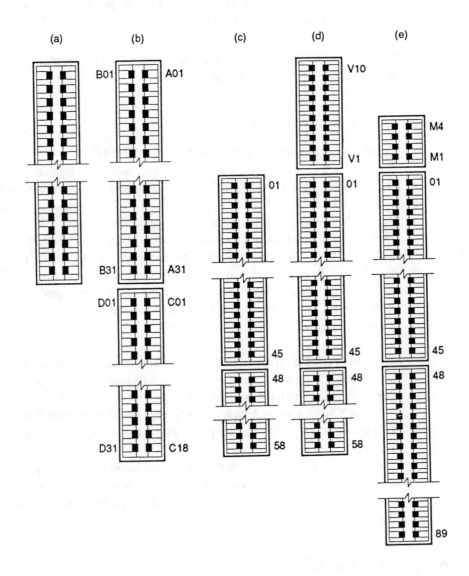

Figure 6.5.   System board adapter slots on ISA and MCA computers. ISA (a) 8-bit adapter slot for PC and XT, and (b) 16-bit adapter slot for AT. Microchannel adapter slots, showing (c) 8-bit section (01-45) with 16-bit extension at bottom; (d) same, with video extension at top; (e) 8-bit section with matched memory section at top, 32-bit extension at bottom. (f) detail view of MCA adapter slots on model 70 system board.

Figure 6.5   (Continued)   (f)

the IBM 3270 Connection Adapter are a perfect match for the 16-bit system board socket shown in Figure 6.5(c), yet the adapter may be inserted into any other adapter socket on the same board. Of course the opposite is not true: a 32-bit adapter will not fit into a 16-bit socket.

There are a few other exceptions, which are described below.

Physically Incompatible Adapters. A few electrically compatible ISA adapters will not fit in an AT dual-slot socket because the second socket prevents the adapter from being properly seated. In this case, one of the single-slot sockets must be used. And of course AT-specific adapters with two edge connectors may not be used in either the PC or the XT.

Some adapters may feature an optional piggyback-mounted card which causes the adapter to take up quite a bit of extra room. A typical example is the IBM Enhanced Graphics Adapter, which can accommodate an add-on graphics memory-expansion card. When using such a card, make sure there is sufficient clearance so that adjacent adapters do not make physical contact with each other.

Regardless of the presence of the add-on memory option, the Enhanced Graphics Adapter should be inserted in slot 1 so that its lower edge does not come into contact with chips on the system board. Although the adapter will function in any other slot, installation elsewhere than slot 1 is not recommended.

In the case of an old-style adapter whose mounting bracket is too wide to fit in an XT or AT, refer to the section on system enhancement at the end of this chapter (page 218).

Electrically Incompatible Adapters.   A few adapters are not compatible with one or more PC systems, even though they may be physically accommodated. Table 6.7 lists various options and adapters that are not compatible with all systems. To avoid system damage, do not use any of the devices listed in the table unless your model is listed in the compatible personal computers column.

EISA and ISA Adapter Compatibility.   As briefly mentioned in Chapter 1, ISA and EISA adapters will fit the adapter slots of either system, but only an ISA adapter will properly function in both systems. Figure 6.6(a) compares the edge connectors on ISA and EISA adapters. On the EISA adapter, the EISA contacts are at the bottom of the edge connector, with ISA contacts located immediately above. Figure 6.6(c) is a much-simplified view of an EISA adapter and system board socket, showing one of several access keys which partially block ISA edge connectors from reaching the bottom of the socket. However, the adapter connectors do make full contact with the ISA pins located near the top of the socket.

By contrast, access notches on an EISA adapter's edge connector permit it to reach the bottom of the socket. As a result, both the EISA and ISA rows make contact with their respective pins in the socket.

CONNECTORS AND CABLES

A variety of internal and external devices are interfaced to the system board via one or more cables and connectors. Representative devices are listed here, along with the required cable connections.

Internal Device Connectors

In every PC, XT, and AT, the speaker and a few other internal devices are mounted near the system board and attached to it via cable. These cables may be easily disconnected for servicing. In each case, the plug/socket combination is keyed so that the device cannot be improperly reconnected. Each connector is briefly described here, and diagnostics information is

(a)

(b)

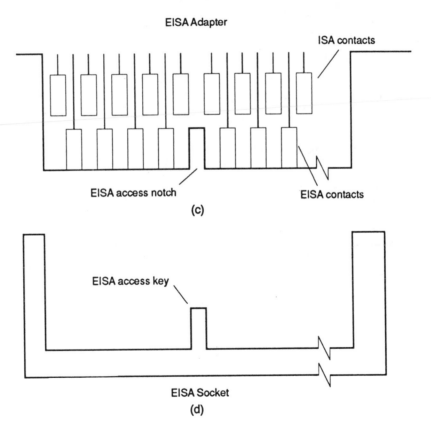

Figure 6.6.   Comparison of edge connectors on (a) EISA and (b) ISA adapters.
Detail of (c) EISA edge connector and (d) system-board socket.

Table 6.7 ISA System Device Compatibility Chart *

IBM part no.	Device description	Compatible computer(s) type (model no.)	note
Memory			
1501001	16Kb memory module kit (9 chips)	PC1 only	
1501011	32Kb memory expansion option	PC1 only	
1501003	64Kb memory module kit (9 chips)	(for 1501013)	
1501012	64Kb memory expansion option	PC, XT	
1501013	64/256Kb memory expansion option	PC, XT	
6450209	128Kb memory expansion option	AT	
78X8955	128Kb memory expansion kit	25	
6450338	128/640Kb memory expansion option	AT	
1501209	256Kb memory expansion option	PC, XT	
6450202	256Kb memory module kit	AT	
6450203	512Kb memory expansion option	AT	
30F5348	512Kb memory expansion kit	25 286-006, -G06	
6450343	512K/2Mb memory expansion option	AT	
30F5360	2Mb memory expansion kit	25 (all)	
Fixed disk and diskette drives, adapters			
1503800	160Kb diskette drive	PC, XT	
1503810	320Kb diskette drive	PC, XT	
6450207	360Kb diskette drive	AT	
4865001	720Kb diskette drive (external)	PC, XT	
4865002	720Kb diskette drive (external)	AT	
6450357	720Kb diskette drive (internal)	AT	
6450206	1.2Mb diskette drive (High Capacity)	AT	
1602500	10Mb fixed disk drive	PC, XT	(a)
6450326	20Mb fixed disk drive	XT 267, 268, 277, 278	
6450205	20Mb fixed disk drive	AT	
6450210	30Mb fixed disk drive	AT 239, 319, 339	
1602513	30Mb fixed disk drive update	AT 68, 69	(b)
1503780	diskette drive (only) adapter	PC, XT	
5161001	expansion unit with 10Mb disk drive	PC	
5161002	expansion unit with 10Mb disk drive	XT	
1602501	fixed disk (only) adapter	PC, XT	(a)
n/a	fixed disk & diskette drive adapter	AT	(c)
Communications			
1502074	asynchronous communications adapter	PC, XT	
1501204	binary synchronous communications adap.	all, except 30 286	
1501206	cluster adapter	PC, XT	
6450215	serial/parallel adapter	AT, 25, 30	
1501205	SDLC (synchronous data link control)	all	

Table 6.7 ISA System Device Compatibility Chart (continued) *

IBM part no.	Device Description	Compatible Computer(s) Type (model no.)	Note
Miscellaneous Devices			
1501005	BIOS update kit	PC only	
6451502	DAC Adapter	30 only	
1501300	Game Control Adapter	all	
6451503	GPIB Adapter	all except 25, 30 286	
1501100	keyboard (83 keys)	PC, XT	
5170099	keyboard (84 keys)	AT	
1501002	math coprocessor	PC, XT	
6450211	math coprocessor	AT	
1501400	prototype card	PC, XT	
6450220	prototype adapter	AT	

* Most, but not all, devices not listed in this table may be used in all ISA systems. In case of doubt, verify compatibility before installation.
(a) Fixed (hard) disk drive must be installed in a PC Expansion Unit, unless PC power supply is replaced with larger capacity device.
(b) Includes required new ROM BIOS modules, which also limit system clock speed to 6 MHz.
(c) Supplied as standard part of AT system, with no individual part number. Separately available on special order only.

found later in this chapter. The cable connections between a diskette or hard disk drive and its adapter are discussed in Chapter 8.

Power Supply. The internal power supply unit provides voltages to the system board, its adapter sockets, and the various internal diskette and hard disk drives. On PC, XT, AT, and some MCA systems, the power supply is connected to the system board via multiconductor connector in the upper right-hand quadrant of the system board. The power leads are a relatively heavy-gauge set of red, white, black, gray (or green), yellow, and orange wires leading from the supply to the system board connector. Similar cables lead from the power supply to each diskette and hard disk drive.

On some MCA systems, the system board/power supply interface is via an edge connector/socket arrangement. In either case, consult Chapter 5 for further details.

Keyboard, Mouse, and Cassette Connectors. At the rear of the system board and accessible from the back panel, a multipin socket is used to connect the keyboard to the system unit. There are five pins on pre-PS/2 system sockets and six on all PS/2 systems. The latter socket is identified by an embossed keyboard layout.

On the PC and all MCA systems, a similar socket is found to the immediate right of the keyboard socket (when viewed from the rear). The PC socket is for use with a cassette recorder, and the MCA socket is for a mouse.

System Keylock and Indicator Lights. On the AT the front panel keylock and green power-on LED (light-emitting diode) are connected to a plug (J20) near the front of the system board (see Figure 6.3(d)). The front panel red hard disk LED is connected to a plug on the hard disk/diskette adapter. On PS/2 systems, the keylock is either on the right-hand side or at the rear of the system unit. On MCA systems, the power-on LED and a yellow hard disk LED are built into the front panel of the system unit.

When either system is turned on, the green power-on LED should come on and stay on until system power is turned off again. The red or amber LED flashes briefly, and then comes on again every time data is written to, or read from, the hard disk. Its function is identical to the in-use light on a diskette drive.

AT keylock troubleshooting is discussed in Chapter 10 (page 434), and an LED test is described later in this chapter.

Speaker. On pre-PS/2 systems, a four-pin plug mounted at the front edge of the system board is used to connect the speaker leads to the system board, using positions 1 and 4 on the plug. As a keying guide, pin 2 has been clipped on the plug, and the corresponding socket hole has been covered. If an internal modem is not equipped with its own speaker, the modem will have to be connected to the system unit speaker, as described in Chapter 12.

On MCA systems, the speaker is mounted on a small removable module, such as the one shown in Figure 6.2(c).

On PS/2 ISA systems, the speaker is replaced by a beeper (in a one-half-inch round metallic housing) mounted directly on the system board, in the lower left-hand corner. On the models 25 and 30, an earphone jack is located at the rear of the system unit, directly to the left of the keyboard socket. When an earphone is plugged in, the internal beeper is disabled.

EISA speaker locations vary according to system layout.

Battery. In the AT and most PS/2 systems, a 3- or 6-volt lithium battery maintains time and date data, as well as system configuration information in a 64-byte section of CMOS (complementary metal-oxide semiconductor) RAM when the computer is turned off. The CMOS contents and location of the battery are given in Table 6.8.

Note that in most EISA systems and the PS/2 models 25 286, 30 286, and 65 SX, the battery and the CMOS RAM are both contained within a

Table 6.8a CMOS Configuration Data *

| CMOS byte | | Contents ** | | |
Hex	decimal	AT	30 286	MCA systems
00 – 0D	00 – 13	real-time clock information	same	same
0E	14	diagnostic status byte	same	same
0F	15	shutdown status byte	same	same
10	16	diskette drives A & B	same	same
11	17	reserved	fixed disk	first fixed disk
12	18	fixed disk drives C & D	reserved	second fixed disk
13	19	reserved	same	same
14	20	equipment byte	same	same
15	21	base memory, low byte	same	same
16	22	base memory, high byte	same	same
17	23	expansion memory, low byte	same	same
18	24	expansion memory, high byte	same	same
19	25	drive C extended byte	reserved	reserved
1A	26	drive D extended byte	reserved	reserved
1B – 2D	27 – 45	reserved	reserved	reserved
2E	46	CMOS checksum; high byte	reserved	reserved
2F	47	CMOS checksum; low byte	reserved	reserved
30	48	expansion memory, low byte	reserved	reserved
31	49	expansion memory, high byte	reserved	reserved
32	50	date century	configuration CRC, low byte	
33	51	information flags	configuration CRC, high byte	
34 – 36	52 – 54	reserved	reserved	reserved
37	55	reserved	date century	same
38 – 3F	56 – 63	reserved	reserved	reserved

  * CMOS not used in PS/2 models 25 & 30.
 ** For further details, see IBM Technical Reference Manual for each system.

Table 6.8b CMOS Battery Locations

Computer	Location of battery
PC	none †
XT	none ‡
AT	inside system unit rear panel, connected to system board via system board socket J21, immediately in front of keyboard socket, J22
25	none ‡
25 286	within clock module (Dallas DS1287) in system board socket ZM35
30	soldered to removable I/O connector board (for clock only)
30 286	within clock module (Dallas DS1287) in system board socket ZM35
65 SX	within clock module (Dallas DS1287) in system board socket U43
other MCA	mounted at the top of speaker module (see Figure 6.2(c)).

  † To add clock function, insert no-slot clock module in empty 24-pin ROM socket, with pins 1, 2, 27, 28 overhanging socket. On top of module, jumper pins 1, 27, 28 to pin 26.
  ‡ To add clock function, insert no-slot clock module in any 28-pin ROM module.

replaceable real-time clock module that fits into a socket on the system board. The PS/2 model 25 does not have an onboard battery, and therefore time and date data are not maintained when the system is turned off. To get around this problem, an accessory clock/calendar module may be installed on the system board. For example, the SMT no-slot clock is housed in a 28-pin DIP module. To install it, temporarily remove the ROM BIOS module in system board socket U17. Insert the clock module in the socket, and then insert the ROM module into the top of the clock module.

External Device Connectors

In the conventional electrical supply system, a universally standard practice dictates that the power source is wired to a female socket, while any device requiring power will have a male plug. Although the opposite convention would be just as effective, the present standard protects the user from receiving an electric shock, for while there is no danger associated with touching the metal prongs on a plug, there is nothing *but* danger in attempting the same thing if there were prongs on an electric outlet instead. So by simply observing the male/female plug/socket convention, the user enjoys the relatively risk-free convenience of being able to install and remove electrical appliances without the assistance of an electrician.

Some other industries, such as professional sound recording, use an inversely arranged wiring practice for audio cables. In the case of audio cables, there is no risk of shock, and the reversed arrangement helps to identify the direction—from the plug to the socket—in which the signal is flowing.

In the computer industry the identification conventions described above are of little value, since the same cable often passes information in both directions. As an obvious example, the line connecting a computer and a modem must carry operating instructions and information in two directions.

A less obvious two-way device is the printer. Before printing begins, the computer inquires whether the printer is ready to receive. If ready, the printer sends a ready signal back to the computer, and printing begins. If the paper or ribbon runs out, another signal is sent from printer to computer to halt transmission until the printer is again ready to receive.

In fact, about the only exception to two-way communication along computer cables is the pre-VGA video display, which always receives data from the system but never sends anything back to it. As for the VGA system, the display returns its status (monochrome or color) to the adapter.

From the above discussion it can be seen that no assumptions about PC signal flow may be made from simply examining the connector. Going one step further, even the number of individual pins or sockets on a connector is no indication of the actual number of wires in use.

Using the external modem as an example, most such devices employ a 25-pin receptacle, although only nine conductors are actually needed for routine operation. In fact, the serial port on various IBM adapters may employ either a 9-pin or a 25-pin receptacle for modem connections, depending on the specific design of the port. Therefore, two cable formats may be found in use: a 25-to-25 conductor cable and a 25-to-9 conductor cable. The appropriate cable is strictly a function of the adapter in use, and there is no difference in the operation of the modem.

Complete details about modem operations are found in Chapter 12, and the above explanation is included here merely as a representative example of what may be encountered when examining the various plugs and sockets seen on IBM and other personal computers.

Connector Descriptions. Figure 6.7 shows many of the connectors that are found on IBM and IBM-compatible adapters, and Table 6.9 gives the polarity for each type of connector. Keep in mind that the actual number of conductors in use may be equal to, but is often less than, the capacity of the connector.

Cable Lengths

For optimum system performance, the cable connecting each external option to its adapter should be kept reasonably short. Although it is not possible to publish a definitive specification for maximum cable length, remember that any cable carrying digital information is susceptible to outside interference, which may affect the accuracy of the transmitted data. For example, if a single bit should change state due to extraneous noise on the line, a transmitted lowercase letter q might be received as one of the following characters:

Bit position 7654 3210	Character	Error bit
0111 0001	q	none
0111 0000	p	0
0111 0011	s	1
0111 0101	u	2
0111 1001	y	3
0110 0001	k	4
0101 0001	R	5
0011 0001	1	6
1111 0001	±	7

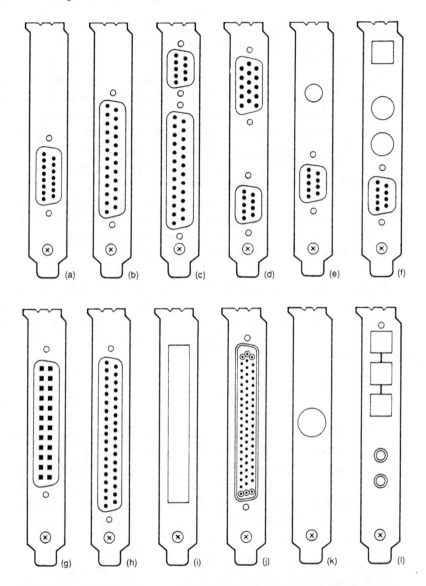

Figure 6.7. Connectors on ISA and MCA adapter cards, showing bracket style used on pre-PS/2 ISA systems. Refer to Table 6.9 for polarity of each connector. The connectors are for the following adapters: (a) Game Control (b) Asynchronous, Binary Synchronous, SDLC Communications, PS/2 serial port (c) Monochrome Display and Printer, Serial/Parallel (d) Professional Graphics (9-pin only), VGA (15-pin only), combination analog/digital video (both) (e) Color/Graphics (f) Enhanced Graphics (g) General Purpose Interface Bus (GPIB) (h) Diskette Drive (i) Data Acquisition (j) Expansion Unit Sender and Receiver (k) Cluster (l) Voice Communications

Table 6.9 Representative Connectors on Adapter Brackets

Adapter card	(*)	Multipin connectors male	female	other connectors
Analog and Digital Video	(d)	—	9	digital (for EGA)
		—	15	analog (for VGA)
Asynchronous Communications	(b)	25	—	
Audio Capture and Playback		—	—	4 mini stereo phone jacks
Binary Synchronous Communications	(b)	25	—	
Cluster, 3270 Connection	(k)	—	—	1 BNC (coaxial)
Color/Graphics	(e)	—	9	1 RCA (phono)
Data Acquisition	(i)	60	—	
Diskette Drive (PC)	(h)	—	37	
Enhanced Graphics	(f)	—	9	2 RCA (phono)
Expansion Unit Adapters	(j)	—	62	
Game Control	(a)	—	15	
General Purpose Interface Bus	(g)	—	24	
Internal Modem		—	—	2 RJ–12 (telephone)
Monochrome Display & Printer	(c)	—	9	for monochrome monitor
		—	25	for parallel printer
Professional Graphics Controller	(d)	—	9 †	
SCSI Host, Bus Master		—	50	
SDLC Communications	(b)	25	—	
Serial/Parallel	(c)	9	25	serial (9), parallel (25)
Video Graphics Array, 8514/A	(d)	—	15 ‡	
Voice Communications	(l)	—	—	3 RJ–11C (telephone)
				2 miniphone

*   cross–reference to Figure 6.7
†   15–pin connector in Figure 6.7(d) omitted
‡   9–pin connector in Figure 6.7(d) omitted

Even an occasional minor error such as this in a data stream sent to the printer is unacceptable in an important document. And if the error occurs during the transmission of, say, critical financial data, the result could be disastrous.

All else being equal, the longer the cable, the greater its susceptibility to outside interference. Conversely, the more outside interference there is, the shorter the cable length must be to preserve data integrity. For this reason, cable extensions should be used with extreme caution. If errors are encountered after installing such an extension, remove it and note the effect. If the errors disappear when the cable is removed, you may simply have exceeded the maximum permissible cable length in a specific environment. The cable itself is not necessarily defective; it's just too long for this application.

Cable Shielding. In interference-prone environments, a shielded cable may offer some improvement in data transmission accuracy. The shield is a metallic braid and/or Mylar foil surrounding the conductors, just underneath the cable's outer insulation. To prevent the shield itself from functioning as an extra conductor, it may be attached to the metal cable plug casing at one end only.

In the case of regular errors during printer operations, or while receiving data via modem, it's a good idea to carefully examine the cable for loose connections.

System Security

Protection against system tampering is available on AT and PS/2 computers, which are supplied with a set of two matching keys. The keys are accompanied by a small tag which gives the key number and in some cases, the address of the key supplier.

Don't lose the tag, for the key number is not found on either key. If a replacement key is needed, contact the key supplier for instructions. If the tag does not give an address, note the format of the key code, and contact the manufacturer listed below.

Key code	Contact
FPSxxxx, MPAxxxx, MSExxxx	Chicago Lock Company
xxxxB	Fort Lock Corp.

AT Security. The key locks the system unit cover in place and also disables the keyboard, thus preventing busy little fingers from gaining access to the system.

PS/2 Security. Here, the system key locks the cover in place, but has no effect on the keyboard. Instead, keyboard and system passwords are used, as described later in the chapter (page 189). The password system may be easily disabled if the system cover is left unlocked. On systems where the battery is mounted above the speaker housing, there are two protruding pins below the speaker. To disable the password, short the pins together. On other systems, a three-pin jumper (J13 on model 30 286) is found on the system board. To disable the password, move the jumper to its alternate position.

Additional Security Measures. For systems which do not provide keyboard locks or passwords, some measure of security against the idle busybody can be arranged by changing the names of a few key DOS internal commands; that is, commands imbedded in the COMMAND.COM file which therefore don't show up in the DOS subdirectory. For example, if DIR is changed to RID, anyone typing the familiar DIR will just get a *Bad command or file name* error message, and you'll have to remember to type RID from now on to see your own directory listings.

To make the change, use the DOS debug or Norton Utilities to examine the end of the COMMAND.COM file for the list of internal command names. Change DIR to RID (or whatever) and then write the changed file back to disk, making sure the new name is the same length as the old. Do *not* practice this on your one-and-only boot diskette or on the hard drive. Instead, format a new diskette and edit its COMMAND.COM file. Then boot with the edited diskette and see if it works. If it does, then it's safe to copy the edited COMMAND.COM to your boot diskette or hard disk. It's certainly not the last word in security, but it might be enough to persuade your colleagues to find someplace else to play.

SYSTEM CONFIGURATION

System configuration simply means setting various hardware (PC and XT) or software (AT, EISA, and MCA) switches to agree with the options that are installed. When the complement of devices is changed, either by addition or removal of an internal or external device, the system board must be reconfigured so as to take that change into account. This is done in one of the following ways:

PC, XT	Set/reset various system board switches.
AT	Run the SETUP program on the diagnostics diskette.
PS/2	Models 25 and 30: no configuration required.
	Other ISA and all MCA systems: run the automatic configuration program on the Starter/Reference diskette.
EISA	Use the Configuration Utilities diskette.

If configuration settings are not correct, one or more devices may not function properly or, in the case of the ISA system display configuration, damage may result. Generally the configuration is performed as each option is put into service, following the instructions that come with it. If you are about to add an option to your personal computer, follow the instructions that are included with that option, as well as any supplementary instructions that may appear in this book in the chapter discussing the option.

It is just as important to remember to reconfigure the system when options are removed. This is especially critical when removing one of two installed displays, since an improper switch setting could damage the remaining display.

SCSI Bus Configuration

If a SCSI device is installed in any ISA, MCA, or EISA system, a SCSI host adapter card must likewise be installed. The 50-conductor SCSI bus links all the SCSI devices in the system, and as part of the configuration procedure the device at either end of the bus must be terminated, as shown in Figure 6.8. In the first example in Figure 6.8, an internal hard disk drive is at one end of the SCSI bus, the host adapter is at the other end, and both are terminated. In the second example, two additional SCSI devices are connected via the host adapter's external socket, and therefore, the adapter is no longer at the end of the bus. Therefore, its terminations must be removed, and the external device now at the end of the bus must be terminated instead, as shown in the figure.

PC AND XT SYSTEM CONFIGURATION

Switch blocks on the system board are used to configure various parts of the PC and XT systems. Each block contains a row of eight miniature

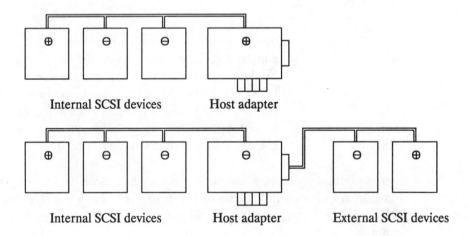

Figure 6.8.   SCSI bus termination requirements. $\oplus$ = termination network installed. $\ominus$ = termination network removed.

switches. The PC has two switch blocks, while the XT has but one, as shown in Figure 6.9. Presumably each switch is already in the proper position for your system, but one or more may have to be repositioned when a modification is made. Table 6.10 lists all possible switch positions for the PC and XT. You may verify at a glance that the switch block settings on your personal computer agree with your system configuration.

On the PC and XT, once all system board switches are in the correct position, the diagnostics diskette should be used to verify that the complete system is in order. Insert this diskette in drive A, turn the power on, and follow the procedures given in the routine diagnostics section of Chapter 3.

AT SYSTEM CONFIGURATION

When the AT was first introduced, some users were surprised to discover that it had neither of the switch blocks described above. Instead, all system configuration is done by software, using the Setup option on the diagnostics diskette. One exception to this is a single display switch (SW1, Figure 6.3(c))

Table 6.10 System Board Switch Blocks used for Configuration

Block 1 (PC and XT)

Switch	Position *	PC	XT
1	0	Drives are installed	POST enabled
	1	are not installed	disabled
2	0	Coprocessor is installed	Coprocessor is installed
	1	is not installed	is not installed
		Memory	
3, 4	00	64K or more	256K
	01	32K	128K
	10	48K	192K
	11	16K	64K
		Display	
5, 6 †	00	mono, mono & CGA	mono, mono & CGA
	01	CGA only, 40 × 25	CGA only, 40 × 25
	10	CGA only, 80 × 25	CGA only, 80 × 25
	11	EGA, EGA + other, none	EGA, EGA + other, none
		Drives Installed	
7, 8	00	invalid position	4
	01	2	2
	10	invalid position	3
	11	less than 2	1

Table 6.10 System Board Switch Blocks used for Configuration (continued)

Block 2 (PC only) Switches	Positions *	Amount of additional memory (Kb) installed on all option cards, in conjunction with	
		64Kb	256Kb system board
1–8	11111000	none	none, 64Kb on system board
	01111000	32	not used
	10111000	64	none, 128Kb on system board
	00111000	96	not used
	11011000	128	none, 192Kb on system board
	01011000	160	not used
	10011000	192	none, 256Kb on system board
	00011000	224	32
	11101000	256	64
	01101000	288	96
	10101000	320	128
	00101000	352	160
	11001000	384	192
	01001000	416	224
	10001000	448	256
	00001000	480	288
	11110000	512	320
	01110000	544	352
	10110000	576	384

* Switch position 0 = OFF (down), 1 = ON (up). Positions not shown are invalid.

† To prevent damage to the display, make sure these switches are set correctly before applying power. See Chapter 10 for further details.

used to select the default video display. See Chapter 11 for more details on this procedure. A second exception takes the form of a small jumper that must be set to agree with the amount of memory installed on the AT system board (see Figure 6.3(d)). This is described in Chapter 7.

When to Configure

The three conditions which require AT system configuration are

First-time operation

Routine configuration or reconfiguration

Configuration after battery replacement

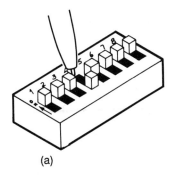

(a)

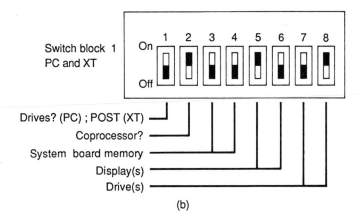

Switch block 1
PC and XT

Drives? (PC) ; POST (XT)
Coprocessor?
System board memory
Display(s)
Drive(s)

(b)

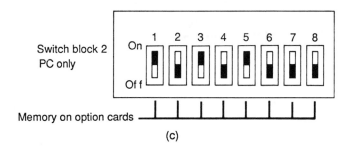

Switch block 2
PC only

Memory on option cards

(c)

Figure 6.9.   Switch block (a) on ISA PC and XT system boards. See Table 6.10 for switch settings. (b) Block 1 on PC and XT; (c) Block 2 on PC only.

In each case, to begin the configuration procedure, insert the diagnostics diskette in drive A and turn the system on.

First-time Configuration. In the case of an AT system that has not yet been configured, the message shown in Figure 6.10(a) is displayed on screen and two beeps are heard. Answer "no" to the prompt, and then follow the routine configuration procedure described next.

Routine Configuration. At the Select an Option menu display (shown in Figure 3.4), choose option 4, Setup.

(a.)

```
xxxxx KB OK
 161-System Optons Not Set-(Run SETUP)

(RESUME = "F1" KEY)

IBM Personal Computer AT
    Setup Program

Have you completed running this
program since connecting the
battery (Y/N).

Type Y or N, then press "ENTER".
?
```

(b.)

```
You have completed your system
Setup. Your system is now ready
to use.

For information on operating your
system go to the "Operating Your
IBM Personal Computer AT section
of your Guide to Operations.

TURN YOUR SYSTEM UNIT OFF.
```

Figure 6.10. First-time AT configuration displays seen (a) when system is powered on, and (b) at the conclusion of the configuration procedure.

Time and Date Set.   To set the AT's internal clock, enter the correct date and time information in response to the prompts. Effective with DOS version 3.3, it is also possible to set date and time without the diagnostics diskette. At the DOS prompt, enter the DATE or TIME command and then press the Enter key. Then change the date or time, as appropriate. When using DOS prior to version 3.3, changes at the DOS prompt are not saved when the system is turned off.

If version 2.0 or 2.1 of the AT diagnostics diskette is run in the diagnostics multiple-test mode described in Chapter 3, the clock will be automatically reset to 13:00. In this case, use option 4 to reenter the correct time before exiting diagnostics. This extra step is unnecessary in subsequent versions of the diagnostics diskette.

Installed Devices.   Once you've changed or verified the date and time, the screen display in Figure 6.11(a) appears. Type N to make further corrections. Otherwise, a display of installed options (Figure 6.11(b)) is seen and you are asked to verify that the list is correct. If it is not, answer *no* and then make the necessary corrections.

To respond to the display seen in Figure 6.11(c), you'll need to know what type of hard disks are installed in your system. If you are unsure about this, refer to the section entitled Drive Types and Parameters in Chapter 9 (page 355), and if necessary, to Tables 9.2 through 9.4.

If you need assistance with any corrections, turn to the appropriate chapter in this book, as indicated here, for further details.

Installed device	Chapter	Section	Page
Diskette drives	8	Drive Systems	297
Hard disk drives	9	Hard Disk Parameters	355
Base memory	7	System Memory Configuration	253
Expansion memory	7	System Memory Configuration	253
Primary display	11	Primary Display Mode	467

Once you have made the necessary corrections to the list of installed options, verify that the list is correct by answering *yes* to the prompt and then follow the configuration exit procedure described below.

However, if a RESUME = "F1" KEY message is seen after you press Enter, it is an indication of some discrepancy between the Setup values and those values the system discovered during its reset. Press function key F1 and then return to the Setup option to make whatever corrections are required. If you are unsure of what's wrong, double-check all the options and be on the lookout for such things as items that do not appear in the screen display, or memory notation that does not agree with what you have installed.

(a.)

You have set your Date and Time to the following:

Current date is:
11-19-1990

Current time is:
15:36:09   *(Note use of 24-hour clock)*

Is this correct (Y/N)
Type Y or N, then press "ENTER"
?

(b.)

Your system may have other options   *(for example, modem,*
installed. They are not required for   *communications card, etc.)*
Setup and are not displayed.

The following options have been set:

Diskette Drive A - High Capacity
Diskette Drive B - Double Sided
Fixed Disk Drive C - Type 12   *(An electronic disk will*
Fixed Disk Drive D - Not Installed   *not appear in this list.)*
Base memory size - 512Kb
Expansion memory size - 1024Kb
Primary display is attached to:
 - Monochrome Display Adapter

Are these options correct (Y/N)
?

(c.)

Enter fixed disk type (1-xx)   *(xx = 15 or greater,*
for Fixed Disk Drive C.   *depending on AT model)*

WARNING

Entering the wrong drive type
causes improper operation of
the fixed disk.
?

(d.)

During system reset, if you
receive the (RESUME = "F1" KEY)
message, go to the Testing Your
IBM Personal Computer AT section
of your Guide to Operations.

Now, press "ENTER" and stand by
while system resets...

Figure 6.11.   Routine AT configuration displays. Use these screen displays as a reference and follow the instructions given in the text.

Configuration After Battery Failure. As mentioned earlier in the chapter, a 3- or 6-volt lithium battery maintains constant power to a 64-byte section of CMOS RAM in which AT configuration data is stored. The data is preserved for as long as the battery lasts, thus obviating the need to run a system setup procedure each time the computer is powered on.

However, when the battery at last fails (it takes about three to ten years), the configuration information is lost unless a new battery is installed within a few hours. To remove and replace the battery, refer to the procedure given in the *Troubleshooting* section of this chapter (page 209). If you have not previously saved the CMOS configuration data as described later in this chapter (below, not applicable to EISA systems), then follow the first-time configuration procedure described above.

Configuration Exit Procedure. At the conclusion of a first-time configuration, the screen display in Figure 6.10(b) is seen. It is not necessary to turn the system off if you wish to use it immediately. Instead, remove the diagnostics diskette and reboot the system, as described below.

At the successful conclusion of a routine configuration procedure, the display in Figure 6.11(d) is seen, indicating the configuration data is correctly stored in the system's CMOS RAM.

System Reboot. With the Setup procedure completed, insert the regular DOS diskette in drive A. This must be done so that the system can reload the DOS diskette's COMMAND.COM file. The file with the same name on the diagnostics diskette has significant differences, and is, in fact, suitable for use only with diagnostics.

On the other hand, if you plan to double-check your configuration by performing the system checkout routine—a good idea, by the way—then simply reboot with the diagnostics diskette still in place and return to Chapter 3 to follow the diagnostics procedures.

CMOS Data Save Program

If the AT is up and running and properly configured with a good battery in place, it's easy to write the CMOS configuration data to a diskette file, so that the data may be retrieved after a failed battery is replaced. By saving the data on diskette, it is not necessary to run the setup program after replacing the battery. The procedure is described here.

Data Save Procedure. Run the BASIC program in Listing 6.2. The program reads the data stored in CMOS and writes it to a file called "CMOS-DATA" on drive A.

Data Replace Procedure. After replacing the battery, turn the system back on again and ignore the error message that was seen in Figure 6.10(a). Press the F1 key, enter BASIC, and then run the program in Listing 6.3. At lines 100–130, the CMOSDATA file is read from diskette. However, since the file contains the date and time stored at the time the file was written, lines 200–250 prompt the user to enter the current date and time. Next, lines 300–350 insert the updated data back into the 64-byte string, and finally lines 400–430 write the original data and the new date and time into CMOS RAM.

The configuration in effect before the battery was replaced is now once again installed, making it unnecessary to run the Setup option on the diagnostics diskette.

PS/2 SYSTEM CONFIGURATION

As with all other IBM personal computers, you must reconfigure a PS/2 system whenever you change its physical configuration, say by adding or removing memory, a math coprocessor, a diskette, or a hard disk drive. After making any such change, two beeps are heard and a $16x$ error code is displayed the next time the system is turned on. As previously mentioned in Chapter 3, the reconfiguration can be postponed simply by pressing the F1 key, after which the DOS prompt should be seen. However, PS/2 system configuration is far simpler than any of the procedures required for its predecessor systems, and it only

Listing 6.2 A BASIC CMOS Data Save Program

```
100 FOR X = 0 TO 63
110 OUT 112, X
120 A$ = CHR$(INP(113))
130 B$ = B$ + A$
140 NEXT X
150 OPEN "CMOSDATA" AS #1 LEN = 64
160 FIELD #1, 64 AS C$
170 LSET C$ = B$
180 PUT #1
190 CLOSE
```

Listing 6.3 A BASIC CMOS Data Replace Program

```
100 OPEN "CMOSDATA" AS #1 LEN = 64
110 FIELD #1, 64 AS C$
120 GET #1
130 CLOSE

200 INPUT "DATE:   Month (1-12):",MO$
210 INPUT "          Day (1-31):",TD$
220 INPUT "         Year  19__:",YR$
230 INPUT "TIME:   Hour (0-23):",HR$
240 INPUT "        Minute (0-59):",MN$
250 INPUT "        Second (0-59):",SC$

300 MID$(B$, 1,1) = CHR$(VAL("&h" + SC$))
310 MID$(B$, 3,1) = CHR$(VAL("&h" + MN$))
320 MID$(B$, 5,1) = CHR$(VAL("&h" + HR$))
330 MID$(B$, 8,1) = CHR$(VAL("&h" + TD$))
340 MID$(B$, 9,1) = CHR$(VAL("&h" + MO$))
350 MID$(B$,10,1) = CHR$(VAL("&h" + YR$))

400 FOR X = 0 TO 63
410 D = ASC(MID$(B$,X+1,1))
420 OUT 112, X: OUT 113, D
430 NEXT X
```

takes a few moments to run the automatic configuration mode as described below.

ISA Models 25 and 30.   As an exception to the rule, ISA models 25 and 30 do not require any configuration. Neither model supports more than 640Kb of memory, and if the first 128Kb is either missing (model 25 only) or defective (both), the system automatically adjusts itself. As a warning, the following message is seen during POST:

```
205-Memory Error       model 25

205 Memory Remap       model 30
```

PS/2 Main Menu

When the system is booted or rebooted with the Starter or Reference diskette in drive A, the IBM logo is displayed on screen at the conclusion of the POST procedure. Press the Enter key to display the Main Menu shown in Figure 6.12. For configuration purposes, select option 3 below. The

(a)

```
┌─────────────────────────────────────────────────────────┐
│ Main Menu                                                 │
├─────────────────────────────────────────────────────────┤
│   1. Learn about the computer                             │
│   2. Backup the Reference Diskette                        │
│   3. Set configuration                                    │
│   4. Set features                                         │
│   5. Copy an option diskette                              │
│   6. Test the computer                                    │
│                                                           │
│                                                           │
├─────────────────────────────────────────────────────────┤
│ Use↑or↓to select. Press Enter.                            │
│ Esc=Quit    F1=Help                                       │
└─────────────────────────────────────────────────────────┘
```

Note the following variations on the Main Menu:
model 30 286
```
    2. Backup the Starter Diskette
    5. Move the system
    6. Test the system
```

model 50/60
```
    6. Move the computer
    7. Test the computer
```

(b)

```
IBM Personal System/2 Model 25 (or 30)
STARTER DISKETTE
Version 1.00

(C) Copyright IBM Corporation, 1987

STARTER DISKETTE MAIN MENU

1.  LEARNING ABOUT YOUR SYSTEM
2.  SERVICES
        System Checkout
        Format Diskette
        Copy Diskette
        Prepare System for Moving
        Set Time and Date

Select a Number and Press ENTER

ESC=Quit
```

Figure 6.12. PS/2 diagnostic main menus: (a) models 25 286, 30 286, and all MCA systems, (b) models 25 and 30.

options are listed here in the order they appear on screen, with diagnostic-related choices described in detail in Chapter 3. PS/2 models 25 and 30 offer options 1 and 2 only.

Option 1.   Learning About Your System   (models 25 and 30)
          Learn About the System   (model 30 286)
          Learn About the Computer   (MCA systems)

No matter what they call it, this is an excellent color/graphics tutorial about the PS/2 system. Onscreen instructions are quite clear and the option presents a well-executed introductory tutorial on hardware, software, and other features.

Option 2.   Services   (models 25 and 30)

An intermediate display (not shown here) explains the purpose of this option. Press the Enter key to display the Services menu itself. Since most of the menu choices are related to diagnostics, refer to Chapter 3 for further details and an illustration of the menu (Figure 3.4(c)). The configuration-related options (0 and 4) are described here.

Option 0. System Checkout. The option begins with a display of installed devices. Since no hardware or software configuration procedures are required, the user need only verify that the displayed list is correct. In response to the *Is the list correct* (Y/N) prompt, enter Y or N and then refer to Chapter 3 (page 59) for information about the diagnostic tests which follow.

Option 4. Set Time and Date. Follow the on-screen prompts to enter first the date and then the time (which appear in the reverse sequence of their order in previous screens).

Option 2.   Backup the Starter Diskette   (model 30 286)
          Backup the Reference Diskette   (MCA systems)

This diagnostic-related option is described in Chapter 3 (page 49).

Option 3.   Set configuration   (model 30 286 and MCA systems)

For all PS/2 systems other than the models 25 and 30, there are two conditions under which system reconfiguration is required:

Configuration required because:

1. You have added or removed a component that requires system reconfiguration. A 16*x* error code is seen when the system is turned on (*x* = 1–5).
2. You wish to reconfigure a component that permits a choice of settings. For example, change the parallel port from 1 to 2.

Take the following action:

When the error code is displayed, insert the Starter/Reference diskette in drive A and press the F1 key (not necessary if diskette is in the drive when you boot/reboot the system). Insert the Starter or Reference diskette in drive A and turn on the power.

In either case, press the Enter key when the IBM logo is seen. If the system recognizes a configuration problem, one of the following error messages is displayed:

Battery Error - 00161   (systems with replaceable battery)
Nonvolatile Memory Error 00161   (systems with clock module)

The message shown in Figure 6.13(a) (or similar) is displayed if the system's CMOS RAM has been without battery power long enough to lose its stored configuration data. This might happen if the battery/speaker module were removed, or if the battery itself is missing or defective. The message is also seen when the computer is powered on for the first time.

In any case, a battery error message (not shown here) lists the conditions that might apply. After reading the complete message, press the Enter key; the automatic configuration routine writes the current configuration data to CMOS RAM. When configuration finishes, press Enter again to reboot the system.

Although the system hardware configuration is now stored in CMOS RAM again, the lost time and date data also need to be reentered. Therefore, after the system reboots itself, the *Date and Time Not Set* error message is seen. For further details, follow the instructions below.

Real Time Clock Module. On the models 25 286, 30 286 and 65 SX (and in most EISA systems), both the battery and the CMOS are packaged in the same module (Dallas DS1287 Real Time Clock), so by default the configuration data gets tossed out with the dead battery. However, the module should live as long as, or longer than, the computer itself, so this is an unlikely problem. However, if the module fails for other reasons, as may be suggested by some of the Other POST Errors described in Chapter 3 (page 34), then the module will have to be replaced, and the system reconfigured.

(a)

```
Nonvolatile Memory Error 00161              Page  1   of  1
─────────────────────────────────────────────────────────
This error appears if you have:

 - A problem with nonvolatile memory

Continue until the system automatically configures
itself to the normal settings.

If this error appears again after the system
has been off for more than 30 minutes, have the
system unit serviced.
─────────────────────────────────────────────────────────
Press Enter to continue.
```

(b)

```
Configuration Error - 00162                 Page  1   of  1
─────────────────────────────────────────────────────────
Be sure all devices attached to the computer are
turned on.

If you have changed the configuration (for example,
added or removed an option), run automatic
configuration.

If you have not changed the configuration, do not run
automatic configuration.  Continue until the Main Menu
appears.  Select "Test the computer" to determine the
cause of this error and what action to take.
─────────────────────────────────────────────────────────
Automatically configure the system? (Y/N)
```

Figure 6.13.   One of these error displays is seen if a PS/2 computer is booted from the Starter/Reference diskette and the system requires configuration.

```
Memory Size Error - 00164                    Page 1  of 1

If you have installed or removed memory, run automatic
configuration.

If you have not installed or removed any memory, do
not run automatic configuration. Continue until the
Main Menu appears.  Select "Test the computer" to
determine the cause of this error and what action to
take.

Automatically configure the system? (Y/N)
```

(d)

```
Adapter Configuration Error - 00165          Page 1  of 1

If you have installed or removed an adapter, run
automatic configuration.

If you have not installed or removed an adapter, do
not run automatic configuration.  Continue until the
Main Menu appears.  Select "Test the computer" to
determine the cause of this error and what action to
take.

Automatically configure the system? (Y/N)
```

Figure 6.13   (Continued)

Date and Time Not Set - 00163 When this message appears, press the Enter key to display the Main Menu, then choose Set Features, Option 4 and next Set Date and Time, Option 1. Both are described below.

Configuration Error 00162
Memory Size Error 00164
Adapter Configuration Error 00165
Depending on the specific configuration error, one of the screens shown in Figure 6.13b–d is displayed. Note the "Automatically configure the system?" prompt at the bottom of the displays. Answer *yes*, or else *no* and then select Option 5 on the Set Configuration menu. In either case, see Option 5 below for further details.

If you answer *no*, or if you wish to make some optional change, such as the port configuration mentioned above, the Main Menu shown in Figure 6.11 appears. Select the Set Configuration option either by pressing 3 or use the cursor-down key to move the highlighted bar to Option 3, and then press the Enter key. In either case, the Set Configuration menu (Figure 6.14) is seen. To make the desired selection, press the appropriate number or use the cursor keys to highlight the option, and then press the Enter key. Each displayed option is described here. As elsewhere in this book, it's a good idea to read through all available options before selecting one of them.

Option 1. View Configuration. The present system configuration is shown on screen. The display is similar to that given in Figure 6.15, except that the brackets and the F5, F6, and F10 function key choices are not seen. Select this choice when you want to review your system configuration, but do not want to make any changes.

Option 2. Change Configuration. For routine configuration applications, it is considerably faster to select the Run Automatic Configuration Option (5) described below. However, the present option must be used if you wish to reconfigure the parallel or serial ports, fixed disk controller, or various other accessories that may be installed in one of the adapter slots on the system board.

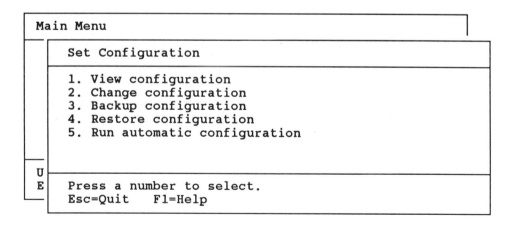

Figure 6.14.   The MCA Set Configuration menu is displayed when this option (3) is selected from the Main Menu (Figure 6.12).

```
┌─────────────────────────────────────────────────────────────┐
│ Configuration                                                 │
├─────────────────────────────────────────────────────────────┤
│ Total System Memory                                           │
│   Installed Memory ................... 2048KB (2.0MB)         │
│   Usable Memory ...................... 1920KB (1.9MB)         │
│                                                               │
│ Built In Features                                             │
│   Installed Memory ................... 2048KB (2.0MB)         │
│   Diskette Drive A Type .............. [1.44MB 3.5"]          │
│   Diskette Drive B Type .............. [not Installed]        │
│   Math Coprocessor ................... Installed              │
│   Serial Port ........................ [SERIAL_1]             │
│   Parallel Port ...................... [PARALLEL_1]           │
│                                                               │
│ Sl>t1 - Empty                                                 │
│                                                               │
│ Slot2 - Empty                                                 │
│                                                               │
│ Slot3 - The IBM 3270 Connection                               │
│   Resources Used ..................... Only Choice            │
│                                                               │
│ Slot4 - Integrated Fixed Disk Controller                      │
│   DMA Arbitration Level .............. [Level 5]              │
│   DMA Burst Pacing Interval........... [24 Microseconds]      │
│   Fairness On/Off .................... [On ]                  │
├─────────────────────────────────────────────────────────────┤
│  Esc=Quit    F5=Previous    F10=Save   ↑  Home    PageUp      │
│  F1=Help     F6=Next                   ↓  End     PageDown    │
└─────────────────────────────────────────────────────────────┘
```

Figure 6.15. To access the Change Configuration menu, select option 2 on the Main Menu (Figure 6.12). Devices enclosed in brackets may be changed by pressing function keys F5 or F6. Configuration of nonbracketed devices is automatic.

A typical screen display is shown in Figure 6.15. However, only 18 lines of this information can be seen at one time. Depending on your system and its complement of adapter cards, you may need to use the Home, End, PageUp, or PageDown keys to display additional information. Then use the cursor-up and cursor-down keys to highlight the line you wish to change. Note, however, that configuration changes can be made only to those items enclosed in brackets.

To change any bracketed item, move the highlighted bar as required, then toggle through the available selections by pressing the F5 or F6 keys. In Figure 6.15, the standard feature selections that may be changed are as follows:

Standard features	Configuration choices
Diskette drive A type	1.44Mb 3.5" or not installed
Diskette drive B type	same, plus external 360Kb 5.25"
Serial port	1, 2, or disabled
Parallel port	1, 2, 3 or disabled
Integrated Fixed Disk Controller:	
DMA arbitration level	1 through 7
DMA burst pacing interval	burst disabled, 24, 31, 16 microseconds
Fairness on/off	on or off

In this PS/2 model 70 example, an IBM 3270 Connection adapter is installed in slot 3, and a fixed disk with integrated controller is in slot 4 (the latter slot designed only for this component). In either case, the appropriate configuration data automatically appears in the slot 3 and 4 positions. And if either of the items were subsequently removed, the display would automatically change to Slot 3 (or 4) - Empty the next time this screen is displayed.

When you have finished making changes, press F10 to save the new configuration.

Note: If you exit instead to the Set Configuration menu and then decide to run the Automatic Configuration option (5), a warning message advises that the changes you made under Option 2 will not be saved as part of the automatic configuration process.

• **Configuration Conflict Caution.** An asterisk seen to the right of a bracketed item in Figure 6.15 warns of a device conflict. As a typical example, if two ports are configured as, say, Serial_2, the warning asterisk appears. To resolve the conflict, simply change one of the ports to Serial_1.

Option 3. Backup Configuration. This option allows you to save your configuration data to a file called SYSCONF (SYStem CONFiguration). The file may be saved on a backup copy of your Starter/Reference diskette for use in the future. See the Restore Configuration option immediately following for additional details.

Option 4. Restore Configuration. If system configuration data is lost due to a battery failure, you may use this option instead of running the Automatic Configuration option (5). This assumes, however, that you have previously run the Backup Configuration option (3), and that the resulting SYSCONF file is on the diskette in drive A. If so, select this option to return the system to its previous configuration.

The Restore Configuration option is especially helpful in the case where you have saved optional configuration changes that will not be recovered during an automatic configuration (port reassignments, for example).

If the SYSCONF file is missing, the following error message will be seen when you attempt to run this option:

```
Error
Unable to restore configuration
because a configuration backup has
not been performed.
Press Enter to continue.
```

Assuming the file is on another diskette, simply put it in drive A, press the Enter key, and again select Option 4. Otherwise you must run either Option 2 or 5 instead.

Option 5. Run Automatic Configuration. If you have added or removed memory, a math coprocessor, diskette or hard disk drive, etc., two beeps are heard and a configuration error code (16*x*) is displayed the next time the system is turned on. Insert the Starter/Reference diskette in drive A and then press F1.

Note that, with the exception of diskette drive type, any other configuration changes you made via Option 2 will *not* be overridden by running the Automatic Configuration option. Thus, if you disabled either port or revised the fixed disk controller options, these changes remain as you left them. However, installed memory, math coprocessor, and diskette drive data will change to reflect the actual configuration every time automatic configuration is run.

Option 4.   Set Features   (model 30 286 and MCA systems)
When this option is selected, a Set Features menu (not shown here) offers the choices listed below. As above, use the cursor keys to move the highlighted bar and then press the Enter key, or simply press the number of the desired selection.

Option 1. Set Date and Time. To enter the correct date and time, use the cursor keys to move the highlighted bar, then type in the correct value. Press the Enter key when you are finished.

Date and time may also be directly set at the DOS prompt. To do so, type DATE or TIME and press the Enter key. Then change the date or time, as appropriate.

Option 2. Set Passwords. To prevent unauthorized use of your computer, three protective mechanisms are provided. These are briefly described here, followed by instructions for their use.

> *Power-on password.* This password must be entered correctly each time the system is turned on. At the conclusion of POST, a password prompt (o─π) is displayed in the upper left-hand corner of the screen. This is your cue to type in your password, which will not be seen on screen. If you enter the wrong password, a o─Xπ symbol is displayed, followed by another password symbol. After three unsuccessful attempts, the system locks up and must be turned off and back on again in order to try again. Once the correct password has been entered, the system continues normal operation, and it will not be necessary to reenter the password if the system is rebooted.

> *Keyboard password.* This provides an additional level of security. With the keyboard password enabled, it is not possible to reboot the system by pressing the Ctrl + Alt + Del keys. And if the system is turned off and back on again, the power-on password will once again be required.

> *Network server mode.* After you have enabled the power-on password feature, the use of this mode permits other computers to access your system's fixed disk, even though your own keyboard may be locked. However, the remote user must correctly enter your own power-on password in order to gain access to your fixed disk.

Select the Set Passwords option to enable one or more of these mechanisms. When you do, the Set Passwords menu is displayed. The five menu selections are described here.

Option 1. Set Power-On Password. Use this choice only if a password is not already in place. At the screen display shown in Figure 6.16, type in the password you wish to use and then press the Enter key. The next time you turn the system on, you will be prompted for the password, as was described above.

Option 2. Change Power-On Password. To prevent anyone from changing your password, this choice simply offers the following instructions: Turn the system off, then back on again. At the password prompt, enter your

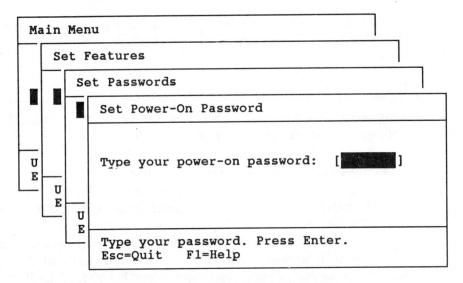

Figure 6.16. To set the power-on password, select the following options: Main Menu option 4 (Figure 6.12), Set Features menu option 2 (not shown), Set Passwords menu option 1 (not shown). When the Set Power-On Password menu appears, enter your password in the highlighted box.

current password, a slash and then the new password. Thus, to change passwords from "This" to "That" type *This/That*↵ at the prompt.

Option 3. Remove Password. Again, turn the system off and back on again. At the prompt, simply enter the password and a slash and then press the Enter key.

Option 4. Install Keyboard Password Program. A screen is displayed to inform you that you must install the keyboard program on the disk or diskette containing your DOS directory. To do so, type Y or y and then enter the appropriate drive letter. When the system is subsequently rebooted, you may enter a keyboard password by typing KP↵, typing in the desired password, and pressing the Enter key again.

The keyboard is now locked and can only be unlocked by once again typing the password and pressing the Enter key. For all subsequent keyboard relocks, simply type KP↵.

To change the keyboard password, type KP/c↵ and then enter a new password.

Note that the keyboard password is lost every time the system is rebooted. Therefore, the next time you try to lock the keyboard, you will be prompted for a new password.

Option 5. Set Network Server Mode. When this choice is selected, an onscreen message explains the purpose of the network server mode (as briefly described above) and a *Set network server mode? (Y/N)* prompt is seen at the bottom of the last screen page of instructions. If you answer *yes*, your computer's hard disk can be accessed by remote systems, even if your own keyboard is locked. Furthermore, your keyboard will be locked if you turn your system off and back on again, but do not boot from a diskette. No power-on password will be required, nor will your keyboard password have any effect.

To regain control of your own system, turn the power off, insert a system diskette in drive A, and turn the power on again.

Option 3. Set Keyboard Speed. When this option is selected, the display shows the two rates at which the keyboard can send characters to the screen:

Screen display	Keyboard rate (characters per second)
Keyboard Speed: [Normal]	10
Fast	30

The default value is enclosed in brackets and highlighted. Use the up or down arrow key to highlight the desired speed and then press the Enter key.

Option 5. Move the system	(model 30 286)
Option 6. Test the system	
Option 5. Copy an option diskette	(models 50/60)
Option 6. Move the computer	
Option 7. Test the computer	
Option 5. Copy an option diskette	(models 70/80)
Option 6. Test the computer	

These options were also described in detail in Chapter 3. Refer to pages 49 and 50 for further information.

EISA SYSTEM CONFIGURATION

EISA systems are supplied with a configuration utility diskette containing the necessary utilities and configuration files, including the following:

File name and extension		Description
CF	EXE	Configuration utility alone
SD	EXE	System setup utilities, including configuration
!(*filename*)	CFG	Configuration files for various EISA and ISA devices
(*filename*)	OVL	Executable overlay file, if required

Additional EISA devices are supplied with their own configuration utility diskette, which contains the necessary configuration file for the device.

Configuration Utilities

The EISA configuration utility performs the following chores:

Reads current configuration from CMOS RAM

Determines presence of EISA adapters

Includes configuration file information in the system configuration

Writes updated configuration information to CMOS RAM

Saves backup configuration file on diskette or hard disk drive

Shows graphic display of system and adapter slot assignments

Shows graphic display of ISA adapter switches and jumpers

Displays system resource map

The Configuration File

These files are in an ASCII format that may be read and edited with any word processor or with the DOS EDLIN or DOS 5.0 EDIT utility. Each file is divided into several sections, such as

CFG section	Contents
BOARD	A description of a system or adapter, with manufacturer's comments, if any
SYSTEM	Information about the system board
IOPORT	The address of the I/O port, if any
SWITCH	Switch settings, if any
FUNCTION & SUBFUNCTION	Configuration functions that may be reviewed and changed by the user during the configuration procedure described below
INCLUDE	Instructions to load an overlay file, if required

The configuration file name begins with !, followed by a three-character manufacturer or generic code, a hexadecimal four-digit product identification number, and a CFG extension, as shown in Table 6.11.

ISA Configuration Files. Note that the table lists a few configuration files that apparently offer ISA support, including some from a company not otherwise known for EISA support. In fact, a diskette library of ISA configuration files is usually included with the regular EISA configuration diskette, for the benefit of users who plan to install ISA adapters in an EISA system.

However, ISA adapters cannot be configured via software, so the data in these files is for information only. If you copy an ISA configuration file into your configuration setup, the configuration display will advise you how to set various switches and jumpers on the ISA adapter, and recommend which

Table 6.11 Representative EISA System Configuration Files

Configuration file	Description
!ACB2322.CFG	Adaptec ACB2322D Hard Disk and Diskette Controller
!ALR7120.CFG	ALR 16–bit VGA with Parallel Port
!ALR7361.CFG	ALR PowerCache 4e EISA System Board
!ALR7461.CFG	ALR PowerVEISA EISA System Board
!BUS4201.CFG	BusTek 32–Bit Bus Master EISA–to–SCSI Host Adapter
!CPQ4001.CFG	Compaq 32–Bit Intelligent Drive Array Controller
!CPQ5000.CFG	Compaq 386/33 System Processor Board
!CPQFA0E.CFG	Compaq 32–Bit 6–Socket System Memory Board
!CPQFB07.CFG	Compaq DeskPro 2400 Baud Modem–1070
!CPQFD17.CFG	Compaq 16–Bit SCSI Option Adapter
!HWP0030.CFG	Hewlett–Packard Enhanced Graphics Adapter Board
!HWP1420.CFG	Hewlett–Packard HPIB Interface
!ISA8202.CFG	AST SixPakPlus Version A
!ISA8500.CFG	DCA IRMA2 Adapter
!ISA8304.CFG	IBM Serial/Parallel Adapter
!ISA8309.CFG	IBM VGA Display Adapter
!ISA9203.CFG	Intel Above Board 286 with 2Mb piggyback
!ISAB700.CFG	Iomega Bernoulli Host Adapter Card
!ISA8712.CFG	Novell NE2000 Ethernet Adapter
!ISA8E00.CFG	Microsoft Mouse Controller
!WDC1007.CFG	Western Digital WD1007V–SE1 Winchester Controller

system board slot to use. Then it's up to you to set the switches and jumpers, as you would do with any conventional ISA system.

Configuration Overlay File. This file includes executable configuration extensions beyond the scope of the configuration file itself. An INCLUDE instruction in the configuration file loads the overlay file, which then handles those parts of the configuration that may be done automatically. For example, default COM port assignments may be set and system memory verified.

Configuration File Listing. Listing 6.4 shows the format of a typical EISA system configuration file, which may be edited by the user who wishes to modify a file, or perhaps write an entirely new one for an adapter whose configuration data is not otherwise available.

If your ISA diskette does not include a configuration file for a specific ISA adapter, and you do not care to try writing one yourself, contact the manufacturer of the EISA computer in which the device is to be installed. If the manufacturer can't help, contact Micro Computer Systems, Inc., the company that wrote most of the ISA files on the library diskette.

Begin EISA Configuration

The configuration procedure described here is based on the ALR Power-Veisa system, with supplementary information on Compaq EISA configuration. Hewlett-Packard EISA systems generally follow the format shown below for Compaq computers.

Screen details, function key assignments, etc., may vary on other systems, so the appropriate user's manual should be consulted for system-specific information.

To begin configuration, copy the EISA configuration utility diskette to a blank diskette, or to an EISA subdirectory on your hard disk. If you have additional EISA devices on hand, turn the power off and physically install each device. Then turn the power back on and log on to the directory containing your EISA files to begin the configuration. Type SD.EXE and press the Enter key when the introductory system logo appears to display a configuration welcome screen such as the one shown in Figure 6.17. Then press the Enter key again to access the Main Menu.

If you execute the CF.EXE utility instead, the procedure branches directly to the Configure Computer section below.

In either case, some EISA system manufacturers recommend that ISA adapters be left out of the system during initial configuration. During

Listing 6.4 A Typical EISA System Configuration File

```
BOARD
  ID="ALR7361"
  NAME="PowerCache 4e EISA System Board"
  MFR="ALR"
  CATEGORY="SYS"
  SLOT=EMB(0)
  LENGTH=380
  READID = yes
  COMMENTS="The PowerCache 4e EISA System board provides
            two asynchronous communication ports, a parallel
            port and up to 128 megabytes of memory.  It also
            supports the Weitek 4167 Numeric Co-processor."
```

```
SYSTEM
  NONVOLATILE=8196              ' Bytes of nonvolatile memory
  AMPERAGE=20000               ' Total +5V current (mA) from
                                 power supply


  SLOT(1)= EISA
     LENGTH=341
     SKIRT = NO
     BUSMASTER = YES           ' (description of other system
                                 board slots follows)

     IOPORT(1) = 0c02h
     IOPORT(2) = 0c03h

FUNCTION = "System Board Peripherals"

   SUBFUNCTION = "Floppy Controller"
   TYPE = "MSD,SYS"
   CHOICE = "Enabled"
      FREE
         IRQ = 6
       SHARE = NO
       TRIGGER = EDGE
     DMA = 2
       SHARE = NO
       SIZE = BYTE
       TIMING= DEFAULT
         PORT = 03f0h-03f5h
         PORT = 03F6h-03f7h
             SHARE = YES
     INIT = PORTADR(0c03h) BYTE 1rrrrrrr
   CHOICE = "Disabled"
   DISABLE = YES
      FREE
     INIT = PORTADR(0c03h) BYTE 0rrrrrrr
```

Listing 6.4 A Typical EISA System Configuration File (continued)

```
SUBFUNCTION = "Parallel Port"
TYPE = "PAR,SYS"
CHOICE = "LPT1"
   LINK
  IRQ = 7
  PORT = 378h-37fh
  INIT = PORTADR(0c03h) BYTE rrrr10rr
```
                              ' *(LPT2 description follows)*

```
SUBFUNCTION = "Serial Port"
TYPE = "SER,SYS"
CHOICE = "COM1"
   LINK
  IRQ = 4
  PORT = 3f8h-3ffh
  1NIT = PORTADR(0c03h) BYTE rrrrrr10
```
                              ' *(similar description of other*
                              COM ports follows)

```
INCLUDE = "ALR7361.OVL"
```
                              ' *(call to load executable overlay*
                              file)

```
══════════════════ Welcome ══════════════════

 This COMPAQ EISA CONFIGURATION utility is provided to
 help you set up (configure) and test (diagnose) your
 computer, and install your operating system.  You should
 use this utility the first time you set up your computer,
 and whenever you want to change or test your computer's
 options.

 If you are configuring your computer for the first time,
 be sure that you have installed your Extended ISA (EISA)
 expansion boards before using this utility.  Your ISA
 boards should NOT be installed at this point.  Use this
 utility to specify which ISA boards and options you plan
 to install. The utility will tell you in which slots to
 install the ISA boards and which ISA jumpers and
 switches should be changed. Make these changes, turn off
 your computer and install the ISA boards.

 Press [Enter] to select <OK>.
```

Figure 6.17. The EISA configuration Welcome screen, as seen on a Compaq computer.

configuration, when you specify the ISA adapters that will be added, the screen will display the recommended switch and jumper settings and suggest the slot in which each adapter should be placed. Follow these directions to ensure the ISA device will not conflict with the EISA components in the same system.

Main Menu

The EISA configuration utility's Main Menu is shown in Figures 6.18(a) and 6.18(b). As each option is highlighted, a help screen explains its purpose. The screen shown in Figure 6.18(c) explains the Configure Computer option.

Learn about configuring your computer   (ALR)
How to configure your computer   (Compaq)
This option displays an overview of the EISA configuration process. Use the PageUp and PageDown keys to scroll through the text, then press the Enter key to return to the Main Menu.

Configure Computer
When this option is selected, the Configure Computer menu shown in Figure 6.19 is seen. If you have not installed any EISA devices in the system board slots, ignore the two Copy Files options.

Copy Files. If you have just installed an adapter card, select the appropriate Copy Files option to copy the device's configuration file into your EISA subdirectory. Then press the Enter key to return to the Configure Computer menu.

Configure Computer: Basic and Advanced Methods. There's a bit of confusion here, since both the menu and two of its options share the same name. In any case, select the advanced method (described here) if you have just installed a new device and copied its configuration file to your EISA subdirectory, or if you wish to make any other configuration changes.

System Configuration Overview. Press the Enter key to display the screen shown in Figure 6.20. The options across the top of the screen are separately described below in the Menu Bar section (page 203).
The overview shows the name of the system board, a graphical view of the system board slots, and the name of any installed adapters that have

(a)

```
╔══════════════════ Main Menu ══════════════════╗
║                                                ║
║   Learn about configuring your computer        ║
║                                                ║
║   Configure computer                           ║
║                                                ║
║   Set date and time                            ║
║                                                ║
║   Exit from this utility                       ║
║                                                ║
╚════════════════════════════════════════════════╝
```

(b)

```
╔══════════════════ Main Menu ══════════════════╗
║                                                ║
║  How to configure your COMPAQ EISA computer    ║
║                                                ║
║  Configure computer                            ║
║                                                ║
║  Set power-on features                         ║
║                                                ║
║  Test or inspect computer                      ║
║                                                ║
║  Install operating system                      ║
║                                                ║
║  Exit from this utility                        ║
║                                                ║
╚════════════════════════════════════════════════╝
```

(c)

```
╔═══════════════════ Help ═══════════════════════╗
║                                                ║
║  To copy configuration (CFG) files to your system
║  configuration diskette and configure your     ║
║  computer, press [Enter].                      ║
║                                                ║
╚════════════════════════════════════════════════╝
```

Figure 6.18.   The EISA configuration Main Menu on an (a) ALR and (b) Compaq display. (c) The Main Menu help screen seen on either system.

```
================= Configure Computer =================
  Copy files from an option configuration diskette

  Copy files from the configuration diskette

  Configure computer - basic method

  Configure computer - advanced method

  Return to the main menu
```

```
==================== Help ====================
To copy option diskettes that were included with
your boards and options, press [Enter].  These
diskettes contain configuration (CFG) files that
need to be copied to your System Configuration
diskette BEFORE you configure your computer.
```

Figure 6.19. The EISA Configure Computer menu and help screen for the first Copy files option.

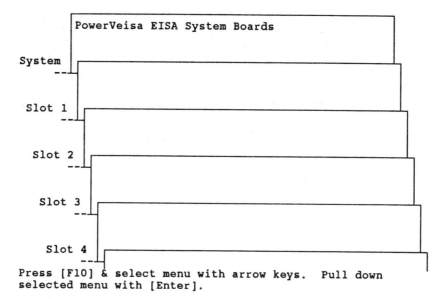

```
                    System Configuration Overview

    System      Edit      View      Settings      Help

These are the boards and options currently detected by your
computer. If this information is correct, select Exit from
the System menu.  To view more detail, press [Enter].
```

```
         | PowerVeisa EISA System Boards

System   |
  --

Slot 1   |
  --

Slot 2   |
  --

Slot 3   |
  --

Slot 4   |
  --
```

```
Press [F10] & select menu with arrow keys.  Pull down
selected menu with [Enter].
```

Figure 6.20. The EISA System Configuration Overview screen.

already been configured. For the moment, ignore any slots that do not display the name of an adapter already in place.

System Configuration Detailed View. Press the Enter key to display the detailed view shown in Figure 6.21 (not available if the Basic Method option was selected at the Configure Computer menu).

To change any part of the displayed system configuration, highlight the appropriate item and press the Enter key. For example, Figure 6.22 shows the Select Drive Type menu, which lists a few of the hard disk drive types supported in ROM BIOS. Toggle through the drive type numbers, then press the Enter key when the desired drive type is highlighted.

Repeat this basic procedure to change any of those options that are in fact changeable, as for example, the hard disk configuration just described, and serial and parallel port assignments. Other options, such as memory and coprocessor presence, are set automatically and cannot be changed via this screen.

When you are finished viewing and/or changing the system configuration, press function key F10 to access the menu bar at the top of the screen, and refer to the Menu Bar section below for further details.

EISA configuration notes:

1. Some early EISA configuration overlay files display the parallel ports as LPT2 and LPT3, since their port addresses (0378h and 0278h) correspond to those used elsewhere by LPT2 and LPT3. Nomenclature notwithstanding, the ports function as LPT1 and LPT2, and appear as such on later versions of the configuration file. See Chapter 13 (page 567) for futher details about parallel port addresses.

2. Although a math coprocessor is contained within the Intel i486 microprocessor package, the EISA system configuration reports the coprocessor as if it were a separate entity (bottom of Figure 6.21).

Return to the main menu. The option is pretty much self-explanatory.

Set date and time

Follow the onscreen prompts to review the date and/or time of day, then press the Enter key to return to the Main Menu.

Exit from this utility

Select this option to exit the configuration utility without saving any changes you have made. The DOS prompt reappears on screen.

```
                 System Configuration Detailed View

  System      Edit      View      Settings      Help

 ┌PowerVeisa EISA System Board─────────────────────────────────┐
 │                                                              │
 │System Board                                                  │
 │                                                              │
 │  System Board Peripherals                                    │
 │    Embedded Hard Disk Controller.......Enabled               │
 │    Floppy Controller...................Enabled               │
 │    Parallel Port.......................LPT1                   │
 │    Serial Port.........................COM1                   │
 │                                                              │
 │  Floppy Diskette Drives                                      │
 │    Diskette A:.........................5.25 Inch, 1.2MB       │
 │    Diskette B:.........................Not Installed          │
 │                                                              │
 │  Hard Disk Drives                                            │
 │    Hard Disk C:........................Type 43               │
 │    Hard Disk D:........................Not Installed          │
 │                                                              │
 │  Installed Memory......................5120   KB             │
 │                                                              │
 │  Available Memory......................4352   KB             │
 │                                                              │
 │  Memory options                                              │
 │    Maximum memory limits...............No Limit              │
 │    ROM BIOS or RAM at 16MB:............ROM BIOS              │
 │                                                              │
 │  ROM BIOS Shadow.......................Enabled               │
 │                                                              │
 │  System Speed                                                │
 │    Speed:..............................Fast                  │
 │    AT Bus Turbo Mode:..................Enabled               │
 │                                                              │
 │  Display Monitor.......................EGA/VGA               │
 │                                                              │
 │  Coprocessor...........................80387                 │
 │                                                              │
 └──────────────────────────────────────────────────────────────┘
```

Figure 6.21.   The EISA System Configuration Detailed View screen. To manually change the configuration, highlight the desired item and press the Enter key.

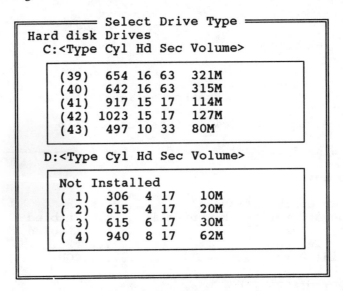

```
============ Select Drive Type ============
Hard disk Drives
   C:<Type Cyl Hd Sec Volume>

   ┌──────────────────────────────────────┐
   │ (39)   654 16 63    321M              │
   │ (40)   642 16 63    315M              │
   │ (41)   917 15 17    114M              │
   │ (42)  1023 15 17    127M             │
   │ (43)   497 10 33     80M              │
   └──────────────────────────────────────┘

   D:<Type Cyl Hd Sec Volume>

   ┌──────────────────────────────────────┐
   │ Not Installed                         │
   │ ( 1)   306  4 17     10M              │
   │ ( 2)   615  4 17     20M              │
   │ ( 3)   615  6 17     30M              │
   │ ( 4)   940  8 17     62M              │
   └──────────────────────────────────────┘
```

Figure 6.22.   The Select Drive Type menu is displayed when either hard disk drive is selected at the Detailed View screen (Figure 6.21).

Additional Main Menu Options

The following additional options appear on the Compaq main menu shown in Figure 6.18b.

Set Power-On Features.   The Power-On Features menu offers the following self-explanatory options:

Set date and time

Set power-on password

Set network server mode

Set NumLock power-on state

Return to the main menu

As each option is highlighted, an on-screen help message explains its function. Press the Enter key, make the desired change, then press the Enter key to return to the menu.

Test or Inspect Computer.   A series of diagnostic routines is available to determine if the computer's options are recognized by the system and are operating properly. In addition, an *inspect* mode displays memory configuration information and other system details.

Install Operating System. Assuming the correct operating system diskettes are on hand, this option may be used for the following installations:

MS-DOS	Novell NetWare 286 or 386
SCO UNIX System V/386	other operating systems
MS OS/2	

You will be prompted for the required diskette as the installation procedure progresses. For detailed information on installing DOS on a hard disk drive, refer to the DOS Installation section of Chapter 9 (page 389).

The System Configuration Menu Bar

The system configuration overview (Figure 6.20) and detailed view (Figure 6.21) both display a menu bar across the top of the screen. To gain access to the five listed options, press function key F10. Use the cursor movement keys to highlight the desired option, then press the Enter key and follow the appropriate directions given here.

System. The pull-down menu displays the options, control key sequences, and descriptions that are listed here.

Option	Control key sequence	Description
Open...		Open an existing SCI (system configuration) file.
Save As...	Ctrl+A	Save the configuration to a specified backup file.
Print...	Ctrl+P	Print configuration information on parallel printer (PRN).
Verify...	Ctrl+V	Verify that the resource has no resource conflicts.
Exit...	Ctrl+X	Return to the Main Menu (actually, to an Exit menu described below).

For future reference, the indicated control key sequence may be used to directly access the listed option from either of the previous menus. Thus, after making configuration changes, you may bypass the System option by pressing Ctrl+A to open an existing system configuration file, or Ctrl+X to proceed to the Exit menu. For additional details about the first four options, select the option and read the on-screen information.

If Exit is selected, an Exit menu lists the following options:

Option	Description
View switch, jumper, and software settings	Select this option to view any settings that have been recommended for ISA adapters. (Refer to the Edit option below for details about adding ISA configuration information.)
Save configuration and exit	The present configuration is saved in CMOS and in a backup file named SYSTEM.SCI. You are prompted to press the Enter key to reboot the system.
Exit	Exit without saving the present configuration changes.

Edit. The Edit pull-down menu lists various options, including the three listed here:

Option	Control key sequence	Description
Add...	Ins key	Add board or option to configuration.
Move...	(none)	Move selected board to another slot.
Remove...	Del key	Remove selected board or option from configuration.

When you select the Add option, the screen displays a list of configuration files currently available in your EISA subdirectory (such as those shown in Table 6.11 above). As a representative example, assume that a Bustek EISA-to-SCSI Host Adapter is to be added to the system. The configuration file supplied with the adapter has already been copied to your EISA subdirectory, and so its name now appears in the displayed listing.

Select the Bustek configuration file name and press the Enter key. Since the file contains a comments section, it is displayed on screen, as shown in Figure 6.23. This is followed by other screens, as appropriate to the device to be installed. For example, since this is an EISA adapter, and there are no other EISA adapters already installed, the next screen suggests installing the adapter in slot 2, although slots 3 and 4 are also available. Make your

```
================== Manufacturer Comments ==================

BusTek 32 Bit Bus Master EISA-to-SCSI Host Adapter
The manufacturer has provided the following comments
about the accessory.  If you would like to view these
comments again they are displayed in the Board
Specifications panel.

This board provides a bus master interface between the
EISA bus and up to seven SCSI peripherals.  As an
intelligent board it offloads the system processor of
SCSI protocol responsibilities and also coordinates
multiple system I/O requests using an industry-standard
host-based mailbox structure.
```

Figure 6.23. Manufacturer's comments contained in a CFG file are displayed during the EISA edit/add procedure.

choice and press the Enter key. The configuration overview screen (Figure 6.20) reappears, and the display now shows the following device description line at the Slot 2 position (or slot 3 or 4, depending on which one you selected):

BusTek 32 Bit Bus Master EISA-to-SCSI Host Adapter

Press the Enter key to again display the detailed view screen (Figure 6.21). Detailed information about the BusTek adapter is now included in the display, as shown in Figure 6.24. As before, you may edit the displayed configuration. For example, to change the SCSI configuration section, highlight the desired item and press the Enter key to display a Change Function menu seen in Figure 6.25. With other adapters, the menu choices will of course be different, as appropriate to the specific device.

When you have finished making changes, again press function key F10 to return to the Menu Bar options. If you are ready to save the configuration, follow the instructions given above in the System section (page 203). Or select one of the other Menu Bar options and refer to the appropriate section here.

```
┌BusTex 32 Bit Bus Master EISA-to-SCSI Host Adapter────────┐
│Mass Storage device                                 Added │
│                                                          │
│ Floppy Subsystem...............Disable Floppy - default  │
│                                                          │
│ Host Adapter Configuration                               │
│   Host I/O Port Address...............330h - default     │
│   Host Interrupt Request..............INT11 - default     │
│   Host BIOS (16K Bytes) Address.......0DC000h - default   │
│                                                          │
│ SCSI Configuration                                       │
│   Host Adapter SCSI ID................ID = 7 - default    │
│   SCSI Parity.........................Enable - default    │
│   SCSI Auto Sense.....................Enable - default    │
│   Adapter Initiate Sync Negotiation...Disable - default   │
│                                                          │
└──────────────────────────────────┐                      │
                          Slot 2    └ⅠⅠⅠⅠⅠⅠⅠⅠⅠⅠⅠⅠⅠⅠⅠⅠⅠⅠⅠⅠⅠⅠⅠⅠ┘
```

Figure 6.24.   Configuration information about each installed device is appended to the Detailed View screen (Figure 6.21).

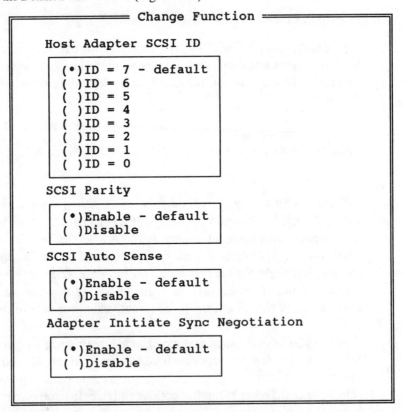

Figure 6.25.   The SCSI host adapter configuration data shown in Figure 6.24 may be modified via this Change Function menu.

View. The following options are offered in the pull-down menu:

Option	Control key sequence	Use to display
Overview	Ctrl+O	Summary of configured boards and options
Detailed by Slot	Ctrl+D	Detailed description of options sorted by slot
Detailed by Type		Detailed description of options sorted by type or function
Switch & Jumper Settings...		Switch and jumper settings
Software Parameters...		Software parameters
Connections... Ctrl+C		External cable connections
Board Specifications		Information about an installed (configured) board
Resources...		Resources for all boards in your configuration

Settings. The pull-down menu offers the following choices:

Auto Verify	The configuration is checked for resource conflicts every time you change the configuration.
Manual Verify	The auto-verify function is disabled.

As a typical example, assume that an IBM ISA serial/parallel adapter is to be added to an EISA system with an existing COM1 port. If the serial/parallel adapter is also configured for COM1 and the auto-verify mode is enabled, a Configuration Changes screen will advise you that your COM1 selection must be changed to COM2. You have two choices: either reconfigure the ISA adapter by hand, or reconfigure the EISA serial port to COM2 by selecting the detailed view screen (Figure 6.21). Then highlight Serial Port.....COM1 and change it to COM2.

With auto-verify disabled, no such notice will appear. However, the detailed view screen will display an asterisk in the left margin of each line in which a resource (device) conflict is detected.

Help. The final choice in the Menu Bar options list offers a wide variety of help screens, with information on just about every aspect of system configuration, on how to access help screens during configuration, and so on.

SYSTEM BOARD TROUBLESHOOTING

This section describes a few of the problems that are traceable to the system board or to a component—such as the speaker—that is connected to it. If such an error is not resolved here, the system board or the suspect component probably requires servicing or replacement.

Speaker Problem

The easiest way to verify that the speaker is functioning is to simply turn the PC on and listen for the beep (two beeps on many IBM-compatible systems) at the end of the POST procedure. If POST concludes successfully, but no sound is heard, then enter BASIC and press Ctrl + G or type either BEEP or PRINT CHR$(7). In each case, a single beep at a frequency of about 800 Hz should be heard.

If no sound is heard, carefully check the connections between the speaker and the system board. The speaker/system board interface is briefly described here:

Computer	Speaker location in system unit	Speaker cable connector labeled
PC	left-hand front	P3
XT	left-hand front	P1
AT	left-hand front	J18
PS/2 ISA	beeper, soldered directly to system board at SP1	
PS/2 55 SX	mounted on adapter guide	
PS/2 60 & 80	bottom front	
PS/2 50 & 70	on removable module	J19 (module socket)
EISA	on front panel	varies

Also make sure the two wires leading to the speaker itself are securely soldered to its terminals.

If a very low-level beep is heard, the speaker is probably defective and will have to be replaced. As a double-check, the following short BASIC program should produce the sound of an equal-tempered octave beginning at A = 440 Hz (the A above middle C on a piano).

```
100 FOR X = 0 TO 12
110 S = 1.059^X
120 SOUND 440 * S, 2
130 NEXT X
```

For a wider-range test, change the 12 in line 100 to 24 to check two octaves, to 36 for three octaves, and so on. In line 120, change 440 and 2 to select a different starting frequency and duration, respectively.

If all sounds are very faint, or if some are louder than others, the speaker is probably defective. But remember this is no hi-fi set; low frequencies will sound more like buzzes than musical tones.

If no sound at all is heard, then either the speaker or its related system board circuitry is defective. To further localize the problem, another speaker—or even a headphone—may be temporarily attached to the system board connector with a pair of alligator-clip leads. Or use the headphone jack on the models 25 and 30. If the new speaker works, then the system speaker is indeed defective; otherwise, there's a problem on the system board that will require servicing.

Math Coprocessor Errors

If the math coprocessor is installed with its notch or beveled edge facing in the wrong direction, the POST procedure will fail, resulting in a blank display screen and no beep. On some early model ATs, the system board coprocessor socket is installed backward, with the notch facing the rear of the system unit. However, the coprocessor should still be installed with its own notch facing forward.

On a PC or an XT, make sure that switch 2 on switch block 1 is in the OFF (0) position, as was seen in Table 6.10. There is an error in some early IBM documentation, where ON (1) is specified as the position indicating a coprocessor is installed. However, OFF (0) is the correct position on all IBM PCs and XTs.

701 Error Code. During PC or XT diagnostic testing, if switch 2 on switch block 1 is in the wrong position, the following error code will be seen if the procedure attempts to check a coprocessor that is in fact not installed:

```
hh:mm:ss
ERROR - SYSTEM UNIT 701
PRESS ENTER TO CONTINUE
```

To eliminate the error, put the switch in the correct position. If a coprocessor is installed and the switch is set correctly, the coprocessor is defective.

An incorrect switch position may also cause a system crash if a software program attempts to access the coprocessor.

Battery Failure

A 161 error code displayed during the POST procedure is an indication that the CMOS RAM has lost its battery power, and system configuration data is therefore lost. If a fresh battery is on hand, turn the system power off, disconnect the battery cable, and gently pull the old battery away from its plastic fastener strip. Reverse the procedure to install a new battery. Next, follow either the first-time configuration procedure (p. 174) or the data replace procedure (p. 178).

Front-Panel LED Failure

Although this section describes how to troubleshoot the LEDs on the AT front panel, the same general comments should apply to any other LEDs found within most PC systems.

LED Test Procedure. If an LED remains dark even though the system seems to be operating properly, the LED may be either disconnected or defective. To double-check, locate the two-conductor cable leading from the LED to a connector on the system board or on an adapter. A few typical examples are given here.

LED	Connected to
AT power-on	J20 on system board
AT hard disk in use	J6 on fixed disk and diskette drive adapter
AT diskette drives	P3 on J3 multiconnector strip
PC 360Kb drives	P9 at rear of drive circuit board
Other drives	varies

The connections listed here are those found on a representative sampling of systems, and may vary on other systems. In case of doubt, simply trace the cable leading from the LED and note the specific connector to which it is attached. Then unplug the connector. With a 6-volt battery and a pair of test leads, connect the negative battery terminal to the black conductor leading to the LED. Connect the other test lead to the positive battery terminal, and briefly touch the other end of this test lead to the colored (usually, red) conductor leading to the LED. If the LED comes on while the test lead is connected, it is of course good, and the trouble is at the board connector or elsewhere in the associated circuitry. Otherwise, the LED is indeed defective and will have to be replaced.

In the case of an AT hard disk LED connected to J6 on an IBM Fixed Disk and Diskette Drive Adapter, the four pins on J6 are wired so that the cable connector can be installed in either direction. Therefore, if the LED does not work, try reversing the connector, on the unlikely chance that the other set of connector pins on the adapter is OK. This check should be tried on other adapters only if you are sure that the adapter pins are wired as described here.

UPDATING AN ISA SYSTEM

This section may be of interest to the ISA system owner who suffers PS/2 envy. There are a number of products available for enhancing the performance of a PC, XT, or AT, and a few representative examples are briefly described here. Some devices bring an old PC up to AT standards, while others allow an ISA computer to hold its own against any PS/2 system.

System enhancement may be as simple as replacing a crystal oscillator with a faster model, or as elegant as installing a new system board with an i486 microprocessor. The discussion begins with a review of the various methods of obtaining a system speedup, and then looks at some of the problems that may be encountered after doing so.

With so many different product types available, it's all but impossible to discuss specific installation procedures in detail. With the exception of a few general notes, the reader is best advised to rely on the time and budget available for the job, and on the documentation accompanying the device. If possible, try to read the instructions before purchasing the device in question, to make sure that they are comprehensible and that the job does not require more technical expertise than is readily available.

System Board Component Replacement

Depending on which device is to be installed, one or more of system board components may need to be removed or replaced. Typical examples are given here.

Crystal Oscillator. The easiest AT speed enhancement is a simple swap of the system crystal for one that runs at a faster rate, and this may be done provided the ROM BIOS date is earlier than 11/15/85.

To determine the date of your system, use the program in Listing 6.1. If the displayed date is earlier than 11/15/85, the original 12-MHz crystal may be swapped for one rated at 16-MHz or higher. The crystal's rating is stamped on its outer case, and should be double the clock rate of the microprocessor.

An AT system with a 16-MHz crystal installed will probably function with little or no problem at all. With a still higher speed crystal in place, one or more of the problems described later in this chapter will probably be encountered.

In AT systems dated on or after 11/15/85 (for example, models 319 and 339), IBM revised the POST procedure to cause a system crash if the original crystal is simply replaced by a faster one.

Varispeed Devices. Some AT acceleration devices circumvent the POST problem just described by maintaining the original clock speed until the POST procedure concludes successfully. Then, the speed automatically increases to a preset maximum. The preset maximum is found by trial and error, by adjusting a rear-panel potentiometer. A typical varispeed device is shown in Figure 6.26.

If a faster crystal is installed in an AT that will accommodate it, it may also be necessary to replace the 80286 microprocessor.

Microprocessor. For many pre-PS/2 speedup devices, the installation procedure requires the removal of the original system board 8088 or 80286 microprocessor. A multipin connector is inserted in its place, and a flat-ribbon cable leads from the connector to an adapter card which contains a new

Figure 6.26. An AT accelerator with a varispeed control. Normal speed is maintained during POST, after which the clock rate increases to a preset maximum. (XcelX 286/287 SpeedInjector courtesy Ariel Computer Corp.)

microprocessor and associated circuit components. A typical example is shown in Figure 6.27. See Table 6.6 above for further details on microprocessor clock rates.

Clock Chip. Some older PC and XT accelerator cards require the removal of the system board 8284 clock chip and also supply a faster MPU for installation on the system board itself, in place of the original one. In the example seen in Figure 6.28, an 8088-2 microprocessor is a direct swap for the old MPU on the system board, and a flat-ribbon cable leads from the system board 8284 socket to the accelerator card.

On some early model systems, the 8284 chip is soldered in place and will have to be desoldered, removed, and replaced with a socket in order to complete the installation. Since this is a rather delicate operation, you may want to have it done by a reputable service facility, especially if it is also necessary to have soldered-in RAM chips removed, as described below. But if this is the case, it might be wise to consider replacing the entire system board instead, as described later in this chapter (page 217).

RAM. At a MPU clock speed greater than 8 MHz, it will probably be necessary to replace old RAM chips with new ones rated at 120 ns (nanoseconds) or faster. On early model PCs, the RAM chips in bank 0 are soldered in place, again requiring some careful desoldering in order to remove them.

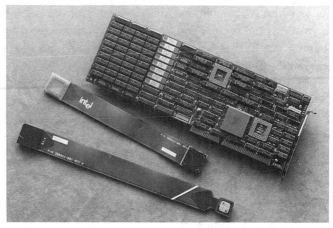

Figure 6.27.   This AT accelerator uses an onboard 80386 microprocessor in place of the system board's 80286, which is replaced by a cable leading to the pin-grid array socket seen at the top-center of the adapter. (Inboard 386/AT courtesy Intel Corp.)

Figure 6.28.   An early PC accelerator supplied with an 8088-2 microprocessor to be inserted in the system board in place of the original 8088. The flat-ribbon cable leading away from the card is plugged into the system board socket formerly occupied by the 8284 clock chip. Speed selection and system reset are via the switch and push-button on the external module. (Microspeed Fast 88)

Given an early model PC with 8284 clock chip and bank 0 RAM soldered in place, it may be worthwhile to replace the entire system board with a new one in which all components are socketed. This can often be done for about the price of having the soldered components removed and replaced with sockets. For further details, consult the system-specific sections immediately following.

ROM BIOS Replacement.   Since the discontinuance of the PC, XT, and AT computers, IBM has not issued additional ROM BIOS updates for these systems. Therefore, even the latest pre-PS/2 BIOS does not support VGA displays, nor the latest diskette and hard disk drives that are otherwise physically and electrically compatible with these systems.

To remedy the situation, a number of other suppliers market updated replacement ROM BIOS chips. IBM compatibility will of course vary just as it does on IBM-compatible computers. However, ROM BIOS from AMI (American Megatrends, Inc.), Award, and Phoenix BIOS Systems are highly regarded for IBM compatibility, and other BIOS systems may or may not be as close a match. If you are not sure about the level of compatibility, seek expert advice before making a purchase.

As a typical example, a non-IBM ROM BIOS chip set may offer its own built-in diagnostics, support for all presently available 3.5" and 5.25" drives, and also provide a drive table with extensive choices of hard disk types. (See Chapter 9 for further details about drive types.) Installation usually involves nothing more than removing the IBM BIOS and inserting the replacement chips in the same slots, then running a setup program. But before removing any chips, carefully note the orientation of the notches on the original chips and make sure each new chip is installed with its notch facing in the same direction as the one on the removed chip. Otherwise the chips will be destroyed as soon as power is applied.

Some replacement chips are labeled "odd" or "high" and "even" or "low," in reference to their starting address. In case of doubt about which system board socket is which, refer to the ROM address notes at the bottom of Table 6.4. Generally, no damage is done if the chips are installed in the wrong sockets, although of course the system will not work.

AMI BIOS Example

When replacement ROM BIOS chips are installed, a new opening display will be seen the next time the system is turned on. As a typical example of the operational differences between IBM and other BIOS systems, this section offers a brief description of a system in which AMI BIOS chips replace original IBM AT chips.

When power is applied, the on-screen memory check display is accompanied by an audible click as each memory increment is checked. A screen advises that the remaining POST memory check may be bypassed by pressing the Escape key. At the conclusion of POST, the system configuration screen shown in Figure 6.29 is seen. To enter the setup or diagnostics modes, press the Delete key and then choose the desired mode.

Setup. The AMI setup screen is shown in Figure 6.30. If the displayed configuration is incorrect, it may be changed by using the cursor movement keys to highlight the desired device, then pressing the PageUp or PageDown keys to toggle through the available options for that device. Press the Escape key to exit the setup mode and save the new configuration. (AMI diagnostics are briefly mentioned in Chapter 3, page 73.)

ROM BASIC. In all IBM personal computers, the complete BASIC interpreter program is the sum of the BASICA.COM file on diskette and a ROM (or "cassette") BASIC module, or modules, on the system board. The locations of these modules were also given in Table 6.4.

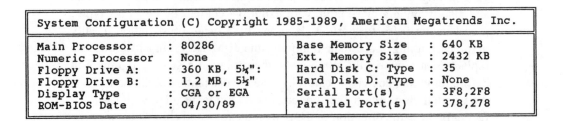

```
System Configuration (C) Copyright 1985-1989, American Megatrends Inc.

Main Processor      : 80286          Base Memory Size   : 640 KB
Numeric Processor   : None           Ext. Memory Size   : 2432 KB
Floppy Drive A:     : 360 KB, 5¼":   Hard Disk C: Type  : 35
Floppy Drive B:     : 1.2 MB, 5¼"    Hard Disk D: Type  : None
Display Type        : CGA or EGA     Serial Port(s)     : 3F8,2F8
ROM-BIOS Date       : 04/30/89       Parallel Port(s)   : 378,278
```

Figure 6.29.   System Configuration report seen at the conclusion of POST on ISA systems with AMI BIOS installed.

```
          CMOS SETUP (C) Copyright 1985-1989, American Megatrends Inc.

Date (mn/date/year):Thu, Aug 27 1990   Base Memory Size : 640 KB
Time (hour/min/sec):14 : 06 : 32       Ext. Memory Size : 2432 KB
Floppy Drive A:     :360 KB, 5¼":      Numeric processor: Not Installed
Floppy Drive B:     :1.2 MB, 5¼"
                                       Cyln Head WPcom LZone Sec  Size
Hard disk C: type  : 35                1024  9   65535 1024  17   77 MB
Hard disk D: type  : Not Installed
Primary display    : VGA or EGA
Keyboard           : Installed          Sun Mon Tue Wed Thu Fri Sat

Scratch RAM option : 1                   1   2   3   4   5   6   7

                                         8   9  10  11  12  13  14

                                        15  16  17  18  19  20  21

Month : Jan, Feb,.....Dec               22  23  24  25  26  27  28
Date  : 01, 02, 03,...31
Year  : 1901, 1902,...2099              29  30   1   2   3   4   5

ESC=Exit, ↓→↑← =Select, PgUp/DgDn = Modify  6  7  8  9  10  11  12
```

Figure 6.30.   When the System Configuration report (Figure 6.29) is seen, press the Delete key to access the CMOS Setup menu seen here. Display is from a PC AT with replacement AMI BIOS installed.

Typically, replacement ROM modules from AMI and others provide the enhanced BIOS features described above, but do not offer a replacement for IBM's ROM BASIC. But given the demise of the audio cassette as a practical storage medium, the absence of a ROM cassette BASIC module should not be a serious consideration to anyone planning an update. In any case, serious BASIC programmers should consider one of the modern BASIC compilers—such as Microsoft QuickBASIC and Borland Turbo BASIC—which make no use of system-board ROM BASIC anyway. Or as another alternative, a completely diskette-based BASIC interpreter program may be used in place of the IBM system.

System Board Replacement

Depending on the required degree of system enhancement, it may be practical to replace the entire system board instead of making one or more of the component replacements just described. For example, the enhancement potential of the original IBM PC was greatly curtailed by its modest power supply and a system board with only five adapter slots. In fact, a well-equipped PC may not even have room for a new CPU mounted on a plug-in adapter card; at first glance, it may seem that the only alternative is to start over again with a new computer.

However, it is reasonably easy to undertake a major overhaul project that will bring an older machine up to or beyond AT performance standards, yet allow many existing components to remain in service. This section describes each component that may be replaced or modified. Although the discussion begins by updating an ancient IBM 64Kb PC, the same general comments can be applied to most PC and XT system updating projects.

The project begins with the purchase of a new system board, or motherboard, with eight adapter slots on it. New eight-slot system boards are readily available from a number of suppliers, and may be supplied with no RAM chips installed.

Most boards designed for PC updating follow the XT layout—one socket for IBM-compatible BIOS and another socket for ROM BASIC (see Figure 6.3(b) and Table 6.4). The board is usually supplied with the former, but not the latter, chip. Obviously, the four-chip BASIC from a discarded PC cannot be used here. The IBM XT BASIC chip may work, but only if the IBM XT BIOS chip is also used, in place of whatever BIOS was supplied with the updated board. On the AT, both BASIC and BIOS are split between modules U27 and U47, which makes it impossible to isolate the BASIC feature.

System Unit Replacement. Since the metal chassis of the original IBM PC will only accommodate five brackets, it will also be necessary to purchase a new system cabinet. To avoid interference with nearby television sets, make sure the new cabinet meets FCC radiation requirements. In the case of a flip-top cabinet, make sure that cables at the rear of the system unit don't get in the way, thereby defeating the advantage of the hinged cabinet style.

Power Supply Replacement. With the availability of three additional slots, the original PC power supply will also have to be replaced. However, this can wait until later on if all slots will not be occupied immediately. To install a new power supply, or transfer the old one from the original PC system unit, follow the general procedures described in Chapter 5.

Adapter Modifications. Some older adapters for the PC used a black mounting bracket that was 15/16-inch wide. This style bracket is too wide to fit in an XT or AT adapter slot, which accommodates a bracket that is just under 3/4 inch in width. If the adapter is otherwise compatible, it should be possible to replace the bracket with a narrower one, if this is available from the adapter's manufacturer. Alternatively, new brackets are available from Globe Manufacturing Sales, Inc., JDR Microdevices, and Olson Metal Products Co.

Table 6.12 lists a few older PC adapters that may be equipped with a 15/16-inch mounting bracket, along with the part number for the appropriate replacement bracket. Recently acquired adapters should fit a new 8-slot system unit with no physical compatibility problems.

Diskette and Hard Disk Drives. Most drives, including 3.5-inch diskette drives, can also be physically installed with no difficulty at all. However, a system speedup may cause various software-related problems, as described below.

Diagnostics Diskette Compatibility. As a final system hardware update note, don't overlook the fact that a new non-IBM system board may not be compatible with the IBM diagnostics diskette. But as noted above, setup and diagnostic procedures are usually built-in features of non-IBM ROM, so this is not a serious consideration.

An Updated IBM PC. Figure 6.31 shows an updated IBM PC in which all of the above modifications were made, and Table 6.13a lists both the original PC components and the replacement devices that were used in the system update. The IBM diagnostics diskette runs successfully on this

Table 6.12 Replacement Brackets for PC Adapter Cards

Adapter	Part number Globe	JDR	Olson
AST MegaPlus	G89	—	—
Asynchronous	G05	BKT-2	—
Blank bracket	G83	BKT-10	XT Blank
Cluster (BNC)	—	BKT-15	—
Color/Graphics	G94	—	—
Diskette drive	G95	BKT-13	XTB37-B
Game control	G30	BKT-8C	—
Monochrome display & printer	G33	BKT-4	XTB2509-A
Serial/Parallel	G33	—	XTB2509-A
1 DB-9 cutout	—	BKT-12	—
2 DB-15 cutouts	—	BKT-4	—
1 DB-15 & 1 DB-25 cutout	—	BKT-8	—

system, and verifies that 640Kb of RAM are installed on the system board. However, the diagnostics program must be started by first booting the system with the regular DOS diskette, as described for IBM-compatible computers in the section entitled Start Diagnostics in Chapter 3 (page 51).

Surpassing AT System Performance. Given the performance specifications of EISA and PS/2 systems, even the formerly fast AT can suffer by comparison. However, there are now a number of ISA and EISA system boards with 386 DX or i486 microprocessors available for system upgrade projects. Figure 6.32(a) shows an upgraded AT system, based around the replacement 33-MHz system board shown in Figure 6.32(b). Table 6.13(b) lists the principal components in the upgraded system.

TROUBLESHOOTING ACCELERATED ISA SYSTEMS

Most early ISA systems tolerate a certain amount of system speedup without any problem. However, the dividing line between "go" and "no-go" varies from one system to another, and is also somewhat dependent on the software in use. Therefore, it's a good idea to be well acquainted with system performance before tackling any speedup enhancements; knowing what to expect under normal operating conditions makes it just that much easier to evaluate a post-speedup problem.

Some of what follows is relevant only to systems in which the original system board remains in place, with enhancements confined to a new microprocessor, crystal, or other speedup device.

To make the simplest diagnosis, disable the enhancement and try again. If the problem is gone, then it's safe to assume it was indeed speed related. If it's not, then the enhancement should be left disabled until the problem is identified and resolved.

Software Problems

If the enhanced system works with most but not all software, the software in use when the problem is encountered is probably speed sensitive. Some typical examples are given here.

Screen Displays. If a game or other program requires a response within a certain time interval, the accelerated interval may simply be too short to allow the user to react. The solution is obvious: return to normal speed to run the program or to play the game. Or if you can, play faster.

Figure 6.31. An early IBM PC1 whose performance has been given a boost with a new system board and the other enhancements listed in Table 6.13a.

Table 6.13a Components Used to Upgrade an IBM PC1

Component	Original	Replacement
System unit (cabinet)	IBM	Soletek LY-2 Flip-Top
System board	IBM	Supreme 10 MHz Multi-Turbo
Adapter slots	5	8
ROM BIOS	IBM	Phoenix
ROM BASIC	IBM	none
RAM	64Kb	640Kb
Microprocessor	Intel 8088	Intel 8088-2
Power supply	IBM	PC Cooling Systems Silencer 150
Keyboard	IBM	Key Tronic KB 101
Monochrome display adapter	IBM	same, with new bracket
Color/graphics adapter	IBM	same, with new bracket
Extended memory adapter	AST MegaPlus	same, with new bracket
Real-time clock	on AST board	same
Internal modem	IBM	same, installed as is
Diskette drive adapter	IBM	same, with new bracket
Diskette drives	A: IBM 360Kb	same, installed as is
	B: IBM 360Kb	Toshiba 720Kb
hard disk drive	C: none	Plus Development Hardcard

Table 6.13b Components Used to Upgrade an IBM AT

Component	Original	Replacement
System unit (cabinet)	IBM	Axxion TA-04FN
System board	IBM	Hauppauge 386MBAT33-02
Adapter slots	8	8
ROM BIOS	IBM	Award
ROM BASIC	IBM	none
RAM	512Kb	640Kb (of 2Mb total)
Microprocessor	Intel 80286	Intel 386 DX (33 MHz)
Power supply	IBM (192 W)	same
Keyboard	IBM	Northgate OmniKey PLUS
Graphics adapter	IBM EGA	Boca Research VGA
Extended memory	IBM adapter	1334Kb on system board
Shadow RAM	none	64Kb on system board
Real-time clock	on system board	on system board
External modem	Hayes 2400	same
Drive adapter	IBM	same
Diskette drives	A: IBM 1.2Mb	Teac 1.44Mb
	B: IBM 360Kb	same, installed as is
Hard disk drive	C: Seagate 4096	same, installed as is
	D: none	44Mb Bernoulli Box II

(a)

(b)

Figure 6.32.   A new cabinet (a) suitable for installing the AT upgrade components listed in Table 6.13b. (Courtesy Axxion Group Corp.) (b) An AT replacement system board with 33 MHz microprocessor (386MBAT33-02 courtesy Hauppauge Computer Works, Inc.)

During diagnostics testing, various screen display tests may fail, even though the display is satisfactory during routine operation. Refer to Chapter 3 (page 65–66) for further details about display diagnostics.

Copy-Protected Software. If there's a problem with a copy-protected program, the solution is again to return to normal speed.

Communications Program. Don't overlook the fact that a communications program that waits for a dial tone, carrier, or other response is marking time according to the system clock speed and is not actually counting the passing seconds. Increasing the software's time-out defaults may solve various time-related communications problems.

Hardware Problems

The speedup-related hardware problem may range from a POST system crash every time the system is powered on, to generally unpredictable behavior later on. To help anticipate problems, boot the system with the diagnostics diskette. At the Select An Option menu, choose Option 0, and then at the System Checkout menu, choose Option 1, Run Tests Multiple Times (see Chapter 3 for further details on running these tests). Let the tests run continuously and be on the lookout for intermittent and/or recurring errors.

Keep in mind that although an error code signifies the indicated device is having a speedup-related problem, it does not necessarily mean that the device is defective at normal speed. A display-related error code may be ignored if the display itself seems to be functioning properly.

If the source of a system crash cannot be localized, try removing all adapters except for the primary display and diskette adapters. If the system now works properly, replace the removed adapters one at a time until the problem reappears. Don't overlook the math coprocessor or the possibility that more than one installed option may be speed sensitive.

A few of the potential trouble areas are briefly reviewed here.

Memory. A memory-related error code may indicate that the RAM is not fast enough to work with the enhanced system. Check the accompanying documentation to determine the requirements for new RAM chips.

Display. Some acceleration devices may create various display errors such as snow, scrolling problems, start-up in 40-column mode, or a graphics memory error. There may also be a problem with an enhanced graphics adapter running in the enhanced mode. The same adapter may operate satisfactorily in its CGA mode.

Hard Disk Drive. Before installing any speedup device, make sure you backup all hard disk files. Then, with the accelerator in place, run extensive write and read tests to make sure the drive system functions properly at the higher speed. If it does not, you may need to reformat and/or return to normal-speed operation.

Math Coprocessor. Try to divide by zero, or find the log of a negative number. If there's a problem, the system may crash and have to be rebooted. Use Table 6.6 as a cross-reference guide to find the math coprocessor that should be used with each microprocessor.

Formatting. Try to format a diskette in each drive. Some apparent drive-related errors may be resolved simply by trying the same operation several times.

Printer. If you use a printer, carefully examine the first few documents produced after a system speedup. Be on the lookout for missing line feeds, sporadically garbled text, and generally inconsistent printer behavior.

Summary

Each problem described above is symptomatic of a device that is being driven beyond its design limitations. The solution is either to replace the device or to slow down until the problem disappears. And so, the best general advice on system speedup is, Proceed with Caution. Run extensive system tests to try to find trouble before it finds you. If the enhancement device permits continuously variable speeds, gradually increase the speed until there's a problem. Then back down until the trouble goes away.

Some accelerators provide a two-position switch, with one position returning the system to its normal speed. Depending on your requirements, you may be able to "down-shift" for those operations that require it. However, on some devices it's necessary to reboot every time the switch position is changed. If pressing the Ctrl + Alt + Del keys doesn't work, the system will have to be turned off and back on again.

Other accelerators may be supplied with a diskette containing a software speed-switching program, which allows the speed to be changed without rebooting.

CHIP-HANDLING PROCEDURES

The remainder of this chapter reviews a few procedures that may be helpful when handling IC chips. First, make sure the computer's power is turned off before removing or installing any memory module kit or other expansion option. Failure to observe this precaution will usually cause damage to one or more components.

Once properly installed, most integrated circuit chips exhibit a remarkably long life. However, it is quite easy to damage a chip during handling. The chip's pins are easy to bend, and great care should be taken to make sure that each pin remains straight and that all are firmly seated in the socket on the system board. A single bent or broken pin is sufficient to put the chip out of service, thereby triggering an error message. In addition, chips are susceptible to static electricity and may be electrically destroyed simply by improper handling.

Chip Removal

In performing any procedure which involves chip handling, carefully observe the following steps as the chip is removed:

1. Make sure that the power switch is off, but that the power cable remains plugged in, thereby keeping the system chassis at ground potential.

2. Touch the system chassis before touching a chip, so as to safely discharge any static electricity.

3. Before removing a chip, note the orientation of the notch on the chip. Make sure the notch on the replacement chip is positioned in the same direction.

4. When a chip is removed from the system board or an adapter, protect it from static electricity by pushing the chip legs into a piece of conductive plastic foam or into a sheet of aluminum foil. As extra protection, the foam or foil should be grounded to the PC chassis by a short jumper wire.

Chip Installation

Using the notches on previously installed chips as a guide, make sure that all newly installed chips are oriented in the correct direction. Chips installed in the wrong direction will not function and will probably be destroyed. Be especially attentive to this when installing an entire bank of new chips on the system board or on a memory-expansion option.

Also note that all chips of the same size look pretty much alike, so if you are about to install chips of uncertain origin, make sure they match those already installed. Installing the wrong chip will not permanently damage the computer, but it will quite likely destroy the chip itself, and system operation may be unpredictable until the chip is removed.

Chip Recovery Notes

In checking and replacing integrated circuit chips, it may have been necessary to remove more than one chip in order to correct a problem. However, it would not be unusual to find that only a few of the removed chips are actually defective. Once your computer is back up and running, the following procedure will help you to identify which of the removed chips are not defective. These may be saved for future use.

During this procedure, make a written note of which chips are being reinstalled, in case one or more must be removed again. Also note that this procedure applies only to groups of identical chips as, for example, those removed from a bank of memory modules.

Divide the removed chips into two equal-sized groups, A and B. Reinstall group A only. If an error message is not seen, then group B contains the defective chip(s). Install half of group B and try again. Or, if the error is in group A, replace half that group and try again. Continue installing/removing half groups until the error is isolated to a single chip, which should be discarded.

If you manage to replace all the chips without encountering an error, then one of the following possibilities should be considered:

1. The original error was caused by an improperly seated chip. Simply removing and reinstalling it cleared up the problem.

2. One of the previously removed chips has an intermittent problem. Keep a record of where the suspect chips are located, and if the same problem recurs, remove and discard all of them, since identifying the specific chip with the problem will be more trouble than it's worth.

Figure 6.33 illustrates how to handle chips while doing routine maintenance. If you plan to install or remove chips, chip-extraction and insertion tools are inexpensive aids that are well worth having on hand.

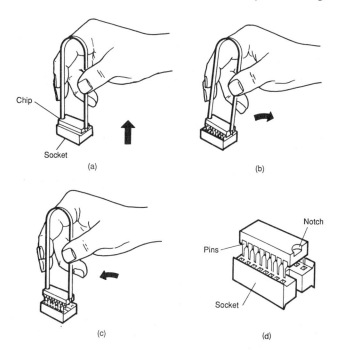

Figure 6.33.   Chip handling procedures. Chip removal (a) is made easier by the use of a chip-removal tool. Note upward pull (b) and gentle rocking motion. Chip replacement (c) requires careful attention to the alignment of the pins with the holes in the circuit board socket. Make sure the notch on the chip (d) is aligned with a similar notch on the circuit board socket.

To remove an integrated circuit chip from its socket, use a chip-removal tool to grasp the chip and gently rock it back and forth while pulling upward. To replace the chip, align its pins with the holes in the socket. Firmly push the chip into place, making sure the notch is aligned with the notch on the socket.

7

MEMORY

Not unlike parts of the human brain in concept if not in complexity, computer memory is the place where data may be stored for retrieval later on. The storage medium described in this chapter is the electronic circuitry within the computer itself, while the following chapters cover magnetic storage on diskette or hard disk systems.

The computer's internal memory capacity may be easily varied by the user, simply by adding or removing memory chips or modules, as described later on in this chapter. Memory-related errors are usually attributable to one of three causes:

1. The computer fails to recognize newly installed additional memory.

2. The computer unsuccessfully attempts to check recently removed memory.

3. There is indeed a memory-related failure.

In the first two examples, the system simply needs to be reconfigured to take the new memory capacity into account, and in the final example, the error code displayed on screen identifies the specific component that has failed. In each of these cases, it is quite easy to get back up and running quickly by following the instructions found here.

Since the significance of system reconfiguration with regard to memory-related problems is often overlooked or misunderstood, this chapter presents a rather detailed examination of the computer's memory system before discussing the actual problems that may occur. The information is presented because most changes in memory capacity will create an apparent system error during POST, until the PC is properly reconfigured. In dealing with such problems, it's always faster and easier to make the necessary corrections than to return the entire system for servicing, especially when that "servicing" consists of nothing more than flipping a few switches, and/or running the setup program.

Chapter Outline

We begin with an overview of computer memory, in order to gain a better understanding of this important part of the total system. The second section reviews what's available in memory-expansion devices.

Once memory capacity has been increased, the system must be configured to take the expansion into account. The System Configuration section describes the necessary procedures.

The Memory Diagnostics section explains how to identify a defective memory chip and shows how to keep the rest of the system up and running until the faulty chip can be replaced with a good one. This is followed by a look at expanded memory diagnostics.

Next, the Memory Configuration Notes may be of use in diagnosing memory-related problems not specifically covered so far. And finally, the chapter concludes with a look at memory problems related to software.

A BRIEF OVERVIEW OF COMPUTER MEMORY

Every personal computer contains two types of memory circuits; ROM (Read-Only Memory) and RAM (Random-Access Memory). Both types are found in IC (integrated circuit) chips and both are briefly described here.

ROM (Read-Only Memory)

These chips contain various standardized instructions which your own program may call upon as required. Since these instructions must never be modified, a ROM chip is designed so that its contents may be read, but may not be replaced by new instructions, thus the name read-only. As an analogy, ROM might be compared to the information on a phonograph record. The user may "read," that is, hear, the same information over and over again, but may not replace it with new information. In either case, the only way to update the information is to physically remove the old version and replace it with a new one.

RAM (Random-Access Memory)

These chips are the electronic scratchpad where your own software's instructions and/or data may be temporarily stored. Here, the analogy is to magnetic recording tape, on which information may be recorded and played back. Later on, new information may be recorded over the previously stored information, which is lost in the process. In computer jargon, *record* and *playback* become *write* and *read*.

The term random-access may be confusing, since an action taken by a computer would appear to be anything *but* random. Perhaps the simplest if not most elegant explanation is that the user may, at random, access any part of this memory. That ROM may also be accessed at random does nothing to help clarify matters, but nevertheless, RAM is popularly used only in reference to memory that may be written and/or read by the user.

Shadow RAM. Since ROM is inherently slower than RAM, some systems speed things up by copying the ROM contents into RAM during system bootup. The RAM is remapped to the ROM addresses, where it effectively replaces, or shadows, the slower ROM. Shadow RAM may also be mapped to areas of unoccupied memory in the upper memory block (see page 234).

Dynamic (DRAM) and Static (SRAM) Memory. Unlike permanent data storage in ROM, the data stored in RAM is lost whenever the system power is turned off. In fact, some RAM chip data disappears almost as fast as it is written, or it would if the data were not dynamically refreshed; that is, the system continually rewrites the data to the chips. As a practical consequence, this DRAM (dynamic RAM) is relatively slow: the system can only read data from such chips during the intervals between refresh cycles.

By contrast, data written to SRAM (static RAM) remains in place for as long as power is applied. Since its stored data does not need to be continually refreshed, SRAM operates considerably faster than DRAM.

CMOS RAM. For laptop computers and other systems which must operate under low-power conditions, CMOS (complementary metal-oxide semiconductor) RAM provides the same features as conventional RAM, though at a cost of some design complexity. The IBM AT and PS/2 MCA systems provide a small segment of CMOS RAM in which configuration data is stored. A system battery supplies the modest power requirement, thus configuration data is not lost when system power is turned off.

Note that a microprocessor using CMOS technology is identified by a "C" in the type number; thus 80C88 indicates the CMOS 8088 CPU found in the IBM PC Convertible.

RAM in Pre-PS/2 Systems. The installation or replacement of individual RAM chips is a simple matter which may be handled comfortably by users with little or no technical skill. Nevertheless, some attention to detail is required, so before attempting any work on individual memory chips, be sure to read the section of Chapter 6 that discusses chip-handling precautions (page 225).

RAM In PS/2 Systems. With the introduction of the PS/2 system, most memory chips are no longer handled individually. Instead, the system board contains several dedicated connectors, each of which accommodates a memory module. The module is a small card with memory chips permanently soldered in place, as shown in Figure 7.1. Typical system board sockets for these modules were shown in one of the detail photos of the PS/2 model 70 system board (Figure 6.2(b), page 136).

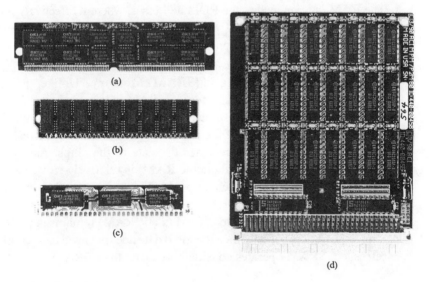

Figure 7.1. Typical memory modules for IBM PS/2 and other personal computers. (a) 2Mb for model 70, (b) 1Mb for model 30 (c) 256Kb for model 30 (d) 2Mb for model 80 (modules courtesy Memory Products and More).

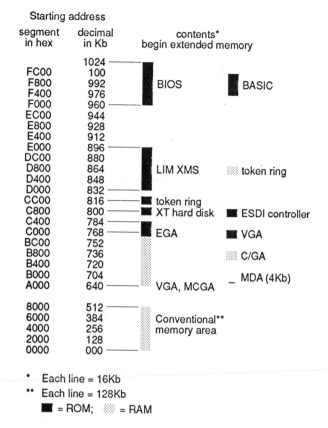

Figure 7.2. A PC memory map, showing details of reserved memory area between end of conventional memory (640Kb) and beginning of extended memory (1024Kb). Vertical bars indicate amount of memory occupied by indicated devices.

Two PS/2 ISA systems do have a small amount of memory (128Kb) installed as individual chips (model 25), or permanently soldered to the system board (model 30).

Categories of Random-Access Memory

Figure 7.2 is a simplified PC memory map, and each memory area seen in the figure is briefly described here. Unfortunately, the computer industry is devoted to descriptive terms that convey almost no meaning, and worse, that look pretty much like other terms with quite different meanings.

Therefore, it may be necessary to read at least a few of the following descriptions several times to distinguish one from another.

Base Memory. The amount of memory actually installed in the conventional memory area.

Conventional Memory. Also called user memory since it is immediately available for user applications, this is the 640Kb area beginning at absolute address zero. On systems claiming onboard memory capacity of, say, 1Mb, the additional 384Kb of memory is automatically remapped to a starting address of 1024Kb.

Video Memory. Also referred to as *graphics memory*, this is the 128Kb area immediately following conventional memory, which is occupied by the RAM on various display adapters. Video memory is discussed in greater detail in Chapter 11.

Reserved Memory. This is the area between 640 and 1024Kb. With the exception of the segment occupied by video memory and ROM on pre-PS/2 systems, IBM reserved it for future applications. In MCA 80286 systems, this block is remapped to the 1024Kb (1Mb) starting address. In 80386 and 80486 systems, the same block is placed at the first address immediately following any other installed extended memory. However, 128K may be set aside for other purposes, and in addition, the 128Kb block between 512K and 640K may also be remapped on some systems.

A 64Kb block of addresses situated between video memory and ROM may be utilized by an expanded-memory device.

Upper Memory Block (UMB). This too is the memory area between 640K and 1024K, as defined by the Microsoft Extended Memory Specification (XMS), which permits part of the area to be filled by shadow RAM. Or expanded or extended memory may be remapped into the unused portions of the upper memory block.

High Memory. This is yet another term used by some software utilities to define the 640–1024Kb memory area.

Extended Memory. The extended memory area comprises RAM installed (or mapped) to begin at 1024Kb (1Mb). It is not available on PC and XT systems, or on PS/2 models 25 and 30. Most DOS applications cannot directly use extended memory, although it may be used by an electronic disk, as described in Chapter 8. In addition, 80386 and 80486 systems may use extended memory as expanded memory, as described later in the chapter.

AT and model 30 286 Extended Memory comprises RAM installed on one or more AT-bus memory expansion cards. The starting address of the first such card must be set at 1024Kb.

High Memory Area (HMA). This XMS term defines the first 64Kb block of memory in the extended memory area, and should not (but probably will) be confused with the *high memory* definition given above. Some programs can make use of the HMA, thus releasing conventional memory for use by other applications.

Extended Memory Block (EMB). If part of the extended memory area is remapped (for example, to UMB) or otherwise engaged (HMA), the remaining area—available for RAM disks and disk caching—is identified as an *extended memory block.*

Expanded Memory. This is additional random-access memory that may be accessed through a 64Kb window located within the reserved memory area. Expanded memory is defined by the Lotus/Intel/Microsoft Expanded Memory Specification, which is briefly described below (page 258).

Expansion Memory. A term loosely applied to any random-access memory used to expand a personal computer's capacity. Due to the similarity between "expanded" and "expansion," it's important to remember that the latter term applies to *any* additional RAM, and is frequently encountered in describing various memory devices that may be installed within the conventional (user) or extended memory area.

RAM Chip Organization

In pre-PS/2 systems, RAM chips were generally 1-bit wide; that is, each chip handled a single bit for each byte of memory. Thus, one would need eight 64 (or 256) K-*bit* chips to handle 64 (or 256) K-*bytes* of memory, plus an additional chip for parity.

In PS/2 systems, each RAM chip may be one, four, or eight bits wide. (Nine-bit wide chips—to include parity—are also manufactured.) Therefore, the chips on a memory module containing, say, 1M byte of RAM, might take any of the configurations in Figure 7.3, where for clarity the chip required for parity checking is not shown. Since parity checking requires 1

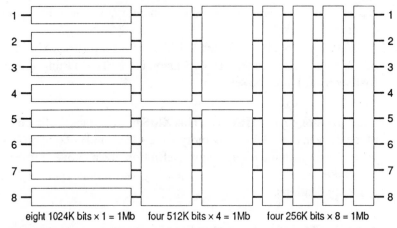

eight 1024K bits × 1 = 1Mb   four 512K bits × 4 = 1Mb   four 256K bits × 8 = 1Mb

Figure 7.3.   Possible chip configurations for a 1Mb memory module.

bit for each byte of memory, an additional 1,024K-bit-by-1-bit chip (or equivalent) would be required for each configuration.

MEMORY-EXPANSION DEVICES

It is generally impractical for the user to expand ROM capacity, since the computer has been designed to make optimum use of the ROM that is already installed on the system board.

ROM Expansion

Having said that, however, a certain amount of ROM expansion is possible within the reserved memory area described above (p. 234). In fact, various portions of this memory area may be utilized by ROM installed on a plug-in adapter, as in these examples:

Adapter	ROM	Starting Address
Enhanced Graphics	16Kb	C000:0000
VGA Display *	24Kb	C000:0000
Hard Disk	8Kb	C800:0000
ESDI Hard Disk	16Kb	C800:0000
Token Ring Network	8Kb	CC00:0000
Cluster	32Kb	D000:0000

* for use with ISA systems

This type of memory expansion takes place automatically, simply by plugging in the adapter containing the ROM, and is not further discussed here.

RAM Expansion

The computer's RAM capacity may be increased in two ways: by adding additional memory to the system board or by installing one or more memory expansion options. IBM nomenclature for the various available devices is summarized here, and Table 7.1 lists representative memory expansion devices.

Memory Module Kit

PC, XT, AT. A memory module kit—a collection of 9 or 18 RAM chips— may be installed on the system board or on a Memory Expansion Option.

PS/2 Systems. A small card or module, with a collection of RAM chips soldered in place, may be installed in a matching socket on the system board or on a Memory Expansion Option or Expanded Memory Adapter. Note that a PS/2 memory module kit may contain two or four such modules. For example, most 512Kb module kits comprise two 256Kb modules.

The capacity of a memory module may be verified by checking the continuity at certain pins with respect to a ground pin on the module. Table 7.2 lists the pin numbers and DC resistance for each available memory module.

Memory Expansion Kit

PS/2 Systems. The expansion module is the same as the memory module kit, except that it is designed for installation on an adapter card only.

Memory Expansion Option, Expanded Memory Adapter

PC, XT, AT. A plug-in adapter card contains one or more banks of sockets for RAM chips.

PS/2 Systems. A plug-in adapter card contains sockets for the PS/2 memory module kits and/or memory expansion kits described above.

Table 7.1a Memory Expansion Devices

Memory chips and module kits

Cat. no.	Memory	for *	Kit description **
1501001	16Kb	PC1	9 chips, for system board expansion
1501003	64Kb	PC2, XT	9 chips, for system board or 64/256Kb expansion option
6450202	256Kb	AT	18 chips, for system board expansion
78X8955	128Kb	25	six chips for system board expansion
30F5348 †	512Kb	25 & 30 286	two 256Kb modules (1497259, 30F5364)
30F5360 †	2Mb	25 & 30 286	two 1Mb modules (1497252, 1497259, 30F5364)
34F2866	4Mb	30 286	two of above, plus 34F2863
6450345	512Kb	‡	two 256Kb modules (6450344)
72X8517	512Kb	50	one module
61X8906	1Mb	60	four 256Kb modules
6450603 †	1Mb	55 SX, 70 (E61, 061, 121)	one module (34F3011, – 77, 6450605, – 09)
6450604	2Mb	50Z, 55SX, P70, 70 (E61, 061, 121)	one module (34F3011, – 77, 6450605, – 09)
6450372	2Mb	‡	one module (6450367)
6450608	2Mb	70 (A&B 21, 61)	one module
34F2933	4Mb	55SX, 65 SX, P70, 70, 80	one module (34F3011, – 77)
6450375	1Mb	80 (041, 071)	one module
6450379 †	2Mb	80 (111 to 321)	one module
6451060	4MB	80 (A21, A31)	one module

   * PS/2, for use on system board of indicated models.
** (cat. no.) identifies adapter card (see Table 7.1b) that also accepts this module.
   † shown in Figure 7.1
   ‡ for use with indicated adapter module only.

Table 7.1b Memory Expansion Devices (continued)

Memory expansion options (adapter cards)

Cat. no.	Memory	For	Option description *
1501011	32Kb	PC, XT	These Memory Expansion Option cards
1501012	64Kb	PC, XT	are supplied with the amount of RAM
1501209	256Kb	PC, XT	indicated. They do not accept additional
6450209	128Kb	AT	RAM chips. For further expansion, one or
6450203	512Kb	AT	more additional cards may be installed.
1501013	64/256Kb	PC, XT	64Kb, plus sockets for three 64Kb Memory Module Kits, for a total of 256Kb.
2685193	2Mb	XT, AT, 30	2Mb expanded memory, parallel port
34F2863	–	30 286	All Chargecard (memory management card), included with 34F2864 & 34F2866
30F5364	0-12Mb	30 286	Twelve sockets for 30F5348 *or* 30F5360, serial & parallel ports, LIM EMS 4.0 support
34F2864 #	3 *or* 12Mb †	30 286	same, with six 30F5348 installed & 34F2863
1497259 §	0-8Mb	50	eight sockets (30F5348, 30F5360)
1497252 §	2 *or* 8Mb †	50	same, with four 30F5348 installed
6450609	2-8Mb	50, 50Z, 55SX, 60	four sockets (6450603, 6450604)
6450344	512K-2Mb	50, 50Z, 60	four sockets (6450345)
6450367 §	2-6Mb	P70, 70	three sockets (6450372)
6450605 §	2-8Mb	P70, 70, 80	four sockets (6450603, 6450604)
34F3077	2-14Mb ‡	P70, 70, 80	four sockets (6450603, 6450604, 34F2933)
34F3011	4-14Mb ‡	P70, 70, 80	same

  * For PS/2, indicated minimum memory is installed; (cat. no.) identifies additional memory modules (see Table 7.1a) that fit this adapter.

  # can only be used with 512Kb on system board. Move additional system board modules (if any) to the adapter card.

  § discontinued

  † For higher capacity replace all 30F5348 with 30F5360 module kits.

  ‡ 14Mb maximum because adapter requires 2Mb on system board.

Table 7.2 MCA Memory Module Capacity and Speed Guide

Module style	Presence detect 0 1 2 3 is at connector pin no.				Ground is at pin no.
30–pin SIP	24	26	–	–	22
72–pin SIP	67	68	69	70	72
3 × 32–pin connector	not implemented				

Memory on module amount speed (ns)		DC resistance at pin number given above, with respect to ground pin (ohms)			
256 Kb	120 or 150	0	∞		
512 Kb	120 or 150	∞	0		
1 Mb	85	0	∞	∞	0
1 Mb	100	0	∞	0	0
1 Mb	120	0	∞	∞	∞
2 Mb	85	∞	0	∞	0
4 Mb	80	0	0	0	0

Multifunction Adapter

PS/2 model 30 286. A multifunction adapter card has serial and parallel ports, plus sockets for memory module kits.

Each memory-expansion alternative is described in detail below. In general, the expansion procedure is a five-step process:

1. If necessary, temporarily remove components and disconnect cables that obstruct access to the system board RAM area or the adapter.

2. Remove the memory-expansion adapter that is to receive more chips or remove the blank bracket at the slot where a new memory expansion adapter is to be installed. On PS/2 systems, remove any memory module that is to be replaced by a higher-capacity module.

3. Insert each new memory module in the appropriate system board or adapter socket, and if required, replace the memory expansion adapter into a system board expansion slot.

4. Set various memory-configuration switches on the system board and/or on the memory-expansion adapter. On AT and PS/2 systems,

use the Setup option on the diagnostics or Starter/Reference diskette to reconfigure the system.

5. Replace any components and reconnect cables that were removed or disconnected in step 1.

Contiguous-Memory Requirements

Within the conventional and extended memory blocks described above, every increment of new memory must be installed contiguously; that is, its starting address must fall immediately above the previously installed memory. For memory on an ISA system board, this means that new RAM chips must be installed in the next available memory bank, as described earlier (page 237). Additional memory on an adapter will not function unless the system board RAM banks are completely full.

AT Contiguous Memory. The AT exception to this rule is that the system hardware does not require the memory address space between 512K and 640K to be filled in order to utilize extended or expanded memory. Furthermore, a suitably configured memory-expansion adapter may take the place of the second 256Kb of system board memory, provided jumper J18 (described on page 245) is properly positioned.

PS/2 Contiguous Memory (80386 Systems). If the POST procedure detects a memory error within the first 512Kb of system board memory, the 1Mb block containing that error is deactivated. If there is another 1Mb of system board memory available, it will take the place of the defective block. If not, the POST procedure fails and the system will not boot.

If a failure occurs beyond the first 512Kb of memory, the diagnostics program on the reference diskette must be run to deactivate the 1Mb block containing the error. In this case, all higher-address blocks are readdressed downward to take the place of the deactivated block.

Extended Memory. Extended memory must begin at 1024Kb (1Mb) and extend upward from there. To meet this requirement, the ISA system memory-configuration switches described later in this chapter are used to make sure that there are neither address overlaps nor gaps in the installed extended memory. On MCA systems, memory above 640Kb is automatically remapped to begin at 1024Kb.

Since so many different combinations are possible, the most that can be said here is to follow the instructions that come with each adapter. However, the following general comments may help to make these instructions more understandable when adding memory to an ISA system. The comments do not apply to PS/2 systems, where memory configuration is automatic.

Consider a PC or XT with a completely filled system board and a 32Kb memory-expansion adapter properly installed. Now let's add a 64Kb adapter. As we shall see later, its configuration switches permit its starting address to be set at any 64Kb increment. However, the presence of the 32Kb adapter might seem to present a problem. The new adapter will either overlap the 32Kb card or begin 32Kb beyond it, and neither alternative is acceptable. The easy solution is to reconfigure the 32Kb card so that its starting address follows the new 64Kb adapter. Of course, it would also be possible to install two 32Kb cards ahead of the 64Kb adapter, but this might lead to a misinterpreted error code in the event of a RAM chip failure. Therefore, the 32Kb card(s) should always follow the 64Kb card(s).

Now, let's install another 64Kb adapter. This must be configured to follow the first 64Kb adapter, and once again each 32Kb adapter must be reconfigured to follow at the end of all 64Kb adapters. This rule applies whether the additional 64Kb is installed in an empty bank on a 64/256Kb adapter or as a separate 64Kb adapter. In any case, the instructions accompanying each memory-expansion adapter will list most, if not all, possible configurations.

The contiguous memory concept is further illustrated in Figure 7.4. Although the 32Kb memory-expansion adapter is no longer available, the concept described in the figure may be applied to almost any combination of currently available expansion adapters.

SYSTEM BOARD MEMORY

PC, XT, and AT Systems

As Figure 7.5 illustrates, there are four rows of nine sockets each in the lower left-hand quadrant of the system board. This is the area in which all system board RAM chips are installed.

Depending on the amount of memory already in place, one or more of these rows may still be available for memory expansion. If all rows are already occupied, then further expansion requires the installation of a memory-expansion adapter containing the additional RAM.

Memory Banks. On the PC and XT, the four rows of nine sockets each are identified as banks 0 through 3, and bank 3 is at the front of the computer. On

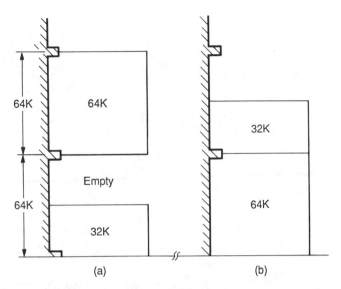

Figure 7.4. Contiguous memory requirements. (a) An illegal configuration because there is an empty memory space between the end of the 32Kb block and the beginning of the 64Kb block, the 64Kb option is not accessible. (b) In this rearrangement, memory is contiguous from the start of the 64Kb block through the end of the 32Kb block; all memory is now accessible.

the AT, the sequence is reversed and the rows are paired: bank 0 comprises the two rows closest to the front, while bank 1 is the next two rows.

In all cases, a bank that is to be put into service must be completely filled with chips or it will not function at all. Furthermore, banks must be filled in ascending order, starting at bank 0. Because of these constraints, a defective chip in bank 0 will prevent the entire system from being used, due to the requirements for contiguous memory discussed earlier. However, as we shall soon discover, a defective chip may be quickly identified and swapped with a good one taken from the installed memory device with the highest starting address. This will enable the system to work at reduced capacity until a replacement chip can be installed.

RAM Chip Orientation. On the PC and XT, an orientation notch on each system board RAM chip points toward the rear of the system unit. The AT also reverses this convention, with each notch pointing to the front of the system unit.

Figure 7.5(a).   On ISA systems, RAM chips are installed in the four rows in the lower left-hand quadrant of the system board. (a) PC, (b) XT, and (c) AT system boards.

PC. The memory capacity of an IBM PC system board varies, depending upon whether it is an early model (PC1) or a later one (PC2). Memory capacity may be verified by reading the label on the leftmost edge of the system board, just above bank 0. There are two possibilities:

Model	System-board label	Interpretation
PC1	16Kb–64Kb CPU	16Kb in each bank, for a total of 64K
PC2	64Kb–256Kb CPU	64Kb in each bank, for a total of 256Kb

As further identification, the 64Kb–256Kb PC2 system has a "B" stamped on the rear panel of the system unit directly above the keyboard input socket. Note that 16Kb and 64Kb chips may not be interchanged.

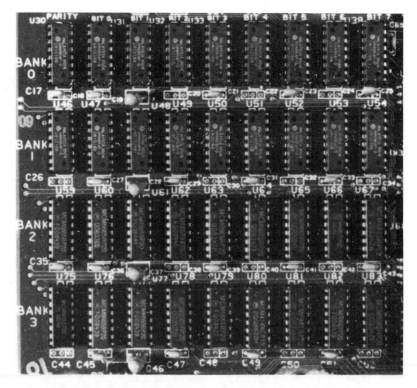

Figure 7-5(b)   (Continued)

AT. Remember that the four 9-chip rows in the AT make up only two banks, 0 and 1. Therefore, the system board must have either 18 or 36 chips installed. No other quantity is valid.

AT RAM Jumper. A small three-pin jumper on the AT system board (see Figure 6.3(d)) determines whether the POST will look for 256Kb or 512Kb of memory on the system board before testing any expansion memory that may be present. The position of the jumper switch is critical in the following two configurations:

1. 256Kb of system board memory only, but with additional memory installed on memory-expansion adapters

2. 512Kb of system board memory

Figure 7-5(c)   (Continued)

In the first case, the jumper between pins 2 and 3 disables RAM bank 1 so that the expansion memory immediately follows the 256Kb in RAM bank 0. This jumper position is required when installing a memory-expansion adapter in an AT with only 256Kb of memory on the system board. On the other hand, if RAM bank 1 is actually occupied with memory chips, then the jumper must be set between pins 1 and 2, so that bank 1 is not disabled. Otherwise bank 1 will be ignored, even when it is fully occupied.

As Figure 6.3(d) indicated, the jumper labeled J18 is at the front of the system board, to the immediate right of the adapter occupying slot 8. To reach the jumper, the adapter in slot 8 must first be removed. If this is the fixed disk and diskette drive adapter, its removal will be made easier by first disconnecting the four-pin plug at the front end of the card. Note the relative position of the plug's two conductors as a guide to correct replacement later on.

With the adapter removed, observe the position of the jumper. If jumper J18 must be moved, do so carefully, and make sure the jumpers to its immediate right have remained securely in place before replacing the adapter. Don't forget to reconnect the four-pin plug described in the preceding paragraph.

PS/2 Systems

System board memory configuration varies significantly from one model to another, and as noted above, any RAM between 640 and 1024K is automatically remapped to a starting address at or above 1024Kb (1Mb). On systems with an 80286 processor, this 384Kb memory segment cannot be used as expanded memory. On systems with an 80386 or 80486 processor it can be used as expanded memory, in conjunction with the DOS 4.00 drivers XMAEM.SYS and XMA2EM.SYS described in Chapter 4 (page 87).

Model 25. The first 128 Kbytes of RAM consist of six chips, four 64Kb × 4-bit and two 64Kb × 1-bit chips, mounted in sockets on the system board. This is followed by 512 Kbytes of RAM in two banks of 256Kb × 9-bit removable 1 × 30-pin SIP modules. If the first 128K is defective or missing, the starting address of the 256Kb RAM modules automatically shifts downward to replace the missing/defective chips.

Model 30. The memory configuration is the same as the model 25, except that the first 128K bytes of RAM are soldered in place.

Model 30 386. Four 1 × 30-pin sockets on the system board are labeled A, B, C, D. Each socket accommodates a 256Kb or 1024Kb RAM module. The system requires the use of either two or four identical modules, as shown here.

Total	Module size (Kb)	
(Kb)	256	1024
512	2	-
1024	4	-
2048	-	2
4096	-	4

Neither an odd number of modules, nor a mix of different capacity modules, will work.

Model 50 (021, R21). There are two 1 × 30-pin sockets on the system board, each of which requires a 512Kb RAM module, for a total of 1024Kb (1Mb).

Model 50 Z (031, 061). There is one 1 × 72-pin socket on the system board, which accepts either a 1Mb or a 2Mb memory module.

Model 55 SX. There are two 1 × 72-pin sockets on the system board, each of which accepts a 1Mb, 2Mb, or a 4Mb memory module, as shown here.

Total (Kb)	Module size (Kb) 1024		2048		4096
2048	2	or	1		-
3072	1	and	1		-
4096	-		2	or	1
5120	1		-		1
6144	-		1	and	1
8192	-		-		2

Model 60. There are four 1 × 30-pin sockets on the system board, each of which requires a 256Kb module, for a total of 1024Kb (1Mb). No other memory configuration is possible.

Model 65 SX. There are two 1 × 72-pin sockets on the system board. Memory configuration is the same as the model 55 SX above.

Model 70 386 (E61, 061, 121). There are three 1 × 72-pin sockets on the system board, each of which accepts either a 1Mb or a 2Mb memory module, as shown here.

Total (Kb)	Module size (Kb) 1024		2048
1024	1		-
2048	2	or	1
3072	1	and	1
4096	-		2
5120	1	and	2
6144	-		3

Model 70 386 (A21, A61) and P70 386. There are four 1 × 72-pin sockets on the system board, each of which accommodates a 2Mb memory module, for a total capacity of 2048, 4096, 6144 or 8192Kb.

Model 70 486 (B21, B61). Memory configuration is the same as the equivalent model 70 386 (A21, A61), since there is no difference in the system board with respect to memory configuration.

Model 80. There are two 3 × 32-pin sockets on the system board, each of which accommodates either a 1Mb or a 2Mb memory module, according to the system model number, as indicated here.

Total	Module size (Kb)			
(Kb)	1024	2048	4096	
1024	1	-	-	(041, 071)
2048	2	-	-	
2048	-	1	-	(111 to 321)
4096	-	2	-	
4096	-	-	1	(A21, A31)
8192	-	-	2	

RAM Module Orientation. A notch at one end of the module (see Figure 7.1) prevents it from being installed backward, with correct notch orientation varying from one computer to another. If in doubt, simply match the module with others already installed (or examine the socket to see which end accommodates the notch).

System Board Memory Comparison

The system board memory capacity for the IBM personal computers listed above is summarized in tabular format in Table 7.3.

System Board Memory Checks

There are three ways to check the amount of valid system board memory.

DOS Base Memory Checks. When the DOS CHKDSK (check disk) command is executed, the base memory—that is, the amount of RAM installed within the 640Kb base area—is reported in the next-to-last line of the screen display. To use this command, insert the DOS diskette in the

Table 7.3a RAM on PC, XT, AT System Boards

Model	Type	RAM banks	Capacity (Kb) each	min-max
PC	1	4×9	16	16–64, in four increments of 16Kb
	2	4×9	64	64–256, in four increments of 64Kb
XT	all	4×9	64	64–256, in four increments of 64Kb
AT	all	2×18	256	256–512, in two increments of 256Kb

Table 7.3b RAM Modules on PS/2 System Boards

Model	Type	Module sockets	Capacity each (Kb)	Total socket capacity (Kb)
25	all	2 †	256 ‡	512 or 640
25 286	all	2	512 or 1024	512 to 4096
30	all	2 †	256 ‡	512 or 640
30 286	all	4 †	256 or 1024	512 to 4096
50	021, R21	2 †	512	1024
50 Z	031, 061	1	1024 or 2048	1024 or 2048
55 SX	all	2 †	1024, 2048, 4096	2048 to 8192
60	all	4 †	256	1024
65 SX	all	2	1024, 2048, 4096	2048 to 8192
70	E61, 061, 121	3	1024 or 2048	1024 to 6144
	A or B 21 & 61	4	2048	2048 to 8192
P70 386	all	4	2048	2048 to 8192
80 §	041, 071	2	1024	1024 or 2048
	111 to 321	2	2048	2048 or 4096
	A21, A31	2	4096	4096 or 8192

† Must be filled in multiples of 2; all 4 required for model 60; all modules must be same capacity
‡ An additional 128K system–board RAM is:
   in sockets on model 25
   soldered in place on model 30
§ Minimum memory configuration for:
   Type 1 (041, 071) may be installed in either connector 1 or 2
   Type 2 (111, 311) *must* be installed in connector 1

default drive, type CHKDSK, and press the Enter key. The display will include this line:

```
655360 total bytes memory
```

The actual number will of course depend on the amount of memory installed, and you may want to divide the number on screen by 1,024 to determine the more familiar "xxxK" memory designation, which in this example is 640 Kbytes.

The much faster MEM command, introduced in DOS version 4.00, may also be used to display the same information (use MEM.EXE in DOS subdirectory). But in this case the amount of base memory is seen as the first line of the display.

BASIC Base Memory Check. When the computer is turned on, base memory information is automatically written into RAM, so the following one-line BASIC program will also give an on-screen display of base memory, in Kbytes.

```
100 DEF SEG = 0: PRINT PEEK(1043) + 256 * PEEK(1044)
```

or, for PS/2 systems,

```
100 DEF SEG = 0: PRINT PEEK(1043) + 256 * PEEK(1044) + 1
```

See the IBM BASIC Manual for an explanation of the DEF SEG statement and the PEEK function.

Needless to say, the amount should agree with that found when using the DOS CHKDSK or MEM commands. In the case of the IBM PC only, an additional line will calculate the amount of expansion memory, if any.

```
110 PRINT PEEK(1045) + 256 * PEEK(1046)
```

To determine the memory on the system board only, the amount of expansion memory may be subtracted from the value found in line 100. All displays are in Kbytes.

On an AT, if the BASIC program displays the number 640, this is an indication that an additional 128Kb of user memory is installed on a memory-expansion adapter.

Visual Check of Memory. If the amount of user memory displayed by CHKDSK and/or the BASIC program does not agree with what you expected it to be, make a visual check of the RAM area to note how many banks have chips in them. Table 7.4 may serve as a guide for what to expect.

Table 7.4 Guide to Visual Check of ISA System-Board Memory

Banks occupied		Total	System board memory (Kb)			
PC, XT	AT	chips	PC1	PC2	XT	AT
0	–	9	16	64	64	–
0–1	0	18	32	128	128	256
0–2	–	27	48	192	192	–
0–3	0–1	36	64	256	256	512

MEMORY-EXPANSION ADAPTERS

To extend the total system memory beyond the capacity of the system board itself, one or more memory-expansion adapters may be installed. The installation is a three-step procedure:

1. Set the configuration switches (if any) on the expansion adapter.
2. Install the expansion adapter in one of the adapter slots on the system board.
3. Configure the system to take the new memory into account.

Remember that the system must be reconfigured again if the expansion adapter is subsequently removed. Table 7.5 lists some typical combinations of expansion adapters. Although the table refers to the old PC and XT systems, the basic concept should apply to any ISA system.

MEMORY CONFIGURATION

When the amount of memory in any IBM personal computer is changed, the system must be reconfigured to take the new capacity into account. With the computer properly configured, all of the installed memory will be checked during the POST procedure and will subsequently be available for use. In the event of an improper memory configuration, one of the following errors occurs:

POST attempts to check memory that does not exist, or

POST checks memory that is not accounted for in the system configuration. In either case, the POST procedure displays an error message.

Table 7.5 Representative Memory Expansion Options

For a total capacity (Kb) of: PC1	PC2, XT	add this	by installing these memory expansion options			or		or		
64	256	0								
96	288	32	32							
128	320	64	32	32		64				
160	352	96	32	32	32	64	32			
192	384	128	64	64		64	32	32	128	
224	416	160	64	64	32	128	32			
256	448	192	64	64	64	128	64		192	
288	480	224	128	64	32	192	32			
320	512	256	128	64	64	192	64		256	
352	544	288	192	64	32	256	32			
384	576	320	192	64	64	256	32	32	256	64
416	608	352	256	64	32					
448	640	384	256	64	64	256	128			
480		416	256	128	32					
512		448	256	128	64	256	192			
544		480	256	192	32					
576		512	256	192	64	256	256			
608		544	256	256	32					
640		576	256	256	64					

  32 = 32Kb expansion option
  64 = 64Kb expansion option, or 64/256Kb option with 1 bank installed
 128 = 64/256Kb option with 2 banks installed
 192 = 64/256Kb option with 3 banks installed
 256 = 64/256Kb option with 4 banks installed

System Memory Configuration

The system must be configured to recognize the amount of installed memory, in one of the following ways.

PC and XT. The system board configuration switches listed in Table 7.6 must be properly set to indicate the amount of memory that is installed. On both systems, positions 3 and 4 on switch block 1 define the amount of memory on the system board. On the PC only, switch block 2 is used in conjunction with the installed memory-expansion adapters. In addition, the switch block on each memory-expansion adapter must be properly set.

In Chapter 6, Table 6.10 showed the correct settings for all system board switch blocks. The correct positions for switches on memory-expansion adapters may be found in the instructions accompanying each card. Note that when any memory-expansion adapter is installed, its correct switch

Table 7.6 System Board Memory Configuration Switches

PC and XT Block 1 Switches *	Amount of memory on system board		
	PC1 (Kb)	PC2 (Kb)	XT (Kb)
xx11xxxx	16		64
xx01xxxx	32		128
xx10xxxx	48		192
xx00xxxx	64	64–256	256

PC only Block 2 Switches *	Total memory	Amount of memory on all option cards in a PC with system board capacity of	
		64Kb	256Kb
11111000	64	none	none
01111000	96	32	not used
10111000	128	64	none
00111000	160	96	not used
11011000	192	128	none
01011000	224	160	not used
10011000	256	192	none
00011000	288	224	32
11101000	320	256	64
01101000	352	288	96
10101000	384	320	128
00101000	416	352	160
11001000	448	384	192
01001000	480	416	224
10001000	512	448	256
00001000	544	480	288
11110000	576	512	320
01110000	608	544	352
10110000	640	576	384

* Switch position 0 = Off (down), 1 = On (up), x = not used for memory configuration. Switch positions not shown are invalid.

positions will be affected by the presence of other expansion adapters within the same system. Therefore, if any adapter is removed, the switch positions on the remaining adapters may need to be changed. Also, the removed adapter may need to be reconfigured if it is to be installed in a different computer.

AT. As noted in Chapter 6, the AT does not require the use of system board switches for memory configuration. Instead, the system is configured by software, using the diagnostics diskette immediately after making any change in the amount of system memory. With the diagnostics diskette in place, turn the power on. If the system was already configured correctly, the Select an Option menu shown in Figure 3.4b would have appeared. However, when a memory configuration error is detected during POST, an error code is displayed on screen, along with the following message:

```
(RESUME = "F1" KEY)
```

When you press the F1 function key, another memory error message appears, followed by various messages about date, time, disk drives, and so on. Answer "yes" to all questions until the following screen is displayed:

```
Base memory is composed of:
- 256Kb on the system board or
- 512Kb on the system board or
- 640Kb of Base memory consisting
  of 512Kb on the system board,
  and 128Kb on the 128Kb Memory
  Expansion Option.
Base memory size is xxxKB
Is this correct (Y/N)
?
```

Again, the actual information displayed will depend on your system, but you should answer *no* if you have just installed an additional bank on the system board and/or you have added the 128Kb memory-expansion adapter. If the 128Kb adapter is to be added to a 256Kb system, don't forget to reposition jumper J18, as described above. If you answered *no*, you will be prompted for the correct base memory size. Otherwise answer *yes*, and in either case, the next screen to be seen is:

```
The Expansion Memory size is
composed of additional memory
adapters not including the 128KB
```

```
Memory Expansion option.
Expansion memory size is xxxKb
Is this correct (Y/N)
?
```

If the correct answer is no, the following screen is displayed next:

```
EXPANSION MEMORY SIZE
0
512
1024
1536
2048

.

.

Enter correct Expansion Memory Size
(0, 512, 1024, 1536, ...).
?
```

Note that IBM's *Expansion Memory* phrase refers to extended memory only. If some memory adapter is installed that uses the Lotus/Intel/Microsoft Expanded Memory Specification, the memory allocated for this purpose should not be counted here. For further details, see the section on expanded memory configuration notes (page 258).

After entering the correct number for extended (not expanded) memory, the new configuration will be displayed so that you can review the changes that you have made. Further corrections may be made by once again answering *no*. Otherwise, the Select an Option menu will be displayed, and you may choose

```
9 - END DIAGNOSTICS
```

or if you prefer

```
0 - SYSTEM CHECKOUT.
```

If you choose Option 0, refer to Chapter 6 for further details on how to proceed with the system checkout. Then return here to continue.

Assuming you have now chosen Option 9, you will see the following screen:

```
PREPARE SYSTEM FOR DESIRED OPERATION
AND PRESS ENTER
?
```

```
┌─────────────────────────────────────────────────────────────┐
│ Memory Size Error - 00164              Page   1 of 1          │
├─────────────────────────────────────────────────────────────┤
│ If you have installed or removed memory, run automatic        │
│ configuration.                                                │
│                                                               │
│ If you have not installed or removed any memory, do           │
│ not run automatic configuration.  Continue until the          │
│ Main Menu appears.  Select "Test the computer" to             │
│ determine the cause of this error and what action to          │
│ take.                                                         │
│                                                               │
│                                                               │
├─────────────────────────────────────────────────────────────┤
│ Automatically configure the system? (Y/N)                     │
│                                                               │
└─────────────────────────────────────────────────────────────┘
```

Figure 7.6.   PS/2 Memory Size Error message seen when system is booted from the Starter/Reference diskette and the memory configuration is incorrect.

Remove the diagnostics diskette and replace it with your regular DOS diskette. Then press Enter and the system will be reconfigured to incorporate whatever memory and other changes you made.

PS/2 Systems. In the event of a memory configuration error, the POST procedure will display a 164 error code and two short beeps will be heard. On some systems the error code is followed by an OK symbol with a backslash and an arrow pointing to an IBM manual. A 201 error code may also be seen.

Insert the Starter/Reference diskette in drive A and reboot the system (or see the MCA System note in Chapter 3 (p. 39) for a temporary work-around alternative). When the IBM logo appears, press the Enter key. When the *Memory Size Error* message shown in Figure 7.6 is displayed, press Y and the system will automatically reconfigure itself to take the new amount of memory into account. During the process, the following message is seen:

```
Automatic configuration is being run.
```

This is followed by:

```
Automatic configuration complete. When Enter
is pressed, the computer restarts itself.

Press Enter to continue.
```

Do so, and immediately remove the Starter/Reference diskette from drive A. The system will reboot itself, taking into account its new memory configuration.

On some PS/2 systems (e.g., model 70, and model 80 type 1) a single memory module may be installed in either connector 1 or 2. A note in the model 70 *Quick Reference Manual* advises "Always install the first memory module kit in the right-hand connector" (labeled J31 on system board). The note should read ". . . the first *additional* memory module kit."

Expanded Memory Configuration Notes

The LIM (Lotus/Intel/Microsoft) Expanded Memory Specification (Version 3.20, September 1985) described a memory management system whereby up to 8Mb of memory could be accessed through a 64Kb RAM window located within the reserved memory area. In LIM version 4.0, the specification was revised to handle up to 32Mb of RAM. In either case, each 1Mb of expanded memory is divided into 64 blocks, or pages, of 16Kb each, and the 64Kb RAM window holds any four of these pages at a time. Earlier in the chapter, Figure 7.2 illustrated how these four expanded-memory pages may be accessed as if they were physically installed within the reserved memory area.

Note that expanded memory has no permanent memory address, and that the four pages which appear to be within the reserved memory area are varying continually, according to the needs of the software program utilizing the memory. Therefore, expanded memory does not lend itself to the routine memory check performed by the POST procedure. Most such memory expansion adapters are supplied with a separate diagnostics diskette which may be used for a thorough checkout of all the expanded memory.

Although there's little reason to do so, expanded memory might be checked during POST by temporarily reconfiguring it as though it were extended memory.

For help in LIM troubleshooting, refer to the Expanded Memory Diagnostics section later in this chapter (page 264).

Reconfiguring Conventional Memory. The performance of some commercially available software may be optimized by allocating up to 384Kb on an expansion memory card to take the place of conventional memory from 256K to 640K. To do so, the AT jumper (J18 in Figure 6.3(d)) must be set in the 256K position.

It may also be possible to transfer some of the expanded memory into the extended memory area. This might be desirable when installing a 2Mb memory adapter in a 256Kb system with no other memory expansion adapters present. In this case, the first 384 would be used to fill out the conventional memory area, with the remainder of the first 1Mb (640Kb) used as an electronic, or virtual, disk in extended memory. This leaves the remaining 1Mb for use as expanded memory.

When memory is assigned as described here, the conventional and extended memory segments will be checked during POST, while the remaining expanded memory area will not be checked.

MEMORY DIAGNOSTICS

In most cases, a defective memory chip will be encountered during the start-up POST procedure. In the event of a ROM or RAM chip failure, a multidigit error code will be displayed on screen. On the PC, the error code may appear briefly and then be replaced by a PARITY CHECK x display. Therefore, if you did not see the error code, turn the system off and back on again. Watch the screen closely and jot the number down before it disappears. Keep in mind that if the failed chip happens to be in one of the first few banks, the error code may come and go before the display has a chance to warm up sufficiently to show the error code. If you have trouble viewing the error code, turn the display on first and let it warm up. Then turn on the system itself and watch for the error code.

ROM Error Codes

During POST, a failed ROM chip will display an error code in the following format:

*xx*00 ROM

   or

*xx*000 ROM

where each x may be any hexadecimal character.

The error code itself indicates the address of the failed ROM chip, which may be further identified by referring to Table 7.7. If the table localizes the failure to a specific chip, its location may be found in one of the system board diagrams seen in Figure 6.3 in the last chapter. However, not all ROM problems can be identified by an error code, since certain ROM failures will

Table 7.7 ROM Error Codes and Messages

Error code	Computer	Location of faulty ROM
C8000 ROM	all	Hard disk drive adapter
CC000 ROM	PC, XT	PC Network
IO ROM CC000	XT 286, AT	PC Network
F600 ROM	PC	U29
F800 ROM	PC	U30
FA00 ROM	PC	U31
FC00 ROM	PC	U32
F*xx* ROM	PC	System board
ROM Error	all	System board
IO ROM *xxxxx*	XT 286, AT	Power–related (Chapter 5)

prevent the system from booting. In this case, there is no easy way to diagnose the problem, and outside servicing will be required.

RAM Error Codes

When the last three numbers in the error code are 201, this is a verification that the fault is in the RAM area. The numbers preceding the 201 are the code that identifies the specific chip that has failed. The complete error code will be displayed in the format seen here:

Computer	Error code format
PC	*xxx* 201
XT	*xxxxx xx* 201
AT and PS/2	*xxxxxx xxxx* 201

where each *x* may be any hexadecimal character (0-9, A-F).

In every case, the first one or two characters indicate the bank or expansion adapter, and the last two or four characters before the 201 point to the specific chip that has failed. If you do not wish to go further, simply make a note of the number so that your service person can make a speedy repair. However, if you are able to localize the error to a specific expansion adapter, you may wish to remove it for servicing, while keeping the rest of the system up and running. In such a case, the system should be reconfigured to take the diminished memory capacity into account.

If you prefer to make the replacement yourself, refer to the sections immediately following for further information. In checking error codes, make sure you follow the sequence as it appears here. In other words, check the system board before checking the memory expansion adapters, and then check each of the memory expansion adapters in the order indicated. The correct checking sequence is important, since a code beginning with the same digit(s) may be applied to more than one adapter. If the adapters are checked out of sequence, the code may not be valid.

Multiple-Chip Error Code. If the final characters in the error code do not agree with any of the numbers in the appropriate figures and charts in the pages following, then more than one chip in the indicated bank needs to be replaced. In an otherwise properly functioning computer, this is quite an unlikely occurrence, unless the chips were just installed and are the wrong kind, improperly seated, or backward. Therefore, make a careful visual inspection before doing anything else.

If the visual inspection fails to turn up an obvious error, then consult the section entitled Multiple-Chip Error Locator (page 273) for information on how to identify the chips causing such a failure. And if this type of error occurs some time after the chips were placed in service, then the problem may lie elsewhere on the board containing the chip sockets. In this case, outside servicing is indicated.

Do not discard any removed chips until you have read the section entitled Chip Recovery Notes in Chapter 6 (page 226).

Memory-Size Error. A *164 Memory Size* error message indicates the system is improperly configured. Disregard any other messages and run the Setup program on the diagnostics diskette before continuing. If the display of system and expansion memory agrees with what you have physically installed in your system, then perhaps one or more configuration switches on an expansion adapter are set incorrectly.

RAM Error Codes on PS/2 Systems

MCA Systems. All RAM chips are permanently soldered in place on one to four removable memory modules. In the event of a memory error, there is little reason to isolate the specific chip that has failed, since the entire module containing that chip must be replaced anyway. In most cases, the easiest procedure is to simply remove all memory modules except the one or two required for minimum configuration operation. Then reinstall the remaining modules (or module pairs) until the memory error reappears. If the error is isolated to a pair of modules, swap the modules one-at-a-time with another pair known to be good in order to find the specific module containing the defective chip.

During POST, the system may lock up part way through the memory check, with a screen display of *n* KB OK (where *n* indicates the amount of memory that was successfully checked before the lockup). For example, in a system with two *x*Kb modules, a lockup at a number less than *x* would indicate a failure on the first module; a number greater than *x* indicates the second module.

ISA Systems. The same general comments apply to PS/2 ISA systems, except that the first 128Kb are either installed on six removable chips (model 25) or soldered in place on the system board (model 30). In either case, if there is an error within the first 128Kb, the two 256Kb memory modules are automatically readdressed downward to take the place of the onboard chip set, which is in turn disabled. In this case, the following error code and message is displayed during POST:

```
205-Memory Error (model 25)
205 Memory Remap (model 30)
```

PARITY-CHECK Error Message

Parity checking is an error-detection procedure in which the correct performance of a block of memory is verified. In each memory bank, eight RAM modules fulfill user memory requirements, while the ninth module is the so-called parity module, whose sole function is to check the performance of the preceding eight modules.

Although the parity check may detect an error, it does not identify the specific RAM module that has actually failed. The best it can do is to identify the general area in which the failure occurred, as seen here:

Screen Display		Meaning
PC, XT, AT	PS/2	
PARITY CHECK 1	110	Failure is on the system board
PARITY CHECK 2	111	Failure is on an expansion adapter

PC Parity-Check Display. As noted earlier, the error code that briefly appears before the PARITY CHECK *x* display identifies the chip that failed. Make a note of that number and then follow the directions on memory-error interpretation given below.

XT and AT Parity-Check Display. If the system is able to identify the specific chip that failed and display the appropriate error code, no parity-check message will appear. Otherwise, the hexadecimal number below the message may give additional information:

```
PARITY CHECK x
xxxxx
```

   or

```
PARITY CHECK x
?????
```

If the line below the parity-check message displays a hexadecimal number, then the error has been localized to a specific memory bank on the system board or on an expansion adapter. In that case, follow the procedures given below, but with this important exception: replace all the RAM chips in the bank containing the error. In other words, don't attempt to further localize the problem to a single chip within the failed bank.

If the five characters in the second line are ?????, try one of the following two procedures, as appropriate.

Screen display	Meaning and procedure
PARITY CHECK 1 ?????	The problem has been traced to the system board, but not to a specific RAM bank. Replace all the RAM chips on the board; if the same message is still seen, the system board itself must be replaced.
PARITY CHECK 2 ?????	The problem is on one of the memory-expansion adapters. Removing all of them and reconfiguring the system for system board memory should only temporarily solve the problem. If so, then reinstall the memory-expansion adapters one at a time, until the message again appears. When the adapter causing the PARITY CHECK 2 message is identified, replace all its RAM chips. If the message persists, the adapter itself must be replaced. If the removal of all memory-expansion adapters does not remove the PARITY CHECK 2 message, outside servicing is required.
PARITY ERROR xxxx:yyyy. SYSTEM HALTED	A message in this format (or similar) is seen on some IBM-compatible systems, indicating a failure at segment:offset xxxx:yyyy.

Segment:Offset Memory Error

If a memory error is reported at a segment:offset that does not cause a similar message during POST, it's possible the problem is actually in expanded memory (described below) but is being reported via an expanded memory driver resident at the displayed location. To verify this, use the DOS 4.00 MEM /PROGRAM command or the MEMMAP.EXE utility described later in the chapter (page 280) to see what program occupies the area where the trouble is being reported.

EXPANDED MEMORY DIAGNOSTICS

As noted above, expanded memory is made accessible through a 64Kb window within the reserved memory area. In order to take advantage of such memory, the user must define the following parameters:

The segment address of the specific memory block (or blocks) to be used for the window

The segment addresses of two 16Kb memory pages required by DOS 4.00

The number of 16Kb pages of expanded memory to be allocated

These parameters must be entered in the XMA2EMS.SYS driver line in a configuration file, as was described in Chapter 4 (page 87). If the line is not already in place, then it must be inserted before expanded memory can be used.

EMS Conflicts

If one or more of the listed address segments conflict with the address of some installed adapter, an EMS (Expanded Memory Specification) conflict message will be displayed on screen shortly after the successful completion of POST. One or more of the following message lines may be displayed:

```
Specified page address conflicts with installed adapter at address nnnn
Possible 16KB page available at address nnnn
Possible 64KB frame available at address nnnn
Press any key to continue . . .
Error in CONFIG.SYS line x
```

One or more of the first few message lines may be repeated several times, thus suggesting various segment addresses (*nnnn*, above) that may be substituted in line *x* of the CONFIG.SYS file to clear up the conflict. Note that in the event of an EMS conflict, the system pauses so that the conflict messages remain on the screen. You may either jot down the displayed segment addresses and take corrective action as described below, or simply press any key to continue booting the system, in which case expanded memory will not be available for use.

64Kb Frame Conflict. If a `64KB frame available` message is seen, substitute the suggested *nnnn* for whatever value currently appears in your configuration file. But if a 64-Kbyte frame is not available, then note how many `16KB page available` messages are seen. In the configuration file, delete the FRAME parameter and in its place write the following line:

`P0=nnnn P1=nnnn P2=nnnn P4=nnnn`

This new parameter list permits up to four 16Kb page segment addresses to be defined. Assuming there are at least four such page segments seen on screen, jot down the addresses and substitute them for each *nnnn* in the line above. If fewer than four pages are available, then truncate the line as required.

P254 or P255 Page Conflict. An EMS conflict may also occur at one of the two 16Kb pages reserved for DOS, as defined by the P254 and P255 parameters in the XMA2EMS.SYS line of the configuration file. This is indicated when one of the `page address conflicts` messages displays a segment that appears after either the P254= or the P255= in the file. In this case, simply substitute one of the suggested `Possible 16Kb page` segments for the segment causing the conflict.

Resume Operations. Once the XMA2EMS.SYS line in the configuration file has been corrected, the system must be rebooted so that the new values will be recognized. After doing so, no further EMS conflict messages should be seen. However, if another conflict message is displayed, then further corrections are required.

Faulty Chip Location Procedures

This section will help you find a failed pre-PS/2 memory adapter, and then lead you directly to the specific chip on that adapter that has failed. However, although a memory-error code is also valid for a non-IBM memory adapter, the figures and tables seen here will be of little use, unless that adapter is physically identical to an IBM adapter. Since this is unlikely,

Table 7.8 Error Code Area Locator *

PC1	PC2	XT	AT	Failed chip is in	See
00xx	0xxx	0xxxx	00xxxx – 03xxxx	system board, bank 0	Fig. 7.8(a)
04xx	1xxx	1xxxx	04xxxx – 07xxxx	system board, bank 1	Fig. 7.8(a)
08xx	2xxx	2xxxxx	– –	system board, bank 2	Fig. 7.8(a)
0Cxx	3xxx	3xxxx	– –	system board, bank 3	Fig. 7.8(a)
10xx – 84xx	40xx – 94xx	40xxx – 94xxx		memory exp. option	Tbl. 7.9 – 12
– –	– –	– –	08xxxx – 09xxxx	128Kb exp. option	Fig. 7.8(b)
– –	– –	– –	10xxxx – 17xxxx	512Kb exp. option 1	Table 7.13
– –	– –	– –	18xxxx – 1Fxxxx	512Kb exp. option 2	Table 7.13
– –	– –	– –	20xxxx – 27xxxx	512Kb exp. option 3	Table 7.13
– –	– –	– –	28xxxx – 2Fxxxx	512Kb exp. option 4	Table 7.13
– –	– –	– –	30xxxx – 37xxxx	512Kb exp. option 5	Table 7.13

* In the column for your computer, find the error code whose first one or two characters match the error code on your screen display. Consult the indicated figure and/or table to identify the specific chip that has failed.

the section below, entitled Memory Code Interpretation, may be of more use in finding the failed chip on any memory adapter not specifically discussed here.

In Table 7.8, find the specific error code that best matches your display. As usual, x may be any hexadecimal character, PC1 refers to an IBM PC with a 16Kb–64Kb system board, and PC2 refers to PCs with 64Kb–256Kb system boards.

The first step is to find the general area in which the failed chip is located, using Table 7.8 as a guide. If the failure is on the system board, then consult Figure 7.7 to find the specific chip that has failed within the indicated bank. Note that the 128Kb adapter is checked as though it were part of the system board. If any other memory-expansion adapter failure is indicated, then each one of these must be checked in the following sequence:

		Location of appropriate guide	
Computer	Checking sequence	Table	Figure
PC, XT	All 32Kb adapters	7.9	-
	All 64Kb adapters	7.10	-
	All 64/256Kb adapters	7.11 and 7.12	7.8
AT	The indicated 512Kb adapter	7.13	7.9

In each case, compare the first character(s) in the specified figure with the error code that was displayed on your screen. When you find the column that matches your error code, read the switch settings listed in that column

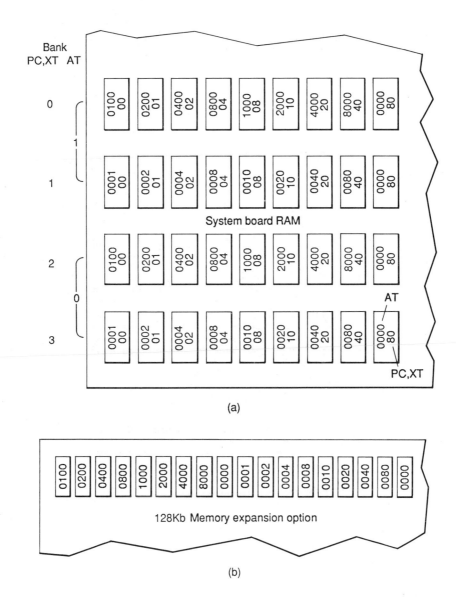

(a)

(b)

Figure 7.7. ISA system board RAM replacement guide. Locate the bank that you identified in Table 7.8. In that bank only, replace the chip whose number matches the final two (PC, AT) or four (AT) characters of your error code. (a) On the AT system board, and (b) on the 128Kb option, a 0000 code requires the replacement of two chips.

Table 7.9 32Kb Memory-Expansion Option Check *

Settings valid for	If the first two characters are	Check these switch settings 1	2	3	4	5
PC1 only	10 or 14	On	On	On	Off	On
	18 or 1C	On	On	On	Off	Off
	20 or 24	On	On	Off	On	On
	28 or 2C	On	On	Off	On	Off
	30 or 34	On	On	Off	On	On
	38 or 3C	On	On	Off	Off	Off
PC1, PC2, XT	40 or 44	On	Off	On	On	On
	48 or 4C	On	Off	On	On	Off
	50 or 54	On	Off	On	Off	On
	58 or 5C	On	Off	On	Off	Off
	60 or 64	On	Off	Off	On	On
	68 or 6C	On	Off	Off	On	Off
	70 or 74	On	Off	Off	Off	On
	78 or 7C	On	Off	Off	Off	Off
	80 or 84	Off	On	On	On	On
PC2, XT	88 or 8C	Off	On	On	On	Off
	90 or 94	Off	On	On	Off	On

* Find the first two characters of your error code. Compare your option's switch settings against those listed in the same row as your error code. If the settings agree, the option must be replaced. If not, check all other 32Kb cards, and then proceed to the next appropriate test (Table 7.10 or 7.11).

Table 7.10 64Kb Memory-Expansion Option Check *

Settings valid for	If the first character is	Check these switch settings 1	2	3	4
PC1 only	1	On	On	On	Off
	2	On	On	Off	On
	3	On	On	Off	Off
	4	On	Off	On	On
PC1, PC2, XT	5	On	Off	On	Off
	6	On	Off	Off	On
	7	On	Off	Off	Off
PC2, XT	8	Off	On	On	On
	9	Off	On	On	Off

* Find the first character of your error code. Compare your option's switch settings against those listed in the same row as your error code. If the settings agree, the option must be replaced. If not, check all other 64Kb cards, and then proceed to the next test (Table 7.11).

Table 7.11 64/256Kb Memory-Expansion Option Check *

Settings valid for	If the first character is	Check these switch settings 1	2	3	4
PC1 only	1 to 4	On	On	On	Off
	5 to 7	On	Off	On	Off
PC2 only	4 to 7	On	Off	On	On
	8 or 9	Off	On	On	On

* Find the first character of your error code. Compare your option's switch settings against those listed in the same row as your error code. If the settings agree, the option has a failing RAM chip, which may be located using Figure 7.9. If not, check all other 64/256Kb cards. If no match is found, then the system board needs servicing.

Table 7.12 64/256Kb Memory-Expansion Bank Check *

If the first character is PC1	PC2	Failed chip is in
1 or 5	4 or 8	Bank 0
2 or 6	5 or 9	Bank 1
3 or 7	6 only	Bank 2
4 only	7 only	Bank 3

* Using the appropriate column above, find the first character of your error code. This identifies the bank containing the failed RAM chip. Locate that bank in Figure 7.9. Find and replace the chip whose number matches the final two characters of your error code.

Table 7.13 512Kb Memory-Expansion Adapter/Bank Check *

First two characters	Adapter	Bank	Switch settings 1	2	3	4	5	6	7	8
10 to 13	1	0	On	On	On	Off	On	On	On	On
14 to 17	1	1	On	On	On	Off	On	Off	On	Off
18 to 1B	2	0	On	On	On	Off	Off	On	On	On
1C to 1F	2	1	On	On	On	Off	Off	Off	On	Off
20 to 23	3	0	On	On	Off	On	On	On	On	On
24 to 27	3	1	On	On	Off	On	On	Off	On	Off
28 to 2B	4	0	On	On	Off	On	Off	On	On	On
2C to 2F	4	1	On	On	Off	On	Off	Off	On	Off
30 to 33	5	0	On	On	Off	Off	On	On	On	On
34 to 37	5	1	On	On	Off	Off	On	Off	On	Off

* Find the first two characters of your error code. On the indicated Adapter and Bank, compare the switch settings against those listed in the same row as your error code. If the settings agree, the bank contains the failed chip, which must be replaced. Refer to Figure 7.10 to locate the specific chip.

and compare them with the switch settings on your expansion adapter. If the settings match, then you have found the faulty adapter. If this is a 32Kb or 64Kb adapter, it must be replaced. If it is a 64/256Kb or 512Kb adapter, further testing may identify the specific chip that has failed. Consult Tables 7.11 and 7.12 and Figure 7.8 for 64/256Kb adapters or Table 7.13 and Figure 7.9 for 512Kb adapters.

If the switch settings on your memory adapter do not match those in the appropriate column, then the adapter is not faulty, and you may proceed to the next one. Switch settings not listed are not relevant for these tests.

To begin, consult the sequence list above to find the first adapter to be checked. Then proceed to the next one, until all tests have been made. If you complete the entire testing sequence without finding a faulty chip, then the problem is likely on the system board, which will require outside servicing.

After locating and correcting an error, run the diagnostics program again. If the same error code is seen, then there may be one of two problems:

1. If you have just replaced a 32Kb or 64Kb memory-expansion adapter, the system board is probably at fault and will require servicing.

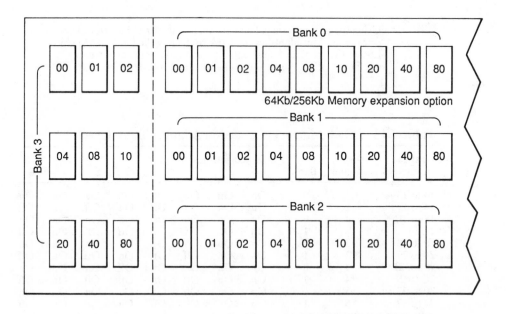

Figure 7.8. 64/256Kb memory-expansion RAM replacement guide. Locate the bank that you identified in Table 7.12. In that bank only, replace the chip whose number matches the final two characters of your error code.

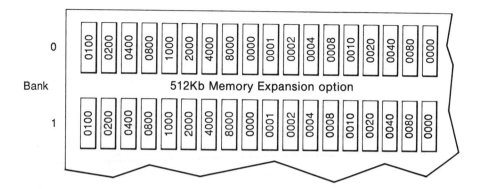

Figure 7.9.   512Kb memory-expansion RAM replacement guide. Locate the bank that you identified in Table 7.13. In that bank only, replace the chip whose number matches the final four characters of your error code. If the code is 0000, two chips must be replaced.

2. If you have just replaced a single RAM chip on a 64/256Kb or 512Kb memory-expansion adapter, it is likely that the first character of the error code was erroneous and directed you to the wrong bank. Replace the equivalent chip in each of the other banks, one at a time, until the problem is corrected.

Whenever a newly installed RAM module does not correct a memory error, don't overlook the fact that the new module itself may be defective. If the same error symptom remains, try installing another RAM module in the same location.

MEMORY CONFIGURATION NOTES

The section deals with various aspects of memory configuration that go a bit beyond routine diagnostics and troubleshooting. This information is presented here in order to assist the reader to relate the switch settings discussed above with those found on various memory adapters not directly discussed in this chapter.

Error Code Interpretation

The displayed memory error code can be interpreted to discover the address at which the faulty chip resides. This may be of some use in finding a failed chip on a non-IBM memory adapter, or when more than one chip in a memory bank has failed, resulting in a multiple-chip error code.

Table 7.8 illustrated the formats used by IBM personal computers to display a memory error code. In every case, the first two characters are a two-byte hexadecimal error code which points to the starting address of the bank in which the failed chip resides. To find the specific bank, ignore the remaining characters and multiply the value of the first two bytes, *BB*, as indicated here.

Computer	Error code	Multiply BB by
PC	*BBxx*	4
XT	*BBxxx xx*	4
AT and PS/2	*BBxxxx xxxx*	64

The following are some specific examples of how to identify the bank containing the failed chip. Of course, the specific adapter containing that bank will depend on the amount of memory on each installed memory adapter.

PC and XT Bank Locator. A memory error code of 0C*xx* (hexadecimal 0C = decimal 12) indicates an error in the bank starting at address 12 × 4 = 48K. On a PC1 system board with 64 Kbytes of system board memory, each bank (labeled 0–4) contains 16Kb, so this code would point to bank 3. On a PC2 or an XT with 256 Kbytes of system board memory, the same error code would indicate a chip in bank 0, since each bank contains 64 Kbytes.

A 50*xx* code would point to a chip in the bank beginning at (decimal) 80 × 4 = 320K, and so on. As noted above, the actual location of this bank depends on what sort of memory-expansion devices are installed in your system.

AT Bank Locator. A memory error code of hexadecimal 24*xxxx xxxx* indicates an error in the bank starting at decimal 36 × 64 = 2304K. In a system containing several 512Kb memory-expansion adapters, this would place the failed chip in the second bank on the third adapter. Of course, it would lie elsewhere if a different set of adapters were installed.

Chip Locator. Once the suspect memory bank has been located, convert the error code's last two (PC and XT) or four (AT) hexadecimal characters into a binary string. For example,

80 = 1000 0000
2000 = 0010 0000 0000 0000

Each binary 1 indicates the position of a chip that has failed.

The user's guide accompanying most memory-expansion devices usually labels the chip positions as 0 through 7, or 0 through 15. In addition, one or two chips are labeled P, for parity. Therefore, in the above examples, the 80 error code points to chip 7, and the 2000 code points to chip 13. In each case, the chip count begins at the extreme right character in the string, which represents chip 0.

If the error code segment just described reads 00 or 0000, then the parity chip(s) in the suspect bank must be replaced.

Keep in mind that the chips on the adapter are not necessarily found in a physically sequential order. For example, the sequence on the IBM 128Kb Memory Expansion Option is 8–15, P, 0–7, P. So although the 2000 error code mentioned above points to chip 13, on the adapter this chip is the sixth one in the row of 18 chips. Therefore, it's important to double-check your adapter's actual layout before attempting a chip replacement.

Multiple-Chip Error Locator. Since the simultaneous failure of more than one memory chip is unlikely, this chapter's charts and figures confine themselves to the codes indicating a single chip failure. However, if more than one chip has indeed failed, then the last part of the error code will simply represent a binary string with more than a single 1 in it. For example, a code of A4, or binary 1010 0100, would indicate that the three chips in positions 7, 5, and 2 are defective.

ISA Memory Board Switch Settings

This section may be of some use to readers who wish to go beyond the memory diagnostics and troubleshooting so far described. However, since automatic configuration has done away with the vagaries of switch settings, PS/2 owners may smugly disregard what follows.

It should be kept in mind that the switch settings discussed here are based on representative samples of available memory expansion devices, and do not necessarily hold for all such devices on the market. If there is a conflict between the procedures discussed here and the documentation for a specific device, then the information presented here should not be followed.

In the figures and charts given earlier in this chapter, the switch settings used to define each memory adapter's starting address are simply the ones supported by IBM documentation. However, most memory-expansion devices—IBM or otherwise—can be configured to start at some other address, subject to the requirement that all memory be contiguous, and that there is no memory overlap.

Starting Address Configuration. In many cases, an eight-position switch block on the adapter is used to define the starting address, by setting the first seven (sometimes only four) switches according to the instructions in the user's manual. Position eight is often reserved for some other function, such as parity enabling, and should not be considered when defining the starting address.

Calculate the starting address by reading the switches from left to right, with each switch representing a descending power of 2. Usually, for calculations, Off = logical 1 and On = logical 0. (Elsewhere in this book, switch settings are usually specified in terms of the physical position, with On represented by 1, and Off by 0.) Therefore, the first seven switches on a single 512-Kbyte Memory Expansion Option are probably found in the following positions:

Switch positions	Read as
On, On, On, Off, On, On, On	0001000

Since this type of adapter is usually intended to start at address 1024K, it may be inferred that 0001000 represents 2^{20} (that is, 1024K). If so, then the starting address for the second such adapter should be 0001100, or $2^{20} + 2^{19} = 1536$K. Figure 7.10(a) illustrates one of the switch blocks on the 512K adapter.

IBM documentation sometimes includes a chart, which identifies the starting address switches with a prefix of A or LA. Thus, switch A17 represents 2^{17} (on some adapters), or switch LA23 is 2^{23} (on others). With still other IBM adapters, this identification appears only on the accompanying logic diagram. Non-IBM manufacturers may or may not publish the numeric values of the addressing switches. Nevertheless, it should be possible to figure out the significance of each switch and to verify it by checking against the table of switch settings found in some documentation.

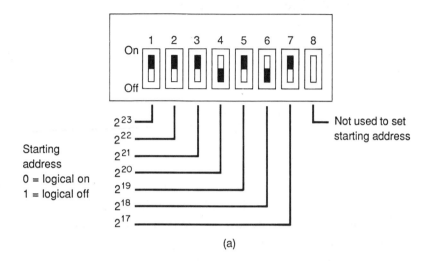

(a)

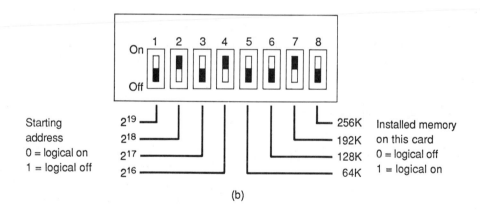

(b)

Figure 7.10. Configuration switches on typical ISA memory-expansion cards. On the 512Kb card (a), the first seven switches set the starting address, which in this example is 1,280K. On the IBM 64/256Kb card (b), the first four switches set the starting address, and the next four specify the amount of memory on the card. Note the reversal of switching logic between the first and the last four switches. As seen here, the starting address is 640K and there are 192 Kbytes of memory on the card.

For calculation convenience, it may be helpful to mentally subtract powers of ten from the exponent, to quickly visualize the address as it would be expressed in Kbytes or Mbytes. Thus,

$$2^{21} = 2097152 \text{ and } 2^{19} = 524288$$
$$2^{11} = 2048Kb \qquad 2^{9} = 512Kb$$
$$2^{1} = 2Mb \qquad 2^{-1} = 0.5Mb$$

The purpose of doing all this is of course to be able to come up with switch settings that may not be listed, or to figure out an adapter's switch settings later on, in the absence of documentation.

On board Memory Configuration. On some boards a few switch positions are set aside to define the amount of memory installed on the board. This setting becomes especially critical if the board is not fully populated with chips, and another board is installed at a higher memory address. The switches allow the unused (or perhaps defective) space to be disabled, thus permitting the next board to start at the correct address, with no memory conflicts.

Taking the IBM 64/256Kb Memory Expansion Option as an example, the first four switches on the block are used for setting the starting address, and the next four specify the amount of installed memory, as shown in Figure 7.10b.

Address-Shifting Techniques

When a memory chip fails and there is no replacement chip on hand, the contiguous memory requirement precludes the use of memory at any address beyond the failed chip. As a temporary solution, disable the bank containing the defective chip by giving it a starting address that is higher than any in current use. Next, move the address of the highest good bank down to take the place of the disabled bank. If the good bank is not the same memory size as the disabled bank, then it may be necessary to reconfigure every bank downward until the memory gap is closed. In any case, there is now a break in contiguous memory immediately after the last good bank of chips, as illustrated in Figure 7.11.

Reconfigure the system, deducting the amount of memory residing in the defective bank. On subsequent system reboots, the POST procedure's memory check will conclude successfully before it reaches the defective bank.

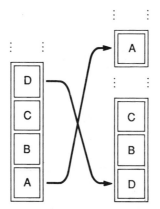

Figure 7.11. An example of memory address shifting to remove a disabled ISA memory bank from the contiguous memory area. If bank A contains a defective chip, switch it to a higher address, and configure bank D to take its place. Then reconfigure the system to recognize only the three contiguous banks of memory seen in the illustration.

Of course, if the defective bank is the only one on the board in the first place, simply remove the board until a good chip can be obtained. Otherwise, if there is more than one set of addressing switches on the bank, the procedure just described can be put to use. For example, the IBM 512Kb Memory Expansion Option consists of two banks (0 and 1) of chips, each with its own switch block. If two such devices were installed, we might refer to the four banks as, say, A through D, as seen here:

Bank identification		Starting address (Kb)
A	bank 0 on adapter 1	1024
B	bank 1 on adapter 1	1280
C	bank 0 on adapter 2	1536
D	bank 1 on adapter 2	1792

Given a failure in bank A, bank D can be used in its place, while banks B and C remain as is. Set the bank D switches for a 1024K starting address, and then set bank A for any starting address greater than 1792K, thus placing it above, and out of, the contiguous memory block.

AT System Board Memory Swapping. If a failure on the AT system board occurs, the obvious solution is of course to borrow a chip from the highest memory bank on an installed adapter, as described above. However, if the failure is in the second bank (bank 1) on the system board, it's also possible to disable the entire bank by moving jumper J18 (seen in Figure 6.3d). Having done so, a 256Kb memory adapter, or either bank of a 512Kb adapter, may be used in its place, simply by configuring its starting address to begin at 256Kb. On the 512Kb adapter switch block shown in Figure 7.10a, this would be accomplished by setting switch position 6 (2^{18}) only to the logical On (down) position.

This alternative might be considered if the failure is traced to the system board itself, rather than to a chip in bank 1.

SOFTWARE-RELATED MEMORY DIAGNOSTICS

Assuming that all system memory is properly installed, that no chips or modules are defective, and that system configuration is correct, there are still no shortage of memory problems that may be traced to the software in use at the time the problem surfaced. For example, given the DOS 640-Kbyte ceiling and the tendency of programs to expand to fill whatever space is available (and then some), most users will soon enough discover one or more variations on the familiar "out of memory" theme, a few of which are mentioned below.

However, if a memory error message seems to be contradicted by the amount of memory that you know is available, it's possible your system is under attack by a computer virus. Refer to the Virus Attacks section of Chapter 9 for more details.

```
Program too big to fit in memory.
```

There's nothing mysterious about this DOS error message; the program you are trying to load is simply too big to fit in the space available.

```
Not enough memory to run program.
```

This message (or similar) may be seen during an otherwise-uneventful word-processing session, when a memory-hungry graphics page preview option is attempted. The system has enough memory for routine operation, but not enough for this option—hence the message.

A less-obvious problem may turn up if an option loads successfully, yet some, but not all, all of its features won't work. However, no advisory message is seen.

```
Insufficient Memory. Remove any RAM-Resident Software.
```

Another variation on the same theme, but here the program at least lets you know what's going on.

```
Critical error: Memory management blown.
```

Despite the fatalistic tone, it's just more of the same. In this case, the message shows up during an attempt to download soft fonts to a laser printer by running an external font-loading program from within a word processor.

No doubt there are many other messages to be seen with other software. But no matter how the message is worded, the bottom line is the same: the system just doesn't have enough free memory to accommodate whatever it is you are trying to do.

TSR Problems

If up until now you thought your system had plenty of memory, the problem may be that one or more TSR (terminate and stay resident) programs have taken up residence in your RAM, thus getting in the way of whatever it is you are trying to do. TSR programs are often loaded via your AUTOEXEC.BAT file, or may be loaded later on, as needed. The problem is that once you are done with the TSR, it often doesn't release its space for other purposes (hence the name TSR).

In such a situation, use the "go to DOS" command (if there is one) and then run the DOS CHKDSK to display the amount of free memory. It is important to do this from within the program you are currently using, since this program is also tying up RAM. And in the case of a word processor, the document itself should be loaded.

You may discover a computing Catch-22: with the program comfortably sitting in RAM and a document loaded for editing, there's not enough room left over for the additional feature you were trying to execute. The solution? Close the document and quit the program to free up the space. But now the feature itself is useless.

Since that's not much of a solution, it might help to examine the contents of your CONFIG.SYS and/or AUTOEXEC.BAT files to see if either file has loaded any space eaters that can be removed to free some memory for other use. A few suggestions are listed below, preceded by a look at a new DOS command which is almost—despite some confusing aspects—a mini-course in memory management. A basic understanding of its capabilities will give the reader a better idea of how to troubleshoot some memory-related problems. But those who would rather not bother can skip directly to the Memory Recovery Techniques section (page 283).

DOS MEM Command

The MEM command, introduced in DOS 4.00, displays information similar to that seen with CHKDSK. However, the utility goes beyond CHKDSK to show extensive memory usage information when involved as seen here:

```
C>MEM /PROGRAM
```

As a typical example, the memory allocation in an IBM AT (640Kb RAM) is shown in Table 7.14. The four columns in the upper section of the table show how space is taken up by the system files, assorted device drivers, COMMAND.COM, and other memory-resident programs installed via CONFIG.SYS and AUTOEXEC.BAT files. The lower left-hand portion is simply a continuation of the same table. The lower right-hand portion shows the same space after loading a popular word processor.

To verify the difference between system memory and available memory, a few lines of math are inserted in the lower left-hand corner of the table and summarized in Table 7.15a. These lines are not seen in the MEM display itself.

Note that decimal 16 must be added to get either sum to agree with the desired value. Furthermore, the sum of any address and size given in the table (starting at address 00BAB0) doesn't add up to the address in the next column. A few more definitions are needed to explain what's going on.

The Memory Block and Memory-Control Block. Storage space is allocated in *memory blocks,* each block named as shown in Table 7.14. Each block begins with a 16-byte MCB (*memory-control block*) describing the contents of the block itself. The *size* column in Table 7.14 indicates how much data is stored in each block, but it doesn't include the block's 16 MCB bytes. Therefore, one must increase each size by hexadecimal 10 (decimal 16), then add that number to the block address to find the address of the next block. In either set of columns, the total system memory is the sum of the free memory starting address, the free memory size, and its 16-byte MCB.

To take a closer look at a memory-control block, the DOS debug utility can display its contents. For example, Table 7.14 shows the starting address of COMMAND.COM as 018880, which is 1888:0000 in segment:offset format. Load DEBUG and then type D 1888:0 to display the following line (or similar):

```
1888:0000 4D 89 18 64 01 3E DD 02-43 4F 4D 4D 41 4E 44 00 M..d....COMMAND.
```

Table 7.14 Example of a DOS MEM/PROGRAM Report

Address	Name	Size	Type	
000000		000400	Interrupt Vector	
000400		000100	ROM Communication Area	
000500		000200	DOS Communication Area	
000700	IBMBIO	0025D0	System Program	
002CD0	IBMDOS	008DE0	System Program	
00BAB0	IBMBIO	00A4B0	System Data	*(System data size is sum of 11 items following, plus 11 MCBs.)*
	ANSI	0011B0	DEVICE=	
	EGA	000BB0	DEVICE=	
	A10-20	000700	DEVICE=	
	VDISK	000890	DEVICE=	
	DRIVER	0000E0	DEVICE=	
	AMDEK	002C50	DEVICE=	
		000380	FILES=	
		000100	FCBS=	
		003410	BUFFERS=	
		000480	LASTDRIVE=	
		000CD0	STACKS=	

Listing continues, as seen here. *

Address	Name	Size	Type
015F70	IBMDOS	000030	-- Free --
015FB0	SCRLK	000040	Environment
016000	IBMDOS	000030	-- Free --
016040	FASTOPEN	002830	Program
018880	COMMAND	001640	Program
019ED0	COMMAND	000100	Environment
019FE0	SCRLK	0001C0	Program
01A1B0	SETVID	0000C0	Environment
01A280	SETVID	000250	Program
01A4E0	MEM	0000B0	Environment
01A5A0	MEM	012FD0	Program
02D580	IBMDOS	072A70	-- Free --
185728		77776	
469616		469616	
16		16	
655360 *(system)*		547408 *(available)*	

(Decimal sum of indicated hex values, plus 16, gives 640Kb system memory and largest executable program size.)

After loading word processor, listing as seen here.

Address	Name	Size	Type
015F70	WS2	000010	Data
015F90	WS2	000010	Data
015FB0	SCRLK	000040	Environment
016000	WS2	000010	Data
016020	WS2	000010	Data
016040	FASTOPEN	002830	Program
018880	COMMAND	001640	Program
019ED0	COMMAND	000100	Environment
019FE0	SCRLK	0001C0	Program
01A1B0	COMMAND	000040	Data
01A200	SETVID	0000C0	Environment
01A2D0	SETVID	000250	Program
01A530	WS2	0000C0	Data
01A600	WS2	03CA70	Program
057080	WS2	03C7D0	Data
057860	WS2	0005A0	Data
(additional WS2 data addresses here)			
05EEE0	WS2	000020	Data
05EF10	WS2	0000D0	Environment
05EFF0	COMMAND	0000F0	Data
05F0F0	COMMAND	001640	Program
060740	COMMAND	0000D0	Environment
060820	MEM	0000E0	Environment
060910	MEM	012FD0	Program
0738F0	IBMDOS	0207C0	-- Free --
0940C0	WS2	00BB10	Data
09FBE0	WS2	000410	Data

547408 largest executable program size   210848 largest executable program size

* Blank lines inserted to aid comparison with righthand columns.

Table 7.15a Summary of Typical MEM Report of Starting Address and Size of Free Memory Area

Report summary	Before loading word processor		After loading* word processor	
	hex	decimal	hex	decimal
starting address †	02D580	185,728	0738F0	473,328
free memory size †	072A70	469,616	0207C0	133,056
To find total system memory:				
add decimal 16	10	16	10	16
CHKDSK total		655,360		606,400

† Data taken from Table 7.14.

Table 7.15b Typical CHKDSK Memory Reports

CHKDSK reports	Total memory (bytes)	Bytes free
After boot up	655,360	547,392
Word processor loaded	606,400	210,832
Document loaded	606,400	176,448

Note that the underlined bytes give the size of the block, as reported by MEM in the *size* column for the COMMAND.COM program. For comparison purposes, the appropriate portion of the column is also underlined.

Largest Executable Program. The MEM command also reports the size of the largest program that may be handled, given the current memory allocation. The figure is the sum of the non-TSR MEM program itself and the free space (IBMDOS) immediately following it, and is also derived at the bottom of Table 7.14. Here, each program's MCB must also be taken into account. But since one of them will be needed for whatever program gets loaded into the available space, the figure shown in the table is the sum of MEM and IBMDOS, plus one MCB only.

The *largest executable program* value displayed by MEM should agree with the *bytes free* given by CHKDSK. Again for comparison purposes, Table 7.15b shows the equivalent values reported by CHKDSK. Note that *in both parts of the table*, the total system memory figure is significantly less when the word processor is loaded, indicating a possible problem in memory management. To account for the missing memory, refer back to Table 7.14, where two memory blocks of data are seen at the bottom of the right-hand set of columns, following the free memory area. The starting address of the first of these blocks (hex 0940C0 = decimal 606,400) corresponds to the *total bytes memory* reported by CHKDSK. In other words, the blocks are lodged at the top of conventional system memory, thus limiting the size reported by CHKDSK.

Again, the DOS debug utility could be used to find out what's in these blocks. In this case, it happens to be nothing: the space has been locked out by a bug in the word processor.

By following the general procedures just described, it should be possible to get a very good idea of how any system uses its memory space, and if necessary, to find areas where space might be released for use by some other application.

Note: For readers who are not using DOS 4.01, *PC Magazine* offers a utility (MEMMAP.EXE) similar to the DOS MEM utility, which may be downloaded via modem.

Memory Recovery Techniques

The MEM utility can be quite valuable in identifying unneeded TSRs and getting an idea of how much space might be recovered by doing away with one or more of them. Generally, this involves editing your configuration and/or batch files, or possibly just rebooting the system to flush out TSRs that were loaded by other applications no longer in use.

A few deletion suggestions are offered here.

CONFIG.SYS file
- Delete device drivers that are not essential.
- Decrease the number of buffers, each of which takes up about 500+ bytes of memory.
- Move all buffers into expanded memory (if available) by appending the /X parameter (see the DOS manual for further details).

AUTOEXEC.BAT file
- Remove any memory-resident programs that you do not need for the particular application you are trying to run. These programs can be loaded later on, prior to use, via another batch file.
- Move TSR programs into expanded or high memory (see Memory-Management Utilities below for details).

Don't overlook the possibility that some previously executed program has not released some of the memory space it occupied. In case of doubt, reboot the system, then reload the program that displayed the memory error message. If the program runs successfully, then the space freed up by rebooting is sufficient to run the program. If not, there is still not enough room for it.

Memory-Management Utilities

In cases where sufficient conventional memory cannot be released for use, a number of third-party memory-management utilities can be used to overcome the 640Kb DOS barrier. By relocating TSRs and other utilities into the area beyond 640Kb, the equivalent amount of conventional memory is made available. One or more of the following options is usually available.

Conventional (User) Memory Extension. On systems with an EGA or VGA display adapter, 96Kb of the first 128Kb of video memory can be appended to the 640Kb conventional memory area. However, doing so restricts the video display to text mode only.

High (Reserved, UMB) Memory. Expanded memory or shadow RAM may be remapped into the 640–1,024Kb area, for use with TSR and other programs, thus freeing space within the conventional memory area.

High Memory Area (HMA). Programs can be loaded into the first 64Kb of extended memory, again releasing space below the 640Kb DOS ceiling.

The successful use of the memory-management utilities summarized above is very much a function of your specific system configuration and the capabilities of the utility itself. In case of doubt, carefully review the hardware and software in order to get an idea of what to expect.

DOS 5.0 Memory Management. Refer to the Memory Management section of Appendix A (page 646) for a review of DOS 5.0 memory management utilities.

8

DISKETTES AND
DISKETTE DRIVES

Before looking at diagnostics for diskettes and diskette drives, the chapter offers a brief review of how computer data is stored on a magnetic surface. To do this we will make some comparisons with the familiar old black vinyl LP (long-playing) phonograph record. But first, we must introduce a few terms that will be frequently encountered later on.

Diskettes and Hard Disks

The terms diskette, flexible diskette, and floppy disk refer to the familiar thin magnetic disk encased in a protective PVC (polyvinyl chloride) jacket or a plastic casing. The term diskette is used throughout this book.

By contrast, the magnetic medium in a hard disk drive is a nonreplaceable rigid disk which is factory installed in the drive. In IBM nomenclature, the device is referred to as a fixed disk, and sometimes as a hardfile. Throughout this book, the term hard disk is used, except when making a specific reference to the name of an IBM product or procedure.

Although more detailed information about hard disk drives will be found in Chapter 9, at least some of the information in this chapter may also be applied to the hard disk. In particular, most of the definitions given below apply to both types of storage systems. And at least one definition— cylinders, which usually applies just to the hard disk—is given here for purposes of comparison with the other definitions. Therefore, the beginning sections of this chapter should serve as an introduction both to what immediately follows and to Chapter 9.

Source and Target Diskettes

When copying files from one diskette to another, the diskette holding the files to be copied is referred to as the source diskette. The diskette that will contain the copied files is the target diskette. Of course, either term applies as well to files copied to or from a hard disk.

Tracks and Cylinders, Sectors and Clusters

On a long-playing record, music is stored in a very fine groove which begins at the outer edge of the disk and spirals inward as the program progresses. A playback stylus tracks the undulations of the groove, and the minute lateral and vertical movements are amplified and then reproduced by loudspeakers. Although the listener can easily skip certain sections of the LP and replay other sections, the disk is designed for continuous start-to-finish playback.

Read/Write Head. Unlike the playback-only stylus of the phonograph, the diskette drive has a read/write head, which resembles the single record/playback head on many tape recorders. The drive mechanism moves this head to the appropriate track where it records, or writes, on a portion of the track called a sector. The same head may also play back, or read, a sector of previously recorded data.

Unlike the LP record, the computer diskette is not turned over to play side B. Instead, there is another head underneath it which is used to read and write data on that side of the diskette.

Figure 8.1 compares the layout of 3.50- and 5.25-inch diskettes, and Table 8.1 gives track-and-sector data for various diskettes used in IBM and compatible personal computers. The terms used in the figure and table are briefly defined here.

Track. In comparison to the continuous spiral groove on the LP, each diskette surface contains a series of 40 or 80 separate concentric magnetic tracks on which data may be written. Diskettes are sometimes identified by track pitch, that is, the number of tracks per inch on each surface. Thus, a 40-track surface has 48 tpi (tracks per inch), and an 80-track surface has either 96 tpi or 135 tpi, depending on the diskette diameter.

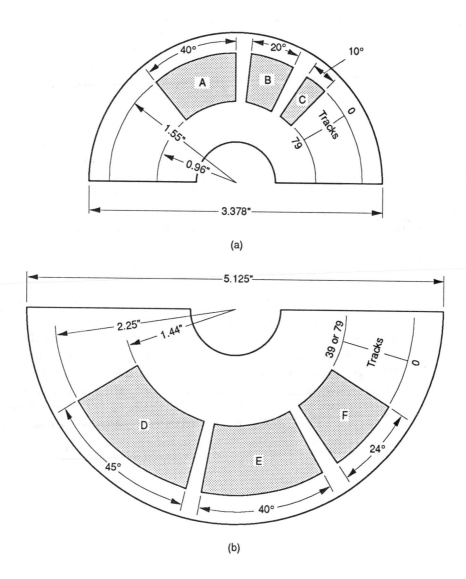

(a)

(b)

Figure 8.1.   Sectors on 3.5-inch and 5.25-inch diskettes. See also Table 8.1.

Table 8.1 Diskette Track-and-Sector Details

Diskette type	Capacity	Diam. (in.)	Tracks per side	Tracks per inch	Sectors per track *	DOS	Label identification: sided/density, other †
Single – sided	100Kb	5.25	(not used by IBM PCs)				single/single
	160Kb		40	48	8 (D)	1.00	single/double
	180Kb				9 (E)	2.00	single/double
Double – sided	320Kb				8 (D)	1.00	double/double
	360Kb				9 (E)	2.00	DD, 40 track, 48 tpi
High capacity ‡	1.2Mb	5.25	80	96	15 (F)	3.00	HD, 80 track, 96 tpi
Double – sided	720Kb	3.50	80	135	9 (A)	3.20	DD, 1MB, 2HC
	1.44Mb				18 (B)	3.20	HD, 2MB
	2.88Mb				36 (C)	5.00	

* (A,B,C) = cross – references to Figure 8.1
† SD = single density   SS = single sided
  DD = double density   DS = double sided
  HD = high density
  tpi = tracks per inch
‡ IBM nomenclature: diskette is also double – sided, high density

Sector. Each magnetic track is divided into 8 (obsolete), 9, 15, or 18 512-byte sectors, and surface space is allocated in whole sector units. Therefore, any file whose length is between 513 and 1,024 bytes will require two sectors for storage. And in order to add just one more byte to a 1,024-byte file, an additional 512-byte sector must be allocated. Thus there is some unavoidable wasted space in the last sector of just about any program written to disk. Furthermore, the sectors occupied by any file are not necessarily contiguous. To understand why, consider a freshly formatted diskette on which several files are to be stored. In this case, the files are written sector-by-sector, and each file does indeed occupy contiguous sectors.

Later on, one of the intermediate files may be edited, making it considerably longer than it was. But now, the new data cannot be written to the next physical sector (or sectors), since this space is already occupied by some other file. So the system seeks out the next available sector, and this may be located just about anywhere on the surface of the diskette. When the diskette is completely filled up, some unneeded files may be erased, thereby freeing up sectors scattered over the entire magnetic surface. Thus, after a certain amount of writing, erasing, and rewriting, the sectors available for the next program will remain scattered over the surface of the diskette. The file allocation table (described below) keeps track of the actual sectors used by each file.

Clusters and Allocation Units. As just noted, a single 512-byte sector is the smallest possible storage unit that can be allocated to a file. In actual practice, a diskette or hard disk drive may allocate this single sector or a *cluster* of two or more sectors at a time. In other words, a small file whose actual size is, say, 400 bytes, may be allocated one, two, four, or eight sectors, depending on cluster size. The amount of space thus utilized is known as an *allocation unit.*

Reserved Sectors

In order to keep track of sectors, clusters, and other diskette management data, several sectors on each surface are reserved for exclusive use by the operating system. Therefore, the amount of space available for program storage is always less than the total capacity of the diskette or hard disk itself. The reserved sectors are briefly described here.

Boot Record. Most of this single sector contains the diskette bootstrap program, which is not further described here. However, the first thirty bytes contain data about the diskette itself, which may be displayed via the DOS debug utility. To do so, log on to the directory (usually, C:\DOS) which contains the DEBUG.COM file. Then type the following lines:

```
C>DEBUG↵
-L DS:0 x 0 1↵
-D DS:0 1D↵
```

To briefly explain the cryptic debug script, the first line is an instruction to begin loading sectors from drive x. Instead of x, type 0 for drive A, 1 for drive B, or 2 for drive C. The 0 following the x means the first sector to be loaded is sector 0, which contains the boot record. Since we're not interested in any other sectors, the final 1 means load one sector only. The next line displays the first 30 (hex 1D) bytes. A readout similar to one of the following two-line displays should be seen on screen:

With a 360Kb system diskette in drive A (x = 0):
```
xxxx:0000 EB 29 90 49 42 4D 20 20-33 2E 31 00 02 02 01 00  .).IBM 3.1.....
xxxx:0010 02 70 00 D0 02 FD 02 00-09 00 02 00 00 00         .p...........
```

With a 720Kb nonsystem diskette in drive B (x = 1):
```
xxxx:0000 EB 34 90 4D 53 44 4F 53-33 2E 33 00 02 02 01 00  .4.MSDOS3.3.....
xxxx:0010 02 70 00 A0 05 F9 03 00-09 00 02 00 00 00         .p...........
```

As the right-hand column shows, part of each boot record identifies the type (IBM or MS) and version of the operating system contained on the diskette. Therefore, the debug script above may be used in lieu of the DOS VER command to identify the DOS version on any diskette (the VER command itself only identifies the version that was used to boot the system).

The displayed ASCII value (if any) of the other bytes has no significance, and bytes whose value is below decimal 32 or above 126 are shown as periods. Table 8.2 describes the contents of these bytes, and the media descriptor byte (underlined above) is further defined in Table 8.3.

File Allocation Table (FAT). The file allocation table, or FAT, contains the information needed to find the clusters assigned to each program listed in the directory. Each FAT entry is 12 bits (1.5 bytes) long for media holding up to 4,096 clusters, and 16 bits (2 bytes) long if there are 4,097 or more clusters. Since all diskette media contain far fewer than 4,096 clusters, each diskette FAT entry is 12 bits in length.

Using a 360Kb diskette as an example, there are 354 data clusters (708 sectors÷2) available to the user, and therefore the FAT must be 354 × 1.5 = 531 bytes long. Three additional bytes are reserved at the head of the FAT for an additional media descriptor byte (described above) followed by FF FF, for a total of 534 bytes. The FAT therefore needs two sectors, even though the second sector holds only 22 bytes. And, since the FAT is so vital

Table 8.2 Boot Record Data Stored in Sector Zero

Hex	Decimal	Contents	Values found on DOS 4.01 5.25" 360Kb diskette (see text)
00–01	00–01	A jump instruction	EB 29 (to bypass system info)
02	02	NOP instruction	90 (NOP = no operation)
03–0A	03–10	Product name and version	49 42 4D 20 20 33 2E 31 (IBM 3.1)
0B–0C	11–12	Bytes per sector	00 02 (= 512 bytes)
0D	13	Sectors per allocation unit	02
0E–0F	14–15	Reserved sectors	01 00 (boot record, other purposes)
10	16	File allocation tables (FAT)	02
11–12	17–18	Entries in root directory	70 00 (= 112 maximum)
13–14	19–20	Total number of sectors	D0 02 (= 720 sectors on diskette)
15	21	Media descriptor	FD (see Table 8.3)
16–17	22–23	Sectors per FAT	02 00 (03 00 IBM DOS 4.xx masters)
18–19	24–25	Sectors per track	09 00
1A–1B	26–27	Heads	02 00
1C–1D	28–29	Hidden sectors	00 00 (for drive partition support)

Table 8.3a Media Descriptor Bytes

Media descriptor	Diskette size	Capacity	Tracks per side	Sectors per track	Sides	Introduced in DOS version
F0 †	3.5"	1.44Mb ‡	80	18	2	4.0
F8	hard disk	varies	varies	varies	varies	2.0
F9	5.25"	1.2Mb §	80	15	2	3.0
	3.5"	720Kb	80	9	2	3.2
FC	5.25"	180Kb	40	9	1	2.0
FD	5.25"	360Kb	40	9	2	2.0
FE	5.25"	160Kb	40	8	1	1.0
FF	5.25"	320Kb	40	8	2	2.0

† F0 may also be used for media types not defined in this table.
‡ 1.44Mb is actually 1.41Mb (80 × 18 × 2 × 512÷1,048,576)
§ 1.2Mb is actually 1.17Mb (80 × 15 × 2 × 512÷1,048,576)

Table 8.3b Bits in Media Descriptor Byte

Bit position	7654 3	2 Removeable media?	1 Sectors per track	0 Sides
	1111 1	0 = no	0 = 9	0 = two
		1 = yes	1 = 8	1 = one
Exceptions				
F9	1111 1	0 = yes	0 = 15	1 = two
F0	1111 0000	0 = yes	0 = 18	0 = two

to system operation, two complete versions are stored in the sectors immediately following the boot record. If one is damaged, the operating system will attempt to use the other one.

Directory. Immediately following the FAT, these sectors store the information that is seen when the DOS internal DIR command is executed.

Reserved Sector Summary

Table 8.4 shows the number of sectors used to store the boot record, FATs, and directory. As an exception to the rule, note that there is only one sector per cluster on the 360Kb and 720Kb IBM DOS 4.xx system diskettes accompanying the DOS manual. Therefore, each FAT is correspondingly larger: the 360Kb distribution diskette requires three sectors per FAT—one more than required on any other 360Kb diskette—and the 720Kb diskette reserves five sectors per FAT—two more than on other 720Kb diskettes.

In either case, the amount of space available to the user is therefore slightly less than on other diskettes. But since these diskettes are permanently write-protected, the diminished space is of no practical consequence. It is mentioned here simply because if CHKDSK is executed on either of these diskettes, the *xxxxx Bytes total disk space* report will show a value that is 1 or 2Kb less than what one might have expected to see, as also recorded in Table 8.4.

The sectors used by the boot record, file allocation tables, and directory of files are located on the outer track(s) of the diskette. Damage to this area can therefore make it impossible to write or read data to or from the diskette. It's almost as if the directory in a large apartment house were vandalized—the tenants may remain secure in their apartments, but they can't be found anymore.

Table 8.4 Sector Usage on 3.5" and 5.25" Diskettes

Diskette type	IBM 4.xx†	other	IBM 4.xx†	other	all	all
Capacity (bytes)	360K	360K	720K	720K	1.2M	1.44M
Size (inches)	5.25	5.25	3.5	3.5	5.25	3.5
Media descriptor byte	FD	FD	F9	F9	F9	F0
Sectors per cluster	1	2	1	2	1	1
File allocation tables	2	2	2	2	2	2
Sectors per FAT	3	2	5	3	7	9
Sectors for						
total FAT	6	4	10	6	14	18
boot record	1	1	1	1	1	1
directory	7	7	7	7	14	14
subtotal	14	12	18	14	29	33
data	706	708	1,422	1,426	2,371	2,847
total	720	720	1,440	1,440	2,400	2,880
Bytes						
subtotal	7,168	6,144	9,216	7,168	14,848	16,896
data ‡	361,472	362,496	728,064	730,112	1,213,952	1,457,664
total	368,640	368,640	737,280	737,280	1,228,800	1,474,560

† These values are found only on IBM DOS 4.xx master 360Kb and 720Kb system diskettes. See text for details.

‡ Figure reported in first line of CHKDSK

Erased Files. When a file is erased by using the DOS ERASE command, it is not in fact actually erased, although this will happen later on if a new file needs to use its space. For the moment, the sectors of the "erased" program are simply marked in the FAT as being available for such reuse. And in the directory, the first character of the file name is overwritten with the hexadecimal digit E5. Because of this, it is often possible to recover an erased program if its space has not yet been occupied by another program. File recovery programs such as Norton Utilities' *Unerase* are readily available for this purpose, but are not discussed in any greater detail in this book.

Recording Density, Capacity, and the Diskette Label

Currently available diskettes are often labeled "double density," "high density," or "high capacity," leaving the user to figure out what it all means, and perhaps to wonder whatever happened to "single density." The actual storage capacity of a diskette is a function of both the recorded density on each track and the number of tracks and sectors on the diskette surface.

Although prolonged immersion in magnetic recording theory is not really essential to the diskette buyer, some frequently encountered terms are nevertheless described here for the benefit of those who may have wondered what those diskette labels really mean. The information presented here was summarized in the right-hand column of Table 8.1 above.

Single Density. Prior to the introduction of the first IBM PC, 5.25-inch diskettes were recorded using a simple FM (frequency modulation) encoding system, as shown in Figure 8.2a. Note that each bit cell begins with a clock pulse. If the data bit itself is a 1, another pulse occurs in the middle of the cell. If the data bit is 0, then there is no additional pulse. Thus a byte of data requires 16 bits (8 clock bits, 8 data bits) for storage. Such a system is now known as *single density* recording.

Double Density. An MFM (modified frequency modulation) system is used on all IBM and IBM-compatible diskettes. Again, a data bit of 1 is indicated by a pulse in the middle of the bit cell; a data bit of 0 by the absence of a pulse. However, the clock pulse is omitted unless a zero data bit is followed by another zero bit, in which case a clock pulse occurs at the beginning of the second zero bit cell, and again at the beginning of all zero bit cells immediately following. This is shown in Figure 8.2b, where it can be seen that the same data byte now requires fewer pulses—at most eight, for a string of consecutive 1s.

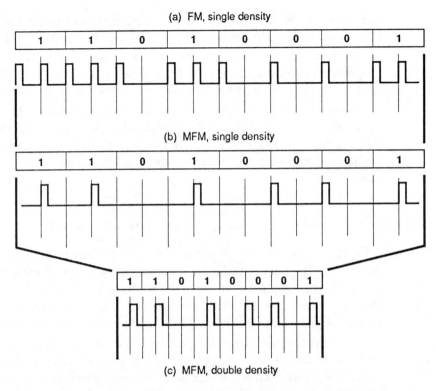

Figure 8.2. Diskette data encoding methods. (a) FM (frequency modulation): every bit cell begins with a clock pulse; there is an additional midcell pulse if the data bit is a one. (b) MFM (modified frequency modulation: the clock pulse occurs only on the second and subsequent zeroes. (c) MFM, double density: although the bit cell length is halved, pulses are no closer than in FM encoding. Therefore, the data density of each track may be doubled. This encoding method is used on all IBM 3.5- and 5.25-inch diskettes.

As a practical consequence, the amount of space taken up by each byte can be cut in half, as shown in Figure 8.2c. Note that the space between each pulse is no less than it was when a series of 1s was recorded using the FM single-density system. The data storage capacity is now double that of the FM system, hence the name *double density*.

High Density. The double-density diskette just described divides each track into nine (formerly, eight) sectors. But due to improvements in magnetic storage technology, it is now possible to divide the same track into more sectors: 15 on 5.25″ diskettes and 18 on 3.5″ diskettes. The same MFM encoding system is used, but the recorded density is compressed as required to fit the greater number of sectors into the same track, resulting in the *high-density* diskette. Because the number of sectors is almost twice that of the double-density diskette, the format is sometimes referred to as *quad density*.

Standard Capacity. This term is introduced here simply as a means to describe the track pitch on the diskettes described above, for purposes of comparison with the high-capacity format which follows. On conventional 5.25-inch diskettes, the standard-capacity pitch is 48 tpi (tracks-per-inch), and there are 40 such tracks (0–39) on each side of the diskette.

High Capacity. The term *high capacity* is used by IBM as a reference to the finer track pitch of 96 tpi, which is used on the 5.25-inch 1.2Mb diskette. The diskette has 80 tracks on each side.

The track pitch on all 3.5-inch diskettes is 135 tpi, and there are 80 tracks per side. Although this certainly ranks as a high capacity too, the term is not used here, perhaps because it would make no distinction between the actual recorded capacities of currently available 3.5-inch diskettes.

Diskette Labels. Labels are often mildly ambiguous in stating the storage capacity of a diskette. For example, a 720Kb diskette is often labeled "1Mb" (or even "2HC" !), while a 1.44Mb diskette is "2Mb." In both cases, the lower value is the number of bytes available to the user, while the higher value is the diskette's total capacity. Table 8.5 illustrates how the latter is actually divided between user and data bytes on a 3.5-inch 1Mb diskette. The same general procedure is followed on all other diskettes and hard disks, although the data-byte allocation varies from one type to another.

The total capacity of a diskette or hard disk is often referred to as its *unformatted capacity*, a bit of a misnomer, since that capacity is only realized when the diskette is formatted. Prior to formatting, the capacity should be given in bpr (bits per radian), which is 7,958 bpr for double-density diskettes.

Formatting

Prior to use for data storage, the magnetic surfaces on a diskette or hard disk must be formatted. This is a two-step procedure, consisting of low- and high-level formatting. The low-level format defines the basic track geometry, while the high-level format sets up the sectors that will be used for the boot record, file allocation tables, and directory, and in addition transfers the COMMAND.COM and hidden files to the diskette or hard

Table 8.5 Allocation of Space on 3.5" 720Kb Diskette *

Each sector contains:	User bytes	Data bytes	Each track contains:	User bytes	Data bytes
1. **Sector Identifier**			**Index Gap** [32 – 146] ‡		146
Identifier Mark					
12 (00) †			**Track Gap** [as required] ‡		182
3 (A1)					
1 (FE)		16	**Sector Bytes**		
			512 × 9	4608	
Address Identifier			146 × 9		1314
Track Address					
1 cylinder number			**Track Total**	4608	1642
1 side number					
1 S (sector number)					
1 SL (sector length)					
2 EDC §		6			
2. **Identifier Gap**					
22 (4E)		22			

Each sector contains:	User bytes	Data bytes	Each diskette contains:	User bytes	Data bytes
3. **Data Block**					
Data Mark					
12 (00)			2 sides		
3 (A1)			80 tracks/side		
1 (FB)		16	160 tracks		
Data Field	512				
2 EDC §		2	**User Bytes**		
			4608 × 160	737,280	
4. **Data Block Gap**					
[78–84] (4E) ‡		84	**Data Bytes**		
			1642 × 160		262,720
Sector Total					
User bytes	512		**Diskette total**		1,000,000
Data bytes		146			

* Nomenclature based on ANSI Draft Proposal X3.169, Project 389 – D
† (*xx*) = hexadecmial value of each indicated byte
‡ [*xx-yy*] = Byte count may vary within bracketed range, with typical value given in the table.
§ EDC = Error Detection Characters

disk. The DOS FORMAT.COM program carries out both levels of formatting on a diskette. However, on a hard disk the two levels are separately executed, as described later in Chapter 9 (pages 384 and 397).

Unless otherwise noted, the word "format" without any qualifiers refers to the entire diskette procedure, or to just the high-level format on a hard disk.

HARDWARE OVERVIEW: DRIVE SYSTEMS AND ADAPTERS

In any IBM PC, and in most compatible computers, several configurations of diskette and hard disk drive systems are possible. In IBM computer nomenclature, the model number indicates—among other things—the quantity of drives that are installed in the system. But of course a system is often expanded after purchase by installing an additional drive or drives. The installation usually requires some hardware/software switching changes, and perhaps an additional drive adapter.

A brief review of various drive systems and adapters is given here. If you need assistance installing or removing a drive from your system, refer to the Drive Installation and Swapping Procedures section at the end of this chapter.

Diskette Drives

A wide variety of diskette drives are available for the IBM family of personal computers. These include 3.50- and 5.25-inch drives in half- and full-height configurations. Table 8.6 lists internal and external diskette drives for the PS/2 series.

5.25-Inch Diskette Drives. A full-height diskette drive for the PC, XT or AT is about 3.4 inches (86 mm) high. A half-height, or "slimline," drive is 1.6 inches (40 mm) high, allowing two such drives to occupy the space required by a full-height drive. On MCA systems, diskette drives are sometimes referred to as "half-high" or "one-third high."

The general appearance of the circuit board on an IBM full-height drive may vary, depending on where it was manufactured. On pre-PS/2 ISA

Table 8.6 IBM PS/2 Diskette Drives *

Location Standard/optional Size Capacity	internal standard 3.5" 720Kb	internal standard 3.5" 1.44Mb	internal optional 5.25" 1.2Mb	external optional 5.25" 360Kb	external optional 5.25" 1.2Mb
25 and 30	•			•	
all others		•		•	•
60 & 80 only		•	•	•	•

* All external drives require additional external drive adapter.

systems, there were three commonly available layouts for 320/360Kb drives, identified as follows:

Type	Serial number begins with
1	A, B, or no letter
2	D
3	E

The type designation has no performance significance, except that a type 3 drive does not support the use of track 40 on the diskette, as described in the section on incompatible software (page 334). Otherwise, the three types are completely interchangeable, and the same PC system may contain drives with different type designations.

A 5.25-inch external diskette drive is available as an accessory option for PS/2 systems.

3.50-Inch Diskette Drives. There were two 3.50-inch external diskette drives available from IBM for the PC, XT, and AT, identified as follows:

Model	For use with
1	PC, XT
2	AT only

The 3.50-inch drives are supported by DOS, beginning with version 3.20. The Model 1 external drive may be connected to the 37-pin socket on the 5.25-inch Diskette Drive Adapter's mounting bracket, which is described below. The Model 2 external drive for the AT requires its own adapter. In addition, both external drives require power connections, illustrated in Figure 8.3.

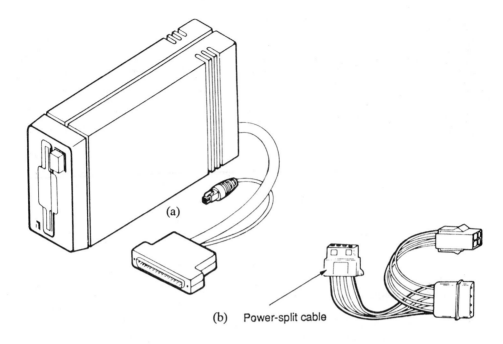

(a)

(b)   Power-split cable

Figure 8.3. External ISA drive power requirements. The external drive receives power via a separate four-conductor cable (a) inserted into a power socket installed on the system unit's rear panel. The socket is powered from a Y connector (b) inserted in any internal drive power line.

Non-IBM External Disk Drives. Various manufacturers market external self-powered disk drives. A typical device may be supplied with its own internal power supply, power cord, and a diskette containing a device driver file. Such a device is also supplied with its own adapter, which is inserted into an adapter slot on the system board, and linked to the drive by a multiconductor cable. The device driver file must be copied to your system diskette, and you must write the name of this driver in your configuration file, as described in Chapter 4. The next time you boot your PC, the external drive(s) automatically assume the next available drive letter(s). Thus, an external two-drive system installed in a PC with three previously installed drives would become drives D and E.

Figure 8.4 shows one of the many external drive systems that may be used with an IBM or compatible personal computer.

Figure 8.4. A CD-ROM system is one of the many external drive systems that may be interfaced with most personal computers. Each such drive will have its own adapter card, interface cable, and device driver software. (Laserdrive-1 photo courtesy Amdek Corp.)

Drive Adapters

All diskette and hard disk drives must be connected to the appropriate drive adapter, and Table 8.7 lists some of the adapters used with ISA and MCA systems. The adapters are discussed in greater detail below. In PS/2 systems, the drive controller hardware is either built into the system board or is an integral part of the drive itself.

5.25-inch Diskette Drive Adapter. Although this adapter for the PC and XT contains the logic to control four diskette drives, IBM supports its use for three drives only—two internal and one external. The internal drives, A and B, connect to a multiconductor flat-ribbon cable, and this is attached to the adapter at the left (internal) end of the adapter. The connector is shown in Figure 8.5a. The drives may be either single- or double-sided types.

An external drive C may be attached to the 37-pin connector on the adapter's mounting bracket, which is also shown in Figure 8.5a.

Fixed Disk Adapter. This adapter card is described in Chapter 9 (page 353).

AT Fixed Disk and Diskette Drive Adapter. This adapter supports four drives: two hard disk and one diskette, or two diskette and one hard disk. A single control/data cable feeds the diskette drives, and another control cable feeds the hard disk drives. Each hard disk drive also has its own data cable. The adapter does not support an external drive. The adapter sockets are shown in Figure 8.5b.

Table 8.7 Representative Adapter Cards for Use with Diskette and Hard Disk Drives

IBM part no.	Name of adapter	Drives supported	Computer
1503780	5.25–inch Diskette Drive Adapter	two internal diskette two external diskette	PC, XT
1602501	Fixed Disk Adapter	two internal hard disk	PC †, XT
	AT Fixed Disk & Diskette Drive Adapter	one internal hard disk two internal diskette or one internal diskette two internal hard disk	AT only
6450244 6451007 6450245	External Diskette Drive Adapters	360Kb external 360Kb, 1.2Mb external 360Kb as external drive B	25, 30 50–80 50, 60, 70, 80
Plus Development Corp. Hardcard Hardcard II		one internal hard disk, mounted on adapter card same	PC, XT XT 286, AT, PS/2 30 286
Iomega	Host Adapter Card	two external Bernoulli	PC, XT, AT

† See text for precaution against installing a hard disk system in an IBM PC with a 63.5–watt power supply.

AT 3.5-Inch External Diskette Drive Adapter. When an external 3.5-inch drive is added to an AT system, this adapter must be installed in one of the adapter slots on the system board.

Other Drive Adapters. Various non-IBM drive systems are supplied with their own adapters. Unless otherwise indicated, such drives are not compatible with an IBM Diskette or Fixed Disk Adapter. Typical examples of drives requiring their own adapters are the Iomega Bernoulli Box and the Amdek Laserdrive-1 CD-ROM system.

Device Driver Requirements

When installing an additional drive system, such as a hard disk, a 3.5-inch diskette drive, a Bernoulli Box, or a CD-ROM system, the new drive will

(a)

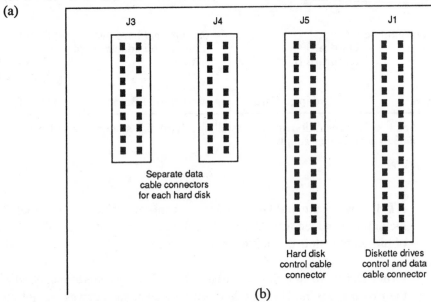

J3

J4

J5

J1

Separate data
cable connectors
for each hard disk

Hard disk
control cable
connector

Diskette drives
control and data
cable connector

(b)

Figure 8.5.   ISA Diskette drive adapter card and connector detail. (a) The adapter
for the 5.25-inch diskette drive supports up to four diskette drives. Two drives (A
and B) connect to a multiconductor flat-ribbon cable at the left (internal) end of the
adapter. Two external diskette drives (C and D) may be connected to the 37-pin
connector on the card's mounting bracket. (b) The AT Fixed Disk and Diskette
Drive Adapter supports four drives (two hard disk, two diskette). One control cable
feeds two diskette drives and another cable feeds two hard disk drives. Each hard
disk drive also has its own data cable.

probably be supplied with its own device driver software. Or the new drive will require the use of the generic diskette driver that is found on the IBM DOS 3.20 diskette. When a third diskette drive is added to an AT, an additional driver is required in order to recognize the additional drive.

If one of these devices is installed in a PC, make sure the name of the appropriate device driver is included in the configuration file on the boot diskette, and that the driver itself is also present. The names of a few representative device drivers were given in Chapter 4 (Table 4.2). If the device driver is not included in the configuration file, the following error message will be seen when the system attempts to access the new drive:

```
Invalid drive specification
```

For further details on this subject, see the section on Device Drivers in Chapter 4 (p. 85).

PROBLEM LOCALIZATION PROCEDURES

If you have a diskette- or drive-related problem, the first step is to determine its origin. There are of course several possibilities, each of which is discussed below:

Drive hardware (the drive itself, its adapter, or the system board)
Diskette
Operating system
Software

If you have already localized the problem to one of these general areas, then refer directly to the appropriate section for further information. Otherwise, continue reading here until you discover the source of the problem.

DRIVE DIAGNOSTICS

If you suspect a drive is defective, the easy way to make sure is to physically swap the drives—easy, that is, if you have a two-drive system or can temporarily borrow a compatible drive from elsewhere. If so, follow the drive-swapping procedures described on page 336. If the problem moves with the drive, regardless of its position, the drive is faulty. But if the problem remains at the drive position, regardless of which drive occupies that position, then both drives may be assumed to be OK.

If so, the problem probably involves the adapter. On systems which use a plug-in diskette drive adapter, try inserting the adapter in any other slot on the system board. If that clears up the problem, put the adapter back in the original slot, just to make sure that the problem wasn't due to an improperly seated adapter. Before doing so, make sure that the contact fingers of the adapter are clean. If not, they may be cleaned by rubbing them with a pencil eraser or by using an electrical-contact cleaning solution.

POST Problem

If an apparently drive-related problem occurs when the system is first turned on, review the POST procedures in Chapter 3 to verify that the problem is indeed in this area. But if POST does conclude successfully and the drive problem appears later on, then it's time to continue with this chapter. Taking the simplest problem first, consider the following screen display:

```
Drive not ready
```

The source of the problem depends upon which drive the system configuration thinks is the boot drive. Try one of the following procedures, as appropriate for your system.

Drive C Is Boot Drive. Insert a system diskette in drive A and try again. If the system now boots successfully from drive A, refer to Chapter 6 for system configuration information. However, if the error message repeats, then there is a problem with drive A that prevents the system from going further. Try removing or swapping the drive to verify the source of the problem. If neither procedure works, then the adapter or system board probably needs servicing.

Drive A Is Boot Drive. Make sure a system diskette is in drive A and that the drive door is closed. If the problem persists, then the drive itself is defective. If possible, try swapping it to verify this.

Start-Up Problems After POST

If the system locks up immediately after POST and displays a message about the command interpreter or operating system, refer to the DOS-Related Diagnostics section later in the chapter (page 319). But if at the successful conclusion of the POST procedure, the system consistently goes into the cassette BASIC mode despite the presence of a good DOS diskette in drive A, the problem may be due to one of the following:

1. The diskette is improperly seated in drive A.
2. Drive A is defective.
3. The drive system—the drive or the adapter—is defective.

Each of these potential trouble spots is reviewed here.

Diskette Seating. From force of habit, users probably follow one of the following two start-up procedures:

1. Insert the boot diskette in drive A, close the drive door, and then turn the power on, or
2. Turn the power on before inserting the diskette.

In most cases it makes little practical difference which sequence is chosen. However, there is the slight possibility that the diskette may not be seated properly if procedure 1 is used, causing the system to go into the cassette BASIC mode. If procedure 2 eliminates the problem, then it should be followed every time the system is turned on.

Defective Drive A Problem. After the POST procedure and just before the cassette BASIC screen appears, the drive A in-use light should come on and the drive motor should be heard spinning. This indicates that the power and signal connections to that drive are in order.

Even if the system has been set up to boot DOS from the drive C hard disk, this sequence should still occur. If it does not, the problem will have to be resolved before continuing. Follow the troubleshooting procedures discussed later on in this chapter.

Defective Drive System (drive or adapter). If the PC still continues to go into the cassette BASIC mode, look carefully for error-code message 601 to appear briefly, just before the BASIC screen display appears. On the

AT, an instruction to press the F1 - Resume key may also be seen, but when this function key is pressed, the BASIC screen is still displayed, as just described.

Error code 601 is a clear indication of a drive-related failure that will require servicing, though you may wish to proceed with more troubleshooting in an attempt to further isolate the problem area.

Hardware Interference Problem. An apparent software-related problem may be caused by a PC display that produces a radiated magnetic field strong enough to interfere with the read/write operations of a drive located immediately below the display. An immediately adjacent printer can do the same thing. In cases of interference, the data read from diskette will appear garbled on screen, and data written to diskette will contain errors. The solution is to move the interference-causing device farther away from the diskette drives.

Inoperative Drive In-Use Light. If a drive operates properly but its in-use light does not come on, the LED (light-emitting diode) is probably defective and will have to be replaced. As a double-check, refer to the LED Test Procedure found in Chapter 6.

Drive-System Interface Checks

In the case of an inoperative drive system, it's possible that one or more of the cables connected to the drive system have worked loose. These should be checked carefully, following the procedures given here.

Drive Connector Check. Table 8.8 lists the cables and connectors used on various diskette and hard disk drives. On all pre-PS/2 system drives, three or four sets of cables lead away from the drive mechanism. On PS/2 systems, cabling varies from one system to another.

The connectors on a representative ISA drive are shown in Figure 8.6. Make sure that all cable connectors are firmly seated where they connect to the drive. The power cables are described in greater detail immediately below.

Drive Power Problems. Note the four color-coded wires running from the power supply to a connector on each drive, which supply the required voltages (5 and 12 volts DC). If a drive appears to be completely inoperative, it may be that this connector has worked loose. Or if unexplained drive-re-

Table 8.8 Diskette and Hard Disk Drive Cables and Connectors

Connector/cable	Purpose	Computer
Single black conductor	Chassis ground connection	PC, XT, AT, 60, 80
4 heavy-gauge wires	DC voltage supply	PC, XT, AT, 60, 80
20-pin flat-ribbon cable	Hard disk data	PC, XT, AT, 60, 80
34-pin flat-ribbon cable	Diskette drive control	PC, XT, AT 25, 30, 30 286 †
	Hard disk control	PC, XT, AT, 60, 80
40-pin flat-ribbon cable	Diskette drive, all functions	25, 30, 30 286 ‡, 55 SX, 60, 80
40-pin edge connector	Diskette drive, all functions	50, 70
SCSI flat-ribbon cable	Hard disk, all functions	65 SX, 80 §
44-pin flat-ribbon cable	Hard disk, all functions	25, 30, 30 286
72-pin edge connector	Hard disk, all functions	50, 55 SX, 70

† Used with one-third-high diskette drives on models 25, 30, 30 286.
‡ Used with half-high diskette drives on models 25, 30, 30 286.
§ For model 80 systems with SCSI drives (−121, −321, −A21, −A31).

lated errors seem to be occurring regularly, but at random intervals, one or more of the power supply connections to the drive may be loose. Carefully check all connections from the power supply to the drive. If necessary, lightly crimp the female connectors for a tighter fit.

A separate set of cables supplies power to each drive, and any power cable set may be connected to any drive. Except in the case of a loose-fitting connector, it is quite unlikely that a power cable set will become defective. Nevertheless, these connectors may be freely interchanged between drives in order to verify the performance of each of them.

BASIC Drive-System Test

The BASIC program seen in Listing 8.1 may be used as a routine check to quickly verify the performance of any diskette or hard disk drive

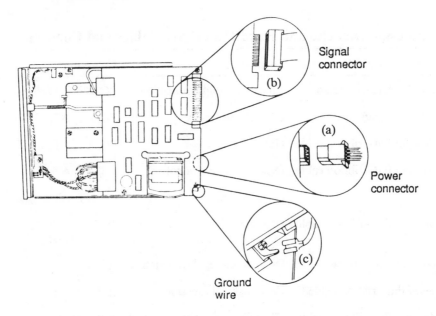

Figure 8.6. ISA drive cable details. The actual positions of the cable connectors may vary from one drive type to another. (a) Four-conductor power cables. (b) Flat-ribbon control and data cable (control only, for hard disk drives). A separate data cable is found on hard disk drives only. (c) Chassis ground connector.

system. First, type BASICA (or GWBASIC in non-IBM systems) at the DOS prompt and then enter each line in the listing. If you input the remarks shown in the right-hand column, don't forget the ' before each one so that remarks will not be read as program. Conclude each line by pressing the Enter key; when you are done, type SAVE "ANYNAME" (or something a little more creative, if you like), and then type RUN.

Listing 8.1 A BASIC Drive-Testing Program

```
100 INPUT A$                     ' to test drive A, enter
                                   A$ = A:TESTFILE
110 OPEN A$ FOR OUTPUT AS #1      ' file opened on designated drive
120 PRINT #1, STRING$(10,88)      ' string of ten Xs written in file
130 CLOSE: CLS                    ' file closed and screen cleared
140 OPEN A$ FOR INPUT AS #1       ' file reopened
150 PRINT INPUT$(10,1)            ' ten characters in file dispayed
160 CLOSE: END                    ' file closed
```

For readers not familiar with BASIC programming, here's a line-by-line summary of what the drive-testing program does. Line 100 displays a question mark on screen, and program execution pauses until you enter the name you want to assign to the test file. In the remarks column in the figure, a name of A:TESTFILE is suggested, with A: designating the drive to be tested. To test drive B, try entering B:ANOTHER or whatever name you prefer to add to the drive B designation.

Line 110 opens a file with the name you specified, line 120 writes a string of ten uppercase letter Xs in the file, and line 130 closes the file and clears the screen. Line 140 reopens the file, line 150 reads and prints its contents on screen, and line 160 again closes the file.

Run the program, and in response to the question-mark prompt, enter the letter of the drive to be tested, a colon, and the file name to be used for the test. Make sure to use a unique file name, since an already existing file with the same name will be lost.

If all goes well, a display of XXXXXXXXXX is seen, which indicates that the drive system successfully wrote a file to diskette or hard disk and then read it back again. Each diskette and hard disk drive may be tested simply by entering the proper drive-letter designation in response to the prompt. To display a different character on screen, change the 88 in line 120 to any other number representing a printable character in the ASCII or IBM extended character set.

Program Troubleshooting. Assuming the program has been correctly entered, any one of the following error messages indicates a problem:

Error message	Meaning
Bad file number in 110	System is in cassette BASIC mode and therefore unable to utilize diskette or hard disk file handling.
Disk not Ready in 110	Drive door is open or diskette is not in drive.
Path not found in 110	Drive and/or path (see Chapter 4) entered in response to input prompt does not exist.

If you are unable to resolve an error such as one of these by taking the obvious action (closing the drive door, making sure a good diskette is in the drive, correcting the drive letter), then servicing of the drive or the adapter is indicated.

DISKETTE DIAGNOSTICS

This section examines a few problems that are a function of the physical diskette itself, not of the software that may or may not be written on that diskette.

If visual inspection of the diskette reveals physical damage, there is little hope that the diskette may be safely used. It should be discarded or, if the information on it is vitally important, referred to a specialist who may attempt to salvage whatever data remains intact.

Invisible damage may also make a diskette almost useless. As noted in Chapter 1, a magnetized paper clip can be more than enough to render a diskette unreadable, and as a result a system that worked earlier now appears to be defective. In a sense, it is—but the system component that has failed is the diskette, not the system hardware.

Diskette Error Messages

Some of the error messages that may be encountered during diskette operations are summarized in Table 8.9. If one of these messages appears, refer directly to the appropriate section of this chapter for further information. For error messages not seen in the table, refer to Appendix A in the DOS Manual (Appendix D in DOS 4.0, B in DOS 5.0).

Abort, Retry, Ignore, Fail Messages

Several error messages to be encountered in this chapter include the following line of options, each of which is briefly described here. Depending on the specific error, *Ignore* or *Fail* may not be displayed. To select the desired option, press the first letter of its name.

```
Abort, Retry, Ignore, Fail?
```

Abort. This "bail out" option simply terminates the operation that caused the error.

Retry. If the error is obvious (drive door open, for example), make the necessary correction and then use this option to try again.

Ignore. The error is ignored and, if possible, program execution continues.

Fail. A DOS system call has failed. If possible, the system continues executing the command or program.

Table 8.9 Diskette-Related Error Messages

Error message	Possible causes
Access denied	Attempt to erase a write–protected file, or to read a file that does not exist.
Attempted write–protect violation	Target diskette is write–protected.
Bad command or file name	DOS conflict, or file does not exist on designated diskette.
Bad or missing Command Interpreter	The boot diskette does not contain a copy of the COMMAND.COM file.
Bad or missing (device name)	A device driver named in your CONFIG.SYS file was not found (see Device Driver section of Chapter 4).
Drive not ready	Drive door is open.
File creation error	Unformatted diskette, or a read–only (write–protected) file with that name already exists on the target diskette.
General Failure error reading drive x	Unformatted or otherwise incompatible diskette.
Format failure	Formatting error on target diskette.
Insufficient disk space	Target diskette does not have enough free space to accept source file.
Unrecoverable format error on target	Formatting error on target diskette.
Unrecoverable read error on drive X: Side x, track xx	The indicated track is defective.
Unrecoverable write error on target	Formatting or other error on target diskette.
Write protect error writing drive A	Target diskette is write–protected.

Routine examples of *Ignore* and *Fail* errors are described in this chapter in the section on track and sector differences below. In other applications there may be some risk of data loss or damage if either option is selected, so use *Abort* or *Retry* if you are not sure how to proceed.

Diskette Format Problems

Still another potential cause of failure is the presence of a diskette that is either unformatted or formatted for a capacity beyond that of the drive. In either case, read or write attempts will produce one of the following error messages.

Error message	Cause of message
General Failure error reading Drive x	Trying to read the diskette
File creation error	Trying to copy a file to the diskette

If you are sure the diskette is new, or does not contain information worth saving, then format it and try again. Otherwise, continue reading here.

Incompatible Diskettes

Problems often arise when a diskette's format is not compatible with the drive in which it is placed. Typical examples—some obvious, others not—are discussed here. In addition to the solutions described within each section below, refer to the File Transfer Techniques section which follows (page 318) for more information.

Table 8.10 lists various diskette drives currently available and the diskette types which should be used in each of them.

Physical Size Difference. The most obvious example is of course the physical incompatibility between a 3.5-inch diskette and a 5.25-inch drive, or vice versa. Unlike the simpler world of audio, there are no drives that take any size computer diskette, so the "solution" to this little problem is easy, and often frustrating—go find a drive that fits the diskette, or try to get a replacement diskette.

Track and Sector Differences. Even when the diskette and the drive size are physically compatible, there may still be a problem. For example, the *General Failure* message seen above is also encountered when drive B attempts to read the directory of a diskette formatted for a higher capacity. The message is of course followed by

Table 8.10 Drive/Diskette Compatibility Chart

Diskette type	Capacity	Compatible drive types are: single-sided 5.25"	double-sided 5.25"	3.50"	high * capacity 5.25"
Single – sided	160/180Kb	Y	Y	N	Y †
Double – sided	320/360Kb	N	Y	N	Y †
Double – sided	720Kb	N	N	Y	N
High capacity	1.2Mb	N	N	N	Y
	1.44Mb	N	N	Y ‡	N

*   All IBM high–capacity drives are double–sided.
†   If a high–capacity drive is used to write data to a normal–capacity diskette, it may not be possible to read that diskette in a normal–capacity drive.
‡   1.44Mb drive required.

DOS 3.00 or earlier
```
Abort, Retry, Ignore?
```

DOS 4.xx
```
Abort, Retry, Fail?
```

If you select Ignore, DOS 3.00 will display

```
Directory of B:\
```

followed by a repeat of the error message. If Ignore is again selected, DOS will try to continue. However, since the drive is still unable to read a high-capacity diskette, the second attempt displays

```
File not found
```

If Fail is selected under DOS 4.00, the message is

```
Volume in drive B has no label
```

again followed by a repeat of the error message. A second *Fail* attempt displays

```
Fail on Int 24 (that is, on Interrupt 24)
```

In either case the solution is to put the diskette in a high-capacity (1.2Mb, 5.25" or 1.44Mb, 3.5") drive and try again. However, this is no solution if the high-capacity drive is on someone else's computer, and you want to run the program on your own system.

Choosing the Right Diskette

In the days of the single-sided diskette drive, many users discovered they could record data on both sides of the diskette simply by cutting another write-protect notch in the protective envelope and flipping the diskette over, just as one would do to play side B on an LP record. Today, the same experimenters have discovered that a 720Kb diskette may be formatted to 1.44Mb in all IBM, and in some other, 1.44Mb drives. Some precautions about doing this are described here.

3.5-Inch Diskette Problems. A 1.44Mb drive can read a 720Kb diskette with no problem, since track pitch (135 tpi = 80 tracks per side) is the same, and the only physical difference is the number of sectors per track (see Table 8.1). However, there is a magnetic difference between 720Kb and 1.44Mb diskettes which is often overlooked. The higher magnetic capacity surface requires—at least in theory—a diskette manufactured to finer tolerances.

Figure 8.7 compares the head and magnetic surface geometry for both diskette and drive types. Note the significant differences in head gap and depth of magnetic coating. As a consequence of these differences, most diskette and drive manufacturers caution against formatting a 720Kb diskette in a 1.44 Mb drive. A much-simplified (but still no doubt confusing) explanation is offered here, and it should be remembered that the same general comments about formatting apply to all subsequent write operations.

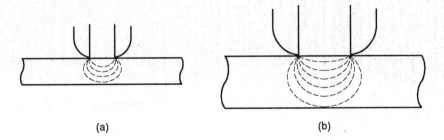

(a)   (b)

Figure 8.7. Head and surface geometry for read/write heads and diskette magnetic surfaces.

(a) 3.5-inch diskettes coating		(b) 5.25-inch diskettes coating	
thickness	coercivity	thickness	coercivity
1.7 μm	650 Oe	2.5 μm	300 Oe
0.9 μm	730 Oe	1.2 μm	690 Oe

When a 1.44Mb diskette is formatted in a 1.44Mb drive, the head gap fully saturates the thin magnetic coating. When the same drive is used to format a 720Kb diskette at 720Kb, (FORMAT A: /F:720), the write current is increased to saturate the greater thickness of the diskette's magnetic coating. However, the drive's own head gap of course does not magically grow larger, so the format is not done under optimum conditions. Nevertheless, the formatted diskette will probably work properly in most, if not all, drives in IBM or other top-quality systems.

Now consider what happens when a 1.44Mb drive is "tricked" into formatting a 720Kb diskette as 1.44Mb. The drive thinks it is formatting the thin magnetic coating of a real 1.44Mb diskette, and so the write current is adjusted accordingly. The surface is not properly saturated, and data written under these conditions is almost guaranteed to deteriorate over time.

The plot thickens. What if a 1.44Mb diskette if accidentally formatted at 720Kb in a 720Kb drive? The large head gap will attempt to saturate the thick magnetic coating that isn't really there. As a consequence, there may be some magnetic bleeding to adjacent tracks, and data integrity will be marginal at best.

So much for theory. In practice, people have been breaking the rules without apparent consequence for a long time now. But nevertheless, the warnings persist, and most diskette manufacturers do not guarantee their product at any other format than the one for which it was designed.

To guard against formatting a 720Kb diskette at 1.44Mb, diskette manufacturers place a second rectangular cutout in the lower right-hand corner (when reading the label) of a true 1.44Mb diskette casing. In some 1.44Mb drives, an LED sensing circuit detects the cutout and adjusts itself accordingly. IBM drives do not include this feature, so it is up to the user to make sure the correct diskette is used. If a 720Kb diskette is formatted at 1.44Mb in an IBM drive, the diskette will be unusable in a drive that does use the sensing feature. In the absence of the cutout, the drive attempts to read the diskette as 720Kb, and thereby fails.

In an emergency, a cutout can be hand carved (carefully!) through the diskette casing, or for large-scale violations of manufacturers' recommendations, a hole punch can be acquired from the Cajun Edge Company.

5.25-Inch Diskette Problems. The same general compatibility characteristics apply to 5.25-inch diskettes; that is, any drive can read from and/or write to diskettes of lesser capacity. There is, however, one important caution to be observed, as described here.

In order to write 1.2 Mbytes of data on a 5.25-inch diskette surface, the track pitch is reduced from 48 to 96 tracks per inch (see Table 8.1). That means the drive's head gap is correspondingly smaller too. The smaller head gap can read a wide 48-tpi track from a 360Kb diskette with no difficulty. And although it can write data back to that diskette at the correct 48-tpi pitch, the width of each track is narrower than that written by a 360Kb drive head. Therefore, consider what happens when a 1.2Mb drive writes new data to a 360Kb diskette previously used in a 360Kb drive. As the new data is written to diskette via the 1.2Mb narrow-gap head, the old data under the head is of course lost. But since the head is narrower than the old track, parts of the original data track may remain on either side of the new track, as shown in Figure 8.8. When the diskette is subsequently read by a 360Kb drive head, the wide head reads both the new data and the leftover remains of the old data. As a result, the diskette is now unreadable in the 360Kb drive, though it can still be read in the 1.2Mb drive.

Again, theory does not always agree with practice: when a portions of a file written to a properly formatted 360Kb diskette in a 360Kb drive are subsequently overwritten in a 1.2Mb drive, the increased write current *may* be sufficient to wipe out the residual data on either side of the new track.

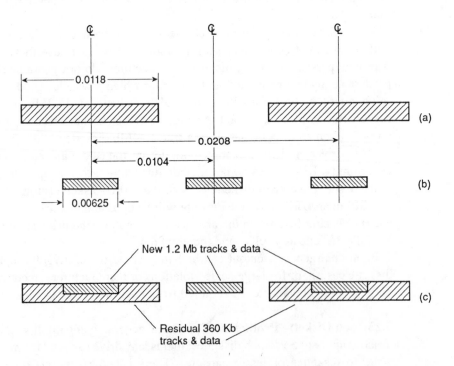

Figure 8.8.   Comparison of track widths and spacings on (a) 360Kb and (b) 1.2Mb 5.25-inch diskettes. (c) Track pattern on a formatted 1.2Mb surface that was previously formatted/written in a 360Kb diskette drive. Dimensions in inches, based on ANSI standards (a) X3.125; (b) X3.126.

Then again, it may not. If you *must* tempt the fates, try a few practice runs first.

For the same reasons as just described, a 1.2Mb drive should not be used to format a diskette to any capacity other than 1.2Mb, even though doing so is possible.

Copy-Related Problems

Various error messages may be seen during an attempt to copy either an entire diskette or just one or more files. Typical messages are listed here and described immediately below:

```
Insufficient disk space
Unrecoverable format (or write) error on target
Unrecoverable read error on drive x:
Invalid drive specification
```

Insufficient disk space. The message indicates that there is not enough room on the target diskette to accommodate the file you are attempting to copy. The solution is simply to copy the file to a diskette with sufficient free space, or to make room on the present target diskette by erasing a file or files that you no longer need. In either case, a DIRectory listing should display *xxxxx* bytes free, and of course *xxxxx* must be equal to, or greater than, the space required by the file you want to place on the diskette.

Note that when the copying of a group of files is terminated by an *Insufficient disk space* error message, the COPY process will look no farther on the source diskette, even though there might still be an uncopied file there that would fit in the remaining space on the target diskette.

Unrecoverable format (or write) error on target. During DISKCOPY, either message indicates a problem with the target diskette. Try formatting this diskette with the DOS FORMAT command. If this attempt also fails, the diskette is probably defective and should be discarded.

Unrecoverable read error on drive *x*: (where *x* is the source diskette drive). If this error message is displayed during the DISKCOPY process, do not interrupt DISKCOPY, and refer to the section on file recovery techniques (page 331) before assuming the worst.

Invalid drive specification. This line is seen when attempting to copy to a target drive that does not exist. If the DISKCOPY command is used, the following lines are also displayed:

```
Specified drive does not exist
or is non-removable
```

The last line is a reminder that DISKCOPY cannot be used to copy to a hard disk.

Other Copying Errors. The *General Failure* error message described earlier is also seen when attempting to use the DOS COPY command to copy a file to a diskette that has been formatted using the Format option on an IBM Diagnostics diskette. As discussed in Chapter 3, the diagnostics Format option is only suitable for use in diagnostics testing, and the regular FORMAT.COM program on the DOS diskette must be used for all other formatting work.

Another copy-related error message may be seen when attempting to DISKCOPY a diskette to a target diskette of a different format. The message displayed is

```
Drive types or diskette types
not compatible
Copy process ended (This line not seen on DOS 4.xx)
```

As an exception to the rule, if a 3.5-inch drive is installed in an ISA system, DOS 3.*xx* will permit a DISKCOPY operation from a 5.25-inch source to a 3.5-inch target. The target diskette will be formatted during DISKCOPY as a 360Kb diskette, and will be recognized as such by CHKDSK. DOS 4.*xx* is too smart to put up with this sort of space-wasting nonsense, and of course neither version is dumb enough to try to DISK-COPY a 720Kb source to a 360Kb target.

To copy all the files from a lower-capacity source diskette in, say, drive B to a higher-capacity target diskette in drive A, first format the target diskette, and then type the following command at the DOS prompt:

```
B> COPY *.* A:↵
```

The COPY command may also be used to transfer the contents of a source diskette to a target diskette of lower capacity, subject of course to the limitations of space on the target diskette.

File Transfer Techniques

Given the proliferation of diskette formats and the fact that most PCs have no more than two drives, it's a pretty safe bet that sooner or later (probably sooner), you will encounter a diskette that is incompatible, either in size or capacity. In fact, this is guaranteed if a PS/2 system is added to an office full of PC, XT, or AT computers. The PS/2's 3.5-inch drives and the latter systems' 5.25-inch drives rule out any diskette swapping.

The obvious solution is to add an external drive to either system. This is certainly not impossible, and is of course the only way to prepare a diskette that needs to be mailed somewhere. But if the two computers are no farther apart than the length of a cable, it may be more efficient—and certainly cheaper—to invest in a data transfer system, such as Rupp Corporation's *FastLynx* or Fifth Generation Systems' *The Brooklyn Bridge*. Each consists of a software program to be installed on both computers, and each includes a cable to run between ports (both serial *or* both parallel) on the two computers.

Using *FastLynx* as an example, a split-screen display shows the desired directories of both computers. A highlighted bar is used to select the file of interest (or all files in the directory), and a function key press copies the file(s) almost instantaneously to the other computer. Files may be copied to and from any diskette, hard disk, or electronic disk, thus obviating the need to keep one of everything in stock.

As another alternative, a file can also be uploaded/downloaded between computers via modem.

DOS-RELATED DIAGNOSTICS

Problems may also be encountered that are not directly attributable to either the drive or to the physical diskette within it. Such problems may be a function of the operating system or of the software in use, and both possibilities are discussed in some detail here.

DOS-Conflict Problem

If your PC's drives appear to be functioning properly, and only one or two diskettes seem to cause a problem not described above, the problem may be a DOS conflict. Now and then a directory listing may display scrambled information, possibly along with a fragment of readable data as well. A typical example will be seen later on in the chapter, in Figure 8.9e. In that figure, the garbled display is a function of a damaged boot record on the diskette. However, when such an uninformative display is seen, there's also a very good chance that the system has been booted with an early version of DOS and that the scrambled-directory diskette was created elsewhere, using a more recent DOS. The solution is to reboot the system with the more recent DOS version.

Generally speaking, DOS is upwardly compatible—that is, new versions of DOS will read diskettes created under earlier versions. Downward compatibility varies. As the above example shows, a system booted under an early DOS version may not read all later-version files properly.

DOS VERsion Command. To double-check the version of DOS used to boot your system, type VER (VERsion) and note the screen display, which should look like one of the following:

IBM DOS Version x.xx	DOS 4.xx
IBM Personal Computer DOS Version x.xx	DOS 2.xx or 3.xx
MS-DOS Version x.xx	Non-IBM version
Bad command or file name	DOS 1.xx

Remember that the displayed version refers to that used to boot the system, which is not necessarily the version on the diskette currently in the drive. In the case of the last message, the system has been booted with DOS 1.*xx* (does not include VER command), and this no doubt accounts for the garbled display.

Table 8.11 supplies some information that may help identify the specific version of DOS on a diskette of unknown origin, provided of course that the diskette's directory is readable on your system. Put the diskette in the default drive, type DIR, and note the number of bytes in the COMMAND.COM listing. Compare this against the COMMAND.COM figures in the first line of the chart. The DOS version listed at the top of that column is the version found on the diskette in question. If this version is later than the version displayed when you typed VER, then reboot the system using the diskette you have just checked.

If none of the above works, try to locate a recent version of DOS, reboot the system, and check the problem diskette again. If it works, the trouble is indeed traceable to a DOS incompatibility.

Of course, none of the above will help find the DOS version of a nonsystem diskette, that is, one that does not contain COMMAND.COM and the hidden files. In this case, the DOS debug utility can be used, as was described earlier in the chapter in the Boot Record section (page 289).

Bad or Missing Command Interpreter. If this message occurs when the system is booted on, DOS can't find the COMMAND.COM file. If you are booting from drive A, make sure COMMAND.COM is on the boot diskette that you are using.

If the system boots successfully and the message occurs when exiting a software program, check the AUTOEXEC.BAT file for the following line:

Table 8.11 DOS Version Chart

DOS	1.00	1.10	2.00	2.10	3.00	3.10
COMMAND.COM	3231	4959	17664	17792	22042	23210
IBMBIO.COM	1920	1920	4608	4736	8964	9564
IBMDOS.COM	6400	6400	17152	17024	27920	27760
Hidden file total	8320	8320	21760	21760	36884	37324
CHKDSK shows it as						
5.25" 160, 180Kb	8704	8704	22016	22528	37376	37888
5.25" 320, 360Kb	–	9216	22528	22528	37888	38912
5.25" 1.2Mb	–	–	–	–	37888	38912

DOS	3.20	3.30	4.00	4.01 †	4.01 ‡	5.00 §
COMMAND.COM	23791	25307	37637	37637	37652	41765
IBMBIO.COM	16369	22100	32810	32816	33901	32297
IBMDOS.COM	28477	30159	35984	36000	37136	36748
Hidden file total	44846	52259	68794	68816	71037	69045
CHKDSK shows it as						
3.50" 720Kb	45056	53248	70656	70656	72704	
3.50" 1.44Mb	–	52736	69632	69632	71680	69632
5.25" 320, 360Kb, 1.2Mb	–	45056	52736	69632	69632	

 † DOS 4.00 after upgrading to 4.01 via CSD 22624, 08 – 03 – 88, or
  DOS 4.01, as issued.
 ‡ DOS 4.00 or 4.01 after upgrading via CSD 25066, 04 – 06 – 89.
 § Microsoft MS – DOS 5.00 (Beta version)

```
SET COMSPEC=(drive letter and path)\COMMAND.COM
```

and make sure that COMMAND.COM is located where COMSPEC expects to find it.

Missing Operating System. In order for the system to boot from a diskette in drive A, the boot diskette must also contain the hidden IBMBIO.COM and IBMDOS.COM system files (or IO.SYS and MSDOS.SYS on IBM-compatible systems). This error message indicates that these hidden files were not found, perhaps because the diskette was formatted without the /S parameter which transfers the hidden files to its root directory. For diskette applications, the quickest fix is to simply format another diskette by typing

```
FORMAT A: /S
```

At the conclusion of the format, copy your CONFIG.SYS and AUTOEXEC.BAT files to this diskette. Or for a more detailed look at other alternatives, see the equivalent sections in Chapter 9 (pages 374 and 375).

SOFTWARE DIAGNOSTICS

The easiest way to rule out a problem caused by the software is simple: just try some other program on the same diskette and see if the problem still exists. If not, it's a pretty safe bet that the problem is indeed software related and that the rest of the system is in good order. The next step is to review the software in an attempt to identify and cure the specific problem. Of course, if a single diskette contains several programs that seem to be causing a problem, then the diskette itself should be suspected. In the case of an error that seems to be a function of the software, a few potential problem sources are discussed here.

System Locks Up

If the system locks up while running a certain software program, reboot the system and try running several other programs. If the problem goes away, then there is something wrong with the program that was running at the time of the lockup. If you wrote the program, then it's up to you to fix it. But if it's a commercially available software package, try to localize the specific conditions under which the lockup occurred and then call the company's technical support for help. Relief from a closed loop of "now press 3" phone messages can sometimes be found by pressing the zero key. With luck, someone with a pulse will eventually answer. With even greater luck, that person will know how to help.

Write-Protection and Error Messages

Here we'll review how a file or group of files may be protected against accidental erasure. The reason for reviewing this information is that attempts to erase or to write over a protected file will display various error messages. Without the following background information, these messages might suggest there is something wrong with the system, when in fact the system is doing just what it is supposed to do under the circumstances.

There are three methods of protecting a program against accidental erasure.

Diskette Write Protection. The contents of an entire diskette may be protected against erasure by means of a notch or a rectangular cutout in the diskette's protective jacket. The status of the notch or cutout determines whether write protection is enabled or disabled, as follows:

Diskette size	Write-protect device	Write protection is enabled	disabled
8″	notch	uncovered	covered
5.25″	notch	covered	uncovered
3.5″	cutout	uncovered	covered

Write protection is easily enabled by placing a protective tab over the notch on a 5.25-inch diskette or by removing same on an 8-inch diskette. And on a 3.5-inch diskette, a sliding tab exposes the cutout for write-protection.

If a diskette is write-protected, then an attempt to write to it will produce the following error message:

```
Write protect error writing drive A
Abort, Retry, Ignore?
```

or in DOS 4.*xx*, the cheery

```
Abort, Retry, Fail?
```

Since this type of protection prevents writing anywhere on the diskette, it of course cannot be used to selectively protect certain files while allowing new data to be written elsewhere on the diskette.

If the write-protect message appears even though write protection is disabled, then the drive requires servicing.

Read-Only File. Using DOS version 3.00 or later, an individual file on a diskette or hard disk may be protected against accidental erasure by designating it as a read-only file. This is possible because along with the name of a file, its size, and date and time of origination, DOS stores a so-called attribute byte, which contains additional information about the file, including whether or not write-protection status is desired. To set the read-only bit within the attribute byte for write protection, the DOS ATTRIBute command is used as described here. Such a file cannot be erased by using the ERASE command or by writing a new file with the same name on the diskette. Trying to do either will display one of these error messages:

Error message	Cause of message
Access denied	Trying to erase a write-protected file or read a file that does not exist.
File creation error	Trying to write a new file, using the name of a write-protected file.

The ATTRIBute Command. To write-protect a file named TEST.XYZ, enter the following command at the DOS prompt:

```
A> ATTRIB +R TEST.XYZ
```

To write-enable the file, type the following:

```
A> ATTRIB -R TEST.XYZ
```

If you are unsure whether a program is a read-only file, type the ATTRIB command, but omit the +R or -R parameter just before the file name. The file name will be displayed on screen, and it will be preceded by the letter R if it is a read-only file. Otherwise just the file name itself will be displayed.

Although a read-only file may be copied, the copy is not write-protected. But of course it can be, by again using the ATTRIB command as just described.

Hidden File. A file may be hidden or unhidden by setting/resetting the hidden-file bit within the file's attribute byte. Beginning with DOS 5.0, the ATTRIB command can be used to do this, as described in Appendix A. With earlier DOS versions, the debug utility program on the DOS diskette may be used instead. Better yet, use the Norton Utilities' *File Attributes* program.

The name of a hidden file is not seen when DIR is typed, although the file still exists on the diskette and it may be executed as before. However, the file can neither be copied nor erased. An attempt to do either will display the following error message:

```
File not found
```

Therefore, if a file can be executed even though it doesn't appear to be present on the diskette, there's nothing wrong; it's just a hidden file. Every IBM DOS system diskette contains two hidden files named IBMBIO.COM and IBMDOS.COM. On MS-DOS diskettes the equivalent files are usually named IO.SYS and MSDOS.SYS. The presence of these files may be verified by attempting to rename some other file to either of these names. Doing so will display the file-creation error message described earlier.

Error Message: Directory Not Empty. If a directory contains one or more files, an attempt to remove the directory will display the following error message:

```
Invalid path, not directory,
or directory not empty
```

Since the DOS ERASE *.* command does not delete hidden files, the presence of such a file may be the cause of this error message. To erase the hidden file, first unhide it using one of the following (or similar) utilities:

ATTR.COM	DOS Power Tools diskette
FA	*File Attributes* in Norton Utilities
ATTRIB.EXE	DOS 5.0 adds an unhide option to this command.

Once all the hidden files have been unhidden, exit the empty directory by typing CD.. and then type RD *(directory name)* to remove the directory.

Data Loss or Damage

In the event of a power failure, information not saved before the power failure is of course lost. But in certain situations you may discover that information saved before the failure also appears to be lost. This problem may occur if a power failure occurs during an interval in which data is being written to disk, in which case you may have noticed that the disk-in-use light was on when the power failed. Unfortunately, this is not a rare event, since many users instinctively try to save their current work as soon as an imminent power failure is anticipated. This is just about the worst time to do so, since it is a certainty (Murphy's Law again) that if power will fail at all, it will do so during a write operation.

When power is restored, note the directory listing for the file that was being written when the system shut down. The file length may read zero or some other number that is not what you expected it to be. This indicates that the directory now has erroneous information about the file, but it does not mean that the file is, in fact, erased.

If you do try to recover a damaged diskette file, first make a backup copy of the complete diskette, using the DOS DISKCOPY command only. This copies the entire contents of the diskette, and DOS does not consult the directory for guidance. If you attempt a simple copy of the damaged file itself and the directory claims the file has some number of bytes less than the real file length, only that number of bytes will be copied. In the worst case, you will now have a copy that really does contain zero bytes—that is, nothing.

Sector Damage

In addition to the power-related problems just described, the data integrity of a diskette or hard disk may be compromised by a variety of other factors, such as writing data to the wrong location during a disk-swap operation and head crashes. Depending on the nature of the error, it may be possible to recover some, most, or even all of the data that for the moment seems to be lost.

If the data loss involves damaged sectors that can be localized to a specific file (or files), the nondamaged sectors may be salvaged by one of the methods described here.

The DOS RECOVER Utility. The RECOVER.COM program sequentially copies good sectors of a damaged file into a new file named FILE*xxxx*, where *xxxx* increments by 1 for each file so recovered. Assuming a bad file named DAMAGED.DOC is on drive A and that RECOVER.COM is in the DOS subdirectory on drive C, the command syntax is

```
A>C:\DOS\RECOVER A:DAMAGED.DOC
```

Perhaps the best suggestion about using this utility is, "Don't." Or if you must, proceed with extreme caution. If you forget to include the name of the file you want to recover, the program recovers everything on the drive, whether it needs recovering or not. It does this by looking in the FAT for contiguous sector groups, and each such group is given a new name. For example, consider the directory listing shown in Figure 8.9a, where the file containing some bad sectors is named DAMAGED.DOC. For purposes of illustration, the QBASIC subdirectory contains two compiled programs and the BATFILES subdirectory contains five small batch files, for a total of 14 files on the diskette.

If RECOVER is executed without specifying the file to be recovered, the new "recovered" directory listing will be as shown in Figure 8.9b. Note that all date and time information has been replaced, the byte counts don't match those in the original directory, and the subdirectories are gone. One could try guessing which recovered file contains which original information, but on any diskette with more entries than this one, it's not going to be fun putting things back together again.

Recovering From RECOVER. Norton Utilities' *Disk Doctor* program can repair most, if not all, of the destruction, as shown in Figure 8.9c. To do so, type NDD A:/RA:FILE. Note that the two subdirectories are restored, although the original names are gone. However, each subdirectory does contain the files originally stored therein, each of which has its original name. These programs are all usable (assuming they weren't damaged in the first place), and with only five files back in the root directory, it will now be easier to figure out which is which.

(a)

```
QBASIC      <DIR>       05-15-90  11:07a
BATFILES    <DIR>       03-01-87   8:56p
COMMAND  COM    37637   06-17-88  12:00p
CONFIG   SYS      329   05-31-90   2:28p
AUTOEXEC BAT      277   05-31-90   2:29p
DAMAGED  DOC    87201   10-20-90   5:48p
TAXDOCS  WS2    92679   04-15-90  11:59p
        7 File(s)       34816 bytes free
```

A>C:\DOS\RECOVER A:

Press any key to begin recovery of the
files(s) on drive A:

12 files(s) recovered

(b)

```
FILE0001 REC      512   06-01-90   9:05a
FILE0002 REC      512   06-01-90   9:05a
FILE0003 REC      512   06-01-90   9:05a
FILE0004 REC      512   06-01-90   9:05a
FILE0005 REC      512   06-01-90   9:05a
FILE0006 REC      512   06-01-90   9:05a
FILE0007 REC    37888   06-01-90   9:05a
FILE0008 REC      512   06-01-90   9:05a
FILE0009 REC      512   06-01-90   9:05a
FILE0010 REC      512   06-01-90   9:05a
FILE0011 REC    40960   06-01-90   9:05a
FILE0012 REC    62464   06-01-90   9:05a
FILE0013 REC    87552   06-01-90   9:05a
FILE0014 REC    93184   06-01-90   9:05a
        14 File(s)      34816 bytes free
```

(c)

```
DIR0000      <DIR>       06-01-90  11:04a
DIR0001      <DIR>       06-01-90  11:07a
FILE0002 COM    37888   06-01-90  11:21a
FILE0003 _DD      512   06-01-90  11:21a
FILE0004 _DD      512   06-01-90  11:21a
FILE0005 _DD    87552   06-01-90  11:21a
FILE0006 _DD    93184   06-01-90  11:21a
        7 File(s)       34816 bytes free
```

(d)

>?(/ILES   <DIR>   03-01-87   8:56p

(e)

Volume in drive A is ü!↑âA↑àa↑çü
Directory of A:\

```
§Wü§Yí§[ ⊥§]296645225  8-22-31  12:11p
↓üü↓Öí↓¢ ⊥↓¥370649257  8-26-63  12:13p
↔╫ü↔┘ í↔█ ⊥↔█444653289  8-30-95  12:15p
        3 File(s)       0 bytes free
```

Figure 8.9. Typical directory listings. (a) Drive A directory, before executing DOS RECOVER command. (b) Same directory listing, after RECOVER. (c) Original directory listing, after running Norton NDD utility. Example of (d) a damaged directory listing and (e) a garbled directory listing.

File not found. The obvious solution to this error message is to double-check the file name or replace the diskette with the one that contains the desired file. However, if the message appears when you attempt a directory listing of a diskette that you know contains valid files, it's possible that the file allocation table is damaged. Unless you're an experienced debugger, this is another occasion to reach for a good third-party file-recovery utility.

Before going further, it's worth checking the directory to see if the file or subdirectory name is damaged. For example, Figure 8.9d shows a damaged directory listing. Note that the directory begins with a few illegal characters, so an attempt to access it will produce the *File not found* error message. As above, the *Disk Doctor* utility will repair the listing, renaming it DIR0000. Create a new directory with the missing name, copy the contents of DIR0000, then erase and remove the DIR0000 subdirectory.

Damaged Boot Record. Figure 8.9e shows a garbled directory display that may be caused by a DOS-conflict problem described earlier (page 319) or by damage to the boot record. In the latter case, no new-and-improved version of DOS is going to help (maybe next year). But again, a utility such as the *Disk Doctor* may be able to restore the boot record.

Programming-Related Problems

Sometimes a program that works on one drive will not work on another, even though both drives work well when other programs are run. One of the following errors may cause the problem.

Path Error. A software problem is often traced to a part of the program that assumes data will be found on a diskette located in a specific drive. An obvious clue is the illumination of the in-use light on the wrong drive. This indicates the program is looking there for information that probably exists elsewhere. In another case, the program may look for data on its own diskette and not find it.

In either of these cases, and depending on the nature of the specific program, a new file name may appear on the diskette in question, with a length of zero bytes, or perhaps some other suspiciously small number. Not finding the file it looked for, the program opened a new file with that name and then wrote nothing, or perhaps something, to it. The new file may be discovered by typing DIR and looking for a file name that was not there previously. If you're uncertain on this point, look for a file showing today's date and the time at which the in-use light was observed.

Finding such a file is a clear indication of a programming problem and not a hardware failure.

The solution is either to relocate the software to another drive or directory, or to revise the program to include the correct PATH information so that the program may find the desired file. If neither solution is possible, try revising the PATH statement in your AUTOEXEC.BAT file to include the path that the software needs.

Improper Drive Support. In addition to the actual drives that are physically installed in the computer, unused drive letters can be temporarily assigned to various subdirectories on a diskette, using the DOS SUBST (substitute) command described in Chapter 4. Also discussed there was the creation of an electronic disk, using the DOS VDISK.SYS program.

If the software currently in use has been written to make use of these substitute and/or electronic drives but your PC has not been configured to take these features into account, the following error message may be seen:

```
Invalid drive specification
```

or, in BASIC,

```
Path not found in xxx
```

where *xxx* is a line number. Either message indicates an attempt to access a drive that does not yet exist. Of course, the BASIC message might also really indicate an unsuccessful attempt to access a path that doesn't exist on a valid drive.

The remedy is to make sure the CONFIG.SYS file on your boot diskette contains one or both of the following lines:

Program line	Purpose
DEVICE=VDISK	To create an electronic disk in RAM
LASTDRIVE=*x*	To designate the last possible drive; default value is drive E, and *x* = any letter in the alphabet after E

In the event that the LASTDRIVE command has been used in order to take advantage of the SUBST command, then presumably an AUTOEXEC.BAT file has been used to assign the new drive letters to various subdirectories;

```
SUBST F: C:\(insert the name of a subdirectory)
```

```
SUBST G: C:\(insert the name of another subdirectory)
```

and so on, up to the last letter specified in LASTDRIVE. For further details on CONFIG.SYS and batch files, see Chapter 4.

Careful attention to the programming details discussed in this section should clear up many apparent system failures that are actually attributable to an electronic or substitute diskette drive.

If the drive or path error refers to a hard disk drive, review the drive partition information found in Chapter 9 (page 348).

Disk Full (or similar) Error Message. The obvious problem here is clearly stated by the message itself. However, some word-processor programs have the annoying habit of announcing this *after* you attempt to save the document you are working on, and then force you either to abandon it or else to erase some other file(s) to make room for it. If there is nothing that can be sacrificed, then the only choice is to abandon the present document. However, and despite the mean-spirited message, there's a good chance that some of it—perhaps most of it—has been saved. To check, quit the word processor and then display a directory listing. Look for a file with a strange name like TM123456.$83 or something equally uninformative. The displayed file time should be that at which you tried to save your document. Rename the file HOPEFUL (or whatever), then get back to your word processor to have a look at it. If it's worth saving, exit the word processor again and copy it to another diskette with more room on it. Also, don't overlook the document backup file—the one with the BAK suffix. If you were making regular saves prior to getting into trouble, this file will have a reasonably close version of the desired document. Rename it to eliminate the BAK suffix and proceed as just described.

If the Disk Full message doesn't seem to make sense (because you thought the diskette had plenty of room), don't forget that many word processors create temporary files that take up space on the diskette. These get in the way of the save operation if they are written to the same diskette as your actual document (as in the case of the TM123456.$83 file mentioned above).

Some word processors can be set up so that temporary files are written to another drive. If you can do this, try routing them to a RAM disk (see Chapter 4, page 86) so they won't get in the way anymore.

If you have the uncomfortable feeling that you are about to get into trouble (it comes with experience), try a temporary exit to DOS from within the document you are working on. Then look at the directory of the diskette you are using. If space is getting tight, copy a few files (not the one you are working on though) over to another diskette. Then erase them to free up some space, return to your document, and save it.

Virus Problems

Although computer viruses do their worst work on hard disks, diskettes are also subject to infection, and are as well a major carrier of viruses from one system to another. If virus damage is suspected, refer to the Virus Attacks and Virus Damage sections of Chapter 9 (pages 378 and 381).

File Recovery Techniques

If you discover a text file that appears to be defective, the following technique may allow you to salvage much of it. As an example, consider a text file that your word-processing program can no longer read. To rule out a completely defective diskette, look at another text file on the same diskette. If there are none, try writing and then reading a brief test file. If either test works, exit the word processor. At the DOS prompt, enter the following command:

```
A> TYPE DAMAGED
```

where DAMAGED is of course replaced by the name of the suspect file. The following error message confirms that the file is indeed damaged:

```
Data error reading drive A
Abort, Retry, Ignore?_
```

Select the Abort option by typing A or a, and then copy the entire diskette containing the defective file, using DOS's DISKCOPY command. You'll see the following message when attempting to copy the defective source file in drive A to a target diskette in another drive:

```
Unrecoverable read error on drive A:
Side x, track xx
```

The message may repeat more than once, depending on how many errors are encountered. At the conclusion of DISKCOPY, the following message is seen:

```
Target diskette may be unusable
```

Despite the ominous tone of these warnings, it's quite possible that the file containing the faulty tracks may indeed be recoverable. Try reading it with your word processor to see if it can be salvaged. If not, the BASIC file recovery program in Listing 8.2 makes a byte-by-byte copy of the damaged file, but substitutes an exclamation mark in place of erroneous non-printable characters. Once the file copy is made, return to your word processor to work on it. With luck, there may be enough of it intact to allow you to restore the garbled sections.

Of course, if the entire file is garbled, the above technique will be of no use. Instead, try reviewing the section immediately following.

Completely Garbled File. As a last software diagnostics resort, don't overlook the fact that a completely garbled text file received from another source may not be written in the format recognized by your word processor.

EBCDIC Files. For example, the EBCDIC (Extended Binary-Coded Decimal Interchange Code) format is a feature of the IBM System/360 and System/370. An EBCDIC file will make no sense at all if it is read as an ASCII file. The following line taken from an early EBCDIC file is shown as it will appear when read properly, and as it is interpreted by a PC using the IBM extended character set:

```
To be or not to be
! û@éà@ûÖ@òûú@úû@éà
```

The PC "interpretation" is not very informative, to say the least. Listing 8.3 presents a short BASIC program to copy an EBCDIC file into a new file in ASCII format. The 128 numeric constants found in the program's DATA statements are the EBCDIC equivalents of the ASCII format. Most

Listing 8.2 A BASIC File Recovery Program *

```
100 CLS
110 OPEN "DAMAGED.DOC" AS #1 LEN = 1
120 FIELD #1, 1 AS A$
130 OPEN "FIXED.DOC" FOR OUTPUT AS #2
140 IF EOF(1) THEN CLOSE:END
150 GET #1
160 B$ = A$: IF A$ < " " AND A$ <> CHR$(10) AND
    A$ <> CHR$(13) THEN B$ = "!"
170 PRINT #2, B$;
180 PRINT B$;
190 GOTO 140
```

   * Change lines 110 and 130 to indicate the names of the damaged file and the
      name you wish to use for the repaired copy file.

word processors have a mode for reading a straight ASCII file, and once the EBCDIC-to-ASCII conversion is done, the file can no doubt be converted into whatever modified ASCII format your own word processor likes.

Archived Files. As another possibility, files downloaded via modem are often received in an archived, or data-compressed, format which is unreadable until expanded. Such files are usually identified by a file name with an ARC suffix. In case of doubt, use the DOS debug utility to load the file. Then, dump the first part of the file to screen. If a readable file name is seen, followed by unreadable data, the file is probably compressed. Several data-expansion utilities are readily available, usually via the same modem bulletin board from which the file itself was downloaded.

Listing 8.3 A BASIC Program to Copy an EBCDIC File to ASCII Format *

```
100 DATA    0,   1,   2,   3,  55,  45,  46,  47
110 DATA   22,   5,  37,  11,  12,  13,  14,  15
120 DATA   16,  17,  18, 255,  60,  61,  50,  38
130 DATA   24,  25,  63,  39,  34,  29,  53,  31
140 DATA   64,  90, 127, 123,  91, 108,  80, 125
150 DATA   77,  93,  92,  78, 107,  96,  75,  97
160 DATA  240, 241, 242, 243, 244, 245, 246, 247
170 DATA  248, 249, 122,  94,  76, 126, 110, 111
180 DATA  124, 193, 194, 195, 196, 197, 198, 199
190 DATA  200, 201, 209, 210, 211, 212, 213, 214
200 DATA  215, 216, 217, 226, 227, 228, 229, 230
210 DATA  231, 232, 233, 139, 225, 155,  95, 109
220 DATA  121, 129, 130, 131, 132, 133, 134, 135
230 DATA  136, 137, 145, 146, 147, 148, 149, 150
240 DATA  151, 152, 153, 162, 163, 164, 165, 166
250 DATA  167, 168, 169, 192, 106, 208, 161,   7
260 DIM X(255)
270 FOR K = 0 TO 127
280 READ A
290 X(A) = K
300 NEXT K
310 OPEN "EBCFILE" FOR  INPUT AS #1
320 OPEN "ASCFILE" FOR OUTPUT AS #2
330 WHILE NOT EOF(1)
340 B$ = INPUT$(1,#1)
350 B = ASC(B$)
360 PRINT CHR$(X(B));
370 PRINT #2, CHR$(X(B));
380 WEND
390 CLOSE: END
```

* Line 310 assumes your EBCDIC file is called "EBCFILE." Change this, and line 320, to suit your requirements.

Of course, EBCDIC and archived files are but two of many possibilities. In case of doubt, try to determine the actual format of the file you are trying to read. Unless it's something truly exotic, chances are your word processor has a file conversion utility that will convert it into something more-or-less readable. Or a data-expansion or other file conversion utility can be used.

Illegal Space in File Name. If you accidentally save a file with a space in its name, the file cannot be erased or renamed. An attempt to do so will display a *too many parameters* error message. To correct the error, rename the file by typing a question mark in place of the space. For example, to fix a file named MY   FAULT.BAS, simply type

```
RENAME MY?FAULT.BAS NEWNAME.BAS↵
```

Incompatible Software

A few software programs use diskette tracks beyond those specified (tracks 0–39) by the American National Standards Institute (ANSI) in one of its standards for 5.25-inch diskettes, that is, track 40 or greater (ANSI X3.125-1985). Although these programs work on some diskette drives, they won't work on others, and an error message may be displayed. A normal-capacity IBM 5.25-inch drive (PC, XT, or AT) whose serial number begins with the letter E is known as a Type 3 drive, and will probably not be able to read these programs. The serial number on this drive type may be seen through the front of the drive, with the door open and the diskette removed. If this appears to be the source of the problem, first call or write the software manufacturer to make sure that track 40 is indeed in use before concluding that the diskette drive is faulty. If track 40 has been used by the program on the diskette, you'll have to replace the software, unless a different type drive is conveniently available.

DRIVE INSTALLATION AND SWAPPING PROCEDURES

The following section describes how to install a new drive in an IBM personal computer, as well as how to swap drives as an aid to troubleshooting.

System-Board Diskette Configuration Procedures

When an additional diskette drive is installed, or an old one is removed and not immediately replaced, the system will have to be reconfigured to take the new drive complement into account. Configuration requirements are summarized here and explained in greater detail in Chapter 6.

If an ancient single-sided diskette drive is replaced by a 5.25-inch double-sided drive, system reconfiguration is not required.

PC and XT. Switches on the system board are used to reconfigure the system. These must be set as indicated in Table 8.12 (see also Table 6.10). The hard disk drive(s) should not be considered when setting these switches.

AT. System reconfiguration requires the use of the diagnostics diskette, as described in the section on AT configuration found in Chapter 6. Reconfiguration is required when changing the number or type of diskette drives or hard disk drives.

PS/2 Systems. System reconfiguration requires nothing more than running the automatic configuration routine found on the Starter or Reference diskette. Simply reboot with this diskette in drive A and follow the on-screen prompts.

Table 8.12 System Board Switch Settings for PC and XT Diskette Drive Configuration

Installed drives	Block 1 switch positions * PC	XT
0	1xxxxx11	n/a
1	0xxxxx11	xxxxxx11
2	0xxxxx01	xxxxxx01
3	0xxxxx10	xxxxxx10
4	0xxxxx00	xxxxxx00

* Switch Positions:
0 = off (down)   x = not used for diskette drive configuration
1 = on (up)   n/a = not available

Drive-Swapping Procedures

To verify that a drive is indeed defective, the positions of drives A and B may be temporarily swapped. In the case of a drive A failure, if the swap restores normal DOS operation, then the drive just removed from position A is indeed defective. If the swap has no effect on the problem, then outside servicing is probably required. By contrast, if a defective drive B is temporarily put in the drive A position, the system should give a positive indication of the failure by going into the cassette BASIC mode when power is again turned on.

When swapping drives, make sure to review the Terminating Resistor Network section below.

Drive-Cable Designations.   On PC, XT, AT, and some PS/2 systems, one flat multiconductor cable leads from the drive adapter to drive B and then continues back to drive A. Within the short cable length between the two drive connectors, the position of some of the conductors is reversed, as seen in Figure 8.10.

The drive connectors on the cable determine the identity of each drive; a drive plugged into the end connector becomes drive A, and a drive plugged into the other connector becomes drive B. A connector may be labeled to indicate the appropriate drive (A or B), or may have an uninformative label (J2 or J3) instead.

In order to swap drives, simply unplug both connectors and replug them to the opposite drives. Each drive connector on the cable is keyed so that it cannot be attached to a drive in the wrong direction. If your PC has two piggy-backed, half-height drives, follow the drive-swapping directions given below since you will have to physically swap the drives themselves, in order to complete the swap.

The sets of four conductors supplying power to each drive, as well as the black chassis ground wire, may be freely interchanged or left as is.

On those MCA systems that do not use the multiconductor cable just described, the diskette drives can be swapped simply by sliding each one out of its own slot and into the adjacent slot.

On pre-PS/2 systems a functioning drive A is required for any operation other than cassette BASIC, so you may wish to make a drive swap if the present drive A appears to be defective. With drive B temporarily assigned to position A, you may continue diskette operation while the defective drive is being serviced. However, read the section on the terminating resistor network (page 342) before sending any drive out for servicing.

PS/2 systems set up to boot from the hard disk will continue to do so even if diskette drive A has been physically removed from the system. Therefore,

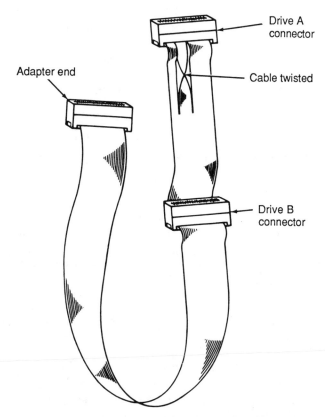

Figure 8.10. Control and data cable detail. Note that the relative positions of a few conductors are swapped in the section between the two drive connectors.

you may wish to disconnect a defective drive A if its presence prevents the system from booting. The error messages will have to be ignored, since the missing drive precludes using the Starter or Reference diskette for reconfiguring. However, if drive B is usable, you can insert the Starter/Reference diskette and type COMMAND to access the automatic configuration screen.

AT Drive-Swapping Notes. On an AT containing one 1.2Mb high-capacity drive and one 360Kb normal-capacity drive, remember that although the designation letters and physical positions of the drives may be swapped, the diskettes used with each drive are not completely interchangeable. If you have been using a 1.2Mb diskette in drive A to boot your system, the diskette will not be usable in a normal-capacity drive temporarily connected to the drive A cable connector. Instead, a normal-capacity boot diskette must be prepared for use in the new drive A.

Drive Removal and Replacement Procedures

After following the appropriate procedures given here, don't forget to reconfigure the system if the total number of diskette drives changes due to the removal or installation of a drive. On the AT, reconfiguration will also be necessary if a high-capacity drive is replaced by a normal-capacity drive, or vice versa.

Drive removal.   Figures 8.11 through 8.13 illustrate various drive systems used in IBM personal computers. Study the appropriate illustration and follow the specific instructions accompanying each figure. The general procedure is as follows:

1. Turn PC off and unplug power cord from wall outlet.
2. Remove system unit cover.
3. Remove drive-mounting screws, if any. In some cases, adapters may need to be removed first. (To avoid damage later, note the size of any screw that is removed, and make sure that it is used in the same location when drive is reinstalled.)
4. Slide drive unit forward slightly.
5. Disconnect all cables leading to drive.
6. Slide drive unit all the way forward, until it is clear of system unit.

Drive Replacement.   Reverse the sequence illustrated in the appropriate drive-removal figure. The general procedure is as follows:

1. Turn PC off and unplug power cord from wall outlet.
2. Remove system unit cover.
3. Slide drive about half way into appropriate slot.
4. Reconnect all cables leading to drive.
5. Slide drive the rest of way into system unit.
6. Reinstall all mounting screws.

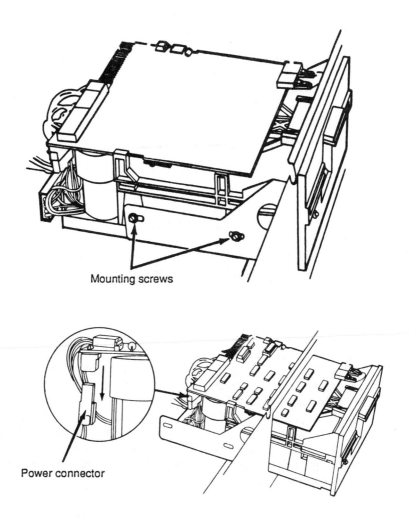

Mounting screws

Power connector

Figure 8.11. PC and XT diskette drive removal procedure. 1. Remove the two mounting screws, either on the left side of drive A or the right side of drive B. To remove the drive A screws, you will have to remove the nearby adapter cards first. 2. Slide the drive forward slightly and disconnect its power, signal, and ground cables. The actual position of each of these connectors may vary from one drive type to another. 3. Slide the drive all the way forward until it is clear of the system unit. 4. If drive unit is to be transported elsewhere, protect read/write heads by sliding cardboard shipping insert into drive slot and then closing drive door. If insert is not available, use a scratch diskette.

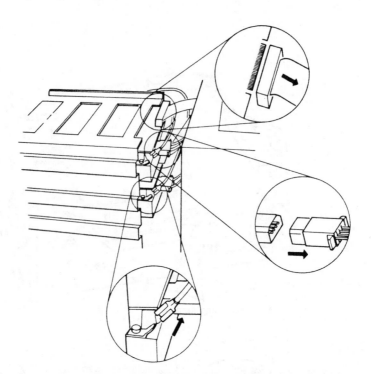

Figure 8.12.   AT diskette drive removal procedure. If you have two diskette drives, you may have to partially remove the upper one to gain access to the connectors for the lower drive. 1. Remove the two mounting screws and clips on either side of the drive. 2. Slide the drive forward slightly and disconnect its power, signal, and ground cables. The actual position of each of these may vary from one drive type to another. 3. Slide the drive all the way forward until it is clear of the system unit. 4. If drive unit is to be transported elsewhere, protect read/write heads by sliding cardboard shipping insert into drive slot and then closing drive door. If insert is not available, use a scratch diskette.

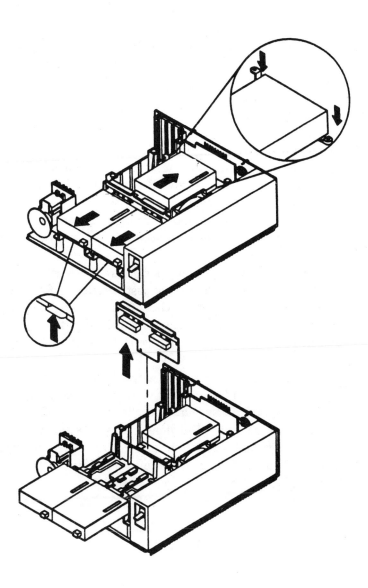

Figure 8.13.   Diskette drive removal procedures on PS/2 table model computers.
1. Depress metal tab under diskette drive. 2. Disconnect attached cables or slide
drive forward to disconnect it from drive adapter card. 3. Slide the drive all the
way forward until it is clear of the system unit. 4. If drive unit is to be transported
elsewhere, protect read/write heads by sliding cardboard shipping insert into drive
slot and then closing drive door. If insert is not available, use a scratch diskette.

Terminating Resistor Network

For proper operation, a terminating resistor network is found on some diskette and hard disk drives. When the system configuration is changed by adding or removing a drive, the network may require attention, as described here.

PC, XT, and AT Systems. A single, 16-pin (14-pin on AT drives) terminating resistor network must be installed on the printed circuit card on the top of the first diskette drive and the first hard disk drive only (i.e., on drives A and C). Typically the resistor may be found in the drive A socket, as seen in Figure 8.14a. If drive B is also installed, its equivalent socket must not contain this resistor.

When swapping drives, move the resistor to the new drive A. When installing a new or recently serviced drive B, remove the resistor if it is found in place.

Some drives may employ an 8-position switch-block termination network instead of the removable resistor just described. If so, turn all drive A switches on and all drive B switches off. Of course, drives with termination switches may be used interchangeably with other drives using a removable resistor. Just make sure that on drive B the switches are off or the resistor is removed.

For hard disk drives, the same logic applies. The terminating resistor must be installed only on hard disk drive C, not on drive D. If a switch-block terminator is used, the switches must be on in block C and off in block D.

In summary, a properly functioning drive A is required for all operations other than cassette BASIC. If the present drive A is defective, drive B may be installed in its place. This permits normal operation to continue while drive A is being serviced. To accomplish this

1. Disconnect all cables from drive A and remove the drive.
2. Attach the drive A cable connector to drive B.
3. Move the terminating resistor from the removed drive A to drive B.

Drive B will now function in place of the removed drive A.

PS/2 Systems. Diskette drives for PS/2 systems do not use a terminating resistor, and hard disk drives may or may not require one either. Generally, a system that can accommodate only one hard disk drive does not need the network. But on a system that may include either one or two hard disk drives, a terminating resistor network should be installed on drive C only. The

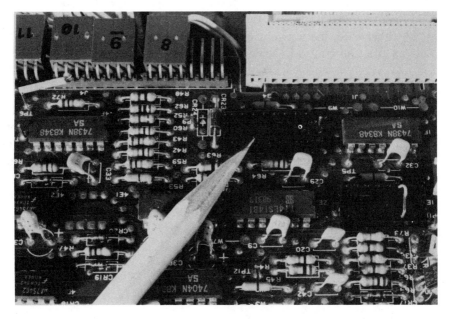

(a)

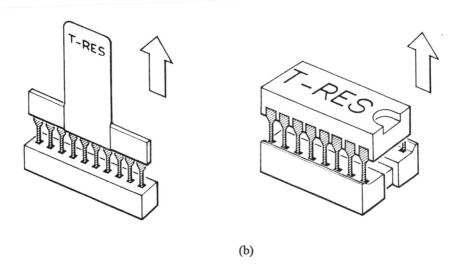

(b)

Figure 8.14. The drive termination network must be installed on drive A and hard disk drive C only. If a removable network is replaced by an 8-position switch block, switches must all be on. On diskette drive B and hard disk drive D, the network/switches must be removed/switched off. (a) plug-in network on an ISA diskette drive. (b) Terminating networks found on some MCA systems.

location and physical description of the network varies from one drive to another, and it may be packaged in either an inline or DIP format. But in either case, the network is clearly labeled "T-RES" as shown in Figure 8.14b, and it must be removed from the second hard disk drive.

Drive Relocation Note

If you need to transport your PC to another location, be sure to protect the head in each diskette drive against colliding with each other. To do so, remove any diskettes in the drives and place a cardboard shipping insert in each drive. If inserts are no longer on hand, use a scratch diskette instead. With the insert or scratch diskette in place, close the drive door. This places the drive heads in contact with the insert and prevents them from striking each other during transit.

9

HARD DISK DRIVES

In contrast to the flexible diskette, the storage medium in a hard disk drive is a set of rigid magnetic disks. Since they are tucked away in a sealed enclosure which makes them both inaccessible and nonremovable ("fixed" in IBM jargon), there is not much to do to fix one if it breaks.

Barring the dreaded head crash, hard disk problems are quite often traceable to software. Or if not, then the vagaries of partitioning, logical disk drives, formatting requirements, the operating system, etc., make it easy to get into trouble, and often difficult to get back out of it. As to the software itself, since there are as many problems as there are programs, this chapter takes the easy (?) way out by not even trying to describe every specific problem that could come up (since this would take a book even bigger than *DOS Power Tools*). Instead, an extensive overview of all the variables that help to confuse things is presented, with the hope that this will help the reader first to pin down, and then to exterminate, any software bug that dares raise its head.

After a longer than usual look at nomenclature, we review the general procedures involved during installation and setup, which in many cases are of no concern if the system is delivered in operable condition. If so, then one might want to skip to the Preventive Maintenance section, to learn a little something about staying out of trouble. This section is followed by a look at Diagnostics—mostly related to the interaction between the operating system (DOS, in this book) and the drive.

The final section on hard disk preparation reviews a few procedures that are required every now and then (or for the very lucky, never). For example, most drives are delivered with low-level formatting already in place, so much of that section can be skipped, except by those who would like to get an idea of what it's all about.

If the operating system has aready been installed on the drive, there's a good chance that the partitioning (if any) is not the way you would have done it. Therefore, the FDISK utility—which is used for partitioning or repartitioning a hard disk—is described in a separate section.

Hard Disk Nomenclature

This section introduces some of the many terms that will be encountered later on in the chapter, or any other time the subject of hard disks comes up. Still more terms are introduced later on, as they show up in the text.

Hard Disk. Since most hard disk drives contain two or more two-sided nonremovable magnetic disks, the term *hard disk* itself is understood to refer to the entire system, not just to one of the disks therein.

Cylinders and Heads. A hard disk system usually consists of a stack of two or more magnetic disks, with each disk surface holding 300 or more magnetic tracks. A cylinder is defined as the complete set of tracks—two per disk—found at any given diameter. The outer cylinder is cylinder zero, and the highest-numbered cylinder is at the inner diameter of the disk. Since the magnetic coating does not stop abruptly at the highest cylinder, the cylinder count simply represents the area certified by the manufacturer as usable.

Each double-sided magnetic disk within the hard disk enclosure requires two heads, so if the head count is an uneven number, one of the disks uses one side only for data storage.

The number of certified cylinders and heads is found on the drive housing label, or in the accompanying user's manual.

Sectors. In contrast to the 9, 15, or 18 sectors on a diskette, each hard disk surface is divided into 17 or more sectors.

Interleave. Assuming the drive's sectors are numbered sequentially according to their physical position, it is often more efficient to read a sector, skip one or more sectors, read another one, skip again, and so on until the disk has made one complete revolution. The reason for this sector *interleave* is that after the system reads say, sector 0, it needs a finite length of time to figure out what to do next. By the time it realizes it should be reading sector 1, it's too late; the sector has already passed under the head. So it must wait until sector 1 comes around again. Thus it takes 17 revolutions to read every sector on a 17-sector track.

Assuming the system needs x sectors worth of time between each read or write operation, an $x{:}1$ interleave can be set up, in which sequential *logical* sectors are spaced x *physical* sectors apart. As a result, it will now take x revolutions to read or write all the sectors on a track.

A few interleave ratios are given below. In each case, the head reads the underlined physical sectors during one revolution, then the group not underlined during the next revolution, and so on until all sectors have been read.

For logical sector number

	0	1	2	3	4	5	6	7	8	9	10	11	12	13	14	15	16	
Interleave	its physical location is at sector																	
1:1	<u>1</u>	2	<u>3</u>	4	<u>5</u>	6	<u>7</u>	8	<u>9</u>	10	<u>11</u>	12	<u>13</u>	14	<u>15</u>	16	<u>17</u>	(worst case)
	<u>1</u>	<u>2</u>	<u>3</u>	<u>4</u>	<u>5</u>	<u>6</u>	<u>7</u>	<u>8</u>	<u>9</u>	<u>10</u>	<u>11</u>	<u>12</u>	<u>13</u>	<u>14</u>	<u>15</u>	<u>16</u>	<u>17</u>	(ideal case)
2:1	<u>1</u>	<u>3</u>	<u>5</u>	<u>7</u>	<u>9</u>	<u>11</u>	<u>13</u>	<u>15</u>	<u>17</u>	2	4	6	8	10	12	14	16	
3:1	<u>1</u>	<u>4</u>	<u>7</u>	<u>10</u>	<u>13</u>	<u>16</u>	2	5	8	11	14	17	<u>3</u>	<u>6</u>	<u>9</u>	<u>12</u>	<u>15</u>	
4:1	<u>1</u>	<u>5</u>	<u>9</u>	<u>13</u>	<u>17</u>	4	8	12	16	<u>3</u>	<u>7</u>	<u>11</u>	<u>15</u>	2	6	10	14	
5:1	<u>1</u>	<u>6</u>	<u>11</u>	<u>16</u>	5	10	15	<u>4</u>	<u>9</u>	<u>14</u>	3	8	13	<u>2</u>	<u>7</u>	<u>12</u>	<u>17</u>	

and so on.

Note that logical sector numbering begins at zero, while actual physical sectors are counted from one (i.e., logical 0–16 = physical 1–17). Each physical sequence listed above represents a sequential read/write of the logical sectors 0–16.

Typical interleaves vary from 1:1 for a drive system fast enough to read or write sequential sectors, to 5:1 for an older XT drive. Sector interleave is set during the low-level format procedure described later in this chapter (page 384), and several interleave ratios are shown graphically near the end of the chapter (Figure 9.19(b)).

Bad Tracks. Even with the most rigorous manufacturing standards, one or more sectors on a hard disk may contain minute magnetic defects, thus rendering a write/read operation impossible, or at least unreliable. Each track containing such a sector is marked as a *bad track*, and a list of bad tracks is usually printed on a label on the drive housing or included with the documentation. The list will give the cylinder and head number corresponding to the bad track, and it may be necessary to manually enter this information during low-level formatting. If the bad track data is unavailable, many third-party disk-management utilities (*SpeedStor*, for example) will test the disk surface and prepare a table listing of the bad tracks.

Partitions and Logical Drives

The magnetic surface of a hard disk may be divided into two, three, or four separate sections, each of which is known as a *partition*. In early versions of DOS, no partition could exceed a capacity of 32M bytes. Furthermore, no operating system could access more than one partition. Therefore, regardless of the total disk capacity, DOS could make use of only 32Mb of its total surface.

The FDISK utility is used to create, change, or delete the DOS partitions and logical drives described here. FDISK itself is covered in detail later in the chapter (page 398).

Primary and Extended Partitions. Later DOS versions broke the 32Mb barrier by permitting two DOS partitions. The *primary* partition was still limited to 32Mb, while a secondary partition on the same surface could be of any size, up to the total remaining capacity of the disk. Although common sense might rule otherwise, the additional section is called an *extended* partition (perhaps *secondary* would have been too logical a choice). DOS version (4.00) removed the 32Mb limitation imposed on the primary partition, which may now also be of any size.

Non-DOS Partition. Additional partitions (3 and 4) can be set up for use by other operating systems. Such partitions are not accessible to DOS. Again, see the FDISK section for more details.

Active Partition. The active partition is the one that is read when the system is powered on. After the computer boots itself, it functions under whatever operating system is in the active partition. The active partition may be set by FDISK or most third-party hard disk utilities.

Logical Drives. In a one-drive system, the primary partition becomes drive C and the extended partition is drive D. However, the extended partition may be further subdivided into two or more logical drives. A *logical drive* is a portion of the extended partition that may be given its own drive letter. Thus, the surface of a single hard disk system might include a primary partition identified as drive C, and one extended partition containing many logical drives (D, E, F, and so on). A logical drive is sometimes referred to as a *volume*.

For an important variation on this drive-lettering sequence, refer to the Dual-Drive Systems section on page 362.

Hidden Sectors: The Partition Table. At the beginning of every hard disk partition and logical drive, sectors are set aside for a *drive partition table,* used for partitioning purposes. These sectors are reported by the Norton Utilities' *Disk Information* program as "hidden sectors," and are the first physical sectors in each partition, located immediately ahead of the boot record sector. The hidden sectors occupy the entire track 0 on side 0.

The hidden sectors are ignored by the DOS debug utility, which considers the boot record to be absolute sector zero, even though the hidden sectors do in fact precede it.

Boot Record. The boot record sector was described in detail in Chapter 8 (page 289), and Table 8.2 gave the contents of the first 30 bytes for a typical 360Kb diskette. The table shows that the last two bytes give the number of sectors reserved for the drive partition, in other words, the hidden sectors.

Using the DEBUG procedures described in Chapter 8, the boot record data for a hard disk formatted under IBM DOS 4.01 as drive C ($x = 2$) is

```
xxxx:0000 EB 3C 90 49 42 4D 20 20-34 2E 30 00 02 08 01 00 .<.IBM  4.0.....
xxxx:0010 02 00 02 28 60 F8 0A 00-11 00 09 00 11 00        ...('.........
```

Again the media descriptor byte (F8) is underlined, and here the last two bytes (11 00) indicate that hex 11 (decimal 17) sectors are reserved for the partition table on the drive being examined (Seagate ST4096).

Partition and Logical Drive Summary

The following section briefly reviews the significant partition and drive changes that have taken place since the introduction of DOS version 2.00.

DOS 2.00 to 3.2. These versions permit up to four partitions, but only one may be used for each operating system. The size limit for the single DOS partition is 32 Mbytes. In lieu of the primary/extended DOS partition capability introduced with DOS 3.3, the SUBST command (see Chapter 4, page 96) can be used to assign drive letters to various directories within the single DOS partition.

DOS 3.3. Two DOS partitions—primary and extended—are allowed. In order to use DOS, the primary partition must be set as the active partition. The primary partition may not be subdivided into logical drives, and it has a size limit of 32 Mbytes. The secondary partition may be subdivided into logical drives, each of which has its own drive letter (D, E, F, . . .). There is no limit to the size of the DOS extended partition. However, no logical drive within the extended partition can be set as active.

DOS 4.00 and 4.01. These versions remove the 32Mb size limit for the primary partition. Other partition characteristics are the same as in DOS 3.3.

DOS 5.0 Partition size may be up to 2 Gb (G=2^{30}=1,073,741,824).

The DOS SHARE Command. The SHARE.EXE utility was added in DOS version 3.00. Starting with version 4.00, SHARE has been enhanced to support partition sizes greater than 32Mb. This feature is not mentioned in the summary of enhanced commands at the front of the DOS manual, but it is included in the command explanation later in the DOS 4.00 manual (page 50). If SHARE is not loaded, some programs stored in a large partition may not execute properly. Share is not needed with DOS 5.0.

If you are using DOS 4.00, the new INSTALL command may be added to your configuration file to load the SHARE utility, as described in Chapter 4 (page 84).

Hard Disk Data Encoding Methods

In Chapter 8, the FM (frequency modulation) and MFM (modified frequency modulation) encoding methods were described (page 293). For hard disk systems where even greater recording density is required, the RLL (run-length limited) encoding system is sometimes used. Although not described in detail here, RLL converts each byte into a unique 16-bit pattern in which the "run length" of zeroes between each 1 bit is limited to a defined range. The encoding scheme permits an even greater data density than MFM encoding. The following table briefly summarizes the information presented in Chapter 8 and adds the RLL parameters.

Encoding method	Brief description
FM	Clock pulse at beginning of each bit cell. Between each clock pulse, no flux reversal = 0, flux reversal = 1. FM was used on single-density diskette media (page 293).
MFM	Similar, but clock pulse only at beginning of second and subsequent 0 bits. MFM is used on all

IBM diskettes and many hard disk systems.

RLL or RLL 2, 7   The run length is limited to 2 to 7 zero bits between each 1.

RLL 3, 9 or ARRL   Same, but 3 to 9 zero bits between each 1 (ARRL = Advanced RLL).

System/Drive Interfaces

IBM and other hard disk drive controllers use one of several types of interface systems, each of which may use either MFM or RLL data encoding. The principal system/drive interfaces are described here, and Table 9.1 lists interface, encoding, and other parameters for a few representative hard disk drives from IBM and third-party sources.

ST506/412. The nomenclature is borrowed from the early Seagate ST506 6Mb and ST412 12Mb hard disk drives. The system interface for these long-since discontinued drives lives on as the "ST506 standard," although it is in fact not a standard in the usual sense of that word. That is, no standards organization has published an ST506 Standard. Seagate itself refers to it as the "ST412 interface."

When an ST506 drive is installed, the system needs to be configured to recognize the drive. This is done by entering the drive type number into CMOS RAM during system configuration. For further details, see the Drive Parameter Table section below.

The physical connection between an ST506 drive and its adapter card is via two cables: a 34-conductor control cable and a 20-conductor data cable. The adapter card connector is illustrated in Figure 9.1a. At the opposite end, the two cables mate with edge connectors on the drive.

ESDI (Enhanced Small Device Interface). Compared to the ST506 interface, the ESDI interface provides a higher data density, typically 34 sectors per cylinder. In addition, the drive parameters may be stored on the drive itself, thus obviating the need for, and limitations of, the ROM BIOS drive table. In addition, bad track information is also stored on, and read from, the disk itself.

Some ESDI drive connectors use a single 40-pin connector similar (except for the extra pins) to connector J1 in Figure 9.1a. On other ESDI drives, the connectors are physically identical to the two ST506 connectors described above. However, the two systems are not logically compatible, so neither drive type will work with the other's adapter card.

Table 9.1a Representative IBM Fixed Disk Drives

Computer Drive part no.	30-x21 6451031	5x-031	5x, 7x-061 6450606	80-311 6450381	65 SX no. 64510xx xx=49	=50	=55
Interface †	ST–506	ST–506	ESDI	ESDI	SCSI	SCSI	SCSI
Encoding	MFM	RLL	RLL	RLL	RLL	RLL	RLL
Transfer rate ‡	7.5	7.5	8.4	10	10.2	10.2	16
Capacity (Mb)	20	30	60	314	60	120	320
Cylinders	610	615	762	915	920	920	949
Heads	4	4	6	7	4	4	14
Sectors/track	17	25	26	36	32	32	48
IBM type no.	26	33	n/a	n/a	n/a	n/a	n/a

    † Table gives manufacturer's nomenclature: ST–506, ST412, ST506/412
      interfaces are identical.
    ‡ Transfer rate is in Mbits per second.

Table 9.1b Representative Other Hard Disk Drives

Manufacturer Model number	Micropolis 1335	Micropolis 1565-8S	Seagate ST225	Seagate ST225R	Seagate ST225N	Seagate ST296N
Interface †	ST506/412	ESDI	ST412	ST412	SCSI	SCSI
Encoding	MFM	RLL	MFM	RLL (2,7)	MFM	RLL (2,7)
Transfer rate ‡	5	15	5	7.5	12	12
Capacity (Mb)	71.3	389	21.4	21.17	21.3	84.9
Cylinders	1024	1632	615	667	615	820
Heads	8	8	4	2	4	6
Sectors/track	17	54	17	31	17	34
IBM type no.	none	n/a	2	n/a	n/a	n/a

    † Table gives manufacturer's nomenclature: ST–506, ST412, ST506/412
      interfaces are identical.
    ‡ Transfer rate is in Mbits per second.

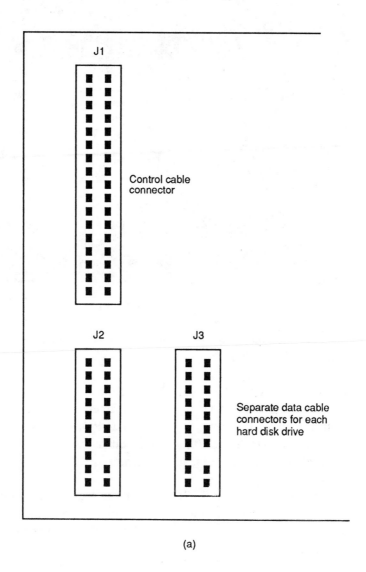

Figure 9.1.   Hard disk drive adapter cards. (a) Connectors on an IBM ISA fixed disk adapter which supports two drives. A single control cable feeds both drives, while each drive has a separate data cable. (b) SCSI host adapter card for EISA system (BusTek BT-742A).

(b)

SCSI (Small Computer System Interface). The distinguishing characteristics of this interface are that it may be called "scuzzy" in public, and
that the interface adapter can accommodate up to seven SCSI devices
connected in parallel. Typical SCSI devices are

Diskette and hard disk systems	Tape systems
SCSI host (the computer)	Printers
Optical memory devices	CD-ROM drives
Communications devices (modems)	Scanners
WORM (write once, read many) systems	

Hard disks using the SCSI system require a SCSI bus master adapter
or host adapter card which must be inserted in an ISA, MCA, or EISA
system slot. A shielded 50-pin socket on the adapter bracket connects
external devices to the adapter. Internal devices are connected to an
unshielded 50-pin socket (IBM uses an edge connector) at the top of the
adapter. A representative SCSI adapter for an EISA system is shown in
Figure 9.1b.

Refer to the SCSI Bus Configuration section of Chapter 6 (page 170) for
information about termination procedures for hard disk drives and other
devices connected to a SCSI adapter.

Drive parameter data is also stored on the drive, so again the ROM BIOS
drive parameter table is not required. And in this case, the interface is
described by a published standard—ANSI (American National Standards

Institute) X3.131-1986, Small Computer Systems Interface. A revised and updated standard (SCSI-II) should be published shortly, and is presently available in a draft version (X3 Project 375-D) from Global Engineering Documents.

Drive Type and Parameter Tables

To establish an accurate data flow between system and drive, the former must know a little something about the latter; specifically the number of cylinders, heads, sectors per track, etc. Hard disk drives using the ST506 and ESDI interface make use of a drive table permanently stored in ROM BIOS on the system board. The table provides space to store data for four (XT) to 47 types of drives. However, IBM has not yet assigned parameters to all 47 types, and the actual number of types stored in the table varies from one computer model to another. Table 9.2a lists the drive types currently assigned by IBM. Table 9.2b indicates the portion of that table found in each IBM computer, and in addition gives the starting address of the table in each computer.

Two additional drive table parameters are briefly described here.

Write Precompensation. In the illustration of track and sector layout shown in Chapter 8 (Figure 8.1), note that the size of a sector gets progressively smaller as the track diameter diminishes. Yet each sector must still accommodate 512 bytes of data. To improve the data-write performance at the smaller diameters, a *write precompensation* circuit boosts the write current when data is written to the inner tracks. The track at which write compensation begins is listed in Tables 9.2a and 9.4.

Landing Zone. The *landing zone,* also listed in Tables 9.2a and 9.4, is an inner cylinder at which the drive's heads should be parked prior to turning the power off. The landing zone cylinder is not used for data storage, and therefore offers some protection against accidental data destruction due to head crashes during the power on/off interval. Remember that cylinder numbers begin at zero, so on drives with 1,024 cylinders (0–1,023) or 1,023 cylinders (0–1,022), a 1,023 landing zone indicates the last cylinder, or one cylinder beyond the last, respectively. On drives where the landing zone cylinder number is considerably higher than the last certified cylinder (IBM types 33 through 37 in Table 9.2a, for example), the parking mechanism simply moves the heads to a safe zone even farther removed from the data storage area.

Table 9.2a IBM Hard Disk Drive Parameters

IBM type	Cylinders	Heads	Sectors per track	Capacity * (bytes)	Write precomp.	Landing zone
1	306	4	17	10,653,696	128	305
2	615	4	17	21,411,840	300	615
3	615	6	17	32,117,760	300	615
4	940	8	17	65,454,080	512	940
5	940	6	17	49,090,560	512	940
6	615	4	17	21,411,840	none	615
7	462	8	17	32,169,984	256	511
8	733	5	17	31,900,160	none	733
9	900	15	17	117,504,000	none	901
10	820	3	17	21,411,840	none	820
11	855	5	17	37,209,600	none	855
12	855	7	17	52,093,440	none	855
13	306	8	17	21,307,392	128	319
14	733	7	17	44,660,224	none	733
15	reserved					
16	612	4	17	21,307,392	all	663
17	977	5	17	42,519,040	300	977
18	977	7	17	59,526,656	none	977
19	1024	7	17	62,390,272	512	1023
20	733	5	17	31,900,160	300	732
21	733	7	17	44,660,224	300	732
22	733	5	17	31,900,160	300	733
23	306	4	17	10,653,696	all	336
24	612	4	17	21,307,392	305	663
25	306	4	17	10,653,696	none	340
26	612	4	17	21,307,392	none	670
27	698	7	17	42,527,744	300	732
27 †	855	5	17	37,709,600	none	855
28	976	5	17	42,475,520	488	977
29	306	4	17	10,653,696	all	340
30	611	4	17	21,272,576	306	663
31	732	7	17	44,599,296	300	732
32	1023	5	17	44,520,960	none	1023
33	614	4	25	31,436,800	none	663
34	775	2	27	21,427,200	none	900
35	921	2	33	31,122,432	none	1000
36	402	4	26	21,405,696	none	460
37	580	6	26	46,325,760	none	640

*   capacity = cylinders × heads × sectors/track × 512
†   PS/2 model 25 only

Table 9.2b IBM Drive Parameter Table Cross-Reference *

Computer	Drive types supported **	Table begins at segment:offset
PC, XT	See Table 9.3	
AT	1 – 14 01/10/84 BIOS	F000:E401
	1 – 23 all others	F000:E401
25	1 – 27	F000:E352
30	1 – 26	F000:E352
30 286	1 – 37	E000:020A
50Z	1 – 33	E000:025E
55 SX	1 – 33	E000:0250
60	1 – 32	E000:025D
65 SX	1 – 33	E000:0262
70	1 – 33	E000:025E
80	1 – 32	E000:02E7

   * For use with hard disk drive ST506 interface.
 ** See Table 9.2a for drive type parameters.

Table 9.3a IBM XT Hard Disk Drive Parameters

Switch table	Cylinders	Heads	Sectors per track	Capacity (bytes)	Write precomp.	Landing zone
XT BIOS dated 11/10/82 only						
00	306	2	17	5,326,848	all	none
01	375	8	17	26,112,000	all	none
02	306	6	17	15,980,544	256	none
03	306	4	17	10,653,696	all	none
XT BIOS dated 1/08/86 or later *						
00 (1)	306	4	17	10,653,696	all	306
01 (16)	612	4	17	21,307,392	all	663
02 (2)	615	4	17	21,411,840	300	615
03 (13)	306	8	17	21,307,392	128	336

   * (*x*) indicates an early IBM drive type. Note that Type 1 write precompensation
       and Types 1 and 13 landing zone values differ from the later drive types listed
       in Table 9.2a.

Table 9.3b IBM 20 Mbyte Hard Disk Adapter Card Switch Settings

Switch table	Binary * equivalent	Switches on adapter card †		XT drive type ‡
00	11	Off	Off	1
01	10	Off	On	16
02	01	On	Off	2
03	00	On	On	13

* 0 = switch on, 1 = switch off
† For Drive 0, use adapter card switches 1 and 2.
  For Drive 1, use adapter card switches 3 and 4.
‡ Drive type data valid only for XT BIOS dated 1/08/86 or later.

Table 9.4a AMI Hard Disk Drive Parameters *

AMI type	Cylinders	Heads	Sectors per track	Capacity (bytes)	Write precomp.	Landing zone
1 − 23	Same as IBM					
24	925	7	17	56,358,400	all	925
25	925	9	17	72,460,800	none	925
26	754	7	17	45,939,712	754	754
27	754	11	17	72,190,976	none	754
28	699	7	17	42,588,672	256	699
29	823	10	17	71,633,920	none	823
30	918	7	17	55,931,904	918	918
31	1024	11	17	98,041,856	none	1024
32	1024	15	17	133,693,440	none	1024
33	1024	5	17	44,564,480	1024	1024
34	612	2	17	10,653,696	128	612
35	1024	9	17	80,216,064	none	1024
36	1024	8	17	71,303,168	512	1024
37	615	8	17	42,823,680	128	615
38	987	3	17	25,772,544	987	987
39	987	7	17	60,135,936	987	987
40	820	6	17	42,823,680	820	820
41	977	5	17	42,519,040	977	977
42	981	5	17	42,693,120	981	981
43	830	7	17	50,570,240	512	830
44	830	10	17	72,243,200	none	830
45	917	15	17	119,723,520	none	918
46	1224	15	17	159,805,440	none	1223
47	user defined					

* American Megatrends, Inc.

Table 9.4b Award Hard Disk Drive Parameters *

Award type	Cylinders	Heads	Sectors per track	Capacity (bytes)	Write precomp.	Landing zone
1 – 23	Same as IBM					
24	977	5	17	42,519,040	none	976
25	1024	9	17	80,216,064	none	1023
26	1224	7	17	74,575,872	none	1223
27	1224	11	17	117,190,656	none	1223
28	1224	15	17	159,805,440	none	1223
29	1024	8	17	71,303,168	none	1023
30	1024	11	17	98,041,856	none	1023
31	918	11	17	87,892,992	none	1023
32	925	9	17	72,460,800	none	926
33	1024	10	17	89,128,960	none	1023
34	1024	12	17	106,954,752	none	1023
35	1024	13	17	115,867,648	none	1023
36	1024	14	17	124,780,544	none	1023
37	1024	2	17	17,825,792	none	1023
38	1024	16	17	142,606,336	none	1023
39	918	15	17	119,854,080	none	1023
40	820	6	17	42,823,680	none	820
41	1024	5	17	44,564,480	none	1023
42	1024	5	26	68,157,440	none	1023
43	809	6	17	42,249,216	none	808
44	820	6	26	65,495,040	none	819
45	776	8	33	104,890,368	none	775
46	user defined					
47	user defined					

* Award Software, Inc.

Table 9.4c ALR/Phoenix EISA Hard Disk Drive Parameters *

ALR type	Cylinders	Heads	Sectors per track	Capacity (bytes)	Write precomp.	Landing zone
1 — 4	Same as IBM					
5	1630	15	52	650,956,800	none	1630
6	615	4	17	21,411,840	none	615
7	1630	8	52	347,176,960	none	1630
8	733	5	17	31,900,160	none	733
9	900	15	17	117,504,000	none	901
10	615	8	17	42,823,680	128	664
11	776	8	33	104,890,368	none	776
12	535	10	29	79,436,800	none	535
13	953	7	34	116,128,768	none	953
14	733	7	26	68,303,872	none	733
15	reserved					
16	953	5	34	82,949,120	none	953
17	977	5	17	42,519,040	300	977
18	977	7	17	59,526,656	none	977
19	1024	7	17	62,390,272	512	1023
20	823	10	34	143,267,840	none	823
21	733	7	17	44,660,224	300	732
22	971	5	26	64,629,760	none	971
23	820	6	17	42,823,680	none	820
24	1024	7	34	124,780,544	none	1024
25	1022	7	34	124,536,832	none	1022
26	1024	4	17	35,651,584	none	1023
27	1024	5	17	44,564,480	none	1023
28	1024	8	17	71,303,168	none	1023
29	615	4	26	32,747,520	612	615
30	845	7	35	105,996,800	none	845
31	989	5	17	43,041,280	128	989
32	1020	15	17	133,171,200	none	1024
33	1024	9	17	80,216,064	none	1024
34	966	9	34	151,345,152	none	966
35	1024	16	63	528,484,304	none	1630
36	1024	5	17	44,564,480	512	1024
37	1024	5	26	68,157,440	none	1024
38	611	16	63	315,334,656	none	612
39	654	16	63	337,526,784	none	1630
40	642	16	63	331,333,632	none	1778
41	917	15	17	119,723,520	none	918
42	1023	15	17	133,562,880	none	1024
43	497	10	33	83,973,120	none	497
44	820	6	17	42,823,680	none	820
45	1024	8	17	71,303,168	none	1024
46	1024	7	26	95,420416	none	1024
47	288	16	63	148,635,648	none	1224
48	user defined					
49	user defined					

* Advanced Logic Research PowerVEISA with Phoenix BIOS

Some drives automatically park the heads over the landing zone when power is turned off, while others require manual parking via software. See the Drive Relocation section (page 366) for further details about head-parking procedures.

Drive-System Interface Techniques

Given the variety of ST506 hard disk drives now available, it's not unusual to encounter a drive whose parameters do not match any of those in the ROM drive parameter table. In this case, there are three alternatives:

1. Choose the closest possible match, but make sure that each parameter in the table is equal to or less than that of the drive itself.
2. Use a commercially available software disk management utility.
3. Install a new ROM BIOS containing a drive parameter table that recognizes the drive type you wish to use. Each choice is briefly described below.

Closest Possible Match.   Drive parameters for a few hard drives and their closest IBM drive types are given here:

	Cylinders	Heads	Sectors /track	Capacity (Mb)	Matched in a ROM table by
Miniscribe 3650	809	6	17	42,249,216	Award, Type 43
IBM Type 3	615	6	17	32,117,760	(see Table 9.4b)
Priam V130	987	5	17	42,954,240	
IBM Type 17	977	5	17	42,519,040	
Seagate ST4096	1,024	9	17	80,216,064	AMI, Type 35
IBM Type 7	1,024	7	17	62,390,272	(see Table 9.4a)

Although these drives will function properly if the system is set up to recognize the closest IBM drive type, this is an impractical solution when available capacity is made significantly lower than it should be.

Disk Management Utility.   If the hard disk drive parameters do not match any of those supported by the IBM drive parameter table, one of several partitioning utilities may be used instead. For example, Figure 9.2 shows a section of the hard disk installation menu in Storage Dimensions' *SpeedStor* utility. Parameters are set by highlighting the manufacturer and specific drive model, and if a corresponding set of drive parameters is not found in the ROM drive parameter table, the utility writes the values into the first

```
           SpeedStor(TM)  Disk Integration Software, version 6.0.1
        Copyright(C) 1985-1989 Storage Dimensions, Inc.  All rights reserved
====================================================================================
                     Please pick the drive model for Drive 1

              Use arrow keys to point, then press ENTER to select.


  Drive     Manufacturer/Model      Cyls  Heads  Secs  Precomp  Lzone  TotalBytes
   1        <Standard Type 35>      1024    9     17    none     1024   80,215,552
                         S e a g a t e   D r i v e   M o d e l s
          ModelName   Cylinders  Heads  Sectors  PreComp  LandingZone  TotalBytes
          ─────────   ─────────  ─────  ───────  ───────  ───────────  ──────────
          ST4038        733        5      17       300       733       31,900,160
          ST4038M       733        5      17      none       977       31,900,160
          ST4051        977        5      17      none       977       42,519,040
          ST4053       1024        5      17      none      1023       44,564,480
          ST4096       1024        9      17      none      1023       80,216,064
          ST138R        615        4      26      none       615       32,747,520
          ST157R        615        6      26      none       615       49,121,280
          ST238R        615        4      26       300       615       32,747,520
          ST251R        820        4      26      none       820       43,663,360
          ST277R        820        6      26      none       820       65,495,040
```

Figure 9.2. A third-party diskette-based hard disk installation menu (*SpeedStor* Disk Integration Software). The desired drive type is selected by moving a highlighted bar to the appropriate line.

hidden sector in the hard disk partition table, for use the next time the system is booted.

New ROM BIOS. As yet another alternative, a set of replacement ROM BIOS modules for IBM systems can be ordered from AMI, Award, or other third-party suppliers. Such modules are standard on IBM-compatible systems. The drive parameter table sometimes matches that of IBM for Types 1 through 24, while type numbers above 24 vary from one supplier to another. One or two drive types are usually left unassigned, for use with drives not covered by the table. Examples of drive tables in third-party ROM BIOS modules for ISA and EISA systems are seen in Table 9.4.

Dual-Drive Systems

If a second hard disk drive is added to a PC, its primary partition automatically becomes drive D, and therefore all logical drives in the drive C extended partition are shifted up one letter. Drive letters for the logical partitions on the second drive begin immediately after the last drive letter used by the first drive. Thus:

	Complete system contains ·		
	one	two drives	
Partition	drive	first	second
primary	C	C	D
extended, with	D	E	H
3 logical drives	E	F	I
	F	G	J

As a result of this slightly confusing convention, the addition of a second hard disk drive may require various PATH commands (see Chapter 4, page 94) to be rewritten in order to find programs whose logical drive has just taken on a new identity, even though the program itself hasn't budged.

HARD DISK INSTALLATION AND SETUP

Most hard disk drives are designed to function properly regardless of physical orientation. However, it's a good idea to perform hard disk formatting procedures with the system in the position in which it will be used.

As part of the configuration procedure, the system must be set up to recognize the installed hard disk. The following section lists a few system-specific notes for various IBM personal computers.

PC, XT, and AT Systems

The hard disk drive is connected to the system with four cables; one each for power, data, control, and chassis ground. Although IBM documentation for the AT actually mentions mounting the system unit in an upright position, no cautions have been published against mounting a PC or an XT system in the same position.

PC and XT. Figure 9.1a gave a detail view of the sockets on the hard disk adapter used with these systems. The adapter supports two ST506 hard disk drives. A single control cable is used to feed both drives, while each drive has a separate data cable.

In the IBM PC, the factory-installed 63.5-watt power supply is not sufficient to power a hard disk drive, which requires a 130-watt power supply. Therefore, IBM states that its Fixed Disk Adapter and Fixed Disk Drive must be installed in an external expansion unit. This limitation may be overcome by replacing the original PC power supply with a higher-capacity unit, as described in Chapter 5.

AT. The hard disk is connected to the Fixed Disk and Diskette Drive Adapter described in Chapter 8 (page 300).

PC, XT, and AT Setup. During the routine configuration procedure described in Chapter 6 (page 170), the list of installed devices will display the fixed disk drive type. Follow the on-screen prompts and, if necessary, enter the correct type number, which should be found on a label on the drive. To make sure the type number on the drive agrees with the parameters in the ROM table, check Tables 9.2a or 9.4 (or your own documentation if these tables do not include your system's ROM).

PS/2 Systems

The hard disk controller interface varies from one system to another, as seen here.

Model	Controller interface is
25	on adapter card (upgrade kit)
30	integrated with drive, no adapter required
30 286	integrated with drive, no adapter required
50	on adapter card
55 SX	integrated with drive, no adapter required
60	on adapter card
65 SX	SCSI bus master adapter
70	integrated with drive, no adapter required
P70	integrated with drive, no adapter required
80	on SCSI bus master or other adapter

The connection may be via one or two flat-ribbon cables to an adapter, or through an edge connector on drives with an integrated controller.

PS/2 Setup. Configuration is handled by the automatic configuration routine on the Starter or Reference diskette.

EISA Systems

A hard disk drive installed in an EISA system may require its own adapter card or make used of a controller built into the drive itself. Since the EISA system is compatible with ISA hardware, any drive adapter card that works in an ISA system may be inserted in an ISA slot on the system board. Or, it may be inserted in an EISA slot if necessary.

EISA Setup. The configuration utility suppied with all EISA systems will display information about the hard disk that is installed in the system. If the information is incorrect, it may be changed by the user, usually by moving a highlighted bar to the appropriate section on the screen and then toggling through the available choices. See the EISA Configuration section of Chapter 6 (page 191) for further details.

Internal "Hard Card" Disk Drives

Hard disk drives are also available from several manufacturers in a configuration in which the drive itself is mounted on its own adapter. The card-mounted disk drive is quickly installed simply by inserting it into an available adapter slot, as shown in Figure 9.3.

A drive letter is assigned to the drive by inserting the name of its device driver in your CONFIG.SYS file, as described in Chapter 4. When the configuration file is read, the drive becomes drive x, where x is the next available drive letter. If the configuration file assigns other letters to other devices, then each assigned letter depends on the sequence in which the drivers appear in the file.

Figure 9.3. A hard disk mounted directly on its own adapter card is installed simply by plugging the card into an adapter slot on the system board. (*Plus Hardcard II* 80 courtesy Plus Development Corp.)

• **Hard Card Caution** Such drives often increase the number of sectors per track at outer cylinder diameters. The low-level formatting procedures described in this chapter are unable to make the necessary adjustments, and so should not be used on any drive whose sector count is not the same on all tracks. In case of doubt, consult the drive manufacturer before doing anything with potentially fatal consequences.

Hard Disk Drive Power Considerations

When installing a new hard disk drive, don't overlook two important variables; the system's power supply and the power requirements of the drive. See Chapter 5 (page 107 and Table 5.4) for further details.

Drive Relocation Notes

The IBM *Guide to Operations* contains a special section devoted to instructions on how to prepare your computer for moving. Unfortunately, people sometimes ignore these instructions, and although some are indeed obvious (turn off the power, remove all connectors, etc.) other less obvious ones are equally crucial to a successful relocation. For example, the read/write heads on hard disk drives must be safely parked to lessen the likelihood that a head crash will damage the disk surfaces during shipment. The heads should also be parked every time the system is turned off, so that a sudden power-off or power-on jolt does not scrape the heads across a sensitive data track.

Head Parking. A head-parking mechanism moves the heads to the designated landing zone—usually an unused cylinder beyond the data storage area. On many recent hard disk systems, the heads are automatically parked—and sometimes even locked in place—each time system power is turned off.

If your hard disk does not automatically park the heads in the landing zone, then the Guide to Operations or User's Manual will advise you to use the diagnostics or Starter/Reference diskette to manually park the heads. Use the diskette as described in the appropriate section listed here.

Computer	Option	See Chapter 3
PC, XT, AT	3. Prepare System for Relocation	page 57
25, 30	3. Prepare System for Moving	page 57
30 286	5. Move the System	page 50
50/60	6. Move the Computer	page 50

Since these procedures are somewhat time consuming, most users probably ignore them during routine off again/on again sessions. However, a number of third-party utilities include a head-parking program that can be easily executed via a small batch file prior to powering down.

If you're not sure whether your drive requires manual head parking, go ahead and park the heads anyway. Doing so does not cause any harm.

Hard Disk Moving Preparation. Before parking the heads prior to moving the system, backup the files as an insurance policy against in-transit data loss. The procedure is described in the Hard Disk Drive Backup Procedures below. After the backup, use the appropriate park procedure as described in Chapter 3, or one of the head-parking utilities available elsewhere.

• **Relocation Caution.** Make sure that the proper IBM diskette is used when performing this procedure. For example, if an XT diagnostics diskette is used to park the heads on an AT hard disk, data will be destroyed.

ROUTINE MAINTENANCE TECHNIQUES

If a monitor or modem dies, it's reasonably easy to get back in business. After an appropriate grieving period, go out and buy another one. But if the loved one was a hard disk, the grieving may go on a lot longer if you didn't have a good insurance policy. Even a 20-Mbyte drive that's only half full has a lot of information on it. If you have to bury all that information along with the drive itself, you will not be pleased. Therefore, the backup procedures described here should be taken seriously.

Hard Disk Drive Backup Procedures

Thanks to the latest developments in magnetic storage technology and Edsel Murphy, the modern hard disk drive never crashes . . . unless there is irreplaceable information on it. Then, the magnitude of the destruction is directly proportional to the value of the data. So, a word to the wise: make backup copies frequently. It's annoying, but not nearly so annoying as trying to reconstruct the last six months worth of information stored on a drive that has just taken your data on a crash dive.

A few backup procedures are briefly described here. The three DOS commands described here are executed via COM files in the DOS subdirectory. For further details consult the appropriate DOS or user's manual.

XCOPY. This DOS command can copy all the files in a directory, as well as all those in any subdirectories found within that directory. The directory/subdirectory structure of the source is preserved on the target, so the latter is a faithful and directly usable copy of the former. The catch is that XCOPY can only be used to copy files to a target whose capacity is equal to, or greater than, the source. In other words, when XCOPY runs out of space on the target diskette, it displays an *insufficient disk space* error and ceases operation. This makes it unusable for copying a source hard disk to a set of target diskettes.

The correct syntax for copying the contents of a drive C directory, including all subdirectories within it, to a backup diskette in drive A is

```
XCOPY C:\(directory name) A:\ /s
```

Omit the /s parameter to copy only those files within the specified directory. Or omit the directory name to copy the entire source drive to another drive of sufficient capacity.

There are many other parameters that may be used with XCOPY to customize the copy process, as described in the DOS manual.

BACKUP. Use this DOS command to backup an entire source drive to a multiple set of diskettes. As each diskette is filled, BACKUP displays a prompt to remove the target diskette and insert a new one. Make sure you do: if not, BACKUP will simply overwrite the previously written target data, thereby losing it.

If subdirectories exist on a target diskette, BACKUP will leave them and their contents intact, using only the space available within the root directory. If necessary, BACKUP formats the target diskettes before use.

Unlike XCOPY target diskettes, the diskettes created by BACKUP are not directly usable. Instead, all files are merged into a single file labeled BACKUP.*xxx*, and the directory paths, filenames, etc., are saved in another file named CONTROL.*xxx*. In each case *xxx* is the number of the target diskette and is incremented by one for each diskette that is required.

If the hard disk is partitioned into two or more logical drives, each drive must be separately backed up.

To copy all the files on hard drive C to a set of diskettes in drive A, type the following line:

```
BACKUP C:\*.* A: /s
```

See the DOS manual for a description of the other BACKUP options.

Note: Effective with DOS 3.30, BACKUP no longer copies the read-only hidden system files or COMMAND.COM from the root directory (but it does copy the latter file if it finds it elsewhere on the disk). Therefore, if a new operating system is installed on the hard disk after BACKUP, a subsequent RESTORE (see below) won't wipe out the new version by overwriting the new system files with the old versions saved during BACK-UP.

RESTORE. This DOS command copies all files stored on diskettes made via the BACKUP command back to the hard disk drive. To begin, insert the first backup diskette in drive A and type

```
RESTORE A: C:\*.* /s
```

As each diskette is copied back to drive C, RESTORE displays a prompt to insert the next diskette in the series.

Repeat the command as required for all other drives to be restored. Note: RESTORE can be followed by a /P (pause) parameter, which displays a *yes?/no?* prompt prior to restoring a read-only file. On versions prior to 3.30, answer "no" if you do not want to restore the backed-up system files (IBMBIO.COM and IBMDOS.COM), as would be the case if you have just installed a newer version of the operating system on the hard disk.

On DOS versions 3.30 and later, BACKUP does not copy the system files, so the /P parameter need no longer be used for this purpose.

Restore Selected Files. The RESTORE command can also be used to extract a single file, or group of files, from a backup diskette in drive A. For example, to copy all the backup files in SUBDIR1 with a DOC suffix, type the following line:

```
RESTORE A: C:\SUBDIR1\*.DOC
```

If RESTORE can't find the files on the backup diskette in drive A, it will prompt you to insert the next backup diskette in the drive.

Third-Party Backup Utilities. A number of utilities are available to make the backup procedure—if still not quite fun—at least a bit less tedious and more user friendly. For example, Figure 9.4 shows the screen display at the end of a backup performed with Fifth Generation Systems' *FastBack Plus* utility.

Backup Summary. XCOPY diskettes are immediately usable and so can be rearranged as you like. You may prefer to XCOPY any source directory that can fit on a single target diskette, or to copy the entire source to a high-capacity target (Bernoulli drive, or similar).

The BACKUP utility compresses source files slightly as it saves them, but not enough to make this a serious consideration. Furthermore, the

```
┌──────────────────────────────────────────────────────────────────────────┐
│ v2.09                F A S T B A C K      P L U S                           │
│ Estimate      Start Backup        Quit                                      │
├────────────────────────────────┬───────────────────────────────────────────┤
│                                │ Backup E: to G:\                          │
├────────────────────────────────┼───────────────────────────────────────────┤
│ Set Name:    E900529A          │ Starting backup of E: on volume 1...      │
│ Set Date:    05-29-90          │ \                                         │
│ Set Time:    10:45:32          │ \QBASIC\                                  │
│ Volume:          1             │ \QBASIC\ADVR\_EX\                         │
│ Track:                         │ \QBASIC\EXAMPLES\                         │
│ Buffers:                       │ \QBASIC\MATHPROG\                         │
│              Estimate   Actual │ \FONTS\                                   │
│ Files:           515      515  │ \NORTON\                                  │
│ Kbytes:         4726     4726  │ \UTILITIES\                               │
│ Volumes:                    1  │ C:\FASTBACK\E900529A.FUL                  │
│ Time:           3:22     2:46  │ ...Backup completed on volume 1.          │
│ Kbytes/Min:     1400     1708  │ C:\FASTBACK\E900529A.VOL volumes updated. │
│                                │ Old history files for drive E: deleted.   │
│ % Complete:              100   │ Marking files as backup up on E:...       │
│                                │ ...File marking completed.                │
├────────────────────────────────┴───────────────────────────────────────────┤
│ →←, FIRST LETTER: Position highlight bar                                    │
│              ENTER: Start operation                                         │
└──────────────────────────────────────────────────────────────────────────┘
```

Figure 9.4.   Third-party backup utility screen display (*FastBack Plus*) at conclusion of backup procedure.

backups are unusable without going through the RESTORE operation, which puts everything back just the way it was, whether that's what you want or not. BACKUP erases everything stored previously on the target drive. This is of no practical consequence when backing up to multiple diskettes, but it could be a consideration when the target is a high-capacity drive with more than enough room for several backups.

The *FastBack Plus* utility takes slightly longer than BACKUP, but is more efficient in its data compression. Furthermore, it does not erase previous backups or other files on the same target. Therefore, the same target drive could store several backups, if space permits.

For comparison purposes, the size of a few backup files and approximate time required for each backup are given here.

	File name	File size	Time
Source files	various	5,394,432	
Backup utility			
DOS BACKUP	BACKUP.001 and	4,839,950	2:30
	CONTROL.001	18,209	
FastBack Plus	E900529B.001	4,085,760	2:46
DOS XCOPY	same names and sizes as source files	4:00

• **Backup Caution.** When backing up a hard disk prior to installing a new version of DOS, make sure *not* to make backups of the hidden files, since restoring these will defeat the DOS upgrade. Both XCOPY and BACKUP do not copy the hidden files. Furthermore, XCOPY does not copy any hidden or read-only files, and BACKUP does not copy a COMMAND.COM file found in the root directory of the source. If using a third-party backup utility, check this point before starting the backup. Note: For DOS versions prior to 3.3, check the XCOPY and BACKUP sections of the DOS manual for variations not covered here.

Fragmented File Correction Techniques

After a certain amount of routine use, the free sectors on a disk surface are apt to be scattered all over its surface. For example, consider what happens when new material is appended to a previously written file. If the sectors immediately following it are already occupied by other files, DOS will have to allocate additional sectors far removed from the old ones. Therefore, the complete file is said to be fragmented; it is now located in fragments wherever DOS could find free sectors. Although this presents no logistical problems to DOS, it does slow down system performance due to the extra time needed to move the head from one sector to another. As part of routine hard disk maintenance, it's a good idea to do some periodic "housekeeping" to remedy the inevitable fragmentation that is just one of those facts of data-writing life.

One way to speed things up is to backup all the files, reformat the drive, and then restore everything, as just described. As the files are written back to disk, they are copied one file at a time into contiguous sectors. In the case of severe sector fragmentation, the process should produce a noticeable speed improvement.

A number of third-party utilities are available for the purpose of rounding up file fragments and placing them in a contiguous set of sectors without going through the backup-format-restore operation. Such utilities work by "sector shuffling"; that is, they move files out of the first few sectors, copy fragmented files into the free space, then move and copy more sectors until the entire drive is reorganized. The utility may be called Optimize Disk (Norton), UnFrag[ment] (Mace Utilities), or some other descriptive term.

Figure 9.5 shows a map of sector usage on a typical hard disk drive, and it shows that the available sector blocks are also fragmented (the Disk Statistics option seen in the screen menu will show the percentage of files that are fragmented too). To reorganize the files, execute the Optimize Disk option seen in the same menu. This moves each file into a set of contiguous

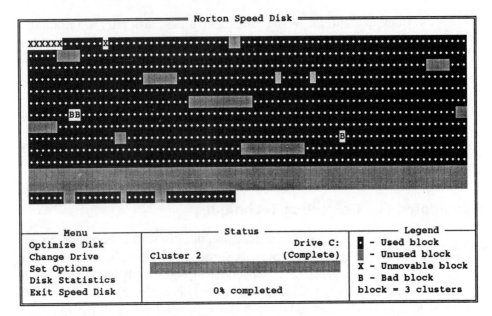

Figure 9.5. Map of typical sector usage, showing unused blocks scattered throughout the disk surface area. (Norton Utilities *Speed Disk*).

sectors, followed immediately by the next file, with all unused sector blocks moved beyond the last written file. At first, an "R" (read) is seen moving through a series of occupied blocks at the beginning of the sector map. The blocks are being read into memory, thus freeing up the space they occupied. Next, a moving "W" (write) shows the same blocks as they are written back to the disk at a more distant location. Then another series of blocks is read and written into the recently vacated area. The read/write operation continues until the fragmented display shown in Figure 9.5 is replaced by one which no longer shows a random scattering of unused blocks.

• **Block Reorganizing Caution:** When using any utility such as the one just described, remember to reboot the system before resuming normal operations. This precaution makes sure that disk caches and other memory-resident programs don't wander off writing data in a sector that now holds something else.

Routine Low-Level Formatting

The word *routine* followed by *low-level formatting* may seem a contradiction in terms, but a few authorities recommend doing a low-level format at regular intervals. In order to understand why this is so, some background information is needed, so further discussion is put off until the Low-Level Formatting section later in the chapter (page 384). The point of mentioning this here is simply to draw attention to that section, even in the absence of a situation which demands low-level formatting.

HARD DISK DIAGNOSTICS

Hard disk problems may be divided into three general categories. First, there are the problems that are not much different from what one encounters in routine diskette operations. For example, much of the Diskette- and DOS-Related Diagnostics sections of Chapter 8 apply to the hard disk too, and so to avoid repetition here, these sections should be consulted for assistance if a problem does not seem to be unique to the hard disk. In case of doubt, continue reading here until you are able to localize the problem to a specific category.

In the second category, the hard disk is assumed to be in good working order, and the problem may be resolved by referring to the Configuration Problems section that follows.

Finally, there is the unfortunate third category in which physical or logical data loss occurs. The obvious physical example is the head crash, which means just about what you think it means: the read/write head makes a forced landing, chewing up part of the magnetic track on which it comes to rest. Less destructive but still traumatic is the logical data loss, in which critical data is overwritten as a result of a system malfunction, a computer virus, or a few careless keystrokes. For more details, the Data Loss section (page 377) describes some of the ways to get in trouble, and the immediately following Data Recovery Techniques offers a bit of help in getting back out of trouble.

Configuration Problems

When power is applied to a PC containing a hard disk, the system first makes an attempt to read a diskette in drive A. If no diskette is found there, then the system attempts to boot from drive C. Assuming all goes well, the boot procedure concludes successfully and POST uncovers no errors. But if all doesn't go well, then one of the following error messages is seen.

Non-system disk or disk error, replace and press a key when ready. If a nonsystem diskette is in drive A, remove it and press any key to try again. If the message repeats, it's possible that drive A is defective, thereby preventing the system from continuing on to drive C. To verify this, disconnect the drive A flat-ribbon signal cable (seen in Fig. 8.6) and turn the power back on again. If the system now boots successfully, then drive A is indeed defective and will need servicing. See Chapter 8 for more details about diskette drives.

If drive A is not the problem, then it's possible that a non-DOS partition on drive C has accidentally been set active, and there is no operating system in that partition. Refer to the Set Active Partition section on page 404 for further details.

No boot device available. This message may be seen on some non-IBM computers if there is no active partition. Again, refer to the Set Active Partition section for details.

Cassette BASIC Screen Appears   (on IBM PCs)
or
NO ROM BASIC
System Halted   (on PCs whose ROM BIOS
                                                          does not contain
                                                          cassette BASIC)

These problems may occur for one of the following reasons.

Drive C is Unrecognized. Drive C is either not installed or the system has not been configured to recognize it. Make sure all connections to drive C are in place and, if necessary, reconfigure the system.

No Active Partition on Drive C. If the error is not traceable to a loose connection or configuration problem, there's a very good possibility that no partition on drive C was set active during an initial installation. To remedy the problem, insert a DOS system diskette in drive A and reboot the system. (If the DOS Install diskette is used, press the Escape key when the IBM logo appears, then press function key F3 to exit to DOS.) At the DOS prompt, run the FDISK utility and set the primary DOS partition active. See the Set Active Partition section on page 404 for further details, and then re-boot the system.

Bad or Missing Command Interpreter. If this message occurs during an attempt to boot from the hard disk, then DOS can't find the COM-MAND.COM file. Make sure the file exists in the DOS subdirectory, and that the CONFIG.SYS file contains the following line:

```
SHELL=C:\DOS\COMMAND.COM /p /e:256
```

If the system boots successfully and the message occurs after exiting a software program, check the AUTOEXEC.BAT file for the following line:

```
SET COMSPEC=C:\DOS\COMMAND.COM
```

or,

```
SET COMSPEC=(some other drive and/or path)\COMMAND.COM
```

and make sure that COMMAND.COM is actually located where COM-SPEC expects to find it.

The /p and /e parameters seen above are described in Chapter 4 (pages 84 and 98).

Missing Operating System. In order for the system to boot from the hard drive, the drive must also contain the hidden IBMBIO.COM and IBMDOS.COM system files (or IO.SYS and MSDOS.SYS on IBM-compatible systems). This error message indicates that these hidden files were not found, perhaps because drive C was formatted without the /S parameter which transfers the hidden files to its root directory. If the drive was formatted with the /B parameter, which reserves space for the system files, then insert a DOS SYS diskette in drive A and transfer the system files by typing

```
A>SYS C:
```

If the drive was not previously formatted with the /B parameter, then only DOS 4.*xx* will allow the SYS command to transfer the hidden files. Other versions may display the error message described immediately below.

No room for system on destination disk. On systems using DOS versions earlier than 4.00, the system files occupy the first two root directory entries and must be transferred prior to copying any other files into the root directory. If this error message is seen when the SYS command is executed, it means that other files are already in the directory, and therefore the SYS transfer was not successful.

About the only way to encounter this error would be during installation of a pre-4.00 version of DOS, if the hard drive was formatted without the system files and then other files and/or subdirectories were set up in drive C. If so, make backup copies of everything on drive C, then erase all of it and execute the SYS C: command described above. Then restore all the files and directories that were removed.

Two beeps and a 162 Error Code. The beeps and error code indicate a system configuration error, which may be corrected by reconfiguring the system as described in Chapter 6. But before doing so, put a DOS system diskette in drive A, reboot, and look for a DOS A> prompt. If it appears, try to log onto drive C. If you can do so, then the configuration error lies elsewhere. But if the screen displays

```
Invalid drive specification
```

then drive C is either disconnected or defective. Turn the power off, check all the drive connections, and then try again. If the problem recurs, proceed with the reconfiguration. Then turn the power off, disconnect the drive, and turn the power back on again. If no further configuration problems show up, then the hard drive is indeed the source of the problem and will need to be serviced or replaced.

Error code	Source
`1780-Disk 0 Failure`	Drive C
or	
`1781-Disk 1 Failure`	Drive D

If the hard disk is defective, or has been removed and the PC is not yet reconfigured, one of these error codes may be seen during the final stage of the POST procedure.

In the case of a missing drive in an ISA system, the POST procedure may pause for 60 or more seconds before displaying the error code. To avoid this long wait, you may want to reconfigure the system before actually removing the drive.

If there is immediate need to use the computer, it may be possible to get around the problem temporarily. The obvious short-term fix is simply to insert a DOS diskette in drive A, and make do with diskettes until the drive can be serviced or replaced.

• **Hard Disk Replacement Caution.** Don't forget to reconfigure an ISA system to account for a new drive with a different type number. Failure to do so will probably damage the data already on the disk. Refer to Tables 9.2a and 9.4 above for a listing of various hard disks drive types. On EISA and PS/2 systems, the drive type (if required) is automatically set during configuration.

Generally Sluggish Performance

If your hard disk seems to be slowing down in its old age, the problem is probably traceable to fragmented files. The solution was described earlier in the chapter, in the Fragmented File Correction Techniques section (page 371).

However, if the sluggish performance begins the day the hard disk is installed, there's a good possibility the interleave ratio (see page 346) is not set correctly and therefore the read/write head is wasting a lot of time waiting for the right sector to wander by.

Interleave is set during low-level formatting, and it's possible the wrong ratio was specified. Some third-party utilities will check the interleave and even recommend an optimum setting. For example, Gibson Research's SpinRite II displays interleave ratios of 1:1 through 8:1, indicates which one is currently installed, and also suggests the optimum interleave. If the two are not identical, the utility can do a low-level format, during which it resets the interleave ratio to the optimum setting. Unlike the usual low-level format, this one is nondestructive; that is, data already stored on the drive is not lost.

Erratic Performance

In case of erratic performance during any type of read operation, do *not* make any attempt to write data to the hard disk. Remember, the head that reads is the same head that writes, so if it's experiencing trouble doing the former, it will surely cause trouble doing the latter. If data gets written to the wrong location, it will not only be useless in itself, but will destroy other data already on the disk. In which case, the following section will be even more relevant.

Data Loss Problems

This section opens on a gloomy note, with a description of the most serious problem to plague the hard disk drive. With some luck and a reasonable amount of care, the reader won't have to take any of the offered advice, and can proceed directly to the little list of other problems that await.

The Head Crash. On a hard disk, there's no chance that a drive door has been left open, so various read error messages may mean that one or more data sectors have been physically damaged. If the message makes its debut after you've kicked the computer by accident (or on purpose), it's a sure thing that a head has collided with the magnetic surface of the disk, thereby demolishing the data in the immediate area. Unfortunately, there are multiple heads on most drives, so whatever force jarred one head has no doubt jarred the others too.

Such failures can range from the minor inconvenience of a damaged sector in an unimportant text file, to the catastrophic loss of both file allocation tables. Or if Edsel Murphy has been really busy, you might have lost the master boot record. But whatever the damage, you should be relieved that you remembered to backup everything just last night.

If a magnetic surface has been physically damaged, it is important to make no attempt to recover the data, *especially* if you did not remember to make that backup last night. If the head is now damaged, or there are loose magnetic oxide particles drifting around inside the drive enclosure, any further rotation of the platters, with or without head movement, could easily cause even more damage.

Needless to say, strange noises are a sure sign that all is not well inside the drive. It's a good idea to get used to the way a drive sounds when it's working properly, and then make note of any audible deviations, although the post-crash racket often leaves little need for such subtle sonic comparisons. But in the absence of an audible clue that trouble is brewing, if there's any doubt about physical damage, turn the system off immediately and unplug all connections to the drive. Then refer to the Data Recovery Service section below for more details.

Electro-Mechanical Problems. The hard disk drive is a rather complex electro-mechanical system, and all things considered, it's a wonder it works at all. But work it does, and usually with no electronic or mechanical glitches. However, if something does go bad inside, it's possible the drive will continue to work, yet not quite the way you would expect it to. For example, a failure in either the electronic or mechanical system could cause the heads to be in the right place at the wrong time. If so, this is no time to be writing data. If there's no reason to suspect a computer virus, then the drive will probably require the attention of a data recovery service, as described later in the chapter (page 382).

Virus Attacks. There are a few social misfits out there whose contribution to society is to destroy the work of others. Some use spray cans in subways, while others write computer virus programs. More or less analogous to its medical equivalent, the virus works its way into a healthy system—in this case, a hard disk—and then either destroys the programs stored there or just generally messes up operations.

The first symptom of a virus infection may be erratic behavior of programs that previously worked properly or an error message that is obviously incorrect. For example, running the DOS FDISK utility (page 398) will display a *program too big to fit in memory* message, even though there is plenty of room for the program. Or a missing command interpreter will be reported, even though COMMAND.COM seems to be available. In still other cases, the virus damages the boot record. In short, anything out of the ordinary may indicate the presence of a virus.

A few virus-prevention techniques are described here, but should not be taken as the last word on the subject. Instead, just consider the next few paragraphs as a very brief overview of the subject.

The first line of defense against virus attack is to be generally suspicious of any program that arrives under dubious circumstances. For example, illegal copies of game programs or utilities—often downloaded via modem or copied from a friend—are but two of several known disease carriers.

Some virus programs damage the boot record and/or infect executable programs, that is, programs whose names end with an EXE or COM extension. Such infected programs may later on spread the infection to other programs. Document files may be subsequently damaged or erased, but are not carriers of the virus itself.

Some viruses do their work by modifying COMMAND.COM, so a degree of protection is possible by simply making this a read-only file. To do so, log on to the DOS subdirectory and make sure that the ATTRIB.EXE and COMMAND.COM files are there. Then type

```
ATTRIB +R COMMAND.COM
```

To verify that the file is now write-protected, type the line again, this time omitting the +R. The COMMAND.COM name will be displayed, preceded by an R.

Unfortunately, this simple bit of preventive medicine does not guarantee immunity against all viruses, so the use of a virus detection utility deserves the serious consideration of anyone who is not absolutely sure of the integrity of every program (or user) that comes near the computer.

As a typical example, Mace Utilities' *Survey* scans every executable file and writes a report file which contains a CRC value for every file on the drive. The next time the utility is run, it compares each file against the report file, and displays a warning message for any file that has been modified. The utility will of course report files that you have intentionally modified, in which case it can be ignored. But if *Survey* discovers a file that was changed without your knowledge, chances are there's a virus at work.

As another line of defense, Mace *Vaccine* is a resident program that continually monitors the COMMAND.COM and system files, as well as the boot record and other reserved sectors. A warning message alerts the user if a potentially damaging write operation attempts to access these areas, in which case the operation can be aborted before the damage occurs.

Parsons Technology's *ViruCide* examines all executable files and displays the name and size of an infected file, and the name of the virus that caused the infection. The program will destroy the virus or simply warn you of its presence, according to the option you have chosen.

Before installing any new program of dubious origin, make a backup copy of the hard disk as insurance against subsequent data damage, virus-induced or otherwise. Also, check the suspect diskette with one of the just-mentioned antiviral programs *before* copying it to your hard disk.

If a virus is discovered the hard way—that is, after damage has already taken place—a detailed report of all observed irregularities may help identify the specific virus causing the grief. Your accurate description of the problems may make it easier to track down the program that introduced the infection. It's a good idea to keep a log (*not* on the computer though) of the dates at which all new programs of dubious origin are downloaded to your hard drive. Chances are, most of your software is from legitimate sources or is the by-product of such software (a word processor or the documents created with it, for example). Therefore, the "suspect list" probably represents a few files at most.

Other Data Loss Problems. Needless to say, head crashes and viruses are not the only things bad that can happen to a hard disk. As noted earlier, it's possible to damage critical data by a momentary power failure during a write operation, or by a few careless keystrokes during debug. As with the head crash, damage may range from trivial to traumatic, and some of the data recovery techniques below may help to make the necessary repairs.

Before continuing, remember that the recovery techniques mentioned here assume there is no damage to the physical or electronic system. If in doubt on this point, proceed directly to the Data Recovery Service comments below.

Data Recovery Techniques

If you have recent backups available, you may prefer to simply reformat the drive, or drives, and then restore the data. But on the off chance that you *didn't* remember to backup everything just last night, there are several remedies to the above problems, based on the extent of the damage.

Head Crash Damage. As noted earlier, physical head crash damage is usually obvious. But in the case of slight damage, it may not be clear if the problem is indeed the result of a crash and its attendant physical damage. In this case, a good hard disk utility can help. A thorough surface scan will point out damaged tracks, and if the reported damage is slight enough, you may decide to do a low-level format and mark off the bad tracks to prevent their subsequent reuse. Refer to the Low-Level Formatting section for further details.

Virus Damage. In the case of a virus attack, if the system is still functioning, do not immediately backup the entire hard disk, as this simply transfers the good, the bad, and the ugly programs to your backup diskettes. Instead, turn the power off (since some viruses will survive a warm reboot), insert a good system diskette in drive A, and turn the power back on again.

If you know the virus has damaged just the boot record sector and you can find the infected program, reboot from a good write-protected system diskette. At the DOS prompt, type SYS C: to transfer good copies of the hidden files and restore the boot sector. As an extra precaution, erase the COMMAND.COM file on the hard disk and replace it with a copy known to be good. Erase the virus-carrying program immediately, so that it doesn't reinfect the boot record the next time the system is rebooted. If you're not sure which program is the culprit, review your list of recently acquired software and apply some Napoleonic justice: eliminate anything that *may* be guilty.

But if you are still not sure of the virus source or of its type, then copy all your nonexecutable programs only (documents, spreadsheets, whatever) to diskette. If you have any EXE or COM programs that you wrote yourself, transfer these to other diskettes and try running each one separately. If appropriate, copy the source code programs only and then recompile them later on, once your hard disk is back in shape. Also copy your batch and configuration files and examine them for integrity via the TYPE command, or by printing them.

Do *not* use a backup utility already stored on your hard disk, as this too may be infected. Instead, use the original write-protected diskette supplied by the software manufacturer. Do not backup any files in the DOS subdirectory. Instead, use the original installation diskettes when you are ready to restore the hard disk.

From the root directory of each logical drive, use the DOS TREE command to display (or print) a copy of your directory tree, as a reference for later reconstruction of the directory structure. If any important document files are missing, use the Norton Utility Unerase function (or similar) to try to recover them.

Next, do a low-level format of the entire hard drive, reinstall your operating system, rebuild your directory structure, and reinstall all your software programs, using legal original source diskettes. Finally, copy your batch, configuration, and document files back to the appropriate subdirectories.

If you have any diskettes that may also have been infected, follow the general instructions given above. Reformat the suspect diskettes before using them again.'

The above brief suggestions are no substitute for a good virus-detection utility. And if your computer is part of a local area network, or communicates with any other computer in any other way, then unless you are absolutely positive that the infection is local, you should consider calling in outside expert help. Simply cleaning up your own part of the total system does nothing to prevent the virus from visiting you again the next time you log on to whatever it was that brought it to you in the first place.

If outside assistance is needed, contact the Computer Virus Industry Association for help.

Sector Repairs. If damaged sectors can be localized to a specific file (or files), the nondamaged sectors may be salvaged by using the DOS RECOVER or other (and better) utilities described in the Software Diagnostics section of Chapter 8 (page 322). And depending on the extent of the damage, some directory and/or FAT repairs can also be attempted. But as mentioned in Chapter 8, use RECOVER only as a last resort. See page 326 for more details.

Damaged Volume Label. If erroneous characters appear in a volume label, the label can be repaired by using the DOS LABEL command to write a new volume label, thereby overwriting the old one.

Reformatting After Data Loss. Once you have saved whatever can be saved, you may want to reformat a damaged drive partition if the nature of the damage prevents simple erasure of a few bad files. Or the entire drive may need a new low-level format, in which new bad sectors are marked to prevent their reuse. If so, refer to the Low-Level Formatting section below for details.

Data Recovery Service. If post-head-crash or virus wreckage is extensive, or you just don't feel comfortable enough to attempt any of the rescue operations described above, there are a number of data recovery services available. In brief, you send the entire drive to a service company and hope for the best. The recovery may include the physical repair of the drive system, the logical repair of the stored data, or both. Such services are often found in the classified listings of computer magazines.

Whatever the cause, a detailed description of all observed problems will go a long way toward expediting the recovery process and will help to keep costs within reason.

Barring the totally catastrophic, the track record of reliable services, such as Ontrack Data Recovery, Inc., is quite high. If you are considering such a service, it's a good idea not to try to fix things yourself first. Recovery service work is often divided into two categories: repairing the real damage and repairing the damage done by the user's repair attempts. In case of doubt, call the recovery service first.

HARD DISK PREPARATION

The following section describes how to prepare a hard disk drive for use as the primary drive in your computer. The complete procedure is divided into five separate operations: DOS upgrades, low-level formatting, partitioning, high-level formatting of each partition, and finally, installation of an operating system (which in this example is DOS).

As described below, low-level formatting is immediately followed by DOS installation, with partitioning and high-level formatting taking place at the appropriate stage within that installation. However, the FDISK utility used for partitioning is described separately so that it may be independently consulted whenever it is necessary to make a change in partitioning.

DOS Upgrades

When installing DOS on a hard disk that already contains an earlier version, the following procedures may be used in place of the complete installation procedure described below. However, if you want to repartition the drive or take advantage of various configuration enhancements, then the complete DOS installation procedures should be followed instead.

From DOS 2.xx to DOS 3.xx or 4.xx. Backup the entire contents of the hard disk and then install the new DOS version and reformat the entire disk surface.

From any DOS 3.xx to a later DOS 3.xx or 4.xx. Use the SYS command to transfer the new hidden files to the root directory on drive C. Then erase all the files in the DOS subdirectory on drive C and copy the new ones to the same subdirectory. If any COMMAND.COM files are at locations other than the DOS subdirectory, make sure these too are replaced with the new version.

From any DOS to DOS 5.0. See Appendix A for details.

Low-Level Formatting

The procedures described here are for *low*-level formatting only. For hard drive applications the DOS FORMAT program is not used for this purpose, although it will be used later on for high-level formatting.

A low-level format prepares the magnetic surfaces of the hard disk by setting the interleave and the number of sectors per track. As part of the process, the low-level format writes a header at the front of every sector. The header contains the sector number and address, gives the number of data bytes to follow, and supplies other information required by the operating system. These header bytes are in addition to the 512 data bytes in each sector, and they account for the difference between the unformatted and formatted capacities of the drive. (See Chapter 8 for a description of sector headers on diskette—the same general concept applies to the hard disk.) In addition, bad sectors are locked out during the low-level format so the operating system will not use them later on for data storage.

Most hard disks are delivered with low-level formatting already in place, so the following steps should not be necessary unless you need to start all over again for any of the reasons described earlier in the chapter. You may also want to do a low-level format at regular intervals, as suggested in the Routine Diagnostics section of the chapter, for the following reason: during the course of routine operation, especially if you regularly clean up fragmented files, the data in every sector will be refreshed. However, the sector header data is *never* refreshed. This means that gradual deterioration of header data over time is not remedied by frequent (or even infrequent) write operations. Once the low-level format is done, the headers remain as is until the next low-level format. Thus, to guard against eventual problems due to header-reading errors, some authorities suggest a low-level format at least once a year. Others say that this shouldn't be necessary. But necessary or no, the low-level format does refresh all the header data and certainly can't do any harm (unless you forget to backup your files before doing it).

But for a routine first installation, it's safe to assume that the hard disk is already low-level formatted, and proceed directly to the Install DOS or FDISK sections described below (pages 389 and 398). However, when low-level formatting is indeed indicated, the utility required for the process may be found in one of several places:

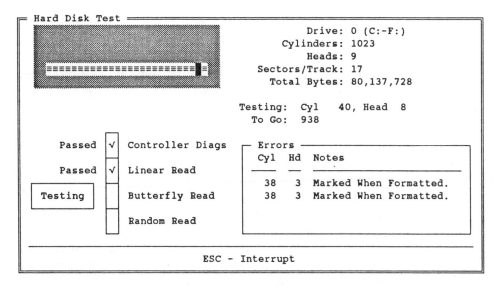

Figure 9.6. Third-party hard disk test utility display (Priam *InnerSpace*).

- IBM ISA systems: on an Advanced Diagnostics diskette
- IBM MCA systems: on the Reference diskette
- EISA systems: in one of the following locations

  most IBM-compatible computers: in the system ROM BIOS

  on some hard disks: in ROM on the disk controller card

  on a separately available utility diskette

To give a general overview of the low-level format procedure, each of these is briefly described below. For more detailed descriptions and accurate step-by-step instructions, consult the appropriate user's manual.

• **Low-Level Format Precautions.** Some low-level format utilities interact with TSR programs and device drivers. Therefore, the format should be done after booting from a system diskette that does not load any memory-resident software. In case of doubt, read the user's manual carefully before beginning the format. And remember that, with the exception of SpinRite II (page 377) or similar nondestructive utilities, a low-level format obliterates all data previously stored on the hard disk. Data recovery is *not* possible via any commercially available utility.

Drive Number Note. Although DOS refers to hard disks as drives C and D, for formatting purposes they are often referred to as drives 0 and 1, respectively (not to be confused with the drive *type* number).

Drive Parameter Check. If you are unsure of the correct value for any of the parameters that are called for during the low-level format procedure, many commercially available diagnostic software packages contain a hard disk test which will display the required information. A typical example is shown in Figure 9.6. In this example, the hard disk was low-level formatted earlier and therefore the test displays bad track cylinder and head data, as seen in the lower right-hand section of the screen. Jot down this information for later use. However, if the drive was not previously formatted, you will need to take this information from the drive housing label.

Initialization. Based in part on its ANSI definition and other usage, *initialization* is the process of resetting addresses and storage contents during low-level formatting. Some utilities therefore use the following terminology:

Term	Meaning
Initialize	low-level format
Format	high-level format

Although this usage is not such a bad idea (it does away with low-level/high-level confusion), keep in mind that initialization is just another way to describe a low-level format operation.

IBM ISA Format Procedure On IBM ISA systems, the low-level format utility is accessed by booting with the Advanced Diagnostics diskette in drive A, then working down through the following menu maze:

Menu	Make this selection
Select an Option	Option 0: system checkout
List of Installed Devices	Answer yes to "Is the list correct?"
System Checkout	Option 0: run tests one time
Select Option Number(s) to Test	Option 17: fixed disk drive(s) and adapter
Fixed Disk Diagnostics	Option 7: format menu
Format Selection	Begin low-level format

IBM MCA Format Procedure   On MCA systems, boot with the Reference diskette in drive A and when the IBM logo appears, press the Enter key to display the Main Menu. Then press Alt + A to access the Advanced Diagnostic menu, which lists two choices:

```
1 System Checkout
2 Format fixed disk
```

Select option 2 to display the Drive Selection menu:

```
1 Prepare Drive C for DOS
2 Return to control program
```

   Select drive C (or D, if a second hard disk is installed and you wish to format it).
   Next, three (!) successive screens will warn you of impending doom and give you the chance to exit before it's too late. You will have to answer

```
Are you SURE you want to continue?

Do you want to STOP now?

ARE YOU POSITIVE YOU WANT TO CONTINUE?
```

After you answer "yes, no, yes," the low-level formatting finally begins. The screen shown in Figure 9.7 is displayed during the procedure, and is overlaid by that in Figure 9.8 at the end of the formatting. Unless you want to low-level format another hard disk, press the Escape key a few times to exit.

```
┌──────────────────────────────────────────────────┐
│ Message                      Page    1 of 1        │
├──────────────────────────────────────────────────┤
│             Preparing drive C                      │
│                                                    │
│                 Phase :     1                      │
│              Cylinder :    79                      │
│      Defective Sectors :    0                      │
│                                                    │
├──────────────────────────────────────────────────┤
│                                                    │
└──────────────────────────────────────────────────┘
```

Figure 9.7.   Display seen during low-level format operation included on IBM MCA Reference diskettes.

```
┌─────────────────────────────────────────────────────┐
│ Instructions                    Page    1 of 1       │
├─────────────────────────────────────────────────────┤
│ Drive C has the following parameters:                │
│                                                       │
│ Tracks :   763  Sectors / Track    :   27            │
│ Heads  :     6  Sectors Marked Bad :    0            │
│                                                       │
│ Approx. Size :    60 MB                               │
├─────────────────────────────────────────────────────┤
│ Enter=Continue                                        │
└─────────────────────────────────────────────────────┘
```

Figure 9.8.   Display seen at conclusion of IBM low-level format operation.

Format in ROM BIOS

The ROM BIOS in some IBM-compatible systems contains extensive diagnostic testing routines, such as those described in Chapter 3. A low-level format option is usually available within the hard disk test section (see Figure 3.11a). When selected, additional screen displays prompt the user to enter the required preliminary information. For example, Figure 9.9 shows the display at the point where the drive type is to be entered. After you enter this and the other necessary information, the low-level format begins.

```
┌──────────────────────────────┐     ┌──────────────────────────────────────────────┐
│      Hard Disk Format        │     │ Type Cyl.  Head Sec W-pcom L-zone  Size        │
├──────────────────────────────┤     ├──────────────────────────────────────────────┤
│ Disk Drive   (C/D)    ? C    │     │   33 1024    5   17   1024   1024    42 MB      │
│ Disk Drive type       ? 35   │     │   34  612    2   17    128    612    10 MB      │
│ Interleave (1-16)     ?      │     │   35 1024    9   17   FFFF   1024    76 MB      │
│ Mark Bad Tracks (Y/N) ?      │     │   36 1024    8   17    512   1024    68 MB      │
│ Start cylinder number ?      │     │   37  615    8   17    128    615    40 MB      │
│ End cylinder number   ?      │     │   38  987    3   17    987    987    24 MB      │
│ Start Head number     ?      │     │   39  987    7   17    987    987    57 MB      │
│ End Head number       ?      │     │   40  820    6   17    820    820    40 MB      │
│ Proceed (Y/N)         ?      │     │   41  977    5   17    977    977    40 MB      │
└──────────────────────────────┘     │   42  981    5   17    981    981    40 MB      │
                                      │   43  830    7   17    512    830    48 MB      │
                                      │   44  830   10   17   FFFF    830    68 MB      │
                                      │   45  917   15   17   FFFF    918   114 MB      │
                                      │   46 1224   15   17   FFFF   1223   152 MB      │
                                      │ USER 1024    9   17   FFFF   1024    76 MB      │
                                      ├──────────────────────────────────────────────┤
                                      │ Move Bar- ↑↓  Select- <RET>   Quit- <ESC>      │
                                      └──────────────────────────────────────────────┘
```

Figure 9.9.   Low-level format displays included in AMI ROM BIOS replacement modules for IBM AT BIOS. The format begins after you enter all the parameters listed in the left-hand box.

Format in ROM on Disk Controller

On some hard disk controllers (Adaptec ACB-2320D, Western Digital WD1009V-MM1, for example), a low-level format program is contained in ROM, usually at sector C800. The DOS debug utility may be used to begin the format procedure, and the user's manual for the drive should contain the necessary instructions.

If you are not sure if your hard disk drive controller includes this program, insert a diskette with the debug utility (DEBUG.COM) in one of the diskette drives and type

```
DEBUG↵
D C800:xxxx↵ (xxxx will vary from one system to another)
```

If the low-level format utility is not present, the right-hand side of the screen will display a long series of FF FF FF . . . (or similar). Figure 9.10 lists a typical debug script for a low-level format using the ROM on the disk drive controller.

Utilities Diskette Format

As noted earlier, many diagnostic software packages contain a low-level format utility. For example, Figure 9.11 is a typical hard disk format screen that may be seen prior to the start of an actual low-level format operation. The drive parameter data in the upper right-hand portion of the screen may be revised if necessary, and the bad track table must be completed by entering the numbers of the bad track cylinders and heads. In the example shown, the information was taken from the hard disk test screen shown earlier (Figure 9.6). To begin formatting, press the Enter key and follow the on-screen prompts.

DOS Installation

At the conclusion of the low-level format operation, the next step is to partition and high-level format the disk and install the operating system. As described below, the installation is carried out on a PS/2 system with a single 3.5-inch diskette drive and one hard disk that has not yet been partitioned. The procedure will vary slightly if 5.25-inch diskettes are used.

To keep the following section within a reasonable length, only the most likely options are described in detail. For more information about options not fully covered here, highlight the option of interest and press the

Debug prompt	Enter the following data
Type DEBUG and press the Enter key to begin. - (the hyphen is the debug prompt)	G=C800:CCC
ADAPTEC 2010/2070A FORMAT PROGRAM Please enter numbers in decimal	
Enter sector interleave (3-9)	4
Enter drive ID (0/1)	0
Use the default Parameters? (Y/N)	N
Number of logical units (1-8)	1
Step pulse rate (0-7)	3
Number of heads (1-16)	number of heads
Number of cylinders:	number of cylinders
Specify the defect byte offset encoding: MFM or RLL (M/R)	M for 2010; R for 2070A
Enter defect list as "cyl/head/byte" or "head/cyl/byte" (C or H)	C
Type defect file name, or press enter	⏎
Enter defect locations as Cyl/Head/Byte	the defect locations
Are above parameters correct (Y/N)	Y
Formatting drive ...	
Verifying format in logical unit 0 cylinder xxx	
Format complete ... Run this program again (Y/N)	N (or Y to format second drive)

Figure 9.10.   A typical low-level format script accessed through the DOS debug utility. The example is for Adaptec 2010 and 2070A hard disk drives.

help key (function key F1) to display a summary of the option. If necessary, read the help screens for all options before making your selection.

SHARE Error Message.   If the hard disk capacity is greater than 32Mb, the following error message will be seen at the conclusion of POST if the

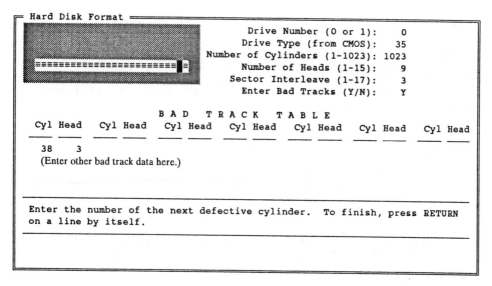

Figure 9.11.   Low-level format display from Priam *InnerSpace* utility diskette.

drive has not already been divided into partitions (page 395) of 32Mb or less:

```
WARNING! SHARE should be loaded for large media
```

If this message appears at any time other than during an initial installation, edit your configuration file so that SHARE.EXE is installed, as described in Chapter 4 (Install Command, page 84). But during installation, the message—which may disappear from the screen before you even notice it—may be ignored.

The SELECT.EXE Program. The DOS version 4.01 SELECT command is used in the following description. Unlike the earlier version, SELECT now installs DOS without losing data already stored on disk, except that previous DOS versions will be updated, unless you specify otherwise.

The new DOS SELECT will not work by typing SELECT at a DOS prompt. Doing so displays the following error message:

```
Invalid parameters on SELECT command line
```

The correct procedure is to insert your DOS Install diskette in drive A and boot or reboot the system.

```
               Specify Function and Workspace

SELECT sets up your computer to run DOS and your programs
most efficiently based on the option you choose.

NOTE:  You can review the results of your choice later
in this program.

Choose an option:

    1. Minimum DOS function; maximum program workspace

    2. Balance DOS function with program workspace

    3. Maximum DOS function; minimum program workspace
```

Figure 9.12.   During the DOS 4.01 installation procedure, this screen prompts you to balance DOS and program workspace, according to amount of installed memory.

IBM DOS SELECT Screen. If you are using the IBM DOS Install diskette, an IBM logo screen appears. Microsoft's Install diskette skips this step, while diskettes supplied with IBM-compatible systems may or may not insert their own logo or message at this point. In any case, press the Enter key to continue.

DOS Welcome Message. An introductory screen displays a *Welcome to DOS* message and advises that you will need a blank diskette to complete the installation procedure. Note that if you are installing from a 5.25-inch drive, a 360Kb diskette is needed even if the drive capacity is 1.2Mb.

Press the Enter key to display the Introduction screen, which lists the various keys you may need to press to indicate your choices. In most cases you can simply press the Enter key to select the default option. If you select the wrong option by mistake, you can usually back up one or more screens by pressing the Escape key.

Press the Enter key again to display the Specify Function and Workspace menu shown in Figure 9.12. If you are unsure which option to choose, select any one of them and press the F1 key for help. The three options are summarized here.

If installed memory is	Select this option
256Kb	1. Minimum DOS function
512Kb	2. Balance DOS function
more than 512Kb	3. Maximum DOS Function

Additional screen displays prompt you to select country and keyboard codes, the drive to install DOS on (presumably C), and the location for the DOS directory. The last screen, shown in Figure 9.13, also prompts you to update all DOS files on the fixed disk. Assuming the disk has not yet been used, or has been recently reformatted (low-level), there are no files on it yet. Nevertheless, select this option and continue. Also select this option if you are updating from a previous DOS version.

The next screen asks for the number of printers, and if you answer 1 or more, the printer selection screen lists various IBM or other parallel or serial printers. Make the appropriate selection and then specify the parallel or serial port that is to be used.

DOS 4.0x Shell Option. At this point, only MS-DOS users are offered the option of installing the MS-DOS shell. Briefly stated, on boot up, DOS-SHELL replaces the vaguely unfriendly C> (or on diskette, A>) prompt with a directory map which may be traversed via cursor keys or mouse. Shell fans may love it; others may not. For more information on its features, see *Introducing the DOS Shell* in your DOS documentation. Then make the appropriate menu choice and continue the installation. If you decide to install the shell and subsequently find you can do without it, simply edit your AUTOEXEC.BAT file to remove the DOSSHELL.BAT line.

The Shell Option menu is not seen during an IBM PC-DOS installation, and DOSSHELL is automatically installed, unless you decide against it, as described immediately below.

```
You can accept the DOS directory name shown or type a new
directory name.

DOS Directory . . . .C:\[DOS                                    ]

To select option 1 below, press Enter.  To change your
option, press the tab key, highlight your choice and then
press Enter.

   1. Update all DOS files on fixed disk

   2. Copy non-system files to directory specified
```

Figure 9.13. During DOS installation, this screen prompts you to specify the directory for the DOS files.

Review Installation Options. The next screen lets you accept the choices you have already made and continue the installation, or you may review and/or modify these and still other selections that are not otherwise noted during installation.

For example, the just-mentioned DOS Shell option is automatically included in IBM PC-DOS installations, unless you review your installation options and delete it. Figure 9.14 shows one of several screens that are displayed if you do decide to review the options. To make a change, highlight the appropriate option and press the space bar to toggle between *yes* and *no* choices.

Prepare the SELECT COPY Diskette. The next screen advises you to have a blank diskette, labeled Select Copy, ready. Press the Enter key and follow the on-screen prompts to alternately swap the Install diskette and your blank Select Copy diskette (not necessary on systems with two diskette drives).

Remember that if your drive A is a 1.2Mb 5.25-inch drive, the Select Copy diskette must still be a 360Kb diskette. An error message will be seen if you insert a 1.2Mb diskette by mistake.

At the conclusion of the complete installation procedure, save the Select Copy diskette for future use. If you decide to reinstall DOS at a later date, the use of the Select Copy obviates the need to repeat all the diskette swapping required during some initial installation procedures.

```
SELECT made these selections for you.  You can accept
these selections or change any of them.  If you change
an item from No to Yes, it will increase the amount of
memory DOS uses.

To change a selection, use the up and down arrow keys to
highlight your choice, then press the spacebar.  To accept
all the selections, press the Enter key.
                                            Choice:
     Code Page Switching                      No
     Expanded Memory support                  No
     Extended display support (ANSI.SYS)      Yes
     File performance enhancements (FASTOPEN) Yes
     GRAFTABL display support                 No
     GRAPHICS PrtSc support                   Yes
     DOS SHARE support                        No
     DOS SHELL                                Yes
     Virtual Disk support (VDISK.SYS)         No
```

Figure 9.14. This screen lets you change some of the options that have been automatically set up during the installation procedure.

DOS Installation Error. If SELECT detects an error during installation, the following message is displayed:

```
An error occurred while installing DOS.
Press Enter to continue, or F3 to exit SELECT.
```

If pressing the Enter key has no effect, and the error is not obvious, then reboot the system and try again. If the error persists, try running the diagnostic procedures on the Starter/Reference or Diagnostics diskette to determine its cause. See Chapter 3 for further details.

On IBM systems, there is no such thing as peaceful coexistence: the error message above is seen if an IBM Select diskette discovers the hard disk already contains a valid non-IBM primary DOS partition. If you are sure this is the problem,

1. Reboot the system, then exit the installation procedure by pressing the Escape key and function key F3.
2. Use DEBUG or the Norton Utilities' FA (File Attributes) to unhide the system files (IO.SYS and MSDOS.SYS or similar) on drive C.
3. Erase the system files and COMMAND.COM on drive C.
4. Reboot the system again and rerun the installation procedure.

If none of the above procedures resolves the installation error, then the system probably needs outside servicing.

Begin Partitioning. At the conclusion of the above procedure, with the Select Copy diskette still in the drive, one of three sets of prompts appears, depending on the present status of the hard disk. In each case, the prompts offer the appropriate partitioning options, and the disk is partitioned according to your instructions.

The three partitioning menus are described below. Partitioning is followed by high-level formatting and then by a prompt to begin copying the Operating diskette files.

Hard Disk Requires Partitioning. If the hard disk has not yet been partitioned, as for example during an initial DOS installation on a new drive, the following choices are offered:

```
1. Let SELECT define partition sizes
2. Define your own partition sizes
```

If you select option 1, you will be prompted to reboot the system by pressing the Ctrl+Alt+Del keys. When you do, the system will do a high-level format of the complete hard disk, as described in the Begin High-Level Formatting section below.

However, if you don't want the entire disk surface to be devoted to a single DOS primary partition, you should define your own partitions at this point by choosing option 2, and then refer to the FDISK section below. If you do select option 2, then when you finish using FDISK, the formatting options offered in the Hard Disk Does Not Require Partitioning section below are displayed. Refer to that section for further details.

Hard Disk May Require Re-Partitioning. If the installation program discovers space not assigned to a partition, the displayed options are

```
1. Leave disk unchanged
2. Define your own partition sizes
```

If you choose the first option, the disk is left as is and installation continues as described below. The second option allows you to review and/or change the partitioning as described in the FDISK section below.

Hard Disk Does Not Require Partitioning. If the hard disk has been partitioned for both a primary and an extended DOS partition (either just now or previously) but has not yet been formatted, the top of the screen will display a drive number (1 for the first drive, 2 for the second). In addition, the *letter* of the first logical drive in the extended partition will be seen, followed by these two options:

```
1. Format fixed disk partition
2. Do not format fixed disk partition
```

To do a high-level format of the indicated partition, select option 1. When you press the Enter key, the next drive letter (if any) appears. Select the desired option and repeat the procedure until all logical drive partitions have been accounted for. At this point, the primary DOS partition will be formatted, followed by a format of every logical drive for which you chose option 1.

If you selected option 2 for any partition, you will have to format it later on, unless of course it was previously formatted and contains information you do not wish to lose (for example, during a format/reinstallation of DOS on the primary partition only).

Begin High-Level Formatting. If high-level formatting is required, this step will begin at the conclusion of the partitioning described above. During the procedure, a *Formatting disk . . .* message is displayed on screen, and in the upper left-hand corner, *xx percent of disk formatted* is shown. You may also see *Attempting to recover allocation unit xxxx* displayed from time to time during the format. The format display repeats for each partition that is to be formatted. However, there is no indication of which partition is currently being formatted.

Copy Operating Diskette Files. At the conclusion of partitioning or of the high-level format, you are prompted to insert the Operating diskette in the drive. This contains the DOS files which are now copied into a DOS subdirectory on drive C. On 5.25-inch drive systems, there are three Operating system diskettes, which must be inserted sequentially, according to the prompts seen on screen.

At the end of this step, the following *Installation Complete* message is displayed.

```
Installation of IBM DOS 4.00 is complete.
```

If this is the first time DOS has been installed on the hard disk, the message continues

```
REFER TO THE "GETTING STARTED WITH DOS 4.00" BOOK
FOR INFORMATION ON USING THE DOS SHELL.
```

But if a previous installation has left an AUTOEXEC.BAT and a CONFIG.SYS file on drive C, these files are left undisturbed and the following lines are displayed:

```
The files AUTOEXEC.400 and CONFIG.400 have been
copied to your fixed disk. The files contain the
options selected for DOS 4.00. To get the options
selected, update your AUTOEXEC.BAT and CONFIG.SYS
files. Refer to the "Getting Started with DOS 4.00"
book for information on updating these files.
```

In either case, the message concludes with

```
Remove all diskettes. Press Ctrl+Alt+Del to
start DOS.
```

If all goes well, the system reboots itself from drive C when you press the Ctrl+Alt+Del keys.

If the longer message above was seen, compare your AUTOEXEC.BAT file with the new AUTOEXEC.400 file that was just created by the installation process. If the old file contains instructions that you want to continue using, add the appropriate lines to the AUTOEXEC.400 file, then erase the old batch file and rename the 400 file as AUTOEXEC.BAT. Follow the same procedure for the two CONFIG files. Then reboot once again to use the two new files. However, if the two 400 files contain nothing new, just erase them and leave the two old files as they were.

If a *non-system disk* error message is seen when the system attempts a reboot, it's because a non-DOS partition is set active and this partition does not contain a valid operating system. Refer to the Set Active Partition section below for instructions on how to set the correct partition to be active.

The rest of this chapter contains information about the FDISK utility, which is probably not needed at this time. But if you wish to change the disk partitioning either now or in the future, this is the place to start reading again.

The FDISK Utility

The FDISK utility is used to divide a hard disk into one or more partitions and/or to set one of the partitions active. Even if you intend to use only one operating system, it's usually a good idea to divide the disk into two partitions; a primary partition to hold the operating system and an extended partition for everything else. The entire area devoted to the primary partition becomes drive C. However, the extended partition can be subdivided into two or more logical drives; that is, incremental parts of this partition can be assigned unique drive letters (drive D, E, F, and so on). This is especially helpful on a large-capacity hard disk drive, since it allows the drive to be treated as if it were two or more smaller drives.

During the DOS installation procedure described above, you may let the SELECT program do the partitioning for you. Although this may at first seem convenient, there's a very good chance that the partitioning will not be suitable for your needs.

For example, SELECT's partitioning may create a single primary DOS drive. Therefore you should define your own partition sizes if you want to create an extended partition which may be subdivided into logical drives. You should also do so if you want to reserve space for one or more non-DOS partitions. In either case, remember to set the primary DOS partition (or one of the non-DOS partitions) active before exiting FDISK. If you overlook this important step, the system will not be able to boot itself on from the hard disk. If this happens, refer to the Set Active Partition section for further details.

FDISK Options. Figure 9.15 shows the first of several FDISK menus. This menu is seen if you run FDISK separately, or if you elect to define your own partitions during the installation procedure. In either case, select option 1 to begin. All four options are described below.

• **FDISK Caution.** If the hard disk has already been partitioned—say, by the Installation procedure described above—you may need to delete the previous DOS partition and/or the logical disk drives that are already installed, in order to set up the partitioning layout that you really want. Needless to say, all information previously stored on the disk must be backed up, since it will be lost during repartitioning. Do the backup first, then select the Delete DOS Partition option (3) below and follow the on-screen prompts. Then select the Create DOS Partition option (1) and continue reading here.

Option 1. Create DOS Partition or Logical Disk Drive

In the following example, a 20Mb hard disk will be divided into two partitions: a 5Mb active DOS partition (drive C) and one 15Mb extended partition. The extended partition will then be subdivided into three logical drives (D, E, F). Needless to say, the numbers seen below should be changed to whatever values are appropriate for your needs.

The first step is to create the primary DOS partition, that is, the partition that will be identified as drive C and contain the DOS subdirectory. To do so, select this option from the FDISK Options menu shown in Figure 9.15. Then select option 1 from the menu shown in Figure 9.16. Each of these options is described below.

Option 1. Create Primary DOS Partition

The first onscreen prompt asks

```
Do you wish to use the maximum available size for a
Primary DOS Partition and make the partition active
(Y/N)............? [Y]
```

```
                    FDISK Options

Current fixed disk drive: 1

Choose one of the following:

1. Create DOS Partition or Logical DOS Drive
2. Set active partition
3. Delete DOS Partition or Logical DOS Drive
4. Display partition information

Enter choice: [1]
```

Figure 9.15.   The FDISK Options menu.

Assuming you will want to divide the disk space into two or more partitions, answer "no" (N or n) to the prompt. This displays the following information:

```
Total disk space is 20 Mbytes (1 Mbyte=1048576 bytes)
Maximum space available for partition is 20 Mbytes (100%)

Enter partition size in Mbytes or percent of disk
space (%) to create a Primary DOS Partition ..:[ 5]
```

Enter the amount of space you wish to devote to the primary DOS partition (drive C) and press the Enter key to display the following:

```
Partition Status        Type    Size in Mbytes  Percentage of Disk Used
C: 1                    PRI DOS       5                  25%
Primary DOS Partition created
```

Press the Escape key to return to the FDISK Options menu shown above in Figure 9.15. A warning note at the bottom of the screen advises that an active partition has not yet been defined. You may do so now (see Set Active Partition below for details) or first define additional partitions by again selecting option 1 to display the Create DOS Partition or Logical DOS Drive menu. This time, select option 2 to begin creating an extended DOS partition.

Option 2. Create Extended DOS Partition

When this option is selected, the following message is displayed:

```
          Create DOS Partition or Logical DOS Drive

Current fixed disk drive: 1

Choose one of the following:

1. Create Primary DOS Partition
2. Create Extended DOS Partition
3. Create Logical DOS Drive(s) in the Extended DOS Partition

Enter choice: [1]
```

Figure 9.16.   The FDISK utility menu choices for creating primary and extended DOS partitions and logical drives within the extended partition.

```
Total disk space   15 Mbytes (1 Mbyte = 1048576 bytes)

Maximum space available for partition is 15 Mbytes
(75%)

Enter partition size in Mbytes or percent
of disk space (%) to create an Extended
DOS Partition................................ :[ 15]
```

If you wish to reserve space for a non-DOS partition, then do not use up all the remaining space at this time and refer to the Set Non-DOS Partition section below for more details. But for now, enter the amount of space you want to use for the extended partition, or just press the Enter key to allocate all available space, as indicated by the following display.

```
Partition Status     Type        Size in Mbytes   Percentage
                                                   of Disk Used
C: 1                 PRI DOS          5               25%
   2                 EXT DOS 1        5               75%

Extended DOS Partition created
```

Option 3. Create Logical DOS Drive(s) in the Extended DOS Partition

If you have just created the extended partition described above, then press the Escape key to proceed directly into this section. However, if the extended partition was created earlier, and it still contains space for more logical drives, then this option can be selected. In either case, the following display is seen:

```
No logical drives defined
```
(or data about existing drives is displayed at the top of the screen)

```
Total Extended DOS Partition size is 15 Mbytes
Maximum space available for logical drive is 15 Mbytes (100%)
Enter logical drive size in Mbytes or percent of disk space (%)...[ 15]
```

To create several logical drives, select a value less than 15 for the present drive, press the Enter key, and repeat this procedure until all available space within the extended partition has been assigned.

The following display shows the end result of subdividing all of the remaining 15Mb space into three logical drives of 6, 4, and 5 Mbytes. Note that the three drives have been assigned drive letters D, E, and F.

```
Drv Volume Label        Mbytes        System        Usage
D:                      6             UNKNOWN       39%
E:                      4             UNKNOWN       26%
F:                      5             UNKNOWN       34%
```

All available space in the Extended DOS Partition is assigned to logical drives.

Note: If a non-DOS partition already occupies space beyond the DOS extended partition, then the *Create Logical DOS Drive(s)* Option (3) cannot be accessed via the menu shown in Figure 9.16 (bug?). Instead, you must delete the entire extended partition (using Option 3, below), recreate it (Option 2, above), then proceed directly into this section to set up all the logical drives you need. Any available extended partition space not assigned now as a logical drive will not be accessible later on.

Set Non-DOS Partition. This option is not directly available via the FDISK utility, and may be ignored if the entire disk surface is to be used by DOS. However, if you do wish to set aside non-DOS partition space for subsequent use by another operating system, you may do so by allocating less than 100 percent of the available space to the primary and extended DOS partitions described above, and then continue reading here.

Many third-party utilities can be used alone, or in conjunction with FDISK, to set up non-DOS partitions. For example, Figure 9.17a shows a display screen within the Partition Manager section of Storage Dimensions' *SpeedStor* utility, after using it to set up two non-DOS partitions. Although the utility might have been used to partition the entire hard disk surface, in this example FDISK was used first to set the primary DOS partition and an extended partition with two logical drives. Then *SpeedStor* divided the remaining space into the two non-DOS partitions labeled SSTOR in the figure. For comparison purposes, Figure 9.17b displays a report on the same drive configuration as reported by the Priam *InnerSpace* Disk Manager.

Note that the *SpeedStor* screen suggests there are now *five* partitions on the disk. However, the displayed DOS partitions 2 and 3 are in fact the two logical drives that show up as such within the single DOS extended partition when FDISK is used to display partition information. Even though FDISK itself cannot set up or erase these non-DOS partitions, it will recognize and display information about them, once they have been installed by some other utility (see option 4, below).

As a final point, the sum of the five partition capacities in the right-hand column is less than the displayed total capacity of 21,272,576 bytes. This is because the Bytes column does not tally the space occupied by each

a)

```
        SpeedStor(TM)  Disk Integration Software, version 6.0.1
      Copyright(C) 1985-1989 Storage Dimensions, Inc.  All rights reserved
```

```
                   P A R T I T I O N   M A N A G E R

   Drive    Manufacturer/Model    Cyls Heads Sectors  TotalBytes  FreeBytes
    1       <system given Params.>  611   4    17     21,272,576         0

                                            Cylinder
  No. Owner DOS Compatibility      Status   Start  End  Sectors     Bytes
  ───────────────────────────────────────────────────────────────────────
   1   DOS  2.0 and later    BOOT (ACTIVE)    0   150  10,251    5,248,512
   2   DOS  3.31 and later   usable         151   240   6,103    3,124,736
   3   DOS  3.31 and later   usable         241   300   4,063    2,080,256
   4  SSTOR 2.0 and later    read/write     301   480  12,223    6,258,176
   5  SSTOR 2.0 and later    read/write     481   610   8,823    4,517,376

                    < no free blocks available >
```

b)

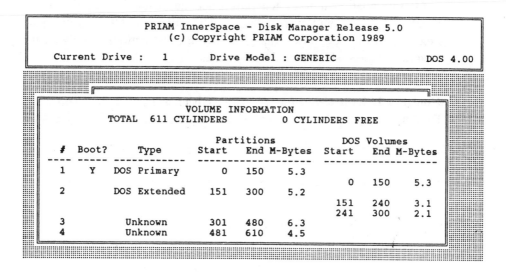

```
        ┌──────────────────────────────────────────────────────────────┐
        │          PRIAM InnerSpace - Disk Manager Release 5.0           │
        │             (c) Copyright PRIAM Corporation 1989               │
        │                                                                │
        │   Current Drive :   1      Drive Model : GENERIC    DOS 4.00   │
        └──────────────────────────────────────────────────────────────┘

                            VOLUME INFORMATION
                 TOTAL   611 CYLINDERS           0 CYLINDERS FREE

                              Partitions          DOS Volumes
         #  Boot?    Type    Start  End M-Bytes  Start   End M-Bytes
        ─── ───── ────────── ────────────────── ───────────────────
         1    Y    DOS Primary    0   150   5.3
                                                   0    150   5.3
         2         DOS Extended 151   300   5.2
                                                 151    240   3.1
                                                 241    300   2.1
         3         Unknown      301   480   6.3
         4         Unknown      481   610   4.5
```

Figure 9.17. Typical disk reports of a hard disk drive with DOS partitions created by the FDISK utility, with non-DOS partitions added by *SpeedStor* Partition Manager: (a) SpeedStor Disk Integration Software, (b) Priam *InnerSpace*.

partition's 17 hidden sectors (see page 406). The apparently missing bytes can be accounted for by multiplying $17 \times 5 \times 512 = 43{,}520$ bytes. For further details about reconciling various reports on hard disk capacity, refer to the Hard Disk Capacity section on page 406.

Option 2. Set active partition

As noted earlier in the chapter, the operating system installed in the active partition is the one that will be used when the computer is booted. To define the active partition from within FDISK, select option 4 on the FDISK Options menu (Figure 9.15). The Set Active Partition menu shown in Figure 9.18 appears. In this example, four partitions (2 DOS, 2 non-DOS) were previously defined using FDISK and *SpeedStor*, as described above and illustrated in Figure 9.17a. Despite FDISK's inability to set up or delete a non-DOS partition, it can set any such partition as active. Therefore, partition 1, 3, or 4 (but not 2) may now be set active. Assuming DOS is to be the operating system, enter a "1" and press the Enter key.

Note that in this example, FDISK shows the last non-DOS partition (SSTOR no. 5 in Figure 9.17a) occupying 26% of the disk, thus creating a hard disk in which 101 percent of the space has been allocated. Unfortunately, this is no high-tech breakthrough, just another one of those rounding errors that show up now and then.

After installation, if the system fails to boot due to the absence of an active partition, reboot from a system diskette containing the FDISK utility (your Select Copy diskette, for example). Follow the instructions just given, and then reboot the system from the hard disk.

Continue DOS Installation. If you have been using FDISK as part of the DOS installation process, then after defining the active partition, press the

```
                    Set Active Partition

Current fixed disk drive: 1

Partition Status Type  Size in Mbytes  Percentage of Disk Used
   C: 1            PRI DOS        5            25%
      2            EXT DOS        5            25%
      3            Non-DOS        5            25%
      4            Non-DOS        5            26%

Total disk space is   20 Mbytes (1 Mbyte = 1048576 bytes)

Enter the number of the partition you want to make active..........: [ ]
```

Figure 9.18.   The FDISK Set Active Partition screen. After you select the active partition, the letter "A" appears in the Status column next to the selected partition.

Escape key to exit and resume the installation process. The following message is seen:

```
You must restart your computer to continue.
Press Ctrl+Alt+Del to continue with DOS installation.
```

When you do so, one of two possible actions will occur. If you elected to devote the entire hard disk surface to a single DOS partition, this partition will be formatted without additional menu displays. Refer directly to the Begin High-Level Formatting section (page 397) above for further details.

However, if you did create an extended partition, you will first be asked for formatting instructions for each logical drive within that partition. Formatting begins after you make your choices. To continue, refer to the Hard Disk Does Not Require Partitioning section above (page 396).

Exit FDISK. If you were using FDISK simply to repartition the extended partition, set an active partition, or view partition information, then press the Escape key twice to return to the DOS prompt.

Option 3. Delete DOS Partition or Logical DOS Drive

If you wish to change the partition or logical disk structure, you must first delete the existing values. To do so, work backward through the list as far as is necessary; that is, first delete the logical drives in the extended partition, then the extended partition itself, and finally, the primary partition. For example, to define three logical drives in a partition presently occupied by two, delete both of them and then use the Create DOS Partition or Logical Disk Drive option (1) above to access the Create Logical Disk Drive(s) option.

Option 4. Display partition information

This option simply displays the current partition status of the hard disk. The display format was shown in Figure 9.18, except that now an "A" is seen in the status column to indicate the partition that has been set active, and the prompt to change the active partition is not seen.

Hard Disk Capacity: Theoretical and Actual

Once the hard disk is partitioned, formatted, and otherwise ready for active duty, there may be some confusion as to why CHKDSK, FDISK, third-party utilities, and the hard disk brochure can't agree on the capacity of the disk. With few exceptions, the brochure always promises more than the utilities can find.

For example, consider a typical hard disk divided by the DOS FDISK utility into two partitions, the second of which is subdivided into three logical drives (D, E, and F). Depending on who you believe, the disk has a capacity of

Bytes	according to
80,216,064	the manufacturer
80,137,728	*SpeedStor* Partition Manager
80,102,912	same, sum of reported bytes in 4 logical drives
79,876,096	CHKDSK, sum of total disk space in same 4 drives
79,691,776	FDISK reports 76M bytes

In the grand scheme of things the spread is not enormous, but it is enough to make one wonder which is the right answer.

They all are. The manufacturer lists the capacity according to the total number of cylinders. The utility reports the number of cylinders available for data storage. It's one less because a complete cylinder is set aside for self-diagnostic purposes.

To get a closer look at what's going on, Table 9.5 resolves the other discrepancies between the above reports. Although the various figures surely won't match anyone else's drive (except by coincidence), applying the same general principles should help the reader figure out where all the bytes have gone.

The drive was first partitioned into a 20Mb primary DOS partition (drive C in Table 9.5a), which FDISK approximated by allocating 256 cylinders. For the first and second 20Mb logical drives (D & E) in the extended partition, FDISK allocated 255 cylinders each, thereby leaving 257 cylinders for the final drive (F). (To assign space by cylinder number instead of Mbytes, a third-party utility such as *SpeedStor's* Partition Manager can be used instead of the DOS 4.01 FDISK utility. Earlier versions of FDISK also allocated space by cylinder number.)

In Table 9.5a, note that for each drive, the reported bytes are less than the product of cylinders × heads (9) × sectors (17) × bytes (512). In fact, each reported amount is short by 8,704 bytes, or 17 sectors. These hidden sectors (seen in Table 9.5a but not accounted for by *SpeedStor*) are set aside at the beginning of each drive for use by the operating system, and contain the drive partition table, among other things.

Table 9.5b compares the *SpeedStor* report for each drive with the figure reported by the DOS CHKDSK command. Again, something is missing—

Table 9.5a Space Utilization on Representative 80.2 Mbyte Hard Drive *

Reported item	Drive C	Drive D	Drive E	Drive F	Totals
First cylinder †	0	256	511	766	
Last cylinder †	255	510	765	1022	
Cylinders – per – drive	256	255	255	257	† 1,023
Diagnostic cylinder					1
Total cylinders					1,024
Reported sectors †	39,151	38,998	38,998	39,304	156,451
Hidden sectors	17	17	17	17	68
Diagnostic sectors					153
Total sectors ‡					156,672
Reported bytes † §	20,045,312	19,966,976	19,966,976	20,123,648	80,102,912
Hidden bytes	8,704	8,704	8,704	8,704	34,816
Diagnostic cylinder bytes					78,336
Total bytes ‡					80,216,064

† Data reported by *SpeedStor* Partition Manager. Other information added.
‡ Sector and byte totals match published specifications (Seagate ST4096).
§ Compare with CHKDSK report in Table 9.5b.

Table 9.5b Comparison of Data and User Byte Reports

Bytes reported	Drive C	Drive D	Drive E	Drive F	Totals
by *SpeedStor*	20,045,312	19,966,976	19,966,976	20,123,648	80,102,912
by DOS CHKDSK	19,988,480	19,910,656	19,910,656	20,066,304	79,876,096
Missing bytes	58,832	56,320	56,320	57,344	226,816
Missing sectors †	111	110	110	112	443

† Compare with DOS and lost sectors reported in Table 9.5c.

CHKDSK is consistently short by the number of bytes and sectors shown in each column.

In Table 9.5c, Norton Utilities' *Disk Information* reports the number of DOS sectors used by the boot record, file allocation tables, and directory. For drive C, the number of DOS sectors matches the missing sectors in Table 9.5b, thus accounting for all the space on this drive. This comparison points out that CHKDSK reports the bytes actually available to the user for data storage, which is of course always less than the number of bytes on the drive itself.

Table 9.5c Summary of Norton Disk Information Reports

Reported item	Drive C	Drive D	Drive E	Drive F	Totals
Clusters †	9,760	9,722	9,722	9,798	39,002
Sectors/cluster †	× 4	× 4	× 4	× 4	× 4
Data sectors †	39,040	38,888	38,888	39,192	156,008
DOS sectors † ‡	111	109	109	111	440
Lost sectors	0	1	1	1	3
Total sectors †	39,151	38,998	38,998	39,304	156,451
Sectors – per – track	÷ 17	÷ 17	÷ 17	÷ 17	÷ 17
Complete tracks	2,303	2,294	2,294	2,312	9,203
Hidden – sectors track †	1	1	1	1	4
Tracks (subtotal)	2,304	2,295	2,295	2,313	9,207
Diagnostic tracks					9
Total tracks					9,216

  † Data reported by Norton *Disk Information*. Other information added.
  ‡ Compare with DOS sectors reported in Table 9.5d.

Table 9.5d DOS Sectors Reported by Norton Disk Information

Sectors	Drive C	Drive D	Drive E	Drive F	Totals
Boot record	1	1	1	1	4
File allocation tables (2)	78	76	76	78	308
Directory	32	32	32	32	128
Total DOS sectors	111	109	109	111	440

However, there's still a little something missing on drives D, E, and F: the math in Table 9.5b shows 110, 110 again, and 112 missing sectors, but in Figure 9.5c, the *Disk Information* DOS sectors report is one sector less for these drives. These sectors are lost by the hard disk system, which must begin each logical drive at the start of a new track. Using drive D as an example, it uses 38,888 data sectors and 109 DOS sectors, for a total of 38,997 sectors. Therefore, there is one sector left over at the end of the drive's final track, and this sector is lost to the user. Table 9.5c adds the lost sector, so that a division of total sectors by sectors-per-track yields an integer number of tracks.

Finally (!), Table 9.5d shows how the DOS sectors are allocated to the boot record, the two file allocation tables, and the directory.

To summarize, each of the figures reported in Table 9.5 is a report of some characteristic of the hard disk drive, though at first glance it is not always clear of what. But by comparing several reports of the same drive capacity, it should be possible to figure out where all the bytes are hiding. Better yet, just take CHKDSK's word for it, since that's the number available for your use.

Format and Partition Summary

Figure 9.19 presents a four-part graphical overview of the entire low-level format, partition, and high-level format operation.

Figure 9.19a shows the magnetic surface of a single hard disk platter prior to low-level formatting. The low-level format (Figure 9.19b) divides this surface into a large number of tracks (only 12 shown), each of which is subdivided into 17 or more sectors. The dashed line in each sector separates the sector header from the 512-byte user area. Each sector header contains, among other things, the logical sector number. As illustrated, the sector interleave was set at 3:1 during the low-level format. (Sector headers were described in Table 8.5 (page 296).)

In Figure 9.19c, the disk surface has been divided (by the solid dark ring) into a primary and an extended partition. The extended partition is subdivided (by the broken dark ring) into two logical drives, and the interleave shown in this illustration is 2:1. The hidden sectors at the beginning of each partition are not shown in the illustration (after all, they *are* hidden).

Finally, in Figure 9.19d, a high-level format of logical drives C and E has set up a boot record, two file allocation tables, and a directory for each drive. Since the interleave was here set at 1:1, the boot record, FATs, and directory occupy contiguous physical sectors. In actual practice, the FATS and directory of course occupy more sectors than those shown in the illustration.

DRIVE REMOVAL AND REPLACEMENT PROCEDURES

Figures 9.20 through 9.22 show hard drive systems installed in several IBM PCs, and the figure legends give instructions for removal of each drive. In addition, the hard drive in a PS/2 model 70 was seen in Figure 8.13. For additional drive removal information, refer to the general procedures described in Chapter 8 for diskette drives (page 338).

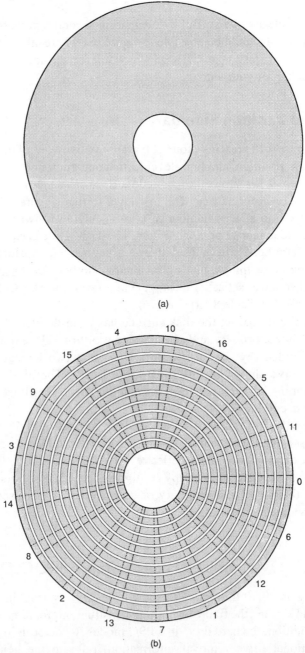

(a)

(b)

Figure 9.19. Hard disk format and partition summary. (a) Disk surface prior to low-level formatting. (b) Low-level format divides magnetic surface into tracks and sectors. Each sector header contains logical sector number (3:1 interleave shown) and other housekeeping data. (c) Tracks divided among three partitions (2:1 interleave shown). (d) High-level format sets up boot record, FATs and directory (1:1 interleave shown).

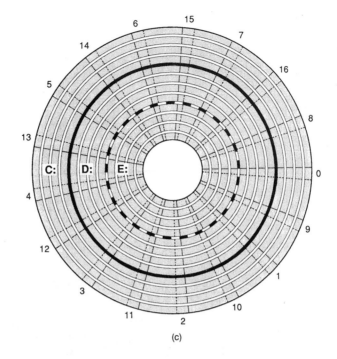

(c)

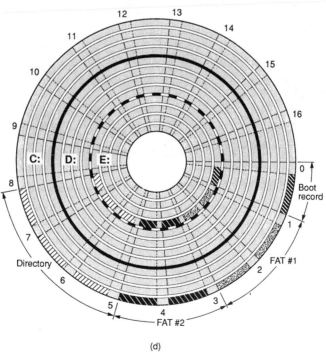

(d)

Figure 9.19   (continued)

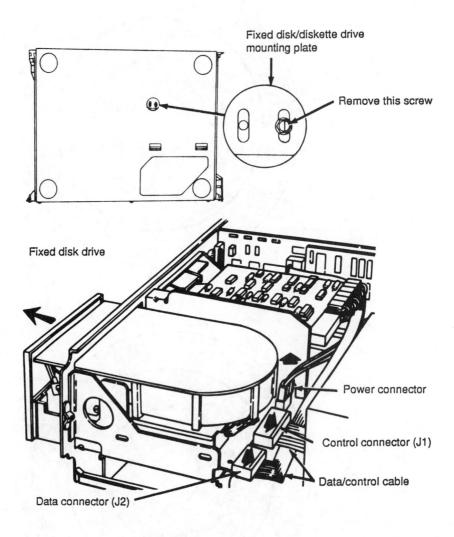

Fixed disk/diskette drive mounting plate

Remove this screw

Fixed disk drive

Power connector

Control connector (J1)

Data/control cable

Data connector (J2)

Figure 9.20. PC (Expansion Unit) and XT hard disk removal procedure. 1. Park the heads. 2. Tilt the system unit up and remove the drive's mounting plate screw, which is accessible from the bottom of the system unit chassis. 3. Remove the system unit cover. 4. Remove the two mounting screws on the side of the drive. 5. Slide the drive slightly forward and disconnect all cables to it. 6. Slide the drive all the way forward until it is clear of the system unit.

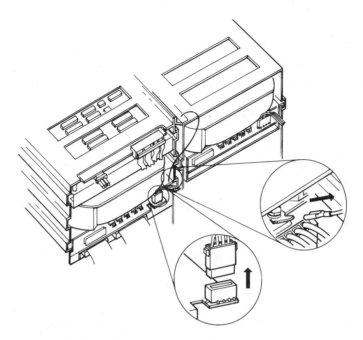

Figure 9.21.   AT hard disk removal procedure. 1. Park the heads. 2. Remove the system unit cover. 3. Remove the two mounting screws and clips on either side of the drive. 4. Slide the drive forward slightly and disconnect all cables to it. 5. Slide the drive all the way forward until it is clear of the system unit.

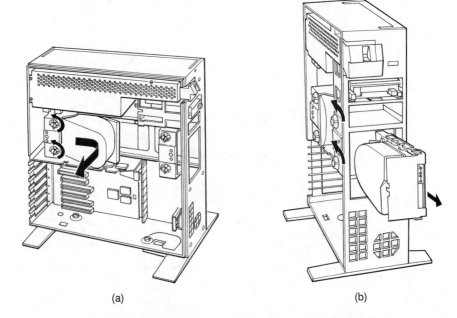

(a)   (b)

Figure 9.22.   Hard disk removal procedure for MCA models 60 and 80. 1. Loosen large nuts holding drive in place. 2. Disconnect all cables leading to drive. 3. (a) Remove drive C by lifting it clear of drive support housing. (b) Remove drive D by sliding it forward.

10

KEYBOARDS AND MICE

KEYBOARDS

Figure 10.1 illustrates several of the keyboard styles that have been used with IBM and other personal computers. Table 10.1 provides a cross-reference guide between keyboard style and PC model number.

Keyboard Style Descriptions

Each keyboard style is briefly described here.

83-Key PC Keyboard. As seen in Figure 10.1(a), this is the keyboard supplied with all PCs and with some models of the XT. There were ten Function keys on the left side of the keyboard, an Escape key in the upper left-hand section of the standard typing area, and a combination numeric keypad/cursor control section on the right.

84-Key AT Keyboard. This was the standard keyboard (Figure 10.1(b)) for almost all models of the AT. Although similar in layout to the 83-key keyboard, there are a few changes. For example, the Escape key is moved to the top of the numeric keypad section and an extra key (Sys Req) is added at the extreme right of the keypad. In addition, three LED status lights

415

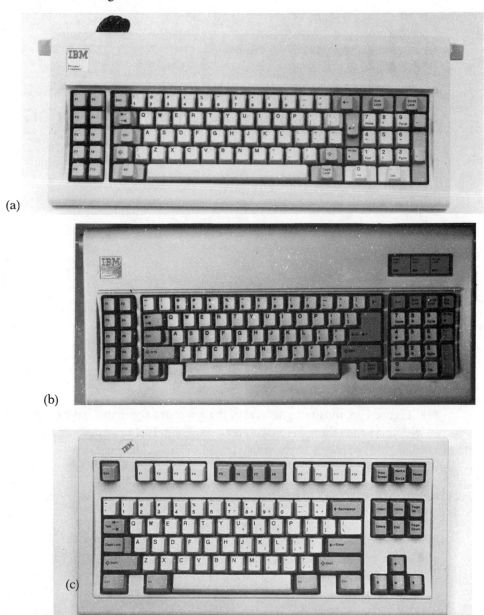

(a)

(b)

(c)

Figure 10.1. Typical keyboards for ISA and MCA systems. (a) original IBM 83-key keyboard (b) 84-key IBM AT keyboard (c) 84-key space saving keyboard supplied with some model 25 systems (d) 101-key IBM enhanced keyboard (e) Replacement keyboard for most ISA and MCA systems (OmniKey PLUS courtesy Northgate Computer Systems, Inc.) (f) Modular keyboard allows user to arrange function keys, numeric keypad, trackball (not shown) to suit personal preference. (Switchboard courtesy Datadesk International, Inc.)

Figure 10.1 (continued)

Table 10.1 Keyboard Cross-Reference Guide

Computer	Model number	Number * of keys	Keyboard fuse ** on system board
PC	all	83	no
XT	68, 78, 86, 87, 88	83	no
	267, 277	83	no
	89, 268, 278, 286	101	no
AT	68, 99, 239, 319	84	no
	339	101	no
25	001, 004, C02, C05	84/85	yes
	all others	101/102	yes
25 286	006, 036	84/85	yes
	all others	101/102	yes
30	all	101/102	yes
30 286	all	101/102	no
50, 55 SX	all	101/102	yes
60, 65 SX	all	101/102	yes
P70	all	101/102	yes
70, 80	all	101/102	no

  * 84/85 and 101/102 are number of keys on US/foreign keyboards.
 ** POST error code 305 indicates blown fuse.

indicate when the Caps Lock, Num Lock, and Scroll Lock functions are enabled.

84-Key Space-Saving Keyboard. Some versions of the model 25 and 25 286 are supplied with this keyboard. Its layout—shown in Figure 10.1c—is similar to the 101-key keyboard described immediately below, except the right-hand numeric keypad is not implemented.

101-Key Keyboard. This keyboard, supplied with some XT and AT models and all PS/2 systems, relocates the function keys in a horizontal row across the top of the keyboard and increases their number from ten to twelve. The Escape key returns to the upper left-hand side of the keyboard, and there are duplicate cursor movement and other keys. IBM documentation sometimes refers to this keyboard as an "enhanced" keyboard. Figure 10.1d shows the enhanced keyboard layout.

Other Keyboard Styles. The enhanced keyboard was not introduced to universal acclaim; not a few users rather liked the earlier layout of function keys on the left side of the keyboard. Consequently, many third-party suppliers have introduced keyboards that combine the functionality of the 101-key design with the user-friendliness of the previous layouts, as shown by the example in Figure 10.1e. Or for those who wish to hedge their bets, a design-it-yourself keyboard is now available, in which each major function group is contained in its own plug-in module, as shown in Figure 10.1f. The modules may be moved to suit user preference and/or the needs of left-handed typists.

KEY IDENTIFICATION

Every key on an IBM keyboard may be described by four identifiers:

The characters seen on the face of the key cap
The character codes associated with each key-cap character
The key's scan code
A decimal key-locator number

Table 10.2 presents a complete cross-reference guide to key characters, scan codes, and location numbers, each of which is described in the next section. Note that on the IBM PC, the scan code matches the key-locator number, since these numbers were specified concurrently. As newer keyboards introduced variations in key placement, the scan codes followed the keys, and so they no longer appear in strict sequential order.

The Key-Cap Character

The alphanumeric character engraved on the key cap is, of course, the obvious identifier from the user's point of view. As on the typical office typewriter, most keys display more than one character. Also, a few characters (. + - * 0–9 and the Shift key) put in an appearance on two physically different keys. Furthermore, the role of many keys may change completely if the system is configured to represent another keyboard layout. Therefore, a more specific designation is required to identify each physical key, without regard to the character displayed when it is pressed.

Table 10.2 Cross-Reference Guide to Key Character, Scan Code, Locator Number *

Key	Esc	1	2	3	4	5	6	7	8	9	0	-	=	←
Hex	01	02	03	04	05	06	07	08	09	0A	0B	0C	0D	0E
Decimal	1	2	3	4	5	6	7	8	9	10	11	12	13	14
83	1	2	3	4	5	6	7	8	9	10	11	12	13	14
84	90	2	3	4	5	6	7	8	9	10	11	12	13	15
101	110	2	3	4	5	6	7	8	9	10	11	12	13	15

Key	Tab	Q	W	E	R	T	Y	U	I	O	P	[	]	Enter
Hex	0F	10	11	12	13	14	15	16	17	18	19	1A	1B	1C
Decimal	15	16	17	18	19	20	21	22	23	24	25	26	27	28
83	15	16	17	18	19	20	21	22	23	24	25	26	27	28
84	16	17	18	19	20	21	22	23	24	25	26	27	28	43
101	16	17	18	19	20	21	22	23	24	25	26	27	28	43

Key	Ctrl	A	S	D	F	G	H	J	K	L	:	"	~
Hex	ID	1E	1F	20	21	22	23	24	25	26	27	28	29
Decimal	29	30	31	32	33	34	35	36	37	38	39	40	41
83	29	30	31	32	33	34	35	36	37	38	39	40	41
84	30	31	32	33	34	35	36	37	38	39	40	41	1
101	58	31	32	33	34	35	36	37	38	39	40	41	1

Key	Shift left	\	Z	X	C	V	B	N	M	,	.	Shift /right	Prt Sc
Hex	2A	2B	2C	2D	2E	2F	30	31	32	33	34	35	36	37
Decimal	42	43	44	45	46	47	48	49	50	51	52	53	54	55
83	42	43	44	45	46	47	48	49	50	51	52	53	54	55
84	44	14	46	47	48	49	50	51	52	53	54	55	57	106
101	44	29	46	47	48	49	50	51	52	53	54	55	57	124

Key	Alt	Sp	Caps lock	F1	F2	F3	F4	F5	F6	F7	F8	F9	F10	Num lock
Hex	38	39	3A	3B	3C	3D	3E	3F	40	41	42	43	44	45
Decimal	56	57	58	59	60	61	62	63	64	65	66	67	68	69
83	56	57	58	59	60	61	62	63	64	65	66	67	68	69
84	58	61	64	70	65	71	66	72	67	73	68	74	69	95
101	60	61	30	112	113	114	115	116	117	118	119	120	121	90

Table 10.2 Cross-Reference Guide to Key Character, Scan Code, Locator Number (continued) *

Key	Scroll Lock	7 (	8	9	-	4	5	6	+	1	2	3	0	Del)
						above keys are in the keypad area								
Hex	46	47	48	49	4A	4B	4C	4D	4E	4F	50	51	52	53
Decimal	70	71	72	73	74	75	76	77	78	79	80	81	82	83
83	70	71	72	73	74	75	76	77	78	79	80	81	82	83
84	100	91	96	101	107	92	97	102	108	93	98	103	99	104
101	125	91	96	101	105	92	97	102	106	93	98	103	99	104

Key	Sys Req	F11	F12
Hex	54	57	58
Decimal	84	80	81
83	n/a	n/a	n/a
84	105	n/a	n/a
101	n/a	122	123

* Find the key of interest in the first (Key) row. Directly below it, read; hexadecimal scan code, decimal scan code, and locator number for 83, 84, or 101 – key keyboard, as appropriate. Keys are listed here in the sequence found on the PC keyboard. Note that PC locator number and scan code are identical. Scan codes for duplicate keys on 101 – key keyboard are listed in Table 9.3.

Keyboard Character Codes

In order to efficiently convey data in a digital format, a unique code is assigned to each character or control code that must be transmitted. This transmission may take place between various devices within a single computer, or between two computers (for example, via modem). In either case, a standard coded character set is used.

Although this character set is not directly utilized in keyboard diagnostics, its use is required for some keyboard reconfiguration applications, and it is often called upon for various routine operations.

ASCII Character Set. The published standard employed by most personal computers is known by the title *Coded Character Sets— 7-bit American National Standard Code for Information Interchange (7-bit ASCII)*, or simply, ANSI X3.4-1986.

The first 128 characters in Figure 10.2 are based on the the 7-bit ASCII character set, and the control characters found within the ANSI standard are listed in Table 10.3.

(a)   **ASCII Control Characters (ANSI X3.4-1986)**

NUL	SOH	STX	ETX	eot	eng	ack	BEL	BS	HT	LF	VT	FF	CR	SO	SI
0	1	2	3	4	5	6	7	8	9	10	11	12	13	14	15
DLE	DC1	DC2	DC3	DC4	NAK	SYN	ETB	CAN	EM	SUB	ESC	FS	GS	RS	US
16	17	18	19	20	21	22	23	24	25	26	27	28	29	30	31

(b)   **ASCII Graphic Characters (ANSI X3.4-1986)**

	!	"	#	$	%	&	'	(	)	*	+	,	-	.	/
32	33	34	35	36	37	38	39	40	41	42	43	44	45	46	47
0	1	2	3	4	5	6	7	8	9	:	;	<	=	>	?
48	49	50	51	52	53	54	55	56	57	58	59	60	61	62	63
@	A	B	C	D	E	F	G	H	I	J	K	L	M	N	O
64	65	66	67	68	69	70	71	72	73	74	75	76	77	78	79
P	Q	R	S	T	U	V	W	X	Y	Z	[	\	]	^	_
80	81	82	83	84	85	86	87	88	89	90	91	92	93	94	95
`	a	b	c	d	e	f	g	h	i	j	k	l	m	n	o
96	97	98	99	100	101	102	103	104	205	106	107	108	109	110	111
p	q	r	s	t	u	v	w	x	y	z	{	|	}	~	DEL
112	113	114	115	116	117	118	119	120	121	122	123	124	125	126	127

(c)   **IBM Extended Character Set**

Ç	ü	é	â	ä	à	å	ç	ê	ë	è	ï	î	ì	Ä	Å
128	129	130	131	132	133	134	135	136	137	138	139	140	141	142	143
É	æ	Æ	ô	ö	ò	û	ù	ÿ	Ö	Ü	¢	£	¥	₧	ƒ
144	145	146	147	148	149	150	151	152	153	154	155	156	157	158	159
á	í	ó	ú	ñ	Ñ	ª	º	¿	⌐	¬	½	¼	¡	«	»
160	161	162	163	164	165	166	167	168	169	170	171	172	173	174	175
░	▒	▓	│	┤	╡	╢	╖	╕	╣	║	╗	╝	╜	╛	┐
176	177	178	179	180	181	182	183	184	185	186	187	188	189	190	191
└	┴	┬	├	─	┼	╞	╟	╚	╔	╩	╦	╠	=	╬	╧
192	193	194	195	196	197	198	199	200	201	202	203	204	205	206	207
╨	╤	╥	╙	╘	╒	╓	╫	╪	┘	┌	█	▄	▌	▐	▀
208	209	210	211	212	213	214	215	216	217	218	219	220	221	222	223
α	β	Γ	π	Σ	σ	µ	τ	Φ	Θ	Ω	δ	∞	φ	ε	∩
224	225	226	227	228	229	230	231	232	233	234	235	236	237	238	239
≡	±	≥	≤	⌠	⌡	÷	≈	°	∙	·	√	ⁿ	²	■	
240	241	242	243	244	245	246	247	248	249	250	251	252	253	254	255

Figure 10.2. ASCII and IBM extended character sets. (a) ASCII control characters, (b) ASCII graphic characters, (c) IBM extended character set (not part of ASCII standard). The ASCII control characters are defined in Table 10.3.

Table 10.3 ASCII Control Characters *

ASCII	Mnemonic and meaning		ASCII	Mnemonic and meaning	
0	NUL	null	16	DLE	data link escape
1	SOH	start of heading	17	DC1	device control 1
2	STX	start of text	18	DC2	device control 2
3	ETX	end of text	19	DC3	device control 3
4	eot †	end of transmission	20	DC4	device control 4
5	enq †	enquiry	21	NAK	negative acknowledge
6	ack †	acknowledge	22	SYN	synchronous idle
7	BEL	bell	23	ETB	end of transmission block
8	BS	backspace	24	CAN	cancel
9	HT	horizontal tab	25	EM	end of medium
10	LF	line feed	26	SUB	substitute
11	VT	vertical tab	27	ESC	escape
12	FF	form feed	28	FS	file separator
13	CR	carriage return	29	GS	group separator
14	SO	shift out	30	RS	record separator
15	SI	shift in	31	US	unit separator
			127	DEL	delete

* Information based on ANSI X3.4–1986.
† Lowercase mnemonics are not defined in IBM PC usage.

IBM Extended Character Set. It is of course possible to define an additional 128 characters (128–255) simply by employing the unused eighth bit within each byte. IBM uses these characters in its extended character set (Fig. 9.2c). Although popularly referred to as an "extended ASCII" code, the additional characters are not in fact part of the official ANSI standard.

Keyboard Scan Codes

A scan code is a unique number that IBM has assigned to each key function, and it does not change from one keyboard style to another, despite the physical relocation of some keys. And although the same character may appear on more than one key, each key has its own unique scan code. Thus, the left and right shift keys have different scan codes, as do the two keys which have the + sign on them.

When any key is struck, a two-byte code is generated. The first byte represents the actual character of interest to the user (for example, A or a, # or 3, M or m), while the second byte is the scan code for the key that was struck. In fact, each keystroke actually produces two scan codes; one when the key is pressed (the make code) and another when it is released (the break code). But only the former is considered in this chapter, since this value is displayed on screen in the event of a keyboard malfunction during the POST procedure.

As an error code, the scan code is an unambiguous reference to the specific key that is defective, regardless of what character or function that key happens to represent at the moment. For example, when the R key is pressed (in BASIC) one of the following displays will be seen:

Keys pressed	Screen display
Ctrl + R	square insert-mode cursor
Shift + R	uppercase R
Alt + R	BASIC keyword RUN (if ANSI.SYS is listed in the CONFIG.SYS file)
R alone	lowercase r

In each case, the scan code for the R key remains decimal 19, and in the event of a malfunction during POST, this code is displayed on screen in its hexadecimal equivalent of 13. Figures 10.3a, 10.3c, and 10.3e give the scan codes for each key on the three IBM keyboards. Table 10.4 is a cross-reference guide to the keyboard character associated with each scan code.

Scan Codes and the 101-Key Keyboard. Certain keys on the 101-key keyboard have a scan code consisting of more than one hexadecimal number. For example, each of the duplicate cursor movement keys has a scan code beginning with a hexadecimal prefix code E0, as indicated in Figure 10.3e. Therefore, if a keyboard error code containing E0 is displayed during POST, the specific key causing the problem may be any one of the 14 keys using this prefix code.

BASIC Scan-Code Program. The short BASIC program seen in Listing 10.1 will display the scan code for any key that is pressed. Begin at the DOS prompt by typing BASIC or BASICA. Then enter the program lines on the left.

When you are finished, type RUN and then press various keys. For example, if the Q, a, A, Z, and 1 keys are pressed, the display below is seen.

	Scan code	
Keystroke	**hexadecimal**	**decimal**
Q	10	16
a	1E	30
A	1E	30
Z	2C	44
1	2	2

To quit the program, press the Escape key.

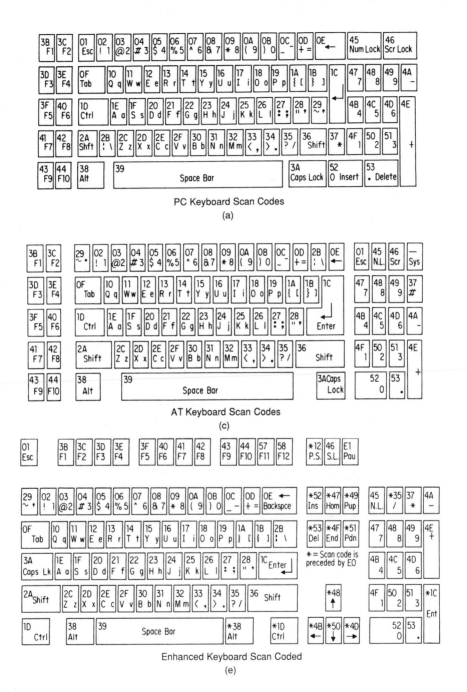

PC Keyboard Scan Codes
(a)

AT Keyboard Scan Codes
(c)

Enhanced Keyboard Scan Coded
(e)

Figure 10.3. Keyboard layouts showing scan codes and key-locator numbers.
Scan codes locator numbers (a) PC (b) PC (c) AT (d) AT (e) 101-key (f) 101-key

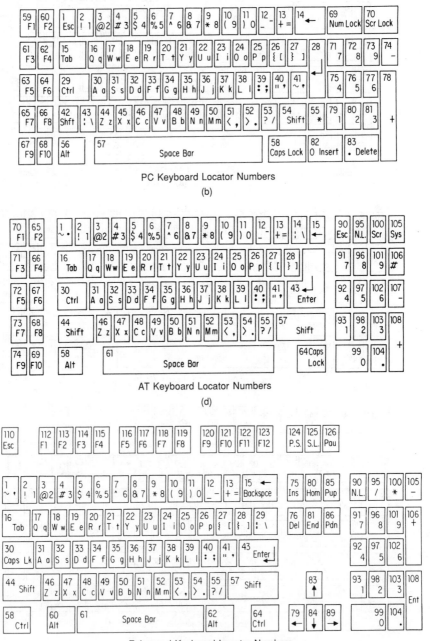

PC Keyboard Locator Numbers

(b)

AT Keyboard Locator Numbers

(d)

Enhanced Keyboard Locator Numbers

(f)

Figure 10.3. *(Continued)*

Table 10.4a Cross-Reference Guide to Scan Code for Each Keyboard Character *

Scan code	Keys	Scan code	Keys	Scan code	Keys	Scan code	Keys
01	Escape	16	U u	2B	| \	40	F6
02	! 1	17	I i	2C	Z z	41	F7
03	@ 2	18	O o	2D	X x	42	F8
04	# 3	19	P p	2E	C c	43	F9
05	$ 4	1A	{ [	2F	V v	44	F10
06	% 5	1B	}]	30	B b	45	Num Lock
07	^ 6	1C	Enter	31	N n	46	Scroll Lock
08	& 7	1D	Ctrl	32	M m	47	7 Home
09	* 8	1E	A a	33	< ,	48	8 Cursor Up
0A	(9	1F	S s	34	> .	49	9 Pg Up
0B	) 0	20	D d	35	? /	4A	– (gray key)
0C	–	21	F f	36	Right Shift	4B	4 Cursor Left
0D	+ =	22	G g	37	PrtSc *	4C	5
0E	Backspace	23	H h	38	Alt	4D	6 Cursor Right
0F	Tab	24	J j	39	Space Bar	4E	+ (gray key)
10	Q q	25	K k	3A	Caps Lock	4F	1 End
11	W w	26	L l	3B	F1	50	2 Cursor Down
12	E e	27	: ;	3C	F2	51	3 PgDn
13	R r	28	" '	3D	F3	0	Insert
14	T t	29	~ '	3E	F4	.	Delete
15	Y y	2A	Left Shift	3F	F5	54	Sys Req (84–key)
						E1	Pause (101–key)

The Key-Locator Number

On some IBM drawings of keyboard layouts, a decimal number is assigned to each key, as illustrated in Figures 10.3b, 10.3d, and 10.3f. The number is a convenient guide to the general physical location of each key. Numbering begins at 1 in the alphanumeric area, then progresses to the function keys, and moves finally to the numeric-keypad/cursor-movement area. On the 101-key keyboard, the locator numbers for the function keys come after those used for the keypad.

Since there are several keyboard layouts in current use on IBM personal computers, the relationship between the key-locator number and the character seen on that key varies slightly from one keyboard style to another. Note that if the characters displayed by a key are changed—for example, on a foreign-language keyboard configuration—the key-locator number is unaffected. Therefore, the number offers a guide to the key location, but not necessarily to the character seen when that key is struck.

Table 10.4b E0 Error Codes on 101-key keyboard

	Duplicate key description	Key locator no. in Figure 10.3(f)	Complete scan code
Gray keys	cursor left	79	E0 4B
	cursor right	89	E0 4D
	cursor down	84	E0 50
	cursor up	83	E0 48
	Delete	76	E0 53
	End	81	E0 4F
	Home	80	E0 47
	Insert	75	E0 52
	Page Down	86	E0 51
	Page Up	84	E0 49
	Pause	126	E1 1D 45 E1 9D C5
	Print Screen	124	E0 2A E0 37
Keypad area	Enter	108	E0 1C
	/	95	E0 35
Other keys	Right Alt	62	E0 38
	Right Ctrl	64	E0 1D

*   In the event of an xx 301 POST error, look in the Scan Code columns to find the hexadecimal error code (xx) seen on the screen. The indicated key is the one that is causing the error. On a 101–key keyboard, an E0 error code indicates a duplicate–key error, but does not identify the specific key causing the problem.

The key-locator number is chiefly of value in advanced keyboard servicing work or as an intermediate guide in comparing a displayed character with its scan code, as described on page 423.

Foreign-Language Configuration

To configure an alternate foreign-language keyboard layout, use one of the methods described below, as appropriate.

Listing 10.1 A BASIC Scan Code Display Program

```
100 WHILE SC <> 1          ' If Escape key is not pressed,
110 K$ = INPUT$(1)         ' wait for a single keystroke, then
120 SC = INP(96)           ' find its scan code and
130 PRINT K$, HEX$(SC), SC ' display keystroke, hex &
                           '   decimal scan code.
140 WEND                   ' Then do another one.
```

The keyboard layout instructions in the DOS 3.30 and 4.00 manuals are close to incomprehensible, and the much-abbreviated summary given here makes no attempt at an English-language translation. Instead it is offered mostly to point out that if a few keystrokes produce unexpected characters, the trouble may be traced to an installed foreign-language keyboard layout.

DOS 3.00 to 3.20. One of five DOS keyboard layout programs may be used. These are found on the original IBM DOS diskette that comes with your PC, and are listed here in Table 10.5. If you are unsure which keyboard configuration is currently in use, the *character displayed* column gives the uppercase and lowercase characters that are displayed by PC key number 40 and AT key number 41 (see Figure 10.2(b), (d), (f)).

To load the desired program listed in the table, type the following command at the DOS prompt:

KEYB*xx*

where *xx* indicates the last two characters in the program name.

Table 10.5 Foreign Language Keyboard Configuration Guide

Keyboard configuration	DOS 3.00–3.20 KEYB*xx*.COM *xx*	DOS 3.30 or later KEYB.COM *xx*	Character displayed when PC key 40 or AT key 41 is pressed (shift) (normal)	
Belgium		BE	%	ù
Canada (French)		CF	‘	‘
Denmark		DK	¥	¢
Finland		SU	Ä	ä
France	FR	FR	%	ù
Germany	GR	GR	Ä	ä
Italy	IT	IT	#	à
Latin America		LA	:	;
Netherlands		NL	±	+ †
Norway		NO	Æ	æ
Portugal		PO	"	›
Spain	SP	SP	:	;
Sweden		SV	Ä	ä
Switzerland (French)		SF	ä	à
Switzerland (German)		SG	à	ä
United Kingdom	UK	UK	@	›
United States	default	US †	"	›

† To return to U. S. configuration
‡ key 40 on AT (: ;)

It is not necessary to type in the COM extension. Once the keyboard-layout program is loaded, press the Alt+Ctrl+F1 and F2 keys to toggle between the standard and custom keyboard layouts.

If the alternate keyboard layout is frequently required, the KEYB*xx* command may, of course, be written into a batch file, using the batch file directions given in Chapter 4. Only one alternate keyboard may be used at a time, and the last one loaded takes the place of any previously loaded alternate layout.

DOS 3.30 or 4.*xx*. Much-expanded foreign-language keyboard support is now provided via a single KEYB.COM utility in the DOS subdirectory. To select the desired layout, type the following command:

KEYB *xx*

where *xx* is the country keyboard layout parameter, as also listed in Table 10.5. Note that this parameter is separated by a space from the KEYB command itself.

Scan Codes and Foreign-Language Keyboards. Note that on keyboards configured for a language other than U.S. English, the identity of some keys is changed to suit the general usage of that language. As one example, the character seen by depressing the letter key closest to the left Shift key is seen here:

Character displayed	Keyboard configuration
Z	U.S. English, U.K. English, Italian, Spanish
W	French
Y	German

But whatever the key-cap designation and whatever appears on screen when this key is pressed, its scan code remains decimal 44, hexadecimal 2C.

KEYBOARD DIAGNOSTICS

Although the keyboard does not readily lend itself to user servicing, there are nevertheless a few diagnostics tests that may be done to determine if it is indeed the keyboard itself that requires attention or some other system component that is at fault.

The most likely keyboard error is the occasional stuck key, a problem which may be easily pinpointed by studying the error code displayed during the POST procedure, at which time every key on the keyboard is checked.

If a problem is encountered, one of the error codes described below appears on screen.

As noted in Chapter 3, the keyboard is also checked as part of the routine diagnostics procedure. During the keyboard test, the user is asked to press each key and verify that the proper character is displayed on screen.

Keyboard Error Codes

In case of a keyboard-related error during the POST procedure or while running the diagnostics diskette, various error codes are displayed.

xx **301.** If POST is able to identify a specific key that is faulty, the following error message is seen:

```
xx 301
```

where *xx* is the scan code for the defective key and 301 is the keyboard error code. Table 10.4 may be used to determine which key is causing the error-code message. Once the key is identified, try pressing it several times in rapid succession to dislodge any dirt particles that may be interfering with its operation. If this doesn't clear up the problem, then the keyboard will have to be serviced.

As noted earlier, an E0 error code indicates one of the duplicate keys on a 101-key keyboard, but does not identify the specific key causing the problem. Table 10.4 also lists all the keys that display an E0 error code.

301 (with no scan code). This indicates that the keyboard is disconnected or otherwise inoperative. Make sure the connector on the keyboard-interface cable is securely inserted in the keyboard socket on the rear of the system unit.

On the IBM PC, make sure the keyboard cable is not plugged into the adjacent cassette-recorder socket, which is located to the immediate right of the keyboard socket.

On PS/2 systems, the keyboard and mouse sockets are side by side and physically identical. Make sure the keyboard is plugged into the left-hand socket (when facing the rear of the system unit).

302. During diagnostics testing (see Chapter 3), this number is written to the error log if the user indicates an error during the keyboard test. In this case, the user's own observation of the specific error will best serve to identify the specific key that is faulty. On the AT, a 302 error code during the POST procedure may indicate that the keyboard is inoperative because the front-panel system key is in the off position.

303 or Greater. This indicates that the keyboard and/or related components on the system board require servicing. To localize the source of the problem, turn off the power, unplug the keyboard, and reboot the system. If a 301 error code is seen, the keyboard itself requires servicing, since unplugging it cleared up the original problem. If the number remains 303 or greater, then the problem is on the system board, which must be serviced.

301 or 303 with Non-IBM Keyboard. In many cases, a replacement keyboard must be configured for the personal computer with which it is to be used. If a keyboard-related error code is seen and/or a continuous series of beeps is heard, the keyboard may be incorrectly configured. For further details, see the section on keyboard replacement (page 436).

Other Keyboard-Related Problems

During routine operations, the keyboard-related problems listed here may be encountered.

Inoperative Keyboard. If the keyboard suddenly appears to be inoperative, don't overlook the following possibilities:

1. The system is sending keystroke characters to another display that is not currently in use.
2. The system is attempting to send output to an external device, such as a printer or modem, that either has not been turned on or is not currently available.
3. The keyboard cable plug has accidentally been disconnected at the system unit rear panel connector.

In the case of a two-display system, turn both displays on to verify that neither is displaying your keystrokes. Also make sure that all external devices are turned on and properly connected. And finally, check the rear-panel keyboard connection.

As an obvious error example, depressing the Shift+PrtSc keys attempts to send the current screen display to the printer. If the printer is disconnected or its power is not on, the system will lock up for some time—from a few seconds to a minute or more, depending on the specific system configuration.

To check for this kind of temporary printer-related system lockup, press the space bar 15 times and verify that the cursor does not move. Each keystroke beyond the fifteenth will produce a warning beep, indicating that the keyboard buffer has received the preceding 15 keystrokes and is temporarily full. This suggests that the keyboard and its associated circuitry are in good order and that the problem lies elsewhere.

If the cursor eventually moves 15 spaces and the keyboard once again functions properly, the system has returned to normal operation.

If this type of problem occurs while a program is running, one of the following messages may be displayed:

```
Device Timeout in xxx
```

or

```
Device Timeout at address xxxx:yyyy
```

where *xxx* is a line number and *xxxx:yyyy* is an address in segment:offset format.

Either message points to a line number or address at which a program instruction is initiating the error. In this case the source of the actual error is at some external device, for example, a printer or a modem that is either malfunctioning or not powered on. But in any case, a keyboard problem seems unlikely.

Incorrect Display of Some Keystrokes. If one or more keys do not display the expected characters, the system is probably configured for a language that does not match the keyboard. In some cases, a custom keyboard configuration may be in use. Since such configurations require some software support, it is all but impossible to encounter them unexpectedly.

As usual, there is one exception that should be noted. Assuming a foreign-language (or custom) keyboard configuration is in use, it is possible to switch between it and the standard local (usually U.S. English) keyboard. This is accomplished by holding down the Ctrl and Alt keys while pressing a function key.

Press	to use
Ctrl+Alt+F1 key	standard local configuration
Ctrl+Alt+F2 key	installed alternative keyboard configuration

Pressing Ctrl+Alt+F1 restores the standard local configuration, while pressing Ctrl+Alt+F2 will have effect only if some other keyboard configuration has been previously loaded into memory. If an alternative keyboard configuration has been loaded into memory and pressing the Ctrl+Alt+F2 has the wrong effect, or no effect at all, then the alternate keyboard layout is probably incorrect or lost from memory.

Keyboard Password Problem. Unlike the AT, the PS/2 system unit key has no effect on the keyboard; it only secures the system unit cover. Instead, a keyboard password is entered to temporarily block access to the computer until such time as the password is reentered or the system is turned off. In the latter case, the keyboard password is lost and a new one must be set the next time you wish to temporarily lock the keyboard.

If there is a problem reactivating the keyboard after a password has been set, chances are it was not typed correctly—either now or when initially entered. In either case, simply turn the system off and back on again. Note that a key symbol o⁻┐ seen when the system is powered on indicates a system (not keyboard) password is in effect. For further details about system security, refer to the *Set Passwords* section in Chapter 6 (page 189).

System Security Notes

In a security-sensitive environment it is important to remember that the front-panel key lock is not a tamper-proof device. With the system locked and the key removed, it is still not that difficult to pry the system unit cover off, disable or unplug the key mechanism, and thereby gain access to the system. Therefore, the lock should be regarded as a convenient means of discouraging idle access and not as foolproof protection against deliberate tampering.

AT Keyboard Lock. As noted earlier, a 302 error may indicate that the AT keyboard is locked. If turning the front-panel key to the unlocked position does not clear up the problem, unplug the keyboard lock assembly from the system board at the J20 jumper location shown in Figure 10.4. Doing so also disables the front-panel power-on light. If the system successfully boots when power is turned back on, then the keyboard lock assembly is defective and will have to be replaced. Otherwise, the fault is on the system board, which will require servicing.

Note that when the keyboard is locked, the system unit cover is also locked in place. Therefore, make sure the keyboard is unlocked before trying to remove the cover. The cover-lock action is mechanical and will not be affected by a faulty or unplugged electric connection.

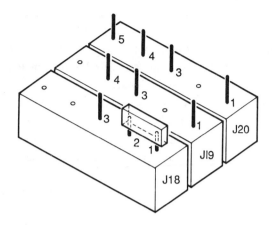

Figure 10.4. To temporarily disable the keyboard lock, disconnect the cable connected to jumper J20 on the AT system board.

AT Key Replacement. The two keys supplied with each AT are accompanied by a key-replacement code, which is located on a tag included with the keys. See the System Security section of Chapter 6 (page 168) for information on ordering additional keys.

Status Lights

The three status lights on AT and PS/2 keyboards alert the user that one or more of the modes described below are enabled. Each light should go on and off as the related key is toggled.

Mode	Description
Caps Lock	All letter keys display uppercase characters when depressed; simultaneously holding down Shift key

	and letter key displays lowercase letter. Punctuation, numeric, and other keys are unaffected.
Num Lock	Eleven white keys in right-hand keypad area become numeric keypad, instead of cursor-movement keys.
Scroll Lock	Various software-dependent scrolling functions are enabled, depending on specific program currently in use; in absence of software making use of this function, Scroll Lock key has no effect on keyboard.

Status-Light Test. The status lights themselves may be tested by running a one-line BASIC program. Begin at the DOS prompt by typing BASIC or BASICA, and then type any convenient line number and the program itself:

```
xxx OUT 96, 237: OUT 96, 7
```

where *xxx* is any line number.

First, make sure all three status lights are out, and then run the program, which turns all the lights on but does not enable the corresponding functions. To execute this program as a direct statement, eliminate the line number and make sure the rest of the line is entirely typed before pressing the Enter key; otherwise, the keyboard will lock up and the system will have to be rebooted.

To restore normal operation, press any one of the three associated keys. This enables the corresponding mode and simultaneously extinguishes the other two lights.

KEYBOARD REPAIR AND REPLACEMENT

Aside from the routine cleaning procedures described in the keyboard-care section of Chapter 2, there is little the user can do to repair a defective keyboard. The keyboard assembly is a sealed unit with many parts, and will fly apart if opened by a nonspecialist.

Key Reassignment

In the event that a specific key becomes inoperative and it is not possible to make an immediate keyboard replacement, another key may be used as a temporary substitute. For example, if the letter A key is out of service, its characters might be temporarily reassigned to the rarely used tilde (~ ‘) key, using the DOS PROMPT command. To do so, first consult Figure 10.2 and note the decimal ASCII values of all four characters:

A = ASCII 65   a = ASCII 97
~ = ASCII 126   ' = ASCII 96

Type the following string of characters at the DOS prompt (in this example, the uppercase A is used) and then press the Enter key. The final character must be lowercase.

```
A>PROMPT $e[126;65p
```

Now whenever the tilde key is pressed, the uppercase letter A is displayed instead of the tilde sign. In other words, ASCII 126 has been replaced by ASCII 65. To restore normal operation, enter the following command:

```
A>PROMPT $e[126;126p
```

The PROMPT command can also be used to make one or more permanent key reassignments by including it in a batch file.

If one of the characters in the PROMPT command requires the use of the key that is defective, hold down the Alt key and enter the ASCII value for the defective character, using the numeric keypad at the right of the keyboard. Release the Alt key after you have entered the ASCII value and the correct character should be displayed on screen.

Keyboard Replacement

A number of replacement keyboards are available from various sources, and—unlike the three IBM keyboards—it's often possible for the same replacement keyboard to be used with almost any IBM or IBM-compatible computer. In this case, the new keyboard may have one or more switches that must be set to configure it for the computer with which it is to be used.

Although the following description specifically refers to the Northgate OmniKey Plus keyboard in Figure 10.1e, the general comments may be applied to other switchable keyboards with appropriate corrections for variations in switching. The keyboard has an eight-position switch block on the underside of the housing. The first four switches must be set as follows:

Computer	Switch positions			
	1	2	3	4
PC, XT	down	up	up	up
AT and PS/2 *	up	up	up	up

* Keyboard is incompatible with PS/2 models 25 and 30 286.

If the keyboard is incorrectly configured, a 301 or 303 error code may be seen during the POST procedure, and/or a continuous series of beeps will be heard.

Mouse Installation and Diagnostics

Two types of mouse device are in common use with IBM and other personal computers, and both are briefly described below.

Serial Mouse

As its name suggests, the serial mouse is interfaced to the computer via a serial port. The obvious advantage is that the mouse can be quickly and directly connected to any PC that has a spare serial port available.

PC, XT, AT Interface. The mouse is connected to the 9-pin (DB-9) male plug on the adapter card containing the serial port. A 9-to-25-pin adapter may be used if your serial port uses a 25-pin connector.

PS/2 Interface. The serial mouse is connected to the 6-pin mouse port, located next to the keyboard socket at the rear of the system unit. If necessary, a DB-9-to-PS/2 adapter can be used to connect a serial mouse to the PS/2 mouse port. The port is the equivalent of the bus mouse port described below.

Bus Mouse

For applications where a serial port is unavailable, a bus mouse may be interfaced to the computer via its own bus interface board, using a 9-pin connector. The bus interface board is installed in any available adapter slot.

InPort Mouse. When the bus interface board is not used, the bus mouse itself is sometimes referred to as an *InPort Mouse* since it may be connected to an InPort connector on various other adapters manufactured by Microsoft and others.

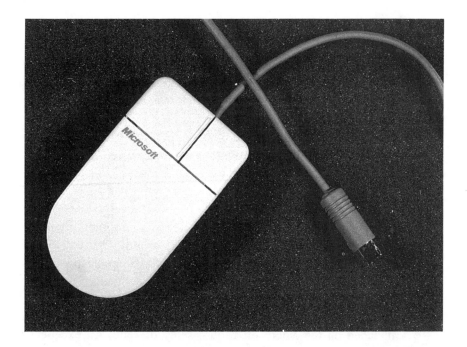

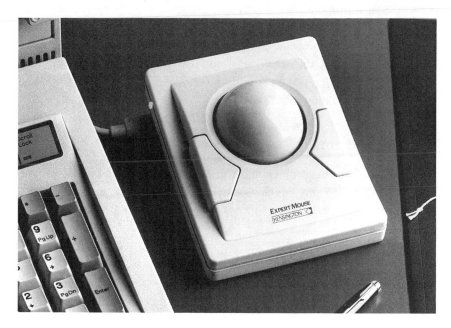

Figure 10.5. Typical pointing devices: (a) mouse (InPort Mouse courtesy Microsoft Corp.), (b) trackball (Expert Mouse courtesy Kensington Microware Ltd.).

MOUSE DIAGNOSTICS

Figure 10.5 illustrates the popular pointing device known as the mouse, and also shows a trackball system that is its functional equivalent. For diagnostic purposes, the comments below should apply equally to both types of design.

In case of a mouse-related problem, don't overlook the obvious—is the mouse cable firmly plugged into its adapter? If so, then the next question is, does your program support the use of a mouse? Not all do, so the simple presence of a properly installed mouse system will do nothing for a program that is not designed to use it.

An optional utility may be available for some programs that do not include mouse support as a regular feature. If so, the utility must be loaded in order to use the mouse. Some support utilities may be included with your mouse software, while others are available from the software company or from an electronic bulletin board that supports the software. As typical examples, mouse support utilities for some versions of WordPerfect and WordStar are included on the Microsoft Mouse setup diskette. An excellent archived utility for WordStar 2000 is available via modem on CompuServe's Word-Star forum (GO WORDSTAR, LIBRARY 9). For more information, contact the appropriate source to find out what's available. Refer to Chapter 12 for general information on modem communications.

If none of the above is of any use, continue reading here to determine whether the problem is with the on-screen cursor or with the operation of one of the mouse buttons.

Cursor Problems

Perhaps the problem most frequently encountered with a mouse has to do with its cursor, which is either dead, dying, or missing in action. Such problems and a few solutions are given here.

Missing or Inoperative Cursor

If the mouse cursor is either missing from the screen, or present but immovable, there's a good possibility the mouse driver or MOUSE.COM program has not been loaded by your configuration or batch file, or via a command at the DOS prompt. To check this, type MOUSE OFF at the DOS prompt and note the display. Using a Microsoft mouse as an example, one of the following messages may be seen.

Error message	The MOUSE.COM utility
`Bad Command or file name`	can't be found in the path
`Mouse Driver Not Installed`	is present, but has not yet been installed
`Mouse Driver Disabled`	is properly installed and has just been removed

Bad Command or file name. Log on to the directory where the mouse utilities are kept and try again. One of the following two messages should now be seen.

Mouse Driver Not Installed. If the mouse driver was not installed in the first place, it can't be un-installed by typing MOUSE OFF, and so the error message lets you know what the problem is. Load the utility by typing MOUSE, then return to the application in which the cursor problem was observed and try again.

Mouse Driver Disabled. The mouse driver was installed properly. Reinstall it by typing MOUSE and then try the application again. Chances are the problem with the cursor still exists and that the mouse needs servicing.

Immovable Cursor in DOS 4.00 SHELL Display. If you have installed DOS 4.00 and are using the DOS Shell, check the DOSSHELL.BAT program in the DOS subdirectory for the following line:

`@SHELLC` `/MOS:PCIBMDRV.MOS`/TRAN/ (additional parameters follow)

Remove the underlined portion of the line if you are not using the IBM PS/2 mouse driver. Then, install your mouse's driver in the configuration file, or MOUSE.COM in your AUTOEXEC.BAT file, as appropriate.

Cursor Movement Problem

Once the cursor has been found and brought to life, the next step is to check its on-screen performance. A few typical problems are reviewed immediately below.

Cursor Sensitivity Misadjusted. If the cursor seems to leap across the screen, or barely moves at all, chances are the mouse sensitivity needs to be adjusted. Again using the Microsoft Mouse as an example, a supplementary CPANEL.COM (control panel) program on an accompanying setup diskette may be used to find the optimum sensitivity setting. First, load

CPANEL and then press the Ctrl+Alt+mouse button (either) to display the panel shown in Figure 10.6. Now use the mouse to adjust its own sensitivity and/or acceleration. Move the mouse around to make sure the new setting is satisfactory for your personal use, then jot it down and exit. To use that sensitivity every time the mouse is used, add the following software switch to the mouse installation line in your batch file:

MOUSE /Sxx, where xx is the desired sensitivity (range 5–100)

Additional customization information will be found in the mouse user's guide.

Erratic Cursor Movement. Within the mouse housing, a small round ball must rotate freely as the mouse is moved about on a flat surface. The ball translates mouse motion into cursor movement, and in the process picks up a fair amount of dust and lint. If cursor movement becomes erratic over time, it's possible that the ball enclosure, or the ball itself, needs cleaning.

Turn the mouse over to see if the ball can be easily removed. For example, on Microsoft and IBM mice, the ball can be removed by sliding a retaining ring in the direction of an engraved arrow. With the ball removed, both it and its enclosure can be cleaned, the latter by blowing or vacuuming. Use a clean cotton swab soaked in denatured alcohol to wipe away embedded dirt, but do *not* use alcohol on a rubber ball as it may deform it. Also, make

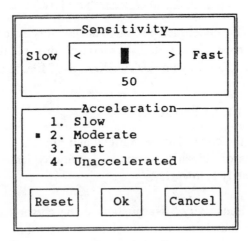

Figure 10.6. An on-screen control panel used to adjust mouse sensitivity and acceleration.

sure the alcohol has completely evaporated before returning the ball to its enclosure.

In case of doubt about removing the ball for cleaning, consult the manufacturer's instructions before reaching for a screwdriver.

Mouse Button Problems

If the mouse cursor moves properly but one or more buttons don't work, or work intermittently, the mouse may be defective and need servicing. But before assuming the worst, try a few tests to verify the problem.

If either button produces a beep instead of enabling the selected option, it's possible that the option is currently unavailable. As an obvious example, a text block can't be copied from a clipboard if the clipboard is empty. On many pull-down menus, an unavailable option is indicated by a different color (often, red) display, or by broken lettering. In either case, an attempt to use that option probably produces a beep instead of the desired action, thus indicating the mouse is working properly.

As a double-check, try to perform the same operation by pressing the equivalent keys on the keyboard. If the keyboard works, then the problem is indeed related to the mouse. Otherwise, some other problem is indicated.

If a problem seems confined to just one button, the following suggestions may help.

Left Button Problem. First, move the cursor to the desired location and click the left button twice in rapid succession. For example, on some menu choices if the button is only clicked once, or if there is a significant delay before the second click, nothing happens. If the double-click still doesn't work, move the cursor to some other menu choice, then back to the desired option and try again. If none of this helps, then the button probably is defective and will require servicing.

Right Button Problem. If the right button has no effect, it may very well be that the button is not supported by the software currently in use. Try some other application in which you know the right button is supposed to do something. For example, in many applications the left button enables an option, after which the right button will disable the same option. In others, the two buttons perform entirely unrelated tasks. Try at least a few such applications before concluding the worst.

Center Button Problem. Few applications make use of more than two mouse buttons, so an inoperative center button may simply mean that there is nothing for it to do. As above, try to find an application that is known to use the button as a double-check of its operation.

For applications that do require a center button, and a mouse that doesn't have one, try pressing both left and right buttons simultaneously.

11

MONITORS AND ADAPTERS

Since the first edition of this book, the reasonably simple choice between a monochrome and a color monitor has been complicated by a bewildering assortment of new video hardware, to say nothing of initials, which now include MDA, CGA, MCGA, EGA, VGA, Super VGA, 8514/A, and so on. In each case (except VGA), the final letter stands for "adapter," as in, say, Enhanced Graphics Adapter. However, in popular usage the initials may describe either part of the complete video system, as in "EGA monitor" and, redundancy notwithstanding, "EGA adapter."

In order to understand computer monitors, it's really necessary to have a good working knowledge of the various video adapters which drive the monitors. But in order to understand what each adapter does, one must first be familiar with monitors. In this chapter, the chicken comes before the egg (unless it's the other way round): adapters are described before monitors. But first comes a detailed look at some video terminology to help sort out the finer points between one video system and another. Much of this can be skipped by the reader who would rather be spared the gory details of pixels, screen masks, dot-clock frequencies, and such.

The system configuration section is reasonably brief, since there isn't much that needs to be done when adding or changing a monitor. Routine diagnostics come next, followed by a troubleshooting section. The Hercules monochrome graphics system is described separately at the end of the chapter.

IBM calls a monitor a "display," which presents a few awkward moments when trying to describe both what it is and what it does in the same sentence. Except in reference to a specific IBM product, this chapter calls a video device a monitor, and what one sees on its screen is the display.

VIDEO SYSTEM TERMINOLOGY

This section introduces most of the terms that will be encountered later on in the chapter. Wherever appropriate, the discussion refers to the specific video category (CGA, EGA, etc.) which best illustrates the characteristic being described. For further details about any adapter or monitor mentioned here, refer to the Adapter Types or Monitor Types sections which follow.

Dot Pitch

A color monitor's CRT (cathode ray tube) screen is internally coated with multiple triads of red, green, and blue phosphor dots, and a shadow mask is placed just behind the screen, as shown in Figure 11.1. The mask is drilled with minute holes—a single hole for each phosphor dot triad. The CRT's electron gun aims a triple beam at the dot triad, and because of the intervening hole in the mask, each beam component can strike only the dot for which it is intended. The *dot pitch* is the spacing between holes in the shadow mask and, by extension, between adjacent dots of the same color. The finer the dot pitch, the sharper the displayed image.

In most color monitor shadow masks, the dot pitch is 0.31 mm (0.012 inch), or about 80 dots per inch.

Pixels and Pels

A *picture element* is the smallest screen area whose color and brightness can be independently controlled. The term is usually abbreviated as *pixel*, or by IBM, as *pel*. The perceived color of each pixel is controlled by varying the intensity of the electron beams which strike the dot triads described above.

Aspect Ratio

Although the relationship between screen width and height varies slightly from one monitor to another, the screen's *aspect ratio*—a comparison of its width to height—is usually close to a 4:3 ratio. Here, as elsewhere

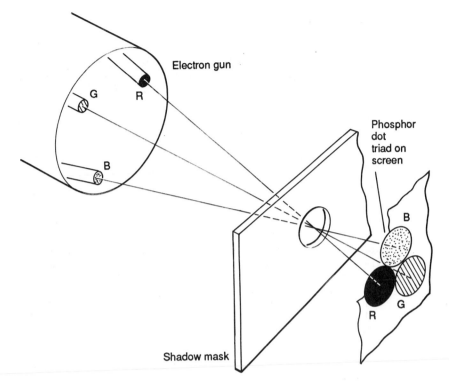

Figure 11.1   Due to the shadow mask, the electron beam strikes only one phosphor in each dot triad on the CRT screen.

throughout this book, the horizontal dimension is given first, for the sake of consistency with the usual 80 × 25 (or 40 × 25, etc.) format used to describe most text display screens.

Until recently the number of horizontal and vertical pixels did not follow the just-mentioned 4:3 aspect ratio. For example, Table 11.1 lists the number of horizontal and vertical pixels used in various display modes. The table also gives the physical size of each pixel on a monitor whose active display area is exactly 10 by 7.5 inches—the perfect 4:3 aspect ratio. Note that in the first few examples, the pixel width is less than its height.

As a practical consequence of this aspect ratio conflict, a "square" box drawn on screen will look like a rectangle, and a circle is drawn as an ellipse, unless the aspect ratio is 4:3, as in the VGA, VGA+, and 8514/A graphics modes also listed in the table.

Table 11.1 Representative Pixel Aspect Ratios and Character Box Formats

Display and mode		Pixels H × V		Aspect ratio H:V	Pixel size (10 × 7.5") H × V (in.)		Character box H × V	Columns × rows	(*)
Mono	7	720	350	4:1.94	.014	.021	9 × 14	80 × 25	(a)
VGA	7	720	400	4:2.22	.014	.019	9 × 16	80 × 25	(b)
CGA	6	640	200	4:1.25	.016	.038	8 × 8	80 × 25	(c)
EGA	F	640	350	4:2.19	.016	.021	8 × 14	80 × 25	(d)
VGA	12	640	480	4:3	.016	.016	8 × 16	80 × 30	(e)
8514/A	–	640	480	4:3	.016	.016	8 × 14	80 × 34 ‡	(f)
VGA+6A †		800	600	4:3	.013	.013	8 × 16	100 × 37 ‡	(g)
8514/A	–	1024	768	4:3	.010	.010	7 × 15	146 × 51 ‡	(h)
8514/A	–	1024	768	4:3	.010	.010	12 × 20	85 × 38 ‡	(i)

* Cross–reference to Figure 11.4
† 7–bit mode number defined by VESA standard
‡ 2–8 pixels unused in some columns, rows
H = horizontal; V = vertical

A BASIC program for checking the screen's aspect ratio is given later in the Aspect Ratio Check section of this chapter (page 483). The character box information in Table 11.1 is described on page 452.

Dot Pitch/Pixel Relationship

The number of color triads across the screen's width and height may be calculated by simply dividing the active screen dimension by the dot pitch. Thus, a screen width of 9.9 inches has 9.9/0.012 = 825 horizontal dots, a number that does not match any of the horizontal pixel values listed in Table 11.1. And even if it did, a screen of some other width would have a different dot count, even though both would allegedly display the same pixel count.

The display screen segment shown in Figure 11.2 may help resolve the apparent conflict. The illustration represents a 12 × 12-pixel area in which the shaded circles show that every other pixel is illuminated. The small circles are the shadow mask dots, through which the electron beam must pass. Every now and then the beam falls squarely on a single dot (indicated by dark shading), but more often than not it doesn't. And when it doesn't,

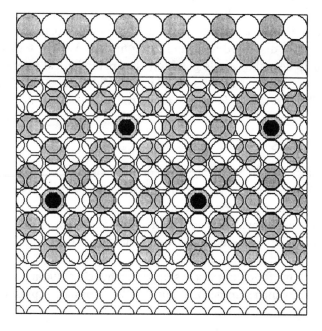

Figure 11.2   CRT screen detail, showing 12 × 12 pixel area (large circles) and shadow mask (small circles). The darker circles indicate the few areas where the electron beam lines up with a single dot.

the beam partially illuminates the appropriate phosphor within two or more dot triads.

Although the beam size changes as required to deliver the appropriate number of horizontal and vertical pixels, the dot pitch of course remains fixed. Therefore, each illuminated pixel may comprise one or more color dots—whatever it takes to meet the specified resolution.

A short BASIC program for checking the pixel/dot mask relationship is given later in the chapter, in the section on routine diagnostic test procedures (page 482).

Monitor Performance Characteristics

This section takes a rather close look at the many often-confusing variables that determine the performance differences between the various monitor types presently available.

Figure 11.3 illustrates the manner in which an image is drawn, one line at a time, on a computer screen. The complete path from upper left to lower right is discussed here, and along the way various terms are introduced to help describe what's going on. The parenthetical references (T1, T2, etc.) are to the timing charts found in the "Video Subsystem" section of the IBM PS/2 *Hardware Interface Technical Reference* manual.

Video Modes

Most monitors are capable of operating in several *video modes,* each distinguished by the parameters described below. As new video hardware systems are introduced, each one adds one or more new modes to those previously available and, with a few exceptions, each new system supports the older video modes as well. The currently available IBM video modes are listed in Table 11.2.

In the following discussion, parenthetical column references are to Table 11.3, which summarizes much of the information presented here.

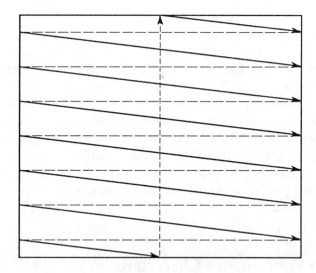

Figure 11.3   Scanning lines on the CRT screen. The electron beam moves left to right (solid lines), then returns to the left during each horizontal blanking interval and to the top of the screen during the vertical retrace interval (dashed lines).

Table 11.2 IBM Video Modes

Video mode * and type		Adapter	Resolution horiz.	vert.	Characters col.	rows	Char. box H	V	Colors **
0	text	CGA	320	200	40	25	8	8	16
		EGA	320	350			8	14	
		MCGA	320	400			8	16	
		VGA	360	400			9	16	
1	text	CGA	320	200	40	25	8	8	16
		EGA	320	350			8	14	
		MCGA	320	400			8	16	
		VGA	360	400			9	16	
2	text	CGA	640	200	80	25	8	8	16
		EGA	640	350			8	14	
		MCGA	640	400			8	16	
		VGA	720	400			9	16	
3	text	CGA	640	200	80	25	8	8	16
		EGA	640	350			8	14	
		MCGA	640	400			8	16	
		VGA	720	400			9	16	
4	graphics	all except MDA	320	200	40	25	8	8	4
5	graphics	all except MDA	320	200	40	25	8	8	4
6	graphics	all except MDA	640	200	80	25	8	8	2
7	text	MDA, EGA	720	350	80	25	9	14	B & W
		VGA	720	400			9	16	
8	graphics	PCjr only	160	200	20	25	8	8	16
9	graphics	PCjr only	320	200	40	25	8	8	4 or 16
A	graphics	PCjr only	640	200	80	25	8	8	2 or 4
D	graphics	EGA	320	200	40	25	8	8	16
		VGA							256
E	graphics	EGA	640	200	80	25	8	8	16
		VGA							256
F	graphics	EGA, VGA	640	350	80	25	8	14	B & W
10	graphics	EGA	640	350	80	25	8	14	4 or 16
		VGA							16 or 256
11	graphics	MCGA, VGA	640	480	80	30	8	16	2
12	graphics	VGA	640	480	80	30	8	16	16 or 256
13	graphics	MCGA, VGA	320	200	40	25	8	8	256
8514/A †									
	graphics	8514/A	640	480	80	34	8	15	16 or 256
	graphics	8514/A	1024	768	85	38	12	20	16 or 256
	graphics	8514/A	1024	768	146	51	7	15	16 or 256

   * Modes 0, 2, 5 same as 1, 3, 4, except CGA modes 0, 2, 5 suppress color at adapter's composite output (RCA jack).
  ** Where two values are listed, the higher value requires additional memory.
   † Internal interface makes all VGA modes available at 8514/A adapter.

Table 11.3 Horizontal and Vertical Video Parameters

Mon. type	Dot clock (MHz)	Horizontal					Vertical				
		pixels	freq. (kHz)	period (μs)	active (μs)	blank (μs)	pixels	freq. (Hz)	period (ms)	active (ms)	retr. (ms)
	a	b	c	d	e	f	g	h	i	j	k
MDA	16.257	720	18.432	54.254	44.289	9.965	350	50.087	19.965	18.989	0.977
CGA	14.318	640	15.700	63.696	44.699	18.997	200	59.922	16.688	12.739	3.949
EGA	16.257	640	21.851	45.765	39.368	6.397	350	60.030	16.658	16.018	0.641
	14.318	640	15.700	63.696	44.699	18.997	200	60.383	16.561	12.739	3.822
	16.257	720	18.432	54.254	44.289	9.965	350	50.087	19.965	18.988	0.977
VGA	25.175	640	31.469	31.778	25.422	6.356	400	70.086	14.268	13.155	1.112
	28.322	720	31.469	31.778	25.422	6.356	400	70.086	14.268	13.155	1.112
	25.175	640	31.469	31.778	25.422	6.356	480	59.940	16.683	15.762	0.922
	25.175	640	31.469	31.778	25.422	6.356	350	70.086	14.268	11.504	2.764
VGA+	36.000	800	35.156	28.444	22.222	6.222	600	56.250	17.778	17.067	0.771
	40.000	800	37.879	26.400	20.000	6.400	600	60.317	16.579	15.840	0.739
	40.000	800	48.090	20.794	15.995	4.798	600	72.010	13.887	12.510	1.376
8514/A	25.175	640	31.469	31.778	25.418	6.360	480	59.940	16.683	15.250	1.433
	44.900	1024	35.52	28.153	22.807	5.345	768	43.480	22.999	22.309	0.690
Compaq †	41	1024	54	18.519			768	66	15.152		
HGS 16-bit 24-bit	25.175	640	31.469	31.778	25.588	6.190	480	59.94	16.683	15.250	1.433
	50.350	640	30.50	32.787	28.477	4.340	480	60.04	16.556	15.647	0.909
	20.000	512	31.64	31.606	25.251	6.355	480	59.93	16.686	15.164	1.522
	44.900	1024	35.52	28.153	22.803	5.350	768	86.95	11.501	10.795	0.706
	64.000	1024	48.48	20.627	16.107	4.520	768	60.60	16.502	15.839	0.663
	36.000	800	35.15	28.450	22.260	6.190	600	56.24	17.780	17.071	0.710

HGS   Hercules Graphics Station: 8–bit except as noted, 64 MHz is non–interlaced.
VGA+ Super–VGA. First two listings document parameters of most current super–VGA hardware. Third listing is proposed VESA standard for future monitors.
†   Compaq does not publish active, blanking, retrace specifications.

Displayed Character Resolution. When characters are displayed in a text mode, the display of each character is created by illuminating certain pixels within a so-called character box. Assuming the monitor is connected to the proper adapter, the horizontal-vertical pixel matrices of the character box are as listed in Table 11.1.

The maximum size of the character within each box is slightly smaller than the box itself, so that there will be a little space around each displayed character. There are however, two exceptions: in the CGA character box, a lowercase letter with a descender (g, j, p, q, y) will touch the top of an uppercase letter immediately below it. And in all modes, the line-drawing symbols in the IBM extended character set will of course butt up against related symbols in adjacent boxes.

Figure 11.4 shows each of these character boxes, as drawn using the pixel dimensions listed in the previous section. Actual dimensions will vary slightly according to physical screen dimensions.

Screen Resolution. The sharpness of a computer screen image is a function of the number of pixels within the display area. As noted earlier in the chapter, the original IBM monochrome monitor was designed to display eighty columns of 9 × 14-pixel characters in each of 25 rows. Therefore, the total pixel count per screen is

80 columns, each 9 pixels wide	720 horizontal pixels
25 rows, each 14 pixels high	350 vertical pixels
total	720 × 250 = 252,000 pixels

Each screen is drawn left to right, top to bottom, in much the same manner as one reads a page of printed text. However, the screen is not drawn one character at a time, but rather one line at a time, with each pixel in that line turned on or off, as required. As noted, 14 lines must be drawn for each row of characters displayed on the monochrome screen.

Graphic displays are also drawn one horizontal line at a time, at resolutions which vary according to the graphics mode in use. Obviously, the more pixels per line, and the more lines per screen, the sharper the resolution will be.

Scan Lines. The lines just described are drawn by a minute electron beam, as described earlier in the chapter. For the purposes of the following explanation, the beam from the three-beam electron gun is described as a single beam.

As the beam travels from left to right across the screen, it scans the horizontal row of color dot triads in its path, turning each color dot within the pixel area on or off, as required. Each transit from left to right is a horizontal *scan line,* or simply, a *line.* The number of lines required to scan the complete screen varies from 200 to 768, depending on the capabilities of the adapter, the monitor, and the video mode in use.

In Table 11.3, the number of scan lines is equivalent to the number of vertical pixels listed in column h.

Frame and Frame Rate. A little movie jargon is borrowed to describe each complete drawing of an entire screen as a *frame.* Although films on

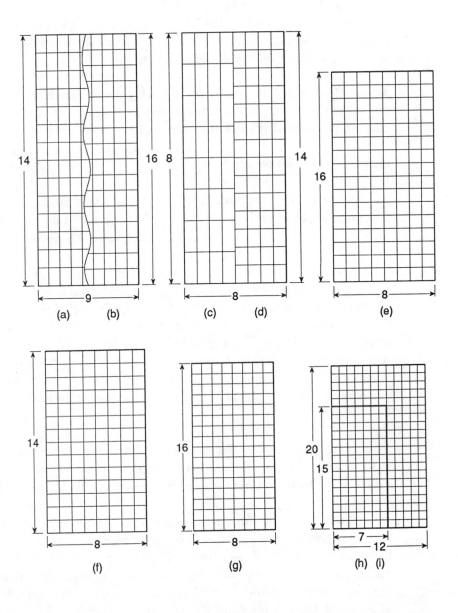

Figure 11.4   Character boxes for various video modes. (a) 9 × 14 MDA and (b) 9 × 16 VGA mode 7; (c) 8 × 8 CGA mode 6; (d) 8 × 14 mode F; (e) 8 × 16 mode 12; (f) 8 × 14 8514/A; (g) 8 × 16 super-VGA mode 6A; (h) 7 × 15 and (i) 12 × 20 8514/A modes.

the big silver screen make do with 24 frames per second, the computer screen's frame rate is two or more times higher, as described below.

Flicker. In the old silent movie days, the shutter opened and closed only 16 times per second, which created a noticeable flicker effect on the screen. On the computer screen, flicker may still be quite noticeable even at the high (by movie standards) monochrome frame rate. The effect is usually accentuated when the monitor is viewed from an angle, so that the display is seen by peripheral vision.

Some monitors use a high-persistence phosphor screen coating, in which case pixel brightness decays gradually after the pixel is illuminated by the moving electron beam. Therefore, the pixel does not have enough time to turn off completely before the beam returns to reenergize it. As a result, the flicker effect is minimized.

Screen persistence may be subjectively evaluated by switching an active monitor off and noting the time it takes for the image to disappear. On a monochrome screen, the phosphor persistence is relatively long, since the text-only screen image does not change quickly. However, on a fast-moving animated color graphics display, a long-persistence phosphor would create a blurred image if old screen colors did not disappear fast enough. Therefore, a shorter persistence phosphor is used, and this may force a compromise, since the phosphor can only be optimized for one frame rate. Therefore, if the monitor is capable of operating at several frame rates (i.e., vertical frequencies), some flicker may be noticeable at the slower frame rates.

Vertical Frequency and Period. In electronic terms, the frame rate becomes the vertical frequency of the display, with each frame requiring one complete cycle. Thus, the frame rate is expressed as a *vertical frequency* of *n* Hz (hertz, or cycles per second). The *vertical period* is the time required to complete one cycle. Both values are listed in Table 11.3 (columns h and i).

Vertical Retrace Interval. In a movie projector, the shutter closes after each frame is displayed. During this period of darkness, the next frame moves into position and the shutter opens again to display it. On the computer screen, each completed frame remains in place while the electron beam returns to the upper left-hand corner to begin drawing the next frame. The *vertical retrace,* or just *retrace*, interval (T1 and column k) is the time it takes to make it back to that corner. The electron beam is disabled during this interval to prevent it from drawing a diagonal line across the face of the screen.

Active Video Interval. The *active video interval* (column j) is the time it takes for the electron beam to move from the top to the bottom of the screen. The interval is equal to the vertical period less the retrace interval. In PS/2 video system documentation, IBM mixes time with space to call this the *active video area* (T2).

Horizontal Frequency and Period. During each active video interval, the electron beam must make several hundred horizontal passes across the screen, as described above. Consequently, the *horizontal frequency* (column c) is considerably higher than the vertical frequency. The *horizontal period* (column d) is the time required to complete one horizontal cycle.

Blanking Interval. As soon as the beam reaches the extreme right-hand side of the screen, it must be moved back to the left-hand side to begin drawing the next line. The time required for this return voyage is the *blanking interval* (T1 and column f), so called because the electron beam is disabled, or blanked, to prevent it from wiping out the pixels in the line just drawn.

Active Horizontal Interval. This is the time during which the electron beam makes a complete horizontal scan of a single line. Similar to the active video interval, the *active horizontal interval* (column e) is equal to the horizontal period, less the blanking interval.

Screen Borders. A color border surrounding the active screen may be turned on or off via software. Assuming the border is off, the horizontal blanking interval begins when the electron beam reaches the right-hand border, and ends when the beam reenters the active area immediately beyond the left-hand border. Accordingly, when the border area is illuminated, the active interval is slightly longer and the blanking interval slightly shorter than with the border off.

Sequential and Interlaced Scanning Modes. In most computer video modes, the electron beam scans the horizontal lines in sequential order, hence the *sequential scanning* term. This is sometimes referred to as *noninterlaced scanning,* to distinguish it from the interlaced mode.

The *interlaced scanning mode* divides each frame into two *fields,* one of odd-numbered lines, the next of even-numbered lines. After completing the first field, the electron beam returns to the top of the screen and then interlaces the next field of lines into the frame. Therefore, the complete picture area is scanned twice during each frame interval which, all else being equal, reduces the sensation of screen flicker.

Interlaced scanning may also be used to cut the horizontal frequency in half, since each vertical interval need only transmit half of the total frame. Therefore, for a given horizontal frequency, interlaced scanning permits doubling the number of lines per frame.

Double Scanning Mode. Compared to the CGA system, the VGA video system doubles the number of scan lines in each frame. Therefore, when a VGA system is operated in a CGA mode, each CGA line is scanned twice, thus improving the clarity of the display, while maintaining compatibility with the CGA mode itself. (The CGA and VGA modes are described in greater detail later in the chapter.)

Bandwidth. In order to draw the desired number of horizontal lines, each containing the specified number of pixels, and to continuously redraw the entire screen, the system bandwidth, or *dot clock* (column a), must be set high enough to transmit the requisite number of dots (pixels) per second. Using the monochrome monitor as an example, the theoretical bandwidth might be calculated by taking the product of pixels per line and lines per frame, and multiplying that by the frame rate, which could be 60 frames per second (60 Hz) if the ubiquitous AC line frequency were used. In other words, bandwidth = 720 × 350 × 60 = 15,120,000 Hz.

However, real-world considerations intrude. The simple calculation ignores both the horizontal blanking and the vertical retrace intervals, which if available for data transmission, would allow more pixels per line and more lines per frame to be transmitted. Taking these times into account, the effective values become 882 (720 + 162) pixels per line, and 368 (350 + 18) lines per frame, or 324,576 pixels per frame. At the time when the monochrome monitor was introduced, the active interval available with a 60-Hz vertical frequency would have pushed the dot-clock frequency beyond 20 MHz, which was too high (read, too expensive) for the available technology. Instead, an oscillator on the monochrome adapter card generates a 16.257-MHz signal, and based on that frequency the horizontal and vertical frequencies are derived from the effective rates as follows:

Horizontal frequency	dot clock/(720 + 162)	18.432 kHz
Vertical frequency	horizontal frequency/(350 + 18)	50.09 Hz

All-Points-Addressable (APA) Mode. In order to transmit lines, circles, or any type of information other than the ASCII and extended character set, the adapter must independently address (that is, control) every pixel within each horizontal line. Therefore, the modes in which such control is possible are often referred to as *all-points-addressable* (APA) graphics.

Alpha-Numeric (Text) Mode. By contrast, when a display of graphics is not required, an alpha-numeric (A/N, or text) mode will transmit just the ASCII and extended character sets shown in the previous chapter (Figure 10.2), or a similar set of characters. Although each character is still transmitted one horizontal line at a time, a text line is defined as the set of horizontal lines required to form a complete text character. For example, if the resolution is 720 × 400 pixels and the character box is a 9 × 16 matrix, then the text format is 80 (720/9) characters per (text) line, and 25 (400/16) lines per screen.

Video Mode Summary. Table 11.3 summarizes most of the video parameters described above, and Table 11.4 lists dot-clock components and their locations on either the system board or a video adapter. The effective values

Table 11.4 Dot-Clock Component Locations

Monitor type	Dot clock (MHz)	Components and location		
MDA	16.257	6845 CRT controller on adapter		
			crystal oscillator	8284 clock generator	frequency trim
CGA	14.318	PC Y1	U11	C1
		XT Y1	U1	C1
		AT † Y1	U18	R1
		OSC output routed to contact B30 on adapter slots 1–8		
EGA	16.257 14.318	6845 CRT controller on adapter See CGA		
VGA	25.175 28.322	Both oscillators in PS/2 system board video subsystem or on separate adapter card.		
8514/A	25.175 44.900	Both oscillators on 8514/A adapter		
other		Oscillator(s) on adapter		

† Oscillator (Y1) is in addition to system clock (Y2).

described above and listed in the table are derived from values stored in the CRTC register and used by the system to determine horizontal and vertical timings.

Video Adapters

Video adapters and monitors may be broadly classified as digital or analog, according to the manner in which the adapter transmits color information to the monitor. As we shall see, this is one high-tech area in which the magic word "digital" suffers by comparison with analog.

Digital Adapters

In digital adapters color and intensity data are transmitted to the monitor via digital code, so the number of colors that can be displayed is a function of the number of available bits. Such systems are sometimes referred to as TTL (transistor-transistor logic).

Table 11.5 lists the conductors used by various digital video adapters. The adapter connector is usually a female 9-pin socket, as shown in Figure 6.7(c–f).

Table 11.5 Conductors Used in Monitor Cables

Cond. no.	Digital monitors				Analog monitors **	
	Monochrome	CGA	EGA	(*)	VGA mono	VGA color
1.	ground	ground	ground		unused	red
2.	ground	ground	secondary red	(5)	mono	green
3.	unused	red	primary red	(2)	unused	blue
4.	unused	green	primary green	(1)	ID bit 2	ID bit 2
5.	unused	blue	primary blue	(0)	self test	self test
6.	intensity	intensity	secondary green	(4)	key pin	red ground
7.	video	reserved	secondary blue	(3)	mono ground	green ground
8.	horizontal	horizontal	horizontal		unused	blue ground
9.	vertical	vertical	vertical		unused	unused
10.					sync ground	sync ground
11.					ID bit 0	ID bit 0
12.					ID bit 1	ID bit 1
13.					horizontal	horizontal
14.					vertical	vertical
15.					unused	unused

* (x) = EGA bit number.
** Self test and ID bit conductors are not implemented on some adapters. IBM VGA & 8514/A adapter sockets are not drilled for pin 9.

Monochrome Display and Printer Adapter (MDA). This alpha-numeric (A/N) adapter was introduced along with the first IBM personal computer. Used in conjunction with the IBM monochrome display (page 464), the adapter supports 25 lines of 80-character text, but cannot be used for graphics applications.

In theory, only one conductor is needed to transmit monochrome video information. However, in practice the MDA uses two conductors in order to vary the intensity of each displayed character.

As its name suggests, the adapter contains a printer port for a parallel printer, both of which are described in Chapter 13.

Hercules Graphics Card. This monitor adapter is used in conjunction with a monochrome monitor in order to produce graphics displays in addition to the conventional IBM extended-ASCII character set.

A detailed description of this card, including diagnostics and troubleshooting, is given later on in this chapter. For the purposes of most routine diagnostics and troubleshooting, the Hercules Graphics Card may be treated as a direct plug-in replacement for the IBM Monochrome Display and Printer Adapter. However, before using the IBM diagnostics diskette, make sure the Hercules Graphics Card is in its DIAG (diagnostics) mode, as described on page 512.

Color/Graphics Monitor Adapter (CGA). This all-points-addressable (APA) adapter was designed for use with the original IBM Color Monitor, also introduced with the first PC. The adapter would also drive a conventional television set.

Color information is transmitted to the monitor over four conductors, which should permit it to display 16 (2^4) colors. However, the adapter could only transmit four colors at a time from a palette of sixteen. Its APA resolution was not very good, and in its so-called high-resolution mode, color selection was limited to two—black and white.

For the sake of graphics trivia, this is the only color device for which IBM uses the word "monitor" instead of "display."

Enhanced Graphics Adapter (EGA). This adapter was a significant improvement over the CGA system. With color information assigned to six conductors the adapter could transmit 16 colors from a palette of 64. The EGA system offers a monochrome-compatible text-mode resolution of 720 × 350 pixels, and in graphics mode, 640 × 200 or 350 pixels.

Analog Adapters

A good example of analog technology is the elegantly simple rotary volume control on a radio. With a minimum of knob twiddling, listening level is infinitely adjustable between the minimum and maximum positions of the knob, as are any other independent variables adjusted by similar controls.

In an analog video adapter, the independent variables are the primary additive colors red, green, and blue—each transmitted on a separate conductor. Given the analog transmission medium, each color is infinitely variable, in theory. But in practice there are no continuously variable knobs to turn; the adapter circuitry limits the color selection to "only" 262,144 (2^{18}) colors, with further limitations imposed by various color modes, as described later in the chapter.

Table 11.5 also lists the conductors used in IBM and other analog video systems. The interface between most analog adapters and monitors is via a cable terminated with a male 15-pin D-connector, as shown in Figure 6.7d. Note that the pins are arrayed in three rows of five pins each, thus distinguishing the VGA connector from the two-row 15-pin connector shown in Figure 6.7a.

Professional Graphics Controller. This IBM video system did not enjoy wide commercial success and has been subsequently replaced by the Video Graphics Array system. It offered 640 × 480-pixel resolution and displayed 256 colors simultaneously, out of a palette of 4,096 colors.

Video Graphics Array (VGA). IBM's PS/2 system introduced a new graphics standard—the video graphics array. The VGA is built into the MCA system board, so a separate plug-in adapter is not required. However, both IBM and other manufacturers now market VGA adapters for ISA and EISA computers.

The video graphics array is capable of transmitting 256 (2^8) separate colors, which may be chosen from a palette of 262,144 (2^{18}) colors.

Multi-Color Gate Array (MCGA). This video subsystem is built into the IBM PS/2 models 25 and 30. It supports the old IBM CGA (but not EGA) modes, plus VGA modes 11 and 13. The MCGA system is sometimes referred to as a Memory Controller Gate Array.

Super VGA (SVGA). Also called *VGA-plus, VGA-1024,* and *extended VGA,* this system is proposed by VESA (Video Electronics Standards Organization) and supports the following display capabilities:

Resolution	Colors
640 × 480	256 (same as VGA)
800 × 600	16
800 × 600	256
1,024 × 768	16 (resolution same as 8514/A, fewer colors)

Unless otherwise noted, the super VGA mode refers to a resolution of 800 × 600 pixels.

8514/A. The IBM 8514/A PS/2 Display Adapter has given its name to a video subsystem that goes beyond VGA to offer 1,024 × 768 pixel resolution. The 8514/A adapter plugs into an MCA video-extension adapter slot (see Figure 6.5d), and the monitor is connected to the 15-pin connector on the adapter, instead of to the built-in VGA port on the MCA system board. The adapter exceeds the super VGA standard by offering 256 colors in its 1,024 × 768 mode.

Although only the 1,024 × 768 mode is directly supported by the 8514/A adapter itself, all the other modes from the existing VGA subsystem are internally routed to the adapter and so to the monitor. The adapter does not support the 800 × 600 super VGA modes described above.

Multiresolution Adapter. Non-IBM manufacturers have used a variety of names to describe those multipurpose adapters that are capable of driving a wide variety of monitors, including a multiscan monitor. This chapter describes all such adapters under the generic term, multiresolution adapter, to avoid confusion with Color Graphics, Enhanced Graphics, or other similar-sounding names. In any case, a multiresolution adapter defines any adapter capable of operating in most, if not all, of the modes described above.

MONITOR TYPES

Within reason, most monitors are downward compatible; for example, both the VGA and EGA monitor will function in CRT mode 7, the old monochrome text-only mode. However, the EGA system duplicates the MDA video parameters (see Table 11.3), while the VGA system does not. Instead, if offers an enhanced mode 7, in which text characters are displayed with slightly better resolution, with two more horizontal lines per character box. The improvement is a function of both the adapter and the monitor itself.

Many of the monitor properties mentioned here are actually a function of the adapter in use, and for optimum performance, each one should of course be used with the adapter for which it was designed. However, most color monitors will function at reduced capability with other adapters. For example, an EGA monitor will function in CGA mode when connected to a CGA adapter. However, a CGA monitor will not be magically upgraded simply by connecting it to an adapter better than CGA.

Needless to say, a digital monitor is incompatible with an analog adapter, and vice versa. Due to the entirely different manner in which the video signal is transmitted, an accidental analog-to-digital connection will not work and could easily damage the monitor, the adapter, or both. In most cases, the 9-pin (digital) and 15-pin (analog) connector formats make accidental mismatches impossible. However, a few analog monitors do use a 9-pin plug, in which case a 9-to-15 pin connector adapter is required, as shown in Figure 11.5. Before using such a device, make sure its pin-to-pin format agrees with the connections on the monitor and the video adapter that are to be connected.

Digital Monitors

The digital monitors described here are designed to work with the digital adapters described above. Although the connectors on the monochrome and

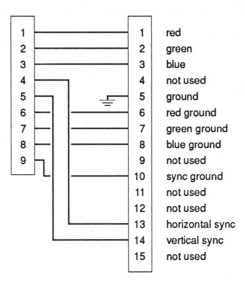

Figure 11.5   Wiring diagram for an 8-to-15 pin analog video adapter.

color monitors are physically compatible, a monochrome monitor will probably be damaged if it is accidentally plugged into a color adapter. Color adapters and monitors may be interconnected, although performance will be limited to the specifications of the weakest link in the video chain.

Monochrome Monitor. The monochrome monitor (i.e., IBM Monochrome Display) made its debut with the original PC, where it would display any color you liked, provided you only liked green. Subsequent monochrome monitors marketed by other manufacturers may display green, amber, or white characters against a black background, or black characters against a white background.

Any monochrome monitor will display graphics (lines, circles, etc.) if used with the Hercules Graphics Card described above.

Color Monitor. The IBM Color Display was introduced with the original PC and was designed for use with the Color/Graphics Monitor Adapter described above. Since the monitor receives its color information from the adapter over four lines, it is capable of displaying 16 (2^4) colors. The monitor's highest resolution is 640 pixels per line and 200 lines per frame.

Enhanced Color Monitor. The enhanced color monitor was a significant improvement over the CGA color monitor described above. With six color transmission lines, the monitor is capable of displaying 64 (2^6) colors, though usually limited to 16 or fewer by the adapter.

Analog Monitors

The analog monitor is designed so that the intensities of the three electron beams are continuously and separately variable. Therefore, the monitor is capable of displaying an infinite number of colors. In practice, the number of colors is limited by the adapter hardware.

As with the digital monitor, maximum horizontal and vertical resolutions are functions of both the monitor design and the adapter in use.

Professional Graphics Display. This was IBM's first analog monitor for PC applications, and its most notable feature was perhaps the price tag. Neither the monitor nor its adapter was widely accepted, except for computer-aided design applications.

Video Graphics Array Monitor. The PS/2 series of computers introduced the video graphics array, which offers some performance improvement over the digital monitors described above. Although the monitor is capable of displaying an infinite number of colors, the VGA adapter will transmit only 256 colors simultaneously, from a palette of 262,144 colors.

In addition to the usual variations in screen size and general picture quality, VGA monitors are available in monochrome and color versions. The former translates a color signal into 64 shades of gray.

Super VGA Monitor. A super VGA monitor is any VGA monitor capable of operation at the 800 × 600 and 1,024 × 768 modes defined by the VESA standard. The 800 × 600 mode requires a multifrequency monitor, while the 1,024 × 768 mode requires a monitor capable of operating in the interlaced mode described earlier in the chapter (page 456).

Note that Compaq Computers supports a noninterlaced 1,024 × 768 mode that is not compatible with the proposed super VGA standard.

8514 and 8515 Color Displays. These monitors are designed to support the high-resolution specifications of the IBM 8514/A Display Adapter described above (page 462). Neither display supports the super VGA 800 × 600 mode.

Analog/Digital Monitors

The monitor types described here may be available with either analog or digital inputs, or in some cases, with both. Needless to say, either type of input must be matched to the appropriate adapter in the computer.

Multiscan Monitor. Also called a multisync monitor, this device can automatically adjust itself to function in most of the modes described above, according to the configuration of the adapter to which it is attached.

RGB Monitor. The *RGB* (red-green-blue) nomenclature simply refers to the three primary additive color signals. Both digital CGA and analog monitors have been called RGB, since both use three separate conductors for the RGB signals. When a monitor specification sheet refers to *RGB inputs,* these are usually three separate coaxial (BNC) input connectors.

Adapter/Monitor Compatibility

Since many video-related problems in ISA systems can be traced to little more than a switch set in the wrong position, this section offers a broad overview of the interface between the PC and the various monitors introduced above. A basic understanding of the requirements for a successful interface can go a long way toward clearing up many problems before or as they occur.

Compatibility Chart. Some problems may arise if an unsupported adapter/monitor combination is inadvertently installed. Table 11.6 sets forth the combinations of adapters and monitors that are available for the IBM personal computer. Note that although certain nonstandard combinations are possible, the resultant display will be somewhat limited. For example, an enhanced color monitor will function as a conventional color monitor if it is attached to the IBM Color/Graphics Adapter, and of course a monochrome monitor will never show colors. However, the nonstandard

Table 11.6 Adapter/Monitor Compatibility Chart

Adapter	Digital Monitors			Analog Monitors	
	Mono	CGA	EGA	VGA	8515
Digital					
Monochrome only	YES	NO	NO	NO	NO
CGA only	NO	YES	yes	NO	NO
EGA only	yes	yes	YES	NO	NO
Monochrome and	YES	NO	NO	NO	NO
CGA	NO	YES	yes	NO	NO
Monochrome and	YES	NO	NO	NO	NO
EGA	NO	yes	YES	NO	NO
CGA † and	NO	YES	NO	NO	NO
EGA	YES	NO	NO	NO	NO
Analog					
VGA	NO	NO	NO	YES	yes
8514/A	NO	NO	NO	yes	YES

YES Standard configuration.
 yes Configuration will work with limitations.
NO Configuration may cause damage to the display and/or the adapter.
  † If a standard color display is connected to a Color/Graphics Adapter, an Enhanced Graphics or multiresolution adapter can only be used to support a monochrome display.

combinations do allow for a gradual system upgrading, one device at a time. Note also that while the combination of a standard color monitor and an enhanced graphics adapter offers up to 16 colors in the 620 × 200 graphics mode, there is no improvement in text resolution, since improved resolution requires both an enhanced graphics adapter and an enhanced graphics monitor.

VGA Adapter/Monitor Compatibility. Within the VGA video system, compatibility problems are now and then encountered between specific adapters and system units, or in certain adapter/monitor pairings. For example, a monitor may only display monochrome with one adapter, yet operate flawlessly with another. Yet the adapter exhibits no such difficulty when used with some other monitor. Assuming both the adapter and the monitor are in fact in good working order, the problem is probably due to a conflict in the monitor identification interface. For further details, refer to the section on VGA Display Problems (page 505).

SYSTEM UNIT CONFIGURATION

EISA and PS/2 owners can skip this section, since neither system board requires physical configuration when a monitor is installed or removed. On the PC, XT, and AT, the system board switches shown in Figure 11.6 configure the system to accommodate the installed monitors. Table 11.7 summarizes the correct system board switch settings for various combinations of monochrome and color monitors.

In the following sections, keep in mind that certain incorrect switch or jumper settings may cause damage to a monitor or to an adapter. Therefore, it is important to verify all switch and jumper settings before turning on the computer for the first time, and to recheck the settings and make necessary adjustments each time the monitor complement is changed.

The Primary Display Mode

The primary display mode is the one you want activated when the system is first turned on. Although many display modes are available through programming, here we will limit the discussion to the three most common start-up modes:

Mode	Line width
Monochrome	80 characters
Color	80 characters
Color	40 characters

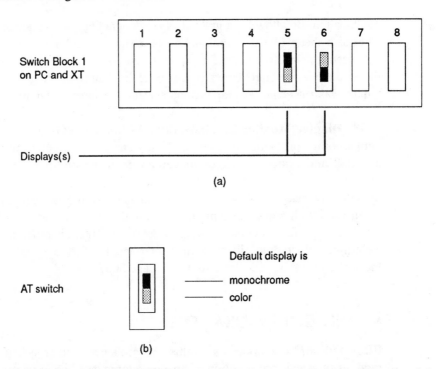

(a)

(b)

Figure 11.6   System board display-configuration switches: (a) Switches 5 and 6 on switch block 1 on the PC and XT. As shown, the primary display is to be driven by the color/graphics adapter in the 80 × 25 mode. (b) The single primary display switch for the AT, shown in the monochrome position.

PC and XT. If a monochrome monitor is used in conjunction with a PC or XT, the system board switches must be set so that it is the primary display. If a color monitor is also a part of the system, the DOS MODE command described in the following section may then be used to switch immediately to either of the color modes listed above.

Note that the two system board switches shown in Figure 11.6 permit only four combinations, which provide for various configurations of monochrome and CGA color monitors. When any other type of monitor is used with a PC or XT, system board switches 5 and 6 must be placed in the on, or up, position (11), indicating that no monitors are installed. Then configure the system as follows:

Table 11.7a PC and XT System-Board Display Configuration Switch Positions

Installed monitor	Switch block 1 positions 5 and 6 *
Monochrome only	00
Monochrome and standard color	00
Standard color only (40 × 25)	01
Standard color only (80 × 25)	10
Enhanced color	11
Enhanced color plus any other	11
No installed displays	11

* 0 = off (down), 1 = on (up). To prevent damage to displays, make sure these switches are set correctly before applying power.

Table 11.7b AT System-Board Display Configuration Switch

Primary display adapter	Switch position *
Monochrome	0
Color/Graphics	1
Enhanced Graphics Adapter	doesn't matter

* 0: toward rear of system board.
1: toward front of system board.

Monitor	Configuration via
EGA	four-position switch block on the adapter (see page 472)
other	switch block and/or jumpers on the adapter (refer to adapter user's guide for details)

If switches on an installed video adapter determine the primary display, then the use of the MODE command in an AUTOEXEC.BAT file is not required.

AT. As described in Chapter 3, the Diagnostics diskette is used for most AT configuration tasks. During system configuration, the user is asked to verify that the active display—the one on which the question is seen—is the active display, which of course it is, since it is the one on which the question appears. If it is not supposed to be, then the single system board switch is set incorrectly and its position must be changed. Or you can use the MODE command to make the switch later on.

When an EGA adapter is installed, the position of the single AT system board switch is unimportant, since the adapter switches take precedence. Therefore, if the active screen is the wrong one, the four switches on the enhanced graphics adapter, rather than the single system board switch, must be reset (see page 471). If there are no switches on the adapter, then the DOS mode command, or a software utility accompanying the adapter, is used to set active screen mode.

You may wish to leave the AT system board switch in the monochrome position (pointing toward the rear of the system board) so that if the second adapter is subsequently removed, the system automatically defaults to the monochrome display.

MODE Command

This command may be used to change from the primary display mode set by the system board switches to one of the other modes. If you prefer to switch from one display mode to another immediately after the POST procedure is completed, type one of the following lines when the DOS prompt appears:

Program line	Meaning
A> MODE CO*xx*	Switch to color display
A> MODE BW*xx*	Same, but with color disabled
A> MODE MONO	Switch back to monochrome display

In the first two commands, *xx* is either 40 or 80, to set the number of characters displayed per line. No *xx* appears in the third command, since the monochrome display width is always 80 characters per line.

The following three-line batch file switches the display mode from monochrome to color, then loads and executes the program named in the second line, which is then seen on the color screen. At the end of the program, the batch file picks up where it left off and returns the system to the monochrome display.

```
MODE CO80
YOURPROG
MODE MONO
```

where YOURPROG is the name of your program.

To write the batch file itself, follow the instructions given in Chapter 4 and give the file a name appropriate to the task. For example, to have the batch file execute automatically every time the system is turned on, name it AUTOEXEC.BAT. If you prefer that it be executed only on command, give it some other name with a BAT extension.

MONITOR ADAPTER CONFIGURATION

Depending on your choice of monitor adapters, it may be necessary to configure the adapter for your system, as described here. Although some of these adapters contain no onboard switches, it may be necessary to reconfigure another already installed adapter to work properly in a system containing two monitor adapters. It may also be necessary to install some software drivers and/or copy some configuration utilities to your backup reference diskette.

Monochrome Display and Printer Adapter

This adapter contains no hardware configuration switches. The monitor attached to it automatically becomes the default monitor, except as noted below in the description of the enhanced and multiresolution adapters. The IBM monochrome display and printer adapter is shown in Chapter 13, Figure 13.2.

Color/Graphics Adapter

This adapter also contains no hardware configuration switches. In the absence of a monochrome adapter, it becomes the default monitor adapter, except as noted below in the description of the enhanced and the multi-resolution adapters.

Enhanced Graphics Adapter

When an Enhanced Graphics Adapter is installed, the primary display mode must be defined by the position of the switches on this adapter.

Switch and Jumper Settings. The switches and jumpers used to configure the IBM enhanced graphics adapter are shown in Figure 11.7. A typical switch block may be seen in the upper right-hand corner of the EGA adapter shown in Figure 11.8(a). Tables 11.8 and 11.9 may be used to set and/or verify the correct positions for these switches, while Table 11.10 gives the correct positions for the jumpers found on a few EGA adapters.

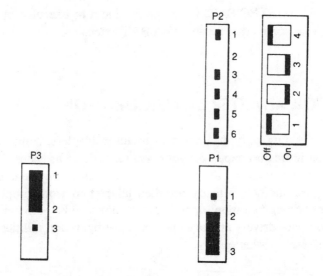

Figure 11.7 Enhanced graphics adapter display-configuration switches and jumpers. The switches define the system's primary and secondary displays. Jumper P1 is the display selector, P2 is the light-pen connector and jumper P3 is the I/O address-port selector. In the illustration, P1 is set for a monochrome or standard color display.

To prevent damage to the adapter or to the attached monitor, make sure these jumpers are correctly positioned before applying power to the system.

Enhanced Graphics Adapter in Early Model IBM PCs. An old IBM PC with a 16/64Kb system board and a serial number below 0300961 may require a BIOS update module in order to support the IBM Enhanced Graphics Adapter. To determine the need for the update, run the ROM BIOS date program given in Chapter 6, Listing 6.1, to display the date of the installed BIOS module. If the displayed date is 10/19/81 or earlier, the updated BIOS module is needed. The new module (IBM part 1501005) must be purchased and installed in position U33 on the system board (seen in Figure 6.2(a)). If the program displays a date later than 10/19/81, the update is not required.

For informational purposes, note that the date of an IBM Enhanced Graphics Adapter may be displayed by changing the first two lines in the program, as indicated in Listing 6.1.

(a)

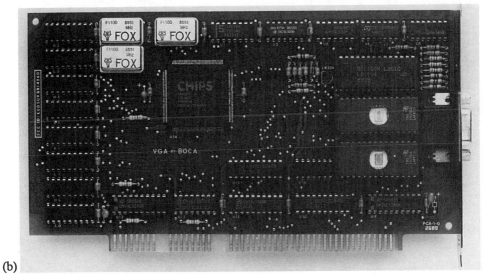

(b)

Figure 11.8 Typical EGA (a) and VGA (b) video adapter cards. Note the three oscillators near the upper left-hand corner of the VGA adapter (MultiEGA and VGA by Boca adapters courtesy Boca Research).

Table 11.8 Enhanced Graphics Adapter Configuration Switch Settings, Part 1 *

Primary display	Secondary display	Installed adapters	Switch ** positions
Monochrome	none	EGA only	0010
Monochrome	none	EGA, CGA	0010
Monochrome	none	MDA, EGA	0111
Monochrome	CD (40 × 25)	EGA, CGA	1010
Monochrome	CD (80 × 25)	EGA, CGA	0010
Monochrome	CD (40 × 25)	MDA, EGA	1111
Monochrome	CD (80 × 25)	MDA, EGA	0111
Monochrome	CD (80 × 25)	MDA, NEC	1100
Monochrome	ECD, normal mode	EGA, MDA	1011
Monochrome	ECD, enhanced mode	EGA, MDA	0011
Monochrome	ECD or Multisync	MDA, NEC	0100
CD (40 × 25)	none	EGA only	1001
CD (80 × 25)	none	EGA only	0001
CD (40 × 25)	none	CGA, EGA	1101
CD (80 × 25)	none	CGA, EGA	0101
CD (40 × 25)	Monochrome	EGA, MDA	1001
CD (80 × 25)	Monochrome	EGA, MDA	0001
CD (40 × 25)	Monochrome	CGA, EGA	1101
CD (80 × 25)	Monochrome	CGA, EGA	0101
CD (80 × 25)	Monochrome	NEC, MDA	1000
CD	ECD	not permitted	
ECD, normal mode	none	EGA only	1110
ECD, enhanced mode	none	EGA only	0110
ECD, normal mode	Monochrome	EGA, MDA	1110
ECD, enhanced mode	Monochrome	EGA, MDA	0110
ECD or Multisync	Monochrome	NEC, MDA	0000
ECD	CD	not permitted	

   * Find the column containing the combination of displays and adapters installed in your system. The switch settings must match those indicated in the same column. Refer to Table 11.6 for jumper positions.

  ** Switch position 0 = off; 1 = on

  CD: Color Display
CGA: Color/Graphics Adapter
ECD: Enhanced Color Display
EGA: Enhanced Graphics Adapter
MDA: Monochrome Display Adapter
NEC: NEC GB–1 with CMII CGA and Hercules Card Compatibility Module.

Table 11.9 Enhanced Graphics Adapter Configuration Switch Settings, Part 2 *

Switch ** position	Adapters	Primary display	Secondary display
0000	NEC, MDA	ECD or Multisync	Monochrome or none
0001	EGA only	CD (80 × 25)	none
	EGA, MDA	CD (80 × 25)	Monochrome
0010	EGA only	Monochrome	none
	EGA, CGA	Monochrome	none
	EGA, CGA	Monochrome	CD (80 × 25)
0011	EGA, MDA	Monochrome	ECD, enhanced mode
0100	MDA, NEC	Monochrome	ECD or Multisync
0101	CGA, EGA	CD (80 × 25)	Monochrome or none
0110	EGA only	ECD, enhanced mode	none
	EGA, MDA	ECD, enhanced mode	Monochrome
0111	MDA, EGA	Monochrome	none
	MDA, EGA	Monochrome	CD (80 × 25)
1000	NEC, MDA	CD (80 × 25)	Monochrome or none
1001	EGA only	CD (40 × 25)	none
	EGA, MDA	CD (40 × 25)	Monochrome
1010	EGA, CGA	Monochrome	CD (40 × 25)
1100	MDA, NEC	Monochrome	CD (80 × 25)
1011	EGA, MDA	Monochrome	ECD, normal mode
1101	CGA, EGA	CD (40 × 25)	Monochrome or none
1110	EGA only	ECD, normal mode	none
	EGA, MDA	ECD, normal mode	Monochrome
1111	MDA, EGA	Monochrome	CD (40 × 25)

    * On a system that is already operational, the EGA switch positions indicate the primary and secondary displays, and may be verified or changed via an access port on the face of the option card bracket. NEC GB – 1 switch settings utilize first four switches on an eight – switch block on the card: external access not possible.

    ** Switch position 0 = off; 1 = on

  CD Color Display

 CGA Color/Graphics Adapter

 ECD Enhanced Color Display

 EGA Enhanced Graphics Adapter

MDA Monochrome Display Adapter

 NEC NEC GB – 1 with CMII CGA and Hercules Card Compatibility Module

Table 11.10 Representative EGA Jumper and Connector Descriptions

Monitor attached to adapter	Adapter Manufacturer *	Connector labeled	Place jumper across pins
EGA	Boca	CM	C – center pin
	IBM	P1	1 – 2
	NEC	P1	1 – 2
	NEC	P7	1 – 2
Multisync	Boca	CM	C – center pin
	NEC	P1	1 – 2
	NEC	P7	2 – 3
Monochrome or CGA	Boca	CM	M – center pin
	NEC	P1	2 – 2
	NEC	P7	– –
Port address jumper	Boca	2XX 3XX	3XX – center pin
	IBM	P3	1 – 2
	NEC	P4	3XX – center pin
Light pen connector	Boca	L.PEN	
	IBM	P2	
	NEC	P2	

* Boca: Boca Research Enhanced Graphics Adapter
  IBM: IBM Enhanced Graphics Adapter
  NEC: NEC GB – 1 Multisync Color Graphics Board

Video Graphics Adapter

The video graphics subsystem is an integral part of the system board in PS/2 systems. For ISA and EISA systems, a video graphics adapter card, such as the one shown in Figure 11.8b, may be used. Most such adapters are supplied with a variety of utilities to emulate non-VGA modes (CGA, EGA, Hercules, etc.). In addition, software drivers are included to support various modes in conjunction with popular word-processing and graphics software packages.

On some VGA adapters, onboard jumper and/or switch block settings determine the operating mode of the adapter. Depending on the settings, the adapter automatically switches to 8- or 16-bit operation according to the slot in which it is placed, or is forced into the 8-bit mode.

The automatic bus-detection feature may not work properly with some computers, in which case the jumper or switch block may be used to force the adapter into the 8-bit mode. A few typical examples of ISA adapter settings are given here.

Adapter	Jumper	Switch	16-bit	8-bit
Boca VGA	J1		1-2	remove jumper
Hercules VGA	none	none	n/a	default mode
Maxon MVGA-16	J1		2-3	1-2
	J2		1-2	2-3
		S6	on	off
Paradise VGA 1024		S4	on	off

8515/A Display Adapter

In order for an MCA system to recognize the 8514/A adapter, the display adapter option files must be copied to your backup reference diskette. These files (@EF7F.DGS, @EF7F.ADF, and SC.EXE) are on the option diskette which accompanies the adapter. Follow the instructions given in the Copy an Option Diskette section of Chapter 3 (page 50). After copying the files, leave the backup reference diskette in drive A, reboot the system, and select the automatic configuration option.

The next step is to install the *display adapter interface code*, which is found on a diskette with that name which also accompanies the adapter. Insert the diskette in drive A and type

```
INSTALL A: C:
```

The installation procedure creates an HDIPCDOS subdirectory and adds the line \HDIPCDOS\HDILOAD.EXE to your AUTOEXEC.BAT file.

To verify that the adapter and its software interface are correctly installed, execute the HDIDEMO.EXE program. Press the Enter key when you get tired of watching the axial spokes change color.

Multiresolution Adapter

As noted earlier, a multiresolution, or multisync, adapter is capable of driving various types of monitors, from monochrome to enhanced graphics and beyond. Generally, a series of switches and jumpers on the adapter must be set to agree with the type of monitor attached to the adapter. For the purposes of diagnostics and troubleshooting, the adapter may then be treated similarly to whatever adapter it replaces. If the multiresolution adapter is configured for a Hercules-mode graphics monitor, then follow the Hercules Graphics Card procedures given on page 510.

Figure 11.9 illustrates the switch settings on a typical multiresolution adapter. Jumper settings were shown in Table 11.10.

From a study of the information given in some of the tables, it can be noted that most such adapters use the same general configuration found on the IBM Enhanced Graphics Adapter. However, the labeling, location, and physical setting of each switch and jumper is quite likely to vary from one adapter to another. Therefore, when relating the settings seen in this chapter to those on an adapter not actually described here, make sure to make whatever changes are required to suit the particular requirements of the adapter in use.

ROUTINE MONITOR DIAGNOSTICS

Once the system is properly configured so that the desired display is seen when the system is turned on, the POST procedure should conclude with a single beep, as described in Chapter 3. In addition, the screen display should be stable and clear, with colors accurately rendered. During routine operation, modifications to the display or displays should function as specified by the operator or by the software that is in use.

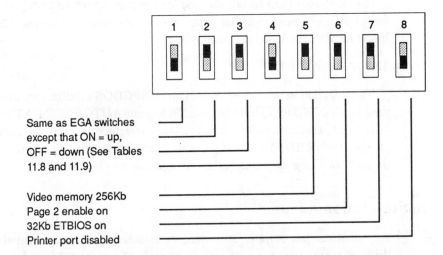

Figure 11.9   The configuration switches on a typical multi-resolution adapter card (NEC GB-1 Multisync Color Graphics Board). As seen here, the board is configured (switches 1-4) to drive a primary multiscan or EGA monitor in the enhanced mode. Switches 5-7 should remain in the ON (up) position at all times. Switch 8 is set to disable the parallel printer port, to prevent conflict with another parallel port in the same system.

If any of these conditions are not met, an error message will be noted. During POST, this may be the sounding of an audio error signal, the display of a numeric error code, or simply visual evidence that the screen display is not satisfactory. During routine operation, a monitor-related problem may be indicated by an error message, which may be accompanied by a single beep. Each of these conditions is described in more detail in the sections following.

In the discussion of monitor diagnostics, the removal of either the monochrome or the color adapter may be suggested. If the removed device is the default adapter, an error signal of one long beep followed by two short beeps (which may be repeated once) may be heard during the next POST procedure. If this audio signal replaces the error that prompted you to remove the adapter in the first place, then the removed device or the monitor attached to it is defective.

Brightness and Contrast Controls

Practically every monochrome and color monitor has at least two user-variable controls on or near the front panel.

Brightness. The brightness control adjusts the intensity of the entire screen display. It should therefore have a noticeable effect on the brightness of the cursor and the DOS or BASIC prompt, even if there is no other on-screen information.

Contrast. On all IBM monochrome, CGA, and EGA monitors, the contrast control is used to vary the difference in brightness between low- and high-intensity colors. However, the variation is accomplished in different ways, as indicated here.

| Monitor type | Colors affected by contrast control | | Cursor brightness |
	Low-intensity colors	High-intensity colors	
Monochrome	varied	unaffected	varied
Color	unaffected	varied	unaffected

Colors of the appropriate intensity must be present in order for the contrast control to have any effect. In IBM BASIC, the COLOR statement may be used to display the colors that will be affected by the contrast control, and these are listed in Table 11.11.

Table 11.11 Standard Colors Affected by Contrast Control

Monitor in use	Color numbers
Monochrome	0–7 16–23 (blinking)
Color	6 8–15 22 24–31

EGA Contrast Tuning Control. On the IBM Enhanced Color Monitor, a rear-panel screwdriver adjustment is also available to set the default contrast values when the front-panel contrast control is pushed in. This control (seen in Figure 11.12) may be used to fine-tune the color contrast by adjusting for the best brown color with the contrast control pulled out.

VGA Contrast Control. On some VGA monitors (IBM 8515, for example), the contrast (sometimes called *background*) control varies the intensity of the black area on the screen, and so it may have little or no apparent effect on color contrast, especially in VGA color modes 12 and 13.

Monochrome Monitor Precautions

When an IBM monochrome monitor is disconnected from its adapter, make sure its power cable is also unplugged from the back of the system unit. To prevent accidental damage to the monitor, unplug its power cord before disconnecting the cable leading from the monitor to the Monochrome Monitor Adapter. Reverse the procedure when reconnecting the monitor. Of course, the main power should be off in both cases.

Follow the above procedure with a non-IBM monochrome monitor if you have any doubt about its circuit details. And avoid plugging the monitor's power cord into the system unit's rear panel AC outlet unless you are sure the monitor does not exceed the power limitations of this outlet. For further details, see Chapter 5.

As you proceed through the various monochrome monitor diagnostics procedures, be especially attentive to unusual sounds or visual displays such as the following:

| High-pitched whistle | This may indicate a configuration error that could damage the monochrome monitor or its adapter. |
| Center-screen spot | This indicates the monitor is receiving power but is not connected to its adapter. |

In cases such as the two just mentioned, turn the power off immediately and take the necessary remedial action. If the problem persists, again turn the power off and have the complete system serviced.

Checking the Secondary Monitor

Since the POST procedure examines only the primary monitor system, a problem in the secondary monitor may not be discovered until that monitor is called upon during subsequent operation of the PC. If you are not sure of the condition of the secondary monitor, you may wish to temporarily reconfigure your system to make it the primary monitor. Then reboot and take note of any errors that occur during POST. These may then be diagnosed according to the primary monitor diagnostics information that follows.

Screen Blanking Utilities

It's possible to damage the monitor by leaving a bright nonmoving image on its screen for an extended period of time, during which the stationary display permanently burns itself into the screen's phosphor coating. To prevent this from happening, the screen brightness should be turned down if the computer is going to remain on but inactive for, say, ten minutes or more. Although an occasional lapse probably won't cause any lasting damage, you'll know things have gone too far if you can read your spreadsheet even when the computer is turned off.

A screen-blanking utility prevents such disasters by turning the screen off if there is no keyboard activity for a certain period of time, typically five minutes. The utility is loaded via the AUTOEXEC.BAT file during system boot up, or may be executed later on, as needed. Most such utilities provide an on/off software switch to disable the screen-blanking function when it is not wanted. For example, if a lengthy graphics program requires no user intervention at the keyboard, the utility might otherwise blank the screen before the display is finished. Or a long file sent or received via modem might apparently disappear if the screen blanks out before the message ends. On the other hand, the blanking function does come in quite handy during certain word-processing sessions which involve long periods of staring at the screen, or off into space.

Screen blanking utilites are sometimes supplied on the utilities diskette accompanying a video adapter, and are generally available through modem bulletin board services. The DIMMER screen-blanking utility is included on the diskette accompanying *DOS Power Tools*.

Routine Diagnostic Test Programs

A few BASIC programs presented here may be useful for testing the display characteristics of most computer monitors.

Pixel Check. The BASIC pixel-check program in Listing 11.1 should display a matrix of 200 columns × 150 rows of equally spaced pixels. The matrix will indeed by seen, and all the pixels will be there, but there will be extra space between some of the columns and rows, as shown in Figure 11.10a. On screen, the visual effect is that black horizontal and vertical bars run through the display, and the spacing will vary from one screen to another, according to the screen dimensions and the actual dot pitch.

Figure 11.10b is a magnified view of two adjacent pixels in Figure 11.10a, as seen if the screen is viewed through a jeweller's loupe. The actual dot patterns vary from one color to another, and some dots will be brighter than others. To the unaided eye, however, the pixels should appear to be of uniform size and brightness, if not quite evenly spaced.

Border Display Check. Few commercially available software programs illuminate the border surrounding the active screen area. The short BASIC program in Listing 11.2 may be used to turn the border on, which may be useful if the active screen area needs alignment. The illuminated borders on either side of the screen should be equal in size, and the border edges should of course be straight.

Listing 11.1 A BASIC Pixel-Check Program

```
100 SCREEN 9                              ' (or SCREEN 8)
110 WINDOW (1, 1) - (2000, 1500)
120 FOR X = 1 TO 2000 STEP 10
130 FOR Y = 1 TO 1500 STEP 10
140 PSET (X, Y), n                        ' n = 1, 2, 4 or 7
                                            (blue, green, red, white)

150 NEXT Y
160 NEXT X
```

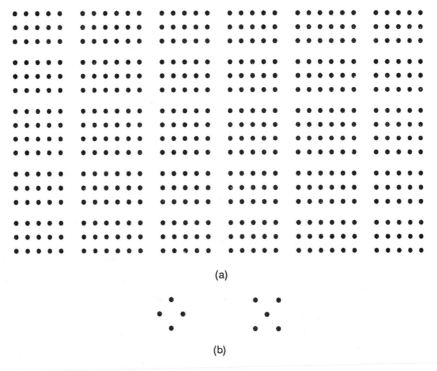

(a)

(b)

Figure 11.10   Detail view of 200 × 150 pixel matrix display, showing (a) some uneven column and row spacing; (b) magnified view of two adjacent pixels.

Aspect Ratio Check. In CGA and EGA color modes, the horizontal-to-vertical pixel ratio (320:200, for example) does not match the 4:3 aspect ratio of the typical monitor screen. Therefore, the aspect ratio of geometric figures will vary according to the display mode, as may be demonstrated by running the three-line BASIC program in Listing 11.3.

Listing 11.2 A BASIC Border-Check Program

```
100 SCREEN m                    ' m = any BASIC screen mode
                                   (see Table 11.16)
110 INPUT c                     ' c = desired border color
120 K = INP(986)
130 OUT 960, 17
140 OUT 960, C
150 OUT 960, 32
```

Listing 11.3 A BASIC Aspect Ratio Program

```
100 SCREEN m: CLS              ' m = any CGA or EGA graphics
                                   screen mode
110 LINE (150,50)-(250,150), 2, B
120 CIRCLE (200,100), 70.7


105 WINDOW (0,0)- (400,300)    ' add this line to correct aspect
                                   ratio distortion
```

The value for *m* in line 100 determines the screen mode, and the next two lines draw a "square" box (that is, 100 × 100 pixels) and then a circle surrounding the box. However, the aspect ratios of both box and circle are distorted, and the distortion varies from one video mode to another.

To compensate for the distorted aspect ratio, line 105 maps the active display into an area whose width-to-length ratio is 4:3. Since this matches the actual aspect ratio of most screens, both the box and the circle will be drawn properly.

Contrast Check. Listing 11.4 gives a short BASIC program that may be used to verify the correct performance of the contrast control and to check the available colors on all color displays.

Run the program and note that as the contrast control is adjusted, the difference in brightness between the two displayed lines varies as described above. If varying the contrast control on an enhanced color monitor has no effect, the control is probably defective. The same problem on a monochrome or standard color monitor suggests a bad connection at pin 6 in the plug on the monitor cable. For further details, see the EGA Test or CGA Test sections later in this chapter.

Since only the first two program lines are needed for the contrast test, program execution pauses at line 120 until any key is pressed.

Color Test. Lines 130–250 in Listing 11.4 are a much-abbreviated version of the COLORBAR.BAS program on the DOS supplemental diskette. After pressing any key, 16 color bars are displayed, and these may be used to verify that the colors are correctly rendered. If not, use the front-panel contrast and brightness controls as required.

When you are finished with the tests, press any key to restore the normal 80-character text format.

Listing 11.4 A BASIC Contrast/Color Test Program

```
100 COLOR 2,0: PRINT "Low Intensity"
110 COLOR 10,0: PRINT "High Intensity"
120 K$ = INPUT$(1)
130 DEF SEG: SCREEN 0,1: WIDTH 40
140 SCREEN 0,1: COLOR 0,0: CLS
150 A = 2: B = 11
160 FOR X = 1 TO 2
170 FOR Y = 0 TO 7
180 FOR Z = A TO B
190 LOCATE Z, Y * 5 + 1
200 COLOR Y + K, Y+K: PRINT STRING$(3,219);
210 NEXT Z
220 NEXT Y
230 A = 12: B = 21: K = 8
240 NEXT X
250 PRINT "Blk  Blu  Grn  Cyn  Red  Mag  B/Y  Wht"
260 K$ = INPUT$(1)
270 SCREEN 0: WIDTH 80
```

Extended Color Tests

For the benefit of readers who would like to take a closer look at the color capabilities of various video systems, the following additional color display tests are offered.

CGA Test. The program given in Listing 11.4 will display two sets of eight identical color bars.

EGA and VGA Tests. This section specifically describes an EGA monitor/adapter combination. Although the visual results are valid on VGA systems operating in an EGA mode, all references to conductors, bits, intensity, etc., apply only to an actual EGA adapter.

In the case of an EGA adapter with at least 64 Kbytes of video memory, or a VGA system operating in EGA mode, the colors displayed by the program in Listing 11.4 may be selected from 64 that are available. To create a palette containing 64 different hues, the EGA adapter employs a 6-bit system, in which the bits represent the colors listed in Table 11.12a.

To transmit the necessary data to the enhanced color monitor, six of the nine conductors (2–7) in the EGA display cable are used, as seen in Tables 11.5 and 11.12a. The 64 combinations are made possible by enabling various 6-bit combinations, although as noted only 16 colors may be displayed simultaneously. Taking a single color as an example, enabling bit

Table 11.12a EGA Colors and Cable Conductors

Bit	Color		Intensity	IBM designation	Conductor
5	red	(r)	low	secondary red	2
4	green	(g)	low	secondary green	6
3	blue	(b)	low	secondary blue	7
2	Red	(R)	normal	primary red	3
1	Green	(G)	normal	primary green	4
0	Blue	(B)	normal	primary blue	5

Table 11.12b EGA Color Numbers and Hues

Color	No.	Hue	Color	No.	Hue
black	0	0	dark gray	8	56
blue	1	1	light blue	9	57
green	2	2	light green	10	58
cyan	3	3	light cyan	11	59
red	4	4	light red	12	60
magenta	5	5	light magenta	13	61
brown	6	20	yellow	14	62
white	7	7	intensified white	15	63

5 only (100000) creates a very dark red, while bit 2 only (000100) is the normal red identified as COLOR 4 in BASIC. For a brighter red, a combination of bits 5, 4, and 3 (red, green, blue) produces the low-intensity white (that is, dark gray) of COLOR 8, and this is added to bit 2 (111100) to produce COLOR 12. Note that the BASIC color number does not always agree with the corresponding bit pattern. The actual hues used for colors 0 through 15 are listed in Table 11.12b.

The contrast control on an IBM (or compatible) enhanced color monitor varies the low-intensity bits only. Therefore it does not affect colors 0 through 5 and 7. Color 6 is affected, because it is actually created by bit pattern 20 (010100), which is a combination of low-intensity green and normal-intensity red. And, of course, all combinations from 8 (001000) to 63 (111111) are affected by the contrast control.

EGA Color Palette Test. The program in Listing 11.5 will display all 64 colors, in seven sets of nine hues each. Each set represents a related family

Listing 11.5 A BASIC Extended Color Test Program *

```
100 GOSUB 160                          ' to do setup
110 GOSUB 400                          ' to select a color group
120 ON S GOSUB 470, 730                ' to read data, or end
130 GOSUB 550                          ' to display palettes
140 GOTO 110
150 ' - - - - - - - Setup - - - - - - - - - -
160 CLS: SCREEN 0
170 LOCATE ,,0
180 DIM A$(32), P(15)
190 A$(32) = "r": CL(0) =  1
200 A$(16) = "g": CL(1) =  2
210 A$( 8) = "b": CL(2) =  4
220 A$( 4) = "R": CL(3) =  1
230 A$( 2) = "G": CL(4) =  2
240 A$( 1) = "B": CL(5) =  4
250 C$(1) = "  Blues  "
260 C$(2) = " Greens  "
270 C$(3) = " Cyans   "
280 C$(4) = "  Reds   "
290 C$(5) = "Magentas"
300 C$(6) = "Yellows "
310 C$(7) = "Whites  "
320 N = 9
330 LOCATE 10, 50
340 FOR X = 0 TO 5
350 PALETTE 10 + X, 2^(5-X)
360 COLOR 10 + X: PRINT CHR$(219);
370 NEXT
380 RETURN
390 ' - - - - - - - Select a color group - - -
400 LOCATE 1,1:COLOR 2:PRINT "Select a color:"
410 K$ = INKEY$: IF K$ = "" THEN 410
420 LOCATE 1,1:PRINT STRING$(20,32)
430 K = VAL(K$)
440 S = 1: IF K = 0 OR K > 7 THEN S = 2
450 RETURN
460 ' - - - - - - - Read Data - - - - - - - -
470 FOR R = 1 TO K
480 FOR P = 1 TO N
490 READ P(P)
500 NEXT P
510 NEXT R
520 RESTORE
530 RETURN
```

Listing 11.5 A BASIC Extended Color Test Program (continued) *

```
540 ' - - - - - - - Display Palettes - - - - -
550 LOCATE 10,35:PRINT C$(R-1)
560 FOR P = 1 TO N
570 PALETTE P, P(P)
580 COLOR P
590 PRINT TAB(20) USING "##";P(P);
600 PRINT ". text ";STRING$(20,219);" ";
610 FOR X = 5 TO 0 STEP -1
620 K = P(P) AND 2^X
630 IF N = 9 THEN COLOR 15 - X ELSE COLOR CL(X)
640 IF K = 0 THEN PRINT CHR$(249); ELSE PRINT A$(K);
650 NEXT
660 NEXT P
670 PRINT
680 COLOR 14
690 PRINT TAB(45) "Bits 543210"
700 PRINT TAB(39) "Conductors 267345"
710 RETURN
720 ' - - - - - - - Restore normal palettes and end
730 RESTORE 940
740 CLS
750 COLOR 7
760 PRINT TAB(29)"Standard IBM Palette"
770 N = 15
780 FOR P = 0 TO 15
790 READ P(P)
800 PALETTE P,P(P)
810 NEXT
820 GOSUB 560
830 K$ = INPUT$(1): CLS
840 COLOR 7
850 END
860 ' - - - - - - - Data statements - - - - -
870 DATA  08, 01,  9, 17, 25, 33, 41, 49, 57:  ' Blues
880 DATA  16, 02, 10, 18, 26, 34, 42, 50, 58:  ' Greens
890 DATA  24, 03, 11, 19, 27, 35, 43, 51, 59:  ' Cyans
900 DATA  32, 04, 12, 20, 28, 36, 44, 52, 60:  ' Reds
910 DATA  40, 05, 13, 21, 29, 37, 45, 53, 61:  ' Magentas
920 DATA  48, 06, 14, 22, 30, 38, 46, 54, 62:  ' Yellows
930 DATA  56, 07, 15, 23, 31, 39, 47, 55, 63:  ' Whites
940 DATA  00, 01, 02, 03, 04, 05, 20, 07:      ' IBM standard
950 DATA  56, 57, 58, 59, 60, 61, 62, 63:      ' colors
```

* For use with an EGA or multi-resolution color adapter only.

of hues (blues, greens, cyans, reds, magentas, yellows, and whites). One set at a time appears on screen, as in the display shown in Figure 11.11. The program is useful in making a routine check of color quality and may also help diagnose a few problems that are not discovered during the POST procedure.

To see any color set, run the program and press any number key from 1 to 7. To the left of each horizontal color bar seen in Figure 11.11 is the number of the displayed hue and to the right of the bar, a six-character display represents the six bits discussed above. Each enabled bit is represented by a letter, and a disabled bit appears as a dot. Each letter and dot is displayed in its appropriate color. Note that turning the contrast control affects only those colors in which one or more of the first three bits (5,4,3) are enabled.

If the standard colors seen on a display are unsatisfactory, it may be possible to select a more suitable hue from within the same color group. For example, a good brown (COLOR 6) is often difficult to achieve. As noted earlier, the color adapter uses bit pattern 20 (low-intensity green plus normal red) for this color. Try using bit pattern 32 (low-intensity red only), by

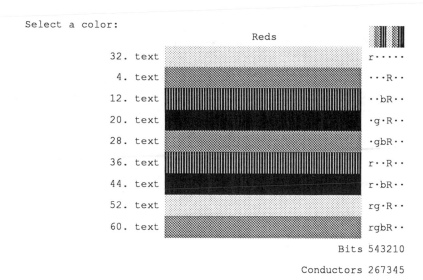

Figure 11.11 Screen display created by the extended color test program in Listing 11.5. Each horizontal color bar is a different hue in the color group. A color bar will be affected by the contrast control on the color display, if one or more of its rgb bits (5, 4, 3) is enabled. Thus, all but one of the reds above will be affected by this control.

changing the 20 in the next-to-last data statement line to 32 instead. Now, when the program concludes, this color will be seen within the standard 15 colors.

To exit the test program, press any key except the numbers 1 through 7. Doing so restores and displays the standard colors 1 through 15, modified by any changes you may have made to the last two DATA lines in the program. Pressing any other key clears the screen and concludes the program.

The PALETTE statement alone, followed by no parameters, may also be used to restore all default color values.

VGA Color Tests. The VGA screen modes 12 and 13 will display 16 and 256 colors, respectively. In each case the colors may be chosen from a palette of 262,144 (64^3) hues. Each displayed color is created by varying the intensity of the three primary additive colors, red, green, and blue. The intensity range for each color is from low = 0 (off) to high = 63. Each displayed color is determined by the following equation:

$$C = R + 256 \times G + 65,536 \times B$$

where

C = the color number, and

R, G, B = 0 to 63—the desired intensities of the red, green, and blue color components.

The modes 12 and 13 tests described below are valid only for use with Microsoft QuickBASIC, version 4.00 or later. Neither IBM BASICA nor GWBASIC supports the SCREEN 11, 12, or 13 statements.

VGA Mode 12 Test. The QuickBASIC program in Listing 11.6 will display a set of 16 vertical color bars, with the color of each one determined by the values given in the DATA statements. The values were arbitrarily chosen, and may of course be changed to any legal value that can be calculated by the equation above. The third and fourth program lines turn the border on.

VGA Mode 13 Test. The program above would require calculating and entering 256 DATA values in order to display that many different colors in mode 13. Instead, the program in Listing 11.7 displays a 16 × 16 matrix of 256 color boxes. Each row of boxes blends one color combination with another, as listed in Table 11.13. The arrows indicate the alternating direction of the displayed blend.

In Listing 11.7, the array values, R(n), determine which color fades in and/or out in row *n*; 1 = color fades in, -1 = color fades out, R() = red, G()

Listing 11.6 A QuickBASIC Video Mode 12 Color Test

```
SCREEN 12
WINDOW (0,0)-(160,1)
K = INP(986)
OUT 960, 17: OUT 960, 1: OUT 960, 32
FOR K = 0 TO 15
READ CLR
PALETTE K, CLR
LINE (X, 0)-(X + 9, 1), K, BF
X = X + 10
NEXT K

DATA       31,       50,       63,     8255
DATA    16191,     8224,     8192,    16128
DATA  1916672,  4144896,  4136960,  4128768
DATA  4128805,  4128831,  4137010,  4144959
K$ = INPUT$(1)
```

= green, and B() = blue. To vary the color blends, change any 1 to -1, or
vice versa. To omit a color, change either value to a zero. In the absence of
a zero, the color intensity remains at minimum or maximum, according to
the value it reached at the end of the most recent for/next loop.

VGA Monitor Identification

A VGA adapter may recognize the type of monitor attached to it by one of
two methods, both of which are described here.

Table 11.13 VGA Video Mode 13 Color Test Pattern *

| | Screen color | | | | Screen color | |
Row	left side	right side	Row	left side	right side
1.	black	→ red	9.	blue/green	→ blue/green/red
2.	red/green	← red	10.	black	← blue/green/red
3.	red/green	→ black	11.	black	→ red/blue
4.	green	← black	12.	red/blue/green	← red/blue
5.	green	→ blue/green	13.	red/blue/green	→ blue/green
6.	black	← blue/green	14.	blue/red	← blue/green
7.	black	→ blue	15.	blue/red	→ green/red
8.	blue/green	← blue	16.	green/blue	← green/red

* Colors displayed by QuickBASIC program in Listing 11.7.

Listing 11.7 A QuickBASIC Video Mode 13 Color Test

```
SCREEN 13: WINDOW SCREEN (0, 0)-(160,160)
CLS : DIM R(16), G(16), B(16)
R = 3: G = 3: B = 3: S = 1

R(0) = 1
G(1) = 1
R(2) = -1: G(2) = -1
G(3) = 1
B(4) = 1
G(5) = -1: B(5) = 1
B(6) = 1
G(7) = 1
R(8) = 1
R(9) = -1: G(9) = -1: B(9) = -1
R(10) = 1:  B(10) = 1
G(11) = 1
R(12) = -1
R(13) = 1:  G(13) = -1
G(14) = 1:  B(14) = -1
B(15) = 1:  R(15) = -1

FOR K = 0 TO 15
FOR L = 0 TO 15
R = R + 3 * R(K)
G = G + 3 * G(K)
B = B + 3 * B(K)
PALETTE P, R + 256 * G + 65536 * B
LINE (X, Y)-(X + 8, Y + 8), P, BF
X = X + 10 * S: P = P + 1
NEXT L
S = -S: X = X + 10 * S: Y = Y + 10
NEXT K

K$ = INPUT$(1)
```

Current Sensing System. In a VGA color system, cable conductors 1, 2 and 3 transmit the primary red, green, and blue data from the adapter to the monitor. For monochrome monitors, only conductor 2 is used (see Table 11.5). Some adapters recognize the presence of a color monitor by sensing the current flow on these lines. If there is no current on lines 1 and 3, the adapter switches to monochrome mode, and colors are displayed as a gray scale.

Monitor ID Lines. As an alternative monitor identification system, conductors 4, 11 and 12 are used by some VGA adapters to identify the type of monitor in use. At the adapter, all three lines are at +5 volts DC, and in the monitor, one or two of these lines are connected to the 0 VDC sync return

Table 11.14 Monitor Identification Bit Configuration in IBM Video Systems *

| Monitor type | IBM model no. | Bit 2 | Bit 1 Conductor † | Bit 0 |
		4	12	11
Monochrome	8503	n/c	0 V	n/c
Color (noninterlaced)	8512, 8513	n/c	n/c	0 V
Color (interlaced)	8514	0 V	n/c	0 V

* Implemented in PS/2 8514/A adapter and PS/2 adapter for ISA systems, but not in MCA video system systems.

† n/c: no connection

line (conductor 10). The ID convention supported by IBM is listed in Table 11.14, and is implemented in the PS/2 8514/A display adapter and in the PS/2 adapter for PS/2 and pre-PS/2 (i.e., PC, XT, AT) ISA systems. This ID system is not currently implemented in the VGA subsystem built into MCA systems.

Some third-party video systems identify these conductors as described by the IBM convention, and some don't. For example, Table 11.15 lists a few of the ways these and other conductors are labeled by various manufac-

Table 11.15 Conductor Assignment in Representative Video Devices

| Cond. no. | Monitors | | VGA Adapters | | |
	IBM (all)	Zenith ZCM-1490	Boca VGA	Maxon MVGA-16	Paradise VGAPlus
1.	red	red	red	red	red
2.	green	green	green	green	green
3.	blue	blue	blue	blue	blue
4.	ID bit 2	n/c	ID bit 2	not used	not used
5.	self test	test	ground	ground	ground
6.	red ground	red ground	ground	red ground	red ground
7.	green ground	green ground	ground	green ground	green ground
8.	blue ground	blue ground	ground	blue ground	blue ground
9.	unused	n/c	ground	not used	not used
10.	sync ground	sync ground	not used	sync ground	sync ground
11.	ID bit 0	mode	ID bit 0	not used	not used
12.	ID bit 1	n/c	ID bit 1	not used	not used
13.	horizontal	horizontal	horizontal	horizontal	horizontal
14.	vertical	vertical	vertical	vertical	vertical
15.	not used	not used	not used	not used	not used

turers. In most cases the ID lines either follow the IBM convention (Zenith, Boca Research) or are not used at all (Maxon and Paradise).

In case of doubt, disconnect the monitor and measure the DC voltage on adapter pins 4, 11, and 12—each should read +5 VDC if the ID convention is implemented, and 0 V if it is not. In the monitor cable, the appropriate 0 V lines should be tied to pin 10 (see Table 11.14). A usually reliable way to determine the monitor status is to look for missing pins in its cable connector. Match the missing pins with the conductors labeled n/c in the table. This may help in a case such as the famous Zenith ZCM-1490 "flat screen" monitor, where the pin 11 "mode" nomenclature is not explained. However, the missing pins 4 and 12 do suggest that the Zenith system follows the IBM convention.

If no pins are missing, then check each pin for continuity with pin 10.

TROUBLESHOOTING DIAGNOSTICS

In diagnosing any problem in which an improper screen display—or no display at all—is seen, the first order of business is to determine whether the monitor itself is at fault. In many cases, the very appearance of on-screen information is sufficient evidence to rule out a monitor malfunction.

For example, if the screen shows recognizable "garbage"—that is, readable letters, graphics characters, or dots that make no apparent sense at all—the actual problem probably lies elsewhere. If the monitor or its associated adapter were actually defective, these characters would not be seen. So it's probably safe to conclude that some other part of the system is faulty, and that the problem is being faithfully reported by a properly functioning monitor.

On the other hand, if the screen display is off center, rolling, skewed, or otherwise distorted, then the problem may indeed be attributed to the monitor or its adapter. And in the event of a completely blank screen, don't overlook the obvious: Is the monitor power cable plugged in? Is the front-panel power switch on? Or, less obviously, is the system's primary monitor not the one you think it is?

Beep Code Error Signals

Two monitor-related audio signals may be encountered during the POST procedure. The first is a specific indication of a monitor problem, while the second is a more general system-error signal which may or may not accompany a monitor problem. In localizing any monitor-related problem, the general error may be replaced by the specific one. Therefore, the sections describing both audio signals should be studied before completing your tests.

If an audio error signal is heard, this problem should be resolved before investigating any other problem that may be noted at the same time.

One long, two or three short beeps (— · ·) or (— · · ·). Either   signal, which may be repeated, indicates the primary adapter is defective, missing, or, in the case of an enhanced graphics adapter, incorrectly configured. In a single-monitor ISA system, the system board configuration switch settings are especially critical, since incorrect settings may cause the system to search for an adapter that isn't really there.

If the audio signal persists, despite double-checking the configuration switches, then reconfigure for another monitor adapter, provided one is available. Or on the PC or XT, configure for zero monitors by putting switches 5 and 6 on switch block 1 in the on position, as seen in Table 11.7a. If either technique clears up the problem, then the first adapter is defective and needs servicing. If the problem persists, then the system board is probably defective.

Two short beeps (· ·). While this audio signal is employed to indicate a variety of errors encountered during the POST procedure, if the signal is accompanied by a blank or otherwise incorrect screen, a monitor-related problem is indicated.

The fault might be on the system board or the monitor adapter or, less likely, in the monitor itself. Turn the power off, disconnect the monitor, remove the adapter, and reboot the system. If the two-beep signal is still heard, then there is a problem on the system board, which will have to be replaced. But if the signal is now the previously described one long beep followed by two short beeps, the missing adapter was noted during an otherwise-successful POST. Either it or the monitor is defective. Reinstall the adapter, leave the monitor disconnected, and reboot the system. If the two-beep signal is again heard during POST, then the adapter is at fault. But if a single beep is heard, the adapter is good and the monitor itself is causing the error signal.

Once the problem is localized to the system board, the adapter, or the monitor, the defective device will require servicing.

During those power-on tests in which the monitor itself remains disconnected, make sure you leave the computer power on until the POST procedure is completed. You can judge this by observing the performance of drive A. With a good system diskette in place, note that the drive-in-use light comes on at the completion of POST. When the drive stops again, type the DIR command. The drive should again spin, indicating the diskette

directory is being read. This suggests that the system is functioning properly, with the exception of the missing monitor, of course.

If typing DIR A: has no effect, try typing PRINT CHR$(7) and then
press the Enter key. If you hear a beep, the system is in the BASIC mode.
If it should not be, then there is an apparent problem with the default
drive (or diskette), in addition to the monitor problem. Try to resolve the
latter problem first, and then proceed to Chapter 8 to resolve the drive
problem.

Error Codes and Messages

Most visible error codes related to the monitor are seen when the user
answers an "Is this correct?" inquiry by typing N or n while running a
diagnostics program. In such a case, the code number displayed after the
user has typed N or n is simply a reminder of the failure noted during testing
and verified by the user. No further discussion of such messages is necessary
here, beyond the following general advice.

The mere presence of a user-indicated error code usually isolates the
location of the error. For example, if most of the tests are satisfactory, the
monitor itself obviously functions properly in the presence of a correct
signal, and the error is therefore on the adapter, rather than the monitor. On
the other hand, if the colors are poorly rendered, then the monitor may
indeed be faulty or simply need minor brightness and contrast adjustments,
as described later in this chapter.

If an error code associated with a user-indicated failure does not clearly
indicate whether the monitor or its adapter is faulty, then both should be
returned for servicing.

Monitor-Adapter Memory Errors

In the sections immediately following, an error code ending in 01 may
indicate a problem with a video memory module on a monitor adapter. In
contrast to system-board-memory error codes, the specific chip is not
identified by the graphics-memory error code. Furthermore, the video
memory chips on IBM CGA and EGA adapters are soldered in place, so the
adapter will require servicing to correct any memory-related error that is
noted. The plug-in memory-module chips on the piggyback expansion card
of the Enhanced Graphics Adapter are not checked during POST, so an
error there will not produce a 2401 error code message.

Note also that video memory chips are not interchangeable with system
board memory chips.

Monochrome Error Codes

The following error codes seen during the POST procedure or when using the IBM Diagnostics diskette indicate an error related to a monochrome adapter.

Error code	Explanation
400	Diagnostics test of Monochrome Display and Printer Adapter concluded successfully.
401	Various monochrome-related errors. During AT diagnostics, if user indicates that two monitors are connected but power to secondary monochrome monitor is actually off, this error code will appear on the primary color monitor. Otherwise, 401 indicates that memory on the monitor adapter is defective. The 401 code accompanied by a distorted display may indicate a video sync failure.
408	User-indicated monitor attributes failure.
416	User-indicated character set failure.
424	User-indicated 80 × 25-mode failure.
432	Parallel-port test failure. Since the Monochrome Display Adapter also contains a parallel-printer connector, this number is seen during monochrome diagnostics if a printer is attached but not turned on. For further details on printer-related errors, refer to Chapter 12.

Color Error Codes

Two numbers are seen for each error-code entry given below. The first (5xx) applies to the Color/Graphics Adapter, and the second (24xx) is for the EGA or VGA adapter.

Error code		Explanation
CGA	EGA/VGA	
500	2400	Diagnostics test of adapter concluded successfully.
501	2401	Either memory on adapter is defective or there is a video sync failure, which will be accompanied by a distorted display.
508	2408	User-indicated monitor attributes failure.
516	2416	User-indicated character set failure.

524	2424	User-indicated 80 × 25-mode failure.
532	2432	User-indicated 40 × 25-mode failure.
540	2440	320 × 200 graphics-mode failure.
548	2448	User-indicated 640 × 200 graphics-mode failure.
556	2456	Light-pen test failure.
564	2464	User-indicated screen-paging test failure.

As noted earlier, a user-indicated error code should help isolate the problem. In the case of poor color rendition, check the following section. If the error indicates any other failure, the adapter needs servicing.

Visual Messages

A visual message can mean just about any monitor-related problem other than the error codes mentioned above, and such a message may show up in one of many formats. For example, the screen may display nothing at all, nothing but a bright spot in the middle, vertical bars, recognizable-but-garbled characters, unrecognizable characters, a rolling display, poor colors, or no color at all.

Off-Center Display. On a color/graphics monitor, the screen display may be shifted to the left or the right for easier readability. At the DOS prompt, type the MODE command

```
A> MODE xx, L, T
```

or

```
A> MODE xx, R, T
```

where xx sets a line width of either 40 or 80 characters, L or R shifts the display left or right, and the optional T displays a single line of characters across the screen for use in verifying that the display is now centered.

This application of the MODE command does not work on monochrome or enhanced graphics monitors, on which the following message will be seen if it is used:

```
Unable to shift screen left (or right)
```

The same message will be seen on the color/graphics monitor display if a further shift would exceed the allowable limit.

Flicker Problem. As noted earlier in the chapter, flicker may be seen if screen persistence is too short for the vertical frequency currently in use.

Unfortunately, there is no cure for the flicker problem, other than buying a new monitor with a longer-persistence screen. Or, if appropriate, experiment with screen colors to minimize the annoyance.

Darkened Screen. In the absence of any sign of on-screen life, make sure the monitor is receiving power—the pilot light, if any, is an obvious clue. Of course, it could be burned out, but this is quite unlikely. If the light is on, then make sure the brightness and contrast controls are not turned all the way down. Some users have a habit of doing this before turning the power off, although it serves no purpose other than confusing the next person to use the system.

If nothing happens when the brightness and contrast controls of a color monitor are turned all the way on, turn the system power off, while leaving the monitor power on. If the monitor now goes bright white, then the problem is on the adapter, which requires servicing or the replacement of a controller chip as described in the Vertical Bars section below. If the display remains dark, then the monitor itself requires servicing. This test is valid for IBM color monitors only, since some non-IBM monitor displays may remain dark when powered on but not connected to an adapter.

• **Monochrome Monitor Caution.** To prevent damage, an IBM monochrome monitor must not be powered on while the system itself is off.

Bright, Center-Screen Spot. On a monochrome monitor, the presence of a bright, center-screen spot indicates that although the monitor is receiving power, the monitor cable is not attached to the adapter. Turn the system off immediately and double-check all connections. If everything looks in order, then the adapter or the monitor itself requires servicing. Since it is not clear which device is at fault, both will have to be taken to a service center.

Vertical Bars. If the monochrome screen display is completely filled with stationary vertical bars, the character generator chip on the adapter may be defective. This type of display may be simulated by running the following one-line BASIC program:

```
100 PRINT CHR$(222);: GOTO 100
```

The screen will soon fill up with vertical bars and, except for the movement at the bottom of the screen, closely resemble the display seen when this chip is defective. The same defect on a color adapter will display an all-white screen.

The character generator chip is located in the plug-in socket at position U33 on both the IBM Monochrome and the IBM Color/Graphics Adapters (not to be confused with the ROM BIOS module in position U33 on the system board). If you have both of these adapters, try carefully swapping the chips. If the problem follows the chip, the chip is indeed defective and must be replaced. Otherwise the adapter itself requires servicing.

• **Character Generator Caution.** The swapping procedure is only valid between the IBM Monochrome Adapter and the IBM Color/Graphics Adapter. The character generators on the Enhanced Graphics Adapter (position U44) and on the Hercules Graphics Card (position U15) may neither be swapped with each other, nor with the IBM Monochrome or Color/Graphics generators.

Garbled Characters. If some or all characters are not what they should be, the character generator chip described above may be defective. Here are two typical examples:

You type this	**Screen displays this (or similar)**
A> DIR	A. DIB
To be or not to be	Do be ob nod do be

Depending on the nature of the problem, other types of distorted character display may be seen. For example, the characters may be split vertically or horizontally, or look like little more than a collection of vertical lines in place of letters, or perhaps just a series of dots.

In any case, type DIR and press the Enter key. The directory listing should still appear, although now in a garbled state. This confirms that the system is working properly, with the obvious exception of the distorted screen display.

If an alternate monitor and adapter are on hand, use the DOS MODE command to switch over to them, and verify that the new display is correct. If it is, then the problem is definitely on the suspect adapter. If a swap of character generators (as described above) transfers the problem to the alternate monitor, then this chip is of course defective. Otherwise, the 6845 controller or some other component on the adapter is defective. Since the character generator is the only removable component on the monitor adapter, the adapter will need to be serviced or replaced. The Hercules controller (position U6) is mounted in a plug-in socket, and so may be easily replaced by the user if defective.

If only a few letters appear to be transposed from their normal position, refer to the section of Chapter 9 entitled Scan Codes and Foreign Language

Keyboards. And if characters are garbled only in certain text files, see the section on Completely Garbled Files in Chapter 8.

Interference Problems

Two types of interference problems are possible. In one example, the magnetic field radiating from a monitor is strong enough to interfere with an adjacent monitor or with diskette operations. In another case, the field some other nearby device is strong enough to cause a wavering or otherwise distorted display.

Horizontal Bars. Horizontal bars moving slowly downward across the face of an otherwise satisfactory display may be caused by interference from an adjacent device. If so, the effect will probably be noted on both displays. As verification, when the secondary monitor's power is turned off, the bars on the primary monitor should disappear, and vice versa. In such a case, the solution is simply to put more distance between the two monitors.

Other Interference Patterns. A large power transformer on any nearby device is a potential problem source. Most PC setups are arranged with sufficient space between the monitor and other devices. In a cramped environment, however, the monitor may find itself too close to a heavy-duty printer, for example, to be protected by its own shielding. If this seems to be the case, the solution is either some rearrangement of the equipment or the use of an external shielding device.

If neither solution is practical, contact the manufacturer of the device causing the problem to see if a better-shielded power transformer is available.

Diskette Problems. If the interference is severe, it may also be serious enough to interfere with diskette operations. The symptom may manifest itself by a garbled display or by garbling data written to diskette. While many monitors are adequately shielded to prevent this from happening, some may need to be moved away from the immediate top of the system unit if diskette operations seem to be affected as described here.

Vertical Screen Problems

As shown in Figure 11.12, two types of rear-panel controls associated with vertical screen problems are found on IBM CGA and EGA monitors. The

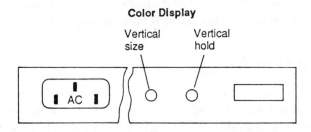

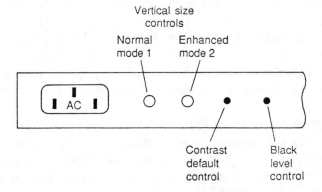

Figure 11.12 Rear-panel controls on IBM standard color and enhanced color monitors.

controls may be used to correct vertical size and movement. Similar controls are not found on monochrome monitors.

Vertical Size. On both color monitors, the vertical screen size may be adjusted as follows. Turn the front-panel brightness and contrast controls fully clockwise. Then turn the rear-panel vertical-size control fully counterclockwise and note the black areas that appear across the top and bottom of the screen. Next, turn the vertical-size control clockwise until these black areas just barely disappear at the corners of the screen. For greatest accuracy, make sure the screen is at eye level while making the final adjustment.

There are two vertical-size controls on the rear panel of the EGA monitor. One is for mode 1 and the other for mode 2 displays. The mode 1 control takes effect when the EGA is configured for normal color mode or when the monitor is being used with a color/graphics adapter. The mode 2 control is active when the EGA is configured for enhanced color mode. For each mode, the opposite mode control is disabled. If you are unsure which is the correct control, turn either one slightly and note the effect, if any. If there is no effect, turn the other control. Remember that if you turn the disabled control far from its current position and leave it in the new position, you will have to readjust the control when and if you change the video mode later on.

For further information, refer to the discussion of normal and enhanced color-mode switches in the EGA configuration section (page 471), and to Figure 11.7 and Table 11.9.

Vertical Hold (Color/Graphics Monitor only). If the display rolls upward or downward, adjust the rear-panel vertical-hold control for a stable image. The control performs the same function as the equivalent control on an ordinary television set.

Vertical and Horizontal Drive Problems

Several TV-like picture distortions are a function of the horizontal and vertical drive signals, which are carried on conductors 8 and 9, respectively, in all 9-pin monitor cables, and in conductors 13 and 14 in analog cables which terminate in a 15-pin plug. For example, a diagonally skewed picture indicates a horizontal drive problem, and a screen full of horizontal lines or other video "hash" is probably a function of the vertical drive signal. In either case, check the connection to conductors 8 and 9 (or 13 and 14) inside the monitor cable plug (unless the plug is a sealed unit). If a loose connection is not discovered, then either the cable, the monitor itself, or its adapter is defective, and will require servicing.

Vertical and/or Horizontal Distortion

If vertical or horizontal distortion is observed in a graphics display, it may be that a program written for a CGA/EGA system is being viewed on a VGA system, or vice versa. If it's possible to modify the program, try adding a line such as line 105 in Listing 11.3 above, which will correct the distortion by forcing the display to follow the 4:3 physical aspect ratio of the typical screen.

EGA Character Sharpness Problem

If the text characters seen on an EGA monitor screen are not as well defined as you would expect, it may be that the default switch settings on the EGA adapter are set to specify the normal mode. To make the desired change, refer to Table 11.9. Note that the achievement of the finer-resolution 8 × 14 character box requires both the EGA adapter and an EGA monitor.

Brightness and Contrast Problems

In the case of a color-related problem not solved by procedures already described, one of the following effects may be noted:

Contrast control has no effect.

Displayed colors are incorrect.

Background is in color when it should be black.

Some colors are missing.

Text in a certain color is distorted or missing.

Most routine brightness and contrast problems can be cleared up by adjusting the appropriate control on the monitor front panel (Figure 11.13). However, if there appears to be a more serious brightness/contrast problem, review the following section before assuming the monitor needs servicing.

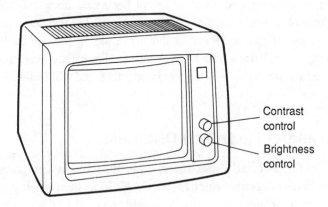

Figure 11.13   Front panel brightness and contrast controls on IBM CGA and EGA monitors.

Brightness. If the screen remains dark even when the brightness control is turned fully clockwise, then it may be assumed that the device needs servicing. However, it is also possible that a software problem has darkened the screen. And if the cursor is not visible, this too could be a software problem. To eliminate all doubts, reboot the system. If a normal screen is seen, the monitor device is presumably in good working order. If not, it is time for servicing.

Contrast. If the contrast control on a CGA or EGA monitor has no effect, there may be a problem with conductor 6. If so, then the program given in Listing 11.4 will display two sets of eight identical color bars. In this case, check the 9-pin plug for a bad connection.

VGA Display Problems

If a VGA color monitor will produce only a black-and-white display, there may be a hardware compatibility problem, either between the VGA adapter and another adapter in the system, or between the VGA adapter and the monitor.

Adapter Conflict. When a VGA adapter is installed in an ISA computer, the system configuration must be set for VGA, EGA/VGA, or EGA, depending on which of these options is available within the configuration utility. If the system is correctly configured and a seemingly nonrelated configuration error is reported during POST, there may be a conflict between the VGA adapter and some other 16-bit adapter.

As a typical example, if an 8/16-bit VGA adapter is set for automatic 8/16-bit bus detection and installed in a 16-bit AT adapter slot, and an older 16-bit memory adapter is also installed, the system may fail the POST memory test and the color monitor may default to a VGA monochrome mode in which colors are displayed as shades of gray. To troubleshoot the problem, reboot the computer with the memory adapter removed. If proper color operation is now observed, then the removed adapter is indeed the source of the conflict. If not, try removing other adapters until the problem is resolved.

If the problem is eventually localized to a specific adapter, remove the VGA adapter and set its jumpers and/or switches as required to force it into an 8-bit mode, as described in the Video Graphics Adapter section (page 476). Then reinstall both adapters, but put the VGA adapter in an 8-bit socket. If this clears up the problem, then there was indeed a conflict between the VGA adapter and the other adapter. The solution is either to replace the other adapter or simply leave the system as is—that is, with the VGA adapter in its 8-bit mode. Depending on your specific applications, the slower video operation may or may not be a practical consideration.

Monitor Current-Sense Conflict. As noted earlier in the chapter (page 492), some adapters recognize the attached monitor by sensing the current on lines 1, 2, and 3. At the monitor, the impedance of each of these lines is usually 75 ohms (measured to the corresponding return line (6, 7, 8). In a color monitor, if one of these impedances should increase significantly— say, due to a loose connection or faulty cable—the VGA adapter might switch to the monochrome mode, and this would cause a configuration error beep code (— · · ·) during POST if the system is in fact configured for a color monitor. In this case, the monitor will display a gray scale instead of color.

To verify that this is the problem, measure the impedance between lines 1-6, 2-7, and 3-8, each of which should be about 75 ohms. If any line varies by more than about ten percent, then either the monitor or the cable is defective. To double-check, try rebooting with the monitor cable disconnected from the adapter. If the system boots successfully (listen for the correct beep code at the conclusion of POST), then there is indeed a problem with the monitor or cable.

Although not recommended by most video hardware manufacturers, another check can be made by reconnecting the monitor after POST concludes successfully. If a good color display is seen, then the impedance is high enough to cause the POST beep code, yet not great enough to affect the actual colors seen on screen. However, if one color is missing completely, then there is of course an obvious fault associated with that line. In either case, the monitor and/or cable need servicing.

If the impedance of each line is correct (i.e., about 75 ohms), and the color display is good, then the problem may be caused by a monitor line ID conflict, as described next.

Monitor ID Line Conflict. As just noted, the above problem could be due to a conflict on the monitor ID lines between the adapter and the monitor. This would occur if line 12 (bit 1) is grounded, thereby signaling the adapter that a monochrome monitor is installed. Review the VGA Monitor ID Lines section (page 492), and if it appears that this may be the source of the trouble, try the reboot procedure just described.

If the evidence suggests an ID line conflict, contact the manufacturer of the adapter and/or the monitor to verify the compatibility problem.

Accelerated System Conflict. If you've just installed a VGA adapter in an older ISA system that had been running in an accelerated mode, don't overlook the possibility of a speed-related problem, although this is unlikely if the system was previously running properly with some other video adapter. In case of doubt, refer to the Troubleshooting Accelerated ISA Systems section of Chapter 6 (page 219).

Monitor Cable Problems

If there is either an open or a short circuit in one of the conductors listed in Table 11.5, or in the associated circuitry, the trouble will not be detected during POST. If the fault is related to conductors 8 and 9 (13 and 14 for VGA), it will be as described in the section on vertical and horizontal drive problems (page 503). However, a problem with one of the other conductors will simply present a display with distorted color values. To identify the specific conductor that is faulty, run the program given in Listing 11.5 and look in the right-hand 6-bit display for a vertical column exhibiting one of the problems described here. The circuit problems described immediately below are valid for EGA adapters only.

Open-Circuit Problem. If an entire vertical column of bits is missing, the number at the bottom of the missing column identifies the missing bit, and immediately below that is the number of the open-circuited conductor.

Short-Circuit Problem. If the small color bar at the top of a column is missing, the number at the bottom of that column again identifies the missing bit, and immediately below that is the number of the conductor that is shorted to ground. The hue in each horizontal color bar will be incorrect if the short-circuited conductor is required for that color bar. Also, text characters in that color will be distorted or missing.

Once the suspected conductor is identified, you may want to check the most likely trouble spot: an open or shorted connection at that pin number within the nine-pin plug at the end of the cable attached to the monitor. If this connection appears to be in good shape, then either the monitor itself or the adapter requires servicing. If another monitor is on hand, try a simple substitution. If the problem remains, then it is the adapter that is faulty. Otherwise, the problem is of course with the monitor that was just removed or its cable.

TV-Set Monitor Problems

If a color television set is used as a monitor, the display will not match the quality of a dedicated computer color monitor. However, some slight improvement may be achieved by turning the color trimmer capacitor on the system board. For the location of this control on IBM PC, XT, and AT system boards, refer to the system board illustrations in Figure 6.2.

For other TV set adjustments, the controls on the set perform their usual functions. The color-bar program discussed on page 484 may be used while adjusting the color rendition.

Note that neither a monochrome nor an enhanced graphics adapter is compatible with a television set. The RCA plugs on the EGA are (or were to be) reserved for future applications, and their specific purpose has not yet been announced by IBM. A television set may only be used in conjunction with a color/graphics adapter.

SOFTWARE-RELATED DIAGNOSTICS

As with other components in the complete system, some apparent video hardware problems are actually a function of the software in use at the time the problem is noted. The problem may be a blank screen or a scrambled image, such as seen on a TV set with a horizontal or vertical hold problem.

If the screen suddenly goes blank or displays a distorted image, especially after installing some new video-related software, turn the system off immediately to minimize the chance of damage. Then turn the system back on again and carefully review the procedure that caused the problem. The chances are that a configuration error was made during installation. If the problem cannot be resolved by reinstalling the application and the suggestions listed below are of no help, then contact the software manufacturer for assistance.

Incomplete or No Display

An apparent problem may occur if a software program assumes a specific device is the primary monitor, when in fact it is not. For example, if the communications software used to support a modem has been configured to display instructions to the user on a color screen, but the system itself is configured for a primary monochrome monitor, these instructions will not be visible. Sometimes an introductory screen is seen briefly on the primary monitor, while the secondary monitor remains blank or shows a meaningless pattern of moving lines or some other unreadable display.

In any case, it appears as though there is a monitor-related problem, when, in fact, there is not. The remedy is to reconfigure something—either the system to match the software or the software to match the system.

In the case of a software program that expects a certain monitor to be active, the MODE command described earlier in this chapter should allow the user to transfer to that monitor. If this transfer clears up the problem, there are three alternatives:

1. Reconfigure the system so that the required monitor is the primary one.

2. Reconfigure the software to accept the user's choice of primary monitor.

3. Insert the MODE command in a batch file that will also be used to load the software program.

Cursor Disappears off Screen

Given the popularity of 43- and 50-line screen displays, it's quite possible for the cursor to "get lost" somewhere beneath the last visible line on the screen. For example, this might happen on a 43-line EGA display when viewing a document with word-processing software set for a 50-line VGA display. If the cursor moves to line 44 through 50, it disappears from view. To correct the problem, use the word-processor installation utility to set the number of display lines to agree with the number actually seen on screen.

Blank Area at Bottom of Screen

When switching between VGA and EGA modes, it's possible to encounter a fairly wide band of unused space near the bottom of a VGA screen. For example, word-processing software properly installed for a 43-line EGA display may not use the entire available screen area on a VGA monitor. If the word processor is reinstalled for a 50-line VGA display, the screen will be fully used, but the text lines may be too small for comfort. Since a 43-line VGA mode is probably not supported, the only alternative may appear to be the old standard 25-line display mode. However, most VGA adapters are supplied with a software utility used to emulate EGA and other display modes, for the sake of temporarily fooling the monitor into behaving like an EGA, Hercules, or other type of monitor.

Given the right video utility software, the EGA display mode is emulated by typing a command such as SETVGA EGA (Boca Research VGA Adapter), SVM EGA (Maxon MVGA-16 Adapter), or similar. Next, execute the word processor or other application in the usual manner. To restore the VGA mode later on, type SETVGA VGA, SVM VGA, or similar. Such utilities usually work only with the adapter for which they were designed, or not at all if the word processor or other application overrides the utility.

Unfortunately, there are no official guidelines here, other than to try it and hope it works. If not, contact the adapter manufacturer, who will swear the problem has never been reported before. Be persistent, and perhaps they will work out a software update for your application. Better yet, invest in Personics' *UltraVision* software, which offers just about any combination of color, screen font, text column, and text row format that might be desired.

Graphics Mode Doesn't Work

If a software program functions properly in the text mode, but does not display graphics screens, it's likely that at some point the program is attempting to enter a video mode not supported by the resident video system. As a typical example, the 1990 CD-ROM edition of the Grolier Electronic Encyclopedia contains artwork and photographic images that can be viewed only on a VGA system. If the computer lacks a VGA adapter and monitor, the text portion of the encyclopedia will be accessible, but an attempt to view a picture will display a message advising that a VGA system is required.

In this case, the message offers sufficient explanation of the problem, and the program continues to function in the text-only mode. A less-sophisticated program may simply crash with an error message such as *Illegal function call at (address or line number)*. In this case, the "solution" is to avoid entering the graphics mode until a VGA system can be installed.

In case of doubt about the video modes supported by any adapter/monitor combination, the following one-line BASIC program will display an error message if the screen mode is not supported.

```
100 SCREEN n: PRINT "This is a test"
```

where *n* is any screen mode listed in Table 11.16. If an error message is displayed, then the equivalent video mode is not supported by the system.

HERCULES GRAPHICS CARD

The graphics capability of the IBM Monochrome Display and Printer Adapter is limited to the display of the handful of line-drawing characters located in the extended character set range from 169 to 254. Therefore, the

Table 11.16 Video Mode/BASIC/DOS Cross-Reference Guide

Video Mode Hex	Decimal	Equivalent BASIC screen mode statement	DOS command
0	0	SCREEN 0, 0: WIDTH 40	MODE BW40
1	1	SCREEN 0, 1: WIDTH 40	MODE CO40
2	2	SCREEN 0, 0: WIDTH 80	MODE BW80
3	3	SCREEN 0, 1: WIDTH 80	MODE CO80
4	4	SCREEN 1, 0	
5	5	SCREEN 1, 1	
6	6	SCREEN 2	
7	7	SHELL "MODE MONO"	MODE MONO
8	8	SCREEN 3 (PC Jr only)	
9	9	SCREEN 5 (PC Jr only)	
A	10	SCREEN 6 (PC Jr only)	
B	11	reserved	
C	12	reserved	
D	13	SCREEN 7	
E	14	SCREEN 8	
F	15	SCREEN 10	
10	16	SCREEN 9	
11	17	SCREEN 11	
12	18	SCREEN 12	
13	19	SCREEN 13	

adapter does not support the various graphics mode commands that may be used elsewhere to draw graphs, charts, or any of the other types of displays that are possible with a color monitor adapter.

To extend graphics capability to the monochrome screen, Hercules Computer Technology, Inc., markets its Hercules Graphics Card. The card allows the user to draw on-screen charts and graphs by making almost every pixel available as a separate data point. The card allows access to the full 720 pixels along the horizontal axis and to 348 (not 350) pixels along the vertical axis. In addition, the card functions as a direct replacement for the regular monochrome monitor adapter, allowing the display of the complete IBM extended character set.

Hardware Description

The Hercules Graphics Card contains 64 Kbytes of video memory, compared to the 4 Kbytes found on the IBM Monochrome Display (and Printer) Adapter. Depending on your system requirements, the card should be used in one of the following configurations:

Hercules Card configuration	Description
Full	All 64Kb is available for use.
Half	32Kb only is available for use, to prevent conflict with a color adapter card in the same system.
Diagnostics	The default mode, allowing the IBM diagnostics programs to be run.

Software switching allows the user or the program to change from one configuation to another, as will be described later on in this chapter.

Full Configuration. In this mode, the card supports two display pages (0 and 1). A page is defined as the 32Kb memory area required to support a full screen—that is, a page—of Hercules graphics. Of course only one page can be seen on the monitor screen at a time, but the pages may be instantaneously swapped via software.

Since two graphics pages require the full 64Kb of memory on the Hercules card, there will be a memory conflict when a color/graphics or enhanced graphics adapter is installed in the same system. The conflict occurs because the second Hercules page occupies the same memory area as the color video memory. Possible memory-conflict problems are discussed on page 513.

Half Configuration. By switching to this mode, only one memory page is available for the Hercules card, so there is no memory conflict with a color adapter. However, if your software program requires the use of both pages, only page 0 will be displayed if the Hercules half mode is selected.

Diagnostics Configuration. When power is first applied, the Hercules Graphics Card is in this mode. With only 4Kb of memory available, the card duplicates the capabilities of the regular IBM Monochrome Display Adapter. That is, only the regular IBM ASCII and extended character sets may be used. The card must be in this mode whenever the IBM Diagnostics diskette is to be used.

Changing Configuration. To select the desired configuration, the Hercules HGC.COM program must be executed, by entering the following command at the DOS prompt:

A> HGC *xxxx*

where *xxxx* is FULL, HALF, or DIAG, as appropriate. Some commercially available software programs which make use of Hercules graphics do this switching automatically. If in doubt, enter the above command line in an AUTOEXEC.BAT file. The same file may also contain a line to switch back to, say, the diagnostics configuration at the completion of your program, as in the following sample batch file:

Batch file	Explanation
MODE MONO	selects monochrome screen, if necessary
HCG FULL	puts Hercules card in its full configuration
YOURPROG	executes your program
HGC DIAG	switches Hercules card back down to 4K memory only
MODE CO80	switches back to color display

Of course, the MODE commands are unnecessary if your system is not using a color monitor as its default monitor device. For more information about batch files, see Chapter 4.

Memory-Conflict Problems

In a system containing a color monitor adapter in addition to the Hercules Graphics Card, when the Hercules system writes data to its second page of memory, one of these effects will be noted.

Color/Graphics Adapter Conflict. The following error message will be displayed on the Hercules-driven monitor, and the system will crash:

```
PARITY CHECK 1

?????
```

The solution is to turn the power off, remove the color/graphics adapter, and reboot the system.

Enhanced Graphics Adapter Conflict. Random characters and colors may be seen on the color display as the Hercules card writes data to its second memory page. However, the performance of the Hercules card itself is usually not affected by the presence of the Enhanced Graphics Adapter, nor is there a system crash.

Software Support

Since so many problems related to the operation of a Hercules Graphics Card are actually a function of software support, a brief software overview is given here. This information may help the user to recognize at least some of the problems that may be encountered in the routine use of the card.

Much commercially available software has been written to take full advantage of the Hercules card. And, for the user who wishes to write his own software, several support programs are available. In the examples seen here, the software is used in conjunction with the standard IBM BASICA.COM program found on the DOS diskette.

Note that the Hercules Graphics Card does not allow the direct use of some regular BASICA graphics statements, such as COLOR, DRAW, LINE, and PSET. To use these statements in conjunction with any IBM DOS prior to version 3.2, the Hercules HBASIC program supplied with the card must be loaded along with BASICA. However, the HBASIC program will not work with DOS versions 3.2 or later. Instead, Hercules separately markets a GRAPH X program for users who write their own software. Table 11.17 summarizes the versions of graphics support currently available for use with the Hercules Graphics Card.

Hercules Card Diagnostics

There are two diagnostics procedures available for checking a Hercules Graphics Card.

IBM Diagnostics. To test the card as nothing more than a plug-in replacement of a conventional monochrome monitor adapter, make sure the Hercules HALF configuration is active, as described on page 512. Then, simply run the regular IBM Diagnostics diskette, as described in Chapter 3. This procedure checks the card's character mode and printer port only.

Table 11.17 Hercules Graphics Card Support Programs

Program name	Identification	For use with DOS version	Machine compatibility
HBASIC1.EXE	Hercules BASIC	1.1 only	IBM only
HBASIC.EXE	Hercules BASIC	2.0 to 3.1	IBM only
GRAPH X †	see note	2.0 or later	IBM or compatible

† Note: GRAPH X is a library of graphics subroutines for use with Assembly Language, BASIC, Fortran, or Pascal.

Hercules Diagnostics. The diskette accompanying the Hercules Graphics Card contains a diagnostics program suitable for checking both screen pages. Before running Hercules diagnostics, your monochrome monitor must be the default device. If necessary, use the DOS MODE MONO command, as described above. Then, switch to the drive containing the Hercules programs, and make sure the following files are listed in the directory:

Hercules files	Purpose
TEST.BAT	Batch file to start the diagnostics
USERDIAG.COM	Support program for the diagnostics
DIAGNSTC.COM	Hercules diagnostics program

The TEST.BAT file contains the names of the two diagnostics programs. If it is missing, simply type the other two file names (but not the COM extensions) in the sequence seen above. Conclude each file name by pressing the Enter key.

If you attempt to execute the DIAGNSTC program before the USER-DIAG program, the following error message is seen:

```
MetaWINDOW Driver not installed
Program terminated
```

If this message appears despite the proper entry of the commands, then there is a problem with the diagnostics software, not with the card itself. But assuming the software is in order, Figure 11.14 shows the single Hercules Diagnostics menu that should appear on screen.

```
The Hercules Graphics Mode Test
Version 1.2 Copyright(C) 1985 Hercules Computer Technology
SELECT AN OPTION

0 - RUN TEST ONE TIME
1 - RUN TEST MULTIPLE TIMES
2 - END TEST

ENTER THE ACTION DESIRED
? _
```

Figure 11.14   The Hercules diagnostics menu.

When you choose either test option, four screens such as the one in Figure 11.15 will be displayed sequentially. If option 0 is selected, you must press any key to toggle between pages 0 and 1. If option 1 is chosen, the pages toggle automatically. In either case, the test may be concluded after four screen displays, by pressing any key. At the conclusion of the test the system returns to the DOS prompt, so it is neither necessary nor possible to select the End Test option, unless you decide at the Main Menu not to run the test in the first place.

The screen displays should of course be well balanced, clear, and sharply defined. If the screen display for either page shows erroneous dots or dashes, there is a problem with that page's memory. The Hercules diagnostics program does not identify the faulty chip, and all chips are soldered in place. Therefore, a memory error will probably require outside servicing.

Troubleshooting

For readers who have the Hercules GRAPH X software diskette, the BASIC program in Listing 11.8 may be of use in diagnosing various screen-related problems. Even if the GRAPH X software is not available, the following paragraphs may still help you to identify the source of some monitor-related problems.

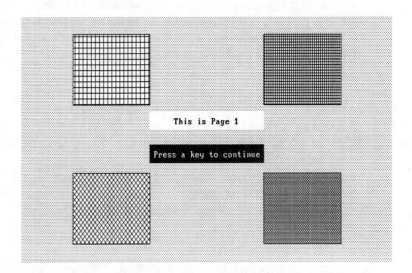

This is Page 1

Press a key to continue

Figure 11.15 One of the page displays seen when the Hercules Diagnostics program is executed.

Listing 11.8 A BASIC Hercules Graphics Card Test Program *

```
100 GOSUB 170                         ' to define variables
110 FOR P = 0 TO 1
120 GOSUB 310                         ' to set up Page P
130 ON P+1 GOSUB 360, 480             ' to draw grid, circles
140 NEXT P
150 GOSUB 540                         ' to toggle between pages
160 ' - - - - - - - - - Define variables
170 DEF SEG = &H3000
180 BLOAD "BAS2GRPH.BIN",0
190 DEFINT A-Z
200 GMODE   = 256 * PEEK( 1) + PEEK( 0)
210 TMODE   = 256 * PEEK( 3) + PEEK( 2)
220 CLRSCR  = 256 * PEEK( 5) + PEEK( 4)
230 GPAGE   = 256 * PEEK( 7) + PEEK( 6)
240 DISP    = 256 * PEEK(11) + PEEK(10)
250 MOVE    = 256 * PEEK(17) + PEEK(16)
260 DLINE   = 256 * PEEK(19) + PEEK(18)
270 CIRC    = 256 * PEEK(27) + PEEK(26)
280 CALL GMODE
290 RETURN
300 ' - - - - - - - - - Page setup
310 CALL DISP(P)
320 CALL GPAGE(P)
330 CALL CLRSCR
340 RETURN
350 ' - - - - - - - - - Draw Grid on Page 1
360 X1 = 0: X2 = 719
370 FOR Y = 0 TO 345 STEP 5
380 CALL MOVE(X1,Y)
390 CALL DLINE(X2,Y)
400 NEXT Y
410 Y1 = 0: Y2 = 347
420 FOR X = 0 TO 719 STEP 5
430 CALL MOVE(X,Y1)
440 CALL DLINE(X,Y2)
450 NEXT X
460 RETURN
470 ' - - - - - - - - - Draw Circles on Page 1
480 X = 360: Y = 174
490 FOR R = 10 TO 350 STEP 10
500 CALL CIRC(X,Y,R)
510 NEXT R
520 RETURN
530 ' - - - - - - - - - Toggle between pages
540 P = 1: Q = 0
550 K$ = "#"
560 WHILE ASC(K$) <> 27
570 CALL DISP(P)
580 K$ = INPUT$(1)
590 SWAP P,Q
600 WEND
610 CALL TMODE
620 END
```

* Program requires the BAS2GRPF.BIN program on the Hercules Graph X
  library diskette

Before running the program, write a CHECK.BAT batch file containing the lines seen below. Do not call this file TEST.BAT or it will erase the existing Hercules file of that name, if this exists in the same directory.

```
MODE MONO
HGC FULL
INT10
BASICA
```

Here it is assumed that the DOS MODE and BASICA programs, as well as the Hercules HGC.COM and INT10.COM files from the GRAPH X diskette, are all on the diskette in the default drive. The BASIC program itself requires the presence of the Hercules BAS2GRPH.BIN file in the default directory. If any of these files is elsewhere, specify the appropriate paths as necessary. (See Chapter 4 for details about the PATH command.)

Once you have completed the batch file, execute it at the DOS prompt, and when the IBM BASICA screen and OK prompt are seen, run the program in Listing 11.8. The screen should display a grid of horizontal and vertical lines, which are immediately replaced by a series of concentric circles. The grid is stored in video memory as page 0, and the circles are in page 1, which remains on-screen, as shown in Figure 11.16. Press any key

Figure 11.16   The page 1 screen displays produced when the BASIC program in Listing 11.8 is run. The grid (not shown) is stored in page 0 memory.

to toggle back and forth between the two pages, and press the Escape key to exit the program. If an enhanced color monitor is attached to an enhanced graphics adapter and turned on, its screen will show a random pattern of colors and graphics characters as soon as the circles appear on the monochrome display. This is because Hercules Page 1 is using the memory area set aside for the color monitor.

Missing Screen Problem. To simulate a memory-related error, replace the HGC FULL line in the batch file with HGC HALF. Now execute the batch file and run the BASIC program once more. This time, only the grid is displayed, and toggling any key has no effect. If HGC DIAG is inserted in the batch file, neither screen will be displayed and the system will crash, requiring a warm reboot.

These deliberate errors demonstrate the errors that will occur if a software program requires more memory than has been allocated by the HGC command. Therefore, in the absence of the expected screen displays, try executing the HGC FULL command before running the program which exhibits the problem. If the problem persists, then either the software needs debugging, or there is a problem on the graphics card which requires servicing. Needless to say, if some other Hercules graphics program runs satisfactorily, the graphics card itself should not be a suspect.

On-Screen "Garbage" Problem. The first 4Kb of Hercules video memory is also used by the text mode buffer. Therefore, if text remains in this area prior to using page 0 for graphics, the top half of the screen display will be contaminated by a series of dots and dashes. This effect may be seen by eliminating line 330 in the BASIC program in Listing 11.8 and running the program once again. The screen should look like that shown in Figure 11.17.

Printer Hardcopy Problem. The GRAPH X diskette also provides a HARDCOPY.COM program for printing Hercules screen displays on a dot-matrix printer. This program is run in conjunction with the PRINTER.DEF file, which provides the printer definition codes required by most IBM and Epson dot-matrix printers.

If your dot-matrix printer does not work properly with the HARDCOPY program, chances are that the PRINTER.DEF file needs to be modified. For example, Listing 11.9 shows the file, along with a version modified for use with the IBM Proprinter. The setup and restore lines are slightly different from those used in the default PRINTER.DEF file found on the Hercules

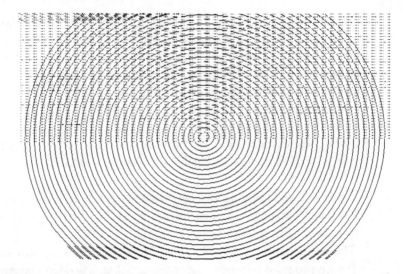

Figure 11.17   If Hercules graphics mode 0 is contaminated by use of the text mode, the top half of the screen display (or hardcopy printout) will be contaminated, as seen here.

GRAPH X diskette. For comparison, the listing also shows the contents of the definition file required for the C. Itoh Prowriter.

The easiest way to create a new PRINTER.DEF file is to copy the existing one, giving the copy a distinctive name such as, in this case, NEW-FILE.DEF. Then edit the lines in the copy, as required. Finally, load the HARDCOPY program by inserting the following line in your batch file:

```
A> HARDCOPY NEWFILE.DEF
```

The command now loads your new definition file in place of the default PRINTER.DEF file that is automatically used when HARDCOPY is not followed by the name of a definition file.

If neither of the Hercules definition files—nor the Listing 11.9 Proprinter modification—works for your printer, then you will have to consult the printer's user's guide to find the necessary codes to replace those found in the definition files. The setup and restore lines are the two most likely to need modification.

Hardcopy "Garbage" Problem.   If the screen garbage problem described earlier is not resolved, of course a printout on paper will exhibit the same garbage problem. But sometimes the problem is seen on the printout, even

Listing 11.9   Hercules Graphics Card Printer Definition File Required by Various Printers *

File Name Use with	PRINTER.DEF Epson and most IBM	PROPRINT.DEF IBM Proprinter	ITOH.DEF C. Itoh Prowriter
width	=8	=8	=8
topbit	=7	=7	=0
setup	=\1B@\1B3\18\41	=\1B3\18\41	=\1B[\1BQ\1BL010\ 1BT16\1BF\41
header	=\1BL\D0\02\41	=\1BL\D0\02\41	=\1BS0720\41
tail	=\0D\0A\41	=\0D\0A\41	=\0D\0A\41
restore	=\1B@\40\41	=\1B2\41	=\1B]\1BE\1BA\41
normal	=1	=1	=1
normal alt	=2	=2	=2
reverse	=3	=3	=3
reverse alt	=4	=4	=4
normal both	=5	=5	=5
reverse both	=6	=6	=6

*   The PRINTER.DEF and ITOH.DEF files are on the Hercules GRAPH X diskette. The PROPRINT.DEF file may be prepared by copying the PRINTER.DEF file and then editing the setup and restore lines.

though the screen display looked clean. This occurs if the software restores the text mode at the conclusion of the program. Doing so automatically contaminates the page 0 memory, creating the problem seen in Figure 11.17. The solution is simply to run off the desired hardcopy before terminating the program which created it.

12

MODEMS AND COMMUNICATIONS

The reliable communication of data between two computers depends on four independent variables:

The message to be sent, via keyboard or from a previously written disk file

The link between the computers

The communications hardware

The communications software

For the purposes of this chapter it is assumed there are no problems with the message to be sent, which is either at the user's fingertips or safely stored on disk or diskette. There's also not too much to be done about the link between the computers, other than to be able to recognize when the link is the cause of trouble.

That leaves the hardware and the software to review here. In this chapter, *software* refers specifically to the program that controls the communications hardware during transmission and reception of data. Since many problems may be traced directly to this software, a close look at some of the programming variables that may affect the reliability of data communication is in order.

HARDWARE OVERVIEW

Telephone System

For sending data between computers, the existing telephone system is the obvious medium of choice. Presumably, this communications network and all the necessary cables are already in place, and the familiar dialing system has long since become second nature to all of us.

However, the phone system is designed for two-way voice communication and is not well suited for the direct transmission of the computer's digital data stream. Before this data can be sent over the phone line, it must first be converted into an audiolike signal that can be accommodated by the relatively narrow bandwidth of the phone lines.

Modem

To convert computer data to audio signal, a modulator is required. This device converts the computer's digital output into an audio signal whose output frequency varies in direct relationship to the input from the computer. At the other end of the signal path, a demodulator converts the audio signal back into computer data. If all goes well, the audio-to-data and data-to-audio conversions are transparent to the computers, so that they operate as if they were directly connected, instead of being separated by a phone line that is perhaps a few thousand miles long.

Since communication is a two-way stream, each operator must have the means to modulate an outgoing signal and demodulate an incoming one. The necessary MOdulator/DEModulator system is, of course, known as a modem.

A modem for a personal computer may be either an internal or an external device. The two types perform identical functions, and the choice is strictly one of personal preference, with each type having the usual advantages and disadvantages of other external and internal devices.

Carrier Signal. To begin communication between modems, the operator of the local modem places a call to the remote modem. When the remote modem answers the call—either automatically or via an operator at the remote location—the remote modem sends out a high-frequency signal indicating it is ready to begin the transfer of data.

During modem operation, the outgoing data signal modulates a carrier frequency, and this is transmitted to the remote modem, where the demodulation process converts the signal back into a data signal usable by the computer. Although further discussion of the process is beyond the scope of this book, this brief mention is made to illustrate the role of the carrier signal.

Near the end of the chapter, various carrier-related problems are discussed, so it may be helpful to remember the general purpose of the carrier in modem communications.

MODEM-TO-COMPUTER INTERFACE

The connection between the modem and the PC will of course depend on whether the modem is an internal or an external device. Both styles are briefly described here.

Internal Modem

An internal modem is completely self-contained and is simply inserted into an adapter slot on the system board. The IBM internal modem does not have its own speaker, so an interface with the PC system speaker must be made in order for the telephone dial tone and the communications carrier signal to be heard. The required connections are shown in Figure 12.1. Many other internal modems do have an onboard speaker, in which case this system interface in unnecessary.

External Modem

An external modem is connected to the PC via cable to a serial port—so called because data is transmitted serially, one bit at a time. (Compare serial transmission to the parallel transmission commonly used for the PC-to-printer communication discussed in Chapter 13.)

Modem Connector. The rear-panel connector on most external modems is a female 25-pin D-shell socket, so called because of its D-like shape. In popular usage, the connector is often incorrectly referred to as an RS-232 plug, after the EIA standard of that number.

Serial Port Connector. The external modem may be connected to the PC via any serial port connector including, but not limited to, the asynchronous communications adapter, binary synchronous communications adapter, serial/parallel adapter, synchronous data-link control communications adapter, and the serial port built into PS/2 and EISA system boards. The port connector is either a male 9-pin or 25-pin plug, as described below.

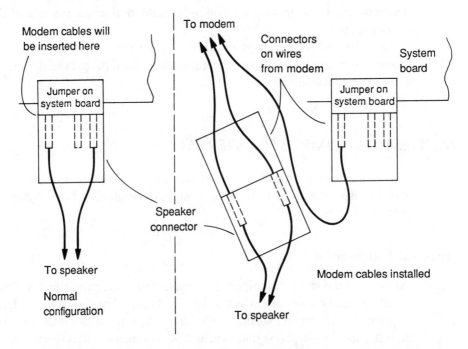

Figure 12.1. System speaker connections required by some internal modems installed in ISA systems. (a) Normal configuration and (b) with modem cables installed. The modem connectors are inserted in the circuit between the system-board jumper and the speaker connector.

The RS-232 Standard

The EIA (Electronics Industries Association) has published the *EIA Standard Interface Between Data Terminal Equipment and Data Communication Equipment Employing Serial Binary Data Interchange (EIA-232-C)*, a standard that defines 25 conductors that may be used in the interface of DTE (data terminal equipment—a personal computer) and DCE (data communications equipment—modem) hardware.

The standard specifies the function of each conductor, but does not designate the physical connector that is to be used. However, the most popular format is the 25-pin connector seen on the rear panel of any Hayes or IBM external modem.

Table 12.1 identifies each RS-232 conductor and indicates which pins are used by various communications devices. Note that the name of each EIA conductor refers to its function at the DTE end of the cable. For example, the DTE "transmit data" conductor is the DCE's "receive data" conductor, and vice versa.

Serial Connectors and Cables

Since not all 25 conductors defined by the EIA standard are required for routine modem operations, some serial communication connectors and cables may provide for less than the full complement, as described below.

Serial Port Connector. The serial port built into EISA and PS/2 MCA system boards and found on many other serial port devices uses a male 25-pin plug, with no electrical connection at some of the pins.

Serial Communication Cable. Several formats of multiconductor cable are available for DTE/DCE communication in which both devices use a 25-pin connector. However, the number of conductors within the cable may be 25 or fewer, as shown in Table 12.1b. In case of doubt, make sure the cable contains the number of conductors (or more) required to link the DTE and DCE.

AT Serial Adapter. The male 9-pin plug on the IBM AT serial adapter provides connections for only the nine EIA conductors required for routine modem operations (2–8, 20 and 22). Instead of following the EIA convention for pins 2 through 8 and then connecting 20 and 22 to 1 and 9, the adapter follows its own standard, and among other things, reverses the function of pins 2 and 3.

AT Serial Adapter Cable. A 9-to-25-pin adapter cable is required to link the 9-pin serial adapter just described to the 25-pin connector on most modems. Most such cables match the adapter's nine pins to the appropriate pins on the modem, as shown by the wiring diagram in Figure 12.2.

Serial Cable Adapter. A 9-to-25-pin adapter may be used as an interface between a 25-pin cable and a 9-pin serial adapter, or between a 9-pin cable and a 25-pin modem socket.

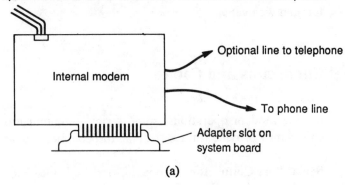

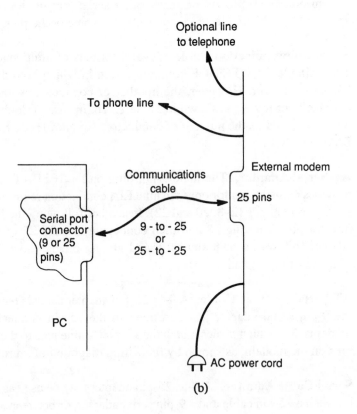

Figure 12.2. Modem interface connections: (a) Internal modem, (b) external modem, and (c) block diagram for a Hayes Smartmodem 2400.

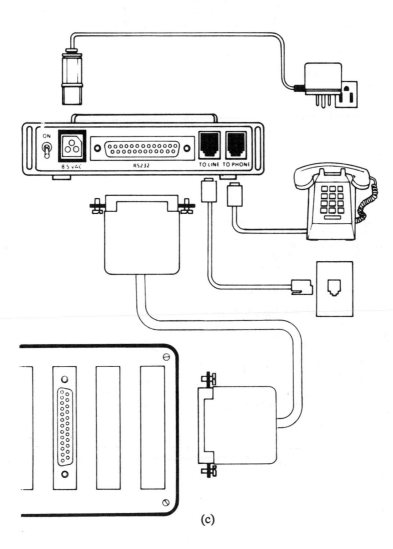

Figure 12.2   (Continued)

Table 12.1a RS-232 Serial Interface Cross-Reference Guide

EIA conductor and function *	XT async (DTE)	AT ** serial (DTE)	PS/2, EISA (DTE)	Modems Hayes (DCE)	IBM (DCE)	null	H-P serial printers § XT	AT
1. Protective ground	1			1	1		1	
2. Transmit data (to DCE)	2	3	2			3		
Receive data (from DTE)				2	2		2	3
3. Receive data (from DCE)	3	2	3			2		
Transmit data (to DTE)				3	3		3	2
4. Request to send	4	7	4	4	4			
5. Clear to send	5	8	5	5	5	20	20	20
6. Data set ready	6	6	6	6	6	20	20	20
7. Signal ground	7	5	7	7	7	7	7	7
8. Received line signal detector	8	1	8	8	8	20		
9. Reserved for data set testing + transmit current loop data (IBM) 9								
10. Reserved for data set testing								
11. Unassigned - transmit current loop data (IBM) 11								
12. Secondary rcvd. line signal detector Select alternate rate †			12	12				
13. Secondary clear to send								
14. Secondary transmitted data								
15. Transmission signal element timing			15	15 ‡				
16. Secondary received data								
17. Receiver signal element timing			17	17 ‡				
18. Unassigned + receive current loop data (IBM) 18 Analog loop test select † 18								
19. Secondary request to send								
20. Data terminal ready	20	4	20	20	20	5, 6, 8		
21. Signal quality detector Remote digital loop test select † 21								
22. Ring indicator		22	9	22	22	22		
23. Data signal rate selector				23 ‡				
24. Transmit signal element timing			24	24 ‡				
25. Unassigned - rcv. current loop return (IBM) 25 Test indicator †					25			

  * Based on *EIA Standard Interface Between Data Terminal Equipment and Data Communication Equipment Employing Serial Binary Data Interchange (EIA-232-C)*.

 ** Male 9–pin socket on AT serial adapters.

 † Bell 212A specification.

 ‡ Used by Smartmodem 2400, not used by Smartmodem 1200.

 § Hewlett–Packard laser printer serial interface shown for comparison purposes. See Chapter 13 for further details.

Table 12.1b RS-232 Conductors Found in Representative Cables

Cable	4-conductor	9-conductor	15-conductor	25-conductor
Connects pins	1, 2, 3, 7	1–8, 20	1–8, 13–15, 17, 20, 22, 24	1–25

Communication Cable Summary. Cables for the modem-to-serial port connections described above are available from IBM and others. A few representative part numbers are listed here.

Manufacturer	Part number	Description	Connector for port	modem
IBM	1502067	serial commun-ication cable	25F	25M
JDR	CBL-DB25-MF			
Radio Shack	26-250			
IBM	6450217	AT serial adapter cable	9F	25M
JDR	CBL-9-Serial			
Radio Shack	26-269			
IBM	6450242	AT serial cable adapter	9F	25M
Radio Shack	26-1388	serial port adapter	9M	25M
	26-265		9F	25F
	26-287		9M	25F

MODEM-TO-PHONE-LINE INTERFACE

Of course, both external and internal modems must be connected to the phone line for communication with the modem at the remote computer. For this purpose, the modem is supplied with a phone-line cable that terminates in a standard phone plug of the type found on any modern one- or two-line phone.

A rear-panel phone jack is found on most personal computer modems. A standard telephone may be plugged into this jack for regular voice communications, while the modem's own phone line plugs into the telephone wall outlet previously used by the phone. This configuration is simply for the convenience of the user, so that the phone line is not completely taken over by the modem. Although the phone may be used in the usual manner when the modem is not in use, it is otherwise not required for data communications work, unless the user prefers to begin communications by speaking to someone at the other end of the line.

Figure 12.3 illustrates the required connections for both external and internal modems.

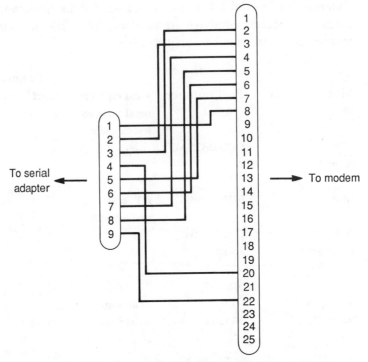

Figure 12.3. IBM AT communications cable wiring details (IBM part number 150267, Radio Shack 26-269, or equivalent).

Phone Line Cable. The interface between the modem and the phone line is identical to that required for the conventional telephone: just run a standard phone cable from the phone jack on the wall to the modem. The typical modem has two jacks on its rear panel, as indicated here:

Rear panel label	**Purpose**
To Line, Telephone Line	to link the modem to wall jack
To Phone, Telephone Set	to install a conventional telephone on same line

MODEM CONFIGURATION

It is not necessary to configure the PC to take the presence of the modem into account, but the modem itself must be configured for the system, so that it will utilize the desired communications port.

Serial Ports: COM1 through COM4

In order to send and receive data, a communications port must be opened, which is not unlike opening a file in order to read or write data in it. DOS versions prior to 3.30 supported two serial ports, identified as COM1 and COM2. Two additional ports, COM3 and COM4, are supported by DOS 3.30 and subsequent versions. Throughout this chapter, most references to COM1 and COM2 can be applied to COM3 and COM4, provided the hardware can be jumpered or switched to address these ports.

The communications software program opens a COM file with the appropriate instruction, usually making the default assumption that COM1 is the port to which the modem is connected, since most modems are configured before shipping to use that port. Of course, both hardware and software may be reconfigured for another serial port if this is required—as it would be if COM1 is already in use for some other application.

Serial Port Addresses. The serial port addresses for COM1 through COM4 are listed here.

Port name	Serial port address
1. COM1	03F8–03FF
2. COM2	02F8–02FF
3. COM3	03E8–03EF
4. COM4	02E8–02EF

ISA System Jumper Configuration. Using the old IBM Internal Modem 1200 as a typical example, two jumpers on the modem's printed circuit board determine whether COM1 or COM2 is used by the modem. When using an external modem, such as the Hayes Smartmodem 2400, you must set system configuration switches on the adapter used with the modem, not on the modem itself.

Figure 12.4 shows the jumper locations and positions for the IBM internal modem and for two representative communications adapters. If you are not already using COM1 for some other purpose (e.g., printer, plotter, or another modem), make sure the jumpers are set for COM1 operation. Otherwise, place them in the COM2 position, and reconfigure your communications software accordingly.

MCA and EISA Configuration. Modems designed for installation in MCA and EISA systems may usually be configured via software. However, if an ISA modem is installed in an EISA system, its jumpers must of course be set to COM1 or COM2 (or, if possible, COM3 or COM4).

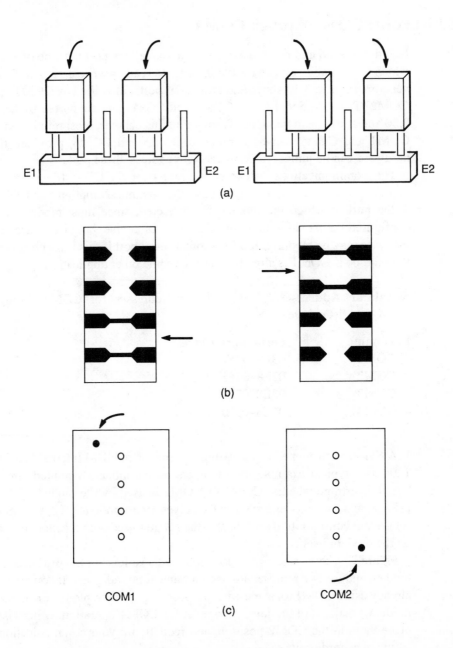

Figure 12.4. Jumpers on representative communications adapters are used for COM1 and COM2 configuration. (a) The IBM Internal modem 1200 uses two jumpers. On the AT Serial/Parallel adapter (b) and the Asynchronous Adapter (c), a single jumper determines the configuration.

COMMUNICATIONS SOFTWARE CONFIGURATION

Although every communications software program is written somewhat differently, all may be configured to take both system-interface and communications protocols into account. The process is usually begun by running the communications program and selecting a configuration option. Various screen menus are displayed, the user indicates the necessary changes, and these changes are written back to the software. The next time the program is executed, the default settings are those selected by the user during this configuration procedure.

Software configuration must take two interfaces into account: the hardware link between the user's computer and modem, and the communications link between the user's modem and the modem at the other end of the phone line. Both procedures are described here in general terms.

System Interface

Modifications to the default configuration are usually made by changing these values in a screen menu selected via an option called configuration or something similar. The communications program documentation will have to be consulted for specific details on how to proceed. Often this is done by moving the cursor to the listing you want to change and then pressing another key to toggle between selections. Here are a few of the listings that may be seen:

Menu listing	Use to select
Communications Port	COM1 or COM2 (add COM3 or COM4 on MCA and EISA configuration software)
Printer Interface	serial or parallel printer
Dialing Method	tone (touch tone) or pulse (rotary dial)
Display	monochrome or color display
Disk Drives	number of drives available for communications purposes

For routine operation, the default values selected by the software publisher are probably correct, with the possible exception of the default display, which may have to be changed to suit your PC configuration.

COMMUNICATIONS PROTOCOL

Since there are many ways to transmit a series of characters across a phone line, the modems at both ends must agree on how this will be done. This is often referred to as the communications protocol, where protocol means an agreement—in this case, a mutually acceptable configuration for transmitting data.

Character Format

One of the most important things to agree on is the character format—the precise number of bits that are to be used for the transmission of each character. Since the standard ASCII character set comprises only seven bits, there is no need to transmit all eight bits used by most computers for internal processing. However, eight bits can—in fact, must—be used to transmit the complete extended-character set or for any other application requiring the transmission of 256 discrete values.

Start/Stop Bits. Since serial data is sent one bit at a time over a single phone line, one or two additional bits may be inserted to mark the beginning and end of each character. Depending on the software, these may be called start bits or start/stop bits.

Parity Bit. In addition, space for a parity bit may be provided as part of an error-checking system, using space, odd, mark, even, or no parity, each of which is briefly described here.

Parity	Explanation
space	The parity bit is always set at 0.
odd	The parity bit's value is 0 if there is an odd number of 1s in the transmitted character. If the number of 1s is even, then the value of the parity bit is set to 1. Thus the quantity of transmitted 1 bits is always odd.
mark	The parity bit is always set at 1.
even	The parity bit's value is 0 if there is an even number of 1s in the transmitted character. If the number of 1s is odd, then the value of the parity bit is set to 1. Thus the quantity of transmitted 1 bits is always even.
none	A parity bit is not transmitted.

Except for the no-parity configuration, an error may be detected if the transmission of bits does not conform to the parity protocol.

A		B		C		D		E		F		G	
p		p		p		p		p		p		p	
1100	0001	1100	0010	0100	0011	1100	0100	0100	0101	0100	0110	1100	0111
⊥		T		C		—		E		F		⊩	

p = parity bit

Figure 12.5. An example of what might happen to a message transmitted under one format and received under another. The character string "ABCDEFG" is sent with seven character bits and odd parity. Not that a parity bit of 1 is transmitted with characters A, B, D and G. Therefore, if the received string is assumed to contain eight character bits, meaningless extended-character set symbols will appear in place of these characters.

The transmitted sequence is always as follows: start bit, character bits, parity bit (if any), stop bit (if any). Table 12.2 lists typical character formats, and Figure 12.5 illustrates what might happen if there were some disagreement between protocols.

A deliberate protocol mismatch might be used to advantage in transmitting a text file (such as Wordstar) in which the final character in each word has its high bit set to 1. By either transmitting or receiving the file with only seven character bits, the high bit is ignored, and all characters are received with their straight ASCII values. However, this also means that various text formatting control characters in the extended character set will be translated into meaningless ASCII characters in the received text. No doubt they can be ignored by the recipient, but it would be better to strip documents of such characters before transmission.

Table 12.2 Typical Character Formats

Kind of bits	Number of transmitted bits per character							
Character	7	7	7	7	8	8	8	8
Parity	0	0	1	1	0	0	1	1
Start	1	1	1	1	1	1	1	1
Stop	0	1	0	1	0	1	0	1
Total	8	9	9	10	9	10	10	11

SOME COMMUNICATIONS NOMENCLATURE

In most modem-related applications, the following terms are commonly encountered, and are frequently either misunderstood or misdefined.

Simplex

In communications jargon, the term refers to a communications channel in which information flows in one direction only. A radio broadcast is a typical example. Simplex communication is not covered in this book.

Duplex

As the term suggests, duplex refers to a two-way communications channel. The two duplex modes in popular use are described here.

Full Duplex. Often simply called duplex, the term describes a communications link that can simultaneously pass data in two directions. A duplex transmission is analogous to the conventional voice telephone system, which allows the parties at both ends to talk and listen simultaneously.

Half Duplex. By contrast, a half-duplex transmission permits communication in only one direction at a time. This may be compared to a CB radio transmission, where only one party may talk at a time. Consequently, the transmission flows first in one direction, and then in the other, but never in both directions simultaneously.

Multiplex. This term is used to describe a communications link in which multiple transmissions are possible. Multiplex is also not covered here.

Echo Modes

There are two ways in which a transmitted character may be displayed on the user's screen.

Local Echo. The sending modem may immediately return, or "echo," each character back to the local display screen, as it is simultaneously being transmitted to the receiving modem. Obviously, this echo mode is required prior to transmission, in order for the user's own keystrokes to be seen to verify that the local system is fully operational.

Remote Echo. Once a communications link has been made between modems, the remote system may echo each received character back to the sender, thus verifying that the entire transmission system is operating properly. Of course, this remote echo mode is only valid in the full-duplex mode, since half-duplex precludes the instantaneous two-way flow of data.

Echo Mode Conflicts. From the above, it should be clear that in a half-duplex system, each modem must be in the local echo mode, and that in a full-duplex system, the two modems must agree on the echo mode. When the brief message "Hello" is transmitted under full duplex, the display seen on the sender's screen depends on the echo mode at each end of the communication chain.

Display seen by sender	Echo mode setting at transmitter	receiver	Display seen by receiver
(blank screen)	Off	Off	Hello
Hello	Off	On	Hello
Hello	On	Off	Hello
HHeelllloo	On	On	Hello

The blank screen appears because the sender expects an echo, but this is not sent back by the receiving modem. The double display (HHeelllloo) appears because the sender does not expect an echo but gets it anyway. But in all cases, the display at the receiving modem is not affected by the echo mode. If either error condition is noted, refer to the section on echo mode changes (page 560).

Baud

Strictly speaking, the baud (after J. M. E. Baudot) indicates the number of discrete signal changes per second. In binary transmission, each such change represents a single bit, so in popular usage the term has become synonymous with bits per second. Although many transmission rates are possible, 300, 1,200, and 2,400 baud are those commonly encountered. Many modems recognize the incoming rate and automatically adjust downward to meet it. However, a modem cannot exceed its own maximum rate, so one with a 300-baud maximum cannot adjust to handle 1,200- or 2,400-baud reception.

MODEM DIAGNOSTICS

Since there is such a wide variety of software available commercially, it's impossible to describe the particular details of a single program here, without thereby alienating the reader who uses some other program. Therefore, whenever communications software support is required for modem diagnostics, the brief BASIC program in Listing 12.1 will be used.

Preliminary Note: If a procedure described below does not seem to produce the expected results, try turning the modem off and then back on again. This should restore any internal settings that may be improperly set as a result of an earlier experiment. In the case of an internal modem, turn the system power off and back on again—do not simply reboot.

Hardware-Related Problems

If the communications software reports that the modem is unavailable, the problem may very well be that the modem is configured for the wrong communications port. As an example, when the Hayes Smartcom II communications software assumes COM1 is to be used, but the modem is configured for COM2 or highter, the following error messages are seen at the bottom of the display screen:

```
                       Smartmodem:       UNAVAILABLE
Smartmodem Not Responding on COM1:       Press F1 To Continue
```

Listing 12.1 A Simple BASIC Communications Program

COM1 version	COM2	COM2	COM4
40 SCREEN 0,0: WIDTH 80			
70 KEY OFF: CLS: CLOSE			
72 OUT &H3FC, 4	&H2FC, 4	&H3EC, 4	&H2EC, 4
73 FOR I = 1 TO 500: NEXT			
74 OUT &H3FC, 0	&H2FC, 0	&H3EC, 0	&H2EC, 0
90 DEFINT A-Z			
110 FALSE = 0: TRUE = NOT FALSE			
130 XOFF$ = CHR$(19): XON$ = CHR$(17)			
160 OPEN "COM1:1200,O,7,,RS,CS,DS" AS #1			
	COM2:	COM3:	COM4:
200 LOCATE ,,1			
400 PAUSE = FALSE: ON ERROR GOTO 9000			
510 B$ = INKEY$: IF B$ <> "" THEN PRINT #1, B$:			
530 IF EOF(1) THEN 510			
570 IF LOC(1) > 128 THEN PAUSE = TRUE: PRINT #1, XOFF$;			
590 A$ = INPUT$(LOC(1),#1)			
620 LFP = 0			
630 LFP = INSTR(LFP+1, A$, CHR$(10))			
640 IF LFP>0 THEN A$ = LEFT$(A$,LFP-1)			
+ RIGHT$(A$,LEN(A$)-LFP): GOTO 630			
660 PRINT A$;: IF LOC(1)>0 THEN 570			
690 IF PAUSE THEN PAUSE = FALSE: PRINT #1, XON$;			
710 GOTO 510			
9000 PRINT "Error Nr.";ERR: RESUME			

Other software will respond in a similar manner, and the solution is to reconfigure the internal modem or the adapter used with an external modem, or to reconfigure the software instead. Follow the general procedure described in the section on modem or software configuration (page 532 or 535), as appropriate.

As a quick configuration check, at the DOS prompt enter the BASIC mode by typing BASIC or BASICA, and then run the following one-line BASIC program:

```
100 OPEN "COMx:" as #1: BEEP
```

where x = 1 to 4, to indicate COM1 to COM4.

If the beep is heard, then the number entered in place of the lowercase letter x agrees with the communications port in use. However, the following error message may be seen:

```
Device Timeout in 100
```

This indicates that no device in your system is configured for the communications port you indicated.

Note that a successful test only verifies that there is some device in your system configured for the indicated port number—it does not tell you that the device is the modem. Presumably it is, but if you have some other device installed in one the COMx positions and the modem in the other, the test is not conclusive.

Device Conflict. A device conflict exists if two devices attempt to use the same port. This could happen if two adapters are installed and both are configured for the same communications port.

The Diagnostics diskette can be used to verify the presence of one or two communications ports, and to ascertain whether or not the modem is interfaced to the proper port. To do this, boot the system with the Diagnostics diskette in place and then select Option 0.

In the PC or XT display of the list of installed devices, look for devices such as those seen here:

```
ASYNC COMMUNICATIONS ADAPTER (or some other serial device)
ALT. INTERNAL MODEM 1200 (or some other ALT. serial device)
```

or

```
ALT. ASYNC COMMUNICATIONS ADAPTER
INTERNAL MODEM 1200
```

In the AT, the list may look like this:

```
SERIAL/PARALLEL ADAPTER
          - SERIAL PORT
ALTERNATE SERIAL/PARALLEL ADAPTER
          - SERIAL PORT
```

The ALT or ALTERNATE prefix indicates that the device's serial port is configured as COM2. When no prefix is seen, the port is configured as COM1. If two serial devices are installed but only one shows up in the list of installed devices, then both are configured for the same port. Here are two examples of what may be seen, and what should be done about it.

Display shows	Problem: both devices are configured as	Solution: reconfigure one of them to become
Device only	COM1	COM2
ALT. device only	COM2	COM1

In this test, note that an external modem will never show up on the list of installed devices. For example, the above AT list indicates a system with two properly configured ports but does not indicate which one the external modem may be connected to. Therefore, a visual inspection must be made. Assuming both ports are unused, simply attach the external modem to the one you want to use, and make sure the communications software is configured accordingly.

MCA and EISA Device Conflicts. Device conflicts (or "resource conflicts") in EISA and MCA systems are usually flagged by an asterisk in the left-hand (EISA) or right-hand (MCA) margin of the configuration utility display.

Diagnostics Diskette for the Internal Modem 1200

The IBM Internal Modem 1200 is supplied with its own diagnostics diskette. The diskette cannot be used to test an external modem, which requires the presence of an adapter for its interface to the PC system. The adapter isolates the modem from the diagnostics diskette, and an 1101 error code is displayed if the internal modem diagnostics program is run in conjunction with an external modem.

There are two diagnostics programs on the internal modem diagnostics diskette. Program USIM212.DGS is new, and US1SRL.DGS is an updated version of the US0SRL.DGS section of the main Diagnostics diskette.

Once these files are added to the main Diagnostics diskette, the internal modem will be tested as part of the regular diagnostics procedure. The merging procedure is described in Chapter 3, in the section on merging diagnostics diskettes (p. 43). To test the internal modem without running all the other tests, use a copy of just the modem diskette itself. Whether modem diagnostics are run separately or as part of a complete system checkout, the following is a description of what will be seen on screen.

To run the internal modem diagnostics tests, boot the system with the diagnostics diskette in drive A. The usual beep should be heard as the system boots on, followed by a higher-pitched beep as each new screen display is seen. If the beeps are not heard, it may be that the speaker/modem connection is faulty. This will be checked in a later test.

The screen display offers various options, and you should select option 0, Run Diagnostics Routines. The next screen will be similar to the one seen here:

```
THE INSTALLED DEVICES ARE
S ASYNC COMMUNICATIONS ADAPTER
S ALT. INTERNAL MODEM 1200
IS THIS LIST CORRECT (Y/N)?
```

The display indicates there are two serial ports in the system unit, and that the internal modem is connected to the COM2 port. If this configuration is incorrect, then turn the system off, reconfigure the modem and the other adapter as required, reboot, and answer the above question with Y or y. The next screen display offers various system checkout options. Choose the following option:

```
0 - RUN TESTS ONE TIME
```

The following display is seen:

```
SYSTEM UNIT 1100
THIS TEST TAKES UP TO TWO MINUTES
PLEASE STAND BY
```

If an error code (11xx) is seen during this test, make a note of the complete code, and return the modem for servicing. Remember that 1100 simply means the test has been completed without the detection of any errors. Make sure to give the service center the list of displayed error codes. For your reference, you can find the list of possible error codes in Appendix C. However, each of these 11xx codes indicates a problem that is not user-serviceable.

Speaker Tests. If no errors are encountered, the next display appears (the Result column indicates the sound that will be heard in response to each option, but is not seen on the screen):

Speaker Tests	Result
0 - Generate sound from SYSTEM	three beeps, then one beep
1 - Generate sound from MODEM	dial tone and three beeps
9 - BYPASS speaker test	

When choosing one of the first two options, it is assumed that you have already verified that the system speaker itself is working by noting the start-up beep and the other beeps mentioned prior to this section. If you did not hear any of these previously discussed beeps, then double-check the speaker connections before choosing one of the options on the screen. If these beeps were heard as expected, then proceed with the modem test.

To make sure the modem is capable of activating the system speaker, select option 0 first and listen for the series of three beeps followed by one beep. If all the previous beeps were heard, failure to hear this particular series of beeps indicates a fault in the modem, which must be serviced.

Next, select option 1 and listen for a dial tone and three beeps, such as those that can be heard by pressing the 2 key on a touch-tone phone three times. The dial tone is heard only if the modem is connected to a working phone line; the three beeps are heard regardless of whether or not the modem is connected.

If this test fails, double-check the connection of the modem speaker leads to the system speaker, using Figure 12.1 as a guide. Once these tests are concluded successfully, select option 9 to end (BYPASS) the speaker tests. The next screen display is:

```
INTERNAL TESTS SUCCESSFUL
0 - Run Problem Determination Tests
9 - EXIT Diagnostic
```

ACE Settings. Select option 0 to display the modem's default ACE (asynchronous communication element) settings, which are displayed as follows:

```
The modem's ACE is set as follows:
 Baud Rate = 1200

 Word Length = 7
 Parity Option = Odd
 Stop Bits = 1
```

```
PROBLEM DETERMINATION TEST OPTIONS


0 - Change the modem's ACE settings
1 - Enter interactive mode
9 - EXIT Diagnostic
```

To change any of these settings, select option 0 and follow the instructions that are seen on screen. Then select option 1 for the following display:

```
INTERACTIVE MODE ENTERED
All keystrokes are sent to the
modem. All characters received
from the modem are displayed.
```

Type any characters on the keyboard and note that these are correctly displayed on screen. Press Ctrl + Break to conclude the interactive keyboard/display test. Then select option 9 to exit this section of the diagnostics program. The following display appears briefly, and then the list of installed devices reappears.

Screen display is	if modem is configured as
SYSTEM UNIT 4800	COM1
SYSTEM UNIT 4900	COM2

As before, any 48xx or 49xx code (other than xx = 00) should be noted, and the modem should be removed for authorized servicing.

External Modem Diagnostics

As noted earlier, the main Diagnostics diskette limits itself to checking the adapter whose serial port may be used for a modem interface. In fact, the external modem itself should be disconnected from the serial port during diagnostics testing.

Wrap Plug. If you are using an IBM communications adapter cable, it came with a wrap plug, as shown in Figure 12.6. Prior to running the diagnostics program, disconnect the modem and substitute the wrap plug in its place. This enables the communications cable itself to be included in the diagnostics testing procedure. If the wrap plug is not available, disconnect the cable at the adapter end instead of at the modem.

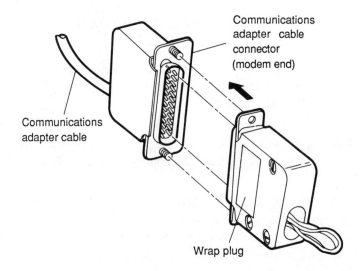

Communications
adapter cable
connector
(modem end)

Communications
adapter cable

Wrap plug

Figure 12.6.   To include the communications cable in the diagnostic diskette tests, unplug the external modem and install the wrap plug in its place.

Modem System Tests

In addition to the diskette-based diagnostics tests described above, many modems have a built-in test facility that may be used to check various segments of the modem/phone line link between two computers. Testing terminology and procedures vary from one manufacturer to another, and even from one modem model to another made by the same manufacturer. Therefore, if the procedures described below do not work, consult your own modem user's manual to find out if the specific test is indeed supported, and if so, if its implementation differs from that described here.

Use of Communications Program.   In order to use either the IBM or AT command sets described below, you must first execute a communications program which supports the set. If this is not available, the IBM modem GTO (*Guide to Operations*) manual offers a BASIC program which may be used instead. The program is listed in the GTO's table of contents as "A Basic Input/Output Program," and it also appears in Appendix C of the IBM BASIC manual. An abbreviated version is offered here, containing some simplifications and omitting those program lines containing remarks only.

The BASIC Input/Output Program Listing.   As can be seen in Listing 12.1, the program is written for use with a modem attached to the COM1 port. If the COM2 port is used instead, substitute the two lines in the right-hand column for those seen in the main listing, and change line 160 accordingly. Line 160 has also been modified to accommodate Hayes-compatible modems, and line 640 has been corrected to agree with a recent IBM errata sheet.

If you plan to use this program, enter the BASIC mode, type in the lines, and save the program on diskette for later use in conjunction with the test procedures described below. If you are testing an IBM modem, use the IBM command set. For most other modems, the AT command set should be used. In either case, a complete command set implements all the functions required for modem communications. Here, however, we shall only discuss those commands needed for test purposes.

IBM Command Set. These commands are used for checking IBM internal and external modems. As described here, the tests will run on either style device. However, the tests may also be run on the external modem via front-panel switches. These switches are described in detail in the GTO manual accompanying the modem, and are not covered further in this chapter.

The IBM command set comprises various two-letter keyboard inputs that the user types to instruct the modem to perform various testing and routine communication tasks. For the tests described here, the letters are always TE followed by a space and a one-digit number. The Diagnostics diskette is not used for these tests.

AT (ATtention) Command Set. Note that the initials have nothing to do with the IBM Personal Computer AT. The following test descriptions are based on observations made while running the tests on a Hayes external Smartmodem 2400, and may be partially or completely supported on various Hayes-compatible modems. For example, IBM modems support most AT commands, but not those used for testing. The Hayes 1200 series supports only three of the tests, and uses a different set of keystrokes to implement each of the commands. To determine which, if any, AT tests will run on your modem, look in its User's Manual to see if the test is listed. If it is, use the keystrokes as described there, in place of those used here. If the test is not described in your manual, it probably won't work.

Test Nomenclature. In these tests, the following nomenclature is used:

local   pertaining to your own system
remote   pertaining to the system at another location

terminal	PC keyboard and display, when used in conjunction with a modem
DTE	data terminal equipment (the PC)
DCE	data communication equipment (the modem)

For the benefit of users who are not experienced in communications work, Table 12.3 offers a simplified set of test names to help clarify what it is that is being tested. For each test, the first part of the descriptive name indicates the location where the test originates, and the word "link" indicates that the communications link—that is, the phone line—is included in the test.

Testing Procedure

This section supplies general background information helpful in running the modem diagnostics tests. It should be read in its entirety before you try any of the procedures described below. When you are ready to run these tests for the first time, remember that the BASIC Input/Output program (or equivalent) must be run first.

Tests 2 through 5 will require the presence of a remote modem and the participation of an operator at the remote location. For the purposes of our explanation, the remote phone number is assumed to be a local number, 123-4567 (the use of a hyphen or a space between the third and fourth digit is optional). Of course, you must change the phone number as required, and begin with 1, or 1 and the area code, if needed. Unless otherwise noted, the

Table 12.3 Modem Test Name Guide

| | Test name used here | Name used to describe test with | |
		IBM command set *	AT command set **
–	Wake–Up	Wake Up Sequence Test	(not described)
0	Local DCE	Analog Loop Self Test	Local Analog Loopback with Self Test
1	Local Terminal	Analog Loop Test	Local Analog Loopback
2	Remote–Terminal Link	Digital Loop Test	Local Digital Loopback
3	Local–DCE Link	Remote Digital Loop Self Test	Remote Digital Loopback with Self Test
4	Local–Terminal Link	Remote Digital Loop	Remote Digital Loopback
5	Remote–DCE Link	Digital Loop Self Test	(not implemented)

   * Taken from IBM modem *Guide to Operations*.
 ** Taken from Hayes Smartmodem 2400 *User's Guide*.

instructions given in each test should be carried out by the local operator only.

It is assumed that the remote system has successfully concluded its own local tests (0 and 1, as described below) before tests 2 through 5 are run. Of course, either the BASIC Communications program or some other communications software must be used at both locations in conjunction with the command set.

In the following procedures, use the IBM command or the equivalent AT command, depending on which modem you are using.

On-Line State. In the on-line state, it is assumed that a communications link is already established, and that the modem is either ready to send or receive data, or is actually doing so. Therefore, if a command is issued at the keyboard, it will be interpreted as just another few keystrokes to be transmitted. Accordingly, you must return the modem to its command state before typing anything that is to be interpreted as a command.

Command State. When a modem is in its command (or local) state, it is ready to receive commands, and is not actually on line, although the link between the two modems may still be active.

To enter the command state, do the following:

IBM tests	Press the Escape key once. In the tests described below, this action also concludes the test.
AT tests	Press the + key three times in rapid succession. In most documentation, this is shown as +++ and is referred to as the escape sequence. If the gray + key produces a beep each time it is pressed, use the other + key instead. If the +++ sequence is entered slowly, it will have no effect. In this case, press the Enter key and then press +++ again, at a faster rate.

Test-Start Procedure. With the exception of the Wake-Up test, begin each of the tests described below by issuing the appropriate test command. The test command sequence is as follows:

IBM tests	Hold down the Control key while pressing the letter N key. When you release the keys, the legend <COM> is displayed on screen. Whenever you see <COM> in the following instructions, it means you should press Ctrl + N as just described.

When <COM> appears on screen, type the letters TE (or te) and the gray number indicated in the test procedure. Do not enter a space between <COM> and TE, but do enter a space between TE and the number. Then press the Enter key. After a brief interval, the word TESTING will appear on screen.

AT Tests   Type the characters AT&T followed by the number of the test. Then press the Enter key. After a brief interval, the cursor should drop down one line on the screen.

Test-Stop Procedure. At the conclusion of each test, return to the command state as previously described.

Local Calling Procedure. To begin the first test requiring the participation of a remote system, dial the remote DCE by entering the dial command, as follows:

IBM command   **AT command**
```
<COM>DI 123-4567     ATD 123-4567 or
<COM>DI 1234567      ATD 1234567
```

where 123-4567 is the phone number of the remote terminal user.

Remote Answering Procedure. When your phone call is received, the remote terminal will display INCOMING CALL, and the remote operator should enter the appropriate Answer command:

IBM command   **AT command**
```
<COM>AN              ATA
```

As soon as this is done, the word CONNECTED should appear on both the local and the remote display screens.

Since these tests require a certain amount of coordination between the operators at the local and remote sites, a second phone line for simultaneous voice communication can be a great help. If this is not practical, then make sure that each operator allows a sufficient amount of time for the other one to enter the required command or take the necessary action.

Direct Modem-to-Modem Testing. If a second DCE/DTE system is available in the same room, it is quite easy to establish a direct connection which completely bypasses the phone system. This has the advantage of ruling out the phone line as a possible source of trouble, allows extended testing without tying up two phone numbers, and permits a single operator to run both the local and the remote system.

Unplug each modem's phone-line cable from the wall socket and link them with an inline coupler. Or simply run a single phone cable between the phone-line jacks on the two modems. To utilize this direct modem-to-modem connection, do not use the dial command as described above. Instead, open the communications link by entering the following command(s) at the local terminal:

IBM command   **AT commands**
```
<COM>OR                 AT&L1
                        ATD
```

Although the INCOMING CALL message is not displayed on the remote terminal when this command is used, the remote operator still uses the normal answer command, and all other commands remain as described below.

Hang-Up Procedure. When tests requiring a link to a remote modem are concluded, either the local or the remote operator may terminate the connection by entering the HA (hang-up) command, as follows:

IBM command   **AT command**
```
<COM>HA                 ATH
```

When either operator enters this command, the legend NO CARRIER appears on the other operator's display.

Running the Tests

At this point you should be ready to run the tests. If you have already used your modem for routine communications since turning the system on, you may wish to turn the power off and back on again to ensure that the modem is returned to its default settings.

Wake-Up Test. Before running diagnostics tests 0 through 5, prepare to "wake up" the DCE by running the BASIC communications program in Listing 12.1. Before running the program, make sure all front-panel switches on an IBM external modem are in the released position, and that the first two LED indicators (PWR and FS) are illuminated. When the program is run, the next two LEDs (DTR and DSR) should also light up.

When the cursor appears, type the following command in uppercase letters only:

IBM command   **AT command**
START   AT

When you press the Enter key you should see a message on screen, as follows:

Screen display with command set
IBM   AT
IBM PC212A   (IBM internal modem)
IBM 5841   (IBM 5841 external modem)
        OK   (any modem)

The display indicates the successful completion of the wake-up test and means that the system is ready for further tests. If the indicated display is not seen, the modem may require servicing. As a quick check, try the following command:

IBM command   **AT command**
<COM>HE   ATI

An IBM modem will display a help screen listing of all the IBM commands. A Hayes modem will display a three-digit product code, such as:

Code   **Meaning**
123   1,200-baud modem, revision 3
246   2,400-baud modem, revision 6

If you are unable to get this far, then the modem probably does require servicing.

Note: A standard format is used for each test below. The first line shows the command that starts the test. The next line shows the response that should be seen. This is followed by a blank line and then the command that ends the test. The test itself is described immediately thereafter.

Test 0: Local DCE Test. The local modem employs its own internal test-pattern generator to test itself for correct operation. No user action is required during this self-test, nothing is seen on screen, and the modem is disconnected from the phone line for the duration of the test.

IBM command	AT command
<COM> TE 0	AT&T8
TESTING	(cursor)
Escape Key	AT&T0

Let the test run for about 60 to 90 seconds, and then end it as indicated above. In either case, a screen display of the number 000 indicates the successful completion of the test. Any other number indicates the number of errors that were detected, and means that servicing is required.

Test 1: Local Terminal Test. This test checks the correct operation of your own DCE/DTE system. The characters the user types on the keyboard are sent through the local modem and immediately back to the local terminal. An error is displayed as an incorrect character.

IBM command	AT command
<COM>TE 1	AT&T1
TESTING	(cursor)
Escape Key	+++
AT&T	0

During the test, type any characters you like. Make sure the resultant screen display is correct and then conclude the test. When using the AT command set, wait for the "OK" prompt before typing AT&T0.

Note: In the tests that follow, it is assumed that you are already connected by phone line to a remote modem. If you are not connected, follow the local calling and remote answering procedures described above.

Test 2: Remote-Terminal Link Test. This test verifies that characters entered at the remote DTE are accurately transmitted to the local DCE and then echoed back to the remote terminal screen. The characters are seen at the remote terminal only.

To begin the test, enter the indicated command at the local—not the remote—terminal.

IBM test	AT test
<COM>TE 2	AT&T3
TESTING	(cursor)
Escape Key	AT&T0

As the word TESTING, or just the cursor, appears on the local screen, the remote operator may also note the appearance of a few random characters. The remote operator must now type a series of characters and verify that they are correctly displayed on the screen at that location. If they are not, there is a problem with the phone line. Note that the characters typed at the remote location are not seen on the local terminal's display. This test will also be used in conjunction with Test 5.

When the test is concluded, the remote operator may again note a few extraneous characters on screen, while the local operator sees the "OK" legend.

Test 3: Local-DCE Link Test. In this test, the local DCE sends a test pattern to the remote DCE, from which it is returned to the local DCE and checked for errors. The test checks the local DCE, the link to and from the local system, and the remote DCE. The test pattern is not seen on screen at either location.

IBM Command	AT Command
<COM> TE 3	AT&T7
TESTING	(cursor)
Escape Key	AT&T0

Let the test run for 60 to 90 seconds and then end it. The following codes may be seen:

Code	Meaning
000	The test concluded successfully.
001-255	Phone-line errors noted.
001-003 (IBM only)	The remote DTE or its cable is faulty.
004-255 (IBM only)	Phone-line errors noted.

Test 4: Local-Terminal Link Test. This test is similar in principle to test 2, the remote-terminal link test. However, the test verifies that characters entered at the local DTE are accurately transmitted to the remote DCE, and then echoed back to the local terminal screen. The characters are seen at the local terminal only.

IBM command	AT command
<COM> TE 4	AT&T6
Escape key	AT&T0

During the test, type any series of characters and verify that they are correctly displayed on your own screen. When you are finished, conclude the test.

Test 5: Remote-DCE Link Test (IBM modems only). This test is similar to the local-DCE link test (test 3), but is not implemented in the AT series of tests. The remote DCE sends a test pattern, not seen on either screen, to the local DCE, from which it is returned to the remote DCE and automatically checked for errors. The test checks the remote DCE, the link to and from the local system, and the local DCE.

To begin this test, the remote operator must first initiate test 2 at that location by entering the following:

```
<COM>TE 2
```

If you are already connected to the remote modem, but lack a second phone line for voice coordination of this procedure, you may find it easier to hang up, redial, wait a prearranged interval during which the remote operator initiates test 2, and then begin the test. In either case, begin it by entering

```
<COM> TE 5
```

If you begin test 5 before the remote operator has the chance to begin test 2, the remote terminal will display a series of uppercase UUUUUUUs for the duration of the test.

Let the test run for a minute or two and then conclude it by pressing the Escape key. The following codes may be seen:

Code	Meaning
000	The test concluded successfully.
001-003	The remote DTE is faulty.
004-998	There is a problem with the phone line.
999	The remote operator did not initiate test 2.

Figure 12.7 summarizes the elements in the complete communications link that are checked by each of the tests described above.

Test Error Resolution. If test 0 or test 1 fails, the problem is probably on your PC's system board, which should be serviced. If your own DCE is unable to dial out or to respond to the remote carrier signal, then it requires servicing.

If the problem appears to be at the remote location, then the equipment there must be checked. An obvious double check at the local level is to try communicating with some other remote system and note the results.

Phone-line problems may be sporadic or chronic. The occasional problem with a noise burst on the phone line may be sufficient to disrupt a test or

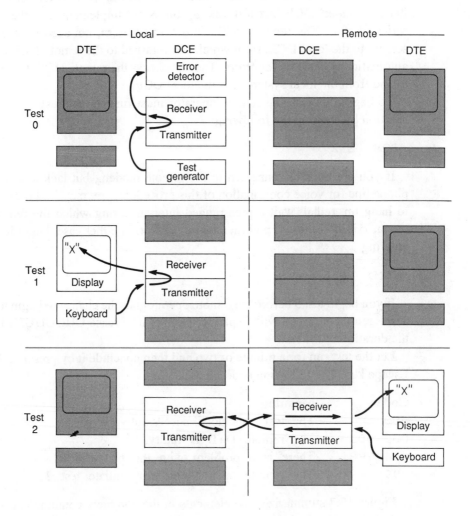

Figure 12.7. Modem tests 0 through 5 check the components of the complete communication link that are seen in the illustrations.

Test 0: local DCE (modem)
Test 1: local terminal
Test 2: remote terminal link
Test 3: local DCE link
Test 4: local terminal link
Test 5: remote DCE link

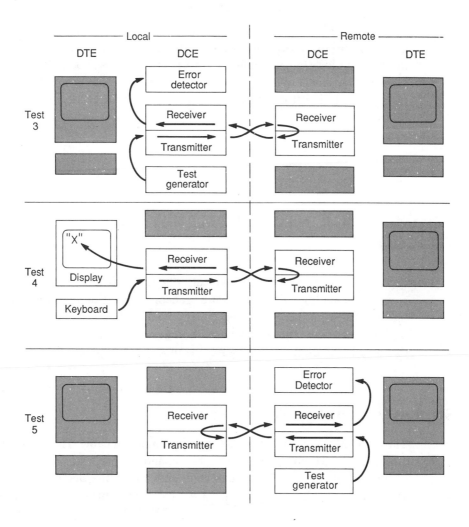

Figure 12.7.   (*Continued*)

any other transmission, yet not lend itself to being remedied by servicing. However, a chronic phone-line problem may require the attention of the phone company. To double-check a line that consistently fails, try using the line for regular voice communication. Noise on the line will verify that it is faulty. But if voice communication remains clear, the problem would seem to be in a DTE or DCE at either end of the line.

To further isolate the problem, consider the obvious: if all transmissions to several different systems fail, the problem is at the local system. If only transmissions to a specific location fail, the problem is at that location. Once the problem location is identified, further localization should be possible. If the DTE segment of the communications system—that is, the PC—functions properly in all its other capacities, then the DCE—the modem—is faulty.

COMMUNICATION LINE PROBLEM-SOLVING TECHNIQUES

Since modem-to-modem communication is done via an audio signal sent over the phone line, it follows that extraneous signals on that same phone line may cause problems, ranging from garbled characters to the termination of the connection. The following section describes a few of the problems that may be encountered during routine modem operations.

Secondary Phone-Line Termination

The standard single-line phone uses a four-conductor cable. The conductors are usually color coded red, green, black, and yellow. The red and green conductors are used as the primary communications line, and the black and yellow are available for other purposes, such as illuminating a line-in-use light on an extension phone or accommodating a secondary phone line.

When a modem is installed on such a phone line, it automatically uses the red and green conductors for communications via the primary phone line. If the black and yellow conductors are in use for a secondary line, an IBM modem will place this line out of service for the duration of the modem communication. Other modems may or may not do the same thing, depending on their internal design.

To prevent interruption of the secondary line, use a two-conductor line (red and green only) between the modem and the phone jack on the wall. Since doing this removes the black and yellow conductors from use by the modem, the telephone jack on its rear panel will now support only the primary phone line. However, a secondary phone installed elsewhere will no longer be disabled when the modem is in use.

Call-Waiting Interruption

Some phones have a call-waiting feature in which a beep is heard during a conversation to indicate that another party is attempting to place a call to the phone with the call-waiting feature. If the beep occurs during modem communications, it will disrupt the transmission.

In many areas of the country, the call-waiting feature can be suspended for the duration of a modem transmission by dialing a special number prior to beginning modem operation. The procedure is as follows. On touch-tone phones, dial *70, and on rotary-dial phones, dial 1170. Listen for a double beep, followed by the usual dial tone. Then proceed with your modem communication in the usual manner.

Ask your local phone company whether this service is available. If it is not, you may be able to prevent the loss of your connection by reconfiguring your communications software for a longer interval between carrier loss and hang-up. Even so, the call-waiting beep may still garble part of your transmission.

Call-forwarding is another option to be considered. With your incoming calls automatically forwarded to another number, the call-waiting-beep problem is eliminated. Of course, this means you—and not the remote user—must originate all modem communications for as long as call-forwarding is in effect.

If none of these solutions works for your system, then you will have to decide whether to cancel the call-waiting feature itself or put up with the possibility of modem errors.

Extension Phone Interruptions

If an extension phone is picked up while modem communications are in progress, it's quite possible that related noise will distort or terminate the transmission. This will certainly occur if the person on the extension attempts to dial out. The solution is simple, if not foolproof. If a modem-equipped phone is part of a multiphone system, alert coworkers to check before dialing.

Carrier-Loss Problems

If phone service is interrupted during modem communications, the loss of the carrier signal is usually indicated by a message such as NO CARRIER or CARRIER LOSS. This may be caused by a variety of problems, from a call-waiting interruption, to noise on the line, to a loose connection at the local or remote facility. Usually the solution is to redial and try again. Recurrent carrier-loss problems, of course, need to be remedied. This requires a series of steps to isolate the source of the problem and then take the necessary corrective action.

Screen-Display Problems

Depending on the echo mode in use, each terminal may display the correct characters, double characters, or nothing at all. For further information, reread the echo mode section in this chapter. The default value for IBM modems is echo mode 1.

Echo mode changes. While using the IBM command set, the echo mode may be changed as follows:

This command	echoes this to the local terminal
<COM>EC 0	nothing
<COM>EC 1	commands only
<COM>EC 2	transmitted data and the <COM> display, but not the command following the <COM> display
<COM>EC 3	everything

For the following echo-related problems, try the echo command given here:

If you see this	Use this command
No transmitted data	<COM>EC 3
Double entries	
for commands (prior to a data	
connection)	<COM>EC 2
for data (after a data connection)	<COM>EC 1
for commands and data (after a data	
connection)	<COM>EC 0

Use of a Null Modem

A null modem is, in fact, no modem at all, but simply a cable connection between the serial ports on two nearby computers. In Table 12.1 note the following pin connections, which are especially significant for null modem operations.

Pin number	Function
2	transmitted data
3	received data

In any DTE/DCE to DCE/DTE system, transmitted data from pin 2 on the local equipment eventually reaches pin 3 on the remote equipment (and, of course, the reverse is also true). In fact, and at the risk of gross oversimplification, the whole communications link is nothing more than a sophisticated way of making sure pins 2 and 3 are connected properly.

When the two computers are in the same area, two-way communication is possible via a multiconductor cable in which the connections between these pins are reversed. The cable runs directly from one serial port to another, completely bypassing the modem interface that is required when a phone line separates the PCs.

The null modem is often nothing more than an adapter plug, such as the one seen in Figure 12.8, which is attached to one end of the cable that will link the two. Note that connections between pins 2 and 3 are reversed, while other conductors are simply linked, as seen in the illustration. The null modem could also be in the form of a cable in which the same reversal takes place at one end. However, this can be potentially confusing if the cable is later mixed up with other cables. By contrast, the null-modem adapter plug is a simple device whose presence at the back of a system unit or between two cables will be easily recognized.

For diagnostics purposes, the null modem can be used to make sure that two computers in the same area and the serial ports of those two PCs are functioning properly, and testing can be done without tying up a phone line. To use the null modem, make the necessary connection between the two serial port connectors, and run the BASIC communications program presented earlier in this chapter (Listing 12.1).

Characters typed at one DTE are seen on the other DTE's display. To see the entered characters at the same DTE where they are being typed in, add the following line to the program at both locations:

```
520 PRINT B$;
```

While using the null modem makes for a less-flexible operation than using actual modems and the IBM command set or other communications

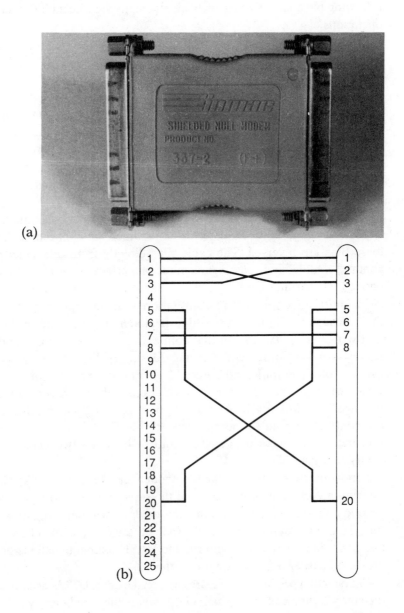

Figure 12.8. A null modem. (a) Typical null modem built into an adapter plug. (b) The pin connections within the plug.

software, the null modem may be of some use in doing preliminary troubleshooting work.

A few representative null modems are listed here.

Manufacturer	Model number	Connectors	
Inmac	530553M-M	25M	25M
	530554F-	F25	F25F
	530555M-	F25M	25F
Radio Shack	24-1496	25M	25F
	26-264	9M	9F

13

PRINTERS

Most of this chapter handles printers and printer problems in a way that applies equally to dot-matrix, printwheel, and laser printers. However, since the laser printer offers facilities (and problems) not available on traditional printers, the separate Laser Printers section beginning on page 593 should be consulted or ignored, as appropriate.

From the perspective of the user, the printer is a one-way communications device; it simply receives data and delivers a printed version of that data. The printer is, however, a two-way communicator, for it also sends information back to the computer. This information consists of various housekeeping functions that keep the computer informed about the status of the printer:

Signal from printer	Meaning
acknowledge	previous data received, ready for more
busy	off line or printing previously sent data
error	error, off line, or out of paper
out of paper	out of paper
select	printer is on/off line

Because of the two-way communications link, some comparisons to the modem may be made. In fact, many of the early sections of this chapter are quite similar in general layout, though of course not in particulars, to several sections in Chapter 12.

Several IBM and Hewlett-Packard printers are used to illustrate various points throughout this chapter. Needless to say, switch settings and test sequences will be somewhat different on other printers. However, the same general procedures still apply, and the appropriate user's manual should be consulted for system-specific details.

PRINTER/COMPUTER INTERFACE

Like the modem, the printer might receive data serially, that is, one bit at a time. However, the printer is usually quite near the PC, so there is little problem in establishing a parallel transmission system in which data is sent one byte at a time. Since a byte comprises eight bits, this means there must be eight data lines between the computer and the printer, plus separate lines for the various housekeeping functions listed above.

A parallel communications link is illustrated in Figure 13.1, where for simplicity only the data links are shown. From the illustration it should be

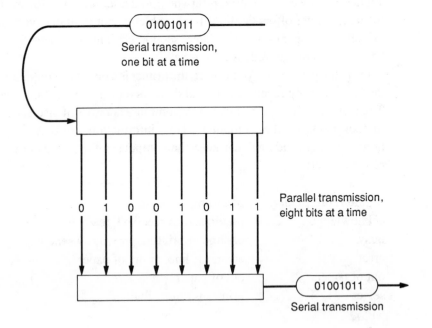

Figure 13.1. Parallel communication allows data to be transmission one byte (eight bits) at a time. For simplicity, only the data links are shown here.

clear that parallel communications via modem between two remote computers would be complex indeed. Transmitting a full byte of data, plus necessary housekeeping information, would require the use of more than eight telephone lines connected to more than eight modems at each end of the link. But when that link is only a few feet in length, a connection such as the one shown in Figure 13.1 is a very practical alternative.

Parallel Printer

The advantage of parallel communication is speed; one byte is transmitted in about the time it takes a serial device to transmit one bit. The disadvantage of requiring more communication lines between devices is of no practical consequence in the typical short-run parallel printer cable, where a single multiconductor cable replaces the entire DCE–phone-line–DCE link described in the previous chapter.

A parallel printer may be connected to the PC via any convenient parallel-port connector. Such a port is found on various adapters, as follows:

This adapter (abbreviation)	provides connections for
ISA Monochrome Display and Printer Adapter (MDA)	Monochrome display and parallel printer
ISA Printer Adapter (PA)	Parallel printer only
AT Serial/Parallel Adapter (S/P)	Parallel printer and serial device
Parallel port	(built into PS/2 (ISA and MCA) and EISA system boards)
Many non-IBM adapters	Various devices

The parallel-port connector is a female-polarity socket, usually located at the bottom of the adapter plate, as shown in Figure 13.2. On PS/2 and EISA systems, a parallel port is usually an integral part of the system board, with its socket at the rear of the system unit. Note that a male-polarity plug with the same pin configuration is used on other communications adapters, such as the IBM Binary Synchronous Adapter and the Asynchronous Communications Adapter described in Chapter 12. However, these devices are not compatible with the parallel printer.

Parallel Port Addresses. The names and customary hexadecimal addresses of the three parallel ports are

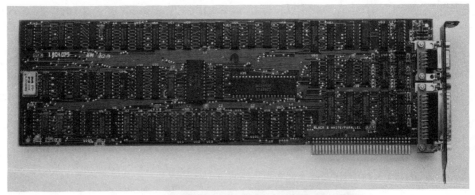

Figure 13.2. Representative ISA system parallel-printer adapters. (a) monochrome display and parallel-printer adapter; (b) printer adapter. (courtesy IBM Corp.).

Printer name	Parallel port address			
	data	status	control	reserved
1. LPT1 or PRN	03BC	03BD	03BE	03BF
2. LPT2	0378	0379	037A	037B
3. LPT3	0278	0279	027A	027B

The parallel printer port on the original IBM Monochrome Display and Printer Adapter was permanently fixed at the LPT1 address. Consequently, additional parallel ports had to be configured as LPT2 and LPT3.

On EISA systems, the built-in parallel port is usually found at the default hexadecimal address 0378, but it may be reset via configuration software to 0278 (but not to 03BC). Consequently, the EISA configuration utility may show an LPT2 and LPT3, but no LPT1 (unless the latter is present on an installed ISA adapter). However, software commands that refer to LPT1 (or PRN) are routed to the address of the first port in the system (regardless of what it's called), so the apparent absence of an LPT1 is of no practical consequence.

Serial Printer

When other design considerations make the serial design more suitable, serial printers such as the IBM Proprinter are used. Data communication to a serial printer approximates communication to a modem, and, in fact, a serial printer may be connected to the serial port described in Chapter 12 or to an asynchronous communications adapter. As Figure 13.3 illustrates, an asynchronous communications adapter resembles the parallel printer adapter shown in Figure 13.2, except that its connector is a male-polarity plug.

Serial port addresses were given in Chapter 12 (page 533).

Printer Cables and Connectors

The following cables and connectors are suitable for most computer-to-printer installations.

I/O Cable. In addition to being called simply "the printer cable," the link between any printer and the printer port is often referred to as either an input/output (or I/O) cable or as a communications cable.

Figure 13.3.   The IBM Asynchronous Communications Adapter may be used as the interface to a serial printer. (courtesy IBM Corp.).

Parallel Printer Cable. The cable between the parallel port and the printer has a 25-pin male connector at the adapter end and a 36-pin male connector at the printer end. The printer connector is often referred to as a Centronics plug, after the company that popularized its early use.

The parallel printer cable and adapter-pin connections shown in Figure 13.4a may be used with most impact and laser printers.

Serial Printer Cable. The cable configuration between a serial printer and the computer varies according to the adapter used in the computer, as shown here.

Computer adapter	Cable connector at computer end	Cable connector at printer end
Asynchronous communications	25-pin female	25-pin male
Serial adapter or port	9-pin female	25-pin male

For connecting most serial impact printers to a serial port, the AT communications cable illustrated in Chapter 12 (Figure 12.3) may be used. For Hewlett-Packard laser printers, the correct pin connections are shown in Figures 13.4b and 13.4c.

Compact Printer Connector Adapter. The special 25-to-16 pin adapter shown in Figure 13.4d is required to connect the 16-pin cable from the serial IBM Compact Printer to the 25-pin connector on the IBM Asynchronous Communications Adapter.

SYSTEM CONFIGURATION REQUIREMENTS

In this section, switch settings and other configuration requirements are discussed, using representative IBM printers as examples. Table 13.1 lists various printers, along with the cable and adapter required for each one.

Printer Configuration

As with the installation of a modem, it is not necessary to configure an ISA system board to take the presence of the printer into account. However, it may be necessary to configure the adapter so that the printer attached to it is recognized as LPT1, LPT2, or LPT3 (Line PrinTer), or, in the case of a serial printer, as COM1 or COM2.

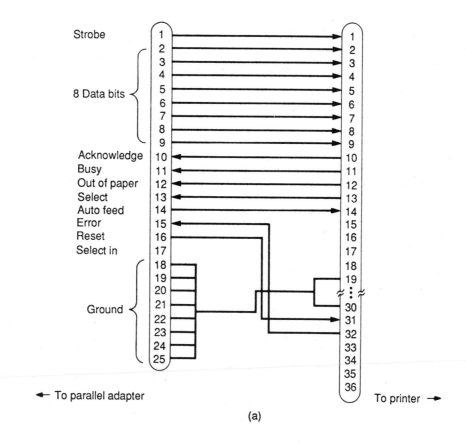

Strobe — 1

8 Data bits { 2, 3, 4, 5, 6, 7, 8, 9

Acknowledge — 10
Busy — 11
Out of paper — 12
Select — 13
Auto feed — 14
Error — 15
Reset — 16
Select in — 17

Ground { 18, 19, 20, 21, 22, 23, 24, 25

← To parallel adapter

To printer →

(a)

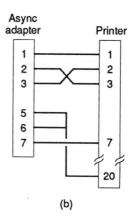

Async adapter   Printer

(b)

Figure 13.4.   Printer cable details. (a) Parallel printer cable (IBM 1525612, JDR CBL-PRINTER, or similar). Hewlett-Packard laser printer serial interface for (b) 25-pin serial port, and (c) 9-pin serial adapter cable. (d) Special adapter for interface between serial IBM Compact Printer and 25-pin serial port (IBM 6450220).

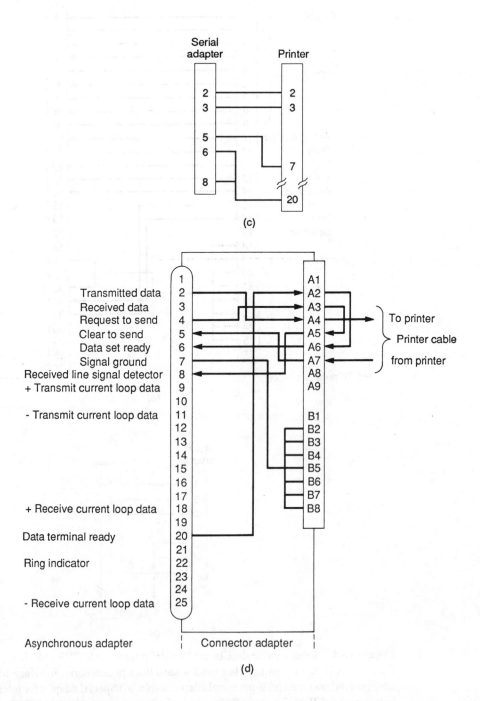

Figure 13.4 (Continued)

Table 13.1a Adapter and Cable Required for Representative Parallel and Serial Printers

IBM model	Name	Print method	Communication method	Adapter	*
3852–1	Color Printer	color ink jet	parallel	parallel	1
3852–2	Color Jetprinter	color ink jet	parallel	parallel	1
5181	Compact Printer	thermal	serial	asynchronous	2 †
5152	Graphics Printer	dot matrix	parallel	parallel	1
3812	Pageprinter	electrophotographic	serial	serial, or	2
				asynchronous	2 †
4201, 2	Proprinter	dot matrix	parallel	parallel	1 ‡
5201	Quietwriter	resistive ribbon	parallel	parallel	1
5223	Wheelprinter 1	printwheel	parallel	parallel	1
5216	Wheelprinter 2	printwheel	parallel	parallel	1 §
			or serial	serial, or	3
				asynchronous	4 †
most	laser printers	laser	parallel	parallel	1
			or serial	serial	3

    * Cross–reference to Table 13.1b.
    † Asynchronous Adapter not compatible with AT.
    ‡ Optional serial interface is available.
    § Wheelprinter 2 takes plug–in parallel or serial interface, which should be specified when ordering.

Table 13.1b Printer Cable Guide

IBM part number	Cable name	Cable connector description at the adapter pins polarity	at the printer pins polarity	*
1525612	PC Printer Cable	25 male	36 male †	1
6450102	Connector Adapter	25 female	16 male	2
6450217	Serial Adapter Cable, or	9 female	25 male	3
6450242	Serial Adapter Connector	9 female	25 male	
1502067	Communications Adapter Cable	25 female	25 male	4

    * Cross–reference to Table 13.1a.
    † 36–pin Centronics plug

Hardware Configuration

If a parallel printer is connected to an ISA system containing a single parallel printer port such as the one on either the IBM Monochrome Display and Printer Adapter or the IBM Printer (only) Adapter, the printer is automatically recognized as occupying the LPT1 position. Hardware configuration is neither necessary nor possible. If a second parallel printer is installed, it should occupy the LPT2 position. The AT permits a third printer to be installed as well.

Up to a point, the printer/port configuration is automatic; the port on the Monochrome Display and Printer Adapter (MDA) is always LPT1, while the port on the Printer Adapter (PA) may be either LPT1 or LPT2, depending on whether or not the former adapter is present. Therefore, the following configurations take effect, depending on which adapters are installed.

When these adapters are installed	The port on the MDA is	The port on the PA is
MDA only	LPT1	—
PA only	—	LPT1
Both	LPT1	LPT2

Primary and Alternate Ports. The parallel port on the AT Serial/Parallel Adapter may be configured as either a primary or an alternate port. These ports sequentially follow the port on the Monochrome Display and Printer Adapter. Therefore, the following configurations are possible.

When these adapters are installed	The port on the MDA is	On the S/P Adapter, the primary port is		alternate port is
MDA only	LPT1	—		—
S/P Adapter only	—	LPT1	or	LPT2
MDA, one S/P	LPT1	LPT2	or	LPT3
MDA, two S/Ps	LPT1	LPT2		LPT3
Two S/Ps, no MDA	—	LPT1		LPT2

As described later in this chapter, two jumpers on the Serial/Parallel Adapter are used to configure its parallel and serial connectors as primary or alternate ports.

EISA and MCA System Configuration

On most configuration utilities, the various available parallel and serial ports are identified as LPT1, LPT2, COM1, COM2, etc. Make sure the appropriate setting agrees with the actual location of your printer.

When using some early EISA configuration diskettes, the configuration screen may show the first parallel port as LPT2, although the port in fact functions as LPT1. An updated configuration diskette should correct the display.

Printer Adapters. Table 13.2 summarizes various ISA parallel and serial adapters, and indicates the configurations that are possible with each. When you install a printer, make sure the jumper on the appropriate ISA adapter card is set in the position specified by the third column of the table.

As noted earlier, MCA and EISA systems usually include one parallel port as an integral part of the system board.

Single-Printer System Configuration. In a single-printer system, the default printer configuration assumes the LPT1 port is occupied by a parallel printer. As a quick check, the BASIC LPRINT statement may be used to send characters to that printer, which does not require further identification.

Two-Printer System Configuration. When two printers are connected to a PC, the respective adapters must be configured so that one printer is LPT1

Table 13.2 ISA Adapter Cards for Use with Parallel and Serial Printers

Adapter	Compatible with	May be configured as	Note
Monochrome Display and Parallel Printer Adapter	PC, XT, AT	LPT1 (fixed)	
Printer Adapter	PC, XT	LPT1 or LPT2 (fixed)	1.
AT Serial/Parallel Adapter	AT only		
serial port		primary or alternate	2.
parallel port		primary or alternate	3.
Asynchronous Communications Adapter	PC, XT	primary or alternate	2.

Notes
1. Port becomes LPT2 if Monochrome Display and Printer Adapter is also present.
2. Primary is always COM1, alternate is always COM2.
3. Primary/alternate ports are LPT1/LPT2, or LPT2/LPT3 if Monochrome Display and Printer Adapter is also present.

and the other, LPT2 (LPT2 or LPT3 on the AT). Using Table 13.2 as a guide, make sure that the jumper on a configurable adapter is set as required. And for EISA or MCA systems, make sure your configuration screen differentiates between LPT1 and LPT2.

Printer Configuration Switches. Many impact printers have a set of internal option switches to change selected factory-set functions. The purpose of these switches varies from one printer to another, according to the specific capabilities of the printer. Figure 13.5 shows the location and Table 13.3 explains the function of the six switches found on the IBM Quietwriter Printer, models 1 and 2. Figure 13.6 illustrates the location and Table 13.4 explains the function of the seven switches found on the IBM Proprinter.

The Quietwriter is a resistive-ribbon parallel printer, while the Proprinter is a dot-matrix parallel printer. On other printers, switches similar to the

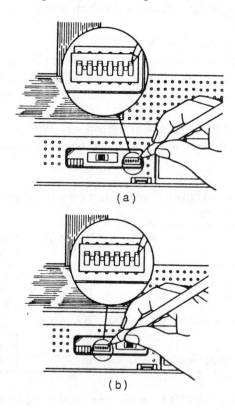

(a)

(b)

Figure 13.5.   Printer-option switches on the IBM Quietwriter (a) model 1 and (b) model 2.

Table 13.3 Positions of Printer Option Switches on IBM Quietwriter Printer

Switch	Function	Description
1. On Off †	form feed	advances paper to top of next sheet advances paper one line
2. On Off †	form length	set for 12–inch paper set for 11–inch paper
3. On Off †	line width	set for 13.2 inches set for 8 inches
4. On Off †	printer table	table 2 table 1
5. On Off †	page break	skips over bottom–of–page perforations does not skip over perforations
6. On Off ‡	ribbon save/ throughput	advances for all characters typed advances for printable characters only

† Factory setting.
‡ Option available on Quietwriter model 2 only.

ones shown in Figures 13.5 and 13.6 are usually found on the printer's system board or behind a side-panel access cover. Consult the user's manual that came with your printer to find the exact location of the internal option switches on your printer.

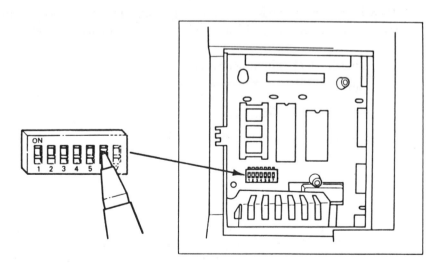

Figure 13.6. Printer-option switches on the IBM Proprinter.

Table 13.4 Positions of Printer Option Switches on IBM Proprinter

Switch	Function	Description
1. On Off †	beeper	heard when out of paper not heard when out of paper
2. On Off †	0 numeral	printed with a slash printed without a slash
3. On Off †	line feed	automatic after a carriage return not automatic after a carriage return
4. On Off †	form length	set for 12–inch paper set for 11–inch paper
5. On Off †	characters	from character set 2 from character set 1
6. On Off †	carriage return	automatic after line feed or vertical tab not automatic after line feed or vertical tab
7. On Off †	reserved	

† Factory setting.

PRINTER SELECTION METHODS

There are several methods of determining which printer will be used. Depending on the requirements of the user, printer assignment may be made via

1. a mechanical switching device
2. cable swapping
3. software switching

Each of these techniques is described here.

Switching Devices

If only one adapter is available, the cable may be routed to a switch with two or more positions, from which a separate cable leads to each printer. Selecting the desired printer is simply a matter of turning a front-panel knob or pushing a button on the switching device. Although this is certainly simple enough, it does rule out the possibility of unattended use of both printers during the execution of a program.

Laser Printer Caution.   Mechanical switching is generally not recommended, since it is possible for voltage and/or current transients to damage the printer interface as the switch is rotated. If a mechanical switch must be used, Hewlett-Packard recommends verifying that printer communication lines are protected during the switching interval or turning the printer off before using the switch.

Cable Swapping

Here, each printer is attached to its own adapter, which is configured as required for default operation. Or again, if only one adapter is available, the alternate printer is simply left unconnected. When it is necessary to make a change, the cables are swapped at the adapter connections. It's not elegant, but it works.

Software Switching

Unlike the communication software associated with most modem operations, the printer does not require its own support program. Instead, it usually operates as part of a larger-purpose program, such as a word processor or a BASIC program containing LPRINT or PRINT#*x* statements. Using the BASIC language as a convenient example, and assuming that two printers are permanently connected to their respective adapters, the following program excerpt readies the printers to receive output from the computer. Each printer is treated as though it were a storage device such as a disk or diskette file. In the first two lines below, a file is opened using the printer's name of LPT1: or LPT2:, where the designations #1 and #2 simply differentiate one printer from the other in subsequent program lines.

```
100 OPEN "LPT1:" as #1
110 OPEN "LPT2:" as #2
```

The next lines send characters to each printer, as indicated.

```
120 PRINT #1, "first line"
130 PRINT #2, "second line"
140 LPRINT "last line"
```

The first line goes to one printer, the second line goes to the other one, and the last line goes to the default printer. In other words, the LPT1 printer prints the "first line" message, the LPT2 printer prints the "second line" message, and the "last line" message goes to LPT1, since that is the default printer.

The only way to reconfigure this program is to swap the #1 and #2, either in lines 100 and 110 or in lines 120 and 130. However, the "last line" message continues to go to the default LPT1 printer, regardless of whether it's designated as #1 or #2.

Needless to say, rewriting every program that sends output to a printer is not a very practical means of operating. There is a much simpler software solution.

BASIC Printer Swapping. A one-line BASIC program will swap the LPT1 and LPT2 designations of two parallel printers. To write the program, type BASIC or BASICA at the DOS prompt, press the Enter key, and then type

```
100 DEF SEG = 0: POKE 1032, 120: POKE 1034, 188
```

Consider a dot-matrix printer attached to an adapter configured as parallel port 1, and a letter-quality printer attached to another adapter configured as parallel port 2. All routine print commands will be sent by default to the dot-matrix printer. But after the above program is run, the same commands will be routed to the letter-quality printer instead. To restore the normal default configuration, change the program as shown here, and run it again.

```
100 DEF SEG = 0: POKE 1032, 188: POKE 1034, 120
```

These one-line programs perform as described, provided the Monochrome Display and Printer Adapter is installed and the AT Serial/Parallel Adapter (if used) is configured to use the primary port. If this is not the case, then the four-line program given below must be used. Every time the program is run, LPT1 and LPT2 are swapped.

```
100 DEF SEG = 0
110 A = PEEK(1032): B = PEEK(1033)
120 POKE 1032, PEEK(1034): POKE 1033, PEEK(1035)
130 POKE 1034, A: POKE 1035, B
```

DOS Printer Swapping. For the convenience of users who need an easy way to switch printers during a word-processing session or whenever it is not convenient to run a BASIC program, a 17-byte assembly language program may be used instead. For readers who are not familiar with assembly language, the BASIC program in Listing 13.1 writes the necessary

Listing 13.1 Printer-Swap Program *

```
100 OPEN "PRT-SWAP.COM" FOR OUTPUT AS #1
110 FOR X = 1 TO 17
120 READ A
130 PRINT #1, CHR$(A);
140 NEXT A

200 DATA 184, 64, 0, 142, 216, 176
210 DATA 120
220 DATA 162,  8, 0, 176
230 DATA 188
240 DATA 162, 10, 0, 205, 32
```

  * Run the program once as shown. Then substitute these lines and run it again.

```
100 OPEN "PRT-NORM.COM" FOR OUTPUT AS #1
210 DATA 188
230 DATA 120
```

bytes into a file called PRT-SWAP.COM which may then be used at the DOS prompt.

  Run the program once, change lines 100, 210, and 230, and run it again. You now have two 17-byte assembly-language programs on your diskette. From now on you may type a command at the DOS prompt to swap printers:

Type this command	the default printer is now the one in
PRT-SWAP	the LPT2 position
PRT-NORM	the LPT1 (normal) position

  Both COM programs should also run from within any word processor that provides either a run-program feature or a temporary exit to the DOS prompt.

  In Listing 13.1, the 17 bytes are seen in the five lines starting at line 200. They are listed as shown to make it easy to swap the values in lines 210 and 230, but you can write all 17 bytes in fewer lines if you prefer. Just be sure to strictly observe the sequences shown.

  The program is valid only for systems meeting the conditions for the one-line BASIC program on page 580. Otherwise, a longer assembly-language program is required, but this is beyond the scope of the treatment given here.

PRINTER DIAGNOSTICS

Printer tests are usually provided on IBM diagnostics diskettes or on third-party diagnostic utilities. In addition, most printers have various self-test procedures that may be run independently of the computer to which they are attached.

Diagnostics Tests

A diagnostics program for a parallel printer is included as part of the main diagnostics program supplied with every IBM personal computer. The serial IBM Compact Printer for the PC and XT is also checked by this diagnostics program.

If two parallel printers are attached, only one can be checked by the diagnostics diskette. Therefore, make sure that the printer to be checked is powered on and that the other printer is not turned on.

On ISA systems, the printer/parallel-port connection is checked during the monochrome display test, provided of course that the Monochrome Display and Printer Adapter is installed. Later in the diagnostics program, test 1400 will check a graphics printer by printing a few lines using various print modes, as shown in Figure 13.7. The printout will vary depending on

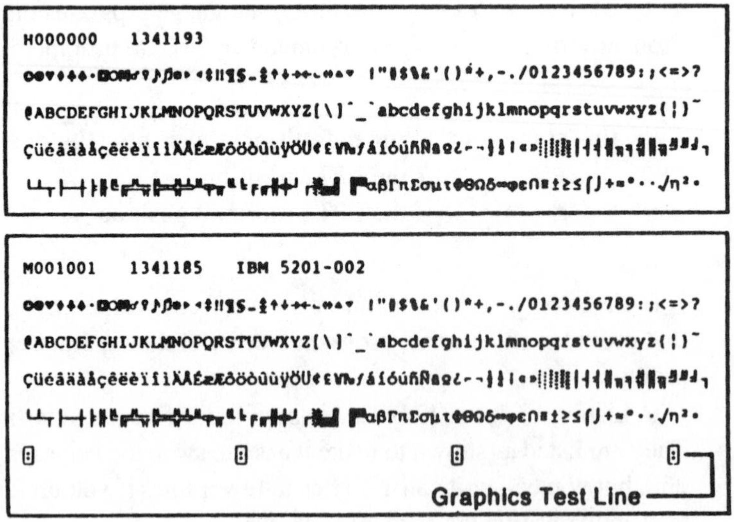

Figure 13.7. During test 1400 on the IBM ISA diagnostics diskette, a printout such as this is generated. The actual printer characters depend on the specific printer in use.

the specific type of printer that is attached. A 14*xx* error indicates a printer-related failure encountered during diagnostics.

Printer Self-Test

In addition to the Diagnostics diskette tests described above, most printers have a so-called self-test mode in which characters are printed continuously for as long as the user runs the test. The printer need not be connected to the computer to run the self-test procedure. A typical self-test printout is shown in Figure 13.8.

The specific self-test procedure varies slightly from one printer to another, but the general sequence is as follows:

Impact Printer Self-Test

1. Turn the printer power off.

2. Depress and hold the Line-Feed key and turn the power on.

3. Release the Line-Feed key when printing begins.

4. Press the Online key to interrupt the test; press it again to resume testing.

5. Turn the power off to conclude the self-test.

```
 !"#$%&'()*+,-./0123456789:;<=>?@ABCDEFGHIJKLMNOPQRSTUVWXYZ[\]^_`abcdefghijklmno
 !"#$%&'()*+,-./0123456789:;<=>?@ABCDEFGHIJKLMNOPQRSTUVWXYZ[\]^_`abcdefghijklmnop
 "#$%&'()*+,-./0123456789:;<=>?@ABCDEFGHIJKLMNOPQRSTUVWXYZ[\]^_`abcdefghijklmnopq
 #$%&'()*+,-./0123456789:;<=>?@ABCDEFGHIJKLMNOPQRSTUVWXYZ[\]^_`abcdefghijklmnopqr
 $%&'()*+,-./0123456789:;<=>?@ABCDEFGHIJKLMNOPQRSTUVWXYZ[\]^_`abcdefghijklmnopqrs
 %&'()*+,-./0123456789:;<=>?@ABCDEFGHIJKLMNOPQRSTUVWXYZ[\]^_`abcdefghijklmnopqrst
 &'()*+,-./0123456789:;<=>?@ABCDEFGHIJKLMNOPQRSTUVWXYZ[\]^_`abcdefghijklmnopqrstu
 '()*+,-./0123456789:;<=>?@ABCDEFGHIJKLMNOPQRSTUVWXYZ[\]^_`abcdefghijklmnopqrstuv
 ()*+,-./0123456789:;<=>?@ABCDEFGHIJKLMNOPQRSTUVWXYZ[\]^_`abcdefghijklmnopqrstuvw
 )*+,-./0123456789:;<=>?@ABCDEFGHIJKLMNOPQRSTUVWXYZ[\]^_`abcdefghijklmnopqrstuvwx
 *+,-./0123456789:;<=>?@ABCDEFGHIJKLMNOPQRSTUVWXYZ[\]^_`abcdefghijklmnopqrstuvwxy
 +,-./0123456789:;<=>?@ABCDEFGHIJKLMNOPQRSTUVWXYZ[\]^_`abcdefghijklmnopqrstuvwxyz
 ,-./0123456789:;<=>?@ABCDEFGHIJKLMNOPQRSTUVWXYZ[\]^_`abcdefghijklmnopqrstuvwxyz{
 -./0123456789:;<=>?@ABCDEFGHIJKLMNOPQRSTUVWXYZ[\]^_`abcdefghijklmnopqrstuvwxyz{|
 ./0123456789:;<=>?@ABCDEFGHIJKLMNOPQRSTUVWXYZ[\]^_`abcdefghijklmnopqrstuvwxyz{|}
 /0123456789:;<=>?@ABCDEFGHIJKLMNOPQRSTUVWXYZ[\]^_`abcdefghijklmnopqrstuvwxyz{|}~
 0123456789:;<=>?@ABCDEFGHIJKLMNOPQRSTUVWXYZ[\]^_`abcdefghijklmnopqrstuvwxyz{|}~
 123456789:;<=>?@ABCDEFGHIJKLMNOPQRSTUVWXYZ[\]^_`abcdefghijklmnopqrstuvwxyz{|}~ Ç
 23456789:;<=>?@ABCDEFGHIJKLMNOPQRSTUVWXYZ[\]^_`abcdefghijklmnopqrstuvwxyz{|}~ Çü
 3456789:;<=>?@ABCDEFGHIJKLMNOPQRSTUVWXYZ[\]^_`abcdefghijklmnopqrstuvwxyz{|}~ Çüé
 456789:;<=>?@ABCDEFGHIJKLMNOPQRSTUVWXYZ[\]^_`abcdefghijklmnopqrstuvwxyz{|}~ Çüéâ
 56789:;<=>?@ABCDEFGHIJKLMNOPQRSTUVWXYZ[\]^_`abcdefghijklmnopqrstuvwxyz{|}~ Çüéââ
 6789:;<=>?@ABCDEFGHIJKLMNOPQRSTUVWXYZ[\]^_`abcdefghijklmnopqrstuvwxyz{|}~ Çüéâäà
 789:;<=>?@ABCDEFGHIJKLMNOPQRSTUVWXYZ[\]^_`abcdefghijklmnopqrstuvwxyz{|}~ Çüéâäà
 89:;<=>?@ABCDEFGHIJKLMNOPQRSTUVWXYZ[\]^_`abcdefghijklmnopqrstuvwxyz{|}~ Çüéâäàç
 9:;<=>?@ABCDEFGHIJKLMNOPQRSTUVWXYZ[\]^_`abcdefghijklmnopqrstuvwxyz{|}~ Çüéâäàçê
```

Figure 13.8. A typical printer self-test printout.

The similar laser printer self-test is described later in the chapter (page 603).

Printer Wrap Test

Some printers permit additional tests to be made. For example, the IBM Quietwriter Printer 5201 includes a printer wrap test whose purpose is to check the printer's internal communications circuits. The wrap plug used in this test is seen in Figure 13.9. To run the wrap test, do the following:

1. Turn the printer power off.

2. Disconnect the printer cable at the printer's rear-panel connector.

3. Insert the wrap plug in the rear-panel connector.

4. Depress and hold the start button, turn the power on, and listen for a beep.

5. Release the start button after the beep.

6. A second beep indicates the wrap test is running.

7. After a few moments, turn the power off to conclude the wrap test.

8. Remove the wrap plug and reconnect the signal cable.

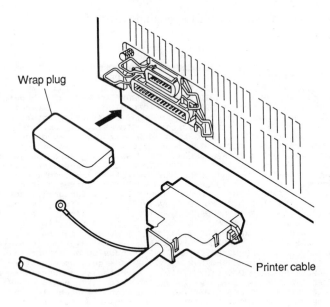

Figure 13.9. During the printer wrap test, the wrap plug replaces the I/O cable at the printer's rear panel.

If the printer beeps continuously at step 6, the wrap test has failed, indicating the printer requires servicing.

PRINT-MODE CONFIGURATION

When any printer is first turned on, certain default print-mode settings are automatically set up. These settings determine the number of characters printed on a line, the vertical spacing between lines, and the style of printing.

Depending on the specific printer, you may wish to make mode changes before printing so that characters are printed in boldface, at near-letter quality (on dot-matrix printers), underlined, compressed, widely spaced, superscripted or subscripted, and so on. The print head may return to the left margin to begin each new line (unidirectional mode) or type the first line left-to-right and the next right-to-left (bidirectional mode).

Although most, if not all, of the print modes described below may be easily set from within any good word-processing program, the discussion may nevertheless be found useful in checking printer performance independently of any software. Assuming the printer correctly responds to the tests given below, any subsequent problems are probably a function of the software in use at the time.

Default Print Mode

Typical default settings for many impact printers include the following characteristics:

> 10 characters per horizontal inch
> 80 characters per line
> 6 lines per vertical inch
> normal print mode (that is, single-strike characters)
> bidirectional print mode enabled

Custom Print Mode

Although the default settings are usually correct for routine print jobs, you may wish to change them to suit a specific task. For example, a spreadsheet may need 100 or more characters per line, thus requiring a compressed print mode. By printing smaller characters, it's also possible to print more lines per vertical inch.

Some software automatically changes various printer default modes as required, but most printers also provide the means for doing this on an as-needed basis, as described in the following paragraphs.

For applications requiring more characters per line—or more lines per inch—than the default setting, many letter-quality printers accommodate a print wheel with smaller-size characters, so that the printed characters do not run together. Laser printers accomplish the same task by using a different font size, along with an accompanying adjustment of the number of lines per inch. In either case, the required command is sent to the printer as described here.

The Escape Sequence. Since printer commands use the same 128-character ASCII set used for conventional printing, each command sequence begins with the so-called ''escape code'' (ASCII 27), which signals the printer that the character(s) immediately following are command codes, not characters to be printed. And, like all good computer code, printer commands are about the next best thing to incomprehensible to the human reader.

The escape code itself may be sent to the printer by a BASIC LPRINT statement, followed by CHR$(27). The next few characters are the command itself, which usually ends in an uppercase letter, followed by a semicolon. The specific examples described here are not for laser printer applications, which are separately covered later in the chapter (page 602).

In the following example, the double-strike mode on an IBM Proprinter is enabled by sending an escape code followed immediately by ASCII 71. The complete BASIC instruction is written as either

```
LPRINT CHR$(27);CHR$(71); or LPRINT CHR$(27);"G";
```

To cancel double-striking, type either

```
LPRINT CHR$(27);CHR$(72); or LPRINT CHR$(27);"H";
```

Characters-per-Inch Code Sequence. The default setting is 10 cpi (characters per horizontal inch). For spreadsheets or other applications that require more characters on each line, the following commands may be used:

BASIC command	to print
LPRINT CHR$(27);CHR$(15);	17.1 characters per inch
LPRINT CHR$(27);CHR$(58);	12 characters per inch
LPRINT CHR$(27);CHR$(18);	10 characters per inch (default)

In order to switch from one of the above nondefault modes to another, some printers require the default mode to be inserted between the two. Thus, to print a line at 17.1 characters per inch followed by a line at 12 characters per inch, the following sequence is required:

```
LPRINT CHR$(15);"This line is at 17.1 cpi"
LPRINT CHR$(18);
LPRINT CHR$(27);CHR$(58);"and this one is at 12 cpi."
```

Lines-per-Inch Code Sequence. The default setting is six lines of type per vertical inch. For purposes of adjusting this spacing, the typesetter's point system is used. Since there are 72 points per inch, divide 72 by the number of lines per inch (lpi) that you require and substitute this quotient for the lowercase letter n in the first of the two BASIC instruction lines given below. The first line stores your instruction, and the second line executes it. If $n = 9$, spacing is 72/9 or 8 lines per inch.

```
LPRINT CHR$(27);CHR$(65);CHR$(n);

LPRINT CHR$(27);CHR$(50);
```

A complete set of print-mode escape-code sequences is found in the Guide to Operations or User's Manual accompanying most printers. Since the codes are not necessarily the same from one printer to another, they should not be buried in a program that is apt to be used to run someone else's printer.

Impact Printer Diagnostics

Once the printer is properly set up and configured to suit the user's specific requirements, errors may be classified in one of several general areas. When a problem occurs, the printer may

fail to operate at all

suspend operation while printing

print incorrect characters, line width, spacing, etc.

perform erratically

Each of these problems is discussed separately below.

Inoperative Printer

Before the printer starts to print, various print-ready checks are made automatically. The printer must be on-line, with paper and ribbon or toner cartridge properly installed. A printwheel printer must have a printwheel installed, and any sort of feeder for continuous forms and separate sheets must be mechanically and electrically in place.

If any of these print-ready checks fails, the printer may indicate the problem by illuminating a front-panel light and/or by sounding a warning beep or series of beeps. The printer will not operate until the error is resolved.

Some problem indicators are quite specific and some aren't. For example, to begin printing, the power-on light must be on and not blinking, the paper-out light must be off, the ready light must be on, and warning beeps must not be heard.

If the power-on light is not illuminated, the problem is clear; but if it's blinking, the problem is not immediately obvious. A warning beep may also require a little investigation to localize the source of the problem.

Inoperative Serial Printer. Most programs are written to direct printer commands to the parallel printer in the LPT1 position. Therefore, a serial printer attached to the COM1 or COM2 port will not respond to these commands.

To redirect parallel printer output to an asynchronous communications adapter, and thereby to the serial printer attached to that adapter, the following two commands must be entered at the DOS prompt (note the four commas in line 1):

```
MODE COM1:12,,,,P
MODE LPT1: = COM1
```

In this example, the first use of the MODE command initializes the asynchronous communications adapter for use with a serial printer. In the next line, the parallel LPT1 output is redirected to the COM1 port.

The first MODE command set the following parameters:

1,200 baud

no parity

7 data bits

1 stop bit

asynchronous communications adapter used

For serial printers that require other parameters, a specific value must be inserted between commas, as appropriate. For further details on this application of the mode command, consult the user's manual for the serial printer, and read the MODE command section in the DOS manual.

Power Problem. If the power-on light does not come on when power is applied, watch and listen for other signs that the printer is indeed receiving power. You should hear some motor noise, and, on conventional (nonlaser) printers, you may note some movement of the print head. If not, check the power cord and also make sure that the wall outlet is working. If this does not indicate the problem, the printer may need servicing.

Installed Devices. If there is no power-related problem, begin by checking various removable devices; ribbon, printwheel, access covers, toner cartridge, and paper-feed devices, if any are attached. A ribbon or toner cartridge must be installed and the former must be neither jammed nor at the end of its travel. A printwheel, if used, must also be properly installed. Access covers must be closed, and paper-feed mechanisms must be mechanically and electrically secure. If any one of these conditions is not met, the printer will not operate. The warning may be a series of beeps, a blinking power-on light, or an error message on a front-panel readout.

If the problem is not immediately obvious, turn the printer power off, remove and reinstall the various devices mentioned above, and carefully check the path the paper takes as it moves through the printer.

Forms-Handling Device. If a forms-handling device is attached, remove it and disconnect the device's cable, if there is one. If this clears up the problem, carefully reinstall the device and try again. If the printer works properly with the accessory removed, then the accessory needs to be serviced. Otherwise the printer itself requires servicing. However, it's a good idea to return both the printer and the accessory, since the problem could be in the electrical or mechanical interface between the two.

Printer Cable Problem. If the printer fails to operate despite all outward appearances of being in good working order, try the self-test procedure described on page 583. If the procedure works, then the problem may be in the printer cable or at the adapter.

Error Codes. If an inoperative printer problem is accompanied by an error code on the computer display, disconnect the printer cable at the adapter end and run the diagnostics program. Watch for an error code that refers to the adapter used to drive the printer. If a printer-related error code is displayed, then the adapter is defective and requires servicing. The error codes of interest are

0432	parallel port on the Monochrome Display Adapter
09xx	Printer Adapter
10xx	alternate printer adapter on the AT Serial/Parallel Adapter
11xx	Asynchronous Adapter
12xx	Alternate Asynchronous Adapter

If the Diagnostics diskette tests run without error detection, reconnect the printer, turn its power on, and run the diagnostics again, this time looking for one of the following errors:

14xx	Graphics Printer
29xx	Color/Graphics Printer
33xx	Compact Printer

If an error code now appears, but the printer passed all its earlier self-tests, the problem is probably in the printer cable. If you have an ohmmeter and are able to check pin continuity, refer to the pin connections in Figure 13.4 or in an equivalent wiring diagram in your printer's manual. Look for shorts and open circuits, or try another cable if one is available. If neither alternative is possible, return the cable along with the printer for servicing.

Print-Interruption Problem

If printing begins normally but halts before the job is done, there are several likely causes which should be checked.

Hardware Problem. Many print operations that terminate prematurely are due to a supply-related problem. Perhaps the ribbon has been damaged or has run out, or maybe no more paper is available. Operation may also be interrupted by paper jamming in the print transport mechanism.

On impact printers, these problems are invariably accompanied by a warning beep and, if lack of paper is the problem, by the illumination of the paper-out light. The obvious solution is to check the ribbon and paper supply, as well as the path the paper takes through the printer.

For laser printers, check the front-panel display for an error message.

Device Error Messages. Depending on the nature of the problem, one of the following error messages may be seen on the computer screen after a print interruption.

This message is seen	in response to this problem
`Device Out of Paper in xxx`	out of paper
`Device Timeout in xxx`	printer taken off line
`Device Fault`	printer power failure

Here *xxx* is the line number or address being executed at the time of the error.

If the paper or time-out problem is identified and resolved before the message is seen, the program will continue running. However, once the error message is displayed, the program has terminated and will have to be rerun after the error is corrected.

Software Problem. A software-controlled print interruption is also possible. For example, the default configuration on a word-processing program may be set for a pause between pages to allow the user to change paper. When using continuous-form paper or a laser printer with a paper supply tray, the software must be reconfigured to print continuously for the duration of the document.

Word-processing software usually provides default settings for a variety of page-formatting options. Typical options include

left margin

justified right margin

top-of-page margin

bottom-of-page margin

characters printed per line

proportional spacing

numbered pages

Most of these variables can be changed by reconfiguring the software, either permanently or before each print job. Depending on the specific software program, there may be a separate installation procedure and program or a series of questions asked before printing begins.

If the printed page does not match your expectations, or if printing pauses—or does not pause—between pages, it may be that the software needs to be corrected. The problem might also be traced to the configuration of the printer itself, as described in the section following.

Print-Mode Problem

If the printer seems to be in good working order, but the general format of each printed character is not correct, one or more print-mode options may be set improperly for the job at hand. This might result in a variety of print errors, many of which were described earlier in the chapter in the section on custom print modes (page 585). To make the necessary correction, follow the directions there or consult the printer manual for other escape-code sequences.

Line Spacing Error. If the error is limited to extra blank lines between the printed lines, don't overlook your word-processing software. Your document may have been saved with double or more spaces between lines. On impact printers, a possible indication that this is the case is the occurrence of unidirectional printing when the bidirectional print mode is specified. In effect, the blank line is being "printed" in the right-to-left direction, so the actual printing is left-to-right only.

Garbled Text. If your printout is completely garbled, don't overlook the possibility that your ASCII-format system is attempting to print an EBCDIC file. If there's any doubt, try printing another file that is known to be in an ASCII format. For more information on solving this problem, see the Completely Garbled File section in Chapter 8 (page 332).

On some impact printers, another possibility is that the installed printwheel does not agree with the printer's front-panel switches. In this case, the solution is simply to find the proper switch combination for the installed printwheel.

On laser printers, it's possible that the desired font is not available and the printer has chosen the closest available match, which may not be close at all if the print job makes use of an extended character set that is significantly different from the one the printer is using.

Erratic Printing Problems

If now and then your printer inserts a few random characters, forgets a line feed, pauses for no apparent reason, or otherwise behaves erratically, the problem may very well be traced back to a PC system that has been accelerated beyond its limitations. For example, a 20-MHz crystal oscillator installed on an old IBM AT system board may cause all of the just-mentioned problems when attempting to print a text file with a word-processing program that otherwise works properly. The solution is to replace the crystal with a 16-MHz (or slower) one. For more information on system-acceleration problems, see Chapter 6.

Graphics Character Errors. On a dot-matrix printer, if text is printed correctly but graphics characters from the IBM extended character set are not, don't overlook the possibility that your word-processing software may be configured for a printer that does not support these characters. If your word processor supports alternate printers, you may be able either to change the default printer driver or simply select the appropriate driver at the beginning of each print job.

Printer Problems and the Hercules Graphics Card   When using a Hercules Graphics Card, it's possible to run off a hardcopy version of the screen display, using software designed especially for that purpose. In this case, for a printer problem not resolved by this chapter, refer to the discussion of the Hercules Graphics Card in Chapter 12.

LASER PRINTERS

In addition to most of what has already been said, the laser printer offers more printing capabilities, and of course more opportunities to get into trouble. Therefore, the following section takes a look at some of the characteristics that are unique to the laser printer.

For printer problems that are not confined to the laser printer, refer to the general Impact Printer Diagnostics section above (page 582) for additional help. And for the benefit of readers who have skipped that discussion, one or two terms are reintroduced here, this time from the perspective of just the laser printer.

Laser Printer Terminology

Given the extensive capabilities of most laser printers, it's really quite easy to run into problems if the printer is not set properly for the job at hand. Although the following section is no substitute for a good course on the fine points of typesetting, it should offer sufficient information to help the reader spot, and possibly avoid, a few potential trouble spots.

Printer Resolution in Dots

Just as each character displayed on the computer screen is made up of pixels (page 446), the same character on the laser-printed page is a series of tiny ink spots, or *dots*. The resolution of the conventional laser printer is 300 dots per inch measured along both the horizontal and vertical axes. There-fore, the diameter of each dot is $1/300^{th}$ of an inch.

Laser Printer Fonts

Unlike the traditional impact printer, where each printable character is embossed on a metal element that strikes the paper, the laser printer's character set is stored as a software font. A *font* is simply a complete set of letters, numbers, symbols, and punctuation marks, all in the same size and style. The laser printer font is the software analog to the famous IBM Selectric typewriter's spherical print element. But of course the latter is far easier to replace than the former (or should be).

Laser printer fonts are available in three formats, each briefly described here. The descriptions are followed by a look at a few important font characteristics.

Internal Fonts. These fonts may be compared to the ROM BIOS modules in the personal computer. That is, ROM modules permanently installed in the printer contain several sets of software fonts. The printer uses one of its internal fonts unless instructed otherwise by a command from the computer.

Cartridge Fonts. To supplement the internal font collection, cartridges with additional fonts stored in ROM may be fitted into slots on the printer front panel, usually just beneath the paper supply tray. The fonts are available for use simply by plugging in the cartridge.

Soft Fonts. Since every print job is different, it's not that unusual to find that the required fonts are not conveniently available in one or two cartridges. The soft font is a font set stored on diskette instead of in cartridge ROM. In order to use it, the diskette-based soft font must be loaded into the printer's RAM. The disadvantage of the soft font is that each desired font must be loaded every time the printer is turned on. However, the advantage is that the user can select just the fonts that are required for a specific print job and that—printer memory capacity permitting—a wide selection of fonts can be loaded from a variety of software sources.

Font Characteristics

Regardless of the source, each laser printer font brings with it an extensive set of parameters, most of which didn't need much thought in the simpler days of the impact printer. However, if one or more of these parameters are incorrect, the resulting print job may not look anything like what was expected. Therefore, a nodding acquaintance with the terms to be described below may help troubleshoot a laser printer problem in which the printer output bears little or no resemblance to what was expected.

Typeface. This is simply the style of the printed characters within each font; perhaps the best known faces are Times Roman and Helvetica. However, these names are trademarks of Linotype, Inc., so similar fonts from other suppliers use slightly different names, as seen here:

	Agfa		
Linotype	**Compugraphic**	**Bitstream**	**Hewlett-Packard**
Helvetica	CG Triumvirate	Swiss	Helv
Times Roman	CG Times	Dutch	TmsRmn

Point Size. The width and height of a printer character are measured in points, and there are 72 points to the inch. However, when a font is identified in points, the size refers to the height of a box in which any ASCII character in that font may be drawn. For example, Figure 13.10 shows a few 12-point character boxes, each of which may contain a letter or symbol from a 12-point character set. Each such character will be less than 12 points in width and height, so that letters in adjacent boxes will not run into each other.

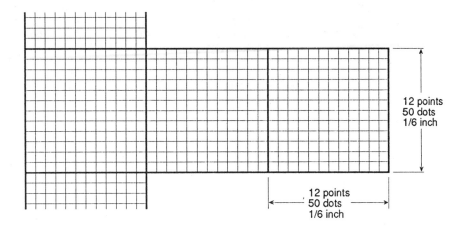

12 points
50 dots
1/6 inch

12 points
50 dots
1/6 inch

Figure 13.10.   Twelve-point character boxes for laser printer fonts.

However, each line-drawing symbol in the IBM extended character set does run the full width or height of the box, in order to butt up against another symbol in an immediately adjacent box. This permits the use of the symbols for continuous line-drawing purposes.

Pitch. This refers to the number of printed characters per horizontal inch (cpi). Older typewriter-style fonts are fixed pitch; that is, each letter or character takes up the same amount of horizontal space. Most laser printer font characters use proportional spacing, in which the allocated horizontal space varies according to the width of the character. For example, the width, in dots, of uppercase letters in a typical 12-point typeface is shown in Table 13.5. The table also gives the width of each character in points. Note that the width of the widest character—uppercase W—is slightly less than 12 points, so that even if another uppercase W follows immediately, there would still be a one-dot space if both letters were set in 12-point (50-dot) character boxes. For narrower characters, the box width is correspondingly less, to visually balance the amount of white space between characters.

Throughout this book, the text is set in a proportional spaced font (Times Roman), while computer listings and sample command lines are set in a fixed-pitch font (Courier). A fixed-pitch font is often referred to as a *monospace* font. For comparison purposes, examples of both are given here.

Table 13.5 Letter Box Widths in a 12-point Soft Font *

Letters	Box width in dots	points	Letters	Box width in dots	points
j †	13	3.12	F	31	7.44
i †	14	3.36	L, l	32	7.68
f	16	3.84	T, t	33	7.92
I	18	4.32	B, w	34	8.16
r	19	4.56	C, E, s	35	8.40
J	22	5.28	Z, c, x – z	36	8.64
v	23	5.52	K	37	8.88
g, X, Y	24	5.76	A, N, R, V	38	9.12
a, e	25	6.00	D, O, Q	40	9.60
k, m	26	6.24	G, H, U	41	9.84
S, n – q, u	27	6.48	M, b, d, h	47	11.28
P	30	7.20	W	49	11.76

* Hewlett–Packard TmsRmn soft font (HP 33412AD)
† Due to font design, the space for letter *i* is greater than for *j*.

IIIII iiiii	proportional spacing
WWWWW wwwww	proportional spacing
IIIII iiiii	fixed pitch
WWWWW wwwww	fixed pitch

As a possible point of confusion, 12-point monospace type is usually set at 10 cpi, while 10-point monospace type is set at 12 cpi, as shown here.

1234567890	12 point, 10 cpi
123456789012	10 point, 12 cpi

Vertical Line Spacing. Although not a property of the font itself, vertical line spacing must be set so that each line of character boxes does not overlap those in the line immediately above it. If 12-point type is used, there may be six character boxes per vertical inch (6 lines × 12 points per line = 72 points = 1 inch). With this choice of point size and line spacing, there will be some vertical space between ASCII characters on each line, and IBM (or similar) line-drawing symbols will merge properly.

For various line spacings, the maximum recommended point size is listed here.

Line spacing (lpi)	point size
2	36
4	18
6 (default)	12
8	9
10	7.2

Figure 13.11 shows the effect of printing a 12-point fixed-pitch font at line spacings of 4, 6, and 8 lines per inch. Note that, in the first example, line-drawing symbols do not merge, and in the final example there is some overlap.

Character Set. For most conventional fonts, the character set is the set of familiar characters found on the conventional typewriter: the letters A–Z, a–z, numbers 0–9, punctuation, etc. However, fonts are also available with characters other than these. As an obvious example, a Greek language font will offer α, β, ε, φ, Δ, and so on. In any case, the term *character set* usually refers to the first 128 character positions in the font, with printable characters beginning at ASCII 32 (or 33, since 32 is a space).

12-point fixed pitch at 4 vertical lines per inch (12 on 18)

12-point fixed pitch at 6 vertical lines per inch (12 on 12)

12-point fixed pitch at 8 vertical lines per inch (12 on 9)

Figure 13.11.   The visual effect of vertical line spacing on a 12-point font. (a) 4 lines per inch (12 on 18), (b) 6 lines per inch (12 on 12), (c) 8 lines per inch (12 on 9).

Symbol Set. The symbol set is the set of printable characters within the font, usually consisting of the ASCII character set, plus the extended characters (128–255) just beyond the ASCII character set, and sometimes a few printable symbols below ASCII 32.

On IBM and most compatible personal computers, the screen font's fixed-pitch extended-character symbol set is a mixed bag of foreign-language characters and line-drawing symbols, as shown earlier in Figure 10.2.

However, these symbols are not used in printer fonts which take advantage of proportional spacing. Although there's no reason why these symbols couldn't be included at a constant character width within an otherwise proportional font, such fonts usually offer either a wider selection of foreign-language characters, extended math symbols, or simply omit the extended character set entirely. For example, the Roman-8 symbol set used in some Hewlett-Packard (and other) font sets includes extensive accented vowels, foreign-language punctuation, currency symbols, etc. Math fonts usually include an extensive set of math symbols not otherwise available, and often replace the conventional ASCII characters with additional math symbols, a Greek alphabet, etc.

Table 13.6 shows three examples of letters and symbols that may occupy the extended character set area above ASCII 127.

Font Orientation. For most print jobs, the printed characters run across the width of the paper, as on this page and in most documents, letters, etc. Since this familiar relationship of print to paper follows the general aspect ratio of a portrait, the orientation is known as the *portrait* mode.

In most traditional landscape paintings, the canvas is wider than it is high, and so it follows that when print is set across the length of the paper (as on a spreadsheet), the printer is in the *landscape* mode.

Printer Configuration

Hewlett-Packard and some other laser printers include both a serial and a parallel interface. In case of doubt, find the rear-panel cable socket(s) and note the socket style, which should be as follows:

Printer socket	Interface
36-pin Centronics	parallel
25-pin male D-plug	serial

The cables used to connect the printer to the computer were described earlier in the chapter in the Printer Cables and Connectors section (page 567). Assuming the correct cable is already installed, follow the appropriate configuration procedures given immediately below.

Serial Configuration. To configure the printer for serial operation, press the ON LINE button once to take the printer off line (the ON LINE indicator light should now be extinguished). Now press and hold the Menu button until the front-panel display reads SYM SET=(*name of a symbol set*). Then press the MENU button to toggle through the various configuration options. If any configuration display varies from that shown here, press the + or – buttons to toggle through the available choices. When the displayed choice is correct, press the ENTER/RESET MENU button to save it. Continue until all configuration options have been displayed and set correctly. Refer to the printer user's manual for more details about each configuration option.

Table 13.6 Representative Laser Font Symbol Sets

Symbol set *	Symbols and extended character set values															

Rmn–8		À	Â	È	Ê	Ë	Î	Ï	´	`	^	¨	˜	Ù	Û	£
math	→	↑	↓	↔	↗	↘	←	⇐	⇒	*	⇓	⇔	↖	↙	↗	∫
IBM	á	í	ó	ú	ñ	Ñ	ª	º	¿	⌐	¬	½	¼	¡	«	»
	160	161	162	163	164	165	166	167	168	169	170	171	172	173	174	175

Rmn–8	¯			°	Ç	ç	Ñ	ñ	¡	¿	¤	£	¥	§	f	¢
math	∞	∈	∋	△	▽	∝	¬	∀	∃	¬	∅	ℜ	ℑ	℘	∫	ℵ
IBM	▒	▓	█	┤	╡	╢	╖	╕	╣	║	╗	╝	╜	╛	┐	┘
	176	177	178	179	180	181	182	183	184	185	186	187	188	189	190	191

Rmn–8	â	ê	ô	û	á	é	ó	ú	à	è	ò	ù	ä	ë	ö	ü
math	±	∓	⊕	⊖	⊗	⊘	⊙	◯	°	•	⨯	≡	⊂	⊇	<	>
IBM	└	┴	┬	├	─	┼	╞	╟	╚	╔	╩	╦	╠	═	╬	╧
	192	193	194	195	196	197	198	199	200	201	202	203	204	205	206	207

Rmn–8	Å	î	Ø	Æ	å	í	ø	æ	Ä	ì	Ö	Ü	É	ï	ß	Ô
math	≺	≻	∼	≈	⊆	⊃	≪	≫	≼	≽	∪	⌐	⊎	∧	⊤	
IBM	╨	╤	╥	╙	╘	╒	╓	╫	╪	┘	┌	█	▄	▌	▐	▀
	208	209	210	211	212	213	214	215	216	217	218	219	220	221	222	223

Rmn–8	Á	Ã	ã	Ð	đ	Í	Ì	Ó	Ò	Õ	õ	Š	š	Ú	Ÿ	ÿ
math	⊣	⌊	⌋	⌈	⌉	⇑	·	⟨	⟩	∣	∥	↕	↨	∩	≀	√
IBM	α	β	Γ	π	Σ	σ	μ	τ	Φ	Θ	Ω	δ	∞	φ	ε	∩
	224	225	226	227	228	229	230	231	232	233	234	235	236	237	238	239

Rmn–8	Þ	þ					—	¼	½	ª	º	«	■	»	±
math	⊔	▽	∫	⊔	⊓	⊑	⊒	§	†	‡	{	×	}	÷	◇
IBM	≡	±	≥	≤	⌠	⌡	÷	≈	°	•	·	√	η	²	■
	240	241	242	243	244	245	246	247	248	249	250	251	252	253	254

* Rmn–8   Roman–8 symbols in Hewlett–Packard TmsRmn soft font.
  math   Math symbols in VS Software GMS F–A soft font.
  IBM   IBM extended character set in Hewlett–Packard internal font.

Printer display for **serial configuration**	**Printer display for** **parallel configuration**
AUTO CONT=OFF	AUTO CONT=OFF
I/O=SERIAL	I/O=PARALLEL
BAUD RATE=9600	
ROBUST XON=ON	
DTR POLARITY=HI	

Parallel Configuration. Follow the same general procedure just described for serial configuration. However, only the two options seen in the parallel configuration column above are displayed.

Conclude Configuration. After making the appropriate choices, press the ON LINE button once to exit the configuration menu and return on line.

LASER PRINTER DIAGNOSTICS

In case of a problem related to a laser printer, the first task is, as usual, to isolate the location at which the problem originates, which may be in one of the following areas:

The printer itself

Computer-to-printer interface

Installed fonts: internal, cartridge, and loaded soft fonts

Software

Each of these areas is discussed below. If it is already known where the problem originates, then refer to the approprite section. Otherwise, continue reading here until the problem area is identified. In case of problems that don't seem to be covered below, refer to the Impact Printer Diagnostics section for additional information that may be useful.

Much of what follows is based on the Hewlett-Packard LaserJet series of laser printers. The printer functions, commands, and general printer nomenclature seen here may vary on other printers, so the appropriate user's manual should be consulted for the equivalent function or command.

PCL: Printer Command Language

For most routine printing operations, the user need not be concerned about how the laser printer figures out font orientation and selection, line spacing, and all the other details. The software application acts as intermediary between user and printer, and somehow or other it manages to get the printer to do whatever it is that needs doing.

Except when there's a problem. Then it may not be entirely clear whether the printer is really at fault or whether it's just not getting the right instructions—in which case the problem originates elsewhere.

As a diagnostic aid, the extensive set of printer commands in Hewlett-Packard's PCL (Printer Command Language) may be used to test the printer independently of software other than PCL itself. Many of the diagnostic tests described below take advantage of PCL, with a little help from BASIC. The command language described here is standard in Hewlett-Packard laser printers; for commands other than those given here and possible variations in other printers, refer to the user's manual for your printer. (So far, PCL is not widely known as "pickle," but that could change.)

The Escape Sequence

Every printer command begins with the escape code described earlier in the chapter (page 586). On the printed page, the escape code itself is often indicated by an ^{E}C symbol, and it is followed by one or more letters, numbers, and/or ASCII symbols which make up the complete command. To send such a command to the printer via the BASIC language, type LPRINT CHR$(27) instead of the ^{E}C symbol, and enclose the rest of the command in quotes, as shown here:

```
LPRINT CHR$(27); "command";
```

The following section describes a series of tests using PCL in short and reasonably simple BASIC programs. If the printer passes the appropriate test, then the print problem lies with the word processor (or whatever) that was in use when the problem was first encountered. However, if the BASIC program produces the same effect, then the printer itself is probably the culprit.

When two or more commands begin with the same character, they can be combined into a single line. For example, the first two lines below set the left and right margins, respectively. Note that each line ends in an uppercase letter. In the third line, the commands are combined, with an important variation; the uppercase "L" is changed to lowercase. In fact, on any multicommand line, only the final letter remains in uppercase.

^{E}C&axL   Set left margin at row x.
^{E}C&ayM   Set right margin at row y.

^{E}C&axlyM   Set left margin at row x and right margin at row y.
where x and y are the row numbers for left and right margins, respectively.

In most of the program listings presented in this chapter, each command is shown on a separate line, to help lessen the problem of trying to make sense out of an already complex command syntax.

Printer Self-Tests

Most laser printers have a self-test function to verify that the printer itself is in good working order. To run such tests, the printer need not be connected to the computer, or if it is connected, it makes no difference whether the computer is on or off.

Turn the printer on and wait a few moments until the ON LINE and READY indicators are illuminated. During the wait interval, the front-panel indicator should display "WARMING UP." When the printer is ready for use, the ON LINE and READY indicators are illuminated and the LCD readout displays "READY."

To begin testing, take the printer off line by pressing the ON LINE button once. The ON LINE light should go off.

Font Printout Test. Press the PRINT FONTS button and release it quickly. After a short pause, two or more pages are printed, showing samples of every currently available font. The front panel displays "06 FONT PRINTOUT" during the test period. Figure 13.12 shows excerpts from a font test of a printer with a few soft fonts loaded in memory and a single plug-in font cartridge installed. In addition, the printer's internal fonts are tested.

Although the figure shows portrait fonts only, the test also prints all installed landscape fonts. The test automatically concludes after printing samples of all available fonts.

Self-Test. Press and hold the PRINT FONTS button until "04 SELF TEST" is displayed on the front-panel readout. The top of the first printed page displays printer system information such as that shown in Figure 13.13. This is followed by repetitive printouts of pages similar to the impact printer self-test printout seen in Figure 13.8. To stop the self-test, press the ON LINE button. The test continues for a few more pages and then printing ceases.

-------- PORTRAIT FONTS --------

FONT ID	NAME			PITCH	POINT SIZE	SYMBOL SET	PRINT SAMPLE

"PERMANENT" SOFT FONTS

S01	CG Times	Bd BOLD		PS	9	8U	ABCDEfghij#$@[\]^'{	}~123 ÀÂ°ÇÑ¡¿£§éëàèêöÅØåæÄÜBÁÐÒ
S02	CG Times	It ITALIC		PS	9·	8U	ABCDEfghij#$@[\]^'{	}~123 ÀÂ°ÇÑ¡¿£§éëàèêöÅØåæÄÜBÁÐÒ
S03	CG Times			PS	9	8U	ABCDEfghij#$@[\]^'{	}~123 ÀÂ°ÇÑ¡¿£§éëàèêöÅØåæÄÜBÁÐÒ
S04	gms12m.sfp			PS	12	0A	ΑΒΓΔΕς η θ ι κ δ χ ς ["] ∂ ' − − ¨ ¨ 1 ↑ ↓ ΔΔ∇ · Ǝ ¬ℜ⊤∓∅∘ • ⊇≤≺~⊂≫≺_⌐⌐
S05	gms9m.sfp			10	9	0A	ΑΒΓΔΕς η θ ι κ δ χ ς ["] ∂ ' − − ¨ ¨ 123 ↑ ↓ ΔΔ∇ · Ǝ ¬ℜ⊤∓∅∘ • ⊇≤≺~⊂≫≺_⌐ (⌐)
S06	TmsRmn			PS	8	8U	ABCDEfghij#$@[\]^'{	}~123 ÀÂ°ÇÑ¡¿£§éëàèêöÅØåæÄÜBÁÐÒ
S07	TmsRmn BOLD			PS	10	8U	ABCDEfghij#$@[\]^'{	}~123 ÀÂ°ÇÑ¡¿£§éëàèêöÅØåæÄÜBÁÐÒ
S08	TmsRmn ITALIC			PS	10	8U	ABCDEfghij#$@[\]^'{	}~123 ÀÂ°ÇÑ¡¿£§éëàèêöÅØåæÄÜBÁÐÒ
S09	tr100rpn.r8p			PS	10	8U	ABCDEfghij#$@[\]^'{	}~123 ÀÂ°ÇÑ¡¿£§éëàèêöÅØåæÄÜBÁÐÒ
S10	TmsRmn BOLD			PS	12	8U	ABCDEfghij#$@[\]^'{	}~123 ÀÂ°ÇÑ¡¿£§éëàèêöÅØåæÄÜBÁÐÒ
S11	TmsRmn ITALIC			PS	12	8U	ABCDEfghij#$@[\]^'{	}~123 ÀÂ°ÇÑ¡¿£§éëàèêöÅØåæÄÜBÁÐÒ
S12	tr120rpn.r8p			PS	12	8U	ABCDEfghij#$@[\]^'{	}~123 ÀÂ°ÇÑ¡¿£§éëàèêöÅØåæÄÜBÁÐÒ
S13	VS Courier			12	10	10U	ABCDEfghij#$@[\]^'{|}-123 íó|┤║┐╕┘┴╚┼╩╦╦╧╦╬║█ απΦ

LEFT FONT CARTRIDGE

RIGHT FONT CARTRIDGE

INTERNAL FONTS

I00	COURIER			10	12	10U	ABCDEfghij#$@[\]^'{	}~123· íó	┤║┐╕┘┴╚┼╩╦╦╧╦╬║█ απΦ
I01	COURIER			10	12	8U	ABCDEfghij#$@[\]^'{	}~123 ÀÂ·ÇÑ¡¿£§éëàèêöÅØåæÄÜBÁÐÒ
I02	COURIER			10	12	11U	ABCDEfghij#$@[\]^'{	}~123 íó	┤║┐╕┘┴╚┼╩╦╦╧╦╬║█ απΦ

Figure 13.12. The PRINT FONT test prints a sample of each currently loaded soft font, plus cartridge and internal font samples. Landscape font samples are also printed.

```
-------- PORTRAIT FONTS --------
```

FONT ID	NAME	PITCH	POINT SIZE	SYMBOL SET	PRINT SAMPLE

INTERNAL FONTS

FONT ID	NAME	PITCH	POINT SIZE	SYMBOL SET	PRINT SAMPLE
I03	COURIER	10	12	0N	ABCDEfghij#$@[\]^`{¦}~123 ¡¢³´¶.¹»½ÄÅÈÉÍÎÐÒÓ×ØÚÞàãè
I04	COURIER BOLD	10	12	8U	ABCDEfghij#$@[\]^`{¦}~123 ÀÂ°ÇÑ¡¿£§êéàèëöÅØåæÄÜßÁÐÒ
I05	COURIER BOLD	10	12	10U	ABCDEfghij#$@[\]^`{¦}~123 íó|┤╢╖╕╣║╗╝╜╛┐└┴┬├─┼╞╟╚╔╩╦╠═╬╧‖ακ♣
I06	COURIER BOLD	10	12	11U	ABCDEfghij#$@[\]^`{¦}~123 íó|┤╢╖╕╣║╗╝╜╛┐└┴┬├─┼╞╟╚╔╩╦╠═╬╧‖ακ♣
I07	COURIER BOLD	10	12	0N	ABCDEfghij#$@[\]^`{¦}~123 ¡¢³´¶.¹»½ÄÅÈÉÍÎÐÒÓ×ØÚÞàãè
I08	LINE_PRINTER	16.6	8.5	8U	ABCDEfghij#$@[\]^`{¦}~123 ÀÂ°ÇÑ¡¿£§êéàèëöÅØåæÄÜßÁÐÒ
I09	LINE_PRINTER	16.6	8.5	10U	ABCDEfghij#$@[\]^`{¦}~123 íó|┤╢╖╕╣║╗╝╜╛┐└┴┬├─┼╞╟╚╔╩╦╠═╬╧‖ακ♣
I10	LINE_PRINTER	16.6	8.5	11U	ABCDEfghij#$@[\]^`{¦}~123 íó|┤╢╖╕╣║╗╝╜╛┐└┴┬├─┼╞╟╚╔╩╦╠═╬╧‖ακ♣
I11	LINE_PRINTER	16.6	8.5	0N	ABCDEfghij#$@[\]^`{¦}~123 ¡¢³´¶.¹»½ÄÅÈÉÍÎÐÒÓ×ØÚÞàãè

```
-------- LANDSCAPE FONTS --------
```

FONT ID	NAME	PITCH	POINT SIZE	SYMBOL SET	PRINT SAMPLE

"PERMANENT" SOFT FONTS

LEFT FONT CARTRIDGE

RIGHT FONT CARTRIDGE

INTERNAL FONTS

FONT ID	NAME	PITCH	POINT SIZE	SYMBOL SET	PRINT SAMPLE
I12	COURIER	10	12	8U	ABCDEfghij#$@[\]^`{¦}~123 ÀÂ°ÇÑ¡¿£§êéàèëöÅØåæÄÜßÁÐÒ
I13	COURIER	10	12	10U	ABCDEfghij#$@[\]^`{¦}~123 íó|┤╢╖╕╣║╗╝╜╛┐└┴┬├─┼╞╟╚╔╩╦╠═╬╧‖ακ♣
I14	COURIER	10	12	11U	ABCDEfghij#$@[\]^`{¦}~123 íó|┤╢╖╕╣║╗╝╜╛┐└┴┬├─┼╞╟╚╔╩╦╠═╬╧‖ακ♣
I15	COURIER	10	12	0N	ABCDEfghij#$@[\]^`{¦}~123 ¡¢³´¶.¹»½ÄÅÈÉÍÎÐÒÓ×ØÚÞàãè
I16	COURIER BOLD	10	12	8U	ABCDEfghij#$@[\]^`{¦}~123 ÀÂ°ÇÑ¡¿£§êéàèëöÅØåæÄÜßÁÐÒ
I17	COURIER BOLD	10	12	10U	ABCDEfghij#$@[\]^`{¦}~123 íó|┤╢╖╕╣║╗╝╜╛┐└┴┬├─┼╞╟╚╔╩╦╠═╬╧‖ακ♣
I18	COURIER BOLD	10	12	11U	ABCDEfghij#$@[\]^`{¦}~123 íó|┤╢╖╕╣║╗╝╜╛┐└┴┬├─┼╞╟╚╔╩╦╠═╬╧‖ακ♣
I19	COURIER BOLD	10	12	0N	ABCDEfghij#$@[\]^`{¦}~123 ¡¢³´¶.¹»½ÄÅÈÉÍÎÐÒÓ×ØÚÞàãè
I20	LINE_PRINTER	16.6	8.5	8U	ABCDEfghij#$@[\]^`{¦}~123 ÀÂ°ÇÑ¡¿£§êéàèëöÅØåæÄÜßÁÐÒ
I21	LINE_PRINTER	16.6	8.5	10U	ABCDEfghij#$@[\]^`{¦}~123 íó|┤╢╖╕╣║╗╝╜╛┐└┴┬├─┼╞╟╚╔╩╦╠═╬╧‖ακ♣
I22	LINE_PRINTER	16.6	8.5	11U	ABCDEfghij#$@[\]^`{¦}~123 íó|┤╢╖╕╣║╗╝╜╛┐└┴┬├─┼╞╟╚╔╩╦╠═╬╧‖ακ♣
I23	LINE_PRINTER	16.6	8.5	0N	ABCDEfghij#$@[\]^`{¦}~123 ¡¢³´¶.¹»½ÄÅÈÉÍÎÐÒÓ×ØÚÞàãè

```
Page Count=14805
Program ROM Datecode=19861203, Internal Font ROM Datecode=19860611
Auto Continue=OFF
Installed Memory=512 Kbytes
Symbol Set=IBM-US
Menu Items:
   Copies=1, Manual Feed=OFF, Font Source=I, Font Number=00,
   Form=60 Lines
Parallel I/O
```

```
 !"#$%&'()*+,-./0123456789:;<=>?@ABCDEFGHIJKLMNOPQRSTUVWXYZ[\]^_`abcdefghijklmno
!"#$%&'()*+,-./0123456789:;<=>?@ABCDEFGHIJKLMNOPQRSTUVWXYZ[\]^_`abcdefghijklmnop
"#$%&'()*+,-./0123456789:;<=>?@ABCDEFGHIJKLMNOPQRSTUVWXYZ[\]^_`abcdefghijklmnopq
#$%&'()*+,-./0123456789:;<=>?@ABCDEFGHIJKLMNOPQRSTUVWXYZ[\]^_`abcdefghijklmnopqr
$%&'()*+,-./0123456789:;<=>?@ABCDEFGHIJKLMNOPQRSTUVWXYZ[\]^_`abcdefghijklmnopqrs
%&'()*+,-./0123456789:;<=>?@ABCDEFGHIJKLMNOPQRSTUVWXYZ[\]^_`abcdefghijklmnopqrst
&'()*+,-./0123456789:;<=>?@ABCDEFGHIJKLMNOPQRSTUVWXYZ[\]^_`abcdefghijklmnopqrstu
'()*+,-./0123456789:;<=>?@ABCDEFGHIJKLMNOPQRSTUVWXYZ[\]^_`abcdefghijklmnopqrstuv
()*+,-./0123456789:;<=>?@ABCDEFGHIJKLMNOPQRSTUVWXYZ[\]^_`abcdefghijklmnopqrstuvw
)*+,-./0123456789:;<=>?@ABCDEFGHIJKLMNOPQRSTUVWXYZ[\]^_`abcdefghijklmnopqrstuvwx
*+,-./0123456789:;<=>?@ABCDEFGHIJKLMNOPQRSTUVWXYZ[\]^_`abcdefghijklmnopqrstuvwxy
+,-./0123456789:;<=>?@ABCDEFGHIJKLMNOPQRSTUVWXYZ[\]^_`abcdefghijklmnopqrstuvwxy
,-./0123456789:;<=>?@ABCDEFGHIJKLMNOPQRSTUVWXYZ[\]^_`abcdefghijklmnopqrstuvwxyz(
-./0123456789:;<=>?@ABCDEFGHIJKLMNOPQRSTUVWXYZ[\]^_`abcdefghijklmnopqrstuvwxyz(|
./0123456789:;<=>?@ABCDEFGHIJKLMNOPQRSTUVWXYZ[\]^_`abcdefghijklmnopqrstuvwxyz(|)
/0123456789:;<=>?@ABCDEFGHIJKLMNOPQRSTUVWXYZ[\]^_`abcdefghijklmnopqrstuvwxyz(|)-
0123456789:;<=>?@ABCDEFGHIJKLMNOPQRSTUVWXYZ[\]^_`abcdefghijklmnopqrstuvwxyz(|)-▪
123456789:;<=>?@ABCDEFGHIJKLMNOPQRSTUVWXYZ[\]^_`abcdefghijklmnopqrstuvwxyz(|)-▪ 
23456789:;<=>?@ABCDEFGHIJKLMNOPQRSTUVWXYZ[\]^_`abcdefghijklmnopqrstuvwxyz(|)-▪ !
3456789:;<=>?@ABCDEFGHIJKLMNOPQRSTUVWXYZ[\]^_`abcdefghijklmnopqrstuvwxyz(|)-▪ !"
456789:;<=>?@ABCDEFGHIJKLMNOPQRSTUVWXYZ[\]^_`abcdefghijklmnopqrstuvwxyz(|)-▪ !"#
56789:;<=>?@ABCDEFGHIJKLMNOPQRSTUVWXYZ[\]^_`abcdefghijklmnopqrstuvwxyz(|)-▪ !"#$
6789:;<=>?@ABCDEFGHIJKLMNOPQRSTUVWXYZ[\]^_`abcdefghijklmnopqrstuvwxyz(|)-▪ !"#$%
789:;<=>?@ABCDEFGHIJKLMNOPQRSTUVWXYZ[\]^_`abcdefghijklmnopqrstuvwxyz(|)-▪ !"#$%&
89:;<=>?@ABCDEFGHIJKLMNOPQRSTUVWXYZ[\]^_`abcdefghijklmnopqrstuvwxyz(|)-▪ !"#$%&'
9:;<=>?@ABCDEFGHIJKLMNOPQRSTUVWXYZ[\]^_`abcdefghijklmnopqrstuvwxyz(|)-▪ !"#$%&'(
:;<=>?@ABCDEFGHIJKLMNOPQRSTUVWXYZ[\]^_`abcdefghijklmnopqrstuvwxyz(|)-▪ !"#$%&'()
;<=>?@ABCDEFGHIJKLMNOPQRSTUVWXYZ[\]^_`abcdefghijklmnopqrstuvwxyz(|)-▪ !"#$%&'()*
<=>?@ABCDEFGHIJKLMNOPQRSTUVWXYZ[\]^_`abcdefghijklmnopqrstuvwxyz(|)-▪ !"#$%&'()*+
ÀÁÈÉÊÌÍ``^``ÛÜ£`Ÿý`ÇçÑñ¡¿®£¥§ƒ¢âêôûáéóúàèòùäëöüÀÎØÅåíøæÀìÒÜÉìÎÕÂÅÅÃÐØÍÌÒÓÓÔÕŠŠÚÝŸÞþ
ÀÁÈÉÊÌÍ``^``ÛÜ£`Ÿý`ÇçÑñ¡¿®£¥§ƒ¢âêôûáéóúàèòùäëöüÀÎØÅåíøæÀìÒÜÉìÎÕÂÅÅÃÐØÍÌÒÓÓÔÕŠŠÚÝŸÞþ
ÀÈÉÊÌÍ``^``ÛÜ£`Ÿý`ÇçÑñ¡¿®£¥§ƒ¢âêôûáéóúàèòùäëöüÀÎØÅåíøæÀìÒÜÉìÎÕÂÅÅÃÐØÍÌÒÓÓÔÕŠŠÚÝŸÞþ
ÈÉÊÌÍ``^``ÛÜ£`Ÿý`ÇçÑñ¡¿®£¥§ƒ¢âêôûáéóúàèòùäëöüÀÎØÅåíøæÀìÒÜÉìÎÕÂÅÅÃÐØÍÌÒÓÓÔÕŠŠÚÝŸÞþ · µ
ÉÊÌÍ``^``ÛÜ£`Ÿý`ÇçÑñ¡¿®£¥§ƒ¢âêôûáéóúàèòùäëöüÀÎØÅåíøæÀìÒÜÉìÎÕÂÅÅÃÐØÍÌÒÓÓÔÕŠŠÚÝŸÞþ · µ¶
ÊÌÍ``^``ÛÜ£`Ÿý`ÇçÑñ¡¿®£¥§ƒ¢âêôûáéóúàèòùäëöüÀÎØÅåíøæÀìÒÜÉìÎÕÂÅÅÃÐØÍÌÒÓÓÔÕŠŠÚÝŸÞþ · µ¶
ÌÍ``^``ÛÜ£`Ÿý`ÇçÑñ¡¿®£¥§ƒ¢âêôûáéóúàèòùäëöüÀÎØÅåíøæÀìÒÜÉìÎÕÂÅÅÃÐØÍÌÒÓÓÔÕŠŠÚÝŸÞþ · µ¶¼-¼
Í``^``ÛÜ£`Ÿý`ÇçÑñ¡¿®£¥§ƒ¢âêôûáéóúàèòùäëöüÀÎØÅåíøæÀìÒÜÉìÎÕÂÅÅÃÐØÍÌÒÓÓÔÕŠŠÚÝŸÞþ · µ¶¼-¼½
``^``ÛÜ£`Ÿý`ÇçÑñ¡¿®£¥§ƒ¢âêôûáéóúàèòùäëöüÀÎØÅåíøæÀìÒÜÉìÎÕÂÅÅÃÐØÍÌÒÓÓÔÕŠŠÚÝŸÞþ · µ¶¼-¼½ ° °
`^``ÛÜ£`Ÿý`ÇçÑñ¡¿®£¥§ƒ¢âêôûáéóúàèòùäëöüÀÎØÅåíøæÀìÒÜÉìÎÕÂÅÅÃÐØÍÌÒÓÓÔÕŠŠÚÝŸÞþ · µ¶¼-¼½ ° °«■»
^``ÛÜ£`Ÿý`ÇçÑñ¡¿®£¥§ƒ¢âêôûáéóúàèòùäëöüÀÎØÅåíøæÀìÒÜÉìÎÕÂÅÅÃÐØÍÌÒÓÓÔÕŠŠÚÝŸÞþ · µ¶¼-¼½ ° °«■»±
``ÛÜ£`Ÿý`ÇçÑñ¡¿®£¥§ƒ¢âêôûáéóúàèòùäëöüÀÎØÅåíøæÀìÒÜÉìÎÕÂÅÅÃÐØÍÌÒÓÓÔÕŠŠÚÝŸÞþ · µ¶¼-¼½ ° °«■»±
`ÛÜ£`Ÿý`ÇçÑñ¡¿®£¥§ƒ¢âêôûáéóúàèòùäëöüÀÎØÅåíøæÀìÒÜÉìÎÕÂÅÅÃÐØÍÌÒÓÓÔÕŠŠÚÝŸÞþ · µ¶¼-¼½ ° °«■»±
ÛÜ£`Ÿý`ÇçÑñ¡¿®£¥§ƒ¢âêôûáéóúàèòùäëöüÀÎØÅåíøæÀìÒÜÉìÎÕÂÅÅÃÐØÍÌÒÓÓÔÕŠŠÚÝŸÞþ · µ¶¼-¼½ ° °«■»±  À
Ü£`Ÿý`ÇçÑñ¡¿®£¥§ƒ¢âêôûáéóúàèòùäëöüÀÎØÅåíøæÀìÒÜÉìÎÕÂÅÅÃÐØÍÌÒÓÓÔÕŠŠÚÝŸÞþ · µ¶¼-¼½ ° °«■»±  ÀÁ
```

Figure 13.13. The SELF TEST prints configuration information plus a continuous test of font characters.

Printer-to-Computer Interface

The connection between the printer and the computer may be the source of a problem if the printer passes the tests described above, yet does not operate properly under the control of the computer. As a quick check, try one of the following tests.

Parallel Printer Test. Simply type the following line at the DOS prompt:

```
ECHO This is a test of the printer > PRN
```

or, from BASIC:

```
LPRINT "This is a test of the printer"; CHR$(12);
```

In either case, the test line should be sent to the printer. If the DOS ECHO command is used, press the ON LINE button to take the printer off line, then press the LINE FEED button to receive a copy of the page with the test line printed on it.

If the test fails, then there is something wrong with either the printer adapter card in the computer or with the printer cable itself. If possible, try swapping the cable and/or the adapter to isolate the problem.

Serial Printer Test. At the DOS prompt, type the lines indicated in the left-hand column below. If the serial printer is connected to a serial port other than COM1, change the COM1 instruction as required.

Type this	Screen display is:
MODE COM1:9600,N,8,1,P↵	COM1: 9600,N,8,1,P
MODE LPT1:=COM1↵	LPT1: rerouted to COM1:
ECHO This is a test of the printer > PRN↵	

Press the ON LINE button to take the printer off line and then press the LINE FEED button to deliver a page with the test line printed on it. If the test fails, check the cable and/or the adapter, as described above.

Installed Font Tests

The tests within this section can be used to check problems with font selection, line spacing, etc., or for routine diagnostic testing of the printer.

Soft Font Test. Unfortunately there is no way (yet) to display a directory listing of the soft fonts currently stored in the printer memory. So if there's any doubt that a certain soft font is indeed installed, the BASIC program in Listing 13.2 may be modified to load any portrait and/or landscape soft font. As shown, the program loads one landscape font (lines 200–220) and one portrait font (300–320) from a FONTS subdirectory on drive C. Next, it prints two sample lines with each font (400–430 and 500–530). To load and print additional fonts, duplicate the appropriate lines in the listing and make sure each additional font is given a new identification number. An ID number is first assigned to a font (lines 200 and 300), then used later on to select the desired font (410 and 510).

Watch the screen while the program is running and make sure that a *1 File(s) copied* message is seen for each soft font sent to the printer. If a *File*

Listing 13.2 Portrait and Landscape Font Test

```
100 CLS
110 LPRINT CHR$(27); "E:"              ' Reset printer.
120 LPRINT CHR$(27); "*c0F";           ' Delete all previous fonts.

200 LPRINT CHR$(27); "*c0D";           ' Font ID is #0.
210 SHELL "COPY/B C:\FONTS\TR100RPN.R8L LPT1:"
                                       ' Load sample landscape font. †
220 SHELL "EXIT"                       ' Return to BASIC program.
230 LPRINT CHR$(27); "*c5F";           ' permanent font (optional).

300 LPRINT CHR$(27); "*c1D";           ' Font ID is #1.
310 SHELL "COPY/B C:\FONTS\TR120RPN.R8P LPT1:"
                                       ' Load sample portrait font. †
320 SHELL "EXIT"                       ' Return to BASIC program.
330 LPRINT CHR$(27); "*c5F";           ' permanent font (optional).

400 LPRINT CHR$(27); "&l10";           ' Set landscape mode.‡
410 LPRINT CHR$(27); "(0X";            ' Select font #0.
420 LPRINT "This line is in landscape mode"
                                       ' Print sample line.
430 LPRINT "and so is this one."       ' Print another line.

500 LPRINT CHR$(27); "&l00";           ' Set portrait mode. ‡
510 LPRINT CHR$(27); "(1X";            ' Select font #1.
520 LPRINT "This line is in portrait mode"
                                       ' Print sample line.
530 LPRINT "and so is this one."       ' Print another line.

600 LPRINT CHR$(12);                   ' Execute form feed.
```

† Change path, subdirectory and font name as required.
‡ The first character following the "&" is lowercase "L" (not 1).

not found—FILENAME message is displayed, then the font with that filename has not been loaded into printer memory. The printer will therefore print the closest match it can find. To correct the error, first check the program listing to make sure the desired file name is spelled correctly and that the path (if any) is also correct. Next, check the appropriate hard disk or diskette subdirectory to make sure the soft font file is actually where it's supposed to be.

If the BASIC program loads and prints the desired soft font, but some other program doesn't, run the BASIC program first and then reload the other program. If the program still does not print properly, then the source of the trouble is the program itself. Refer to the Software Diagnostics section below for more information.

Vertical Line Spacing Test. The program in Listing 13.3 prints four sets of test lines, at vertical spacings of 2, 4, 6, and 8 lines per inch, as shown by the sample printout in Figure 13.14. A vertical distance of one inch should be measured between the bottom of the upper reference line and the bottom line of each group.

The printer command used in line 120 can only be used with line spacings that are evenly divisible into 48. To test other spacings, use the VMI (vertical motion index) command, which will set line spacings in increments of $1/48^{th}$ inch over a range from 0 to 336 (7 inches between lines). Use the following command to execute the VMI command in BASIC:

```
LPRINT CHR$(27); "&lxC";
```

where

l = lowercase ''L'' (not 1), and

x = vertical motion index.

Listing 13.3 Vertical Line Spacing Test

```
100 FOR X = 2 TO 8 STEP 2
110 ST$ = "&l" + MID$(STR$(X), 2) + "D"
120 LPRINT CHR$(27); ST$;            ' Set vertical line spacing at X lpi
130 LPRINT "___Reference Line"
140 FOR Y = 1 TO X
150 LPRINT "___"Line"; Y; "@"; X; "lines per inch."
160 NEXT Y
170 LPRINT
180 NEXT X
190 LPRINT CHR$(12);
```

_____ Reference line	_____ Reference line
	_____ Line 1 at 6 lines per inch
	_____ Line 2 at 6 lines per inch
_____ Line 1 at 2 lines per inch	_____ Line 3 at 6 lines per inch
	_____ Line 4 at 6 lines per inch
	_____ Line 5 at 6 lines per inch
_____ Line 2 at 2 lines per inch	_____ Line 6 at 6 lines per inch

_____ Reference line	_____ Reference line
	_____ Line 1 at 8 lines per inch
_____ Line 1 at 4 lines per inch	_____ Line 2 at 8 lines per inch
	_____ Line 3 at 8 lines per inch
_____ Line 2 at 4 lines per inch	_____ Line 4 at 8 lines per inch
	_____ Line 5 at 8 lines per inch
_____ Line 3 at 4 lines per inch	_____ Line 6 at 8 lines per inch
	_____ Line 7 at 8 lines per inch
_____ Line 4 at 4 lines per inch	_____ Line 8 at 8 lines per inch

Figure 13.14.   The program in Listing 13.3 prints this test of vertical line spacing.

Column and Row Test. The program in Listing 13.4 prints an 80-character horizontal ruler line across the top of the page, using rows 1 and 2 and a vertical column of numbers down the left margin, as shown in Figure 13.15. Since the vertical column exceeds the length of a standard letter-size sheet, the final few numbers should appear at the top of the second sheet of paper. The page break should occur between lines 62 and 63.

Shading Level Test. As a quick check of the printer's ability to print various degrees of shading, type the following BASIC line:

```
LPRINT CHR$(176); CHR$(177); CHR$(178); CHR$(219)
```

This prints the indicated four IBM extended characters: three shaded (light, medium, heavy) blocks and one solid black block (see Figure 10.2).

For a more extensive test, the program in Listing 13.5 prints six (½″ × 1″) rectangles of progressively darker shading levels, as shown in Figure 13.16. Uneven shading, especially around the edges of a rectangle, usually indicates a toner problem. Refer to the Toner Cartridge section for further details.

Envelope Print Test. The program in Listing 13.6 will verify a laser printer's ability to print an envelope. First run the program, then insert an

Listing 13.4 Row and Column Test *

```
100 LPRINT CHR$(27); "E";              ' Reset printer.
110 LPRINT CHR$(27); "&12A";           ' Set page size for letter.
120 LPRINT CHR$(27); "&10L";           ' Disable perforation-skip mode.
130 LPRINT CHR$(27); "&11E";           ' Top margin = 1.
140 LPRINT CHR$(27); "&170F";          ' Text length = 70 lines.
150 LPRINT CHR$(27); "&a0L";           ' Left margin = 0.
160 LPRINT CHR$(27); "&a80M"           ' Right margin = 80.

200 FOR X = 0 TO 7                     ' Print ruler line across page.
210 LPRINT CHR$(X);"|.........";
220 NEXT X
230 FOR X = 48 to 55                   ' Print 0 - 7 under ruler line.
240 LPRINT CHR(X); "            "       ' Add 9 spaces after each number.
250 NEXT X

300 LPRINT CHR$(27); "&a3r0C";         ' Set cursor at row 3, column 0.
310 FOR Y = 3 TO 9                     ' Print 3 - 9 in left margin.
320 LPRINT "__ "; USING "##"; Y
330 NEXT Y
340 FOR TENS = 1 to 7                  ' Print 10 - 79 in left margin.
350 FOR UNITS = 0 to 9
360 LPRINT "__ "; USING "##"; 10 * TENS + UNITS
370 NEXT UNITS
380 NEXT TENS

400 LPRINT CHR$(12);                   ' Execute form feed.
```

* Lines 110-140: The character following "&" is lowercase "L" (not 1).

Figure 13.15

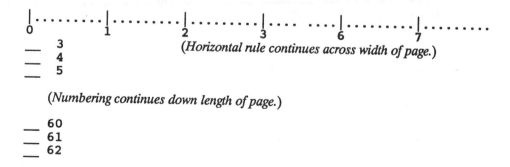

Figure 13.15. Listing 13.4 prints a horizontal rule across the page and indicates the number of printable lines on the page.

Listing 13.5 Shading Level Test *

```
100 FOR X = 1 TO 6
110 X$ = MID$(STR$(X * 300), 2)        ' X position = 300, 600, 900, etc.

200 READ DATA$                          ' Read DATA for shading value.
210 CURSOR$ = "*p" +  X$ + "x100Y"      ' Cursor position is X = X$, Y =
100.
220 SHADE$ = "*c" + DATA$                ' Shading is "*c" plus DATA$.

300 LPRINT CHR$(27); CURSOR$;            ' Set cursor at X$, 100.
310 LPRINT CHR$(27); "*c200A";           ' Rectangle is 200 dots wide.
320 LPRINT CHR$(27); "*300B";            ' Rectangle is 300 dots high.
330 LPRINT CHR$(27); SHADE$;             ' Select shading level.
340 LPRINT CHR$(27); "*c2P";             ' Fill rectangle with shading.
350 NEXT X
360 LPRINT CHR$(12);                     ' Execute form feed.

400 DATA 1G, 11G, 36G, 56G, 81G, 100G
```

    * Line 400 DATA values are for 2%, 20%, 55%, 80%, 100% shading levels.

Listing 13.6 Envelope Print Test *

```
100 LPRINT CHR$(27); "E";                ' Reset printer.
110 LPRINT CHR$(27); "*c0D;              ' Font ID is #0
120 SHELL "COPY/B F:\FONTS\TR100RPN.R8L LPT1:
                                         ' Load return address font. †
130 SHELL "EXIT"                         ' Exit to BASIC.
140 LPRINT CHR$(27); "*c1D";             ' Fond ID is #1.
150 SHELL "COPY/B F:\FONTS\TR120BPN.R8L LPT1:
                                         ' Load recipient's address font. †
160 SHELL "EXIT"                         ' Exit to BASIC.

200 LPRINT CHR$(27); "&l81a1o3H";        ' Page length, landscape mode,
                                           manual feeder
210 LPRINT CHR$(27); "9";                ' Reset margins.
220 LPRINT CHR$(27); "&a10L";            ' Set left margin at 10.
230 LPRINT CHR$(27); "(0X";              ' Select Font #0

300 LPRINT "Your Name"
310 LPRINT "Your Street Address"
320 LPRINT "Your City, State and ZIP"

400 LPRINT CHR$(27); "&a88L";            ' Reset left margin at 88.
410 LPRINT CHR$(27); "(1X";              ' Select Font #1

500 LPRINT: LPRINT
510 LPRINT "Occupant"                    ' Print recipient's address.
520 LPRINT "Street Address"
530 LPRINT "City, State and ZIP

600 LPRINT CHR$(12);                     ' Execute form feed.
610 LPRINT CHR$(27); "E";                ' Reset printer.
```

    * Line 200: "&", lowercase "L", 81a, numeral "one", lowercase letter "O", 3H.
    † Change path, subdirectory and font name as required.

Figure 13.16.   Listing 13.5 prints a series of rectangles at various shading levels. Uneven edge shading indicates a toner problem.

envelope in the manual feeder at the top of the paper supply tray. The program prints the return address in the upper left-hand corner, then drops down two lines and prints the recipient's address.

The indicated fonts print the return address in a 10-point regular typeface, and the recipient's address in 12-point boldface.

Other Printer Tests. The general techniques shown above may be modified to test various other printer parameters. The general procedure is to search the printer command table in your printer user's manual for the desired command, then write a BASIC program line to execute that command. Add an LPRINT CHR$(12); command at the end of the listing to print the final page of the test, or press the FORM FEED button on the printer at the conclusion of the test.

Software Diagnostics

If the laser printer passes all the tests described above, yet still has a problem when used with some application program, then it's quite possible that the software in use is not sending the proper commands to the printer. However, there are almost as many ways to specify printer commands as there are application programs with laser printer support, so the suggestions offered here will have to be modified by reading the appropriate user's manual.

Printer Uses Wrong Font. Don't overlook the obvious: was the desired font loaded into printer memory? If it was, then check the document to make sure the appropriate command is inserted at the correct location.

Page Length Errors. When printer documentation refers to a 66-line page, it means that at 6 lines per vertical inch, the length of a standard

11-inch sheet of paper is 66 lines. It does *not* mean that 66 lines can be printed on it. In fact, the following one-line BASIC program will show how many lines can be printed:

```
100 FOR X = 1 TO 66: PRINT "This is line";X: NEXT X
```

On most laser printers, only 60 lines will be printed, since there is a default half-inch margin at the top and bottom of the page.

Some word processors suggest a lines-per-page setting of 62, with top and bottom margin settings of at least one line each to stay within the 60-line limit. If you try to "cheat" by setting both margins to zero, you may fool the screen but not the printer; that is, the display may show 62 lines per page, but only 61 of them get printed. There may be page creep on multipage documents, with unequal top and bottom margins from one page to another.

To guarantee WYS(OS)IWYG(OP), or, What You See (On Screen) Is What You Get (On Paper), make sure your page format commands don't exceed the margin limits of the printer.

If you specify a page header and/or a footer, each may separate itself from the text by one blank line, in addition to the printed header/footer itself. For example, Figure 13.17 shows a typical word-processor page layout for an 11-inch, 66-line sheet of paper (a). The word-processor document format is set for 62 lines per page (b) at a vertical line spacing of 6 lines per inch, with one-line top and bottom margins. These margins fall within the printer's own half-inch margin areas (c), leaving ten inches, or 60 lines, available for printing (d). In the illustration, a header and footer of one line each are automatically separated from the main text by a blank line; thus, 56 lines remain for the document itself.

If the document were reformatted to print the lines double-spaced—that is, at 3 lines per inch, one might expect 28 lines of text. However, since the margins and headers also use the new 3 lpi spacing, there are only 25 lines in the main text area. An attempt to readjust the page for 28 lines of text will probably make a mess out of the page layout. To avoid wasting this extra margin space, format the document for the conventional 62 lines/6 lines-per-inch settings, then add a 3 lines-per-inch command at the top of the first page. This allows the 28 text lines (half the usual number) while leaving the margins as is.

LASER PRINTER TROUBLESHOOTING

In case of a laser printer problem either not solved by, or unrelated to, the printer diagnostic section above, the next step is to check all the usual trouble spots. Make sure that the paper supply tray is loaded, there are no paper

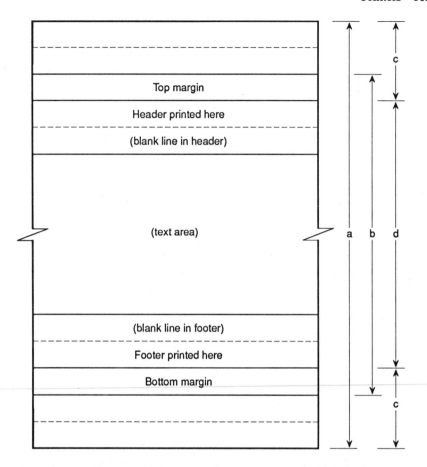

Figure 13.17.   Typical word processor page layout shows (a) 66-line page length (11 inches at 6 lpi), (b) document format set at 62 lines per page, (c) non-print areas at top and bottom of page, and (d) area available for document lines (58 as shown).

jams, the printer is on line, and so on. Most of these problems are accompanied by a front-panel warning display.

Printer Error Codes and Messages

Some error codes (00–16) seen on the laser printer front panel are accompanied by a self-explanatory text message. However, error codes of 20 and above simply display the number and the uninformative word ERROR or SERVICE. These error codes are briefly explained here.

Error Codes

In most cases, the correct procedure is to press the Continue/Reset button to resume normal operation. However, if the same error code continually reappears, then the printer needs servicing.

20 ERROR. This is an out-of-memory error. It appears if you try to download soft fonts beyond the printer's memory capacity, or when that capacity is insufficient to accommodate the page composition. If possible, download fewer fonts. But if the problem is chronic, your production requirements are such that additional memory should be installed.

21 ERROR. This error code is a result of sending graphics instructions that are too complex for the printer to handle. For example, the error code appears if the application software attempts to address the same physical position too many times. Press the CONTINUE/RESET button to resume printing, with some data loss to be expected. If possible, simplify the program that is causing the problem.

22 ERROR. There is an I/O compatibility problem between the printer and the computer. Carefully review your printer configuration, especially serial mode settings, if in use. If so, make sure the printer configuration agrees with the commands being sent by the computer.

40 ERROR. This message can appear if the computer is turned on or off while the printer is on line, or if the printer and computer baud rate do not agree. In the former case, press the CONTINUE/RESET button; in the latter, correct the baud rate at the printer or computer, as appropriate.

41 ERROR. There is a problem related to the laser beam detector. Press CONTINUE/RESET to reprint the page and continue.

42 or 43 ERROR. There is a problem with a card installed in the optional interface slot. If pressing the CONTINUE/RESET button does not clear the error message, then remove the card and try again.

50 ERROR. The fusing area is overheating. Turn the printer off and allow it to cool off. Make sure the surrounding environment is not blocking air circulation to the printer.

51 ERROR. There is a malfunction in the laser beam system or within the toner cartridge. If replacing the cartridge does not cure the problem, then the printer requires servicing.

52 ERROR. The scanning-mirror motor has failed. This may be accompanied by unusual motor noise or no noise at all.

55 ERROR. There is a problem with one or more circuit boards, or with the wiring that connects them.

61 or 62 ERROR. Printer ROM error.

xx **ERROR.** (*xx* is a number not listed above.) Press CONTINUE/RESET to resume operations. Check the next few printed pages for data loss. If the same error code appears frequently, the printer needs servicing.

Service Codes

In most cases, an error code followed by the word SERVICE indicates a problem that will require a service call. However, in a few cases the procedures described here may help to localize, or possibly correct, the condition that caused the message to be generated.

63 SERVICE. This message indicates an internal memory-check error. Turn the printer off and back on again. If the message is seen again, remove the expandable memory board (if any). If this eliminates the message, then the memory problem is on the removed board. Otherwise, the printer itself needs servicing.

64 or 65 SERVICE. Memory-related error.

67 SERVICE. Hardware error. If a font cartridge is installed, remove it and reinsert it.

68 SERVICE. Setup error. Reenter your setup data, using the front-panel buttons.

69 SERVICE. There is a nonmemory problem on a card installed in the optional interface slot. Try reseating the card or remove it and test the printer alone. Depending on the outcome, the card or the printer needs servicing.

xx SERVICE. (*xx* is a number not listed above.) There is an internal service error. Turn the printer off and back on again. As above, the printer needs servicing if the error code reappears.

Print Quality Problems

The source of some print quality problems is the choice of paper. Remember that the laser ink-fusing process requires very high temperatures and a clean environment. Paper that does not stand up well to heat or that has frayed edges—however slight—or other seen or unseen blemishes may cause problems, some of which are more obvious than others.

Your printer documentation should include a chart of recommended paper specifications. Before buying paper in bulk, make sure its specifications lie within a range that is suitable for the printer. For routine printing jobs, a laser printer should produce acceptable results with any good-quality paper suitable for photocopying purposes. Such paper should have the following visible characteristics:

Dust free, no shavings, clean edges

Long grain (running parallel to the long edge)

Uniform moisture content

No visible curl

Uses heat-resistant laser ink (if preprinted)

16 to 35 lb. weight (Hewlett-Packard recommendation)

3.7 to 7.5 mil thickness (Hewlett-Packard recommendation)

Paper with the following characteristics should be avoided:

Textured (classic laid), extra smooth, very shiny, coated (erasable bond), wrinkled, multiform, carbonless, perforated edge, porous

Thermographic (imitation engraved) letterheads

Engraved, embossed (unless designed specifically for laser printer use)

Inked (ink must withstand 200°C (424°F) for 0.1 second)

Less than 16 lb., greater than 35 lb. weight

A few papers that have been used with success are listed here.

Stuart F. Cooper (premium quality laser bond paper, envelopes)

Gilbert Neu-Tech (general-purpose cotton bond paper, envelopes)

Canon NP (quality photocopy paper)

Xerox 4024 DP (28 lb.) (for camera-ready documents)

Hammermill Laser Plus (with wax holdout for paste-up art)

In case of doubt, try an experimental ream (or less) and examine the paper for creasing, smears, ink spots, and other blemishes both before and after use.

Paper-Related Problems

Many of the problems described here are directly related to the paper in use. If any of these problems is encountered, try printing a few sheets of photocopy paper, which may serve as a good reference source. Also, make sure the paper was not just received from a remote location where it was stored at some extreme temperature or humidity. If the storage environment is suspect, try to bring the paper into the printing area a day or two in advance of use.

Don't overlook the fact that air conditioning or heating systems may be turned down during off hours, thus affecting the paper. If possible, store a few reams in an area where there are no extreme fluctutations in the environment.

Letterhead Smeared. As noted earlier, there may some letterhead smearing if the ink does not stand up to the heat of the laser printer. Discontinue using such paper immediately, since the ink will surely foul the printer's fusing roller.

Ink Spots. If paper that appears to be of good quality emerges with tiny ink spots on it, the paper's moisture content or conductivity may be the source of the problem. If possible, try some other type of paper under the same general operating conditions.

If the problem is confined to only one paper type or to just a few reams, it's quite possible that the paper is from a defective production run (it does happen). Make a close visual inspection of the paper, looking for minute paper dust particles, edge imperfections, etc. However, many imperfections not noticed by the untrained eye are still sufficient to cause problems in the printer.

Obviously, if all paper comes out of the printer with ink spots on it, then there is an internal problem with the printer itself—probably with the toner cartridge. Turn the printer off and clean it thoroughly, according to the manufacturer's instructions. Then try another toner cartridge. If the problem persists, the printer probably needs servicing.

Toner Cartridge Problems

A few problems traceable to the toner cartridge are described here. In most cases, such problems may be resolved by cleaning or replacing the cartridge.

Vertical Black Streaks. If one or more fine black lines appear on every printed page, the photosensitive drum inside the toner cartridge is probably scratched and will have to be replaced.

However, if a smeared vertical black line is seen, one or more of the following parts needs cleaning.

Printer part	Cleaning procedure
Fuser roller	Remove the fuser roller's cleaning pad, carefully clean the roller, and then replace the cleaning pad.
Fuser roller cleaning pad	Clean the pad or replace if necessary.
Primary corona wire	Remove the toner cartridge. Clean its internal corona wire with the small wire-cleaner brush stored inside the printer. (See printer user's manual for detailed instructions.)

Horizontal Black Streaks. If the nonprinted side of the paper shows black stains running horizontally, the internal transport rollers probably need cleaning. The fuser roller cleaning pad may also need cleaning.

Faded Print. If a printout shows faded print areas running the length of the paper, the supply of toner in the toner cartridge is probably running low. Check the printer front-panel display for a "TONER LOW" warning message. Remove the cartridge, slowly rock it back and forth a few times to redistribute the remaining toner, then reinsert it. The warning message continues to be displayed, but it should be possible to print another 50 or more sheets. Replace the toner cartridge when the above solution no longer works.

If the faded print problem affects just a few printed characters here and there on the paper, the paper itself is defective. Its moisture content or some other manufacturing defect prevents the faded areas from accepting toner. It's also possible that the transfer corona wire in the printer (not in the toner cartridge) is dirty. Clean the corona wire and try using paper from another source.

Print is Too Dark/Too Light. If print quality is even but consistantly too dark or too light, simply adjust the print density control inside the printer, as required.

Toner Spill. It should never happen, but if you've bought a reconditioned toner cartridge from someone who is still learning how to do it the right way, it's a possibility. If the spill is not severe, gently pat the spill area with a lightly moistened household sponge to pick up the ink powder. Use a mini vacuum cleaner with caution: the fine ink particles may pass right through the vacuum's filter and foul its motor. On the other hand, considering the relative cost of a vacuum cleaner and a laser printer, you may decide to sacrifice the life of the former to preserve the health of the latter. Next time, buy better cartridges. Or invest in a laser printer vacuum cleaner designed to clean up toner particles (Hewlett-Packard 92175V or similar).

Replacement Fuser Roller Cleaning Pads. A replacement cleaning pad for the fuser roller is supplied with most toner cartridges. However, the pad often gets clogged with fused ink before it's time to replace the toner cartridge, so you may want to keep a small supply of extra pads on hand. The part numbers (not listed in the regular H-P catalog) are

LaserJet (original)   FG1—2377—020CN
LaserJet II and III   RG1—2377—030CN

For other printers, consult the manufacturer if the part number is not readily available.

Paper Movement Problems   Figure 13.8 illustrates the paper path though a typical laser printer. Note that paper may be fed out a rear access door or delivered face down to a built-in holding bin on the top of the printer. In the latter case, the additional path length may cause a problem for envelopes and marginal-quality paper.

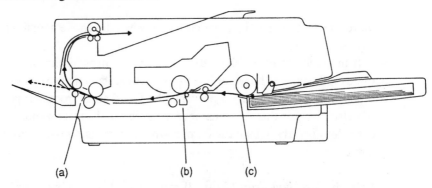

(a)   (b)   (c)

Figure 13.18. The paper path through a Hewlett-Packard LaserJet series II printer, showing (a) fusing assembly area, (b) transfer guide under toner cartridge, (c) paper feed rollers. Dashed-line path indicates rear-access exit recommended for envelopes.

If there is a chronic problem moving paper through the printer, the fault may lie with the mechanical system or with the paper itself. If the cause is not obvious, both should be investigated.

Paper Jamming. In most cases, the cure requires nothing more than opening the printer cover, removing the jammed paper, and resuming operations. In some cases, the paper may be cleared from the front of the printer by removing the paper supply tray and then pulling out the jammed sheet. Note, however, that you must open the top cover and close it again in order to resume operation, even if this action is not required to free the paper jam itself.

If paper jamming problems recur and the paper itself does not seem to be at fault, note the location at which the jams occur. Look for damaged or dirt-clogged rollers, improperly seated toner cartridge, etc. If the problem is at the rear of the printer, open the rear access door and try another print run. If the paper feeds properly, then the fault is in the additional path to the top of the printer. Otherwise, the trouble is before this point. In either case, if the problem cannot be resolved, the printer requires servicing.

Creased Paper. If healthy-looking paper emerges from the printer with creases in it, it's likely the paper's moisture content is the culprit. As a double check, open the printer's rear access door and run a few more sheets through the printer. Also inspect the sheets remaining in the paper supply tray for slight creases. If all paper comes out creased, then the printer needs servicing.

Envelope Feed Problems. For a variety of reasons, feeding an envelope through a laser printer is sometimes a problem. Due in part to uneven paper thickness, flap glue with poor heat tolerance, and the complexities of the travel path, the envelope often comes out creased, or worse, it doesn't come out at all.

The first line of defense is to use a laser-proof envelope (Cooper Laser Bond or similar). Again, open the rear access door to keep the travel path as simple as possible. If jamming persists, take the end of the envelope that enters the printer first, and run it between two fingers while lightly squeezing it. It's not high-tech, but it works (usually). If it doesn't, try to find someone who remembers how to use a typewriter. Refer to the Envelope Print Test section above (page 610) if there is some doubt about the envelope-printing program in use.

14

A SHORT GUIDE TO MORE HELP

There are those times in the life of a computer owner when a book is just not good enough. You've managed to isolate a problem to some piece of hardware, read the appropriate chapter page-by-page, waded through all the tables, stared at the figures, but you still need a little more support. At times like this, there are a few alternatives—some more obvious than others.

The User's Manual

When all else fails, read the instructions. Unfortunately, there is a fatal flaw in this little piece of well-worn advice; often enough, it's the instructions themselves that fail. However, it's a good idea to have at least a passing familiarity with the manual before calling the company's tech support line. Every so often—not always, but now and then it happens—the answer to your question is right there in black and white. You will not be pleased when, after spending hours trying to penetrate the company's phone system, the service technician tells you to have a look at page seven in your manual.

Telephone Technical Support

If you have determined that the manual doesn't have the information you need, the next step is the company's tech support line—if you don't mind spending half a lifetime playing touch-tone tag with an announcement system designed by a crazed BASIC programmer who hasn't quite figured out the endless loop.

Once you penetrate the system, the level of support ranges from superb to wretched, and you'll just have to experiment to find out which companies are worth calling and which aren't. However, to say a word or two in defense of the enemy, a lot of calls are unnecessary. The information you need *may* be in the manual (see above), so you should at least make sure that it isn't before placing that call.

If a call is warranted, do some homework first. The more specific details you supply, the easier it is to get the help you need. At the very least, have the version or serial number handy, and be ready to describe the rest of your system in some detail. Get the name of the person who promises to call you back later, so that when he doesn't you can ask for him the next time you call. That at least saves having to explain the problem all over again.

Diagnostic Software

A number of excellent software utility programs are available to help diagnose many of the problems that sooner or later come up. Although hard disk file recovery programs are perhaps the most visible, don't overlook the other utilities which may be helpful in the diagnosis, if not always in the cure, of other hardware problems. Although this is not the place to review such software, the utilities mentioned in the previous chapters have all been put to good use in preparing this book and in keeping at least a few nearby computers up and running.

PC Magazine is an excellent source for software utilities that will prove useful in many applications. The utilities are usually available for downloading via modem. For further details, refer to the *Utilities* column in the magazine or use CompuServe (GO PCMAGNET) as described below (page 627).

Another good source for utility programs are the diskettes accompanying *DOS Power Tools* (Bantam, 2nd edition, 1990).

IBM Technical Publications

For most IBM hardware products, there is a wealth of technical information available directly from IBM itself. The information is found in various maintenance, service, and technical reference manuals. The manuals are not cheap, are often enough incomprehensible—and you will probably have to buy more than one, for the information is usually divided between three volumes: maintenance reference, maintenance service, and technical reference.

The manuals contain a wealth of information for the serious technical reader, but are definitely not in the easy-reading category. The content and format varies from one manual to another, so that information readily available for one system will not be found for another. A few examples of obstacles to be encountered are given here. To find the battery in a PS/2 MCA system, look up "battery" in the index; to find it in a PS/2 ISA system, you're on your own (or see Table 6.8 in this book). Timing diagrams are given for the PS/2 MCA video subsystem, with various timings indicated as T1, T2, and so on. It's up to you to figure out the significance of each one. The same information is presented in an entirely different format in the documentation accompanying the plug-in VGA and 8514/A adapters, making it difficult if not impossible to make comparisons. Decimal-place accuracy varies from none (integer value only) to three decimal places. Pixel dimensions for characters are published for MDA, CGA, and EGA modes, but not for VGA or 8514/A systems. And so on.

Many of these obstacles to understanding can be hurdled by the reader who is expert enough to fill in the blanks, or who can figure out what the text really meant to say. For the less-experienced reader, the manuals may be a bit too hard to handle.

An IBM Technical Directory lists the publications currently available. The directory or the publications themselves may be ordered by mail or by phone from IBM (see Appendix D).

CompuServe Information Service

Fortunately, there is a reasonably painless way to get expert assistance fast. All you need is a computer (that works), a modem (ditto), and a subscription to CompuServe. To fully explain its workings is a book-length subject, and in fact there are several good ones already on the market, including *How To Get The Most Out of CompuServe,* by Charles Bowen and David Peyton (Bantam, 4th edition, 1989).

To describe CompuServe here in as few words as possible, some comparisons with the traditional voice telephone network can be made. The latter's information-gathering powers are of course well known, but so are its weaknesses. First, you must know who to call. Second, you must have an extraordinary combination of patience, perserverance, and plain old good luck to establish voice contact with someone with a pulse. Third, that person must be ready, willing, and able to give your problem the attention you think it deserves. Unfortunately, the successful completion of a voice call to tech support is about as likely as hitting it big in Las Vegas: it happens, but not that often.

To complete the CompuServe comparison: First, you don't have to know who to call; second, you don't have to worry about getting through; and third, you don't have to keep your fingers crossed that your problem will get careful attention.

Here's an overview of how it works, followed by a few typical examples. The CompuServe network is divided into multiple divisions, not unlike the directory tree on a hard disk. To reach the specific department where your question can be answered, simply dial CompuServe, identify yourself and proceed to the division, and finally to the specific department, where your problem can be resolved. But don't expect an on-the-spot answer, for that's not how the system is set up. Instead, leave your message and then come back in a day or so to pick up the responses.

The reason the system offers such excellent service to the frazzled computer user is that, in most cases, it is *not* the usual tech support facility staffed by a handful of overworked technicians who must answer the same questions day after day. Instead, each department (or in the language of CompuServe, each *forum*) is "staffed" by a large and enthusiastic group of people who are only there because of a genuine interest in problem solving. Some are former neophytes who wandered by with a question, stuck around, and eventually began answering questions themselves. Others are computer professionals who use the forum as an information exchange. Still others are company engineers to whom the forum is a means to stay in continuing touch with the marketplace. In any case, there's probably someone around who can answer just about any question that comes up.

Let's assume you have two questions: one about a QuickBASIC test program, the other about a problem with the interface between a monitor and an IBM-compatible computer. As a new user, you're not quite sure how to find the answers you need. Therefore, just type GO COMPUTERS and press the Enter key to display a menu which lists the selections seen in Table 14.1.

Note: Although the menus shown in Tables 14.1–14.7 summarize currently available software and hardware options, the actual on-screen format varies from that seen in the tables.

The Microsoft Forum. Since your QuickBASIC question is related to software, select Option 1, Software Forums, which displays the menu choices listed in Table 14.2. Choose Option 29, The Microsoft Connection, to access the list of topics shown in Table 14.3a. The next step is to select Option 5, the Languages and Systems Forum. Table 14.3b shows the final list of selections, one of which (2) is BASIC and QuickBASIC. At this point,

Table 14.1 The CompuServe GO COMPUTERS Menu

Topic	Topic
1. Software Forums (Table 14.2)	6. Personal File Area
2. Hardware Forums (Table 14.4)	7. Research/Reference
3. Magazines/Electronic Newsstand	8. CompuServe Software/Graphics
4. Science/Technology	9. Electronic Mall Merchants
5. SOFTEX (sm) Software Catalog	10. Online Today

you'll be invited to officially join the forum, which requires nothing more than entering your name. And now that you have found your way to the right place, next time you can bypass the intermediate steps just described by simply typing GO MSSYS, which is the modem equivalent of this forum's direct-dial phone number.

Having done this, you may post your question, then return in a day or so to read the answers.

The IBM Users Network. Now let's tackle the hardware problem. Referring back to Table 14.1, select Option 2, Hardware Forums, which leads to the hardware forum choices shown in Table 14.4. Select option 12, IBM Users Network, to display the menu choices listed in Table 14.5. A few of these forums are described below. For further details, log on to the forum of interest and follow the on-screen prompts.

New Users Forum. This is the place to ask all those "I don't want to sound dumb, but . . ." questions. Remember, everyone in the New Users Forum is an ex-beginner, and the only reason they're here is to help others leap the techno-hurdles that come up from time to time. To skip all the intermediate steps described above, you may proceed directly to this forum by typing GO IBMNEW after logging on to CompuServe.

Hardware Forum. The hardware forum is divided into the sections listed in Table 14.6. To get help with a video-related problem, leave a message under section 3, Video.

Vendor Forums. Each of these forums is supported by a software manufacturer, so company representatives are on hand to answer questions, offer technical support, pass on operating tips, etc. In addition, experienced users exchange information and may be an excellent resource for problem solving. The forums are divided into three groups (A, B, C), and at press

Table 14.2 The Computer Software Forum Menu

Forum	Forum
1. Access Technology	26. LDOS & TRSDOS
2. ACIUS	27. Lotus Development Corporation
3. Adobe	28. LOGO
4. AI Expert	29. Microsoft Connection (Tbl. 14.3a)
5. Aldus	30. Microware Online Support
6. Ashton–Tate	31. MIDI & Music
7. Ask3Com	32. Nantucket Reference Center
8. Autodesk	33. Novell NetWire
9. Banyan Systems Inc.	34. Oracle
10. Borland International	35. OS9 Operating System
11. CADKEY	36. Portable Programming
12. Computer Consultants	37. PC Magnet
13. CDROM	38. PC Week Extra!
14. Computer Language	39. SAMNA Corporation
15. CP/M	40. Software Publishers Assoc.
16. Crosstalk	41. SPC
17. Data Access Corp.	42. Symantec
18. DATASTORM	43. TAPCIS
19. Desktop Publishing	44. UNIX
20. Digital Research	45. WordPerfect Support Group A
21. Dr. Dobb's Journal	46. WordPerfect Support Group B
22. Forth & Creative Solutions	47. WordStar
23. Fox Software	48. World of Lotus
24. InfoWorld Online Reviews	49. Xerox Desktop Software
25. Javelin & EXPRESS	

time, the companies listed in Table 14.7 were participating. The list is subject to frequent change, so it's a good idea to review the vendor list periodically.

Forum Libraries. In addition to the day-by-day information exchanges described above, most forums also have a library section which contains files of frequently requested information, utility programs related to the subject of the forum, and so on.

Forum Manners. To get the most out of CompuServe or any other online service, it helps to brush up on your electronic manners. For example, the people who are going to help you will be paying for the privilege of doing so. Both you and they are billed for on-line time, so if there's the slightest chance you will be back looking for more information later on, take the trouble to respond to anyone who helps you out now. Or don't come back again.

Table 14.3a The Microsoft Connection Menu

Topic	Topic
1. About the Microsoft Connection	7. Windows 3rd Party Applications A
2. Information on Microsoft	8. Windows 3rd Party Applications B
3. Excel	9. Knowledge Base
4. Applications	10. Software Library
5. Languages/Systems (Tbl. 14.3b)	11. Microsoft Wants Your Input
6. Windows	

Table 14.3b The Microsoft Languages and Systems Menu

Topic	Topic
1. General & New Uploads	9. Presentation Manager
2. BASIC & QuickBASIC	10. Program Help, Miscellaneous
3. Microsoft C	11. QuickC
4. Assembler/M Editor	12. Macintosh QuickBASIC
5. QuickPascal & Pascal	13. FORTRAN
6.	14. Non–technical Customer Service
7. MS–DOS Utilities	15. COBOL
8. OS/2	

Table 14.4 The Computer Hardware Forum Menu

Forum	Forum
1. Apple II/III	10. Epson
2. Apple Macintosh	11. Hewlett–Packard PC
3. Ask3Com	12. IBM Users Network (Table 14.5)
4. Atari Users Network	13. Intel Corporation
5. CDROM	14. Practical Peripherals
6. Commodore & Amiga	15. Tandy Users Network
7. Computer Club	16. Texas Instruments
8. DEC Users Network	17. Toshiba
9. Desktop Publishing	18. Zenith

632 The PC Configuration Handbook

Table 14.5 The IBM Users Network

Forum	Forum
1. Overview & Suggestion Box	9. Bulletin Board
2. Top 10 Help Files	10. PC Vendor A (Table 14.7)
3. New Users & Fun	11. PC Vendor B (Table 14.7)
4. Hardware (Table 14.6)	12. PC Vendor C (Table 14.7)
5. Software Applications	13. File Finder
6. Systems & Utilities	14. IBM PC Junior
7. Programming	15. IBM European Users
8. Communications	16. IBM Special Needs

Each forum is a place for the public discussion of whatever the topic is, so that all may benefit from the exchange of information. You'll learn a lot by reading public messages addressed to others, and they will learn from your messages. So don't expect an answer to be posted privately to your CompuServe mail box to spare you the bother of coming back to the forum to pick up your messages. Make up your mind up front: do you want to join a support group, or don't you? If yes, then do it, be welcome, and don't forget to acknowledge anyone who helps out. If no, then try going down one of the other help routes described above.

Equipment Rental

If all else fails and you must send a critical piece of hardware back to the manufacturer for repair, don't overlook the possibility of renting a replacement device to keep the system up and running for the duration of the repair. Try the local yellow pages under *Computers—Renting and Leasing* for the name of a local rental service. Or call a national rental service such as GE Rental and Leasing.

Table 14.6 IBM Hardware Forum Sections

Section	Section
0. General, new uploads	6. Laptops
1. Disk & Disk Utilities	7. Compatibles
2. Printers & Printer Utilities	8. Village Inn
3. Video	9. PS/2
4. General Hardware	10. Mainframe HW/SW
5. PC–AT	11. Hot Topic

Table 14.7 The PC Vendor Forum

Company Name	PCVEND*n*	Company name	PCVEND*n*
Brightbill–Roberts	C	Mansfield Software Group	A
Broderbund	A	Multisoft Corporation	A
ButtonWare	A	Mustang Software	A
ChipSoft, Inc.	B	Norton Computing, Peter	A
Ctrlalt Associates	A	PDC Prolog	B
Custom Technologies	A	Personics Corp.	B
DacEasy	B	Primavera Systems	B
Digitalk, Inc.	C	Quarterdeck	B
Enable Software, Inc.	A	Quicksoft	B
Foresight	A	Spectra Publishing	B
J. P. Software	B	TOPS	A
Knowledge Garden	A	TurboPower Software	B
Korenthal Assocs.	B	Vericomp	C
Magee Enterprises	A	Vestronix	B

It pays to shop around, since rental prices fluctuate wildly, depending on the local market and sometimes on the tone of desperation in your voice. If the rental hardware is to be delivered to your doorstep, make sure you know what the delivery charges will be and be prepared to pay a similar amount to return the hardware at the end of the rental period.

In most cases, the rental period ends when the equipment reaches the rental agency. Therefore, make sure you know the daily rental rate before consigning the return shipment to a slow-moving cross-country truck.

Appendix A
DOS 5.00

Microsoft's latest disk operating system—MS DOS version 5.00—is briefly summarized in this appendix. The description is based on several preproduction beta test versions, in which some of the newest commands were not yet fully implemented. Consequently, these notes will no doubt need some revision when the final DOS 5.00 production version is released, shortly after the publication of this book.

Although DOS 4.00 did not exactly take the world of personal computing by storm, all the new bells and whistles of DOS 5.00 will probably persuade those with earlier versions that it's now time to upgrade.

DOS 5.00 User's Guide

Not the least attraction of DOS 5.00 is its entirely new documentation, much of which is written in English. The *User's Guide and Reference* has more than 600 pages and is divided into the following sections:

Part 1   **MS-DOS Fundamentals**
             1 MS-DOS and Your System
             2 Command Line Basics
             3 Shell Basics

In addition to the extensive background provided by Parts 1 through 3, the Commands chapter (14) offers detailed information about each command—far more than found in earlier DOS documentation.

Installation Overview

The installation procedure for DOS 5.00 is quite a bit simpler and faster than for previous versions. This brief summary assumes that an earlier version of DOS is already installed on a formatted and partitioned hard disk. If this is not the case, then the procedure described here will be supplemented by additional screens, such as those described in the DOS installation procedure in Chapter 9 (page 389).

To begin, insert the DOS Setup diskette 1 in drive A, type SETUP, and press the Enter key twice to display the screens shown in Figures A.1 and A.2. If you need to back up your hard disk before installing DOS 5.00, do so now by selecting the *Back up the hard disks* option seen in Figure A.2.

The next screen (Figure A.3) displays a few of the installation options that may be changed if you wish to do so. If you are not sure if the displayed choices are correct, highlight any option and press the Enter key to display more information, or press function key F1 for a help screen. When you are ready to continue the installation, highlight the *No Changes* option and press the Enter key to display the next screen (Figure A.4).

Figure A.1

```
Microsoft(R) MS-DOS(R) Version 5.00
═══════════════════════════════

    Welcome to Setup.

    Setup prepares Microsoft MS-DOS Version 5.0 to run on
    your computer.  Each screen has basic instructions for
    completing a step in the installation. If you want
    additional information and instructions about a screen
    or option, press the Help key, F1.

    Before you begin, prepare a floppy disk by labeling it:

    RECOVERY #1

    These disk(s) will be used to save your current
    system files.

    To learn how to use Setup, press F1.
    To continued the installation, press ENTER.
    To exit without installing MS-DOS 5.00, press F3.

ENTER=Continue   F1=Help   F3=Exit
```

Figure A.2

```
Microsoft(R) MS-DOS(R) Version 5.00
═══════════════════════════════

Before installing MS-DOS 5.00, you should back up all of
your hard disks.  Setup includes a recovery program that
restores your original system if an error occurs during
installation.  The backup copies can be used to restore
your original system at a later time.

Use the ARROW keys to select the option you want
and press ENTER.

    ┌─────────────────────────────────────────────┐
    │ Back up the hard disks.                      │
    │ Do not back up the hard disks.               │
    └─────────────────────────────────────────────┘
```

Figure A.3

```
Microsoft(R) MS-DOS(R) Version 5.00
═══════════════════════════════════════
```

    Setup has determined that your system includes the
    following hardware and software components.

    ┌───┐
    │   │
    │   Manufacturer : MS-DOS   │
    │   DOS path   : C:\DOS   │
    │   MS-DOS Shell : Run the Shell on Startup   │
    │   Display type : VGA   │
    │   │
    │   No Changes   : This list matches my system.   │
    │   │
    └───┘

    If all the items in the list are correct, press ENTER to
    indicate 'No Changes.' If you want to change an item
    in the list, use the ARROW keys to select it. Then press
    ENTER to see alternatives for the item.

Figure A.4

```
Microsoft(R) MS-DOS(R) Version 5.00
═══════════════════════════════════════
```

    ┌───┐
    │   │
    │   Setup is ready to install MS-DOS Version 5.00 If you │
    │   choose to continue, you will not be able to interrupt│
    │   the installation until it is complete.   │
    │   │
    │   To install MS-DOS Version 5.0 now, press Y.   │
    │   To cancel the installation, press F3.   │
    │   To review your configuration selections, press any   │
    │   other key.   │
    │   │
    └───┘

Figure A.5

```
Microsoft(R) MS-DOS(R) Version 5.00
═══════════════════════════════════════
```

Copying DOS Files

MS-DOS 5.0 is now being set up.

Setup installs a basic MS-DOS 5.00 system. See the
MS-DOS 5.00 User's Guide to learn about additional features.

You may want to read Chapter 13, 'Optimizing Your System',
in the User's Guide. This chapter describes how to
fine-tune MS-DOS to achieve maximum performance for your
system.

    x% Complete

To begin the actual installation process, press the Enter key once more to copy the DOS 5.00 files to your hard disk. During the installation procedure, the screen shown in Figure A.5 is seen, and you will be prompted to switch diskettes by displays similar to those shown in Figures A.6a and A.6b. At the conclusion of the installation, the display shown in Figure A.6c is seen. Remove the diskette in drive A and press the Enter key to reboot the computer under DOS 5.00.

DOS 5.00 FEATURE SUMMARY

The remainder of this appendix is devoted to a review of some of the features introduced or significantly enhanced in DOS 5.00. Refer to the new DOS 5.00 *User's Guide* for further details about these and other DOS commands.

Attribute Command (ATTRIB)

In every file header, the byte following the file name and extension is the *file attribute byte,* in which each bit defines a file parameter. The ATTRIBute command allows the following file attribute bits to be changed:

Figure A.6

(a)

```
     Insert the disk labeled
          RECOVERY #1
          into drive
               A:

     When ready, press ENTER.

     WARNING:  All existing files
     on this disk will be deleted.
```

Figure A.6

(b)

```
        Insert the disk labeled
  MS-DOS 5.00 Install  x Disk
            into drive
               A:

  When ready, press ENTER.
```

Figure A.6

(c)

```
     The setup is now complete. Please remove
  any floppy disks from your drives and press
  ENTER to start MS-DOS 5.00.
```

Attribute bit	determines whether
archive	data has been written to the file since the last backup session
hidden	the file name appears in the directory listing
read-only	the file is write-protected
system	the file is a system file

If the attribute bit is set (1), the file possesses the attribute defined by that bit; if the bit is cleared (0), that attribute is disabled. To set or clear a file attribute, type the ATTRIB command, followed by a plus (set) or minus (clear) sign, and the name of the file, as shown here:

ATTRIB command	result
ATTRIB +p (*file name*)	Set the attribute bit defined by *p*.
ATTRIB -p (*file name*)	Clear the attribute bit defined by *p*.
ATTRIB	Display all file attributes of all files in the current directory.
ATTRIB /S	Display files in this directory and in its subdirectories.
ATTRIB ± p (*file name*) /S	Set (+) or clear (-) the attribute bit defined by *p* for all files with *file name* in this directory and in its subdirectories.

The last example above may be useful for modifying all files with a common extension, as for example, all *.SYS files.

Replace the *p* above with one of the following parameters. To change more than one file attribute, simply repeat the ±*p* parameter, as required.

Attribute parameter	Purpose
+A	Set archive bit
-A	Clear archive bit
+H	Set hidden-file bit
-H	Clear hidden-file bit
+R	Set read-only bit
-R	Clear read-only bit
+S	Set system-file bit
-S	Clear system-file bit

DIRectory Command Enhancements

The DIRectory command can be followed by several new parameters. In each case the format is as follows:

DIR /p

where *p* is the desired parameter. To specify additional parameters, simply repeat the /p as appropriate.

Attributes (/A:p). This parameter displays only those files whose attribute is specified by the letter following the colon.

Attribute parameter	displays
/A:A	files ready for archiving (for backup)
/A:-A	files that have already been archived
/A:D	directory names only
/A:-D	file names only (no subdirectories listed)
/A:H	hidden files
/A:-H	files that are not hidden
/A:R	read-only files
/A:-R	files that are not read-only
/A:S	system files
/A:-S	all files except system files
/A	all hidden, system, and regular files

Bare (show file names only) (/B). This parameter displays a bare directory listing; that is, one in which only the file name and extension are displayed. If the /B parameter is used together with /W (wide), the latter parameter is ignored.

Search Subdirectories (/S). The */S* parameter shows the contents of the current directory and all its subdirectories. Or you may use it to search for one or more files lost in the maze of directories and subdirectories. For example,

Search parameter	displays
/S	all directory and subdirectory listings
/S *filename.ext*	a specific file
/S WS*.*	all files beginning with WS
/S *.EXE	all files with an EXE extension

The search may be narrowed as required. For example, to search an entire drive, type the command from the root directory. Or log onto any subdirectory to confine the search to just that directory and its own subdirectories. If the search parameter finds the desired file or files, the directory containing the file(s) is displayed, followed by the names of the files. This is followed by the name of the next directory (if any) and its files, and so on, until all instances of the searched item have been found.

The search parameter is helpful for flushing out all the backup files that accumulate over time. Just log onto the root directory and type

```
DIR /S *.BAK
```

Or type a specific file name to make sure that the same name does not exist in two separate locations.

Combination Bare Name and Search (/B/S). When the above two parameters are both appended to the DIRectory command, each line displays the complete path name followed by the name (only) of the appropriate file.

Sort Order (/O:*p*). The directory listings may be sorted as specified by a letter following the colon, as indicated here.

Sort parameter	directory is sorted
/O:D	by date and time; earliest first
/O:-D	by date and time; latest first
/O:E	alphabetically by extension
/O:-E	alphabetically by extension, in reverse order
/O:G	with directories grouped before file names
/O:-G	with directories grouped after file names
/O:N	alphabetically by file name
/O:-N	alphabetically by file name, in reverse order
/O:S	by size; smallest first
/O:-S	by size; largest first

Preset Directory Display. If you would like to use one or more of the above parameters every time you execute the DIRectory command, simply add the *directory command* (DIRCMD) environment variable to your AUTOEXEC.BAT file. For example, to display your directory listings sorted in reverse alphabetical order, include hidden files, and pause when the screen is full, add the following line to the batch file:

```
SET DIRCMD=/O:-N/A/P
```

The next time the system is rebooted, the DIR command will display the directory listing as specified by SET DIRCMD.

Wide Directory Listing. As a final minor improvement, when the DIR command is followed by the /W (wide) parameter, all displayed directories are enclosed in square brackets, as shown in this sample line from a wide directory listing.

```
COMMAND.COM      [DOS]      [MACE]      GENS386.SYS      IBMCDROM.SYS
```

DOSKEY

When the DOSKEY utility is loaded, it maintains a record of your recent DOS commands, which may be recalled by pressing the up and down arrow keys or the PageUp and PageDown keys. To use the utility, either type DOSKEY at the DOS prompt or add the command to your AUTOEXEC.BAT file.

After DOSKEY has been loaded, and several DOS commands have been issued, you can toggle through these commands by pressing one of the following keys:

Press this key	to go to
Up arrow	the previous command
Down arrow	the next command
PageUp	the earliest command
PageDown	the latest command

Repetitive presses of an up or down arrow key will toggle forward or backward through the entire list, one command at a time. When the first (or last) command is reached, the next key press will return to the top (or bottom) of the list, and subsequent key presses will again toggle through the list.

EDIT

For those who need more editing power than is available in the ancient DOS EDLIN, DOS 5.00 offers a new full-screen editor for creating ASCII files. To begin editing, simply type EDIT, optionally followed by the name of the file you wish to edit. The EDIT screen is quite similar to the Microsoft

QuickBASIC program, and EDIT recognizes keystroke combinations used by Microsoft Word and WordStar.

To use the maximum number of lines possible on your monitor display configuration, type EDIT /H at the DOS prompt.

FORMAT

When the DOS 5.00 FORMAT utility is used, it creates a hidden restore file (UNFORMAT.DAT) on the formatted disk. This file will be used for file restoration in the event of a subsequent accidental reformatting.

If you attempt to format a drive that does not have sufficient room for the restore file, the following warning message is seen:

```
There is not enough room to create a restore file
You will not be able to use the unformat utility
Proceed with Format (Y/N)?
```

If you wish to proceed with formatting but still have the option to unformat later on, answer *no* (N or n) and make room for the UNFOR-MAT.DAT file by transferring a few files elsewhere. Then repeat the FORMAT instruction.

Format 2.88-Mbyte Diskettes.   The DOS 5.00 FORMAT utility will also format 3.5-inch 2.88-Mbyte diskettes, on suitably equipped diskette drives.

HELP SCREENS

For a brief on-screen summary of any DOS command, type the command and follow it with the /? parameter. For example, type the DIR command as shown on the first line below to display a summary of the parameters now available.

```
C>DIR /?
Displays a list of files in a directory.
DIR [pathname] [/p] [/w] [/a:attributes] [/o:sortorder] [/s] [/b]
/p Pause after each screen page of display.
/w List Files in columns with up to five filenames on each line.
/a:attributes Displays only files with the attributes you specify.
/o:sortorder Displays files sorted in the specified order.
/s Displays files in the specified directory and all subdirec-
tories.
/b Lists filenames, one per line, without any file information.
```

LOADHIGH

The LOADHIGH command is described in the Memory Management section immediately following.

Memory Management

One of the most noteworthy features of DOS 5.00 is its conservation of the first 640Kb of RAM—a few years ago, a vast uncharted sea of memory, but now reduced to a little bit-pond that frequently dries up completely.

The HIMEM Utility. The new HIMEM.SYS utility is an extended-memory manager that, among other features, allows most of the operating system to be loaded into the high memory area (HMA) of extended memory (see page 235). The utility can be used with 80286, 386 SX and DX, and i486 systems, and frees a considerable amount of low memory for use by other applications.

To take advantage of this feature, add the following lines to your CONFIG.SYS file:

```
DEVICE = C:\DOS\HIMEM.SYS
DOS = HIGH
```

The first line installs the high-memory manager and the second line loads part of DOS into the high memory area. As a typical example of memory savings, the following lines show a few DOS 5.00 CHKDSK reports, both before and after adding the above lines to a CONFIG.SYS file:

CHKDSK shows	DOS 5.00 CONFIG.SYS file details
656384 total bytes memory	
502624 bytes free	without HIMEM.SYS or DOS = HIGH lines
563362 bytes free	with HIMEM.SYS or DOS = HIGH lines
637104 bytes free	same, but with no other device drivers installed, and prior to loading any TSRs

Upper Memory Block (UMB) Support. DOS 5.0 can conserve even more conventional memory by loading device drivers, terminate-and-stay-resident programs, and other programs into the upper memory block area between 640Kb and 1Mb (see page 234).

When UMB support is enabled, DOS adds the upper memory block area to the conventional DOS memory, thus making it available for use by device drivers and other programs. To take advantage of this feature, add or modify the following line in your CONFIG.SYS file:

```
DOS = UMB
```

or

```
DOS = HIGH, UMB
```

With the UMB feature enabled, the next step is to load your device driver(s) or a conventional program into the upper memory block area.

To load a device driver into the UMB area, modify the appropriate DEVICE line in your CONFIG.SYS file, as seen here:

DEVICEHIGH=(*path and name of device driver*)

Some device drivers expand to take up more space than the size indicated by a directory listing would indicate. If the expanded space exceeds that available in the UMB area, there could be a device error or a system crash. If this happens, the DEVICEHIGH line can be revised to include a size parameter. To find the required size, first load the device driver in the usual manner. Now execute the DOS MEM /PROGRAM (page 280) command to display the amount of memory occupied by various installed programs, including the device driver of interest. Finally, modify the DEVICEHIGH line to include this value, as follows:

DEVICEHIGH SIZE=*xxxx* (*path and name of device driver*)

In either of the above examples, the device driver will be loaded into low memory if there is not enough UMB space available for it.

To load a TSR or other program into the UMB area, use the LOADHIGH command from the DOS command line, or within an AUTOEXEC.BAT file, as shown here:

LOADHIGH (*program name*)

Space permitting, the LOADHIGH command loads the named program into the UMB area and makes any unallocated UMB space available to that program.

Not all programs are compatible with the LOADHIGH command, so do a little experimenting to determine if your program runs properly from within the UMB area. In case of any unpredictable results, try the same operation with the program loaded in conventional memory. If this cures the problem, then the program is indeed incompatible with UMB. If not, then there is some other problem which should be resolved before trying LOADHIGH again.

As a final caution, note that although the LOADHIGH command can be executed from within a batch file, it cannot be used to load a batch file itself into the UMB area.

MIRROR

The MIRROR utility saves information that will be helpful later on, when it becomes necessary to recover files lost by erasing or formatting. The utility works by loading a terminate-and-stay-resident MIRROR program which monitors all erasure activity. When a file is subsequently erased, information about that file is written to a *delete tracking file* named PCTRACKR.DEL. The tracking file is written to each disk drive specified by the MIRROR command, as shown here:

```
MIRROR /TC /TD
```

In this example, the MIRROR command will track file erasures on hard drives C and D. The command line should be written in your AUTOEXEC.BAT file, ahead of any other TSR programs. Every time the system is booted, MIRROR saves a copy of the file allocation table and root directory for the specified drive(s). The information is written to a read-only file named MIRORSAV.FIL.

The MIRROR utility can also save hard disk partition information to a diskette, for subsequent use by the REBUILD and UNFORMAT utilities, should the need arise. To use this feature, type the following command at the DOS prompt:

```
MIRROR /PARTN
```

Now press the Enter key to display the following message:

```
The partition information from your hard disk drive(s)
has been read.  Next, the file PARTNSAV.FIL will be
written to a floppy disk. Please insert a formatted
diskette and enter the name of the diskette drive.
What drive? A
```

Assuming drive A is correct, just press the Enter key. Otherwise, change the drive letter as required before pressing the Enter key.

For details on the file recovery process, refer to the UNDELETE, UN-FORMAT, and REBUILD utilities, and to the latter two utilities for restoring the partition table.

QuickBASIC Interpreter

The old familiar GWBASIC has been replaced by Microsoft's QuickBASIC Interpreter. The program offers many of the features of the complete QuickBASIC program, although it is not possible to compile the BASIC programs created with the interpreter. For that, you'll need to buy the complete program, which is sold separately.

REBUILD

The REBUILD utility will restore a disk erased by the FORMAT command, or erased files in the root directory. To begin, type REBUILD x: at the DOS prompt, where x is the appropriate drive letter. A warning message advises you that the utility should only be used to recover from the accidental use of the DOS FORMAT or RECOVER commands, and asks

```
Are you SURE you want to update the SYSTEM area
of your drive x (Y/N)?
```

If you answer *yes*, the following message is seen at the conclusion of a successful restoration:

```
The SYSTEM area of drive x has been rebuilt.
You may need to reboot the system.
```

Reboot the system and log onto the restored drive to verify that all is well.

To restore a corrupted hard disk partition table, type REBUILD /PARTN at the DOS prompt. You will be prompted to insert the diskette containing PARTNSAV.FIL into drive A (or specify some other drive). Do so, and then press the Enter key to display a summary of the partition table that will be rebuilt on your hard drive, such as the one shown here.

Type	Total_size		Start_partition			End_partition			
	Bytes	Sectors	Cyl	Head	Sector	Cyl	Head	Sector	Rel#
DOS16 Boot	32M	65504	0	1	1	31	63	32	32
DOS16	30M	61408	32	1	1	61	63	32	32
DOS16	30M	61408	62	1	1	91	63	32	32
DOS16	23M	47072	92	1	1	114	63	32	32

```
Options: Q - quit, take no action.
         1 - restore partition records for fixed disk # 80h.
Which option? Q
```

To continue, press the 1 key. You will be asked if you're really sure this is what you want to do. If so, type YES and again press the Enter key to actually do the restoration. When the operation is completed, press the Enter key one more time to reboot the system.

SETVER

Once DOS 5.00 is installed, if an application displays a *Wrong DOS version* error message, the SETVER command can be used to modify a DOS version table stored in the MSDOS.SYS hidden file. To view the existing table, type SETVER without any parameters and press the Enter key. This displays a table of existing programs and the DOS version required for each one, as shown by the following examples:

```
EXCEL.EXE       4.10
MSCDEX.EXE      4.00
IBMCACHE.SYS    3.40
NET.COM         3.00
METRO.EXE       3.31
```

If your version of, say, WHATEVER.EXE demands DOS 3.10, you can add this information to the table by entering the following command:

```
SETVER WHATEVER.EXE 3.10
```

To make sure you're properly impressed by the gravity of fooling around with version numbers, the following message is displayed:

WARNING! Lying about version numbers to a program may have bad effects. Microsoft will not be
held responsible in this event.

Version table successfully updated. The version
change will take effect the next time you restart your system.

To verify that the table has indeed been updated, type SETVER again and press
the Enter key to display the revised table. Note that although the above warning
message indicates that the change has already been written to the version table,
you must reboot the system in order for it to take effect. So if you decide you
don't want to keep the change in the table, delete it before rebooting by typing

SETVER WHATEVER.EXE /DELETE

Note: Although SETVER modifies the version table in the hidden
MSDOS.SYS file, neither the length of the file nor its file creation date
are changed.

SETVER and Virus Detection Utilities. As described in Chapter 9 (page
379), some virus-detection utilities display a warning message if a file has been
recently modified, while others monitor the system files for tampering. Since
the SETVER command modifies the MSDOS.SYS system file, such utilities
will either report this file as a possible suspect for virus infection or warn you
of impending attack as SETVER is about to revise the version table.

If virus detection is a consideration, you may want to run a routine virus
check before using the SETVER command, to make sure no files are
corrupted. Then use the SETVER utility as required, and follow it up by
immediately running the virus check once again, this time ignoring the
warning message. Or if an online virus detection utility prevents SETVER
from doing its work, temporarily disable it until SETVER is finished.

UNDELETE

As the name suggests, the UNDELETE command will, within reason,
restore files that have been deleted (erased). For best results, a deleted file
should be undeleted before other files are written to disk. If it is not, there
is the chance that a new file will overwrite the space formerly reserved for,
and still occupied by, the deleted file. Once this happens, the deleted file is
really deleted, and the UNDELETE command will be useless.

Assuming the MIRROR utility (see p. 648) was installed prior to deleting
the file that needs to be undeleted, type UNDELETE /LIST at the DOS

prompt to display information stored in the delete tracking file. A typical example is shown here.

```
Delete Tracking file contains     x deleted files.
Of those,     x files have all clusters available,
              x files have some clusters available,
              x files have no clusters available.

DOS directory contains            x deleted files.

Of those, x files may be recovered.


Using the Delete Tracking file.

AUTOEXEC.BAK    216    9/10/90 10:53a ...A    Deleted: 11/25/90
```

(Directory information on other deleted files seen here)

In the above example, UNDELETE has found *x* deleted files, the first of which is an AUTOEXEC.BAK file. To undelete just this one file, type

```
UNDELETE AUTOEXEC.BAK
```

A screen similar to that shown above will be displayed, followed by

```
All of the clusters for this file are available.

Do you want to recover this file? (Y/N)
```

Assuming that you do, type Y and press the Enter key.

Even if the MIRROR utility was not installed prior to deleting a file, the UNDELETE command can still be used. In this following example, the deleted AUTOEXEC.BAK file described above will again be used as an example. The lines ending with an Enter key symbol indicate entries made by the user.

```
UNDELETE↵
Delete Tracking file not found.

    DOS Directory contains     x deleted files.
    Of those,     x files may be recovered.

Using the DOS Directory.

    ?UTOEXEC.BAK 216 9/10/90 10:53a ...A Deleted 11/25/90
Do you want to undelete this file (Y/N)
Y↵
Enter the first character of the filename.
A↵
File successfully undeleted.
```

The above sequence repeats for every other deleted file that is found.

UNFORMAT

The UNFORMAT utility may be used to restore files lost due to an accidental reformatting. The command may also be used to rebuild a corrupted partition table, provided that you previously saved partition information to diskette, as described in the MIRROR section above (page 648).

The UNFORMAT and REBUILD utilities are quite similar, and the documentation for both should be read carefully before using either command.

Appendix B
Glossary and Acronyms

ACE (Asynchronous Communications Element) Settings   In an IBM modem, the settings for baud rate, word length, parity, and stop bits.

ABIOS (Advanced BIOS)   In a PS/2 MCA system, the additional BIOS used to support addressing above 1 Mbyte for OS/2 and other operating systems.

Active Interval   In a monitor display, the time during which the moving electron beam is turned on, thereby energizing the phosphor dots on the screen.

Active Partition   On a hard disk, the partition containing the operating system, and used to boot the system on power up.

Adapter   Any printed-circuit board that plugs into one of the slots on the system board. In PS/2 systems, a *Feature Card*.

Address   The logical location at which a byte of memory is found. Thus, the first hundred bytes of RAM will be found at addresses 0 through 99, and so on. If a system has 64K-bytes of random-access memory installed, its address range is from 0 to 65535. The address of the next block of memory must be set to begin at 65536—that is, at a 64K-byte starting address.

All-Points-Addressable (APA) Mode   Any video mode in which each point, or pixel, may be separately controlled.

Alpha-Numeric Mode   Any video mode in which control is limited to the display of a complete character, composed of a matrix of horizontal and vertical pixels.

ASCII (American national Standard Code for Information Interchange)   A 7-bit code used to convey data within and between computers. The code defines 128 (2^7) control and graphic characters, which may be represented by the decimal numbers 0 to 127. In the ASCII standard, a graphic character may be a punctuation mark, the digits 0–9, and the upper- and lowercase letters A–Z.

ASCII, Extended   *See* Extended Character Set.

Aspect Ratio   The ratio of active screen width to height, or of horizontal to vertical pixels.

Asynchronous   In data communication, the description of a method of transmission in which the signal itself contains information to indicate the beginning and the end of each command. Compare with Synchronous.

AT (Attention) Command Set   The command set used by Hayes-compatible modems. In this context, AT has nothing to do with the IBM Personal Computer AT.

Attribute Byte   A byte that contains information about various attributes of a file. The value of the Attribute byte defines the file as hidden, system, read-only, etc.

ATTRIBute Command (DOS)   A command that allows the user to set or clear the read-only attribute. In DOS 5.00 the archive, hidden and system attributes may also be set or cleared.

AUTOEXEC.BAT File   An optional file on the boot diskette, containing various instructions that the user wishes to have performed automatically when the system is turned on. After executing the CONFIG.SYS file, DOS looks for an AUTOEXEC.BAT file; if it is found, the instructions within it are executed. These instructions may change the default directory or display, load a word-processing program, or perform many other tasks that would otherwise require the user to enter the same keystrokes every time the system is turned on.

Bandwidth   The frequency, in hertz (cycles per second), required to transmit the required number of pixels per frame.

BASIC   Beginner's All-Purpose Symbolic Instruction Code. A general-purpose programming language, designed to be easy to learn, remember, and use. It features simple constructions and a minimum of special rules, and is oriented toward interactive use.

Basic Input/Output System   *See* BIOS.

Batch File   Any file with an extension of BAT that is used in a manner similar to the AUTOEXEC.BAT file. The difference is that a batch file with a name other than AUTOEXEC.BAT is not executed automatically. Instead, the user must type the name of the file and then press the Enter key to execute the batch file.

Baud   A unit which defines the number of times a data signal changes state each second. Despite popular usage, it is not synonymous with bits per second, although the two are usually equal in PC communications applications.

Beep Code   A series of audible beeps used to signify various error conditions, usually during POST.

Binary   Pertaining to the base-2 system of numerical notation in which only the digits 0 and 1 are used.

BIOS (Basic Input/Output System)   A set of program routines written to handle various rudimentary (basic input/output) functions. The hidden IBMBIO.COM diskette file contains additions and changes to the BIOS found in the system board ROM chips that cannot be modified by the user. Do not confuse the "basic" in BIOS with the language of the same name.

BIT (BInary digiT)   In binary notation, the smallest increment of data, represented by a 0 or 1.

Blanking Interval   In a monitor, the time during which the electron beam is turned off, so that the beam may return to the left side of the screen without overwriting the existing display.

Boot   When a personal computer is turned on, a small program built in to the system hardware is used to load a slightly larger program from the DOS diskette, or from the primary DOS partition on the hard disk drive. This program loads a still larger program as the system pulls itself up (that is, on) "by its bootstraps." To boot the system means to start this process, either by turning the power on (cold boot), or if it is already on, by holding down the Control (Ctrl) and Alternate (Alt) keys while pressing the Delete (Del) key (warm boot, or reboot). The required keystroke action is usually abbreviated as Ctrl+Alt+Del.

Boot Diskette   A system diskette (q.v.) used to boot the computer when it is turned on. The boot diskette may also contain CONFIG.SYS and AUTOEXEC.BAT files.

Bus Mouse   A mouse whose interface to the computer is via a dedicated mouse adapter, instead of a serial port. *See also* Serial mouse.

Byte   A binary character consisting of 8 bits, usually operated on (stored or retrieved) as a single unit.

Carrier   The continuous tone produced by a modem and modulated by the transmitted data.

Cassette BASIC   *See* ROM BASIC.

Cache Memory   A reserved section of RAM in which frequently accessed disk/diskette sectors are stored.

CBIOS (Compatibility BIOS)   In a PS/2 system, that portion of the BIOS that is compatible with the BIOS found in ISA system computers.

Character Box   The matrix of horizontal and vertical pixels within which each character is displayed on screen.

Character Set   The set of printable characters found on the conventional typewriter; the letters A–Z, a–z, numbers 0–9, punctuation, etc. The term usually refers to the ASCII printable characters or other characters assigned to ASCII positions 32–126.

Check Sum   One or more bytes in which the sum of values stored elsewhere is written.

Check Sum Error   A condition in which the check-sum byte(s) value does not agree with a new summation of the values used to create the check sum in the first place. The error indicates that the stored data is probably inaccurate.

CMOS (Complementary Metal Oxide Semiconductor)   Pertaining to the formulation of RAM designed for low-power operation, used in many PCs to store configuration data. With power continuously supplied by a small battery, configuration data is not lost when system power is turned off.

CMOS RAM   A section of RAM generally used for storing configuration data. Since CMOS RAM requires very little power, a small battery preserves the stored data when system power is turned off.

Command Set   The commands comprising a modem's command language, used to control various modem functions. Hayes' Smartcom and similar communication software packages use the AT (Attention) command set recognized by Hayes-compatible modems. IBM modems support the AT command set as well as an IBM command set.

CONFIG.SYS file   An optional file on the boot diskette, containing the names of specific system-configuration files. When the system is turned on, DOS looks for this file, and if it is found the instructions within it are executed, thus loading various device drivers, setting the number of buffers, and performing other start up tasks.

Configure   To set various hardware or software switches to indicate the various options and adapters that have been installed in a PC.

Configuration   The specific complement of options (memory, adapters, displays, printers, etc.) that are installed in a PC.

Crash   The abrupt termination of a program due to a hardware or software problem.

Contiguous Memory   Any memory area within which all addresses are occupied by random-access memory.

Control Signal   Any signal which transmits information required for hardware control (for example, carriage return, line feed, modem commands).

Conventional Memory Random-access memory installed between absolute addresses 0 and 640Kb.

Ctrl+Alt+Del An instruction to hold down the Control and Alternate keys and press the Delete key before releasing them. Doing so reboots the system.

Current A measure of the rate at which electricity flows through a circuit. Measured in amperes, and popularly abbreviated as amps (A). The amount of current varies according to the electrical requirements of the system, and the larger the system, the greater the total current flow.

Cylinder On a hard disk system, the set of tracks (two per disk) that are all of the same diameter.

Data Signal Any signal which transmits readable information between two devices. *See also* Control Signal.

DCE (Data Communication Equipment) A modem.

DEBUG A versatile DOS utility program that may be used to examine and change the contents of memory, to read and write disk sectors, to write small assembly-language programs, etc.

Decimal Pertaining to the familiar base-10 system of numerical notation, in which the digits 0 through 9 are used.

Default A device, directory, or mode of operation that the computer employs in the absence of instructions to the contrary. Thus, on start up the defaults may be drive A, root directory, monochrome display, printer 1 (of 2 or more), modem 2, etc.

Device Driver A program that must be loaded in order to provide a software interface between some device (electronic disk, enhanced keyboard, etc.) and the PC system. The device driver is loaded by including its name in the CONFIG.SYS file.

Diagnostics Diskette The diskette that is supplied with the Guide to Operations Manual, and used in conjunction with various diagnostics procedures described in that manual, as well as in this book.

DIP (Dual Inline Pin) Referring to any chip with two parallel rows of pins. *See also* SIP.

DIP (Dual Inline Pin) Switch A group of switches (usually eight) set in an IC-like package with two (dual) parallel rows of pins.

Disable To set up a condition that prevents a future action from taking place. Thus, if the NumLock mode is disabled (by toggling the NumLock key) the numeric keypad may not be used to enter the numbers printed on the key caps. Instead, the cursor movement functions are enabled. Compare with Enable.

Diskette A flexible magnetic disk, permanently enclosed in a protective PVC or hard plastic jacket. Often called a floppy disk.

Display The cathode-ray tube device used as the visual interface between the PC system and the user. A monitor.

Distribution Diskette The diskette on which an operating system, utility, or other program is received.

DOS (Disk (or Diskette) Operating System) The set of programs that are required to support the basic operations of the computer system. Since DOS is continually upgraded with new functions, it is made available on diskette instead of being permanently fixed in ROM. When the system is turned on, DOS is booted into the system from the system diskette on which it is stored.

DOS Diskette Any diskette containing the COMMAND.COM file and the hidden IBMBIO.COM and IBMDOS.COM files.

Dot Clock In a video system, the oscillator that defines the system bandwidth. So called because the oscillator speed determines the number of pixels, or dots, sent to the screen per unit time.

Dot Pitch On a CRT screen, the distance between adjacent phosphor dots of the same color.

Double Scanning A video convention in which each horizontal line is scanned twice.

DRAM (Dynamic RAM) RAM in which stored data must be continually refreshed. See also SRAM.

Drive The turntable-like device into which a disk or diskette is inserted for data storage and retrieval.

DTE (Data Terminal Equipment) A PC, when used in communications applications.

Duplex Pertaining to a data communication link in which information may be simultaneosly transmitted in both directions. Often called full duplex, to distinguish it from half duplex.

EBCDIC (Extended Binary-Coded Decimal Interchange Code) An 8-bit code used to convey data within and between computers. The code was developed by IBM for its System/360.

Echo In communications jargon, the appearance of transmitted characters on the user's display screen. The characters are displayed (echoed) from the user's own terminal, or are echoed back from the remote terminal.

EISA Extended Industry Standard Architecture. A system proposed as an updated version of the ISA (q.v.) architecture found in the original IBM PC, XT, and AT computers.

Electronic Disk An area of random-access memory that has been reserved to function as though it were a physical diskette. An electronic disk offers much faster read and write operations than a physical diskette. In IBM jargon, an electronic disk is referred to as a virtual disk.

Enable   To set up a condition that permits a future action to take place. Thus, if the NumLock mode is enabled (by toggling the NumLock key) the numeric keypad may be used to enter the numbers printed on the key caps. Compare with disable.

Error Code   A number displayed on screen which indicates the PC has detected a system error.

Error Message   A phrase displayed on screen to describe an error which is usually software-related.

Error Signal   A sequence of beeps heard over the system speaker, which indicates the PC has detected a system error.

Escape Code   An ASCII code sequence in which an Escape character (ASCII 27) is used to signify that the following characters represent an instruction to the device, rather than characters to be printed or displayed.

ESDI (Enhanced Small Device Interface)   A disk interface system which allows higher-speed operations than the ST-506 system.

Expanded Memory   Any random-access memory installed on a device which conforms to the Lotus/Intel/Microsoft Expanded Memory Standard.

Expansion Memory   Any random-access memory installed to expand the RAM capacity of a personal computer. Usually understood to refer to conventional and extended memory.

Extended Character Set   An 8-bit code used in IBM personal computers and elsewhere to supplement ASCII with an additional 128 characters, consisting of various non-English letters, graphics symbols and other characters not found in the ASCII character set. Frequently referred to (incorrectly) as *Extended ASCII*.

Extended Memory   A contiguous block of random-access memory whose starting address is at 1Mb (1024Kb).

FDISK   The DOS utility used to set up or modify the partitions on a hard disk.

Feature Card   IBM nomenclature for any adapter card used in a PS/2 system.

File Attribute Byte   *See* Attribute byte.

Flicker   The visual effect noted when the frame rate is slow enough to be perceived by the unaided eye. So named after the very noticeable flicker seen in silent movies.

Floppy Disk   Deprecated term for a 5-inch flexible magnetic disk. A diskette.

Font   A complete set of letters, numbers, symbols, and punctuation marks, all in the same size and style.

Format, High-Level   The process of defining the sectors to be used for the boot record, file allocation tables, and directory, and transferring the COMMAND.COM and hidden files to diskette or hard disk.

Format, Low-Level   Preparation of the magnetic surfaces of a hard disk by setting the interleave and the number of sectors per track. As part of the process, the low-level format writes a header at the front of every sector.

FORMAT.COM   The DOS command used to format a diskette (high- and low-level) or a hard disk (high-level only). A similar DFORMAT.COM file on the diagnostics diskette is used only in conjunction with various diagnostics procedures.

Frame Rate   The number of frames displayed per second on a computer display, as defined by the Vertical Frequency.

Gang of Nine   The original supporters of the EISA system: AST, Compaq, Epson, Hewlett-Packard, NEC, Olivetti, Tandy, Wyse, and Zenith.

Graphics Memory   *See* Video memory.

Half Duplex   Pertaining to a data communication link in which information may be transmitted in only one direction at a time. *See also* Duplex.

Hard Disk Drive   A storage device in which the storage medium is a permanently installed magnetically coated rigid aluminum disk. In IBM jargon, a hard disk drive is referred to as a fixed disk, and occasionally, as a hardfile.

Hexadecimal   Pertaining to the base-16 system of notation, in which the digits 0-9 and letters A-F express the hexadecimal equivalents of decimal numbers 0-15. When context does not make clear whether 0-9 are decimal or hexadecimal, an "&H" prefix or "H" suffix is often added to hexadecimal notation.

Hidden File   A file whose name is not displayed in the directory listing even though it is in fact present on the fixed disk or diskette. By hiding the file name, it cannot be erased or copied with the COPY command. Hidden files (such as IBMDOS.COM and IBMSYS.COM) are copied by DIS-KCOPY and are written to a diskette or hard disk formatted with the /S option. (See the FORMAT.COM command in the DOS manual for further details.)

High Memory Area   The first 64Kb block of memory in the extended memory area.

Horizontal Blanking   *See* Blanking interval.

Horizontal Frequency   The frequency, in hertz (cycles per second) at which the electron beam moves across the face of the screen display.

IBM Command Set   *See* Command Set.

Install   To both physically add a device, and logically configure the device and the system as required. The logical portion of the installation may require hardware switches to be set, and/or software switching via an installation diskette accompanying the new device.

Interlaced scanning   A video screen writing convention in which one frame refreshes the odd-numbered scan lines and the next writes the even-numbered lines. *See also* Noninterlaced video.

ISA (Industry Standard Architecture)   The system architecture introduced in the first IBM personal computer (PC) and subsequently used in the XT and AT.

Kbytes and kilo   The uppercase "K" is understood to represent 2^{10}, or 1024. This should not be confused with lowercase "k," which is the abbreviation for kilo or thousand, exactly. Thus, 64Kb is actually 65,536 (64 × 1,024)—not 64,000—bytes.

LED (Light-Emitting Diode)   A special-purpose semiconductor device used as an indicator (power on, device in use, etc.) lamp.

LIM (Lotus/Intel/Microsoft) Expanded Memory Standard (version 3.20 September 1985)   A specification for expanding the memory-addressing capability of Intel microprocessors found in IBM and IBM-compatible personal computers.

Mbytes and mega   The uppercase "M" is understood to represent 2^{20}, or 1 048 576. This will no doubt be confused with uppercase "M," which is also the abbreviation for mega or million, exactly. Thus, 60Mb is actually 62 914 560 (60 × 1 048 576)—not 60,000,000—bytes.

MCA (Micro Channel Architecture)   The bus architecture system introduced by IBM in its PS/2 system (models 50–80).

MCGA (Multi-Color Graphics Array)   The video subsystem built into the IBM PS/2 models 25 and 30. It supports the old IBM CGA (but not EGA) modes, plus VGA modes 11 and 13.

Memory   That part of a computer in which data is stored for later retrieval. The contents of memory may be permanently fixed (ROM) or changeable as needed (RAM).

Memory Block   Any section of memory allocated in paragraphs (16 bytes) to a program or to any other form of data storage.

Memory Control Block (MCB)   The paragraph (16 bytes) at the head of every memory block which contains data about the contents of the memory block itself.

MFM (Modified Frequency Modulation)   Data encoding scheme in which a data bit of 1 is indicated by a pulse in the middle of the bit cell; a data bit of 0 by the absence of a pulse. The clock pulse is omitted unless a zero data bit is followed by another zero bit, in which case a clock pulse occurs at the beginning of the second zero bit cell, and again at the beginning of all zero bit cells immediately following.

Modem (MOdulator/DEModulator)   The interface hardware device between a phone line and the computer, used for data communications between two computers. So called because the modem modulates the transmitted signal and demodulates the received signal.

Mouse   A cursor-movement controller, or pointing device, in which the position of an on-screen cursor is controlled by moving the device across a nearby flat surface.

Nominal Value   The value (nominal voltage, for example) at which a device is designed to operate. The actual value may vary within a specified range.

Noninterlaced Scanning   The usual video screen-writing convention in which all scan lines are refreshed during each frame. Also called sequential scanning.

Offset   In a memory address given in the segment:offset format, the two-byte number that identifies the starting address by indicating its relative position (offset) with respect to the segment address.

Option   In IBM jargon, a printed-circuit board that plugs into an adapter slot on the system board, providing sockets for RAM chips. Sometimes used to describe any installable system-enhancement device.

Page   The block of memory required to store the data for a full screen display.

Paragraph   16 bytes.

Parallel   In data transmission, a description of the method in which the 8 bits in a byte of data are transmitted simultaneously, thus requiring eight separate data lines. Thus a parallel printer requires eight conductors, plus others for various support functions. Compare with Serial.

Parity   In a computer, the convention of adding a 1 bit to a byte so that the total number of bytes is always even (even parity) or odd (odd parity).

Parity Error   A condition in which the required even or odd parity is not maintained, thereby indicating that the stored data is probably incorrect.

Partition   Any section of a hard disk which may be treated as if it were a separate drive. Each partition has its own identifying drive letter.

Period   The time interval for one complete frequency cycle.

Persistence   A relative measure of the length of time a phosphor dot remains illuminated after being energized by a moving electron beam.

Pitch   In typesetting, the number of printed characters per horizontal inch, generally used to describe type faces in which each character occupies the same width on the page or screen.

Pixel (Picture ELement)   On a display screen, the smallest area whose color and intensity can be separately controlled. Although the picture element is considered to be a point, it is actually composed of three phosphor dots—red, green, blue—that may be individually controlled to create the desired color. IBM documentation refers to a pixel as a *pel.*

Point   In typesetting, the unit of measure for type size. There are 72 points per inch.

POS (Programmable-Option Select)   In IBM PS/2 50–80 computers, a system in which an adapter card (IBM *Feature Card*) contains a unique ID number. When such a card is installed, the ID is available to indicate the presence of the card.

POST (Power-On Self Test)   The series of system checks that are performed every time a personal computer is powered on.

Power   A measure of the electrical energy consumed by a device. Measured in watts (W).

Primary display   The video display that is automatically placed in service when the system is first powered on.

Prompt   The on-screen display of the current drive letter, followed by the "greater than" > symbol and a blinking cursor. Thus A> or C> are the usual DOS prompts. In BASIC, the prompt is the blinking cursor, with "OK" on the line immediately below.

RAM (Random-Access Memory)   That portion of memory in which the user may write instructions. The lowest RAM addresses are used to temporarily store the disk operating system when the PC is turned on.

RAM Disk   *See* Electronic Disk.

Read   To scan data stored on disk or diskette, or in memory.

Read-only File   Any file whose attribute byte has been set so that new data cannot be written to the file.

Reserved Memory   The memory area between 640Kb and 1024Kb.

Resolution   On a monitor display, a measure of the number of horizontal and vertical pixels (or lines) per frame. The more of each, the greater the screen resolution.

Retrace Interval   In a monitor, the time during which the electron beam is turned off, so that the beam may return to the top of the screen without overwriting the existing display.

RLL (Run Length Limited)   A data encoding scheme in which each byte is converted into a unique 16-bit pattern in which the "run length" of zeroes between each 1 bit is limited to a defined range. The encoding scheme permits an even greater data density than MFM encoding.

ROM (Read-Only Memory)   Memory whose contents are fixed during the manufacturing process and cannot be changed by the user (except by physical replacement of the ROM).

ROM BASIC   A primitive version of the BASIC language imbedded in ROM in IBM personal computers. Also called "Cassette BASIC," since the only supported storage medium was tape—usually a standard audio cassette tape.

ROM BIOS   That portion of read-only memory containing the BIOS.

Root Directory   The base, or main, directory on a disk or diskette. Often the root directory contains nothing but the names of subdirectories.

Scan Code   A unique numeric value assigned to each key on the keyboard, without regard to the characters which that key represents. Thus, the scan code for the numeral-2 key is 3, the letter-R key is 19, and so on.

Scan Line   On a video display, a single horizontal trace of the electron beam across the face of the screen.

Scratch Diskette   Any diskette that has not yet been formatted or whose contents are no longer needed. Such a diskette may be reformatted, used for testing purposes, inserted in a drive during transport, etc.

SCSI (Small Computer System Interface)   An expansion-bus system used as an interface between the personal computer and a hard disk and other devices.

Sector   A subdivision (usually of 512 bytes) of a track, operated upon as a unit when transferring data to and from a storage device.

Sector Header   A group of bytes at the head of each sector in which information about the sector is stored (sector number, data bytes to follow, etc.).

Segment   Any starting address that is evenly divisible by 16 (hexadecimal 10), and written with the least-significant digit omitted. The segment must therefore be multiplied by decimal 16 to find its actual, or absolute, address.

Segment: Offset   The 4-byte format used to define any address within the memory area from addresses 0 to 1024Kb. To find the absolute address, multiply the segment by 16 and add the offset.

Sequential Scanning   *See* noninterlaced scanning.

Serial   In data transmission, a description of the method in which the 8 bits in a byte of data are transmitted sequentially over a single data line. A modem is a serial device, since a phone line transmits only one signal at a time. Compare with parallel.

Serial Mouse   A mouse whose interface to the computer is any serial port. *See also* Bus Mouse.

Shadow Mask   In a cathode-ray tube, a screen placed near the interior surface of the display screen. The electron beams must pass through precision holes drilled in the mask, thus preventing each one from striking a colored phosphor dot other than the one for which it is intended.

Shadow RAM   A segment of RAM in which ROM data is written. The RAM is then remapped, or shadowed, to the ROM addresses, where it operates at a higher speed than the disabled ROM.

SIMM (Single Inline Memory Module)   A plug-in card containing RAM chips mounted on one or both sides of the card. An edge connector on the card interfaces with a matching socket on the system board. *See also* SIPP.

SIP (Single Inline Pin)   Referring to any chip in which all leads are arranged in a single inline row. *See also* DIP.

SIPP (Single Inline Pin Package)   A plug-in card containing chips and/or other components mounted on one or both sides of the card. A single row of inline pins on the card interfaces with a matching socket on the system board. *See also* SIMM.

SRAM (Static RAM)   RAM in which stored data remains in place as long as power is applied. *See also* DRAM.

Subdirectory   Any directory whose name is found in a higher-level directory; thus the root directory may contain the names of several subdirectories, each subdirectory contains the names of sub-subdirectories, and so on. At each level, the directory may also contain the names of programs stored in that directory. The lowest-level directory will contain nothing but file names, since there are no further directories beneath it.

Super VGA   A video standard proposed by VESA (q.v.), which adds an 800 × 600 video mode.

Symbol Set   The complete set of printable characters within a font, usually consisting of the ASCII character set, plus the extended characters (128–255) just beyond the ASCII character set, and sometimes a few printable symbols below ASCII 32.

Synchronous   In data communication, the description of a method of transmission in which the signal is sent in synchronized blocks, usually under the control of a separate timing signal. Compare with asynchronous.

System Board   The large printed-circuit board within the system unit, containing the microprocessor, base memory, math coprocessor (if any), and support circuitry. In addition, the system board features five (PC) or eight (XT, AT) adapter slots to accommodate various plug-in adapters, as well as keyboard and speaker connectors. Also called a mother board.

System Diskette   Any diskette containing a copy of an operating system, which for DOS comprises the COMMAND.COM file and the two hidden files (IBMDOS.COM and IBMBIO.COM, or similar). Also called a boot diskette.

System Files   The three files that must be present on a system diskette. These are COMMAND.COM and the IBMDOS.COM and IBMBIO.COM hidden files. On non-IBM systems, the latter two files will have somewhat different names.

System Unit   The system board, power supply, internal drives, and adapters as a complete system, as well as the metal cabinet in which these devices are installed.

Technical Support   In computer mythology, a friendly service available to all users from a manufacturer.

Toner Cartridge   In a laser printer (or photocopy machine), the removable container holding the toner.

Track   On a storage medium, a single concentric circle of magnetic data. Diskettes used by IBM personal computers may have 40 or 80 tracks per side, each divided into 8, 9, or 15 sectors.

Upper Memory Block (UMB)   The memory area between 640Kb and 1,24Kb, as defined by the Microsoft Extended Memory Specification.

VESA (Video Electronics Standards Association)   An industry association of manufacturers supporting the Super VGA mode.

Vertical Retrace   *See* Retrace interval.

Vertical Frequency   The frequency, in hertz (cycles per second) at which the screen display is refreshed. Thus, the vertical frequency defines the number of frames per second.

Video Memory   The 128-Kbyte area immediately following conventional memory, occupied by RAM on various video adapters. Also called graphics memory.

Virtual Disk   *See* Electronic disk.

VGA (Video Graphics Array)   The video subsystem introduced with the IBM PS/2 series of personal computers. It emulates all previous video modes and introduces several 1,024 × 768 modes.

Voltage   A measure of the difference in electrical potential between the two conductors in a power line. Measured in volts (V) and often in kilovolts (kV). Personal computer-related devices require a constant voltage, which in the United States is nominally 115 volts.

Wild Card   An asterisk or question mark, when used to signify any word, or any character, respectively. For example, DIR *.BAK displays a directory listing of all backup files, while DIR A????? will show all file names of six or fewer charaters that begin with "A."

Write   To record data on a disk or diskette, or in random-access memory.

Appendix C

Error Messages And Error Codes

As a guide to locating the chapter and section in which various errors are discussed, this section lists most of the error messages and error symptoms that are covered in this book. Omitted here are a few of those errors which by their very nature indicate the appropriate chapter.

	Refer to	
Error Message or Symptom	**Chapter**	**Section**
Access denied	8	Read-Only File, Table 8.9
Attempted write-protect violation	8	Start-up Problems, Table 8.9
audio (various beeps)	3	Table 3.1
audio signals	11	Beep Code Error Signals
Bad command or file name	8	DOS VERsion Command, Table 8.9
Bad file number in *xxx*	8	Program Troubleshooting
Bad or missing Command Interpreter	8	Table 8.9
Bad or missing (device name)	8	Table 8.9
Copy process ended	8	Other Copying Errors
Data error reading drive A	8	File Recovery Techniques
Device Timeout in *xxx*	12	Hardware-Related Problems

Path not found in *xxx*	8	Program Troubleshooting, Improper Drive Support
start-up error	3	Error Messages within POST
system locks up	5	System Locks Up
system reboots itself	5	System Reboots Itself
system shuts down (during operation)	5	System Shuts Down during Routine Operation
system shuts itself off (at start-up)	5	System Shuts Itself Off
Target diskette may be unusable	8	File Recovery Techniques
unable to shift screen left (right)	11	Off-Center Display
Unrecoverable format error on target	8	Copy-related Problems, Table 8.9
Unrecoverable read error on drive A	8	File Recovery Techniques, Copy-related Problems, Table 8.9
Unrecoverable write error on target	8	Copy-related Problems, Table 8.9
whistle, high-pitched	11	Monochrome Display Precautions
Write Protect Error Reading Drive A	3	Erroneous Error Codes
Write Protect Error Writing Drive A	8	Start-up Problems, Write Protect Tab, Table 8.9

COMPLETE LIST OF ERROR CODES

The following section contains a listing of numeric error codes collated from a variety of sources. Many of these codes require the use of an IBM Advanced Diagnostics diskette and may not be seen if a failure occurs during routine operation.

The list is presented here as a reference tool for those readers who have the necessary advanced diagnostics resources to go beyond the routine procedures covered elsewhere in this book. Due to the sheer size of the list, it must be emphasized that the accuracy of every code seen below has not been verified.

Notes:

*x*00, *xx*00, *xxx*00 = no errors

000–999 seen at the conclusion of an AT (Hayes) or IBM modem test is discussed in Chapter 11, in the section entitled Test Procedure.

01*xx*   System Board

101	interrupt failure
102	BIOS ROM checksum error (PC, XT); timer (AT, MCA)
103	BASIC ROM checksum error (PC, XT); timer interrupt (AT, MCA)
104	interrupt controller (PC, XT); protected mode (AT, MCA)
105	timer (PC, XT); keyboard controller (MCA)
106	system board
107	system board adapter card or math coprocessor; Hot NMI test (MCA)
108	system board; timer bus (MCA)
109	DMA test; memory select (MCA)
110	system board memory (ISA); system board parity check (MCA)
111	adapter memory (ISA); memory adapter parity check (MCA)
112*	adapter; watchdog time-out (MCA)
113*	adapter; DMA arbitration time-out (MCA)
114	external ROM checksum (MCA)
115	80386 protect mode
121	unexpected hardware interrupt
131	cassette wrap test (PC)
132	DMA extended registers
133	DMA verify logic
134	DMA arbitration logic
151	real-time clock (or CMOS RAM)
152	system board (ISA); real-time clock or CMOS (MCA)
160	system board ID not recognized (MCA)
161	system options (dead battery) (CMOS chip lost power)
162	system options (run Setup) (CMOS checksum or CRC error)
163	time and date (run Setup) (Clock not updating)
164	memory size (run Setup) (CMOS does not match system)
165	adapter ID mismatch (MCA)
166	adapter time-out; card busy (MCA)
167	system clock not updating (MCA)
199	user-indicated device list not correct

* if seen during advanced diagnostics, replace device being tested when error code appeared on screen.

02xx   Memory (see also 110, 111, and 164 above)

201   memory error (number preceding 201 indicates specific location; see Chapter 8 for further details)

202   memory address line 0–15

203   memory address line 16–23; line 16–31 (MCA) 204 relocated memory (PS/2)

205   error in first 128K (PS/2 ISA); CMOS (PS/2 MCA)

207   ROM failure

211   system board memory; system board 64K (MCA)

215   memory address error; 64K on daughter/SIP 2 (70)

216   system board memory; 64K on daughter/SIP 1 (70)

221   ROM to RAM copy (MCA)

225   wrong speed memory on system board (MCA)

03xx   Keyboard

301   keyboard did not respond correctly, or stuck key detected (a hexadecimal number preceding 301 is the scan code for the stuck key) keyboard interface (MCA)

302   user-indicated error from keyboard test (PC, XT)

302   keyboard locked (AT, models 25, 30)

303   keyboard/system board interface

304   keyboard or system unit error; keyboard clock (MCA)

305   keyboard fuse on system board (50, 60, 80); +5V error (70)

341   keyboard

342   keyboard cable

343   enhancement card or cable

365   keyboard (replace keyboard)

366   interface cable (replace cable)

367   enhancement card or cable (replace)

04xx   Monochrome Display

401   memory, horizontal sync frequency or vertical sync test

408   user-indicated display attributes

416   user-indicated character set

424   user-indicated 80 × 25 mode

432   monochrome card parallel port test

05xx   Color/Graphics Display

501   memory, horizontal sync frequency or vertical sync test

508   user-indicated display attributes

516	user-indicated character set
524	user-indicated 80 × 25 mode
532	user-indicated 40 × 25 mode
540	user-indicated 320 × 200 graphics mode
548	user-indicated 640 × 200 graphics mode
556	light pen test
564	user-indicated screen paging test

06xx   Diskette Drives and/or Adapter

601	diskette/adapter test failure; drive or controller (MCA)
602	diskette test (PC, XT); diskette boot record (MCA)
603	diskette size error
606	diskette verify function
607	write protected diskette
608	bad command; diskette status returned
610	diskette initialization (PC, XT)
611	timeout; diskette status returned
612	bad NEC; diskette status returned
613	bad DMA; diskette status returned
614	DMA boundary error
621	bad seek; diskette status returned
622	bad CRC; diskette status returned
623	record not found; diskette status returned
624	bad address mark; diskette status returned
625	bad NEC seek; diskette status returned
626	diskette data compare error
627	diskette change line error
628	diskette removed
630	drive A: index stuck high
631	drive A: index stuck low
632	drive A: track 0 stuck off
633	drive A: track 0 stuck on
640	drive B: index stuck high
641	drive B: index stuck low
642	drive B: track 0 stuck off
643	drive B: track 0 stuck on
650	drive speed
651	format failure
652	verify failure
653	read failure
654	write failure
655	controller

656	drive
657	write protect stuck protected
658	change line stuck changed
659	write protect stuck unprotected
660	change line stuck unchanged

07xx   Math Coprocessor

702	exception errors test
703	rounding test
704	arithmetic test 1
705	arithmetic test 2
706	arithmetic test 3
707	combination test
708	integer store test
709	equivalent expressions
710	exceptions
711	save state
712	protected mode test
713	voltage/temperature sensitivity test

09xx   Parallel Printer Adapter

901	data register latch
902	control register latch
903	register address decode
904	address decode
910	status line wrap connector
911	status line bit 8 wrap
912	status line bit 7 wrap
913	status line bit 6 wrap
914	status line bit 5 wrap
915	status line bit 4 wrap
916	interrupt wrap
917	unexpected interrupt
92x	feature register

10xx   Alternate Printer Adapter

10xx	adapter test failure
1002	jumpers (models 25, 30)

11xx   Communications Devices Asynchronous Communications Adapter System Board Asynchronous Port (MCA) 16550 Internal Modem (PS/2)

1101	adapter test failure
1102	card-selected feedback
1103	port 102 register test
1106	serial option
1107	communications cable or system board (MCA)
1108	IRQ 3
1109	IRQ 4
1110	modem status register not clear 16550 chip register
1111	ring-indicate 16550 control line internal wrap test
1112	trailing edge ring-indicate 16550 control line external wrap test
1113	receive and delta receive line signal detect 16550 transmit
1114	receive line signal detect 16550 receive
1115	delta receive line signal detect 16550 transmit and receive data unequal
1116	line control register: all bits cannot be set 16550 interrupt function
1117	line control register: all bits cannot be reset 16550 baud rate test
1118	transmit holding and/or shift register stuck on 16550 interrupt-driven receive external data wrap test
1119	data ready stuck on 16550 FIFO
1120	interrupt enable register: all bits cannot be set
1121	interrupt enable register: all bits cannot be reset
1122	interrupt pending stuck on
1123	interrupt ID register stuck on
1124	modem control register: all bits cannot be set
1125	modem control register: all bits cannot be reset
1126	modem status register: all bits cannot be set
1127	modem status register: all bits cannot be reset
1128	interrupt ID
1129	cannot force overrun error
1130	no modem status interrupt
1131	invalid interrupt pending
1132	no data ready
1133	no data available interrupt
1134	no transmit holding interrupt

1135	no interrupts
1136	no received line status interrupt
1137	no receive data available
1138	transmit holding register not empty
1139	no modem status interrupt
1140	transmit holding register not empty
1141	no interrupts
1142	no IRQ4 interrupt
1143	no IRQ3 interrupt
1144	no data transferred
1145	maximum baud rate
1146	minimum baud rate
1148	timeout error
1149	invalid data returned
1150	modem status register error
1151	no DSR and delta DSR
1152	no DSR
1153	no delta DSR
1154	modem status register not clear
1155	no CTS and delta CTS
1156	no CTS
1157	no delta CTS

12*xx*   Alternate Communications Devices
Asynchronous Communications Adapter (ISA)
Dual Asynchronous Communications (DAC) Adapter (MCA)
16550 Internal Modem

12*xx*	Same as 1100–1157 ISA systems, except for PS/2 codes listed below
1202	jumpers (models 25, 30)
1202 or 06	any serial device, but most likely Dual Async Adapter
1208 or 09	any serial device, but most likely Dual Async Adapter
1212	dual async adapter or system board
1218 or 19	dual async adapter or system board
1227	dual async adapter or system board
1233 or 34	dual async adapter or system board

13*xx*   Game Control Adapter

1301	adapter failure
1302	joystick test

14*xx*   Color/Graphics Printer

1401	printer test failure

1402	not ready; out of paper
1043	no paper; interrupt failure
1404	matrix printer test failure; system board time-out
1405	parallel adapter
1406	presence test

15xx   SDLC (Synchronous Date Line Control) Communications Adapter

1501	adapter test failure
1510	8255 port B
1511	8255 port A
1512	8255 port C
1513	8253 timer #1 did not reach terminal count
1514	8253 timer #1 output stuck on
1515	8253 timer #0 did not reach terminal count
1516	8253 timer #0 output stuck on
1517	8253 timer #2 did not reach terminal count
1518	8253 timer #2 output stuck on
1519	8273 port B error
1520	8273 port A error
1521	8273 command/read time-out
1522	interrupt level 4 (timer and modem change)
1523	ring indicator stuck on
1524	received clock stuck on
1525	transmit clock stuck on
1526	test indicate stuck on
1527	ring indicate not on
1528	receive clock not on
1529	transmit clock not on
1530	test indicate not on
1531	data set ready not on
1532	carrier detect not on
1533	clear-to-send not on
1534	data set ready stuck on
1535	carrier detect stuck on
1536	clear-to-send stuck on
1537	level 3 (transmit/receive) interrupt
1538	receive interrupt results error
1539	wrap data miscompare error
1540	DMA channel 1 transmit error
1541	DMA channel 1 receive error
1542	8273 error-checking or status-reporting error

1547	level 4 stray interrupt
1548	level 3 stray interrupt
1549	interrupt presentation sequence time-out

16xx DSEA (Display Station Emulation Adapter)
In case of 16xx error, try removing non-IBM adapters and then repeat test.

1604 or 08	DSEA or system twin-axial network problem
1624 or 34	DSEA
1644 or 52	DSEA
1654 or 58	DSEA
1662	interrupt level switches set wrong or defective DSEA
1664	DSEA
1668	Same as 1662
1669 or 74	if with early version of diagnostics diskette, replace with version 3.0 or later.
1674	station address switches set wrong or defective DSEA
1684 or 88	feature not installed, device address switches set wrong, or DSEA

17xx Fixed (Hard) Disk/Adapter

1701	drive not ready (PC, XT)
	fixed disk/adapter test (AT, PS/2)
1702	time-out (PC, XT); fixed disk/adapter (AT, PS/2)
1703	drive (PC, XT, PS/2)
1704	controller (PC, XT),
	adapter, or drive error (AT, PS/2)
1705	no record found
1706	write fault
1707	track 0 error
1708	head select error
1709	bad ECC (AT)
1710	read buffer overrun
1711	bad address mark
1712	bad address mark (PC, XT);
	error of undetermined cause (AT)
1713	data compare error
1714	drive not ready
1730	adapter
1731	adapter
1732	adapter
1750	drive verify

1751	drive read
1752	drive write
1753	random read test
1754	drive seek test
1755	controller
1756	controller ECC test
1757	controller head select
1780	hard disk drive C fatal; time-out
1781	hard disk drive D fatal; time-out
1782	hard disk controller (no IPL from hardfile)
1790	drive C nonfatal error (can attempt to run IPL from drive)
1791	drive D nonfatal error (can attempt to run IPL from drive)

18xx   Expansion Unit (PC, XT only)

1801	Expansion Unit POST error
1810	enable/disable
1811	extender card wrap test failure while disabled
1812	high-order address lines failure while disabled
1813	wait state failure while disabled
1814	enable/disable could not be set on
1815	wait state failure while enabled
1816	extender card wrap test failure while enabled
1817	high-order address lines failure while enabled
1818	disable not functioning
1819	wait request switch not set correctly
1820	receiver card wrap test or an adapter card in expansion unit
1821	receiver high-order address lines

20xx   BSC (BiSynchronous Communications) Adapter)

2001	adapter test failure
2010	8255 port A
2011	8255 port B
2012	8255 port C
2013	8253 timer #1 did not reach terminal count
2014	8253 timer #1 output stuck on
2015	8253 timer #2 did not reach terminal count
2016	8253 timer #2 output stuck on
2017	8251 data-set-ready failure to come on
2018	8251 clear-to-send not sensed
2019	8251 data-set-ready stuck on
2020	8251 clear-to-send stuck on
2021	8251 hardware reset

2022	8251 software reset command
2023	8251 software error-reset command
2024	8251 transmit-ready did not come on
2025	8251 receive-ready did not come on
2026	8251 could not force overrun error status
2027	interrupt—no timer interrupt
2028	interrupt—transmit: replace card or planar
2029	interrupt—transmit: replace card only
2030	interrupt—transmit: replace card or planar
2031	interrupt—transmit: replace card only
2033	ring-indicate stuck on
2034	receive-clock stuck on
2035	transmit clock stuck on
2036	test indicate stuck on
2037	ring indicate not on
2038	receive clock not on
2039	transmit clock not on
2040	test indicate not on
2041	data-set-ready stuck on
2042	carrier detect not on
2043	clear-to-send not on
2044	data-set-ready stuck on
2045	carrier detect stuck on
2046	clear-to-send stuck on
2047	unexpected transmit interrupt
2048	unexpected receive interrupt
2049	transmit data did not equal receive data
2050	8251 detected overrun error
2051	lost data set ready during data wrap
2052	receive time-out during data wrap

21xx   Alternate BiSynchronous Communications Adapter

| 21xx | Same as 2000–2052 |

22xx   Cluster Adapter

| 22xx | adapter test failure |

23xx   Plasma Monitor Adapter

| 23xx | adapter test failure |

24xx   Enhanced Graphics Adapter
System Board Video (MCA)

2401	adapter test failure
2402	monitor if colors change, otherwise system board
2408	user-indicated display attributes
2409	monitor
2410	system board
2416	user-indicated character set
2424	user-indicated 80 x 25 mode
2432	user-indicated 40 x 25 mode
2440	user-indicated 320 x 200 graphics mode
2448	user-indicated 640 x 200 graphics mode
2456	light pen test
2464	user-indicated screen paging test

25xx   Alternate Enhanced Graphics Adapter

25xx	adapter test failure

26xx   PC/370-M Adapter

2601 to 75	memory card
2677 to 80	processor card
2681	memory card
2682	processor card
2694	processor card
2695	memory card
2697	processor card

27xx   PC/3277 Emulation Adapter

27xx	emulator test failure

28xx   3278/79 Emulator, 3270 Connection Adapter

28xx	adapter test failure

29xx   Color/Graphics Printer

29xx	printer test failure

30xx   LAN (Local Area Network) Adapter

3001	adapter test failure (ROM)
3002	RAM
3003	digital loopback
3005	4V or 12V
3006	interrupt conflict

3007	analog
3008	reset command
3015	refer to *PC Network Service Manual*
3020	replace adapter with jumper W8 enabled
3040	LF translator cable
3041	refer to *PC Network Service Manual*
30*xx*	Primary PC Network Adapter
3001	adapter test failure
3002	ROM
3003	ID
3004	RAM
3005	HIC
3006	{+/- sign} 12V dc
3007	digital loopback
3008	host-detected HIC failure
3009	sync fail and no-go bit
3010	HIC test OK and no-go bit
3011	go bit and no CMD 41
3012	card not present
3013	digital fall-through
3015	analog
3041	hot carrier on other card
3042	hot carrier on this card

31*xx* Alternate LAN Adapter

31*xx*	same as 3000–3041
3115 or 40	LF translator cable

32*xx* PC Display Adapter

32*xx*	adapter test failure

33*xx* Compact Printer (PC, XT only)

33*xx*	printer test failure

35*xx* Enhanced Display Station Emulation Adapter

3504	adapter connected to twin-axial cable during off-line test
3508	work station address in use by another work station, or diagnostic diskette from another PC was used
3509	diagnostic program failure; retry on new diskette
3540	work station address invalid, not configured at controller; twin-axial cable failure or not connected; or diagnostic diskette from another PC was used

| 3588 | feature not installed or device I/O address switches set wrong |
| 3599 | diagnostic program failure; retry on new diskette |

36xx   IEEE 488 Adapter

3601	adapter test failure (base address and read registers incorrect, following initialization)
3602	write to SPMR
3603	write to ADR or IEEE 400 adapter addressing problems
3610	adapter cannot be programmed to listen
3611	adapter cannot be programmed to talk
3612	adapter cannot take control with IFC
3613	adapter cannot go to standby
3614	adapter cannot take control asynchronously
3615	adapter cannot take control asynchronously
3616	adapter cannot pass control
3617	adapter cannot be addressed to listen
3618	adapter cannot be unaddressed to listen
3619	adapter cannot be addressed to talk
3620	adapter cannot be unaddressed to talk
3621	adapter cannot be addressed to listen with extended addressing
3622	adapter cannot be unaddressed to listen with extended addressing
3623	adapter cannot be addressed to talk with extended addressing
3624	adapter cannot be unaddressed to talk with extended addressing
3625	adapter cannot write to self
3626	adapter cannot generate handshake error
3627	adapter cannot detect DCL message
3628	adapter cannot detect SDC message
3629	adapter cannot detect END with EOI
3630	adapter cannot detect EOT with EOI
3631	adapter cannot detect END with 0-bit EOS
3632	adapter cannot detect END with 7-bit EOS
3633	adapter cannot detect GET
3634	mode 3 addressing not functioning
3635	adapter cannot recognize undefined command
3636	adapter cannot detect REM, REMC, LOK, or LOKC
3637	adapter cannot clear REM or LOK
3638	adapter cannot detect SRQ
3639	adapter cannot conduct serial poll
3640	adapter cannot conduct parallel poll

3650	adapter cannot DMA to 7210
3651	data error on DMA to 7210
3652	adapter cannot DMA from 7210
3653	data error on DMA from 7210
3658	uninvoked interrupt received
3659	adapter cannot interrupt on ADSC
3660	adapter cannot interrupt on ADSC
3661	adapter cannot interrupt on CO
3662	adapter cannot interrupt on DO
3663	adapter cannot interrupt on DI
3664	adapter cannot interrupt on ERR
3665	adapter cannot interrupt on DEC
3666	adapter cannot interrupt on END
3667	adapter cannot interrupt on DET
3668	adapter cannot interrupt on APT
3669	adapter cannot interrupt on CPT
3670	adapter cannot interrupt on REMC
3671	adapter cannot interrupt on LOKC
3672	adapter cannot interrupt on SRQI
3673	adapter cannot interrupt on terminal count on DMA to 7210
3674	adapter cannot interrupt on terminal count on DMA from 7210
3675	spurious DMA terminal count interrupt
3697	illegal DMA configuration setting detected
3698	illegal interrupt level configuration setting detected

38xx Data Acquisition Adapter

3801	adapter test failure
3810	timer read test
3811	timer interrupt test
3812	delay, BI 13 test
3813	rate, BI 13 test
3814	BO 14, ISIRQ test
3815	BO 0, count-in test
3816	BI STB, count-out test
3817	BO 0, BO CTS test
3818	BO 1, BI 0 test
3819	BO 2, BI 1 test
3820	BO 3, BI 2 test
3821	BO 4, BI 3 test
3822	BO 5, BI 4 test
3823	BO 6, BI 5 test
3824	BO 7, BI 6 test

3825	BO 8, BI 7 test
3826	BO 9, BI 8 test
3827	BO 10, BI 9 test
3828	BO 11, BI 10 test
3829	BO 12, BI 11 test
3830	BO 13, BI 12 test
3831	BO 15, AI CE test
3832	BO STB,
	BO GATE test
3833	BI CTS,
	BI HOLD test
3834	AI CO, BI 15 test
3835	counter interrupt test
3836	counter read test
3837	AO 0 ranges test
3838	AO 1 ranges test
3839	AI 0 values test
3840	AI 1 values test
3841	AI 2 values test
3842	AI 3 values test
3843	analog input interrupt test
3844	AI 23 address or value test

39xx   Professional Graphics Controller Adapter

3901	adapter test failure
3902	ROM1 self-test
3903	ROM2 self-test
3904	RAM self-test
3905	cold start cycle power
3906	data error in communications RAM
3907	address error in communications RAM
3908	bad data detected while read/write to 6845-like register
3909	bad data detected in lower hex-E0 bytes while read/writing 6845-like registers
3910	PGC display bank output latches
3911	basic clock
3912	command control error
3913	vertical sync scanner
3914	horizontal sync scanner
3915	intech
3916	LUT address error
3917	LUT red RAM chip error

3918	LUT green RAM chip error
3919	LUT blue RAM chip error
3920	LUT data latch error
3921	horizontal display
3922	vertical display
3923	light pen
3924	unexpected error
3925	emulator addressing error
3926	emulator data latch
3927	base for error codes 3928–3930 (emulator RAM)
3928	emulator RAM
3929	emulator RAM
3930	emulator RAM
3931	emulator H/V display problem
3932	emulator cursor position
3933	emulator attribute display problem
3934	emulator cursor display
3935	fundamental emulation RAM problem
3936	emulation character set problem
3937	emulation graphics display
3938	emulation character display problem
3939	emulation bank select error
3940	display RAM U2
3941	display RAM U4
3942	display RAM U6
3943	display RAM U8
3944	display RAM U10
3945	display RAM U1
3946	display RAM U3
3947	display RAM U5
3948	display RAM U7
3949	display RAM U9
3950	display RAM U12
3951	display RAM U14
3952	display RAM U16
3953	display RAM U18
3954	display RAM U20
3955	display RAM U11
3956	display RAM U13
3957	display RAM U15
3958	display RAM U17
3959	display RAM U19

3960	display RAM U22
3961	display RAM U24
3962	display RAM U26
3963	display RAM U28
3964	display RAM U30
3965	display RAM U21
3966	display RAM U23
3967	display RAM U25
3968	display RAM U27
3969	display RAM U29
3970	display RAM U32
3971	display RAM U34
3972	display RAM U36
3973	display RAM U38
3974	display RAM U40
3975	display RAM U31
3976	display RAM U33
3977	display RAM U35
3978	display RAM U37
3979	display RAM U39
3980	PGC RAM timing
3981	PGC read/write latch
3982	SR bus output latches
3983	addressing error (vertical column of memory; U2 at top)
3984	addressing error (vertical column of memory; U4 at top)
3985	addressing error (vertical column of memory; U6 at top)
3986	addressing error (vertical column of memory; U8 at top)
3987	addressing error (vertical column of memory; U10 at top)
3988	base for error codes 3989–3991 (horizontal bank latch errors)
3989	horizontal bank latch errors
3990	horizontal bank latch errors
3991	horizontal bank latch errors
3992	RAG/CAG PGC
3993	multiple write modes, nibble mask errors
3994	row nibble (display RAM)
3995	PGC addressing

44*xx*	**5278 Display Attachment Unit and 5279 Display**
44*xx*	test failure

45*xx*	**IEEE Interface Adapter (IEEE 488)**
45*xx*	adapter test failure

46xx   ARTIC Multiport/2 Interface Adapter
4611   adapter
4612 or 13 memory module
4630   adapter
4640 or 41 memory module
4650   interface cable

48xx   Internal Modem
48xx   modem test failure

49xx   Alternate Internal Modem
49xx   modem test failure

56xx   Financial Communication System
56xx   system test failure

70xx   Chip Set (Phoenix BIOS only)
7000   CMOS failure
7001   shadow RAM failure (ROM not shadowed to RAM)
7002   CMOS configuration data error

71xx   Voice Communications Adapter
7101   adapter test failure
7102   instruction or external data memory
7103   PC to VCA interrupt
7104   internal data memory
7105   DMA
7106   internal registers
7017   interactive shared memory
7108   VCA to PC interrupt
7109   DC wrap
7111   external analog wrap and tone output
7114   telephone attachment test

73xx   3.5-inch Diskette Drive
7301   diskette drive/adapter test failure
7306   diskette change line error
7307   write-protected diskette
7308   bad command
7310   track zero error
7311   time-out
7312   bad NEC

7313	bad DMA
7314	DMA boundary error
7315	bad index
7316	speed error
7321	bad seek
7322	bad CRC
7323	record not found
7324	bad address mark
7325	bad NEC seek

74xx   8514/A Display Adapter/A

74xx	adapter test failure
7426	monitor
744x to 7x	8514 memory module

76xx   PagePrinter

7601	adapter test failure
7602	adapter card
7603	printer
7604	printer cable

84xx   PS/2 Speech Adapter

| 84xx | adapter test failure |

85xx   2Mb Memory Adapter

85xx	adapter test failure
850x or 1x	80286 Expanded Memory Adapter/A (model 50)
852x	80286 Expanded Memory Adapter/A, memory module (model 50)

86xx   PS/2 Pointing Device (Mouse)

8601	pointing device; mouse time-out (MCA)
8602	pointing device; mouse interface (MCA)
8603	system board; mouse interrupt (MCA)
8604	pointing device or system board

89xx   MIDI Adapter

| 89xx | adapter test failure |

100xx Multiprotocol Communications Adapter

| 10002 or 06 | any serial device, but most likely multiprotocol adapter |
| 10007 | multiprotocol adapter or communications cable |

10008 or 09 any serial device, but most likely multiprotocol adapter
10012   multiprotocol adapter or system board
10018 or 19 multiprotocol adapter or system board
10042 or 56 multiprotocol adapter or system board
101xx   Modem and Communications Adapter/A
101xx   system board
10102   card-selected feedback
10103   port 102 register test
10106   serial option
10108   IRQ 3
10109   IRQ 4
10110   16450 chip register
10111   16450 control line internal wrap test
10113   transmit
10114   receive
10115   transmit and receive data not equal
10116   interrupt function
10117   baud rate test
10118   interrupt driven receive external data wrap test
10125   reset result code
10126   general result code
10127   S registers write/read
10128   echo on/off
10129   enable/disable result codes
10130   enable number/word result codes
10133   connect results for 300 baud not received
10134   connect results for 1,200 baud not received
10135   local analog loopback 300-baud test
10136   local analog loopback 1,200-baud test
10137   no response to escape/reset sequence
10138   S register 13 incorrect parity or number of data bits
10139   S register 15 incorrect bit rate
104xx   ESDI Fixed Disk or Adapter
10450   write/read test
10451   read verify test
10452   seek test
10453   wrong device type indicated
10454   controller failed sector buffer test
10455   controller
10456   controller diagnostic command
10461   format error
10462   controller head select

10463	write/read sector error
10464	drive primary map unreadable
10465	controller ECC 8-bit
10466	controller ECC 9-bit
10467	soft seek error
10468	hard seek error
10469	soft seek error count exceeded
10470	controller attachment diagnostic error
10471	controller wrap mode interface
10472	controller wrap mode drive select
10473	error during ESDI read verify test
10480	drive C, ESDI adapter or system board
10481	drive D seek failure, ESDI adapter or system board
10482	ESDI fixed disk adapter
10483	ESDI fixed disk adapter; controller reset; drive select 0
10484	controller head select 3 selected bad
10485	controller head select 2 selected bad
10486	controller head select 1 selected bad
10487	controller head select 0 selected bad
10488	controlled rg-cmd complete 2
10489	controlled wg-cmd complete 1
10490	drive C format; read failure; controller
10491	drive D format; read failure
10499	controller
107xx	5.25-inch External Diskette Drive or Adapter
107xx	drive or adapter test failure

112xx SCSI Adapter

112xx	adapter test failure

129xx Processor Card for model 70, type 3

12901	processor portion of processor board
12902	cache portion of processor board

149xx Plasma Display and Adapter

14901 or 02	system board or plasma display
14922	system board or display adapter
14932	display adapter

165xx 6157 Streaming Tape Drive or Tape Attachment Adapter

165xx	adapter test failure
16520	streaming tape drive

16540	tape attachment adapter
166xx	Primary Token-Ring Network PC Adapter
166xx	adapter test failure
167xx	Alternate Token-Ring Network PC Adapter
167xx	adapter test failure

194xx Adapter Memory Module

| 194xx | adapter test failure |

210xx SCSI Fixed Disk and Controller

| 210xx | disk or controller test failure |

215xx SCSI CD-ROM System

| 215xx | CD-ROM system test failure |

Abbreviations Used in List of Error Codes

ADSC	ADdress Status Changed
AI	Analog Input
AO	Analog Output
APT	Address Pass Through
ARTIC	Real-Time Interface Coprocessor
BI	Binary Input
BO	Binary Output
CE	Convert Enable
CMOS	Complementary Metal-Oxide Semiconductor
CO	Command Output, Convert Out
CPT	Command Pass Through
CRC	Cyclic Redundancy Check
CTS	Clear To Send
DAC	Dual Asynchronous Communications
DCL	Device CLear
DEC	DEvice Clear
DET	Device Execute Trigger
DI	Data In
DMA	Direct Memory Access
DSEA	Display Station Emulation Adapter
DSR	Data Set Ready
DO	Data Out
ECC	Error Checking and Correction
EOI	End Of Identify

EOS	End Of String
EOT	End Of Transmission
ERR	ERRor
ESDI	Enhanced Small Device Interface
FIFO	First In, First Out
GET	Group Execute Trigger
GPIB	General Purpose Interface Bus
H/V	Horizontal/Vertical
ICL	Interface CLear
IEEE	Institute of Electrical and Electronics Engineers
IPL	Initial Program Load
IRQ	Interrupt ReQuest
IS	Interrupt Status
ISA	Industry Standard Architecture
LAN	Local Area Network
LOK	LOcKout
LOKC	LOcKout Changed
LUT	Look-Up Table
MCA	Micro Channel Architecture
MIDI	Musical Instrument Digital Interface
NEC	Nippon Electronic Company (drive controller)
PGC	Professional Graphics Controller
RAG/CAG	Row Address Generator/Column Address Generator
REM	REMote
REMC	REMote Changed
SDC	Selected Device Clear
SDLC	Synchronous Data Link Control
SIP	Single Inline Package
SPMR	Serial Poll Mode Register
SR	Shift Register
SRQ	Service ReQest
SRQI	Service ReQuest In
STB	Strobe
VCA	Voice Control Adapter

Appendix D
Directory Of Companies And Products

For the convenience of readers who seek additional information, this appendix lists the companies, organizations and products and services mentioned in the text. In many cases, the listed company produces products other than those few that are cited here. The list is for informational purposes only, and implies no endorsement of products mentioned, nor of other products and services offered by any company.

Companies mentioned in book	Product
ALR—Advanced Logic Research, Inc. 9401 Jeronimo Irvine, CA 92718 (800) 444-4ALR	EISA computers
AMI—American Megatrends, Inc. 3800 Monroe Avenue Pittsford, NY 14534 (716) 248-3627	ROM BIOS
American National Standards Institute 1430 Broadway New York, NY 10018 (212) 642-4900	ANSI Standards

Award Software, Inc.   ROM BIOS
130 Knowles Drive
Los Gatos, CA 95030
(408) 370-7979

Axxion Group Corp.   Tower Cases
3 Butterfield Trail
El Paso, TX 79906
(915) 722-0088

BusTek Corporation   SCSI host adapters
2255G Martin Avenue
Santa Clara, CA 95050
(408) 492-9090

Cajun Edge   hole punch for 3.5"
117 S. Oak Street, Suite C   diskettes
Hammond, LA (70403)
(800) 448-2970

Chicago Lock Company   replacement keys
4311 West Belmont Avenue
Chicago, IL 60641
(312) 282-7177

Compaq Computer Corp.   EISA computers
P. O. Box 692000
Houston, TX 77269
(713) 374-1564

CompuServe Information Service   CompuServe subscription
P. O. Box 20212
Columbus, OH 43220
(800) 848-8990

Computer Virus Industry Association   virus information
4423 Cheeney Street
Santa Clara, CA 95054
(408) 727-4559
(408) 988-4004 (modem
   BBS for virus information)

Stuart F. Cooper Co. 1565 East 23rd Street Los Angeles, CA 90011 (800) 421-8703	laser printer bond paper
Dallas Semiconductor 4350 Beltwood Parkway South Dallas, TX 75244 (214) 450-0400	clock modules
Datadesk International, Inc. 9314 Eton Avenue Chatsworth, CA 91311 (818) 998-4200	modular keyboard
Department of Commerce, U. S. U. S. Government Printing Office Washington, DC 20402	*Electric Current Abroad* booklet
Fifth Generation Systems 10049 N. Reiger Road Baton Rouge, LA 70809 (800) 873-4384	Brooklyn Bridge FastBack Plus Mace Utilities
Fort Lock Corp. 3000 North River Road River Grove, IL 60171 (708) 456-1100	replacement keys
GE Rental and Leasing (800) 437-3687	computer rental service
Gibson Research Corp. 22991 La Cadena Laguna Hills, CA 92653 (714) 830-2200	SpinRite II
Gilbert Paper Co. 430 Ahnaip St. Menasha, WI 54952 (414) 722-7721	laser printer paper

Global Engineering Documents 2805 McGaw Avenue Irvine, CA 92714 (800) 854-7179	draft version of SCSI-II standard
Globe Manufacturing Sales, Inc. 1159 Route 22 Mountainside, NJ 07092 (800) 227-3258	adapter brackets
Hammermill Paper Co. 1540 East Lake Road Erie, PA 16533 (814) 870-5000	Laser Plus paper
Hauppauge Computer Works, Inc. 91 Cabot Court Hauppauge, NY 11788 (516) 434-1600	replacement system boards
Hayes Microcomputer Products, Inc. 705 Westech Drive Norcross, GA 30092 (404) 449-8791	modems

Hewlett-Packard
(800) 367-4772
   (laser printer dealer information)
(800) 835-4747
   (laser printer service information)
(208) 323-2551
   (LaserJet technical support)
(800) 752-0900
   (EISA computer dealer information)
	laser printers, EISA
	   computers

IBM Technical Directory P. O. Box 2009 Racine, WI 53404 (800) 426-7282	technical publications

Intel Corporation
3065 Bowers Avenue
Santa Clara, CA 95051
(408) 765-8080

microprocessors,
math coprocessors

Iomega Corp.
1821 W. 4000 S.
Roy, UT 84067
(800) 777-4241

Bernoulli Box

JDR Microdevices
2233 Branham Lane
San Jose, CA 95124
(408) 559-1200

adapter brackets,
system upgrade supplies

Kensington Microware Ltd.
251 Park Avenue South
New York, NY 10010
 (800) 535-4242

surge suppressors, trackballs

Mace *See* Fifth Generation Systems

Mace Utilities

Memory Products and More
Division of Zomaya Group, Inc.
(800) 222-8861 (dealer information)

memory modules

Microcomputer Accessories, Inc.
5405 Jandy Place
P. O. Box 66911
Los Angeles, CA 90066
(800) 521-8270

vacuum cleaners

Micro Computer Systems, Inc.
2300 Valley View Lane, Suite 800
Irving, TX 75062
(214) 659-1514

EISA and ISA configuration
 files

Micropolis Corp.
21211 Nordhoff Street
Chatsworth, CA 91311
(818) 709-3300

hard disks

Microsoft Corp.   DOS (disk operating system)
One Microsoft Way   Microsoft Mouse
Redmond, WA 98052
(206) 882-8080

Northgate Computer Systems   keyboards
P. O. Box 41000
Minneapolis, MN 55441
(800) 548-1993

Parsons Technology   Virucide
375 Collins Road NE
Cedar Rapids, IA 52402
(800) 779-6000

Peter Norton Computing, Inc.   Norton Utilities
100 Wilshire Blvd.
Santa Monica, CA 90401
(213) 319-2010

Olson Metal Products Co.   adapter brackets
1001 Crossroads
Seguin, TX 78155
(512) 379-7000

OnTrack Data Recovery, Inc.   hard disk data recovery
6200 Bury Drive   service
Eden Prairie, MN 55346
(800) 872-2599

PC Power & Cooling, Inc.   replacement power supplies
31510 Mountain Way
Bonsall, CA 92003
(619) 723-9513

Personics Corp.   UltraVision
68 Great Road
Maynard, MA 01754
(508) 897-1575

Phoenix Technologies Ltd. 846 University Ave Norwood, MA 02062 (617) 551-4000	ROM BIOS
Plus Development Corporation 1778 McCarthy Blvd. Milpitas, CA 95035 (800) 624-5545	hard card
Priam Corporation 350 East Plumeria Drive San Jose, CA 95134 (408) 434-9300	hard disks
Quarterdeck Office Systems 150 Pico Boulevard Santa Monica, CA 90405 (213) 392-9071	QRAM and QEMM 386
Radio Shack 500 One Tandy Center Fort Worth, TX 76102 (consult phone book for nearest local store)	computer accessories
Rupp Corporation 835 Madison Avenue New York, NY 10021 (212) 517-7775	FastLynx
Seagate Technology, Inc. 920 Disk Drive Scotts Valley, CA 95066 (800) 468-3472	hard disks
SMT—Systems Manufacturing Technology, Inc. 310 Via Vera Cruz San Marcos, CA 92069 (800) 326-1638	ISA system clock modules

VESA: Video Electronics Standards
   Organization
1330 South Bascom Avenue
San Jose, CA 95128
 (408) 971-7525

video standards

Xerox Corp.
(800) 822-2200 (dealer information)

copier paper

Index

NOTES

A letter immediately following a page number indicates the page reference is to: *f*, a figure; *p*, a program listing: or *t*, a table.

Some error codes and PS/2 model numbers are enclosed in parentheses, to distinguish them from the page numbers which follow.

Page references to a complete chapter are printed in boldface.

712   Index

PQI Series STABILINE® Power Quality Interfaces

PQI Series STABILINE® Power Quality Interfaces divert and attenuate electromagnetic interference, spikes and transients before they can reach sensitive electronic equipment. Unique, state-of-the-art multi-stage suppression/filtration design utilizes hybrid technology to offer a choice of "Good", "Better" and "Superior" performance levels. All units are light-weight and packaged in attractive, fire-rated ABS plastic housing with convenient access to AC and telephone line input and output connections. Circuit allows bidirectional protection from source or load power disturbances. Feature 205 V peak clamping level; 95 joule energy dissipation capability; less than

1 ns single stage response time; 3000 A surge withstand. Types with "D" suffix have telephone line multi-stage transient protection for use with FAX/modems. Let-through voltage for normal/metallic (line-to-line) and common longitudinal (line-to-ground) is 200 V peak, 200 mA maximum (steady state condition). Response time is less than 1 ns; withstand FCC part 68 metallic waveforms without failure.

All types except those with "D" suffix have circuit breakers. All Series 2000 and 3000 types have on/off pilot light. All PQI Series units are CSA approved and UL 1449 listed (clamping level 330 V).

| Type | Nom. Volt. | Max. Amps. | Receptacles | | | Circuit Breaker | Each |
| | | | NEMA AC | | RJ11 | | |
			Qty.	Style	Qty.		
Series 1000 — Good Performance							
PQI-1115	120	15	4	5-15R	—	Yes	75.00
PQI-1115D	120	15	2	5-15R	2	No	89.00
Series 2000 — Better Performance							
PQI-2115	120	15	4	5-15R	—	Yes	149.00
PQI-2115D	120	15	2	5-15R	2	No	179.00
Series 3000 — Superior Performance							
PQI-3115	120	15	4	5-15R	—	Yes	199.00
PQI-3115D	120	15	2	5-15R	2	No	229.00

Superior Electric
DANA

STABILINE® Uninterruptible Power Supplies

UPSY Series STABILINE® Uninterruptible Power Supplies provide a reliable source of clean, continuous, sine wave AC power for computers and other voltage sensitive equipment. These true on-line UPS systems regulate voltage, protect equipment from noise and provide battery backup in event of utility power failure. Operate at extremely high frequency and utilize MOSFET semiconductor components. Typical operating times for 120 V, 60 Hz types range from 5, 10 or 30 minutes at full load; 10, 25 or 60 minutes at half load. Times can be extended by turning off non-critical devices. Have RS232 signal level interface DB-9 connector to interact with commercial computer operating systems to facilitate orderly system shut-down. Feature low velocity forced air cooling, low audible noise, protection from short circuits, overloads and excessive battery discharge. Input connection on 120 V, 60 Hz types is by an 8-foot cordset with a NEMA 5-15P plug and a UPS input plug IEC-320 connector. Operating temperature range is 0°C to 40°C. Assemblies do not draw from battery power until voltage drops below 96 VAC for longer battery run time and overall system life. Use of pulse width modulation (PWM) concept results in small size, light weight, quiet operation and high efficiency. Cabinet versions are UL listed and CSA approved.

| AC Input Single Phase | | Output | | | Internal Battery Backup Time (Min.) | | Cabinet Models | | Rack Mount Models | |
AC Voltage	Current (Amps.)	Voltage (±)3%	Max. Amps.	Max. Load (VA)	Full Load	Half Load	Type	Each	Type	Each
96-132	5	120	3.3	400	5	10	UPSY61004	1150.00	UPSY61004R	1250.00
96-132	5	120	3.3	400	30	60	UPSY61004L	1295.00	UPSY61004LR	1395.00
96-132	10	120	6.7	800	10	25	UPSY61008	1695.00	UPSY61008R	1795.00
96-132	12	120	10.4	1250	10	25	UPSY61012	2695.00	UPSY61012R	2795.00

Superior Electric
DANA

Add Mainframe Performance to Your New System!

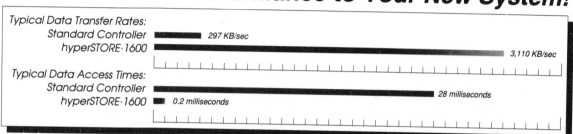

Typical Data Transfer Rates:
Standard Controller — 297 KB/sec
hyperSTORE·1600 — 3,110 KB/sec

Typical Data Access Times:
Standard Controller — 28 milliseconds
hyperSTORE·1600 — 0.2 milliseconds

Today's 16- and 32-bit PC's have many times the CPU power of yesterday's mainframes. But much of this power is wasted . . . waiting on slow disk drives. The fact is that virtually all common applications are disk-bound! PSI opens this disk bottleneck by bringing mainframe technology to the desktop in the form of our hyperSTORE line of high-performance intelligent disk controllers. Data throughput can be increased over ten times while data access time drops by an order of magnitude. hyperSTORE controllers are available in a variety of configurations to fit most computers, disk drives, and budgets.

hyperSTORE Feature Highlights

· Up to 50GigaBytes of on-line storage
· Support for 28 physical disk drives
· 512KB to 20MB of local cache memory
· Field-upgradable controller software
· Works in any 286, 386, or i486 system
· Concurrent support for any interface:
  MFM, RLL, ESDI, SCSI, or AT/IDE